A TREATISE

ON THE

LAW OF TAXATION,

INCLUDING

THE LAW OF LOCAL ASSESSMENTS.

BY THOMAS M. COOLEY, LL. D.,
One of the Justices of the Supreme Court of Michigan, and Jay Professor of Law in the University of Michigan.

THE LAWBOOK EXCHANGE, LTD.
Clark, New Jersey

ISBN 9781584773825

Lawbook Exchange edition 2003, 2013

The quality of this reprint is equivalent to the quality of the original work.

THE LAWBOOK EXCHANGE, LTD.
33 Terminal Avenue
Clark, New Jersey 07066-1321

Please see our website for a selection of our other publications and fine facsimile reprints of classic works of legal history:
www.lawbookexchange.com

Library of Congress Cataloging-in-Publication Data

Cooley, Thomas McIntyre, 1824-1898.
A treatise on the law of taxation, including the law of local assessments/by Thomas M. Cooley.
p. cm.
Originally published: Chicago: Callaghan and Co., 1876.
Includes bibliographical references.
ISBN 1-58477-382-0 (cloth: alk. paper)
1. Taxation—Law and legislation—United States. 2. Tax assessment—Law and legislation—United States. I. Title: Law of taxation. II. Title.

KF6298.C6 2003
343.7304—dc21
2003054550

Printed in the United States of America on acid-free paper

A TREATISE

ON THE

LAW OF TAXATION,

INCLUDING

THE LAW OF LOCAL ASSESSMENTS.

BY THOMAS M. COOLEY, LL. D.,

One of the Justices of the Supreme Court of Michigan, and Jay Professor of Law in the University of Michigan.

CHICAGO:

CALLAGHAN AND COMPANY,

LAW BOOK PUBLISHERS.

1876.

ATWOOD & CULVER,
STEREOTYPERS AND PRINTERS,
MADISON, WIS.

PREFACE.

THE following pages have been prepared with a view to present in a shape for practical use, the general rules which must govern the action of all authorities acting in matters of taxation. Had a similar task been previously undertaken, the writer would gladly have been spared the labor; but Mr. Blackwell's Treatise on Tax Titles covers the ground only in part, and Judge Dillon, though he has done valuable service in the same direction, has not, in his work on Municipal Corporations, deemed it advisable to go beyond what seemed necessary to a legitimate and perspicuous presentation of that subject. Other writers have had occasion to discuss only particular topics in the law of taxation, leaving a comprehensive examination of the general subject to be still entered upon.

The decisions in this country on the subject of taxation have become so numerous, that it would be impossible to give abstracts of them all, within any reasonable compass. The author has thought it preferable, instead of attempting a digest of them, to group the references about the controlling principles. The tax systems of the several states are so dissimilar, that a mere digest of the cases is exceedingly liable to mislead, by giving, as a general rule of law, what is only a conclusion from a local law or custom. There are, or should be, general principles underlying all the cases; and an understanding of these will enable one to make use of decisions under the various tax systems, without confusion.

The subject of taxation seems to invite some consideration of questions of political economy; but these have been passed by after bare mention, as not being necessarily involved in a discussion of the legal points. They present considerations for the legislature in framing tax laws; but courts and ministerial officers must enforce tax laws as they are, whether based on sound or unsound principles of political economy.

The preparation of any treatise on taxation necessarily involves the presentation of disputed points, and the expression of opinions upon them. This has been done in the following pages. It has not been the purpose, however, to take any positions which it was not believed the authorities would justify; and if this has been done in any instance, the references which are made to authorities will doubtless enable the reader to detect the error. Possibly it may be thought, that on some points, too much importance has been attached to those fundamental principles which restrict the power to tax. But when one considers how vast is this power, how readily it yields to passion, excitement, prejudice or private schemes, and to what incompetent hands its execution is usually committed, it seems unreasonable to treat as unimportant, any stretch of power — even the slightest — whether it be on the part of the legislature which orders the tax, or of any of the officers who undertake to give effect to the order. Especially is this so, when it is understood how little restraint there can be on the ignorant action of assessors, acting with jurisdiction, and how very seldom an effectual remedy can be administered where fraud or corruption exists. And as the benefits of republican government have been reached through the efforts of the people to establish and maintain the legitimate restraints upon the power to tax, it seems unwise in a high degree, to slight or disregard any of the checks which the law has provided, whether those which are entrusted to the hands of the judiciary, or those which are the lawful right of the people themselves, who are to bear the burden of the particular tax.

THOMAS M. COOLEY.

UNIVERSITY OF MICHIGAN,
Ann Arbor, January, 1876.

TABLE OF CONTENTS.

CHAPTER I.

TAXES, THEIR NATURE AND KINDS.

CHAPTER II.

THE NATURE OF THE POWER TO TAX.

CHAPTER III.

LIMITATIONS UPON THE TAXING POWER.

CHAPTER IV.

THE PURPOSES FOR WHICH TAXES MAY BE LAID.

CHAPTER V.

THE PURPOSE MUST PERTAIN TO THE DISTRICT TAXED.

CHAPTER VI.

EQUALITY AND UNIFORMITY IN TAXATION.

CHAPTER VII.

APPORTIONMENT OF TAXES.

CHAPTER VIII.

OFFICIAL ACTION IN MATTERS OF TAXATION.

CHAPTER IX.

THE CONSTRUCTION OF TAX LAWS.

CHAPTER X.

CURING DEFECTS IN TAX PROCEEDINGS.

CHAPTER XI.

THE VOTING OF THE TAX.

CHAPTER XII.

THE ASSESSMENT OF PROPERTY FOR TAXATION.

CHAPTER XIII.

THE COLLECTOR'S WARRANT.

CHAPTER XIV.

THE COLLECTION OF THE TAX.

CHAPTER XV.

THE SALE OF LANDS FOR UNPAID TAXES.

CHAPTER XVI.

REDEMPTION OF LANDS FROM TAX SALES.

CHAPTER XVII.

PROCEEDINGS AT LAW TO RECOVER LANDS SOLD FOR TAXES.

CHAPTER XVIII.

TAXATION OF BUSINESS.

CHAPTER XIX.

TAXES UNDER THE POWER OF POLICE.

CHAPTER XX.

TAXATION BY SPECIAL ASSESSMENT.

CHAPTER XXI.

LOCAL TAXATION UNDER LEGISLATIVE COMPULSION.

CHAPTER XXII.

THE REMEDIES OF THE STATE AGAINST COLLECTORS OF TAXES.

CHAPTER XXIII.

ENFORCING OFFICIAL DUTY UNDER THE TAX LAWS.

CHAPTER XXIV.

THE REMEDIES FOR ILLEGAL AND UNJUST TAXATION.

TABLE OF CASES.

B.

C.

D.

E.

F.

G.

H.

I.

J.

K.

M.

N.

O.

P.

S.

T.

U.

V.

W.

Y.

Z

LAW OF TAXATION.

CHAPTER I.

TAXES, THEIR NATURE AND KINDS.

Definition. Taxes are defined as being the enforced proportional contribution of persons and property, levied by the authority of the state for the support of the government, and for all public needs.[1]

They are the property of the citizen, demanded and received by the government to be disposed of to enable it to carry into effect its mandates, and to discharge its manifold functions.[2] The jus-

[1] Opinions of Judges, 58 Me., 591. "The public revenues are a portion which each subject gives of his property in order to secure and enjoy the remainder." Montesq. Spirit of the Laws, b. 13, ch. 1. "What are taxes but the revenue collected from the people for objects in which they are interested; the contributions of the people for things useful and conducive to their welfare." *Agnew*, J., in Hilbish *v.* Catherman, 64 Penn. St., 154, 159. Blackwell, in his Treatise on Tax Titles, p. 1, defines taxes as "burdens or charges imposed by the legislative power of a state upon persons or property, to raise money for public purposes." Substantially the same definition is given by *Field*, Ch. J., in Perry *v.* Washburn, 20 Cal., 318, 350. And see Hanson *v.* Vernon, 27 Iowa, 28, 47, per *Dillon*, J.; Matter of Mayor, etc., of New York, 11 Johns., 77, 80; Mitchell *v.* Williams, 27 Ind., 62; Loan Association *v.* Topeka, 20 Wall., 655, 664, per *Miller*, J.; Philadelphia Association, etc., *v.* Wood, 39 Penn. St., 73, 82, per *Lowrie*, Ch. J.; Glasgow *v.* Rowse, 43 Mo., 479, 489, per *Wagner*, J.; Exchange Bank of Columbus *v.* Hines, 3 Ohio State, 1, 10, per *Bartley*, Ch. J.; Judd *v.* Driver, 1 Kan., 455, 462, per *Kingman*, J. In People *v.* McCreery, 34 Cal., 432, 456, it is said a tax is "a charge levied by the sovereign power upon its subjects. It is not a charge upon its own property, nor upon property over which it has no dominion." Per *Rhodes*, J.

[2] Opinions of Judges, 58 Me., 591; Davison *v.* Ramsay County, 18 Minn., 482. "Tax legislation means the making of laws that are to furnish the measure of every man's duty in support of the public burdens, and the means of enforcing it." Philadelphia Association, etc. v., Wood, 39 Penn. St., 73, 82. per *Lowrie*, Ch. J.

tification of the demand is to be found in the reciprocal duties of protection and support between the state and its citizens, and the exclusive sovereignty and jurisdiction of the state over the persons and property within its territory. The citizen and the property owner owes to the government the duty to pay taxes, that the government may be enabled to perform its functions, and he is supposed to receive his proper and full compensation in the protection which the government affords to his life, liberty and property, and in the increase to the value of his possessions by the use to which the money contributed is applied.[1]

Taxes differ from subsidies, in being regular and orderly,[2] and they differ from the forced contributions, loans and benevolences of arbitrary and tyrannical periods, in that they are levied by authority of law, and by some rule of proportion which is intended to insure uniformity of contribution, and a just apportionment of the burdens of government. In an exercise of the power to tax, the purpose always is, that a common burden shall be sustained by common contributions, regulated by some fixed general rule, and apportioned by the law according to some uniform ratio of equality.[3] While therefore the power is great and imperative, it is not arbitrary; it rests upon fixed principles of justice, which have for their object the protection of the tax payer against exceptional and invidious exactions,[4] and it is to have effect through estab-

[1] People *v.* Brooklyn, 4 N. Y., 419, 422, per *Ruggles*, J.; McKeen *v.* Delaware Division Canal Company, 49 Penn. St.. 524, per *Agnew*, J.

[2] Jacob's Law Dic., "Tax;" Bouvier's Law Dic., "Tax;" Tyson *v.* School Directors, 51 Penn. St., 9. Tribute is often used as synonymous with tax, but the more ordinary meaning is, an exaction demanded by a conqueror, or by some external authority whose power is too great to be resisted; an exaction from "strangers" rather than from the "children." Matthew 17: 26. Lawless and arbitrary exactions are sometimes called tribute when made by the constituted government; as in the remonstrances of the Spanish Cortes to their sovereign against such demands. Hallam's Middle Ages, ch. IV.

[3] *Robertson*, Ch. J., in Sutton's Heirs *v.* Louisville, 5 Dana, 28, 31; *Dixon*, Ch. J., in Knowlton *v.* Supervisors of Rock Co., 9 Wis., 410, 421; *Christiancy*, J., in Woodbridge *v.* Detroit, 8 Mich., 274, 301; Grim *v.* School District, 57 Penn. St., 433.

[4] "Whenever the property of a citizen shall be taken from him by the sovereign will, and appropriated without his consent, to the benefit of the public, the exaction should not be considered as a tax unless similar contributions be made by that public itself, or shall be exacted rather by the same public

lished rules, operating impartially. The equity of a particular exaction cannot support it, unless it is made in accordance with law.[1] Neither can the apparent injustice of a particular tax defeat it, when it is demanded under general rules, which the wisdom of the legislature has prescribed for the general good.[2]

To some taxes a particular designation is applied by which they are commonly known and distinguished from other taxes. Thus, the word *duty* has a meaning nearly synonymous with tax, but in ordinary use it means an indirect tax, imposed on the importation, exportation or consumption of goods. As thus employed it has a broader meaning than *custom*, which is a duty imposed on imports or exports.

The term *impost* also signifies any tax, tribute or duty, but it is seldom applied to any but the indirect taxes. An *excise* duty is an inland impost, levied upon articles of manufacture or sale, and also upon licenses to pursue certain trades or to deal in certain commodities. The term *toll*, in its application to the law of taxation, is nearly obsolete. It was formerly applied to duties on imports and exports, but tolls as now understood are confined almost exclusively to charges for permission to pass over a bridge, road or ferry owned by the party imposing them.[3]

The taxing power an incident to sovereignty. The power of taxation is an incident of sovereignty, and is coextensive with that of which it is an incident. All subjects, therefore, over

will from such constituent members of the same community generally as own the same kind of property." *Robertson*, Ch. J., in Lexington *v.* McQuillan's Heirs, 9 Dana, 513, 517.

[1] However equitable it may be, a tax is void unless legally assessed. Joyner *v.* School District, 3 Cush., 567, 572. As when it is demanded contrary to agreement with the state, but to pay debts for which the state is liable for the party taxed. Northern Missouri R. R. Co. *v.* Maguire, 20 Wall., 46.

[2] It is no objection to a tax that the party required to pay it derives no benefit from the particular burden: e. g., a tax for school purposes levied upon a manufacturing corporation. But in truth benefits always flow from the appropriation of public moneys to such purposes, which corporations in common with natural persons receive in the additional security to their property and profits. See Amesbury Nail Factory Co. *v.* Weed, 17 Mass., 52.

[3] See State *v.* Haight, 30 N. J., 447, 448. This case holds that railroad fares are not tolls.

which the sovereign power of the state extends are, in its discretion, legitimate subjects of taxation; and this may be carried to any extent to which the government may choose to carry it.[1] In its very nature it acknowledges no limits, and the only security against abuse must be found in the responsibility of the legislature which imposes the tax to the constituency who are to pay it. The judiciary can afford no redress against oppressive taxation, so long as the legislature, in imposing it, shall keep within the limits of legislative authority.[2] Even a wrongful government, if it main-

[1] *Marshall*, Ch. J., in McCulloch *v.* Maryland, 4 Wheat., 316, 428, 429; Providence Bank *v.* Billings, 4 Pet., 514, 563; Charles River Bridge *v.* Warren Bridge, 11 Pet., 420; Nathan *v.* Louisiana, 8 How., 73; Howell *v.* State, 3 Gill, 14; Atkins *v.* Hinman, 2 Gilm., 437, 449; Cheaney *v.* Hooser, 9 B. Monr., 330, 339; Perkins *v.* Milford, 59 Me., 315; People *v.* Brooklyn, 4 N. Y., 419; Tallman *v.* Butler County, 12 Iowa, 531; Davenport *v.* Railroad Co., 16 Iowa, 348; State *v.* Bell, 1 Phil., N. C., 76, 85; Pullen *v.* Commissioners of Wake County, 66 N. C., 361; Bridge Proprietors *v.* State, 21 N. J., 384, 386; S. C. on appeal, 22 N. J., 593; People *v.* Lawrence, 41 N. Y., 137, 141; Matter of Van Antwerp, 56 N. Y., 261; People *v.* Coleman, 4 Cal., 46; Taylor *v.* Palmer, 31 Cal., 240; State *v.* Commercial Bank, 7 Ohio, 125; Hanna *v.* Allen County, 8 Blackf., 352. "Power to tax is granted for the benefit of the whole people, and none have any right to complain if the power is fairly exercised and the proceeds properly applied to discharge the obligations for which the taxes were imposed. Such a power resides in the state government as part of itself, and needs not to be reserved when property of any description is granted to individuals or corporate bodies." *Clifford*, J., in North Missouri Railroad Co. *v.* Maguire, 20 Wall., 46, 60: "The declaration * * * that, 'no man's property shall be taken or applied to public use without the consent of his representatives, and without just compensation being made,' concedes no new right to the state, but only regulates its exercise. This is a right inseparably connected with sovereign power with or without its recognition by the constitution." *McClure*, J., in Extension of Hancock Street, 18 Penn. St., 26, 30: see Bank of Pennsylvania *v.* Commonwealth, 19 Penn. St., 144. "By all the well settled and acknowledged principles relating to the power of sovereign states, they have the power to tax all persons or property within their jurisdiction." *Poland*, J., in Catlin *v.* Hull, 21 Vt., 152, 161; Blue Jacket *v.* Johnson County, 3 Kans., 299; Hagar *v.* Supervisors of Yolo, 47 Cal., 222; Coite *v.* Society for Savings, 32 Conn., 173.

[2] "The judicial cannot prescribe to the legislative department of the government limitations upon the exercise of its acknowledged powers. The power to tax may be exercised oppressively upon persons, but the responsibility of the legislature is not to the courts but to the people by whom its members are elected. So, if a particular tax bear heavily upon a corporation or class of corporations, it cannot, for that reason only, be declared contrary to the con-

tains order, receives the obedience of the people, and exhibits a capability of supporting itself by force of arms, may lay taxes, though if overthrown before a levy is collected, the whole proceedings must fall to the ground with the authority that instituted them.[1]

Classification of taxes. Taxes are said to be

Direct, under which designation would be included those which are assessed upon the property, person, business, income, etc., of those who are to pay them; and

Indirect, or those which are levied on commodities before they reach the consumer, and are paid by those upon whom they ultimately fall, not as taxes, but as part of the market price of the commodity. Under the second head may be classed the duties upon imports, and the excise and stamp duties levied upon manufactures.[2] The individual states have always derived their principal revenue from direct taxes, and the federal government from those which are indirect,[3] but the power of each to levy taxes of

stitution." Veazie Bank *v.* Fenno, 8 Wall., 533, 548, per *Chase*, Ch. J. See Carroll *v.* Perry, 4 McLean, 25; Weston *v.* Charleston, 2 Pet., 449, 466; Lane County *v.* Oregon, 7 Wall., 71, 77; Coite *v.* Society for Savings, 32 Conn., 173; Kirby *v.* Shaw, 19 Penn. St., 258; Pittsburgh, etc., Railroad Co. *v.* Commonwealth, 66 Penn. St., 73; Hanna *v.* Allen County, 8 Blackf., 352; State *v.* Newark, 26 N. J., 519; Tallman *v.* Butler County, 12 Iowa, 531; State *v.* Stephens, 4 Texas, 137, 139; Gibson *v.* Mason, 5 Nev., 283, 306; Young *v.* Hall, 9 Nev., 212, 224; Williams *v.* Cammack, 27 Miss., 209, 219. "The sovereign right to lay and collect taxes grows out of the paramount necessities of government; an urgent necessity which admits no property in the citizen whilst it remains unsatisfied." *Nisbet*, J., in Parham *v.* Justices of Decatur, 9 Geo., 341, 352.

[1] So held of a government set up in an attempted revolution which failed. O'Byrne *v.* Savannah, 41 Geo., 331.

[2] Wayland's Pol. Econ., b. 4, ch. 2, § 1. See also 1 Kent's Com., 254; Story on Const., § 950-957; 1 Montesq. Spirit of the Laws, b. 13, ch. 7; Tucker's Pol. Econ., ch. 14; Rogers' Pol. Econ., ch. 22. The term "direct taxes" is employed in a peculiar sense in the federal constitution in the provision requiring such taxes to be apportioned according to representation, and they are, perhaps, limited to capitation and land taxes. Hylton *v.* United States, 3 Dall., 171; Pacific Insurance Co. *v.* Soule, 7 Wall., 433; Veazie Bank *v.* Fenno, 8 Wall., 533, 544.

[3] One chief reason for resorting to indirect taxes is that this method enables the government, in the language of Turgot, "to pluck the goose without mak-

both descriptions is only restrained by certain principles of government, and by constitutional provisions which will hereafter be referred to.

Maxims of policy. Writers on political economy lay down certain principles which should govern the imposition of taxes, but these are guides rather to the legislature than to the courts. The author of the "Wealth of Nations," in particular, has enumerated certain maxims, the substance of which may be stated as follows: 1. That the subjects of every state ought to contribute to the support of the government as nearly as possible in proportion to the revenue which they respectively enjoy under its protection. 2. The tax which each is to pay ought, as respects the time and manner of payment, and the sum to be paid, to be certain and not arbitrary. 3. It ought to be levied at the time and in the manner in which it is most likely to be convenient to the contributor to pay it; and 4. It ought to be so contrived as both to take out

ing it cry out," since those who pay do not perceive, or at least do not reflect, that a part of what they pay as price is really paid as a tax. Montesqueiu says: "There are two states in Europe where the imposts are very heavy upon liquors; in one the brewer alone pays the duty, in the other it is levied indiscriminately upon all the consumers; in the first, nobody fee! the rigor of the impost, in the second, it is looked upon as a grievance. In the former, the subject is sensible only of the liberty he has of not paying, in the latter, he feels only the necessity that compels him to pay." Spirit of the Laws, b. 13, ch. 7. The merchants and others who were the customers of Jewish money lenders in lawless times are supposed to have delighted in the plunder of the usurers, though they themselves were compelled to make it good in the additional interest demanded of them to compensate for the risks to which the lenders were exposed. Hallam's Middle Ages, ch. 8, pt. 2.

Indirect taxation may be as just as any other, provided it is justly laid. To make it just, it must reach everything of the class on which it is levied. If it reaches a part only, it must generally be unjust, because, while increasing the price of that portion which is taxed, it enables the producers of or dealers in that portion which is not taxed, to demand a similar price, and thus operates as a bounty to one class of the community at the expense of other classes. This is a perpetual difficulty attending the imposition of duties on imports, when the laws are not strictly enforced; the smuggler either undersells the honest dealer, or, if he sells at the same price, adds the amount of the duties to his own profits, and to that extent has an advantage in the market.

and to keep out of the pockets of the people as little as possible over and above what it brings into the public treasury.[1]

[1] The following are the maxims in Mr. Smith's words:

"I. The subjects of every state ought to contribute to the support of the government as nearly as possible in proportion to their respective abilities; that is, in proportion to the revenue which they respectively enjoy under the protection of the state. The expense of government to the individuals of a great nation is like the expense of management to the joint tenants of a great estate, who are all obliged to contribute in proportion to their respective interests in the estate. In the observation or neglect of this maxim consists what is called the equality or inequality of taxation. Every tax, it must be observed once for all, which falls finally upon one only of the three sorts of revenue above mentioned [rent, profit, wages], is necessarily unequal, in so far as it does not affect the other two. In the following examination of different taxes, I shall seldom take much further notice of this sort of inequality, but shall, in most cases, confine my observations to that inequality which is occasioned by a particular tax falling unequally upon that particular sort of private revenue which is affected by it.

"II. The tax which each individual is bound to pay ought to be certain and not arbitrary. The time of payment, the manner of payment, the quantity to be paid, ought all to be clear and plain to the contributor and to every other person. Where it is otherwise, every person subject to the tax is put more or less in the power of the tax gatherer, who can either aggravate the tax upon any obnoxious contributor, or extort, by the terror of such aggravation, some present or perquisite to himself. The uncertainty of taxation encourages the insolence and favors the corruption of an order of men who are naturally unpopular, even where they are neither insolent nor corrupt. The certainty of what each individual ought to pay is, in taxation, a matter of so great importance, that a very considerable degree of inequality, it appears, I believe, from the experience of all nations, is not near so great an evil as a very small degree of uncertainty.

"III. Every tax ought to be levied at the time or in the manner in which it is most likely to be convenient to the contributor to pay it. A tax upon the rent of lands or of houses, payable at the same term at which such rents are usually paid, is levied at the time when it is most likely to be convenient for the contributor to pay, or when he is most likely to have the wherewithal to pay. Taxes upon such consumable goods as are articles of luxury, are all finally paid by the consumer, and generally in a manner that is very convenient for him. He pays them by little and little, as he has occasion to buy the goods. As he is at liberty, too, either to buy or not to buy, as he pleases, it must be his own fault if he ever suffers any considerable inconvenience from such taxes.

"IV. Every tax ought to be so contrived as both to take out and to keep out of the pockets of the people as little as possible, over and above what it brings into the public treasury of the state. A tax may either take out or keep out of the pockets of the people a great deal more than it brings into the

Of these maxims, the wisdom of which has secured for them universal acceptance,[1] the second embodies a rule of absolute right from which the authorities are not at liberty to depart; the first and third address themselves to the legislature which frames the revenue laws; the fourth also appeals to the legislative wisdom, and is perhaps less observed than either of the others, especially in those states which have never burdened themselves with heavy debts or been tempted into wild and extravagant expenditures. In such states a tendency has been apparent to heavy accumulations of money in the state treasury; accumulations not only unjust to the people whom they deprive of the use of the money taken from them for considerable periods, but especially impolitic, as they tempt those having the custody of them to a use of them in loans — possibly in speculations — which, when not strictly within the law, is always demoralizing and often leads to defalcations. The maxim which is alluded to would justify

public treasury in the four following ways: First. The levying of it may require a great number of officers, whose salaries may eat up the greater part of the produce of the tax, and whose perquisites may impose another additional tax upon the people. Secondly. It may obstruct the industry of the people, and discourage them from applying to certain branches of business which might give maintenance and employment to great multitudes. While it obliges the people to pay, it may thus diminish, or perhaps destroy, some of the funds which might enable them more easily to do so. Thirdly. By the forfeitures and other penalties which those unfortunate individuals incur who attempt unsuccessfully to evade the tax, it may frequently ruin them, and thereby put an end to the benefit which community might have received from the employment of their capital. An injudicious tax offers a great temptation to smuggling; but the penalties of smuggling must arise in proportion to the temptation. The law, contrary to all the ordinary principles of justice, first creates the temptation and then punishes those who yield to it; and it commonly enhances the punishment too in proportion to the very circumstance which ought certainly to alleviate it; the temptation to commit the crime. Fourthly. By subjecting the people to the frequent visits and the odious examination of the tax gatherers, it may expose them to much unnecessary trouble, vexation and oppression; and though vexation is not, strictly speaking, expense, it is certainly equivalent to the expense at which every man would be willing to redeem himself from it. It is in some one or other of these four different ways that taxes are frequently so much more burdensome to the people than they are beneficial to the sovereign." Wealth of Nations, b. 4, ch. 2.

[1] See Mill's Pol. Econ., b. 5, ch. 2, § 2; Tucker's Pol. Econ., ch. 14; Rogers' Pol. Econ., ch. 21.

any state in having its treasury in condition at all times to meet all possible calls upon it, but it would condemn emphatically any exactions from the people in advance of any needs of the government.[1]

All these maxims assume that the taxation is laid for the purpose of obtaining a revenue. Within the definitions given, the burden would not be taxation, if revenue were not the purpose. But in laying taxes other considerations not only are but ought to be kept in view; the question being always not exclusively how a certain sum of money can be collected for public expenditure, but how, when, and upon what subjects it is wise and politic to lay the necessary tax under the existing circumstances, having regard not merely to the replenishing of the public treasury, but to the general benefit and welfare of the political society, and taking notice, therefore, of the manner in which the laying and collection

[1] Provision is made by law in some states that the moneys in the treasury may be deposited in banks at a low specified interest. The rate is so low as to constitute a temptation to bankers to obtain it, and the fact that the office of state treasurer is generally regarded as a prize beyond what the salary would make it, is strong presumptive evidence that that officer expects to make some profit to himself, either by obtaining a bonus from the favored bank that receives the deposits, or by making loans at a higher rate than he would be expected to account for to the state. That such loans are regarded as impolitic is evidenced by the fact that under the statutes of a number of the states, they would constitute criminal embezzlement; but that they are frequently made is commonly believed. Yet it is within the observation of all who have watched the course of public affairs, that legislation has sometimes been so shaped as to increase the already impolitic accumulations in state treasuries, and tax payers have been hastened up in making their payments by the imposition of heavy penalties for delay, when even the ordinary interest exacted from the tax payer would have accorded better with state policy than collecting the money in advance of state needs, in order that it might be deposited in banks at a rate still lower. The impolicy of such legislation has been intensified in some cases by provisions for which it is difficult to account; so unjust are they, and of such doubtful validity. Allusion is here made to laws imposing a penalty, payable to the state, on those who shall redeem their lands from a tax purchase made by an individual; as if the state had an interest in preventing any citizen who, by poverty or other cause, had failed to pay his taxes in season, from saving his estate by a later payment. That these heavy penalties have sometimes prevented redemptions which otherwise would have been made—especially in the case of special taxes, like those for building school houses or constructing drains—is not to be doubted.

of the tax will affect the several interests in the state. And upon this it may be observed that:

1. In the laying of taxes, one purpose had in view may be to encourage one branch of industry or trade, though at the expense of another; as where a tax is laid upon certain fabrics received from abroad by the exchanges of commerce for the sake of encouraging the domestic producer of similar articles, on whose industry the tax operates as a bounty.[1] Such a burden, however, may be so heavy that the market will not warrant its being paid, and in such case, instead of producing revenue it merely prohibits importation. But a law which, under the name of taxation, has for its purpose only to embarrass and perhaps to destroy a certain branch of commerce, if enacted by a state, would look to the general police power for its justification, and if enacted by the general government would seem more properly to derive its force from the authority conferred upon the government to regulate commerce and the intercourse with foreign countries, than to an authority conferred for revenue purposes, which such a law would not aim or tend to subserve.[2]

[1] Tucker's Pol. Econ., ch. 14. Mr. Justice *Story* in his Treatise on the Constitution, § 965, asserts very broadly the power to tax for other purposes than for revenue. He says: "The absolute power to levy taxes includes the power in every form in which it may be used, and for every purpose to which the legislature may choose to apply it. This results from the very nature of such an unrestricted power. *A fortiori*, it might be applied by congress to purposes for which nations have been accustomed to apply it. Now, nothing is more clear from the history of commercial nations, than the fact that the taxing power is often, very often, applied for other purposes than revenue. It is often applied as a regulation of commerce. It is often applied as a virtual prohibition upon the importation of particular articles, for the encouragement and protection of domestic products and industry; for the support of agriculture, commerce and manufactures (Hamilton's Reports on Manufactures in 1791); for retaliation upon foreign monopolies and injurious restrictions (See Mr. Jefferson's Report on Commercial Restrictions, in 1793; 5 Marshall's Life of Washington, ch. 7, pp. 482 to 487; 1 Wait's State Papers, 422, 434); for mere purposes of state policy and domestic economy; sometimes to banish a noxious article of consumption; sometimes as a bounty upon an infant manufacture, or agricultural product; sometimes as a suppression of particular employments; sometimes as a prerogative power to destroy competition and secure a monopoly to the government. (See Smith's Wealth of Nations, b. 5, ch. 2, art. 4.)"

[2] Chief Justice *Marshall* says in McCullough *v.* Maryland, that "the power

2. They may be intended to discourage trades and occupations which may be useful and important when carried on by a few persons under stringent regulations, but exceedingly mischievous when thrown open to the general public and engaged in by many persons. An example is the heavy tax imposed in some states and in some localities of other states on those who engage in the manufacture or sale of intoxicating drinks. Two purposes are generally had in view in imposing such a tax: to limit the business to a few persons, in order to more efficient and perfect regulation, and also to produce a revenue. As no one will pay the tax who does not expect to be reimbursed the expense from the profits of sales, it is obvious that the heavier the tax the fewer can afford to pay it, and it may be made so heavy that no one can afford to pay it, and then it becomes prohibitory. A tax laid for the double purpose of regulation and revenue must be grounded in both the police and the taxing power; but the grant of a power to tax would not authorize the imposition of a burden in its nature and purpose prohibitory.[1]

to tax involves the power to destroy." And again, "if the right to tax exists, it is a right which in its nature acknowledges no limits. It may be carried to any extent within the jurisdiction of the state or corporation which imposes it, which the will of such state or corporation may prescribe." Weston *v.* Charleston, 2 Pet., 449. The learned Chief Justice in these cases was arguing against the existence of the power; and the idea he expresses so forcibly is that the power to tax is so vast, and rests upon reasons which at times are so imperative that it may be exercised again and again, as the exigencies of the state may demand, until the property taxed is exhausted or the privilege taxed can no longer be exercised. This statement has abundant illustrations in history, of people absolutely impoverished by taxation, and even, in individual cases, sold into slavery because they could not meet the demands of the state upon them. It may justly be questioned, whether this strong statement, which was put forth as a defense against an injurious tax, will fairly justify an affirmative exercise of power that has not revenue in view, but is only called a tax in order that it may be employed as an instrument of destruction. In other words, whether the unavoidable incident to the exercise of a power to demand and collect revenue, can lawfully be the inducement to the exercise of the power when revenue is not contemplated or sought.

[1] So held in *Ex parte* Burnett, 30 Ala., 461. The early case of State *v.* Doon, R. M. Charl., 1, affirmed the right to levy a tax of $1,000 on faro tables for the purpose of prohibition, though the payment of the tax would not legalize the use of the tables.

Taxes in kind. Taxes are generally demanded in money, and any tax law will be understood to require money when a different intent is not expressed.[1] But if the condition of any state, in the judgment of its legislature, shall require the collection of taxes in kind — that is to say, by the delivery to the proper officers of a certain proportion of products — or in gold or silver bullion, or in anything different from the legal tender currency of the country, the right to make the requirement is unquestionable, being in conflict with no principle of government, and with no provision of the federal constitution. Instances of taxes in kind occurred in the colonial period,[2] and statutes requiring state taxes to be paid in gold and silver, to the exclusion of legal tender treasury notes, have been fully sustained in several of the states.[3] Labor is sometimes required as a tax, but such requirement has usually been confined to the labor needed to keep the highways in repair, and it is a peculiar tax, to some extent at least in the nature of a police regulation; and the ordinary tax regulations do not embrace a burden of this nature, except as it may be expressly named.[4]

[1] Amenia *v.* Stanford, 6 Johns., 92; Bryan *v.* Sundberg, 5 Tex., 418; Judd *v.* Driver, 1 Kan., 455.

[2] Lane County *v.* Oregon, 7 Wall., 71; Williams's Case, 3 Bland Ch., 186, 255; 2 Rives' Life of Madison, 146. An early tax by the French government in Canada was of a certain proportion of all the beaver skins and moose hides. Parkman's Old Regimé, 302.

[3] Perry *v.* Washburn, 20 Cal., 318, 350; State Treasurer *v.* Wright, 28 Ill., 512; Trenholm *v.* Charleston, 3 S. Car. (N. S.), 347, 349; Whittaker *v.* Haley, 2 Oregon, 128; Lane County *v.* Oregon, 7 Wall., 71. It has been decided that a state cannot compel state script to be received in payment of county, school and district taxes; it not being money, and the creditors of the municipalities not being compellable to receive it in payment. Wells *v.* Cole, 27 Ark., 603.

[4] In Sawyer *v.* Alton, 3 Scam., 127, 130, a provision of the constitution that "the mode of levying a tax shall be by valuation, so that every person shall pay a tax in proportion to the value of the property he or she has in his or her possession," was held not to prevent the levy of a poll tax payable in labor. In Town of Pleasant *v.* Kost, 29 Ill., 490, 494, a highway assessment on property, payable in labor, was held not to be in the proper sense a tax. And see Fox *v.* Rockford, 38 Ill., 451; State *v.* Halifax, 4 Dev., 345. In Overseers of Amenia *v.* Overseers of Stanford, 6 Johns., 92, 93, where the question was whether one who had worked out a highway poll tax had gained a

Taxes not debts. Taxes are not debts in the ordinary sense of that term, and their collection will in general depend on the remedies which are given by statute for their enforcement. Where no remedy is specially provided, a remedy by suit may fairly be implied, but when one is given which does not embrace an action at law, a tax cannot in general be recovered in a common law action as a debt.[1] Taxes are not demands against which a setoff is admissible,[2] their assessment does not constitute a technical judgment, nor are they "contracts between party and party, either express or implied; but they are the positive acts of the

settlement under a statute which made the settlement depend on the payment of a tax, it is said, "Taxes, in the popular and ordinary sense of the term (and in that sense laws are generally to be read), mean pecuniary contributions; and when the word *paid* is added by way of defining it, the sense becomes more clear and certain." It was therefore held that a settlement was not gained by working out a highway assessment. And see Starkesboro *v.* Heinesburgh, 13 Vt., 215. An assessment of four dollars or two days' work on each male resident over 21 and under 60, was held to be a poll tax, and as such forbidden by the constitution of Nevada. Hassett *v.* Walls, 9 Nev., 387.

[1] Ruddock *v.* Gordon, Quincy's Rep., 58; Andover Turnpike *v.* Gould, 6 Mass., 39, 44; Pierce *v.* Boston, 3 Met., 520; Crapo *v.* Stetson, 8 id., 393; Appleton *v.* Hopkins, 5 Gray, 530; Dunlap *v.* Gallatin County, 15 Ill., 7; Dennis *v.* Maynard, id., 477; Camden *v.* Allen, 26 N. J., 398; Webster *v.* Seymour, 8 Vt., 135, 140; Shaw *v.* Pickett, 26 id., 482; Packard *v.* Tisdale, 50 Me., 376; Carondelet *v.* Picott, 38 Mo., 125: Perry *v.* Washburn, 20 Cal., 318; Richards *v.* Stogsdell, 21 Ind., 74; McCall *v.* Lorrimer, 4 Watts, 351; Miller *v.* Hale, 26 Penn. St., 432; Lane County *v.* Oregon, 7 Wall., 71, 80. Compare Durant *v.* Supervisors, 26 Wend., 66. In Baltimore *v.* Howard, 6 H. & J., 383–394, it is said by *Buchanan*, Ch. J., that if an act authorizes a tax but gives no remedy for its collection, assumpsit will lie for its recovery. Other cases recognize the right to maintain an action for taxes, and treat the statute remedy as cumulative merely. See Dugan *v.* Baltimore, 1 Gill & J., 499; in which the court say the imposition and assessment of the tax "created the legal obligation to pay on which the law raised an *assumpsit*," notwithstanding the statute gave a special remedy. And see State *v.* Steamship Co., 13 La. An., 497. It has been decided in Vermont that if a tax be duly assessed against a *feme sole* who afterwards marries, the husband's property, including the personal property acquired by the marriage, is not liable to be distrained for the satisfaction of the tax. Sumner *v.* Pinney, 31 Vt., 717. Taxes do not draw interest as contracts, but only when it is expressly given. Haskell *v.* Bartlett, 31 Cal., 281; Himmelman *v.* Oliver, 34 id., 246.

[2] Trenholm *v.* Charleston, 3 S. Car. (N. S.), 394; McCracken *v.* Elden, 34 Penn. St., 239; Pierce *v.* Boston, 3 Met., 520; Johnson *v.* Howard, 41 Vt., 122; Himmelman *v.* Spanagel, 39 Cal., 389.

government through its various agents, binding upon the inhabitants, and to the making and enforcing of which their personal consent individually is not required."[1] And the law abolishing imprisonment for debt has no application to taxes, the remedy for the collection of which may include an arrest if the legislature shall so provide.[2] The repeal of a tax law before the tax is collected puts an end to the tax itself, where no rights are reserved in the repealing act, and nothing in the act indicates a contrary intent.[3]

Taxation and protection reciprocal. The protection of the government being the consideration for which taxes are demanded, all parties who receive or are entitled to that protection, may be called upon to render the equivalent.[4] The protection may be either to the rights of person, or to rights in property, and taxes may consequently be imposed when either person or property is within the jurisdiction. But a personal tax cannot be assessed against a nonresident,[5] neither can the property of a non-

[1] Pierce *v.* Boston, 3 Met., 520, per *Shaw*, Ch. J.; Perry *v.* Washburn, 20 Cal., 318; Webster *v.* Seymour, 8 Vt., 135, 140; Johnson *v.* Howard, 41 Vt., 122.

[2] Appleton *v.* Hopkins, 5 Gray, 530; Harris *v.* Wood, 6 T. B. Monr., 641.

[3] Howe *v.* Starkweather, 17 Mass., 240; Fenelon's Petition, 7 Penn. St., 173; Augusta *v.* North, 57 Me., 392; Mitchell *v.* Board of Trustees, 71 N. C., 400; Abbott *v.* Britton, 23 La. An., 511; McQuilkin *v.* Doe, 8 Blackf., 581; Mount *v.* State, 6 id., 25; Ross *v.* Lane, 3 S. & M., 695. In Warren R. R. Co. *v.* Belvidere, 35 N. J., 584, it was decided that the tax might still be collected.

[4] The right to tax an individual results from the general protection afforded to himself and his property. Vattel, b. 1, ch. 20. See Eggleston *v.* Charleston, 1 S. Car. Const. Rep., 45; Bank of U. S. *v.* State, 12 S. & M., 456; De Pauw *v.* New Albany, 22 Ind., 204.

One who is not taxed is just as much entitled to the protection of government as one who is. Every resident of the state, and every owner of property therein is liable to taxation, and it is this liability that entitles him to protection, and not the fact that he is actually taxed. Some persons are never taxed, because they do not come within any of the rules which the state has prescribed for the apportionment of its burdens. But the state prescribes these rules in the discretion of its legislature; and it prescribes them in contemplation of its obligation to give impartial protection to all persons. If one in his person, business or property comes within these rules, he must pay the tax; if he does not, he is guilty of no neglect of duty, and chargeable with no fault for not paying one. Youngblood *v.* Sexton, Sup. Ct. Mich., Oct. Term, 1875.

[5] Dow *v.* Sudbury, 5 Met., 73; Herriman *v.* Stowers, 43 Me., 497; People *v.* Supervisors of Chenango, 11 N. Y., 563; St. Paul *v.* Merritt, 7 Minn., 258.

resident be taxed unless it has an actual *situs* within the state, so as to be under the protection of its laws.[1] The mere right of a foreign creditor, to receive from his debtor within the state the payment of his demand, cannot be subjected to taxation within the state. "It is a right that is personal to the creditor where he resides, and the residence or place of business of his debtor is immaterial. The power of taxation, however vast in its character, and searching in its extent, is necessarily limited to subjects within the jurisdiction of the state. These subjects are persons, property and business. Whatever form taxation may assume, whether as duties, imposts, excises or licenses, it must relate to one of these subjects. It is not possible to conceive of any other, though as applied to them, the taxation may be exercised in a great variety of ways. It may touch property in every shape, in its natural condition, in its manufactured form, and in its various transmutations. And the amount of the taxation may be determined by the value of the property, or its use, or its capacity, or its productiveness. It may touch business in the almost infinite forms in which it is conducted, in professions, in commerce, in manufactures, and in transportation. Unless restrained by provisions of the federal constitution, the power of the state as to the mode, form and extent of taxation is unlimited, where the subjects to which it applies are within her jurisdiction."[2] These are conceded or adjudged principles, and have ceased to be the subject of discussion or argument. Corporations, it is also conceded, may be taxed like natural persons on their property and business. But debts owing to foreign creditors by either corporations or individuals, are not the subject of taxation. The creditor cannot be taxed, because he is not within the jurisdiction, and the debts cannot be taxed in the debtors' hands, through any fiction of the law which is to treat them as being, for this purpose, the property of the debtors. They are not property of the debtors in any sense; they are the obligations of the debtors, and only possess value in the

[1] That personalty may be taxed where it is, though the owner is a nonresident; see ch. III. Personal allegiance has no necessary connection with the right of taxation. An alien may be taxed as well as a citizen. See Witherspoon *v.* Duncan, 4 Wall., 210.

[2] State Tax on Foreign Held Bonds, 15 Wall., 300, 319. See Oliver *v.* Washington Mills, 11 Allen, 265.

hands of the creditors. With them they are property, "but to call them property in the hands of the debtors is simply to misuse terms."[1] Shares in a corporation are also the shares of the stockholder wherever he may have his domicile, and if taxed to him as his personal estate, can only be so taxed by the jurisdiction to which his person is subject, whether the corporation be foreign or domestic.[2]

If it were practicable to do so, the taxes levied by any government ought to be apportioned among the people according to the benefit which each receives from the protection the government affords him; but this is manifestly impossible. The value of life and liberty, and of the social and family rights and privileges cannot be measured by any pecuniary standard;[3] and by the general consent of civilized nations, income or the sources of income are almost universally made the basis upon which the ordinary taxes

[1] Case of State Tax on Foreign Held Bonds, 15 Wall., 300, 319, 320, per *Field*, J., overruling several Pennsylvania cases. See also Hayne *v.* Deliesseline, 3 McCord, 374; Oliver *v.* Washington Mills, 11 Allen, 268.

[2] Great Barrington *v.* County Commissioners, 16 Pick., 572; Newark City Bank *v.* The Assessor, 30 N. J., 13; State *v.* Branin, 23 N. J., 484; State *v.* Bentley, 23 id., 532; Whitsell *v.* Northampton County, 49 Penn. St., 526; *post* ch. III. This statement must, however, be subject to the qualification that a foreign corporation must always accept the privilege of transacting business in a state, on such terms as the state may see fit to exact.

[3] Mr. Thorold Rogers says, in his Treatise on Political Economy, that if taxation were determined by the comparative protection accorded to individuals, women and children should pay a higher rate than strong and healthy adults, since they have more need of assistance; and, if the law be effectual, get more. And this, he shows, was in fact the theory of medieval (feudal) finance. "The lord protected his vassal, the vassal assisted his lord by his service or by his purse. But minors under the English military tenures, and women under some forms of the military assize, were in the hands of guardians, who were enabled to take the rents or profits of their estates, without account, during legal incapacity. The reason given was that there was no reciprocity of service in these cases, and the plea might be justified, because, in an age of violence, weakness taxes the energies of defense more than it excites the sentiment of pity. A more generous and less utilitarian theory has gradually prevailed. It is held that for practical purposes, and under the conditions of organized society, the strongest is too much indebted to the security which a wise and just government gives, to allow any such comparison between his condition and the condition of the weakest, as shall tend to lay a heavier impost on the latter." Ch. 21. See also Mill, Pol. Econ., b. v. ch. 2, § 3.

are estimated. This is upon the assumption, never wholly true in point of fact, but sufficiently near the truth for the practical operations of government, that the benefit received from the government is in proportion to the property held, or the revenue enjoyed under its protection;[1] and though this can never be arrived at with accuracy, through the operation of any general rule, and would not be wholly just if it could be, experience has given us no better standard, and it is applied in a great variety of forms, and with more or less approximation to justice and equality. But, as before stated, other considerations are always admissible; what is aimed at is, not taxes strictly just, but such taxes as will best subserve the general welfare of the political society.[2]

[1] "The idea of property consists in an established expectation, in the persuasion of being able to draw such or such an advantage from the thing possessed, according to the nature of the case. Now this expectation, this persuasion can only be the work of the law. I cannot count upon the enjoyment of that which I regard as mine, except through the promise of the law which guaranties it to me. It is law alone which permits me to forget my natural weakness. It is only through the protection of the law that I am able to inclose a field, and to give myself up to its cultivation with the sure though distant hope of harvest." * * "Property and law are born together and die together. Before laws were made there was no property; take away laws and property ceases." Bentham, Theory of Legislation. Works, Edinb. ed., vol. I, p. 308. And speaking of the right to property, he justly adds: "It is that right which has vanquished the natural aversion to labor; which has given to man the empire of the earth; which has brought to an end the migratory life of nations; which has produced the love of country and a regard for posterity." See Wayland, Pol. Econ., b. 4, ch. 3, § 1; Rogers' Pol. Econ., ch. 21.

[2] An early Maryland law recited that, "fines, duties or taxes may properly and justly be imposed or laid with a political view for the good government and benefit of the community." Upon this Chancellor *Bland* comments as follows: "A citizen may have a fine imposed upon him as a punishment for his misdemeanor or crime; a duty may be imposed as a means of insuring good conduct, and in aid of the police, as in the form of a duty for a license to keep a tavern, to retail spirituous liquors, to keep a billiard table, etc.; a treble tax may be imposed with a political view, as upon non-jurors during a war, etc." Williams's Case, 3 Bland Ch., 186, 257. In the same case the learned Chancellor refers to statutes of the colony which taxed bachelors as such. This was not because they had more to be protected by the government than other persons, but probably from a variety of reasons, one of the most influential being that presumptively, they were better able to bear the burdens of government, than men with families dependent upon them, or unmarried females whose income would commonly be less.

The taxes governments have been accustomed to lay. In modern times, governments have been accustomed to levy a great variety of taxes; sometimes relying upon a single kind for all the needs of the state, and sometimes levying a number of different kinds with a view to distribute the burden more equally or more to the general acceptance. None of these can invariably operate justly, but all have advantages that may make one desirable under one set of circumstances, and another the best when circumstances have changed. Those which have been most common will be briefly referred to.

Capitation Taxes. These are not a common resort in modern times,[1] and only in a few cases could they be either just or politic. As they regard only the person, they must be shared equally by all, except under governments where privileged orders are recognized, and where they might be graded according to the orders to which the several persons taxed belong. If the tax is graded by property, it is obviously something besides a capitation tax.

Land Taxes. These may be measured by the production, by the rent, or by the value. The first method has seldom been resorted to in enlightened periods.[2] To some extent it would operate as a discouragement to industry; and, while it might not be burdensome to the cultivators of very productive estates, it might preclude poor lands, whose production would barely pay for cultivation, from being cultivated at all; in other words, would be equal to the whole rental value. A tax, measured by rents, will usually come nearer to being a tax on the actual revenue of the land proprietor; and this standard is more common. A variety of land taxes, under different names, has been levied in Eng-

[1] The taxes assessed by this name have not always been taxes levied on persons, but sometimes taxes exacted from districts or provinces, and measured by the *capita*. Such were the capitation taxes levied under the Roman Empire, in apportioning which among individuals, one might represent several *capita*, according to his wealth in land, while others escaped the tax entirely. Gibbon's Decline and Fall, ch. 17.

[2] It was made use of under the Roman Empire. Gibbon's Decline and Fall, ch. 17. It has been occasionally employed in recent times. Tithes for the support of the Established Church in England were so measured.

land, merging at last in a general land tax, measured by rent, and apportioned to the municipal divisions. As, however, this tax is based upon valuations made in the fourth year of William and Mary (1692), it is extremely unequal, and perhaps only continues to be acquiesced in because a very small portion only of the whole revenue is raised by it.[1] In this country, land taxes are commonly laid by value. This is subject to some objections. In order to insure equality, it is necessary, in a new and rapidly improving country, that there should be frequent valuations, and this requires a great official force, and involves heavy expense. The apportionment of this expense among towns or other small divisions of territory, the people of which are allowed to choose the officers, reconciles them to the burden, and, in many of the states, a new valuation is made annually.[2] An objection, theoretically more serious, is, that a tax by assessed value is often (where the land is poor and unproductive; or where it is wild and uncultivated) a tax which is paid from capital instead of from revenue. A tax to be thus paid cannot long continue, and is seldom to be purposely laid; but, in particular instances, almost any tax will be such. And in this country, where a considerable portion of the community invest in lands with a view to profit from the rise in value, unproductive and uncultivated lands cannot be exempted from taxation because of the hardships of individual cases, without exempting a large portion of the wealth of the state now legitimately invested where it is insuring large profits to the owner.

Taxes on Houses. These, except where the houses are treated as appurtenances to the lands, have been measured by rents, and

[1] 1 Bl. Com., 307; 1 Broom & Hadley's Com., 368, 372.

[2] In the light of the experience we have of the American system, it is interesting to note what is said by Adam Smith: "A land tax assessed accordding to a general survey and valuation, how equal soever it may be at first, must, in the course of a very moderate period of time, become unequal. To prevent its becoming so would require the continual and painful attention of government to all the variations in the state and produce of every different farm in the country," * * "an attention so unsuitable to the nature of government, that it is not likely to be of long continuance, and which, if it is continued, will probably, in the long run, occasion much more trouble and vexation than it can possibly bring relief to the contributors." Wealth of Nations, b. v, ch. 2, pt. 2.

sometimes by hearths and windows. A hearth tax was obnoxious, because, among other reasons, it involved inquisitorial visits of officers to inspect rooms; and both hearth and window taxes tended to limit among the poor the use of these conveniences, so important not only to comfort, but to health. Both are now abolished in England.

Taxes on Income. These may be on all incomes, or on all with such exemption as will enable the tax payer in a frugal manner to support himself and his family. The latter is the course usually adopted, and in some cases incomes in excess of the exemption have been taxed a larger percentage as they increased in amount. The reasons which favor this discrimination would also justify a heavier proportionate tax on the thrifty classes in other cases; and the principle once admitted there is no reason but its own discretion why the legislature should stop short of imposing the whole burden of government on the few who exhibit most energy, enterprise and thrift. Such a discrimination is a penalty on the possession of these qualities. But any income tax is also objectionable, because it is inquisitorial, and because it teaches the people evasion and fraud. No means at the command of the government has ever enabled it to arrive with anything like accuracy at the incomes of its citizens, and they resist its inquisitions in all practical modes, not only because they desire to avoid as far as possible the public burdens which they are certain are not to be equally imposed, but also because they are not willing that their private affairs and the measure of their prosperity should be exposed to the public.[1] The taxes imposed on incomes by the United States during and immediately following the late war were escaped by a large proportion of those who should have paid them, and the assessors' returns were a wholly inadequate indication of the annual private revenue of the country. In the United States, also, such a tax is unequal because those holding lands for the rise in value escape it altogether — at least until they sell, though their actual increase in wealth may be great and sure.

Taxes on Employments. A tax on the privilege of carrying on

[1] Gibbon refers to torture employed under the Empire to ascertain the profits of employments. See Decline and Fall, ch. 17. Its employment upon the Jews in England is a familiar fact in history.

a business or employment will commonly be imposed in the form of an excise tax on the license to pursue the employment; and this may be a specific sum, or a sum whose amount is regulated by the business done or income or profits earned. Sometimes small license fees are required, mainly for the purpose of regulation, but in other cases substantial taxes are demanded because the persons upon whom they are laid would otherwise escape taxation in the main, if not entirely. Instances of hawkers, peddlers, auctioneers, etc. will readily occur to the mind. The form of a license, though not a necessary, is a convenient form for such a tax to assume, because it then becomes a condition to entering upon the business or employment, and is collected without difficulty. But it is equally competent to impose and collect the tax by the usual methods.[1]

Taxes on the Carriage of Property. There are various methods of imposing these; as by licensing the business, by taxing the vehicles employed, by tonnage duties, etc. As to tonnage duties, the powers of the states are restricted as is elsewhere shown.

Taxes on the Wages of Labor. These, in a country where wages are only sufficient to supply the absolute needs of life, would necessarily fall on the employer; but when the accumulations of labor are relied upon for a competency and even for wealth, the burden might be more felt by the laborer. In modern times such taxes have been unusual.

Taxes on Servants, Horses, Dogs, Carriages, etc. These are intended as taxes on luxury and ostentation, and can seldom prove

[1] In Ould *v.* Richmond, 23 Grat., 464, 468, a city tax on lawyers was contested for the reason, among others, that the persons taxed held a *license* from the state to practice law, and the municipal tax went to nullify it. *Anderson*, J., says: "Whilst a lawyer's license authorizes him to practice law in any court of the commonwealth, and it is not in the power of any municipality to deprive him of that right, or to take away his license, it is a civil right and privilege to which are attached valuable immunities and pecuniary advantages, and is a fair subject of taxation by the state, or by a municipal corporation where he resides and enjoys the privilege. It is a vested civil right; yet it is as properly a subject of taxation as property to which a man has a vested right. I cannot perceive that there would not be as much reason for saying that a man's property is not taxable, because he has a vested right to it, as for saying that a lawyer's license is not taxable because he has a vested right to it." And see Youngblood *v.* Sexton, Mich. Sup. Ct., Oct. 1875.

burdensome. Each person assesses himself in determining how many he will employ or own. The same may be said of taxes on plate and articles of display, when taxed directly.

Taxes on the Interest of Money. These are objectionable for the same reasons that apply to income taxes. They lead to the same evasions, and to some others which it is impossible to check or circumvent. They are seldom levied *eo nomine.*

Taxes on Dividends are more easily collected and do not usually involve inquisitorial proceedings. Dividends come from corporations whose proceedings are usually semi-public, and while the privacy of individuals is not invaded, neither are the demands of the government liable to serious evasions. This is a common method of raising revenue.

Taxes on Legacies and Inheritances.[1] These are laid in diminution of a new capital which now comes to the hands of parties on the death of former owners; and in theory they should not be burdensome. In fact, however, except when they are upon gifts by will to others than the immediate family, or are on collateral inheritances, they are likely to be felt severely. The property held by the head of the family, is usually, for all purposes of supplying comforts and enjoyments, the property of all the family; and a tax upon their succession to it on his death, comes in a time of unusual necessary disbursements to increase the embarrassments and burdens which accompany the loss of their main reliance and support. Sometimes these taxes are levied on testamentary gifts and collateral successions only.

Taxes on Sales, Bills of Exchange, etc. These when laid on the instruments by means of which business is transacted, and imposed in the form of stamp duties, have the high recommendation

[1] In Eyre *v.* Jacobs, 14 Grat., 422, a tax on collateral inheritances was objected to as opposed to the requirement that taxation of property should be uniform. But the tax was sustained as not being a tax on property, but on the privilege of succeeding to the inheritance. The tax is spoken of in the case by *Lee*, J., as one of great antiquity, imposed upon the Romans as early as the days of the Emperor Augustus, and often in early times by nations of Europe, as well as in modern times. See also Williams's Case, 3 Bland. Ch., 186, 259. A similar objection to such a tax in Tyson *v.* State, 28 Md., 577, was also overruled.

that the cost of collection is but a small percentage of the sum realized, and few evasions of payment are practicable. They are besides paid in small sums, as business transactions take place from time to time, and are therefore not much felt. Indeed on many accounts they are the least objectionable taxes that can be levied; and the repeal of the most of those which were levied by federal authority in this country is probably due to the strong interest in favor of taxation calculated to aid particular branches of trade.

Taxes on Newspapers. These would be likely to be imposed in the form of stamp taxes. The objections are very obvious, and were thought to be conclusive in this country even when the need of revenue was the greatest.

Taxes on Legal Process. These are usually imposed with a view to adjusting, on an equitable basis, as between suitors and the public, the expenses of the administration of justice. They may be imposed as stamp fees on process, fees for permission to enter a suit, etc.[1]

Taxes on Consumable Luxuries. Articles like spirituous and malt liquors, tobacco, etc., are generally subjected to heavy taxation as constituting mere luxuries, so that however severe may be

[1] There are express constitutional provisions for such taxation in Georgia, Nebraska, Nevada and Wisconsin. That they may be laid without any such express authority, see Harrison *v.* Willis, 7 Heiskell, 35. The right is easier defended than the policy, as the tax, if heavy, may in some cases be equivalent to a denial of justice. The heaviest taxes of this description have been those indirectly imposed in the form of fees to judicial officers. For several centuries such fees in England constituted the principal compensation of the judges: the regular salaries even of those of the highest courts being insignificant. Adam Smith found an advantage in this, for he says it happened that each of the superior courts of Westminster "endeavored by superior dispatch and impartiality, to draw to itself as many causes as it could. The present admirable constitution of the courts of England was perhaps originally in a great measure formed by this emulation, which anciently took place between their respective judges, each judge endeavoring to give in his own court the speediest and most effectual remedy which the law would admit for every sort of injustice." Wealth of Nations, b. v, ch. 1, pt. 2. These insignificant salaries continued until the 17th century. At times in this country an idea has prevailed that the courts should be made self-supporting; and in the case of the justices' courts this is now the general rule, at least as regards their civil jurisdiction.

the tax, it will never, of necessity, prove burdensome to the needy classes. The taxes are laid in various forms; on the importation, the manufacture, and the sale. In the United States the inclination of late has been to make the tax on spirituous liquors as heavy as can be collected; but experience demonstrates that a point may be reached where any accession to the tax, by increasing the temptations to fraud and evasion, will tend to lessen the amount collected. Indeed the same may be said of all taxes; the higher they are, the more numerous will be the frauds, perjuries, betrayals of official trust, and evasions of public duty; and when they reach a point where the chances of profit by clandestine manufacture or importation are in excess of the chances of loss by detection, added to the tax, the revenue will be certain to fall off very rapidly even though consumption is not diminished. It has recently been proved by the experience of the federal excise laws that a tax of fifty cents a gallon on spirits may be more productive than one of four times that amount. Great Britain at one time had a similar experience with taxes on tea.

Taxes on Exports. These, if the articles exported are a necessity to foreign countries, tend to transfer to such countries a part of the burden of supporting our own government. If not a necessity, they diminish exportation and production. In either case they will usually be impolitic; in the latter, almost certainly, and in the former by inviting retaliatory legislation by the countries affected. In this country the states cannot levy export duties, without the consent of congress, except for the purposes of inspection,[1] and congress is also probibited to lay any tax or duty on articles exported from any state.[2]

Taxes on Imports. These have generally been the chief reliance of the federal government for its revenue. They have been laid on almost every conceivable article of use, taste or ornament, and upon almost every possible theory and principle. Some tariff laws have perhaps been framed with a view to the just distribution of the burden, and for revenue purposes only; others, while having revenue mainly in view, have laid heavier duties on arti-

[1] Const. U. S., art. I, § x.

[2] Const. U. S., art. I, § ix.

cles which would come in competition with home manufactures, while others, in some of their duties, have discarded the idea of revenue entirely, and looked solely to protection. We have thus had revenue tariffs, protective tariffs, and revenue tariffs with incidental protection. All have discriminated more or less against articles of mere luxury, but articles of prime necessity have, under some, been taxed very heavily, on the supposition that the burden imposed would be more than made up to those who shared it, by the incidental advantages they would receive from the building up of manufactures at home. Whether the result has answered expectation is a question foreign to the purpose of the present work.

Taxes on Corporate Franchises. These have been a source of large revenue in some states, while others have only placed corporations on the same footing with individuals, and taxed them on their property, or imposed some specific tax intended as an equivalent for a property tax. A tax on a corporate franchise may or may not be just or politic. If the business is one of which corporations have a monopoly, a tax on their franchises, however heavy, would not be burdensome, because the result would only be to add to the cost of whatever the corporations supplied to the public, so that the tax would really be paid by the community at large. If on the other hand, the business is one open to free competition between corporations and individuals, and in respect to which corporations would enjoy no especial privileges or advantages, a tax upon the privilege of conducting the business under a corporate organization would be wholly unreasonable and unjust, because it would give individuals and partnerships an advantage in the competition; and their competition, keeping down prices, would prevent corporations from indirectly collecting any portion of the tax from the public, and leave them to bear the whole burden of a demand which, under such circumstances, must prove ruinous. While, therefore, a tax on the corporate franchises of banks of issue, which are not subject to competition, might be entirely just, one on the corporate organization of a trading company, with which every individual might compete, would usually be wholly unjust, and if continued, must result in the abandonment of a business which, under such circumstances, would be carried on at a ruinous disadvantage.

Taxes on the Value of Property. These have been the main reliance of the states. A common method of raising revenue has been to levy annual taxes on the value of all the real and personal property of the inhabitants, with limited exceptions, and irrespective of the income which, by means of the property, is or may be realized. This seems at first view to be just, and in the belief that it is just, it has been steadfastly adhered to notwithstanding the many and very serious difficulties attending it. These difficulties pertain, for the most part, to the taxation of personal property, which is subject to the following very important objections:

1. It cannot be assessed without inquisitorial process of some kind, instituted for the purpose of ascertaining that which is not open to public inspection, and which the individual, except under the compulsion of such process, would not consent to disclose.[1] Few persons will voluntarily make a complete exhibit of

[1] The reader will find valuable information on this score in the accounts which the current histories of England give of taxation in that country under the house of Plantagenet. A very interesting account of taxation under Edward I is found in Audrey's National and Domestic History of England, b. 6, ch. 18. The assessment and valuation of articles was so minute and particular as to give us no small insight into the domestic life of that day, and into the extent of the comforts and conveniences enjoyed by different classes of society. Lingard, in his History of England, b. 4, ch. 2, has the following which relates to taxation under Edward III:

"The most ancient method of raising a supply was by a talliage on movable property, varying, according to circumstances, from a fiftieth to a seventh, and descending from the highest classes down to the villeins; and it is interesting to observe how rapidly the art of taxation improved in every succeeding reign.

"Under John, each individual was permitted to swear to the value of his own property, and the bailiffs of prelates, earls and barons swore in the place of their lords. The oaths were received by the itinerant justices who, for that purpose, proceeded regularly from hundred to hundred; and, according to the returns of the justices, the tax in its due proportion was levied by the sheriffs.

"By Henry III, every man was compelled to swear, not only to the amount of his own movables, but to that of the movables belonging to his two next neighbors; and, if the accuracy of his statement was disputed, the truth was inquired into by a jury of twelve good men of the county. The commissioners were not the justices, but four knights appointed by the justices; and they were instructed to inquire into the value of every species of personalty, with the exception of church ornaments, books, horses, arms, gold, silver, jewels, furniture, the contents of the cellar and larder, and hay and forage for private use.

their affairs to the public, and still fewer, perhaps, have their affairs in such shape that public officers can make an inventory of their personal possessions, including property in the hands of others or at a distance, and debts owing to them, without the assistance of the owners in preparing it. Statutes have recognized this difficulty, and provided for a list to be presented by the tax payer under oath, or allowed the assessor to tax every person according to his own judgment, leaving the person taxed to reduce the amount by his own oath if he shall see fit, and be able to do so. This is objectionable, not only as taking away a desirable privacy in business and family concerns, but also as holding out a strong temptation to false swearing in matters where a false oath would be difficult if not impossible of detection.[1]

"Under the Edwards, the commissioners were appointed immediately by the crown. They called before them the principal inhabitants of each township, and bound four, six or more of them, by oath, to inquire into the value of the movables possessed by each householder on the day mentioned in the act, which was generally the feast of St. Michael. By movables, they were to understand not only corn, cattle and merchandise, but money, fuel, furniture and wearing apparel; and, if any such articles had been sold, removed or destroyed since the day specified, they were yet to include them within the amount. The exceptions allowed were few. The knights and esquires did not return their armor, horses or equipments, their plate of gold, silver or brass, their clothes or jewels, or those which belonged to their wives; and persons of inferior rank were exempted from payment for one suit of clothes for the husband and another for the wife, one bed, one ring, a clasp of gold or silver, a silk sash or girdle for daily use, and a cup of silver or porcelain. It is evident that, in these inquiries, as the temptation was great, so also were the means of concealment. But the ingenuity of the commissioners kept pace with the artfulness of the defaulters. Each year new regulations were issued from the exchequer, and, sometimes within a short period, the amount of tax from the same township was nearly doubled. This growing evil occasioned numerous remonstrances. The people complained that the collectors entered their houses and searched every apartment; that they defrauded the king, and that they received bribes to spare some, while at the same time, through pique and resentment, they aggrieved others."

[1] This difficulty has always existed. Latimer, in his sermon at Stamford, in the time of Henry VIII, inveighs against it in this language: "When the parliament, the high court of this realm, is gathered together, and there it is determined that every man shall pay a fifteenth part of his goods to the king then commissioners come forth, and he that in sight of men, in his cattle, corn, sheep and other goods, is worth an hundred marks or an hundred pound, will set himself at ten pound; he will be worth to the king but after ten pound. Tell me, now, whether this be theft or no?"

2. The assessment of personalty holds out constant and very powerful temptations to defraud the state by concealing the knowledge of every thing which the tax payer believes cannot easily be discovered. This is so well understood that it is scarcely expected that citizens will voluntarily state what they possess, or that officers will make much if any effort to discover. Indeed, the assessment of personal property reaches so small a proportion of the amount really protected by government, that it might almost be said that laws for the purpose remain on the statute books rather as incentives to evasion and fraud in the dealings of the citizen with the state than as a means of realizing a revenue for public purposes.

3. Such taxes are usually unjust in their discrimination between residents and nonresidents who enjoy the same protection of the laws. This will be manifest from an illustration: If money is loaned at ten per centum, and the tax upon credits is one per centum of the capital, the resident capitalist may count upon an income of nine per centum upon his investments. But the nonresident who could not be taxed in the state upon his loans which are made there and protected and enforced by its laws, would, upon the like investment, count upon ten per centum; and this difference would not only be a serious discrimination against the citizen, but it would, and does, encourage further evasions and frauds, and particularly the loaning of moneys in the names of nonresidents in order to escape taxation. It also presents an inducement to citizens, whose investments do not require personal attention, to take up their residence abroad; any saving of the tax being equivalent to an addition of that amount to their incomes.

4. Taxation of personalty leads to duplicate taxation in various ways. Other taxes besides those by valuation reach such property, being laid in the shape of duties, excise and license fees, etc.; and, moreover, when property is moved from one jurisdiction into another, where the time fixed for assessment is different, it may for that reason be twice assessed for a tax on valuation for the same period of time.

5. Such taxation requires a large addition to the force of revenue officers which otherwise would be sufficient, and it renders necessary more frequent assessments than would be requisite

were taxation confined to that property, or those subjects which are more permanent in characteristics and ownership. To make it just, it is generally thought necessary that the tax payer's debts should be deducted; and this complicates the difficulty of ascertaining what his estate is, and leaves every man, in effect, to make his own assessment, or subjects him to the arbitrary and capricious action of the assessors.[1] These are objections which every one feels and appreciates; others, which are more obscure, need not be mentioned. A tax on land is not open to these objections. Whenever the law seeks to tax land and personalty with equality, the general result is, that land pays much the greater proportion of the tax, because this can all be reached, and all be taxed; no inquisitorial proceedings are required to discover it, and no frauds or evasions can conceal it from view. These and other reasons have led some political economists to advocate the omission of personalty from the customary taxation by value, and the raising of the ordinary state revenue by a tax laid exclusively on land and a few other subjects which, like land, are open to constant public observation and inspection, and in respect to which neither would harsh sifting processes be required, nor evasions be practicable, nor frauds invited. Such a tax, it is claimed, while nominally falling upon a few, would in fact be diffused through the whole community, and collected from all by being added to the price of what is produced and distributed by the classes taxed, just as we have found that a tax upon any common article of consumption is paid in the end by the consumer, and is no more burdensome to the dealer who nominally pays it than it is to any other member of the community of consumers. Adam Smith declared, that "no tax can ever reduce for any considerable time the rate of profit in any particular trade, which must always keep its level with other trades in its neighbor-

[1] Many statutes leave the assessors to estimate the personal estate, but allow the tax payer to reduce an excessive valuation by a statement under oath. Under the almost universal custom of valuing property at from one-fourth to one-third its estimated value, this privilege to the tax payer becomes of no avail. A man having an estate of $30,000, may be taxed upon that sum, and be without redress, because he cannot make oath that he is not worth so much, when if the general valuation is at one-third only, he should be taxed on but $10,000.

hood."[1] And, indeed, in this country, during and after the great civil war of 1861–5, it was generally found that a heavy tax upon any particular article of consumption gave the business that produced it a new and vigorous impulse of prosperity.[2]

Taxes on Amusements. These constitute a very considerable source of income to the cities and villages of the country, and sometimes to the state itself. When the amusements are of a public nature, like theatrical and other exhibitions and shows, concerts, games of skill or chance, publicly performed, whether for profit or otherwise, races, etc., they seem to be as proper subjects of taxation as property or ordinary business. In fact such a tax is in the nature of a tax on luxuries, and therefore as unobjectionable as a tax can well be. The limit to the right to tax amusements, if any exists, has never been judicially pointed out, but when the public are invited to share them, the right must be clear. On the other hand it would seem that strictly private and family amusements ought to be considered wholly exempt, except possibly when they involve such expense as to be beyond the enjoyment of the people generally, and for that reason to be properly taxable as luxuries.

The foregoing by no means embraces all the subjects of taxation; some others will be referred to as we proceed, but the enumeration here made may be sufficient for our present purposes. Even marriages have sometimes been taxed; though as a rule the

[1] Wealth of Nations, b. v, ch. 11, p. 11, art. 4.

[2] Mr. David A. Wells has treated this general subject with ability in many publications. A pamphlet embodying the remarks of Mr. Isaac Sherman before the N. Y. Assembly committee of Ways and Means, October, 1874, is exceedingly instructive and valuable. It is highly probable that if personalty were wholly exempted from taxation by value, the burden of state taxes would be no more unequal than now, and that the general tone of public morality, on the score of taxation, escaping the schooling in evasions which is now had, would be higher. In our enumeration of taxes, we have not included charges for postage. These, though called taxes abroad, are in this country looked upon rather as reasonable charges for a branch of transportation which the government undertakes. They are not burdens upon the people, because they regularly fall below the cost.

fees imposed in the case of marriages have been only such as were supposed sufficient to cover the cost of proper regulations.[1]

[1] In the British internal revenue law in force near the close of the great wars with Bonaparte, marriage licenses were taxed ten shillings if ordinary and five pounds if special. The marriage certificate was also taxed five shillings. That law was very carefully prepared, with a view to producing as much revenue as possible without serious hardships. The discriminations against luxuries were properly very considerable. Thus, the keeper of one pleasure horse was taxed 2*l.* 17*s.* 6*d.*, but for two he was charged 9*l.* 4*s.*, and for every additional horse 6*l.* more or thereabouts. One carriage with four wheels was taxed 12*l.*, and two 26*l.* For one male servant the tax was 2*l.* 8*s.*, for ten it was 62*l.* No tax was charged on incomes less than 50*l.*; from that to 150*l.* a gradually increasing tax was imposed, and incomes above 150*l.* paid ten per cent. Occupations and legal instruments were specially taxed; the taxes on indentures of apprenticeship ranged from 15*s.* up to 50*l.*, and articles of clerkship in the office of an attorney or solicitor in the higher courts were taxed 120*l.* The window tax was 6*s.* 6*d.* on a house with six windows and 34*l.* 10s. on one with fifty.

CHAPTER II.

THE NATURE OF THE POWER TO TAX.

In the creation of three distinct departments of the government, and the apportionment of power between them, the authority to tax necessarily falls to the legislative. This is manifest from the slightest consideration of what taxation is. It is the making of rules and regulations under which the necessary revenues for all the needs of government are to be apportioned among the people and collected from them. While the principles of the British constitution remained unsettled and in dispute, the authority to lay and collect taxes was claimed for the executive, but only as a branch of the supreme authority, which was his by divine right, to rule at discretion.[1] When this arrogant claim was repudiated and abandoned, it became one of the most inflexible principles of government that the executive could levy no taxes whatsoever except in the execution of laws that had been made for his observance. Indeed, the principle goes farther than this. It is, that taxes are a *grant* of the people who are taxed, and the grant must be made by the immediate representatives of the people. All revenue laws in Great Britain must, therefore, originate with the popular house of parliament; a body very tenacious of its privileges, and disposed to class as revenue laws whatever will, even indirectly, bring revenue to the state.[2] Following this pre-

[1] "This power," said the attorney general in Hampden's Case, "is innate in the person of an absolute king, and in the person of the kings of England. All magistracy, it is of nature ; and obedience and subjection, it is of nature. This power is not any way derived from the people, but reserved unto the king when positive laws first began. For the king of England, he is an absolute monarch; nothing can be given to an absolute prince but what is inherent in his person. He can do no wrong. He is the sole judge, and we ought not to question him. Where the law trusts, we ought not to distrust." Hallam's Const. Hist., ch. 7; 3 State Trials, 826; Broom's Const. L., 306, and notes.

[2] 4 Inst., 29; 1 Bl. Com., 169; Vattel, b. 1, ch. 20, § 241. The house of lords is not permitted to amend money bills, and the commons deny the power even to reject them. See resolutions of 5th and 6th July, 1860.

cedent, the federal constitution requires all bills for raising revenue to originate in the house of representatives,[1] and there are corresponding provisions in the constitutions of nearly one half the states.[2] While such provisions are of little or no importance in this country, where the members of both branches of the legislature are equally responsible to the people, the requirement that executive officers shall confine themselves strictly to executive duties, is one of the most valuable principles of the government. Indeed, the division of the powers of government is the most important of the checks and balances by means of which the benefits of orderly government are secured and perpetuated; and the least encroachment by one department on the powers of the other is usurpation, for which the law is supposed to provide the adequate remedy. Executive and ministerial officers enforce the tax laws; but, in doing so, they must keep strictly within the authority those laws confer, and they cannot add to or vary, in the slightest degree, any tax lawfully levied.[3] They neither have, nor can have any "roving commission to levy and collect taxes from the people without authority of law but [they] can only do so in the manner prescribed by the law, which should be the governing rule for their conduct in levying taxes * * in all cases."[4] So inflexible is this rule, that even the legislature itself, as will be more fully shown hereafter, cannot clothe them with its own authority for this purpose.[5] Where the people have located the power, there it must remain and be exercised.

The power not judicial. It is still more manifest that the power to tax is not judicial. "It is the province of the judicial

[1] During the second session of the forty-first congress, there was much discussion as to what constituted a bill for raising revenue, but nothing was settled.

[2] In the constitutions of Alabama, Arkansas, Delaware, Georgia, Indiana, Kentucky, Louisiana, Massachusetts, Maine, Minnesota, New Hampshire, New Jersey, Oregon, Pennsylvania, South Carolina and Vermont.

[3] State *v.* Bentley, 23 N. J., 532; State *v.* Flavell, 24 id., 370.

[4] Barlow *v.* The Ordinary, 47 Geo., 639, 642, per *Warner*, Ch. J.

[5] See the next chapter. The legislature cannot confer upon a state board a discretionary authority to add to the amount which the statute authorizes to be collected by state tax. Houghton *v.* Austin, 47 Cal., 646.

power to decide private disputes between or concerning persons, but of legislative power to regulate public concerns, and to make laws for the benefit and welfare of the state."[1] "The legislative makes, the executive executes, and the judiciary construes the laws."[2] The legislature must therefore determine all questions of state necessity, discretion or policy involved in ordering a tax and in apportioning it; must make all the necessary rules and regulations which are to be observed in order to produce the desired returns, and must decide upon the agencies by means of which collections shall be made. "The judicial tribunals of the state have no concern with the policy of legislation. That is a matter resting altogether in the discretion of another coördinate branch of the government. The judicial power cannot legitimately question the policy or refuse to sanction the provisions of any law not inconsistent with the fundamental law of the state."[3] And it is as incompetent for the legislature to confer the power to tax upon the judiciary as upon the executive.[4] If the legislature shall

[1] *Richardson*, Ch. J., in Merrill *v.* Sherburne, 1 N. H., 199, 204.

[2] *Marshall*, Ch. J., in Wayman *v.* Southard, 10 Wheat., 1, 46. See Greenough *v.* Greenough, 11 Penn. St., 489, 494; Bates *v.* Kimball, 2 Chip., 77; Newland *v.* Marsh, 19 Ill., 376, 382; Beebe *v.* State, 6 Ind., 501, 515; Jones *v.* Perry, 10 Yerg., 59, 69; People *v.* Supervisors of New York, 16 N. Y., 424, 432

[3] *Redfield*, Ch. J., in Powers *in re.*, 25 Vt., 261, 265.

[4] Hardenburg *v.* Kidd, 10 Cal., 402. "The court of sessions under the constitution can only exercise powers of a judicial character. The legislature is incompetent to confer upon the court any other powers. The assessment of taxes is not a judicial act; it partakes of no element of a judicial character. It is a legislative act; it requires the exercise of legislative power, which for certain governmental purposes in the county may be devolved upon a board of supervisors, but cannot be delegated to any branch of the judicial department." *Field*, J., p. 403. In Heine *v.* Levee Commissioners, 19 Wall., 655, 661, a bill in equity was filed to compel the respondent to levy a tax for the payment of overdue corporation bonds. The bill was dismissed. *Miller*, *J.*, says, "The power we are here asked to exercise is the very delicate one of taxation. This power belongs in this country to the legislative sovereignty, state or national. In the case before us the national sovereignty has nothing to do with it. The power must be derived from the legislature of the state. So far as the present case is concerned, the state has delegated the power to the levee commissioners. If that body has ceased to exist, the remedy is in the legislature, either to assess the tax by special statute, or to vest the power in some other tribunal. It certainly is not vested, as in the exercise of an original jurisdiction, in any federal court. It is unreasonable to suppose that the

abuse its powers and transcend its legislative functions by the enactment of that which is called a tax law, but which is not such in fact, then indeed the abuse may be arrested by the judicial arm;[1] but the interference does not proceed on the idea of any authority of the judiciary over the subject of taxation. The judiciary interposes on the application of any party whose rights are threatened by an unlawful exercise of authority; and it is immaterial with whom or what department the unlawful action originates, or by what name it is designated. But so long as the legislation is not colorable merely, but is confined to the enactment of what is in its nature strictly a tax law, and so long as none of the constitutional rights of the citizen are violated in the directions prescribed for enforcing the tax, the legislation is of supreme authority. Taxes may be and often are oppressive to the persons and corporations taxed; they may appear to the judicial mind unjust and even unnecessary, but this can constitute no reason for judicial interference.[2]

legislature would ever select a federal court for that purpose. It is not only not one of the inherent powers of the court to levy and collect taxes, but it is an invasion by the judiciary of the federal government of the legislative functions of the state government. It is a most extraordinary request; and a compliance with it would involve consequences no less out of the way of judicial procedure, the end of which no wisdom can foresee."

[1] Maltby *v.* Reading etc. R. R. Co., 52 Penn. St., 140, 145. See Gault's Appeal, 33 id., 94; N. Y. & Erie R. R. Co. *v.* Sabin, 26 id., 242; Wharton *v.* School Directors, 42 id., 358; Brodnax *v.* Groom, 64 N. C., 244; Pullen *v.* County Commissioners, 66 id., 361; McCulloch *v.* State of Maryland, 4 Wheat., 316, 428; Providence Bank *v.* Billings, 4 Pet., 514, 563; Veazie Bank *v.* Fenno, 8 Wall., 533, 548; Heine *v.* Levee Commissioners, 19 id., 655; People *v.* Brooklyn, 4 N. Y., 419; Weber *v.* Reinhard, 73 Penn. St., 370; Sharpless *v.* Mayor of Philadelphia, 21 id., 147; Bank of Pennsylvania *v.* The Commonwealth, 19 id., 144; Perkins *v.* Milford, 59 Me., 315, 318, per *Appleton*, Ch. J.; DePauw *v.* New Albany, 22 Ind., 204; Gibson *v.* Mason, 5 Nev., 283; Waters *v.* State, 1 Gill, 302; Alcorn *v.* Hamer, 38 Miss., 652, 751; Blackwell on Tax Titles, 4th ed., ch. 1 and cases cited. "The courts have no more power to assess, or command the assessment of taxes than the legislature has to adjudge or command the adjudication of lawsuits." *Reese*, J., in Justices of Cannon County *v.* Hodenpyle, 7 Humph., 145, 147. The case was one of an application for *mandamus* to compel the county court to levy a tax to pay county debts. And see Delaware R. R. Tax, 18 Wall., 206.

[2] See Veazie Bank *v.* Fenno, 8 Wall., 533, 548, per *Chase*, Ch. J.; Weston *v.* Charleston, 2 Pet., 449, 466, per *Marshall*, Ch. J.; Delaware Railroad Tax, 18

Tax legislation may be colorable merely, either because the purpose for which the tax is demanded is not a public purpose, or because of the absence of some other essential element in taxation. When that is the case, the judiciary is the efficient check, and it must protect individuals and protect the public against what, in such a case, would be an attempt at lawless exactions.[1]

In some of the states the county courts or county justices are empowered to make the county levies. But these, although exercising inferior judicial functions, are really administrative boards, possessing an authority corresponding to that which is exercised in other states by county commissioners or boards of supervisors. Their action in ordering taxes is *quasi* legislative, and governed by the same rules as other legislative action.

In some states, also, tax proceedings are reviewed and confirmed by the courts before any sales of property are ordered or demands conclusively fixed against individuals. But this again is not legislative. Such a review is supposed to be favorable to the taxpayer, as it gives him an opportunity to take the opinion of the court upon the legality of the demand made upon him, without waiting until the collector comes and seizes his person or his property. The proceeding is the institution of a suit on behalf of the state against each individual tax-payer or item of property taxed, and it calls upon the court to apply the law to the issues which such a suit presents. Of the judicial nature of such a review no question could well be raised.

Law of the land. There is a constitutional guaranty which has come to us from Magna Charta, which declares that no person

Wall., 206; Williams *v.* Cammack, 27 Miss., 209; State *v.* Bell, 1 Phil. (N. C.), 76, 85; Bridge Proprietors *v.* State, 21 N. J., 384, 386; S. C. on appeal, 22 id., 593; Dailey *v.* Swope, 47 Miss., 367.

[1] Tyson *v.* School Directors, 51 Penn. St.. 9; Covington *v.* Southgate, 15 B. Monr., 491, 498; Tide Water Co. *v.* Costar, 18 N. J. Eq., 518; Hammett *v.* Philadelphia, 65 Penn. St., 146; S. C., 3 Am. Rep., 615; Sedgw. Stat. & Const. Law, 414. On this clear principle, that the power to tax was legislative and not judicial, and that the valuation of property for the purposes of taxation was an incident to the taxing power, it was held in Auditor of State *v.* Atchison, etc., R. R. Co., 6 Kan., 500, that the supreme court could not be made an appellate tribunal to review the valuations of railroad property made by the board of county clerks.

shall be deprived of life, liberty or property, except by the judgment of his peers or the law of the land. The alternative provisions of this guaranty have sometimes been supposed to mean the same thing, and the guaranty itself to entitle every person to have any demand made upon him submitted to the determination of a jury of the vicinage. Such a construction applied in tax cases would work a thorough and radical change in the principles on which taxation is now supposed to rest. It would cripple the legislative power, and subject the action of the department whose function it is to make laws on its own views of the questions of public interest and public policy which the laws involve, to a review and possible reversal at the hands of a jury. It would not so much strengthen the judicial department as it would weaken the legislative; for the courts themselves, though juries sit with and as a part of them, are compelled to recognize a large degree of independence in the action of these assistants. Such independence is often useful, and never can be seriously detrimental when a verdict determines a single controversy only; but to make juries the assessors of the claims of the state upon individuals, could only introduce anarchy; one jury reaching one conclusion regarding the public needs and the justice of its demands, and another another, until the state would be without general rule, and must fall to pieces from the incurable inefficiency of its government. Such a construction of a clause agreed upon as an important provision in a charter of government can never have been intended.[1]

It has long been settled that while one is to be protected in his

[1] This is now agreed on all hands. See Cruikshanks *v.* Charleston, 1 McCord, 360; State *v.* Mayhew, 2 Gill, 487, 497; Harper *v.* The Commissioners, 23 Geo., 566; State *v.* Frazier, 48 id., 137. In Harris *v.* Wood, 6 T. B. Monr., 641, it is remarked that taxes are recoverable not only without a jury, but without a judge, and the assessment of ministerial officers has been made to operate as an execution on the citizen, and the collector could distrain, and any public collector could be subjected to judgment on motion for the amount. "This process is not founded on a judgment; it issues without a judgment, and it is for this very reason that it is adopted. The state cannot wait the tedious process of getting a judgment. If she were compelled to do this, her honor might be compromitted, and the rights of her citizens jeoparded. Hence she clothes her collecting agents with the power to issue process *at once* which will *at once* command her means." Per *Nisbet*, J., in Doe *v.* Deavors, 11 Geo., 79, 86.

interests by the "the law of the land," he is entitled to "the judgment of his peers" only in those cases in which it has immemorially existed, or in which it has been expressly given by law. The clause recited from Magna Charta does not imply the necessity for judicial action in every case in which the property of the citizen may be taken for the public use. On the contrary, a legislative act for that purpose, when clearly within the limits of legislative authority, is of itself the law of the land. And an act for levying taxes and providing the means of enforcement is, as we have seen, within the unquestioned and unquestionable power of the legislature.[1] It is therefore the law of the land, not merely

[1] This subject was much considered in Weimer *v.* Bunbury, 30 Mich., 202, 212. The following is an extract from the opinion:

"There are, unquestionably, cases in which expressions have been used implying the necessity for a common law trial before, in any instance, a man can be deprived of his property; but they will be found on investigation to be cases calling for no such sweeping statement. If any court has ever decided that judicial proceedings are of constitutional necessity in appropriating property under the power of taxation, the case has not been brought to our attention, and has been overlooked in our investigations. This would be most extraordinary if the necessity existed; for tax systems similar to our own have prevailed ever since our government was founded; and it cannot be said that tax laws are usually so popular as to disarm every person of any legal objections which he might suppose available to relieve him of their burdens. On the contrary, no laws are contested more vigorously, and with none are people more critical in looking after defects and infirmities. It may be safely asserted, without fear of contradiction, that if the collection of the revenue could only be made through legal proceedings, the true principle would not have been left to so late a discovery, but the wheels of government would long ago have been blocked by litigious parties until an entirely new system could be substituted. And it need hardly be said that any new system in which courts should be made the administrators of the revenue would necessarily be so cumbrous, and so subject to impediments and delays, as to make a constitutional provision requiring it a great public inconvenience.

"There is nothing technical, or, we think obscure, in the requirement that process which divests property shall be due process of law. The constitution makes no attempt to define such process, but assumes that custom and law have already settled what it is. Even in judicial proceedings we do not ascertain from the constitution what is lawful process, but we test their action by principles which were before the constitution, and the benefit of which we assume that the constitution was intended to perpetuate. If there existed, before that instrument was adopted, well known administrative proceedings which, having their origin in a legislative conviction of their necessity, had been sanctioned by long and general acceptance, we are no more at liberty to

in so far as it lays down a general rule to be observed, but in all the proceedings and all the process which it points out or provides for in order to give the rule full operation. As has been well said, "the mode of levying as well as the right of imposing taxes is completely and exclusively within the legislative power, which, it is to be presumed, will always be exercised with an equal regard to the security of the public and individual rights and convenience. The existence of government depending on the prompt and regular collection of revenue must, as an object of primary importance, be insured in such a way as the wisdom of the legislature may prescribe. There is a tacit condition annexed to the ownership of property that it shall contribute to the public revenue in such mode and proportion as the legislative will shall direct; and if the officers entrusted with the execution of the laws transcend their powers to the injury of an individual, the common law entitles him to redress. But to pursue every delinquent liable to pay taxes through the forms of process and a jury trial would materially impede, if not wholly obstruct, the collection of the revenue."[1] There is no room for the supposition that in a matter of this public importance, where promptness in collection is always desirable, and often imperative, dilatory proceedings of this nature were within the contemplation of the people when consent-

infer an intent in the people to prohibit them by implication from any general language, than we should be to infer an intent to abridge the judicial authority by the use of similar words. The truth is, the bills of rights in the American constitutions have not been drafted for the introduction of new law, but to secure old principles against abrogation or violation. They are conservatory instruments rather than reformatory; and they assume that the existing principles of the common law are ample for the protection of individual rights, when once incorporated in the fundamental law, and thus secured against violation.

"We are, therefore, of necessity driven to an examination of the previous condition of things, if we would understand the meaning of due process of law, as the constitution employs the term. Nothing previously in use, regarded as necessary in government and sanctioned by usage, can be looked upon as condemned by it. Administrative process of the customary sort is as much due process of law as judicial process. We should meet a great many unexpected and very serious embarrassments in government if this were otherwise."

[1] *Taylor*, Ch. J., in Cowles *v.* Brittain, 2 Hawks, 204, 207; *Crockett*, J., in Hagar *v.* Supervisors of Yolo, 47 Cal., 222, 233.

ing to any general provision of the constitution.[1] It is safer, and, as we believe, more correct, to say that our constitutions have been framed and agreed upon in view of an immemorial practice and rule of government under which the whole subject has been entrusted to the legislative department; and they are to be understood and construed in the light of that practice wherever the people have not expressly undertaken to change it.[2]

[1] See Cowles *v.* Brittain, 2 Hawks, 204, 207; State *v.* Allen, 2 McCord, 55, 60, per *Nott*, J.; Sears *v.* Cottrell, 5 Mich., 251; High *v.* Shoemaker, 22 Cal., 363; Harper *v.* The Commissioners, 23 Geo., 566; Tift *v.* Griffin, 5 id., 185, 191.

[2] Mr. Blackwell, in his Treatise on Tax Titles, p. 26, insists that the constitutional provision we have referred to, renders judicial proceedings requisite in every case before an individual can be deprived of his property under the revenue laws. He concedes, however, that it does not require such proceedings in the ordinary understanding of the term. "The power to levy a tax," he says, "properly belongs to the legislative power. The collection of it involves the exercise of judicial and executive functions. The legislature levy the tax, direct that a demand shall be made upon the owner of the land for the tax charged against it, and if payment is refused, authorize the collector to seize the body or goods of the delinquent; and in case satisfaction is not had in the one or the other of these modes, power is conferred upon the collector to sell and convey the land itself. Now, before the power to sell the land can exist under the law, the fact of the levy and nonpayment of the tax, the demand, and return of no goods, or that the body cannot be found, must exist. These facts must be ascertained to exist before the power of sale attaches. Whether the power to decide the question of delinquency is vested by law in the regularly constituted judicial tribunals, or in those specially instituted for that purpose, or in the collector himself, can make no kind of difference; it is the exercise of judicial power, and the officer who sells performs an executive function; so that in point of fact, the legislative, judicial and executive departments of the government, all aid in the execution of the taxing power. The legislature declare what facts shall constitute a cause of forfeiture; the judiciary ascertain the facts, apply the rule of law prescribed, and pronounce a judgment of condemnation." But in this there is surely some confusion of terms. Where the statute requires no intervention of the ordinary judicial tribunals in the assessment and collection of taxes, there is commonly in the proceedings very little that is even *quasi* judicial. An assessment by values certainly is so, and the law generally is framed on that theory, and gives parties assessed an opportunity to be heard. But under most of our laws the subsequent proceedings are purely ministerial. What is there in the nature of judicial action when a county officer, looking over the lists in his office, draws off the description of lands not there credited with payment of taxes, and proceeds to advertise and sell them? If this is a "decision of the question of delinquency," and is judicial, any act of any officer which is to be perfo med as a step in regular proceedings is judicial also. The sheriff as

CHAPTER III.

LIMITATIONS UPON THE TAXING POWER.

Vast as is the power of the government to levy taxes upon its citizens, there are nevertheless limitations upon it of a very distinct and positive character, which inhere in the very nature of the power itself. Some of these limitations are commonly declared in the written constitutions, but the declaration is rather from abundant caution than from any necessity, as the limitations are equally imperative whether thus declared or not.[1] In some cases the courts in the exercise of their ordinary jurisdiction may and do enforce the restrictions; in others it is beyond their power to

much exercises judicial power, when he sells property on the assumption that a judgment has not been paid to himself or to some other person authorized to receive payment, as does the officer who performs the function of determining what land shall be sold for taxes. In either case there is nothing which resembles judicial proceedings; no hearing of parties; no judgment by the officer; not even any discretion allowed him for the exercise of judgment. It would seem, that if we can get around a requirement of judicial action so easily as this, by calling something judicial that can only be made so by annihilating all distinctions, we may also avoid any other constitutional requirement, by calling whatever is done the equivalent of that which has been required. This may be easy, but it is not safe. Any requirement of judicial action is something of more substance than is here supposed. As to this safeguard of "the law of the land" in tax proceedings, neither the practice of governments nor the decisions of courts warrant us in saying that it includes a judicial finding of delinquency before a sale can be made. It means, beyond any question, regular and orderly proceedings, under the general law, by the proper department of government; and means nothing more.

[1] "Taxation is bounded in its exercise by its own nature, essential characteristics and purpose." *Agnew*, J., in Matter of Washington St., 69 Penn. St., 352, 363. "In our time a French writer has recorded that after attending a debâte in our House of Commons, he observed to an English statesman that he had heard no assertion of the general principles of constitutional freedom. The answer was, 'we take that for granted.'" Knight's England, vol. 3, p. 417. It is observable in the state constitutions that while they enter with considerable minuteness into declarations of individual right, many of the most important principles of government are usually not declared at all, but simply taken for granted.

do so. Whether this may be done in any given case will depend upon whether the question which the case presents is or is not judicial.

The public good. Taxes are only to be imposed for the public good. But what persons or property the public good will require to be taxed, and when the tax shall be laid, and to what extent the burden shall be imposed, are obviously not judicial questions, but questions which address themselves to the judgment and discretion of the legislative department. They must be determined by the legislature, whose conclusion respecting them must be final.[1]

Public purposes. It is the first requisite of lawful taxation that the purpose for which it is laid shall be a public purpose. The decision to lay a tax for a given purpose involves a legislative conclusion that the purpose is one for which a tax may be laid; in other words, is a public purpose. But the determination of the legislature on this question is not, like its decision on ordinary questions of public policy, conclusive either on the other departments of the government, or on the people. The question, what is and what is not a public purpose, is one of law; and though unquestionably the legislature has large discretion in selecting the object for which taxes shall be laid, its decision is not final. In any case in which the legislature shall have clearly exceeded its authority in this regard, and levied a tax for a purpose not public, it is competent for any one who in person or property is affected by the tax, to appeal to the courts for protection. This subject will receive a more full consideration further on.[2]

Territorial limitations. It has already been seen that persons and property not within the territorial limits of a state cannot be taxed by it.[3] In such a case the state affords no protection,

[1] *Ante*, ch. II.

[2] *Post*, ch. IV.

[3] *Ante*, p. 14. The lands of an Indian tribe are not taxable. The N. Y. Indians, 5 Wall., 761. Nor the Indians themselves when not citizens. State *v.* Ross, 7 Yerg., 84.

and there is nothing for which taxation can be an equivalent.[1] But where a person is resident within a state, his personal property in contemplation of law accompanies him, and he may be required to pay taxes upon it wherever it is situate,[2] while the real estate of a nonresident is always taxable where it is.[3] It is competent also for any state to provide that tangible personal property situate within it may be taxed there irrespective of the residence of the owner; and sometimes state laws provide for such taxation.[4] The case of corporations is in some respects pe-

[1] Where the shares in a corporation are taxable to shareholders, it is not competent to tax the corporation itself on the shares of nonresident shareholders. State *v.* Thomas, 26 N. J., 181.

[2] Inhabitants of Great Barrington *v.* County Com'rs, 16 Pick., 572; State *v.* Branin, 23 N. J., 484; State *v.* Bentley, id., 532; Newark City Bank *v.* The Assessors, 30 id., 13; Nashua Savings Bank *v.* Nashua, 46 N. H., 389; Bemis *v.* Boston, 14 Allen, 366; Commonwealth *v.* Hays, 8 B. Monr., 1, 2; Wilkey *v.* Pekin, 19 Ill., 160; Rieman *v.* Shepard, 27 Ind., 288; Johnson *v.* Oregon City, 2 Oreg., 327; Same *v.* Same, 3 id., 13; Griffith *v.* Carter, 8 Kan., 565; Blood *v.* Sayre, 17 Vt, 609. But not in a state where it is merely passing through. Hays *v.* Steamship Co., 17 How., 596; Hoyt *v.* Commissioners of Taxes, 23 N. Y., 224; Parker Mills *v.* Commissioners of Taxes, 23 id., 242; State *v.* Engle, 34 N. J., 425; Chauvenet *v.* Commissioners, 3 Md., 259; Hooper *v.* Baltimore, 12 id., 464; Whitsell *v.* Northampton Co., 49 Penn. St., 526; McKeen *v.* Same, id., 519; Union Bank *v.* State, 9 Yerg., 490; Conley *v.* Chedic, 7 Nev., 336. A mortgage must be taxed to the owner where he lives, not where the land mortgaged is. Latrobe *v.* Baltimore, 19 Md., 13. Investments by residents of the state in bonds and stocks of foreign corporations may be taxed within the state. Worthington *v.* Sebastian, 25 Ohio St., 1. It is competent to provide by law for taxing shares in corporations at the place where the business is carried on. Tappan *v.* Merchants' National Bank, 19 Wall., 490.

[3] Witherspoon *v.* Duncan, 4 Wall., 210; Turner *v.* Burlington, 16 Mass., 208; Jones *v.* Columbus, 25 Geo., 610.

[4] Hood's Estate, 21 Penn. St., 106, 114; Maltby *v.* Reading R. R. Co., 52 id., 140; State *v.* Falkinburge, 15 N. J., 320; Wilson *v.* New York, 4 E. D. Smith, 675; Hoyt *v.* Commissioners of Taxes, 23 N. Y., 224; People *v.* Ogdensburg, 48 id., 390; Howell *v.* State, 3 Gill, 14; Rieman *v.* Shepard, 27 Ind., 288; Catlin *v.* Hull, 21 Vt., 152; Blackstone Manuf. Co. *v.* Blackstone, 13 Gray, 488; Leonard *v.* New Bedford, 16 id, 292; Steere *v.* Walling, 7 R. I., 317; Hartland *v.* Church, 47 Me., 169; Desmond *v.* Machias, 48 id., 478; Mills *v.* Thornton, 26 Ill., 300; St. Louis *v.* Ferry Co., 40 Mo., 580; People *v.* Insurance Co., 29 Cal., 533; Green *v.* Van Buskirk, 7 Wall., 139, 150. The same is true of business carried on within a state or municipality by nonresidents. See Corfield *v.* Coryell, 4 Wash. C. C., 371; Harrison *v.* Vicksburg, 3 S. & M., 581;

culiar. They may be taxed for their franchise, and they may also be taxed as persons where their business is carried on.[1] And as no state is under obligation to permit a foreign corporation to carry on business, or exercise franchises within its territory, the permission to do so may be granted under such restrictions, or allowed on such conditions regarding taxation as the state may think proper or prudent to impose.[2]

Taxation and representation. There is a maxim in our government that the representatives of the people must impose the taxes the people are to pay. The form it sometimes takes is, "taxation and representation go together." The maxim is familiar in English law, where it became established as the result of a long, and at times bloody, controversy between the representatives of the people on one side, and the crown on the other. The meaning there was the same that had been contended for in other countries; that the imposition of taxes was essentially a legislative power, and the sovereign could levy none except as they were granted by the representatives of the realm.[3] In America

Worth *v.* Fayetteville, 1 Winst., 70; State *v.* City Council of Charleston, 2 Speers, 623; Padelford *v.* The Mayor of Savannah, 14 Geo., 438; Pearce *v.* Augusta, 37 id., 597; Shriver *v.* Pittsburg, 66 Penn. St., 446. Compare Bennett *v.* Birmingham, 31 id., 15.

[1] People *v.* Utica Ins. Co., 15 Johns., 358, 382, per *Thompson*, J.; Ontario Bank *v.* Bunnell, 10 Wend., 186. If it is made a provision in the charter of a corporation that its shares shall be taxed at the domicile of the owner "their taxability at such locality is annexed as an incident to the shares, and it does not matter where the domicile of the owner may be. The tax may then be enforced through the corporation, by requiring it to withhold the amount from the dividends payable thereon." *Field*, J., in Minot *v.* Railroad Co., 18 Wall., 206, 230.

[2] Ducat *v.* Chicago, 48 Ill., 172; Fireman's Benevolent Association *v.* Lounsbery, 21 id., 511; Fire Department of Milwaukee *v.* Helfenstein, 16 Wis., 136; People *v.* Imlay, 20 Barb., 68; opinion of *Taney*, Ch. J., in Bank of Augusta *v.* Earle, 13 Pet., 519; Cincinnati Mutual Health Assurance Co. *v.* Rosenthal, 55 Ill., 85; Fire Department *v.* Noble, 3 E. D. Smith, 440; Same *v.* Wright, id., 453; Degroot *v.* Van Duzer, 20 Wend., 390; Commonwealth *v.* Melton, 12 B. Monr., 212, 218; Tatem *v.* Wright, 23 N. J., 429; Paul *v.* Virginia, 8 Wall., 168; Liverpool Ins. Co. *v.* Massachusetts, 10 id., 566; Ducat *v.* Chicago, 10 id., 410.

[3] See Clermont's note to Fortescue's *De Laudimus*, p. 28; also Bates' Case, 2 State Trials, 371; S. C., Broom's Const. Law, 247; Hampden's Case, 3 State

the corresponding contest assumed a different phase, and the maxim took on a different meaning as a rallying cry in the contest for independence. The American colonies insisted upon the right of the colonial legislatures to vote the local taxes; disputing any such right in the parliament of Great Britain, which was a body in which the colonists had and could have no representatives. That body, it was claimed, could legitimately exercise over them the authority only of an imperial legislature to regulate external concerns, and those of the empire at large, leaving internal concerns to the control of their own representatives. What the maxim really meant was, that the local legislature must make the local laws; it was violated in the particular of taxes, and consequently brought that subject prominently to notice, though the principle itself was general. The same principle has sometimes been appealed to as if it meant that *no person* could be taxed unless in the body which voted the tax he was represented by some one in whose selection he had a voice; but it never had any such meaning, and never could have, without excluding from taxation a very large proportion of all the property of the state. If the privilege of voting for representatives in the government were the only or even the principal benefit received from government, there might be the highest reason in exempting the nonvoting infant or alien from taxation; but this privilege to any particular individual, as compared with the protection of life, liberty and property, is really insignificant. And so long as all persons cannot participate in government, the limits of exclusion and admission must always be determined on considerations of general public policy. It is not doubted that, so far as can be prudently and safely permitted, all who are to pay taxes should be allowed a voice in raising them; if for no other reason, because those they vote they will more willingly and cheerfully pay.[1] But the maxim that taxa-

Trials, 825; S. C., Broom's Const. Law, 306, and note, 370. Similar but less successful contests for the same principle in France and Spain are narrated by Mr. Hallam and other writers.

[1] The aim of all the contests from which have sprung the liberties of England and America has been to establish and defend the principle of self taxation, as that which must constitute the main security against oppression. Mr. Burke insists upon this in his speech on Conciliation of America. And see Works of Madison III, 105. The sense of the oppression of any burden is

tion and representation go together is only true when understood in a territorial sense which embraces the state at large; every person in the state being represented in its legislative body, and that body determining the taxation not only for the state at large, but also, within certain limits, for each division and municipality of the state.[1] The local right is subordinate to this general authority.

greatly increased if they who are to bear it, are to do so, not voluntarily but at the command of others. Locke expresses this idea when, in his Treatise on Civil Government, he says, of a burden imposed as compared to one voluntarily assumed, that "it may be all one to the purse, but it worketh diversely to the courage." This is well illustrated in English history; for heavy taxation dates from the time when the right of the commons to grant the taxes became finally settled. But the chief importance in the right of those who pay taxes to vote them, consists in this: that in monarchical countries it constitutes the only substantial and continuous check upon tyranny, and in any country the only security against robbery under the forms of law. As the Spanish Cortes said in one of their remonstrances, "there remains no other privilege or liberty which can be profitable to subjects if this be taken away." Hallam's Middle Ages, ch. IV. The idea is well expressed by *Lawrence*, J., in Harward *v.* Drainage Co., 51 Ill., 130. See also Gage *v.* Graham, 57 id., 144; People *v.* Hurlburt, 24 Mich., 44. It is very justly laid down that a tax law is to be so construed as to harmonize with the principle that the people are not to be taxed except with their own consent or that of officers truly representing them. Keasy *v.* Bricker, 60 Penn. St., 9. In Indiana it has been decided that where the boundaries of a township have been extended after it has voted aid to a work of internal improvement, the territory brought in cannot be subjected to the tax so voted. Alvis *v.* Whitney, 43 Ind., 83.

[1] In Steward *v.* Jefferson, 3 Harr., 335, 336, Mr. James A. Bayard, of counsel, objected to a school district tax, voted by the inhabitants of the district, claiming that it was void. "A citizen of the state who does not reside in the district may, by the act, be taxed without having the right to vote, and when he can derive no benefit from it; as he can neither send his own children nor other children. This violates the first principle of republican government, that, as to citizens, taxation goes with and is dependent on representation." But the court affirmed the tax without discussion. That the property of persons who have not the right to vote is taxable, see Wheeler *v.* Wall, 6 Allen, 558; Smith *v.* Macon, 20 Ark., 17. In State *v.* Ross, 7 Yerg., 74, 77, *Catron*, Ch. J., has something to say about the tyranny of taxation without representation, but the case did not call for it. In Marr *v.* Enloe, 1 Yerg., 452, where the power to authorize a county court to levy taxes for county purposes was denied, stress was laid on the fact that the members of the court were not elected by the people. Upon the general right of the people to tax themselves through their representatives, see Pope v. Phifer, 3 Heis., 682; Sanborn *v.* Rice Co., 9 Minn., 273; People *v.* Hurlburt, 24 Mich., 44; People *v.* Chicago, 51 Ill., 58; People *v.* Batcheller, 53 N. Y., 128; State *v.* Leffingwell, 54 Mo., 458. It has often

To what extent the federal government may rightfully levy taxes in districts not represented in the federal legislature, is perhaps not entirely clear. In the District of Columbia, which by the national constitution was set apart for federal purposes and placed under the exclusive jurisdiction of congress, the power is unlimited, and whoever becomes a resident of the district must do so with the understanding that he can participate in the gov-

been decided that a state may compel a municipality to tax itself for police purposes. See Taylor *v.* Board of Health, 31 Penn. St., 73; People *v.* Mehaney, 13 Mich., 481. And for highways and other like purposes of general concern. See Harrison Justices *v.* Holland, 3 Grat., 247. But these subjects will be elsewhere considered. Tax laws are undoubtedly to be construed, if possible, so as not to impose taxes without the consent of the people taxed, or their immediate representatives: so held of a tax for military bounty purposes. Keasy *v.* Bricker, 60 Penn. St., 9: and see Lexington *v.* McQuillan's Heirs, 9 Dana, 513, 517; Madison Co. *v.* The People, 58 Ill., 456, 463; Hampshire *v.* Franklin, 16 Mass., 75, 83; Cheaney *v.* Hooser, 9 B. Monr., 330; Maltus *v.* Shields, 2 Met. (Ky.), 553. And we shall endeavor to show further on, that, in some cases, this assent is necessary.

That a stranger, coming into a town, becomes liable to a license tax as an "inhabitant and member of the corporation," see Plymouth *v.* Pettijohn, 4 Dev., 391; Whitfield *v.* Longest, 6 Ired., 268. "It is just that it should be so; for, as the defendant has, in the security of his property, the benefit of the night watch and of the other police establishments, he ought to contribute reasonably towards their expenses." Per *Ruffin*, Ch. J., in Wilmington *v.* Roby, 8 Ired., 250, 254; and see Edenton *v.* Copeheart, 71 N. C., 156. In Falmouth *v.* Watson, 5 Bush, 660, 661, *Hardin*, J., in discussing an act of the legislature which empowered the town of Falmouth to impose a license tax not exceeding $100 on the sale, by retail, of all spirituous, vinous or malt liquors in said town, *or* within *one mile* thereof, said: "It is insisted for the appellee that the power, which this enactment purports to confer on the trustees of the town, to exact a license fee for the privilege of keeping a tavern or vending ardent spirits outside of, although near, the town limits, is within the interdiction of the fourteenth section of article 13 of the state constitution, viz.: 'Nor shall any man's property be taken or applied to public use without the consent of his representatives, and without just compensation being previously made to him.' Had the exercise of the power complained of been the imposition of an ordinary tax merely on the property of the appellee, situated within the corporate limits of the town, for municipal purposes, we should not doubt the correctness of the objection; or even if the exaction of the sum in controversy, in consideration of a trade license, had been made for local revenue purposes alone, though not in the usual form of taxation, we should regard it within the constitutional prohibition; for the legislature could not delegate to the corporation the right to either license for compensation or tax a privilege to be enjoyed beyond its limits, except a police regula-

ernment only to the extent that congress may permit.[1] There can be no doubt also of the right of the federal government to levy stamp taxes and imposts of every description, by laws which shall have uniform operation throughout all the states and territories within the jurisdiction of the general government. But taxes for territorial purposes, corresponding to the taxes which are levied by the states for state purposes, it is theoretically at least the right of the people of the territory, when organized with a local legislature, to levy and expend for themselves. It is not to be supposed that the right will be denied by the general government, and if it should be, and the local taxes be imposed and expended by the direct interposition of congressional authority, it is not too much to say that such action would be inconsistent with the maxim of government now under consideration, whether valid in law or not.[2]

The power not to be delegated. The power to impose taxes, like any other branch of the legislative authority, must be exercised by the legislature itself, and cannot be delegated to ministe-

tion having reference to the comfort, safety or welfare of society within its local jurisdiction. Cooley's Const. Lim., 577. But, in our opinion, the exaction of a fee of $100 for the privilege of vending ardent spirits in such proximity to the town as to render its exercise liable to affect the good order or peace of the local community, did not infringe any constitutional right of the appellee. The privilege granted to him was one which public policy requires should be subjected to such legal restraints and regulations as will, as far as practicable, prevent its abuse to the detriment of society. The legislature, having the general power to do this, properly delegated that power to the local government of the community immediately interested. The authority so conferred on the trustees does not appear to have been abused by an excessive or unreasonable exaction, and the rights of the appellee were certainly not invaded by a compulsory one." A city ordinance, taxing wagons used in the city for pay, cannot apply to wagons owned by those residing outside who employ them in hauling into and out of the city. If it could, it would be taking property for private use — for the use of that particular community of which the owner formed no part. St. Charles *v.* Nolle, 51 Mo., 122.

[1] Loughborough *v.* Blake, 5 Wheat., 317, 324. See also Kendall *v.* United States, 12 Pet., 524.

[2] Upon the subject of territorial powers of taxation, the following cases are instructive: Miners' Bank *v.* Iowa, 12 How., 1; Vincennes University *v.* Indiana, 14 id., 268; Williams *v.* Bank of Michigan, 7 Wend., 539; Swan *v.* Williams, 2 Mich., 427.

rial officers, or even to another department of the government.[1] This is a principle which pervades our whole political system, and when properly understood, admits of no exception. The

[1] Dillon Mun. Corp., §§ 60, 567, 618, and notes; Cooley's Const. Lim., 117, 205, and cases cited; Thompson *v.* Schermerhorn, 6 N. Y., 92; St. Louis *v.* Clemens, 52 Mo., 133; Hyde *v.* Joyes, 4 Bush, 464; People *v.* Clark, 47 Cal., 456. Each of these was a case in which a municipal corporation undertook to delegate to an administrative officer the power to determine the plan and extent of a municipal improvement for which a tax was ordered; and it was held there was no power to do so. Subsequent acts of affirmance by a city council could not vitalize such action. Hyde *v.* Joyes, *supra.* And see Randolph *v.* Gawley, 47 Cal., 458; Mercer County Court *v.* Navigation Co., 8 Bush, 300, 307. But it is no delegation of the taxing power to refer to the city engineer and a committee of the council to determine when repairs in a street improvement are needed, and how much of the old improvement can be used in making them. Covington *v.* Boyle, 6 Bush, 204. The following cases may also be referred to: Bellinger *v.* Gray, 51 N. Y., 610, decides that the duties imposed by the tax laws upon boards of supervisors, of examining the assessment rolls and equalizing the valuation of the real estates in the different towns and wards, and of estimating and putting down in the assessment rolls the respective sums to be paid as taxes, are *quasi* judicial, and cannot be delegated, but must be performed by the boards as such; after they have determined what changes are to be made, the mere *act* of changing is clerical, but the rolls must be completed before the warrants required to be issued are annexed thereto. In Scofield *v.* Lansing, 17 Mich., 437, it appeared that the city charter required the common council (as a condition precedent to raising a tax) to declare by an entry on their minutes, what portion of the expense of an improvement should be assessed to the owners of premises benefited thereby, and specifying the amount to be assessed. *Held*, that this duty could not be delegated to commissioners to perform, as the determination of those facts was vital to the levy. The following cases are also in point here: Under the act for the establishment of common schools, the inhabitants of the school district, at their regular meeting, must vote a precise and definite sum as a tax on the inhabitants of the district for building a school house. They cannot at their meeting delegate to the trustees a discretionary power as to the aggregate amount of tax to be collected. Robinson *v.* Dodge, 18 Johns., 351; Trumbull *v.* White, 5 Hill, 46. A city cannot delegate to its ministerial officers the power to tax, though they may be authorized, under general regulations, to issue licenses when the taxes are paid. See East St. Louis *v.* Wehrung, 46 Ill., 392. The following cases have discussed to some extent what constitutes a delegation of the power to tax: State *v.* Sickle, 24 N. J., 125; Menser *v.* Risdon, 36 Cal., 239; Brooklyn *v.* Breslin, 57 N. Y., 591; McInery *v.* Reed, 23 Iowa, 410; Ould *v.* Richmond, 23 Grat., 464, 471; Foss *v.* Chicago, 56 Ill., 354; Warren *v.* Grand Haven, 30 Mich., 24; Johnson *v.* Saunderson, 34 Vt., 94. The subject was largely considered in Houghton *v.* Austin, 47 Cal., 646.

people create a legislative department for the exercise of the legislative power, and they vest it with no authority to relieve itself of the responsibility by a substitution of other agencies. But it is never assumed by the people that the legislature can take such supervision of all the infinite variety of interests in the state, and of all local as well as general affairs, as to be able to determine in every instance precisely what is needed in matters of taxation, and precisely what purposes shall at any time, under the particular circumstances, be provided for. There is a difference between making the law and giving effect to the law; the one is legislation and the other administration. We conceive that the legislature must, in every instance, prescribe the rule under which taxation may be laid; it must originate the authority under which, after due proceedings, the tax gatherer demands the contribution; but it need not prescribe all the details of action, or even fix with precision the sum to be raised or all the particulars of its expenditure. If the rule is prescribed which, in its administration, works out the result, that is sufficient; but to refer the making of the rule to another authority, would be in excess of legislative power. An illustration or two may possibly sufficiently explain the principle. The legislature, with the utmost propriety, may provide for a court of claims or a state board of audit, whose adjudications against the state shall be final upon it; and may direct that the amounts awarded shall go into the general levy for the year. Here is a rule to be properly worked out by a proper agency. A like provision for the adjustment of claims against counties, cities and townships may also be made. A fund for contingent expenses may be put at the disposal of the executive or of other state officers, to be used for public purposes not previously enumerated in detail by the legislature. But to leave to a court of claims or any state officer or board the power to determine whether a tax should be laid for the current year, or at what rate, or upon what property, or how it should be collected, and whether lands should be sold or forfeited for its satisfaction; all this prescribes no rule, and originates no authority; it merely attempts to empower some other tribunal to prescribe a rule and set in motion the tax machinery. And this is clearly incompetent. The legislature must make the law, but it may prescribe its own regulations regarding the ministerial agents that are to execute it.

One clearly defined exception to the general rule exists in the case of municipal corporations in the levy and collection of local taxes. Immemorial custom which tacitly or expressly has been incorporated in the state constitutions, has made them a part of the general machinery of state government, and in their case the state does little beyond prescribing rules of limitation, within which, for local purposes, the power to tax is left to them with authority subordinate to that of the state to make rules for its regulation and execution.[1]

[1] Caldwell *v.* Justices, 4 Jones Eq., 323; Taylor *v.* Newbern, 2 id., 141; Thompson *v.* Floyd, 2 Jones Law, 313; Wingate *v.* Sluder, 6 id., 552; Commissioners *v.* Patterson, 8 id., 182; Wilmington *v.* Roby, 8 Ired., 250; Steward *v.* Jefferson, 3 Harr., 335; Lockhart *v.* Harrington, 1 Hawkes, 408; Cheaney *v.* Hooser, 9 B. Monr., 330; Slack *v.* Railroad Co., 13 id., 1, 9; Battle *v.* Mobile, 9 Ala., 234; Stein *v.* Mobile, 24 id., 591; Osborn *v.* Mobile, 44 id., 493; Harrison *v.* Vicksburg, 3 S. & M., 581; Smith *v.* Aberdeen, 25 Miss., 458; Hope *v.* Deaderick, 8 Humph., 1; Trigally *v.* Memphis, 6 Cold., 382; Bull *v.* Read, 13 Grat., 78; Case of County Levy, 5 Call, 139; People *v.* Kelsey, 34 Cal., 470; Washington *v.* State, 13 Ark., 752; State *v.* Noyes, 10 Fost., 279, 292; Burgess *v.* Pue, 2 Gill, 11; Alexander *v.* Baltimore, 5 id., 383; Kinney *v.* Zimpleman, 36 Texas, 554, able opinion by *Walker*, J.; St. Louis *v.* Laughlin, 49 Mo., 559; St. Louis *v.* Savings Bank, 49 id., 574; People *v.* Hurlburt, 24 Mich., 44, 108; Butler's Appeal, 73 Penn. St., 448; Cooley's Const. Lim., 191 and cases cited. For an early case denying the power of the legislature to delegate to county boards the power to tax, see Marr *v.* Enloe, 1 Yerg., 452. In the subsequent case of Hope *v.* Deaderick, 8 Humph., 1, the right to empower local bodies to levy local taxes was fully sustained. In Arbegust *v.* Louisville, 2 Bush, 271, 275, 276, *Williams*, J., speaking of an extension of city boundaries which was complained of as permitting unjust local taxation of suburban property, says: "Whatever may be said of the intrinsic justice of such measures, there is no power in the courts to control this, when the taxing power is conferred in good faith, to uphold local government, and give police regulations to the population, and not merely to embrace taxable property for revenue purposes in order to lighten the burdens of others." See also Swift *v.* Newport, 7 Bush, 37. In the colony of Massachusetts, the right to raise money by taxation of the interests of the proprietors of a town seems to have been conferred on the proprietors as a corporation, and they enforced the tax by sale of such interests, but they did not sell interests set off in severalty. Bott *v.* Perley, 11 Mass., 169. The case of Anderson *v.* The Kerns Draining Co., 14 Ind., 199, is one difficult to be reconciled with the general principle asserted in the text, that the power to tax cannot be delegated. The Kerns Draining Co. was a corporation formed under a general statute of that state, which permitted as-

The power affected by contracts. There are cases in which state legislatures have pledged the state in a more or less formal manner, that on some particular subject of taxation the state should refrain, either wholly or for some definite period, from levying any taxes whatever, or should levy them only to a certain extent. Whether such a pledge could bind the state has been made the subject of controversy. The general rule is that one legislative body cannot by its own action narrow the scope of the legislative power, but with the same amplitude that it comes to

sociations voluntarily to incorporate themselves for the purpose of the construction of levees and drains, and authorized them when incorporated to take property for the purpose of such levees and drains, and to tax those who were benefited for the expenses. Anderson, being thus taxed for benefits accruing from a drain, resisted payment, but a judgment against him was supported. *Perkins*, J., does not allude to the question of the power of the legislature to make such a delegation of authority, but confines his attention to the question whether the purpose is a public purpose. If the drain is constructed to promote the public health, he assumes the purpose to be public; and as the record does not show the contrary, he assumes that to have been the object and affirms the judgment. With great respect for that eminent judge, if such a power to tax can be given by general law to any persons who will organize to take it, we do not see why the levying and collecting of the whole revenue of the state may not be farmed out after the manner of arbitrary rulers in former periods. In Harward *v.* St. Clair and Monroe Levee and Drainage Co., 51 Ill., 130, 135, the supreme court of Illinois deny the right of the legislature to confer upon a private corporation the power to tax. While basing the denial in the main on a clause of the constitution which, in conferring the power to tax on municipal corporate authorities, they understand was intended to exclude its exercise locally by any other authorities, it is justly said by *Lawrence*, J., "The power of taxation is, of all the powers of government, the one most liable to abuse, even when exercised by the direct representatives of the people; and if committed to persons who may exercise it over others without reference to their consent, the certainty of its abuse would be simply a question of time. No person or class of persons could be safely entrusted with irresponsible power over the property of others; and such a power is essentially despotic in its nature, and violative of all just principles of government. It matters not that, as in the present instance, it is to be professedly exercised for public uses, by expending for the public benefit the tax collected. If it be a tax, as in the present instance, to which the persons who are to pay it have never given their consent, and imposed by persons acting under no responsibility of official position, and clothed with no authority of any kind by those whom they propose to tax, it is, to the extent of such tax, misgovernment of the same character as our forefathers thought just cause of revolution." The case of Cypress Pond Draining Co. *v.* Hooper, 2 Met. (Ky.), 350, is equally em-

one body, it must pass to the successor.[1] Pledges, therefore, or stipulations by one legislature regarding the future levy of taxes, though they may under some circumstances charge the conscience of the members or their successors, are not limitations on legislative power, but may be observed or disregarded as it shall be thought the public necessity or policy may require. An exception, however, is held to exist in case of an agreement by a state, entered into for a consideration, to refrain from exercising this power; that provision of the federal constitution which forbids the state passing laws which impair the obligation of contracts, applying as well to contracts by the state itself as to those between individuals. And therefore, where a state exchanged lands with an Indian tribe, and stipulated by legislative act that those conveyed to the Indians should not thereafter be subject to any tax, this stipulation was held to be binding as a contract, and available on behalf of those who subsequently by legislative permission became purchasers from the Indians.[2] A number of cases, for

phatic against the right to delegate any such power of local taxation. The Drainage Co. Case in 11 La. An., 338, was one in which it is not surprising that the court could not all agree in the conclusion. In that case the legislation permitted a private corporation to drain the low lands near New Orleans at the expense of the proprietors, though the assessment upon the proprietors was made not by the corporation but by assessors. The court at first held this assessment unconstitutional, but a change of two members taking place in its composition, it was then sustained as only an ordinary case of assessment on a basis of benefits. Of course the state cannot confer upon a municipality a power to tax which she does not herself possess: e. g., to tax the agencies of the federal government. O'Donnell *v.* Bailey, 24 Miss., 386. In some of the state constitutions, however, there are express limitations on the power of the state to tax which do not in terms apply to municipalities.

[1] Cooley's Const. Lim., 125-127, 280-284.

[2] New Jersey *v.* Wilson, 7 Cranch., 164. Compare Armstrong *v.* Athens Co., 16 Pet., 281. In Home of Friendless *v.* Rouse, 8 Wall., 430, an act which, for the purpose of encouraging the establishment of a charitable institution, declared that its property should be exempt from taxation, was held to be a contract. So an exemption from taxation, for ten years, of lands which had been donated to the state for reclamation, was held not subject to repeal as to all lands sold. McGee *v.* Mathis, 4 Wall., 143. So where a bonus was paid for a corporate charter, the state agreeing not to impose any further tax upon the corporators during the existence of their charter under the act, it was held that a tax on the stockholders by reason of their shares was in violation of this agreement. Gordon *v.* The Appeal Tax Court, 3 How., 133; followed in

which this has been the precedent, are referred to in the note, but it is conceded in all of them that there must be a consideration to the state for the relinquishment, or the elements of a contract will be wanting. An exemption, from motives of state policy merely, may be withdrawn at any time when the like motives incline the legislature in the opposite direction;[1] and in any case the intention of the state to bind itself by an exemption, must be clear, as all presumptions are against it.[2]

Wendover *v.* Lexington, 15 B. Monr., 258, 264. An act exempting the stock of a railroad company and its real estate from taxation for 36 years was sustained as a contract, in Tomlinson *v.* Branch, 15 Wall., 460; as was a perpetual exemption in Humphreys *v.* Pegues, 16 Wall., 244: see also Pacific R. R. *v.* Maguire, 20 Wall., 36. That a license tax cannot be imposed on a franchise which a corporation has acquired by a surrender of valuable rights, was decided in Lucas *v.* Lottery Commissioners, 11 G. & J., 490. That the franchise to set up a lottery is not a contract, see Moore *v.* State, 48 Miss., 147: but see also Broadbent *v.* Tuscaloosa, etc., Association, 45 Ala., 170.

[1] Christ's Church *v.* Philadelphia, 24 How., 300; East Saginaw Salt Manuf. Co. *v.* East Saginaw, 19 Mich., 259; S. C. in error, 13 Wall., 373. In the first of these cases was considered a legislative act which provided that "the real property, including ground rents, now belonging, and payable to Christ's Church Hospital, in the city of Philadelphia, so long as the same shall continue to belong to the said hospital, shall be and remain free from taxes." Held, that the exemption so given was a mere privilege, *bene placitum*, and might be revoked at the pleasure of the sovereign authority. And the privilege being recalled by a subsequent act, the property of the hospital became taxable like any other. In the second case a legislative act had provided that companies and corporations formed, or that might be formed, for the boring for and manufacturing salt in the state of Michigan, should be entitled to certain benefits conferred by the act, one of which was that " all property, real and personal, used for the purpose mentioned, shall be exempt from taxation for any purpose." This was considered a mere bounty law, dependent for its continuance upon the dictates of public policy, and the voluntary good faith of the legislature. In Home of the Friendless *v.* Rouse, 8 Wall., 430, the exemption, which was held irrepealable, was contained in the charter of the corporation. It was objected that no consideration for the exemption was shown, but it was replied by the court that none was necessary beyond the benefits to the community, which it is to be assumed were anticipated from the corporation. On the general subject, see Hagar *v.* Supervisors of Yolo, 47 Cal., 222; Ramsey *v.* Hoeger, Sup. Ct. Ill. (1874), 6 Chicago Legal News, 318.

[2] "The right to levy and collect taxes is a necessary incident of every government, essential to its very existence, and is never presumed to have been surrendered or abandoned except by clear words, and for what is deemed, at the time, by the law-making power, an adequate consideration. The surrender

It having been authoritatively determined that the charter of a private corporation is a contract between the commonwealth and the corporators, it follows that whatever stipulations it contains regarding taxation of the corporate franchises or property are irrepealable.[1] An exception to this sweeping statement exists

cannot be extended by implication; and if one tax is expressed, it cannot be presumed to extend to others. No power to tax need be reserved; it exists and remains unless expressly yielded." Jones, etc., Manuf. Co. *v.* Commonwealth, 69 Penn. St., 81, 137. See also Commonwealth *v.* Bird, 12 Mass., 443; Dale *v.* Governor, 3 Stew., 387; Brainard *v.* Colchester, 31 Conn., 407, 410; Easton Bank *v.* Commonwealth, 10 Penn. St., 442, 450; Herrick *v.* Randolph, 13 Vt., 525, 531; People *v.* Roper, 35 N. Y., 629; People *v.* Commissioners of Taxes, 47 id., 501; Bradley *v.* McAtee, 7 Bush, 667; S. C., 3 Am. Rep., 309; Nor. Mo. R. R. Co. *v.* Maguire, 49 Mo., 490; S. C., 8 Am. Rep., 141; Pacific R. R.Co. *v.* Cass Co., 53 Mo., 17; Wendover *v.* Lexington, 15 B. Monr., 258, 262; Baltimore & Ohio R. R. Co. *v.* Marshall Co., 3 W. Va., 319; Stein *v.* Mobile, 17 Ala., 234; S. C., 24 id., 591; State *v.* Bank of Smyrna, 2 Hous., 99; Erie R. R. Co. *v.* Commonwealth, 66 Penn. St., 84; Gilman *v.* Sheboygan, 2 Black, 510, 513; Armstrong *v.* Athens Co., 16 Pet., 281; Lord *v.* Litchfield, 36 Conn., 116; S. C., 4 Am. Rep., 41; Bridge Proprietors *v.* State, 21 N. J., 384, 386; S. C. on appeal, 22 id., 593; Bangor *v.* Stetson, 56 Me., 274; Portland, etc., R. R. Co. *v.* Saco, 60 id., 196, 198; People *v.* Lawrence, 41 N. Y., 137; Academy of Fine Arts *v.* Philadelphia, 22 Penn. St., 496; Miller *v.* Kirkpatrick, 29 id., 226; Macon *v.* Central R. R. and Banking Co., 50 Geo., 620; Smith *v.* Macon, 20 Ark., 17; Providence Bank *v.* Billings, 4 Pet., 514, 563; Philadelphia, etc., R. R. Co. *v.* Maryland, 10 How., 376, 393; Minot *v.* Philadelphia, etc., R. R. Co., 18 Wall., 206; Nor. Mo. R. R. Co. *v.* Maguire, 20 id., 46; Erie Railway *v.* Pennsylvania, 21 id., 497. Naming a rate of taxation, but not expressly limiting it, does not preclude its being raised. State *v.* Parker, 32 N. J., 426: compare Louisville R. R. Co. *v.* Louisville, 4 Bush, 478; Erie R. R. Co. *v.* Commonwealth, 66 Penn. St., 84; St. Louis *v.* Boatmen's Ins. and Trust Co., 47 Mo., 150. "While it were better for the interest of the community that this power should on no occasion be surrendered, this court has always held that the legislature of a state, unrestrained by constitutional limitation, has full control over the subject, and can make a contract with the corporation to exempt its property from taxation, either in perpetuity or for a limited period of time. If, however, on any fair construction of the legislation, there is a reasonable doubt whether the contract is made out, this doubt must be solved in favor of the state. In other words, the language used must be of such a character as, fairly interpreted, leaves no room for controversy." Bailey *v.* Pacific R. R. Co., 7 Chicago Legal News, 266 (Sup. Ct. U. S., per *Davis*, J.).

[1] Piqua Bank *v.* Knoop, 16 How., 369; Dodge *v.* Woolsey, 18 id., 331, 339; Home of the Friendless *v.* Rouse, 8 Wall., 430; Washington University *v.* Rouse, id., 439; Wilmington, etc., R. R. Co. *v.* Reid, 13 id., 264; Humphreys *v.* Pegues, 16 id., 244; Illinois Central R. R. Co. *v.* McLean Co., 17 Ill., 291.

where, by the charter, the right of amendment or repeal is expressly reserved, as well as where, by the constitution of the state, all charters are granted subject to that right. Where such is the provision of the constitution, it is a limitation upon the powers of the legislature, of which every person must take notice, and there is no room for the implication of a contract in restraint of the taxing power.[1] Municipal charters are not contracts, but are granted for public purposes, and amended or repealed at the discretion of the legislature.[2]

Exemption of agencies of government. No state can impose taxes on persons, property, or other subjects of taxation, which are not within its jurisdiction. This is selfevident, but it has peculiar application in this country under the federal constitution, which apportions the sovereign authority between the state and the nation, and gives to each over certain subjects an exclusive jurisdiction. Whatever pertains to this exclusive jurisdiction is excluded from the taxing power of the other as much as if it were beyond its territorial limits. The rules upon this subject, as they have been laid down by the authorities, appear to be the following:

1. Every person within a state owing temporary or permanent allegiance to it; all property of every description within the state and entitled to the protection of its laws; every private franchise, privilege, business or occupation, is subject to be taxed by the state, in return for the benefits received and anticipated from state government and protection. But they are also on precisely the same grounds subject to be taxed by the federal government, whenever its necessities or policy shall be thought to require it.[3]

[1] State *v.* Miller, 30 N. J., 368; Same *v.* Same, 31 id., 521; State *v.* Newark, 35 id., 157, 162; Iron City B'k *v.* Pittsburgh, 37 Penn. St., 340; Commonwealth *v.* Fayette Co. R. R. Co., 55 id., 452; Union Improvement Co. *v.* Commonwealth, 69 id., 140; West Wisconsin R. R. Co. *v.* Supervisors of Trempealeau, 35 Wis., 257; Tomlinson *v.* Jessup, 15 Wall., 454; Trask *v.* Maguire, 18 id., 391.

[2] Dartmouth College *v.* Woodward, 4 Wheat., 518, 629, per *Marshall*, Ch. J.; Dillon on Mun. Corp., §§ 49, and 8, 9, 10; Cooley's Const. Lim., 276; Story on Const., 4th ed., ch. XXXIV, and cases cited.

[3] It is said in Lane County *v.* Oregon, 7 Wall., 71, that with the exception of the restrictions expressly imposed by the constitution of the United States,

2. It is the theory of our system of government that the state and the nation alike are to exercise their powers respectively in as full and ample a manner as the proper departments of government shall determine to be needful and just, and as might be done by any other sovereignty whatsoever. This theory by necessary implication excludes wholly any interference by either the state or the nation with an independent exercise by the other of its constitutional powers. If it were otherwise, neither government would be supreme within what has been set apart for its exclusive sphere, but on the other hand, would be liable at any time to be crippled, embarrassed, and perhaps wholly obstructed in its operations at the will or caprice of those who for the time being wielded the authority of the other. And that an exercise of the power to tax might have that effect is manifest from a consideration of the nature of the power. Any "power which in its nature acknowledges no limits,"[1] and which, even in a lawful and legitimate exercise may be carried to the extent of an absolute appropriation of the property or destruction of the franchise or privilege upon which it is exerted,[2] must be incapable of being admitted within its sovereignty by another, with due regard to a safe and independent exercise of its own authority. If this be so, then under the constitution of the United States which contemplates an independent exercise by state and nation severally of their constitutional powers, it must follow as a necessary and inevitable conclusion, —

3. That the means or agencies provided or selected by the federal government as necessary or convenient to the exercise of its functions cannot be subjected to the taxing power of the states.

the state power of taxation in respect to property, business and persons within its limits remains entire. There is nothing in the constitution which contemplates authorizing any direct abridgment of this power by the national legislature.

[1] Per *Marshall*, Ch. J., in Weston *v.* Charleston, 2 Pet., 449, 466; Lane County *v.* Oregon, 7 Wall., 71; Bank of Commerce *v.* New York, 2 Black, 620; Carroll *v.* Perry, 4 McLean, 25; Cheaney *v.* Hooser, 9 B. Monr., 330, 339; Veazie Bank *v.* Fenno, 8 Wall., 533, 548; State *v.* Bell, 1 Phil. (N. C.), 85. Compare Berney *v.* Tax Collector, 2 Bailey, 654.

[2] McCullough *v.* Maryland, 4 Wheat., 316, 431, per *Marshall*, Ch. J.; Veazie Bank *v.* Fenno, 8 Wall., 533, 548, per *Chase*, Ch. J.

The states cannot tax a bank chartered by congress as the fiscal agent of the government,[1] they cannot tax the loans of the United States contracted under the power conferred upon the government to borrow money,[2] nor the revenue stamps issued by the United States,[3] nor the salary or emoluments of federal officers.[4] It also follows,—

4. That the federal government is also without power to tax the corresponding means or agencies of the states, or the salaries of state officers; the state in the exercise of its functions being entitled to the same immunity from congressional interference that the nation is from that of the state.[5] And a state municipal corporation, being only a portion of its sovereign power, created as a convenient if not a necessary part of the machinery of state

[1] McCullough *v.* Maryland, 4 Wheat., 316, 368; Osborn *v.* Bank of United States, 9 id., 738. Property occupied for the United States, but not owned by it, was held taxable to the owner in Speed *v.* St. Louis County Court, 42 Mo., 382. And the fact that the government has an interest in real estate does not preclude the taxation of other interests to the owners. State *v.* Moore, 12 Cal., 56.

[2] Weston *v.* Charleston, 2 Pet., 449; Bank of Commerce *v.* New York, 2 Black, 620; Bank Tax Case, 2 Wall., 200; Van Allen *v.* Assessors, 3 id., 573; People *v.* The Commissioners, 4 id., 244; Bradley *v.* People, id., 459; The Banks *v.* The Mayor, 7 id., 16; Bank *v.* Supervisors, id., 26. Compare State *v.* Jackson, 33 N. J., 450; Commonwealth *v.* Hamilton Manuf. Co., 12 Allen, 298; Commonwealth *v.* Provident Inst., id., 312; Coite *v.* Society for Savings, 32 Conn., 173. A tax on the franchise of a corporation whose capital is in part invested in United States securities, is not a tax on such securities. Society for Savings *v.* Coite, 6 Wall., 594; Provident Institution *v.* Massachusetts, id., 611; Hamilton County *v.* Massachusetts, id., 632. A city cannot tax state bonds unless specially authorized. Augusta *v.* Dunbar, 50 Geo., 387.

[3] Palfrey *v.* Boston, 101 Mass., 329. Or its treasury notes. Montgomery County *v.* Elston, 32 Ind., 27.

[4] Dobbin *v.* Commissioners of Erie County, 16 Pet., 435. In Melcher *v.* Boston, 9 Met., 73, a clerk in a post office was held taxable by the state on his income.

[5] Ward *v.* Maryland, 12 Wall., 418, 427, per *Clifford*, J.; The Collector *v.* Day, 11 id., 113; Railroad Co. *v.* Peniston, 18 id., 5; Friedman *v.* Siegel, 10 Blatch., 327; Warren *v.* Paul, 22 Ind., 276, 279; State *v.* Garton, 32 id., 1; Fifield *v.* Close, 15 Mich., 505; Union Bank *v.* Hill, 3 Cold., 325; Smith *v.* Short, 40 Ala., 385; Jones *v.* Keep's Estate, 19 Wis., 369; Sayles *v.* Davis, 22 id., 225; Moor *v.* Quirk, 105 Mass., 49; S. C., 7 Am. Rep., 499; Cooley's Const. Lim., 484, and cases cited. A railroad wholly owned by a state and operated by it, not taxable under the U. S. revenue laws. Georgia *v.* Atkins, 1 Abb., U. S., 22.

government, is as much exempt from the taxation of the federal government, in all its revenues and property, as the state itself.[1]

5. A tax upon persons may possibly, in some cases, tend to embarrass the operations of either national or state government, in which case it would be void unless imposed by the government which was liable to be inconvenienced by it. And, on this ground, it has been held, that a state tax of a certain sum on every person leaving the state by public conveyance was invalid; the tendency being to embarrass the functions of the national government, by obstructing the travel of citizens and officers of the United States in the business of the government and the transportation of armies and munitions of war.[2]

6. It is customary for the federal government, in receiving a new state to the union, to require from it — and probably without

[1] United States *v.* Railroad Co., 17 Wall., 322. A state may tax its own municipal organizations, or their corporate property, if it shall see fit, but there is always a presumption against the intention to do so. Compare Wayland *v.* County Commissioners, 4 Gray, 500, with Stein *v.* Mobile, 24 Ala., 591; State *v.* Gaffney, 34 N. J., 133; Directors of Poor *v.* School Directors, 42 Penn. St., 21, 25; and Louisville *v.* Commonwealth, 1 Duv., 295. The grant in general terms to a city of the power to tax will not authorize the city to tax state or county property. Piper *v.* Singer, 4 S. & R., 354; Nashville *v.* Bank of Tennessee, 1 Swan, 269. See People *v.* McCreery, 34 Cal., 432, 456; People *v.* Doe, 36 Cal., 220; People *v.* Austin, 47 Cal., 353. It has been held in Massachusetts that lands of a county used for county purposes are exempt from all taxation, whether imposed for general purposes or for local improvements. Worcester County *v.* Worcester, 116 Mass., 193.

[6] Crandall *v.* Nevada, 6 Wall., 35. The like principle was recognized in State *v.* Jackson, 33 N. J., 450, where a bounty voted to relieve a town from a draft was held invalid, as tending to defeat the legislation of congress on the subject. That case was decided by a divided court, and the decision is opposed to the current of authority. In State Treasurer *v.* Philadelphia, etc., R. R. Co., 4 Houston, 158, a law which imposed a state tax on railroad companies of ten cents on every passenger carried within the state, excepting soldiers and sailors of the United States, was held to be not a tax upon the business of the carrier, measured by the number of persons carried, but a tax upon the persons carried, to be collected by the carrier for the state, and, consequently, so far as it operated upon persons entering into, departing from, or passing through the state, was, in effect, a regulation of commerce between the states, and, consequently, within the decision in Crandall *v.* Nevada. The case is reasoned by Chancellor *Bates* with his accustomed ability, but it will be seen from the statement of the case, that some of the objections to the Nevada act could not be made to this.

necessity,[1]— a stipulation that the public domain, lying within its limits, shall not be taxed by the state. The disability remains effective until the United States has made sale, or other disposition, of the lands, but it then terminates, notwithstanding the title may not have passed by the actual execution and delivery of patent of conveyance; the land being actually severed from the public domain by the sale itself.[2] But this principle will not apply in any case until the right to a patent is complete, and the equitable title fully vested in the party without anything more to be paid or any act to be done, going to the foundation of the right.[3] Nor will it apply where, as one of the conditions of the grant, the lands not sold by the grantee within a time named are to be open to preemption and settlement like any portion of the public domain.[4]

7. Railroads owned and controlled by private corporations are in a certain sense public conveniences and agencies, but they constitute no branch or part of the government, and are not properly governmental agencies, even though the government may employ them for the transportation of its troops, its mails, etc., or for other purposes. The corporations owning them are consequently entitled to claim no exemption based on any implication that they are essential to the operations of the government.[5] And the same

[1] See Blue Jacket *v.* Johnson County, 3 Kansas, 299. A possessory interest in the public lands for mining purposes may be taxed as being a species of property. People *v.* Shearer, 30 Cal., 645; People *v.* Cohen, 31 Cal., 210.

[2] Carrol *v.* Perry, 4 McLean, 25; Witherspoon *v.* Duncan, 21 Ark., 240; S. C., 4 Wall., 210; Puget Sound Agricultural Co. *v.* Pierce County, 1 Wash. Ter. Rep., 180; Carrol *v.* Safford, 3 How., 441; Astrom *v.* Hammond, 3 McLean, 107; People *v.* Shearer, 30 Cal., 645; Hull *v.* Dowling, 18 Cal., 619; Iowa Homestead Co. *v.* Webster County, 21 Iowa, 221; McGoon *v.* Scales, 9 Wall., 23. See U. P. R. R. Co. *v.* McShane, 18 Int. Rev. Rec., 68.

[3] Railway Company *v.* Prescott, 16 Wall., 603, in which case one of the conditions of the grant was, that the cost of the government surveys, selections, etc., should be prepaid by the grantee before the lands should be conveyed.

[4] Railway Company *v.* Prescott, 16 Wall., 603. Compare this with Tucker *v.* Ferguson in the same court, 7 Chicago Legal News, 78 (1875).

[5] Thompson *v.* Pacific R. R., 9 Wall., 579. Compare People *v.* Central Pacific R. R. Co., 43 Cal., 398; Huntington *v.* Same, 2 Sawyer, 503; Inhabitants of Worcester *v.* Western R. R. Corp., 4 Met., 564, 568; Boston & Me. R. R. *v.* Cambridge, 8 Cush., 237. In the case of the Union Pacific R. R. Company,

is true of any other private corporation, notwithstanding the fact that the government may find it convenient to make use of the corporation for its purposes, just as a private individual might be employed for the same or any other purpose if the government had need of his services.[1]

Taxes on commerce. The federal constitution provides[2] that no state shall, without consent of congress, lay any imposts or duties on imports or exports, except what may be necessary for executing its inspection laws. Under this provision a state law imposing a stamp duty on bills of lading of gold and silver to be carried out of the state has been held invalid as constituting a tax on exports.[3] But the provision has no application to articles transported merely from one state into another.[4] The same clause of the constitution forbids the states without the consent of congress to lay any "duty of tonnage." The precise meaning of this phraseology has been the subject of some controversy. Vessels are taxable as property, and possibly the tax may be measured by the capacity, when they are taxed only as prop-

chartered by congress. and in which the government has important interests with some power of control, the states have no power to tax. U. P. R. R. Co. *v.* Peniston, 18 Wall., 5. A state bank chartered for the benefit of the state, and with the faith and credit of the state pledged for its support, is not subject to taxation by a municipal corporation. Nashville *v.* Bank of Tennessee, 1 Swan, 269.

[1] The national banking law permits the banks organized under it to be taxed, only limiting taxation to a particular mode, and prohibiting its being in excess of that of state banks. The permission thus given to tax removes any implied exemption that might otherwise exist. See Union Nat. Bank *v.* Chicago, 3 Bissell, 82. The right of congress to inhibit the taxation of national banks except as it shall provide, is assumed in many cases. See Flint *v.* Boston, 99 Mass., 141. The right to tax a railroad company is not affected by the fact of its property being mortgaged to the United States. Thompson *v.* Pacific R. R. Co., 9 Wall., 579.

[2] Art. 1, § 10, par. 2.

[3] Almy *v.* California, 24 How., 169. See what is said of this case by Mr. Justice *Miller* in Woodruff *v.* Parham, 8 Wall., 123, 137. A stamp tax on foreign bills of exchange was sustained in Ex parte Martin, 7 Nev., 140.

[4] Woodruff *v.* Parham, 8 Wall., 123. It was held in Jackson Iron Co. *v.* Auditor General, Mich. Sup. Ct., 1875, that a tax on iron ores of one and a half cents a ton if taken out of the state for smelting, while if reduced within the state they were exempt, was a tax on commerce and therefore void.

erty and not as vehicles of commerce;[1] but any such distinction must be somewhat questionable. It has been often held that a tax on vessels at a certain sum "per ton" was forbidden.[2] And it seems that a tax of a certain sum upon every vessel arriving in port is to be regarded as a duty of tonnage, though demanded irrespective of the vessel's capacity.[3] The federal constitution also provides that congress shall have power to regulate commerce with foreign nations, and among the several states and with the Indian tribes.[4] The constitution, and the laws made in pursuance thereof being supreme over the several states, the power of regulation cannot be interfered with, limited or restrained by any exercise of state authority. When therefore it is held that a power to tax is, at the discretion of the authority which wields it, a power which may be carried to the extent of an annihilation of that which it taxes, and therefore may defeat and nullify any authority which may elsewhere exist for the purpose of protection and preservation, it follows as a corollary that the several states cannot tax the commerce which is regulated under the supremacy of congress.[5]

But a tax on property that may be the subject of commerce under congressional regulation, is not a tax on commerce. Neither is a tax on property that has been the subject of such commerce, where it is taxed only as property, and in common with all other property within the state.[6] An importer of foreign goods, in his

[1] Lott *v.* Mobile Trade Co., 43 Ala., 578. See Steamship Co. v. Port Wardens, 6 Wall., 31; State Tonnage Tax Cases, 12 id., 204.

[2] Sheffield *v.* Parsons, 3 Stew. & Port., 302; Harbor Master *v.* Railroad Co., 3 Strob., 594; State *v.* Charleston, 4 Rich., 286; Lott *v.* Morgan, 41 Ala., 246; Johnson *v.* Drummond, 20 Grat., 419. See Gibbons *v.* Ogden, 9 Wheat., 1, 186; Hays *v.* Steamship Co., 17 How., 596; Sinnot *v.* Davenport, 22 id., 227; Steamship Co. *v.* Port Wardens, 6 Wall., 31. The point is authoritatively determined in Cannon *v.* New Orleans, 20 id., 577.

[3] Steamship Co. *v.* Port Wardens, 6 Wall., 31. It is not, however, incompetent for a state to authorize a city to collect a wharfage charge on all vessels touching at its wharves. Marshall *v.* Vicksburg, 15 Wall., 146.

[4] Art. 1, § 8, par. 3. In Foster *v.* County Commissioners, 7 Minn., 140, it was decided that a state tax upon a licensed trader within an Indian reservation would be in conflict with this provision of the constitution.

[5] McCulloch *v.* Maryland, 4 Wheat., 316, 425, per *Marshall*, Ch. J.

[6] Brown *v.* Maryland, 12 Wheat., 419, 437; Waring *v.* The Mayor, 8 Wall., 110; Purvear *v.* Commonwealth, 5 id., 475, 479.

capacity as such, is not the subject of state taxation, and cannot be required to pay a license fee as importer;[1] and his sales are exempt from state taxation, because he purchases, by the payment of the duty, a right to dispose of the merchandise as well as to bring it into the country; and the tax, if it were admissible, would intercept the import, as an import, in the way to become incorporated with the general mass of property, and would deny it the privilege of becoming so incorporated until it should have contributed to the revenue of the state.[2] But when the importer has sold the imported package, or has otherwise mixed the goods with the general property of the state by breaking up the package, a state tax which then finds the articles already incorporated with the mass of property by the act of the importer, is not a tax upon commerce.[3]

A tax upon freight taken up within a state and carried out of it, or taken up out of a state and brought within it, is held to be a tax upon the commerce between states, even though no distinction is made between freight carried wholly within the state, and that brought into or carried through or out of it.[4] The same has been held of a tax upon *the use* of locomotives and cars employed on a railroad which runs from one state into another. As property, locomotives may be taxed, but not their use as vehicles of commerce between states.[5] A tax upon the masters of vessels engaged in foreign commerce, of a certain sum on account of every passenger brought from a foreign country into the state, is a tax upon commerce.[6] On the other hand, a tax on exchange and

[1] Brown *v.* Maryland, 12 Wheat., 419, 437. And see Low *v.* Austin, 13 Wall., 29.

[2] Waring *v.* Mayor, 8 Wall., 110, 152, per *Clifford*, J., citing Brown *v.* Maryland, 12 Wheat., 419, 448, and Almy *v.* California, 24 How., 169, 173. See State *v.* Allmond, 2 Houston, 612; Hinson *v.* Lott, 40 Ala., 123; S. C. in error, 8 Wall., 148.

[3] Brown *v.* Maryland, 4 Wheat., 419, 437; Waring *v.* Mayor, 8 Wall., 110. Articles imported may be taxed after they have passed from the hands of the importer, even though they remain in the original packages. Waring *v.* The Mayor, 8 Wall., 110. See Low *v.* Austin, 13 Wall., 29; Kenney *v.* Harwell, 42 Ga., 416.

[4] Case of State Freight Tax, 15 Wall., 232. See also Erie Railway Co. *v.* State, 31 N. J., 531.

[5] Minot *v.* Philadelphia, etc., R. R. Co., 2 Abb. U. S., 323; S. C., 18 Wall., 206.

[6] Passenger Cases, 7 How., 283.

money brokers,[1] a tax on legacies to aliens,[2] a tax on the gross receipts of a railway company,[3] have been held not to be taxes on commerce, and consequently not an interference with the constitutional powers of congress.

Taxes in abridgment of the privileges and immunities of citizens. The federal constitution provides that the citizens of each state shall be entitled to all the privileges and immunities of citizens of the several states.[4] Among these privileges and immunities is that of being exempt in other states from higher taxes or impositions than are paid by the citizens of such other states.[5] Under this provision, while it is entirely admissible to levy taxes upon the business or property of nonresident traders within the state,[6] it is not competent to require them to take out a license and to pay therefor a sum greater than that demanded of residents.[7] Different methods of procedure may be expedient in order to secure uniformity of taxation as between residents and nonresidents, and these are not objectionable if uniformity is the purpose, and they have a tendency to secure it.[8] Corporations are not citizens within the meaning of the clause of

[1] Nathan *v.* Louisiana, 8 How., 73.

[2] Mager *v.* Grima, 8 How., 490.

[3] Tax on Railway Gross Receipts, 15 Wall., 284, 289.

[4] Art. 4, § 2, par. 1.

[5] Corfield *v.* Coryell, 4 Wash. C. C., 371, 380, per *Washington*, J.; Wiley *v.* Parmer, 14 Ala., 627; Scott *v.* Watkins, 22 Ark., 556, 564; Oliver *v.* Washington Mills, 11 Allen, 268.

[6] Duer *v.* Small, 4 Blatch., 263; Commonwealth *v.* Milton, 12 B. Monr., 212, 218.

[7] Ward *v.* Maryland, 12 Wall., 418; State *v.* North, 27 Mo., 464; Crow *v.* State, 14 id., 237. In State *v.* Welton, 55 Mo., 288, a tax was sustained which was levied on those dealing in articles "not the growth, produce or manufacture of the state." The court held it not to be within the rule of Ward *v.* Maryland, and not to be a tax on the produce of other states, but only on the business. The same decision was made in State *v.* Hodgdon, 41 Vt., 139.

[8] To provide a different method for assessing the lands of nonresidents for taxation from that provided for residents — e. g., to assess the latter on lists handed in by themselves, and the former on an appraisement by residents in the vicinity — does not infringe on the privileges and immunities of nonresidents. Redd *v.* St. Francis Co., 17 Ark., 416.

the constitution here considered, and it is no violation of the privileges and immunities of citizens of other states to require a corporation, of which they are stockholders, to submit to such taxation as the state shall see fit to impose as a condition of doing business therein.[1]

Taxes which impair the obligation of contracts. No state can pass any law impairing the obligation of contracts.[2] It has never been held incompetent, under this provision, to tax, as personal property, contracts for the payment of money, or which have a money value; and the right to do so may be assumed.[3] But these, it seems, can only be considered as the property of the owner where he has his domicile, and, consequently, are only taxable there. To tax in one state contracts owned in another, is held to impair their obligation, and, consequently, to be inadmissible, even though they are made and payable in the state imposing the tax, and are secured by mortgage in that state.[4]

[1] Tatem *v.* Wright, 23 N. J., 429, and other cases cited, *ante*, p. 43.

[2] Const. of U. S., art. 1, § 10, par. 1.

[3] See Catlin *v.* Hull, 21 Vt., 152.

[4] State Tax on Foreign-held Bonds, 15 Wall., 300. The act of the legislature which came under consideration in this case required the treasurer to retain five per cent. of the interest payable to its creditors, and pay it into the treasury of the commonwealth. *Field*, J., says: "The power of taxation, however vast in its character and searching in its extent, is necessarily limited to subjects within the jurisdiction of the state. These subjects are persons, property and business. Whatever form taxation may assume, whether as duties, imposts, excises or licenses, it must relate to one of these subjects. It is not possible to conceive of any other, though as applied to them, the taxation may be exercised in a great variety of ways. It may touch property in every shape; in its natural condition, in its manufactured form, and in its various transmutations. And the amount of taxation may be determined by the value of the property, or its use, or its capacity, or its productiveness. It may touch business in the almost infinite forms in which it is conducted, in professions, in commerce, in manufactures, and in transportations. Unless restrained by provisions of the federal constitution, the power of the state as to the mode, form and extent of taxation is unlimited, where the subjects to which it applies are within her jurisdiction.

"Corporations may be taxed like natural persons, upon their property and business. But debts owing by corporations are not property of the debtors in any sense; they are obligations of the debtors, and only possess value in the hands of the creditors. With them they are property, and in their hands they may be taxed. To call debts property of the debtors is simply to misuse terms.

Other restraints on the power of taxation. It is customary for the people in framing constitutions for the states to impose other restrictions on the power of taxation, some of which we shall take occasion to consider hereafter. With the exception of those already mentioned, and such as may thus be expressly imposed, the power is limited in extent only by the will of the government itself. No limitations or restrictions upon the exercise of this essential attribute of government can be raised by implication; but the intention to limit or abridge it must be expressed in clear and unambiguous language.[1]

All the property there can be, in the nature of things, in debts of corporations, belongs to the creditors to whom they are payable, and follows their domicile, wherever that may be. Their debts can have no locality separate from the parties to whom they are due. This principle might be stated in many different ways and supported by citations from numerous adjudications, but no number of authorities and no forms of expression could add anything to its obvious truth, which is recognized upon its simple statement.

"The bonds issued by the railroad company in this case are undoubtedly property, but property in the hands of the holders, not property of the obligors. So far as they are held by nonresidents of the state, they are property beyond the jurisdiction of the state. The law which requires the treasurer of the company to retain five per cent. of the interest due to the nonresident bondholder, is not, therefore, a legitimate exercise of the taxing power. It is a law which interferes between the company and the bondholder, and under the pretense of levying a tax, commands the company to withhold a portion of the stipulated interest and pay it over to the state. It is a law which thus impairs the obligation of the contract between the parties. The obligations of a contract depend upon its terms and the means which the law in existence at the time affords for its enforcement. A law which alters the terms of a contract by imposing new conditions or dispensing with those expressed, is a law which impairs its obligations; for, as stated on another occasion, such a law relieves the parties from the moral duty of performing the original stipulations of the contract, and it prevents their legal enforcement." See also Railroad Co. *v.* Jackson, 7 Wall., 262; Oliver *v.* Washington Mills, 11 Allen, 268. Compare Catlin *v.* Hull, 21 Vt., 152. In Commonwealth *v.* Hamilton Manufacturing Co., 12 Allen, 298, it was decided that the fact that a part of its stockholders are residents of another state would not exempt a corporation from the payment in full of an excise tax measured by the market value of its stock. It was held by the supreme court of South Carolina in Jenkins *v.* Charleston, 7 Ch. Leg. News, 78 (1874), that the stocks of the state or its municipalities might be taxed within the state, though owned by nonresidents; and that the case was not within the case of State Tax on Foreign-held Bonds, *supra.*

[1] Lane County *v.* Oregon, 7 Wall., 71, per *Chase*, J.; State *v.* Parker, 32 N. J., 426, 435, per *Depue*, J.; Eyre *v.* Jacob, 14 Grat., 422, 426, per *Lee*, J. *Ante*, p. 54.

CHAPTER IV.

THE PURPOSES FOR WHICH TAXES MAY BE LAID.

The general rule. All definitions of taxation imply that it is to be imposed only for public purposes,[1] and whatever difference of opinion may exist regarding the admissibility of taxation in particular cases, the fundamental requirement, that the purpose shall be public, will be conceded on all sides. Nor will any question be made, that the right and the duty to determine in the first instance what are and what are not public purposes, is devolved upon the legislative department. It falls there of necessity, because the taxing power is a branch of the legislative, and the legislature cannot lie under the necessity of requiring the opinion or the consent of another department of the government before it will be at liberty to exercise one of its acknowledged powers. The independence of the legislature is an axiom in government; and to be independent, it must act in its own good time, on its own judgment, influenced by its own reasons, restrained only as the people may have seen fit to restrain the grant of legislative power in making it. The legislature must, consequently, determine for itself in every instance, whether a particular purpose is or is not one which so far concerns the public as to render taxation admissible.

But it is also generally admitted, that the legislative determination on this subject is not absolutely conclusive. It may be sufficiently so to put the administrative machinery of the state in

[1] This is as true under one form of government as under another. In Sidney's Treatise "On Government," where he has occasion to refer to the doctrine of courtiers, that the revenue voted to the king is to be spent as he thinks convenient instead of being devoted strictly to public purposes, he very truly remarks, that this "is no less than to cast it into a pit of which no man ever knew the bottom. That which is given one day is squandered away the next; the people is always oppressed with impositions to foment the vices of the court; these daily increasing, they grow insatiable; and the miserable nations are compelled to hard labor in order to satiate those lusts that tend to their own ruin." Ch. 3, § 6.

motion, but when the exaction is made of an individual, and the power of the state is made use of to compel submission, he has always the right to invoke the protection of the law. And an appeal to the law for protection of personal property must necessarily render the question, which lies at the foundation of the demand, a judicial question, upon which the courts cannot refuse to pass judgment. It has been forcibly, and yet very truly said, that an unlimited power in the legislature to make any and every thing lawful which it might see fit to call taxation, would, when plainly stated, be an unlimited power to plunder the citizen.[1] In asserting the right, in any particular case, the legislature merely asserts its jurisdiction to act; but questions of jurisdiction are not usually concluded by a decision in its favor made by the party claiming it; they remain open, and may be disputed anywhere. This is as true of courts as it is of the legislature; jurisdiction comes from the law, and is not obtained by any tribunal through a simple assertion that it exists. When, therefore, the question of the validity of taxation becomes judicial, if it shall appear that the exaction is made for a purpose not public, the right of the individual to protection is clear. Such an exaction is not within the competency of the legislative power, and the attempt to enforce it, however honestly made, could only be an attempt to take property from its possessor under an authority which the law of the land does not recognize. "The theory of our governments, state and national," it has been truly said, "is opposed to the deposit of unlimited power anywhere. The executive, the legislative and the judicial branches of these governments are all of limited and defined powers. There are limitations on such power which grow out of the essential nature of all free governments. Implied reservations of individual rights, without which the social compact could not exist, and which are respected by all governments entitled to the name. * * Of all the powers conferred upon government, that of taxation is

[1] Tyson *v.* School Directors, 51 Penn. St., 9; Washington Avenue, 69 Penn. St., 352; S. C., 8 Am. Rep., 255; Talbot *v.* Hudson, 16 Gray, 417, 421; Freeland *v.* Hastings, 10 Allen, 570, 575; Hooper *v.* Emery, 14 Me., 375, 379; Allen *v.* Jay, 60 Me., 124, 139; S. C., 11 Am. Rep., 185; People *v.* Township Board of Salem, 20 Mich., 452, 459; S. C., 4 Am. Rep., 400; Morford *v.* Unger, 8 Iowa, 82, 92; Hanson *v.* Vernon, 27 Iowa, 28.

most liable to abuse. Given a purpose or object for which taxation may be lawfully used, and the extent of its exercise is in its very nature unlimited. It is true that express limitation on the amount of tax to be levied or the things to be taxed may be imposed by constitution or statute, but in most instances for which taxes are levied, as the support of government, the prosecution of war, the national defense, any limitation is unsafe. The entire resources of the people should, in some instances, be at the disposal of the government. The power to tax is, therefore, the strongest, the most pervading of all the powers of government, reaching directly or indirectly to all classes of the people. * * This power can as readily be employed against one class of individuals and in favor of another, so as to ruin the one class and give unlimited wealth and prosperity to the other, if there is no implied limitation of the uses for which the power may be exercised. To lay with one hand the power of the government on the property of the citizen, and with the other to bestow it on favored individuals to aid private enterprises and build up private fortunes, is none the less a robbery because it is done under the forms of law and is called taxation. This is not legislation. It is a decree under legislative forms."[1]

Presumption in favor of legislation. It is not inconsistent with this doctrine that in every instance the highest consideration should be paid to the determination of the legislature that a tax should be laid. It is not lightly to be assumed that its members have come to the examination of the subject with any other than public motives, or that they have failed to give it due investigation or reflection. The presumption on the other hand must always be that they have considered it with honesty and fair purpose, and that their action is the result of their deliberate judgment. And with all these presumptions tending to support the legislative action, it would seem but reasonable and proper that the courts should support it when not clearly satisfied that an

[1] *Miller, J.*, in Loan Association *v.* Topeka, 20 Wall., 655, 663. And see Freeland *v.* Hastings, 10 Allen, 570, 575; Hooper *v.* Emery, 14 Me., 375, 379; Allen *v.* Jay, 60 Me., 124; S. C., 11 Am. Rep., 185; Gove *v.* Epping, 41 N. H., 539; Crowell *v.* Hopkinton, 45 N. H., 9; Curtis *v.* Whipple, 24 Wis., 350; People *v.* Flagg, 46 N. Y., 401; Tyler *v.* Beacher, 44 Vt., 648, 651.

error has been committed. This is the general rule in constitutional law when the validity of legislation is involved,[1] and it is applicable with peculiar force to the case of a legislative decision upon the purpose for which a tax may be laid.

For in the first place, there is no such thing as drawing a clear line of distinction between purposes of a public and those of a private nature.[2] The question is embarrassing to legislatures, and is equally embarrassing to the courts. All attempts to lay down general rules whereby the difficulties may be solved have seemed, when new and peculiar cases arose, to add only to the embarrassment instead of furnishing the means of extrication from it. Money for a particular purpose may be raised by tax, it is said in one case, if there be the *least possibility* that it will be promotive in any degree of the public welfare.[3] "A tax law," it is said in another case, "must be considered valid unless it be for a purpose in which the community taxed has no interest; when it is apparent that the burden is imposed for the benefit of others, and where it would be so pronounced at first blush."[4] And still

[1] Story on Const., § 1482, and notes; Sedg. on Const. and Stat. L., 414; Cooley, Const. Lim., 182, and numerous cases cited in notes.

[2] *General Purposes of Taxation.* These are enumerated by Adam Smith, as follows: 1. The defense of the commonwealth. This includes the expenses of forts, arsenals, ships of war, a standing army and its equipment, the arming and disciplining of the militia, military roads and means of transportation of troops, etc. 2. The administration of justice. 3. The expense of public works and public institutions, of which he enumerates — (a.) Public works and institutions for facilitating the commerce of the society — (b.) Institutions for the education of youth — (c.) Institutions for the instruction of people of all ages. 4. The expense of supporting the dignity of the sovereign.

Dr. Wayland enumerates more perfectly the purposes for which the public funds are most commonly expended, as follows: 1. The expenses for the support of civil government, including in these the compensation of judicial, legislative and executive officers. 2. Expenses for the purposes of education, classified by him as common education and scientific education. 3. Expenses for maintaining religious worship, which, however, he considers inadmissible. 4. Expenses for the improvement of coasts and harbors, and whatever is necessary for the security of external commerce, and for roads, canals, etc. 5. Expenses of pauperism. 6. The expenses of war.

[3] Booth *v.* Woodbury, 32 Conn., 118, 128, per *Butler*, J.

[4] Sharpless *v.* Philadelphia, 21 Penn. St., 147, 174, following, Cheaney *v.* Hooser, 9 B. Monr., 330, 345. And see Guilford *v.* Supervisors of Chenango, 13 N. Y., 143, 149.

another presents the same idea in language but little different: "To justify the court in arresting the proceedings and in declaring the tax void, the absence of all possible public interest in the purpose for which the funds are raised must be clear and palpable; so clear and palpable as to be perceptible by every mind at first blush."[1] These are very strong and sweeping assertions, but they are supported by many others equally emphatic and comprehensive, which are to be met with in the adjudications of courts.[2] The very emphasis, however, with which the principle is declared renders it peculiarly liable to mislead, unless it is examined in the light of the adjudicated cases in which it has been applied, generally with explanations, and often with necessary qualifications.[3]

Grade of the government which taxes. In considering the legality of the purpose of any particular tax, a question of first importance must always concern the grade of the government which assumes to levy it. The "public" that is concerned in a legal sense in any matter of government, is the public the particular government has been provided for; and the "public purpose" for which that government may tax is one which concerns its own people, and not some other people having a government of its own, for whose wants taxes are laid. There may, therefore, be a public purpose as regards the federal union, which would not be such as a basis for state taxation, and there may be a public purpose which would uphold state taxation, but not the taxation which its municipalities would be at liberty to vote and collect. The purpose must in every instance pertain to the sovereignty with which the tax originates; it must be something with-

[1] Brodhead *v.* Milwaukee, 19 Wis., 624, 652, per *Dixon*, Ch. J. And see Speer *v.* School Directors, 50 Penn. St., 150.

[2] "The exercise of the taxing power must become wanton and unjust — be so grossly perverted as to lose the character of a legislative function — before the judiciary will feel themselves entitled to interpose on constitutional grounds. To arrest the legislation of a free people, especially in reference to burdens self-imposed for the common good, is to restrain the popular sovereignty, and should have clear warrant in the letter of the fundamental law." Schenley *v.* Alleghany City, 25 Penn. St., 128, 130, per *Woodward*, J.

[3] This is forcibly put by *Dixon*, Ch. J., in Whiting *v.* Sheboygan etc. R. R. Co., 25 Wis., 167, 180.

in its jurisdiction so as to justify its making provision for it. The rule is applicable to all the subordinate municipalities; they are clothed with powers to accomplish certain objects, and for those objects they may tax, but not for others, however interesting or important, which are the proper concern of any other government or jurisdiction. State expenses are not to be provided for by federal taxation, nor federal expenses by state taxation, because in neither case would the taxation be levied by the government upon whose public the burden of the expenses properly rests. To provide for such expenses would consequently not be a purpose in which the people taxed would in a legal sense be concerned. This is the general rule; some apparent exceptions there unquestionably are, where the nation and the state have common interests and a common duty, such as may require the action of both, and would justify the levy of a tax by either or both to accomplish the one object. An illustration would be the case of a tax for the common defense against the public enemies, which might be levied by each, because the purpose would in a strict sense be public as to both.

The grade of the government is also important for another reason. A municipal government is one of delegated and limited powers, whose authority is generally to receive a somewhat strict construction, and which must find the purposes for which it may tax clearly confided to its charge by the state. It is not sufficient that a purpose may seem to belong properly to its jurisdiction, or that the court may believe it ought to have had authority over it; but it must be seen that the authority has been conferred in fact. It is otherwise with the state, which has all the power of taxation not withheld from exercise in the making of the state and federal constitutions, and in support of whose action consequently the most liberal intendments are to be made. It is otherwise with the federal union also; for though its powers are not general like those of the state, but are limited and defined by the federal constitution, yet as they concern the most important matters of government, and relate to subjects not of domestic concern merely but of international intercourse, and to other matters which sometimes call for broad and comprehensive views, and make a policy of liberal expenditures wise and statesmanlike, it would be neither reasonable nor prudent to subject its action in the matter of taxation to critical rules. That which it decides to be an object of public expenditure must generally be so accepted, and error in its action must be corrected by discussion and through public opinion and the elections.

General expenses of government. Every government must provide for its general expenses by taxation; and in these are to be included the cost of making provision for those public needs or conveniences for which, by express law or by general usage, it devolves upon the government to make provision. As regards the federal government, a general outline of these is to be found in the federal constitution. That government is charged with the common defense of the union, and for that defense it may raise and support armies, create and maintain a navy, build forts and arsenals, construct military roads, etc. It has a like power over the general subject of post offices and post roads, and over other subjects enumerated in the federal constitution and subjected to its authority. It may contract debts, and it must provide for their payment. For all these purposes it may levy taxes, and its power in so doing to select the subjects of taxation and to determine the rate and the methods is as full and complete as can exist in any sovereignty whatsoever, with the exceptions which are prescribed by the constitution itself.

These exceptions are the following:

1. That duties, imposts and excises must be uniform throughout the United States.[1]

2. A capitation or other direct tax must be laid in proportion to the federal census or enumeration, according to which the representation of the states in the popular branch of congress is determined.[2]

3. No tax or duty can be laid on articles exported from any state.[3]

To these express restrictions is to be added the following, which is always implied:

[1] Const. of U. S., art. I, § 8, par. 1; Veazie Bank *v.* Fenno, 8 Wall., 533, 541, per *Chase*, Ch. J.

[2] Const. of U. S., art. I, § 9, par. 4; Veazie Bank *v.* Fenno, 8 Wall., 533, 541, per *Chase*, Ch. J.

[3] Const. of U. S., art. I, § 9, par. 5. A tonnage duty laid on foreign vessels is not a tax on exports. Aguirre *v.* Maxwell, 3 Blatch., 140.

4. No tax can be laid on a state, or its agencies of government, nor any which can tend to impair the sovereign powers of the states, or impede the exercise of their essential functions.[1]

Some taxes levied by the federal government are directly calculated and intended to benefit private individuals. For an illustration, it gives bounty land or pensions to those who have performed military or naval services for the country, notwithstanding it has made no promise, and is consequently under neither a legal nor a moral obligation to do so. But the primary object in all such bounties is not the private but the public interest. To show gratitude for meritorious public services in the army and navy by liberal provision for those who have performed them, is not only proper in itself, but it may reasonably be expected to have a powerful influence in inciting others to self-denying, faithful and courageous services in the future, when the government, which is so ready to be generous as well as just, shall have need of their assistance. The same may be said of a like recognition of valuable public services rendered by other persons: the question in every case is not one of power, but of prudence and public policy.

Imposts laid on any other consideration than the production of revenue have been often objected to as being only colorably taxation, and therefore not warranted by the taxing power. But where the impost produces revenue, it is a tax, and it cannot be invalid merely because, if laid in some other way or at some other rate, the revenue would have been greater.[2] Nor can the motives

[1] *Ante*, pp. 56–59, and cases cited.

[2] "No doubt all taxation should be general and, as far as practicable, equal. Legislation either to benefit or burden particular classes under the idea that it is for the good of the state at large, infringes upon the natural and guarantied right of acquiring, possessing and protecting property, subject to fair and equal contributions to the just and necessary expenses of government in the exercise of its proper and legitimate functions. A government which assumes the office of controlling and directing the lawful industry of the citizens into the channels which it may choose to deem best, assumes what does not legitimately belong to it. Some states in modern times, in undertaking to find work for the people, have discovered that it was a sure way to make work for themselves. But we cannot sit in judgment upon the wisdom or expediency of laws. An act of the legislature must clearly transcend the limits of the power confided to that department of government, or more properly

which have influenced the selection of objects for taxation, or determined the rate, be inquired into for the purpose of invalidating it: proper motives in the legislature are always conclusively presumed.[1] If therefore it should be conceded that a tariff of duties discriminating between articles of merchandise in order to protect or encourage particular branches of home industry, was unwise, impolitic, or contrary to the spirit of the federal constitution, it could not for that reason be treated as invalid. Of public policy in matters of federal taxation the congress must judge, and the spirit of the constitution is supposed to address itself to the legislature rather than to the courts. Every tax must discriminate, and only the authority that imposes it can determine how and in what directions. The motives that influence the members of a legislative body raise questions between them and their constituents alone.[2] Indeed it is only when a burden is imposed which it is impossible to bear; one which is laid not for the purpose of producing revenue, but in order to accomplish some ulterior object which the general government lacks the power otherwise to accomplish, that a case is presented which really can be said to be fairly debatable on the score of power. Such a burden, it may be said, comes under no definition of the word "tax" which is recognized in public law. It demands no contributions for the service of the state; it adds and is expected to add nothing to the public revenue. It annihilates that upon which it is levied, and it differs from confiscation only in this, that confiscation seizes something of value, and appropriates it to the needs of the government, thus making it useful, while this seizes it for the purpose of destruction only. But even in such cases, it is held that the presumption

speaking, it must violate some prohibition, either express or necessarily implied, either of the federal or state constitution, before it can be pronounced by the judicial department to be unconstitutional and void." *Sharswood*. J., in Durach's Appeal, 62 Penn. St., 491, 495. As to the general right of congress to tax, see United States *v*. McKinley, 4 Brewster, 246.

[1] Goddin *v*. Crump, 8 Leigh, 120, 154; People *v*. Draper, 15 N. Y., 532, 545, 555; Sunbury & Erie R. R. Co. *v*. Cooper, 33 Penn. St., 278; Wright *v*. Defrees, 8 Ind., 298, 302; Baltimore *v*. State, 15 Md., 376; Newman, ex parte, 9 Cal., 502; Lyon *v*. Morris, 15 Geo., 480; McCardle, ex parte, 7 Wall., 506, 514; Johnson v. Higgins, 3 Met., Ky., 566; Flint etc., Plank Road Co. *v*. Woodhull, 25 Mich., 99, 103; State *v*. Hays, 49 Mo., 604, 607; State *v*. Fagan, 22 La. An., 545.

[2] See Story on Const., § 1677; Veazie Bank *v*. Fenno, 8 Wall., 533, 548.

that correct motives have controlled the legislative action must preclude the judiciary from inquiring into the purpose of the legislation.[1]

Public purposes in general. For the most part the term public purposes is employed in the same sense in the law of taxation and in the law of eminent domain. But both in the legislation of the country and in the judicial decisions some differences have been recognized, and, as we think, with good reason. An appropriation under the right of eminent domain is only a forced sale which one is compelled to make for the public good. As the consideration paid on such sale is pecuniary, and is supposed to be equal to the full value of what is taken, no injustice results to him whose property is appropriated. On the other hand, no pecuniary consideration is paid when money is demanded under the power of taxation; and if the money is taken in order to be appropriated to private purposes, the benefits which the tax payer might be presumed to receive from its being used for the needs of the government, to enable it to protect and defend him with its other citizens, are not realized. In such a case the supposed consideration to the individual for taking his property wholly fails. A more liberal construction of public purposes is consequently admissible in the law of eminent domain, where an error in the direction of too great liberality could not be seriously detrimental, than in the law of taxation where a like error would result in the most serious injustice.

There are provisions in a number of the state constitutions under which one needing a private way across the land of another may have the way established against the will of the owner, by making out his necessity to the satisfaction of a proper public officer, or of a jury, and by paying such damages as shall be assessed against him. This is an extension of the law of eminent domain,[2] but it has its foundation in public policy, and the appro-

[1] Veazie Bank *v.* Fenno, 8 Wall., 533, 548. That the right to tax may be carried to the extent of destruction is strongly protested against in Berney *v.* Tax Collector, 2 Bailey, 654, 672, per *Harper*, J.

[2] In a few cases it has been held that private roads might be laid out by compulsory proceedings without any such constitutional permission. Harvey *v.* Thomas, 10 Watts, 63; Case of Pocopson Road, 16 Penn. St., 15; Sherman *v.* Buick, 32 Cal., 241.

priation is supposed to accomplish a public purpose in bringing into use a parcel of real property which otherwise would be or might be practically inaccessible. A proposition to make such a private way at the public expense by means of an exercise of the power of taxation would, by general consent, be pronounced wholly inadmissible, as being a proposition to appropriate the public revenues to a private purpose. The difference in the two cases is felt and appreciated the moment they are stated, and the wisdom of recognizing it in legislation has also been very generally felt. There are also some cases in which, without the aid of constitutional provisions, it has been held that private property may be appropriated under the law of eminent domain, in order to enable private parties to establish and carry on their business enterprises, notwithstanding it would be incompetent to aid the same enterprises by payments from the public treasury. An illustration is the case of lands appropriated for the purpose of creating a reservoir for water, by means of which a water power may be made available in private hands for manufacturing purposes. The right to make the appropriation has been sustained, on the ground that, within the meaning of the law of eminent domain, land is taken for the public use whenever its taking is for the general public advantage, and that the establishment of power for manufacturing purposes is an object of such great public interest — especially where manufacturing is one of the great industrial pursuits of the commonwealth — as fully to justify the declaring it a public use and to authorize for the purpose the appropriation of private property by individuals or corporations.[1]

[1] Hazen *v.* Essex Company, 12 Cush., 475, 477, per *Shaw*, Ch. J.; Great Falls Manuf. Co. *v.* Fernald, 47 N. H., 458, per *Perley*, Ch. J. The following cases are to the same effect: Fiske *v.* Framingham Manuf. Co., 12 Pick., 67; Boston & Roxbury Mill Corporation *v.* Newman, 12 id., 467; Harding *v.* Grodlett, 3 Yerg., 41. The courts of Wisconsin have sustained such laws. Newcomb *v.* Smith, 1 Chand., 71; Thein *v.* Vœgtlander, 3 Wis., 461, 465; Pratt *v.* Brown, id., 603. But with some hesitation of late; see Fisher *v.* Horicon Co., 10 id., 351; Curtis *v.* Whipple, 24 id., 350; note of Judge *Redfield* to Allen *v.* Inhabitants of Jay, 12 Am. Law Reg., 493; S. C., 60 Me., 124; also 11 Am. Rep., 185. They have also been sustained in other states: Olmstead *v.* Camp, 33 Conn., 532; Jordan *v.* Woodward, 40 Me., 317; Miller *v.* Troost, 14 Minn., 365; Venard *v.* Cross, 8 Kan., 248; Harding *v.* Funk, id., 315; Burgess *v.* Clark, 13 Ired., 109; M'Afee's Heirs *v.* Kennedy, 1 Lit., 92; Smith *v.*

On the other hand, the right to exercise the power of taxation in aid of the manufacturing enterprises of private persons or corporations has seldom been asserted, and whenever asserted has been most emphatically denied. The views of the learned Chief Justice of Maine on this subject have been so clearly and pointedly stated, in response to an inquiry by the executive — whether the legislature has authority, under the constitution, to pass laws enabling towns, by gifts of money or loans of bonds, to assist individuals or corporations to establish or carry on manufactures — that it is deemed advisable to present the material portions of his negative reply in the note.[1]

Connelly, 1 T. B. Monr., 58; Shackelford *v.* Coffey, 4 J. J. Marsh., 40; Crenshaw *v.* Slate River Co., 6 Rand., 245; Ash *v.* Cummings, 50 N. H., 591.

[1] "The line of demarkation may not always be clear and distinct and well defined between what is for public and governmental and what for private purposes — between the general legislation for the whole people and the special for the individual. But the questions proposed leave no doubt as to the special phase of legislation to which they refer. They are obviously limited by and embrace what is special and private, excluding by their very terms whatever may or can, by the most enlarged and liberal construction, be regarded as relating to municipal, governmental or public objects of any description whatsoever." * * * "Individuals and corporations embark in manufactures for the purpose of personal and corporate gain. Their purposes and objects are precisely the same as those of the farmer, the mechanic or the day laborer. They engage in the selected branch of manufactures for the purpose and with the hope and expectation not of loss but of profit. By the very assumption of the interrogatories, they are engaged in private and corporate undertakings for private and corporate emolument. All municipal, police, educational, public or governmental purpose, whether of peace or of war, is excluded from our consideration by the manifest purpose of the inquiry." * * * "The inquiry is whether the legislature can authorize a town, by a majority or any other vote, to give away the property of an unwilling minority to an individual or manufacturing corporation whom or which such majority may select as donees. The question relates only to manufactures; but if the right of confiscating the private property of an individual for the purpose of giving it away to one branch of industry can be conferred upon towns, one does not easily see where or what bounds can be imposed or limitations made. The general benefit to the community resulting from every description of well directed labor is of the same character, whatever may be the branch of industry upon which it may be expended. All useful laborers, no matter what the field of labor, serve the state by increasing the aggregate of its products — its wealth. There is nothing of a public nature any more entitling the manufacturer to public gifts, than the sailor, the mechanic, the

An equally pointed denial of the right is met with in the opinion of an eminent federal judge, in a recent case, in which a town, under an authority which the legislature had attempted to confer, had voted its bonds in aid of a private manufacture.[1] The like doctrine was afterwards affirmed in the federal supreme court. After consideration of the general nature of the power to tax, the court declare it to be "beyond cavil that there can be no lawful tax which is not laid for a *public purpose*. It may not be easy to draw the line, in all cases, so as to decide what is a public purpose in this sense, and what is not. It is undoubtedly the duty of the legislature, which imposes or authorizes municipalities to impose a tax, to see that it is not to be used for purposes of a private interest instead of a public use; and the courts can only be justified in interposing when a violation of this principle is clear and the reason for interference cogent. And in deciding whether, in a given case, the object for which the taxes are assessed falls upon the one side or the other of this line, they must be governed mainly by the course and usage of the government, the objects for which taxes have been customarily and by long course of legislation levied, what objects or purposes have been considered necessary to the support and for the proper use of the government, whether state or municipal. Whatever lawfully pertains to this, and is sanctioned by time and the acquiescence of the people, may well be held to belong to the public use, and proper for the maintenance of good government; though this may not be the only criterion of rightful taxation.

"But in the case before us, in which the towns are authorized to contribute aid, by way of taxation, to any class of manufactures, there is no difficulty in holding that this is not such a public purpose as we have been considering. If it be said that a benefit results to the local public of a town by establishing manu-

lumberman or the farmer. Our government is based upon equality of rights. All honest employments are honorable. The state cannot rightfully discriminate among occupations, for a discrimination in favor of one branch of industry is a discrimination adverse to all other branches. The state is equally to protect all, giving no undue advantage or special or exclusive preference to any." Opinions of Judges, 58 Me., 590.

[1] Commercial National Bank *v.* Iola, 2 Dillon, 353. See National Bank of Cleveland *v.* Iola, 9 Kan., 689; Opinions of Judges, 58 Me., 590, 596.

factures, the same may be said of any other business or pursuit which employs capital or labor. The merchant, the mechanic, the innkeeper, the banker, the builder, the steamboat owner are equally promoters of the public good, and equally deserving the aid of the citizens by forced contributions. No line can be drawn in favor of the manufacturer which would not open the coffers of the public treasury to the importunities of two-thirds the business men of the city or town."[1]

Further authorities in support of the position that there is a distinction in the meaning of *public use*, as employed in the law of eminent domain and of taxation, would seem unnecessary. Custom must have great influence in determining the proper limit of either power; but it is manifest that the adjudications recognize certain incidental benefits to the public as constituting such a public interest as will justify an exercise of the eminent domain which, in the case of the power of taxation, are not admitted as constituting any basis whatever for its employment. Few cases have undertaken to point out the distinction,[2] but the courts have acted upon it in many cases.

[1] Per *Miller*, J., in Loan Association *v.* Topeka, 20 Wall., 655, 664. See also Allen *v.* Jay, 60 Me., 124; S. C., 11 Am. Rep., 185. Taxation in aid of private enterprises is properly characterized by *Dickenson*, J., in Opinions of Judges, 58 Me., 590–603, as taxation "to load the tables of the few with bounty that the many may partake of the crumbs that fall therefrom."

[2] See, however, Whiting *v.* Sheboygan etc. R. R. Co., 25 Wis., 167, 190, per *Dixon*, Ch. J. In People *v.* Town Board of Salem, 20 Mich., 452, 477, the following remarks are made in response to the argument in favor of the right to tax, drawn from the admitted right of eminent domain for the purpose in question: "Reasoning by analogy, from one of the sovereign powers of government to another, is exceedingly liable to deceive and mislead. An object may be *public* in one sense and for one purpose, when, in a general sense, and for other purposes, it would be idle and misleading to employ the same term. All governmental powers exist for public purposes, but they are not necessarily to be exercised under the same conditions of public interest. The sovereign police power which the state possesses is to be exercised only for the general public welfare, but it reaches to every person, to every kind of business, to every species of property within the commonwealth. The conduct of every individual and the use of all property and of all rights is regulated by it, to any extent found necessary for the preservation of the public order, and also for the protection of the private rights of one individual against encroachments by others. The sovereign power of taxation is employed in a great many cases where the power of eminent domain might be

An enumeration of the purposes which are recognized as justifying taxation is not needful, and is scarcely practicable. The most of them pass unchallenged. To preserve the public order; to provide for the enforcement of civil rights and the punishment

made more immediately efficient and available if constitutional principles would suffer it to be resorted to; but each of these powers has its own peculiar and appropriate sphere, and the object which is *public* for the demands of one is not necessarily of a character to permit the exercise of another. * * * * "If we examine the subject critically, we shall find that the most important consideration in the case of eminent domain, is the necessity of accomplishing some public good which is otherwise impracticable; and we shall also find that the law does not so much regard the means as the need. The power is much nearer akin to that of the public police than to that of taxation; it goes but a step further, and that step is in the same direction.

"Every man has an abstract right to the exclusive use of his own property for his own enjoyment, in such manner as he shall choose; but if he should choose to create a nuisance upon it, or do anything which would preclude a reasonable enjoyment of adjacent property, the law would interfere to impose restraints. He is said to own his private lot to the center of the earth, but he would not be allowed to excavate it indefinitely, lest his neighbor's lot should disappear in the excavation. The abstract right to make use of his own property in his own way is compelled to yield to the general comfort and protection of the community, and to a proper regard to relative rights in others. The situation of his property may even be such that he is compelled to dispose of it, because the law will not suffer his regular business to be carried on upon it. A needful and lawful species of manufacture may so injuriously affect the health and comfort of the vicinity that it cannot be tolerated in a densely settled neighborhood, and, therefore, the owner of a lot in that neighborhood will not be allowed to engage in that manufacture upon it, even though it be his regular and legitimate business. The butcher, in the vicinity of whose premises a village has grown up, finds himself compelled to remove his business elsewhere, because his right to make use of his lot as a place for the slaughter of cattle has become inconsistent with the superior right of community to the enjoyment of pure air and the accompanying blessings and comforts. The owner of a lot within the fire limits of a city may be compelled to part with the property, because he is unable to erect a brick or stone structure upon it, and the local regulations will not permit one of wood.

"Eminent domain only recognizes and enforces the superior right of the community against the selfishness of individuals in a similar way. Every branch of needful industry has a right to exist, and community has a right to demand that it be permitted to exist; and if, for that purpose, a peculiar locality, already in possession of an individual, is essential, the owner's right to undisturbed occupancy must yield to the superior interest of the public. A railroad cannot go around the farm of every unwilling person, and the business of transporting persons and property for long distances by rail, which

of crime; to make compensation to public officers and to others who perform services for the public; to protect public property; to erect and keep in repair the necessary public buildings; to pay the expenses of legislation and of administering the laws; all these are purposes which, in a consideration of the law of taxation, call

has been found so essential to the general enjoyment and welfare, could never have existed if it were in the power of any unwilling person to stop the road at his boundary, or to demand unreasonable terms as a condition of passing him. The law interferes in these cases and regulates the relative rights of the owner and of the community with as strict regard to justice and equity as the circumstances will permit. It does not deprive the owner of his property, but it compels him to dispose of so much of it as is essential on equitable terms. While, therefore, eminent domain establishes no industry, it so regulates the relative rights of all that no individual shall have it in his power to preclude its establishment. * *

* * "But when we examine the power of taxation with a view to ascertain the purposes for which burdens may be imposed upon the public, we perceive at once that necessity is not the governing consideration, and that in many cases it has little or nothing to do with the question presented. Certain objects must of necessity be provided for under this power, but in regard to innumerable other objects for which the state imposes taxes upon its citizens, the question is always one of mere policy, and if the taxes are imposed, it is not because it is absolutely necessary that those objects should be accomplished, but because on the whole it is deemed best by the public authorities that they should be. On the other hand, certain things of absolute necessity to civilized society the state is precluded, either by express constitutional provisions, or by necessary implication, from providing for at all; and they are left wholly to the fostering care of private enterprise, or private liberality. We concede, for instance, that religion is essential, and that without it we should degenerate to barbarism and brutality; yet we prohibit the state from burdening the citizen with its support, and we content ourselves with recognizing and protecting its observance on secular grounds. Certain professions and occupations in life are also essential, but we have no authority to employ the public moneys to induce persons to enter them. The necessity may be pressing, and to supply it may be, in a certain sense, to accomplish a "public purpose;" but it is not a purpose for which the power of taxation may be employed. The public necessity for an educated and skillful physician in some particular locality may be great and pressing, yet if the people should be taxed to hire one to locate there, the common voice would exclaim that the public moneys were being devoted to a *private* purpose. The opening of a new street in a city or village may be of trifling public importance as compared with the location within it of some new business or manufacture; but while the right to pay out the public funds for the one would be unquestionable, the other by common consent is classified as a private interest, which the public can aid as individuals if they see fit, while they are not permitted to employ the machinery of the government to that end. Indeed,

for no comment, as each and all are absolutely indispensable in orderly government. All these may therefore be passed by while attention is directed to cases not so clear, the determination of which will sufficiently indicate the bounds which usage in representative government has prescribed as the proper limit to a lawful expenditure of the public moneys.

Religious instruction. This to individuals is an object of the very highest moment, and formerly it was thought to be the duty of government to provide for it. The more enlightened opinion of the present day refers it exclusively to the voluntary action of the people.[1] It is expressly forbidden by many of the state con-

the opening of a new street in the outskirts of a city is generally much more a matter of private interest than of public concern; so much so that the owner of the land voluntarily throws it open to the public without compensation; yet even in a case where the public authorities did not regard the street as of sufficient importance to induce their taking the necessary action to secure it, it would not be doubted that the moment they should consent to accept it as a gift, the street would at once become a public object and purpose, upon which the public funds might be expended with no more restraints upon the action of the authorities in that particular, than if it were the most prominent and essential thoroughfare of the city.

"By common consent also a large portion of the most urgent needs of society is relegated exclusively to the law of demand and supply. It is this in its natural operation, and without the interference of government, that gives us the proper proportion of tillers of the soil, artisans, manufacturers, merchants and professional men, and that determines when and where they shall give to society the benefit of their particular services. However great the need in the direction of any particular calling, the interference of the government is not tolerated because, though it might be supplying a public want, it is considered as invading the domain that belongs exclusively to private inclination and enterprise. We perceive, therefore, that the term "public purpose," as employed to denote the objects for which taxes may be levied, has no relation to the urgency of the public need, or to the extent of the public benefit which is to follow. It is, on the other hand, merely *a term of classification, to distinguish the objects for which, according to settled usage, the government is to provide, from those which by the like usage, are left to private inclination, interest or liberality.*

"It creates a broad and manifest distinction — one in regard to which there need be neither doubt nor difficulty — between public works and private enterprises, between the public conveniences which it is the business of government to provide and those which private interest and competition will supply whenever the demand is sufficient."

[1] Cooley, Const. Lim., ch. 13 and cases referred to in the notes. Dr. Wayland justly observes that "The only ground on which taxes for the support of

stitutions that public moneys shall be appropriated to religious worship. It is true that in selecting the objects of taxation, buildings and other property made use of for that purpose are generally exempted from the lists. This is done without discrimination between sects, and is generally defended upon the ground that public worship is a public benefit which may properly be encouraged in this indirect way. The discrimination is opposed by some persons, but whether or not it is proper or politic, it cannot be declared unwarranted by the general principles of government. As already observed the question what taxes shall be levied and upon what classes of persons or property is always one of public policy which the legislature must solve. But another view is not entirely without plausibility. Whoever contributes to the support of churches, also contributes to pay the taxes, if any, which are imposed upon them. But as most persons who pay taxes at all do, in some form, and with some regard to their ability, contribute to the support of churches, it is of little importance to the general public whether taxes are levied on church property or not, as whatever is collected from such property, while it goes to diminish what will be collected from individual property, will at the same time increase to the same extent what the individuals pay for the support of religious instruction, so that the burden in the one case will be substantially the same as in the other. We do not say that this view is strictly correct, but it is perhaps safe to say that the inequality occasioned by the exemption of church property from taxation is not so great as without reflection one would be likely to suppose.

Secular instruction. It may be safely declared that to bring a sound education within the reach of all the inhabitants

religion can be defended is that its existence is necessary for the support of civil government, and that it can be sustained in no other manner than by compulsion. The first assertion we grant to be true; the second we utterly deny. Hence we do not believe that any taxation for this purpose is necessary. All that religious societies have a right to ask of the civil government is, the same privileges for transacting their own affairs which societies of every other sort possess. This they have a right to demand, not because they are religious societies, but because the exercise of religion is an innocent mode of pursuing happiness. If these be not granted, religious men are oppressed, and the country where such oppression prevails, let it call itself what it may, is not free." Wayland, Pol. Econ., b. 4, ch. 3, § 2.

has been a prime object of American government from the very first. It was declared by colonial legislation, and has been reiterated in constitutional provisions, to the present day. It has been regarded as an imperative duty of the government; and when question has been made concerning it, the question has related not to the existence of the duty, but to its extent. But the question of extent is one of public policy, and addresses itself to the legislature and the people, not to the courts.[1] And the tendency on the part of the people has been steadily in the direction of taking upon themselves larger burdens in order to provide more spacious, elegant and convenient houses of instruction, and to place within the reach of all a more generous and useful education. And this is usually done by the direct action of the public; the state or its municipalities constructing and owning the edifices, and supporting the schools, academies, colleges and universities.

[1] See the very interesting case of Cushing *v.* Inhabitants of Newburyport, 10 Met., 508. Also Stuart *v.* Kalamazoo, 30 Mich., 69. That a tax for the support of free schools is within a general grant of the power to tax for "municipal purposes," see Horton *v.* School Commissioners, 43 Ala., 598. Dr. Wayland, in speaking of the liberality of construction in determining the purposes of taxation, says: "It must not, of course, always be expected that the product created by consumption (in public expenditure) will be a visible, tangible, material substance. Thus we see no physical, tangible product as the result of taxes for the support of civil government. But we receive the benefit in security of person, property and reputation; or in that condition of society which, though it be incapable of being weighed and measured, is absolutely essential both in individual happiness and individual accumulation. The same may be said in substance concerning the taxes paid for general education. Here, whether the tax payer receives his remuneration in instruction given to his own children or not, he yet receives it in the improvement of the intellectual and social character of his neighbors, by which his property is rendered more secure, the labor for which he pays is better performed, and the demand for whatever he produces is more universal and more constant. The same may be said of the public expenditure by which the moral and social character of a community is elevated, the taste of a nation refined, and an impulse given to efforts for the benefit of man. With this view, no one could oppose the expense incurred in bestowing upon public edifices elegance, or even, in some cases, magnificence of structure, in the public celebration of remarkable eras, and in the rewards bestowed upon those who have by their discoveries enlarged the boundaries of human knowledge, or by their inventions signally improved the useful arts." Pol. Econ., pt. 4, ch. 3, § 1.

In some states a practice has prevailed, while making liberal provision for instruction in public schools, to also give assistance to institutions owned and controlled by private corporations or by religious bodies or denominations. The legal right to do this has received but little attention. In one case in Massachusetts, under a constitutional provision which required moneys raised for public schools to be applied to those only which were under the order and superintendence of the public authorities, it was denied that the legislature could lawfully authorize a town to take moneys which had been raised for the public schools and appropriate them in support of a school founded by a charitable bequest, under which the order and superintendence of the school was vested in trustees who, though a majority were to be chosen by the inhabitants of the town, were yet limited to the members of certain religious societies.[1] And in Wisconsin the authority of the legislature to empower a town to tax its citizens in aid of the erection of buildings for an educational institution to be owned and controlled by a private corporation was denied on general principles. "It strikes us," say the court, "at the first blush, that this is not the levy and collection of money for public purposes, as clearly as if the institute were not an incorporated body, but a mere association of private individuals resolved upon the establishment of a like institution. If it were such an institution, or a grammar or classical school, or a seminary built up and established by individual enterprise, as by persons engaged in the profession of teaching, or by others, and owned and controlled by those contributing towards it, and the emoluments belonging to them, we apprehend that no one would contend that the people [of the town] might be taxed for the purpose of donating the moneys to it. The fact that it is an institution incorporated by act of the legislature does not change its character in this respect. It is but a most frivolous pretext for giving to a corporation, where there is no certain and definite personal responsibility, money exacted from the tax payers, which a just and honorable man engaged in the same business would hesitate to receive though paid without opposition, and to enforce the payment of which, against the will of the tax payers, he would never

[1] Jenkins *v.* Andover, 103 Mass., 94.

think of resorting to coercive measures, provided the same were lawful. It can no more be supported by taxation than if it were unincorporated, or a private school or seminary of the kind above supposed." [1]

It has been decided to be competent for the legislature to authorize a town to tax itself in aid of the erection of buildings for a state educational institution to be constructed within it.[2] In that case the purpose, as regards the state at large, was clearly public, but the locality was allowed to assume a special burden on the ground of special and peculiar benefits. A case in New York perhaps goes further, inasmuch as it sustains the authority of the legislature to require a village to render such assistance.[3] While it is perhaps entirely proper to regard the incidental benefits to the locality as constituting a just basis for an exceptional tax upon it, no such ruling would be admissible where the building itself was not to be one owned and controlled by the public, and where consequently the sole ground for any taxation would be the incidental benefits to flow from a private undertaking. This has been so clearly shown in a case from which we have already quoted, that we copy from the opinion instead of attempting any statement of the general doctrine in our own language:

"That is not the kind of public benefit and interest which will authorize a resort to the power of taxation. Such benefits accrue to the people of all communities from the exercise in their midst of any useful trade or employment, and the argument, pursued to its logical result, would prove that compulsory payment or taxation might be made use of for the purpose of building up and sustaining every such trade or employment, though carried on by private persons for private ends, or the purposes of mere individual gain and emolument. That there exists in the state no power to tax for such purposes, is a proposition too plain to admit of a controversy. Such a power would be obviously incom-

[1] Curtis *v.* Whipple, 24 Wis., 350, 353, per *Dixon*, Ch. J.

[2] Merrick *v.* Amherst, 12 Allen, 500. See also Marks *v.* Trustees of Pardue University, 37 Ind., 155; Burr *v.* Carbondale, Sup. Ct. Ill., 1874, 6 Chicago Legal News, 350.

[3] Gordon *v.* Cornes, 47 N. Y., 608. In that case, however, there was to be a grammar school in the state building, free to the children of the village. Compare State *v.* Haben, 22 Wis., 660.

patible with the genius and institutions of a free people; and the practice of all liberal governments, as well as all judicial authority, is against it. If we turn to the cases where taxation has been sustained as in pursuance of the power, we shall find in every one of them that there was some direct advantage accruing to the public from the outlay, either by its being the owner or part owner of the property or thing to be created or obtained with the money, or the party immediately interested in and benefited by the works to be performed, the same being matters of public concern; or because the proceeds of the tax were to be expended in defraying the legitimate expenses of government, and in promoting the peace, good order and welfare of society. Any direct public benefit or interest of this nature, no matter how slight, as distinguished from those public benefits or interests incidentally arising from the employment or business of private individuals or corporations, will undoubtedly sustain a tax. In thus endeavoring to define how the public must be beneficially interested in order to justify the raising of money by taxation in cases like the present, we of course do not intend to include all purposes for which money may be so raised. Taxes may be levied and collected for charitable purposes, but these constitute a peculiar ground for the exercise of the power which does not exist here.

"So claims founded in equity and justice in the largest sense, and in gratitude, will support a tax; such claims, however, and we think all others where taxation is proper, except claims founded in charity, may be referred to the general principle above spoken of, of public interest in, or benefits received by the transaction out of which the claims arose."[1]

Public charity. The support of paupers and the giving of assistance to those who by reason of age, infirmity or disability, are likely to become such, is by the practice and the common consent of civilized countries a public purpose. The laws not only exempt from taxation the limited means of such persons, but they go further, and provide public funds with which to furnish them retreats where they can be supplied with the necessaries, and to a reasonable extent, with the comforts of life. Hospitals are also provided where dependent classes can receive medical aid

[1] Curtis *v.* Whipple, 24 Wis., 350, 354, per *Dixon*, Ch. J.

and assistance, and asylums where the deaf, the dumb and the blind may be supported and taught, and where the insane may be kept from doing or receiving harm, and can have such careful and scientific treatment, with a view to their restoration, as they would not be likely to receive elsewhere. He would be a bold man who in these days should question the public right to make provision for these benevolent objects. And this provision might not only be made by the establishment of institutions for the purpose, but private institutions might undoubtedly be aided with public funds in consideration of services to be rendered to the public and expenses to be incurred by them in assisting and relieving the same necessitous and dependent classes.[1] The buildings and property of charitable bodies may also, with the utmost propriety and justice, be exempted from taxation, as by implication public buildings for the same purpose are exempted.[2]

Private business enterprises. However important it may

[1] But it is not competent to levy taxes to be paid over to individuals or associations simply because they are charitable. So held in a case where the legislature had required the agencies of foreign insurance companies to pay over two per centum of their receipts to an association for the relief of disabled firemen. "If the legislature may command such a contribution as this, we are unable to see why they may not command every citizen to contribute, not only to this association, but to every charitable association; and indeed, to every man who spends his money and means in a charitable way. There are associations for all sorts of charity — why may not the legislature require us to contribute to them all, if they may require this class of people to contribute to this one? We cannot answer this question." *Lowrie*, Ch. J., in Philadelphia Association etc. *v.* Wood, 39 Penn. St., 73, 82.

[2] In Directors of the Poor *v.* School Directors, 42 Penn. St., 21, 25, in which it was claimed that a public poor house was taxable for school purposes under general words in the statute, *Lowrie*, Ch. J., uses the following vigorous language: "Tax the poor house to support the schools? Why this would be to take the poor *taxes* to support the schools; and the people must be taxed to pay the officers who perform such foolish service. If we require the townships, counties, towns, cities and state, and the road, school and poor authorities to tax each other, we shall furnish fees enough for several hundred officers engaged in transferring from one public body to another the taxes which it has collected for its public purposes. These poor taxes must be collected to support the schools and roads, and *school* taxes to support the poor and so on all around. Surely it is not too much to say that this is absurd. The public is never subject to tax laws, and no portion of it can be without express statute. No exemption law is needed for any public property held as such."

be to the community that individual citizens should prosper in their industrial enterprises, it is not the business of government to aid them with its means. Enlightened states leave every man to depend for his success and prosperity in business on his own exertions, in the belief that by doing so his own industry will be more certainly enlisted, and his prosperity and happiness more likely to be secured. It may therefore be safely asserted that taxation for the purpose of raising money from the public to be given or even loaned to private parties, in order that they may use it in their individual business enterprises, is not recognized as for a public use. In contemplation of law it would be taking the common property of the whole community and handing it over to private parties for their private gain, and consequently unlawful. Any incidental benefits to the public that might flow from it could not support it as legitimate taxation.[1]

[1] Allen *v.* Jay, 60 Me., 124; S. C., 11 Am. Rep., 185. See a valuable note to this case by Judge *Redfield*, 12 Am. Law Reg., N. S., 493. In it reference is made to the recent case of Lowell *v.* Boston, 111 Mass., 454, as follows: "The foregoing opinion and the still more recent decision of the supreme judicial court of Massachusetts, in the case of Lowell *v.* The City of Boston, seems to justify the expectation that some limits will hereafter be placed to the power of interested parties through the legislature to carry forward *private enterprises* by means of taxation. The case of Boston grew out of an act of the legislature, at a special session called largely for that purpose, by which the city was authorized to issue bonds not exceeding $20,000,000, at five per cent. interest when payable in gold, or six per cent. if payable in currency; the avails of these bonds to be loaned to the owners of land upon which buildings were destroyed by the great fire of November last. Commissioners were appointed to manage the loan, and were required to take a first mortgage upon the land at less than three-fourths its value, as security for the money advanced, at seven per cent. interest. Here there was a case where there could be no reasonable danger of loss, and a high probability of some gain to the city by means of the larger rate of interest paid by the borrowers than that paid by the city. There could be no fair question either that such a proceeding would afford great accommodation to the property owners on the burnt district, and that it would greatly conduce to the speedy restoration of that portion of the city, and thus naturally to the increase of the wealth and business prosperity of the city, and to some extent, to the greater convenience, accommodation and prosperity of the inhabitants of the city generally. And still the court, unanimously, so far as we learn, came to the conclusion that the statute was void, and perpetually enjoined all proceedings under it." A town cannot raise money by tax to distribute among its citizens according to numbers. Hooper *v.* Emery, 14 Me., 375, 379. Towns cannot raise moneys for the pur-

Moral obligations. There are some cases in which taxation has been allowed for the benefit of private persons on considerations not of charity so much as of justice. Any exercise of the powers of government is liable to cause injury to particular individuals. When the injury is merely incidental, these individuals have no legal claim to indemnification. Nevertheless, it seems eminently proper and just, in some exceptional cases, to recognize a moral obligation resting on the public to share with the persons injured the damage sustained; and this can only be done by means of taxation. All governments are accustomed to recognize and pay equitable claims of this nature under some circumstances; claims, for instance, for the destruction of private property in war, and sometimes for incidental injuries occasioned by the construction of a public work, or for loss in performing a contract to construct it.[1]

In these cases the legislature is not confined in making compensation within the strict limits of common law remedies, but it may recognize moral or equitable obligations, such as a just man would be likely to recognize in his own affairs, whether by law required to do so or not. The principle is clear, but it has sometimes been employed with considerable severity against municipal corporations in compelling them to recognize claims which appeared to the legislature more just than to those who were required to pay them.[2]

pose of abating a particular class of taxes — *e. g.*, poll taxes upon its male inhabitants — and consequently cannot appropriate public moneys for that purpose. Cooley *v.* Granville, 10 Cush., 56.

[1] See Friend *v.* Gilbert, 108 Mass., 408. This principle was carried very far in Brewster *v.* Syracuse, 19 N. Y., 116.

It has been decided that a municipal corporation has power to defend and indemnify its officers where they have incurred liability in the *bona fide* discharge or attempt to discharge their duty. See cases cited in next note. In Briggs *v.* Whipple, 7 Vt., 15, 20, *Williams*, Ch. J., says: "Towns must always indemnity the collector against any damage he may sustain, where a recovery is had against him on account of the want of power to lay the tax, or any illegality in granting the same." This is certainly the statement of a sound principle in morals, but it is not clear that the collector would have a legal remedy against the town in case of its failure to indemnify.

[2] It was held (without discussion) in Wilkinson *v.* Cheatham, 43 Geo., 258, that in providing for the removal of a county seat the legislature had power to cause commissioners to be appointed to assess the damages suffered by in-

Amusements and celebrations. To furnish amusements to its citizens is not one of the functions of government. But to provide public parks or other grounds which shall be open to the public use and occupation for healthful recreation and enjoy-

dividuals in consequence, and to levy a county tax to pay the same. This was certainly going a great way. On much stronger grounds officers who have been subjected to liability in performing or in the attempt to perform public duty, have been held justly entitled to indemnity from the public funds. Nelson *v.* Milford, 7 Pick., 18, 23; Hadsell *v.* Hancock, 3 Gray, 526; Fuller *v.* Groton, 11 id, 340; Baker *v.* Windham, 13 Me., 74; Pike *v.* Middleton, 12 N. H., 278; Briggs *v.* Whipple, 6 Vt., 95; Sherman *v.* Carr, 8 R. I., 431; Bancroft *v.* Lynnfield, 18 Pick., 566, 568. It was held in Beals *v.* Supervisors of Amador, 35 Cal., 624, that the legislature, having apportioned the debts of a county on dividing it, might subsequently require the payment of interest upon it; this being only just. Also that the power was not affected by the circumstance that a debt by assignment had become the property of an individual, who would reap the benefit of the legislation.

In Blanding *v.* Burr, 13 Cal., 343, 349, *Field*, J., speaking of a case in which a city had been required to issue its bonds for equitable demands upon it, for which no legal remedy existed, says: "The question presented is not one of power in the legislature to impose upon the corporation the payment of claims for which no consideration has been paid, but of power to provide for claims, meritorious in their character, for which an equivalent has been received, and from the payment of which the corporation could only escape on strict technical grounds. That the legislature can provide for the payment of claims, invalid in the forum of the law, but equitable and just in themselves, would seem unquestionable. It may become, for example, of the highest importance to a municipal corporation, that counsel should be employed to defend its rights of property assailed by different parties, but its charter may not confer authority to employ the counsel or to meet his charges. Professional services, rendered under such circumstances, would not constitute a legal charge upon the corporation, but that it would be competent for the legislature to authorize the payment of the charge, and the imposition of a tax for that purpose, no one will deny. Or, take a still stronger case: a city has issued, in pursuance of law, its bonds, the annual interest is maturing, and the sources of revenue on which it relied to pay the same have failed, and it has no power to borrow the money within the requisite time, but individuals possessing the means come forward and, at the request of its authorities, advance the necessary money to protect the honor and good faith of the city. A claim for reimbursement would not, under the circumstances, in face of positive prohibitions of the charter to raise money except in a particular way, be valid and binding, but that the legislature could authorize its payment, and the raising of the means by taxation without trenching on any constitutional restrictions, is clear."

In Guilford *v.* Supervisors of Chenango, 13 N. Y., 143, 149, *Denio*, J., says: "The legislature is not confined in its appropriation of the public moneys, or

ment is not only proper but highly commendable, and in large towns may almost be said to be absolutely necessary.[1] The great public parks of the world are great public blessings, in which the poor participate with the rich, and from which they, perhaps, derive the larger share of positive benefit. How far a state or a town should go in making these attractive, the legislative wisdom must provide, and it will be likely to err but seldom in the direction of liberality so long as careful provision is made for an honest expenditure of public funds.[2]

Government sometimes provides for the celebration of important events or eras. Cities or towns have no authority to do this, at least without express legislative permission. Such are the decisions in cases where public money has been voted to celebrate the declaration of independence, or the closing military success in the revolutionary war.[3] It is not very clear that the power could be conferred upon them if the legislature were disposed to do so.

of the sums to be raised by taxation in favor of individuals, to cases in which a legal demand exists against the state. It can thus recognize claims founded in equity and justice in the largest sense of these terms, or in gratitude or charity. Independently of express constitutional restrictions, it can make appropriations of money whenever the public well-being requires, or will be promoted by it, and it is the judge of what is for the public good. It can moreover, under the power to levy taxes, apportion the public burdens among all the tax paying citizens of the state, or among those of a particular section or political division. It is well settled that the authority to raise money by the exercise of the taxing power is not in conflict with the constitutional provision protecting private property from seizure. The two principles coëxist in the constitution, and it is not difficult to distinguish between them."

[1] In Attorney General *v.* Burrell, 31 Mich., 25, a town was held to have authority under its general power to purchase and hold land for town purposes, to buy and hold a public square.

[2] "It is difficult to name a limit beyond which taxes will not be borne without impatience, when they appear to be called for by necessity and faithfully applied. * * But the sting of taxation is wastefulness." Hallam's Middle Ages, ch. 1, pt. 2.

[3] Hodges *v.* Buffalo, 2 Denio, 110; Tash *v.* Adams, 10 Cush., 252; New London *v.* Brainard, 22 Conn., 552; Gerry *v.* Stoneham, 1 Allen, 319; Hood *v.* Lynn, id., 103, 107; Dillon's Mun. Corp., § 110.

In the case last cited, the following remarks are made by *Bigelow*, Ch. J., regarding the force of usage in the construction of town powers: "It was urged by the counsel for the respondents, that the appropriation in the present

Highways and roads. One of the most important functions of government is the making provision for public roads for the use of the people. The variety of these is great, and the modes of construction and operation are different. No question is made of the competency of the legislature to levy taxes for the common highway, the improved turnpike and macadamized road, the planked or paved street, the canal, the tramway or the railway. Any or all of them may be constructed by the state, or, under state authority, by the municipal subdivisions of the state within whose limits they may be needed.[1] They may be supported and kept in repair by taxation of the state or of proper districts, or private corporations may be invested with the franchise of constructing them and taking tolls for their use. Upon these points, also, no question arises. The differences of opinion

case might be justified and sustained on the ground of usage. But the answer to this argument is twofold. In the first place, there is no evidence in the case of the existence of any such usage or custom in the towns or cities of this commonwealth. It is not even alleged in the answer of the respondents. Certainly, the court cannot take judicial cognizance of it. But even if such usage was alleged and proved, it would not alter the case. An unlawful expenditure of the money of a town cannot be rendered valid by usage, however long continued. Abuses of power and violations of rights derive no sanction from time or custom. A casual or occasional exercise of the power by one or a few towns will not constitute a usage. It must not only be general, reasonable and of long continuance, but, what is more important, it must also be a custom necessary to the exercise of some corporate power, or the enjoyment of some corporate right, or which contributes essentially to the necessities and conveniences of the inhabitants. The usage relied on in the present case, if established, would not satisfy either of these last named requisities, which are necessary to give it validity. It is said by this court, in a recent case, that there are many things in the management of town affairs, which are done without objection and pass by general consent, which cannot, when objection is made and they are brought to the test of judicial investigation, be supported as strictly legal. Sikes *v.* Hatfield, 13 Gray, 353. The present case is an illustration of the truth of this remark."

[1] In Philadelphia *v.* Field, 58 Penn., 320, it was held competent for the legislature to provide for the construction of a free bridge over the Schuylkill, opposite one of the streets of Philadelphia, and to require the expense to be borne by taxation of the city. The cases of Thomas *v.* Leland, 24 Wend., 65; Norwich *v.* County Commissioners, 13 Pick., 60; Hingham, etc., Corporation *v.* Norfolk County, 6 Allen, 353, and Board of Wardens *v.* Philadelphia, 42 Penn. St., 209, were cited with approval. Some of these will be referred to hereafter.

which are met with, regarding taxation for public conveniencies of this nature, have principally arisen in those cases in which the legislature has permitted or required the municipal corporations or subdivisions of the state to become stockholders in private corporations organized for the purpose of constructing them, or to make loans or donations to such corporations in order to assist them in their enterprises. On the one hand, it has been insisted, that the state cannot subject itself and its property, as a corporator, to the risks of a business conducted and managed in part, perhaps mainly, by individuals for their own benefit; and that if it can do so in one business, because of benefits that may flow to the public in consequence of their being supplied with convenient facilities for travel and transportation, there is no reason in the nature of things why it may not do so in any other case where benefits to the public might reasonably be anticipated in consequence of their being furnished any other valuable conveniences or facilities. The public, it has also been claimed, could not be taxed in aid of such private corporations, because the benefits anticipated from them would be purely incidental, not differing in their nature from those which might flow from the establishment of a mill for the manufacture of bread stuffs, or from any other manufactory of a useful kind, or from any useful and necessary private business; and, consequently, could not, on the principles already stated and universally recognized as sound, constitute any basis for taxation. On the other hand, the argument has been, that corporations for the construction of turnpikes, canals, railroads, etc., had a duplicate nature, and were both public and private; that the taking of property for them was universally recognized as being for a public use; that the ways they constructed or proposed to construct were *quasi* public highways on which the public at large were entitled to equal and impartial accommodations, and that for all these reasons there was a public interest in their construction which constituted them public purposes within the meaning of the law of taxation, and rendered the question of public assistance to them a question purely of policy and not at all one of power.

The question concerns first, the power of the state, and, second, the power of the municipal bodies. So far as the state at large is concerned, a large preponderance of decisions is in support of the authority to aid these corporations by an exercise of the power to tax, and this by taking stock in such corporations, or by making to them loans or donations.[1] As to the municipal bodies, it is conceded that they have no such power unless it is specially conferred by the legislature; the general authority to construct streets, roads and bridges not comprehending such a case.[2] It is also conceded that any special authority must be strictly pursued, or the action of the municipality under it will be invalid. But when the legislature has thought proper to confer the power, and care has been observed to keep strictly within it, in the municipal action, the same cases already referred to sustain the action as standing on the same ground, and as being supported by the same reasons which would support the like action when taken by the state itself.[3]

[1] "Improvement of coasts and harbors, and all that is necessary for the security of external commerce, must be done by the public. Internal improvements, such as roads, canals, railroads, etc., may, in general, be safely left to individual enterprise. If they would be a profitable investment of capital, individuals will be willing to undertake them. If they would be an unprofitable investment, both parties had better let them alone. The only case in which a government should assume such works is that in which their magnitude is too great to be intrusted to private corporations. Whenever they are undertaken, the principles on which the expenditure should be made are the same as those which govern the expenditure of individuals." Wayland's Pol. Econ., b. 4, ch. 3, § 2.

[2] Bullock *v.* Curry, 2 Met. (Ky.), 171; Stokes *v.* Scott County, 10 Iowa, 166, 173; State *v.* Wapello County, 13 id., 388; La Fayette *v.* Cox, 5 Ind., 38. A considerable number of cases in which proceedings of municipal bodies in aid of railroads have been held to vary from the special authority, and consequently invalid, recognize and proceed upon this principle.

[3] Talbot *v.* Dent, 9 B. Monr., 526; M'Clenachan *v.* Curwen, 3 Yeates, 363; Commonwealth *v.* McWilliams, 11 Pa. St., 61; Goddin *v.* Crump, 8 Leigh, 120; Thomas *v.* Leland, 24 Wend., 65, and cases collected in Cooley's Const. Lim., 119, note. In Loan Association *v.* Topeka, 20 Wall., 655, 660, from which liberal extracts have already been made, Mr. Justice *Miller* gives the following condensed statement of the arguments for and against municipal aid to railroads: "The subject of the aid voted to railroads by counties and towns has been brought to the attention of the courts of almost every state in the Union. It has been thoroughly discussed in those courts. It is quite true that a preponderance of authority is to be found in favor of the proposition that the legislatures of the states, unless restricted by some special provision of their constitutions, may confer upon these municipal bodies the right to take stock in corporations created to build railroads, and to lend their

It has been decided that an assessment for making and opening a road where no road has in fact been laid out, and where, consequently, the land is the subject of private ownership, and no highway would exist when the money was expended, would be illegal and void.[1] It has also been held that a city has no authority

credit to such corporations. Also, to levy the necessary taxes on the inhabitants, and on property within their limits subject to general taxation, to enable them to pay the debts incurred. But very few of these courts have decided this without a division among the judges of which they were composed, while others have decided against the power altogether.

"In all these cases, however, the decision has turned upon the question, whether taxation, by which this aid was afforded to the building of railroads, was for a public purpose. Those who came to the conclusion that it was, held the laws for that purpose valid. Those who could not reach that conclusion held them void. In all the controversy, this has been the turning point of the judgments of the courts. And it is safe to say that no court has held debts created in aid of railroad companies, by counties or towns, valid on any other ground than that the purpose for which the taxes were levied was a public use, a purpose or object which it was the right and the duty of state governments to assist by money raised from the people by taxation. The argument in opposition to this power has been, that railroads built by corporations organized mainly for purposes of gain — the roads which they built being under their control and not that of the state — were private and not public roads, and the tax assessed on the people went to swell the profits of individuals and not to the good of the state or the benefit of the public, except in a remote and collateral way. On the other hand, it was said that roads, canals, bridges, navigable streams, and all other highways had, in all times, been matter of public concern. That such channels of travel and of the carrying business had always been established, improved and regulated by the state, and that the railroad had not lost this character because constructed by individual enterprise aggregated into a corporation.

"We are not prepared to say that the latter view of it is not the true one, especially as there are other characteristics of a public nature conferred on these corporations, such as the power to obtain right of way, their subjection to the laws which govern common carriers, and the like, which seem to justify the proposition. Of the disastrous consequences which have followed its recognition by the courts, and which were predicted when it was first established, there can be no doubt."

[1] Philbrook *v.* Kennebeck, 17 Me., 196; and see People *v.* Supervisors of Saginaw, 26 Mich., 22. The same reasons would render void all subscriptions to internal improvements which are made without any precautions to secure the construction of the works, and which contemplate the payment of the money or the delivery of the securities subscribed in reliance only on the good faith and business prudence of the corporators. In some cases, large sums thus subscribed and paid have been wholly misappropriated.

to assess on abutters upon a street the expense of a bridge over a mill race running through the center of the street, and owned by private parties. The duty of the owners of the race to restore the street which they occupied to a passable condition, could not thus be transferred to the public, or to any portion of the public.[1]

Municipal water and gas works. The propriety and necessity of provision by taxation for a supply of water for the extinguishment of fires, and for the general use of the inhabitants of large towns, is not disputed. Costly expenditures are sometimes made in the construction of public works for these purposes, and large sums are in some instances paid to corporations or individuals who furnish or contribute to furnish the public supply.[2]

[1] People *v.* Rochester, 54 N. Y., 507.

[2] Mayor of New York *v.* Bailey, 2 Denio, 433; West *v.* Bancroft, 32 Vt., 367; Rome *v.* Cabot, 28 Ga., 50; Wells *v.* Atlanta, 43 id., 67; Dillon's Mun. Corp., §§ 97, 371, note, 438, note. In Van Sicklen *v.* Burlington, 27 Vt., 70, 75, in which it was held competent for a town in its corporate capacity to vote money for procuring apparatus for the extinguishment of fires, and to aid fire companies formed for the purpose, the following remarks are made by *Isham*, J.: "There is no doubt that towns or municipal corporations, as well as private corporations, are limited to the exercise of such powers as are expressly given them; that is, the inhabitants of a town cannot by a vote impose a tax, or appropriate their funds, for objects entirely foreign to their political or municipal duties — such as to build a county jail, 10 Vt., 506; to repel the public enemies of the country, 13 Mass., 272; or to build a county road, 11 Pick., 396. But when the object is within their duty and jurisdiction as a municipal corporation, they may exercise such powers as will enable them fully to discharge the duties devolving upon them. Our statute on this subject is nearly a transcript of that of Massachusetts. In that state it is provided by statute, that 'towns may vote money as they shall judge necessary for the support of the ministry, schools, the poor, and other necessary charges arising within the same town.' On the question whether this latter and general clause is limited to the objects previously specified, Ch. J. *Shaw*, in the case of Willard *v.* Newburyport, 13 Pick., 230, observed, 'that it seems very clear that this statement was not intended to be an enumeration of objects and purposes for which towns may raise money, but the expression of a few prominent objects by way of instance, and a general reference to others, under the term of other necessary charges.' On the same construction, the general words in our act, that money may be voted 'for the prosecution and defense of their common rights and interests, and for all other necessary and incidental charges,' must not be limited to the objects specially mentioned in that act, but will be extended to other matters that fall within their rights and duties. It has always been found difficult to define the limits within which towns may act, or give any definite rules by which we may ascertain when their votes will.

Cities may also be authorized to construct gas works in order to furnish their citizens with light, as well as to supply the corporate needs,[1] or they may be empowered to contract for the corporate wants with private corporations or persons.[2] The more common objects for which towns and cities customarily levy taxes we pass over as not requiring enumeration.[3]

Military bounties. The general government having authority to declare war and conduct warlike operations, no question

be deemed illegal. Ch. J. *Shaw* observed, 'that perhaps no better approximation to an exact description can be made, than to say that it embraces that large class of miscellaneous subjects affecting the *accommodation and convenience* of the inhabitants, which have been placed under the municipal jurisdiction of towns by statute or usage.'"

[1] See Western Saving Fund Society *v.* Philadelphia, 31 Pa. St., 175; Same *v.* Same, id., 185.

[2] See Wilson *v.* La Porte, 33 Ind., 258.

[3] A tax to repair a meeting house, and to pay the sexton for ringing the bell, is *prima facie* not a town purpose, but it may be shown by the vote to levy it to be such, by showing that it is to be done as compensation for the use of the meeting house for town purposes. Woodbury *v.* Hamilton, 6 Pick., 101. A town may appropriate money for the repair of a fire engine used by the town but owned by individuals. Allen *v.* Taunton, 19 id., 485. And for the repair and regulation of clocks used for the benefit of the citizens of the town generally. Willard *v.* Newburyport, 12 id., 227.

To what extent municipal corporations may be legally justified by their general grant of power in levying taxes to defray the expense of procuring legislation for their benefit, has in some cases been made a question. The bounds of such authority, must, it is conceived, be very much restricted. Probably no case which comes within the principle of the early Rhode Island tax to raise for Mr. Roger Williams £100, to remunerate him for obtaining the colonial charter (Arnold's Rhode Island, vol. 1 p. 205) would be questioned. Some attention to the interests of a local community at the state capital is frequently essential, and no reason is apparent why the expense may not be considered a proper municipal charge. See Bachelder *v.* Epping, 8 Fost., 354. Compare Frankfort *v.* Winterport, 54 Me., 250. But *lobby* services are services a municipality has no right to employ and no power to pay. The practice is immoral and corrupting, and will not be tolerated in the law. The subject is fully and satisfactorily considered and discussed by *Chapman*, J., in Frost *v.* Belmont, 6 Allen, 152, who in denying the right of a town to pay for lobby services in procuring its charter, cites with approval the cases of Pingrey *v.* Washburn, 1 Aiken, 264; Gulick *v.* Ward, 10 N. J., 87; Wood *v.* McCann, 6 Dana, 366; Clippinger *v.* Hepbaugh, 5 W. & S., 315; Harris *v.* Roof, 10 Barb., 489; Sedgwick *v.* Stanton, 14 N. Y., 289; Fuller *v.* Dame, 18 Pick., 472. And see Hatzfield *v.* Golden, 7 Watts, 182.

can exist of its right to levy taxes in order to pay bounties for military services performed or promised. The several states may with as little question do the same. But it is no part of the duty of a township, city or county, as such, to raise men or money for warlike operations; and under the general grant of municipal powers, they are without authority to impose upon their people any burden by way of taxation for any such purpose.[1] No reason is perceived, however, which should preclude them, under the proper legislative sanction, from devoting their funds to this purpose to any extent that may be necessary to enable them to secure a voluntary performance of any duty which may rest upon their inhabitants to contribute their proportion to the public defense. And so are the authorities. The several municipal divisions of the state, under proper enabling legislation, may promise and pay bounties to those who will volunteer to fill any call made upon their people for their proportionate contribution to the public armies in time of actual or threatened hostilities.[2] They may also pay bounties to those who have voluntarily entered the public service from or as representing their lo-

[1] Stetson *v.* Kempton, 13 Mass., 272; Gove *v.* Epping, 41 N. H., 539, 545; Crowell *v.* Hopkinton, 45 id., 9; Baldwin *v.* North Brandford, 32 Conn., 47; Webster *v.* Harwinton, id., 131; Cover *v.* Baytown, 12 Minn., 124; Petersburg *v.* Noss, 52 Penn. St., 448; Meek *v.* Bayard, 53 id., 217; Fiske *v.* Hazzard, 7 R I., 438; People *v.* Supervisors of Columbia, 43 N. Y., 130; Alley *v.* Edgecombe, 53 Me., 446; Wahlschlager *v.* Liberty, 23 Wis., 362; Wilson *v.* Buckman, 13 Minn., 441; Dillon on Mun. Corp., 103. Furnishing a uniform for a voluntary military company is not within the compass of "town charges." Claflin *v.* Hopkinton, 4 Gray, 502.

[2] Speer *v.* School Directors, 50 Pa. St., 150, 159; Waldo *v.* Portland, 33 Conn., 363; Bartholomew *v.* Harwinton, id., 408; Fowler *v.* Danvers, 8 Allen, 80; Lowell *v.* Oliver, id., 247; Cass *v.* Dillon, 16 Ohio St., 38; Opinions of Judges, 52 Me., 590, 595; Washington County *v.* Berwick, 56 Pa. St., 466. Where the municipality has taken action for the payment of such bounties in advance of legislative authority, it may be conferred retrospectively. Booth *v.* Woodbury, 32 Conn., 118; Crowell *v.* Hopkinton, 45 N. H., 9; Shackford *v.* Newington, 46 id., 415; Ahl *v.* Gleim, 52 Pa. St., 432; Weister *v.* Hade, id., 474; Grim *v.* School District, 57 id., 433; Coffman *v.* Keightly, 24 Ind., 509; Board of Commissioners *v.* Bearss, 25 id., 110; Comer *v.* Folsom, 13 Minn., 219; State *v.* Demorest, 32 N. J., 528; Taylor *v.* Thompson, 42 Ill., 9; Barbour *v.* Camden, 51 Me., 608; Hart *v.* Holden, 55 id., 572; Burnham *v.* Chelsea, 43 Vt., 69; Butler *v.* Putney, id., 481; Lowell *v* Oliver, 8 Allen, 247.

cality in advance of any such promise.[1] And they may raise moneys by tax in order to refund to individuals any sums advanced by them to relieve the municipality from a draft, or to fill its assigned quota of a call, on an understanding, based upon informal corporate action, that the sums should be refunded when legislation could be had permitting it,[2] and perhaps also where the advancements were made without any such informal action.[3] But they cannot be empowered to refund to individuals sums which such individuals may have paid in order to procure substitutes in military service, for themselves as individuals, in an impending draft. Such payments being made by the parties in their own interest, the repayment of them by the public could be nothing else than an appropriation of public moneys to a private purpose.[4]

The public health. It is not doubted that the preservation of the public health is a public purpose of prime importance. Sanitary regulations are indispensable in large towns, but they may be made for every locality. The right to provide for draining low lands for the purpose is well settled,[5] and the right to protect low lands from overflow may also be justified on the same reasons.

[1] Brodhead *v.* Milwaukee, 19 Wis., 624, 652. See also Freeland *v.* Hastings, 10 Allen, 570; Cass *v.* Dillon, 16 Ohio St., 38; State *v.* Richland, 20 id.. 362; Veazie *v.* China, 50 Me., 518; Kunkle *v.* Franklin, 13 Minn., 127.

[2] Weister *v.* Hade, 52 Pa. St., 474. See People *v.* Sullivan, 43 Ill., 412, 413; Johnson *v.* Campbell, 49 id., 316; Susquehanna Depot *v.* Barry, 61 Pa. St., 317. Compare Gregg *v.* Jamison, 55 id., 468.

[3] Kelley *v.* Marshall, 69 Pa. St., 319; Freeland *v.* Hastings, 10 Allen, 570, 585. See Hilbish *v.* Catherman, 64 Pa. St., 154; Micheltree *v.* Sweezey, 70 id., 278; Cass *v.* Dillon, 16 Ohio St., 38; State *v.* Harris, 17 id., 608; Perkins *v.* Milford, 59 Me., 315.

[4] Freeland *v.* Hastings, 10 Allen, 570; Tyson *v.* School Directors, 51 Penn. St., 9. See also Crowell *v.* Hopkinton, 45 N. H., 9; Miller *v.* Grandy, 13 Mich. 540; Pease *v.* Chicago, 21 Ill., 500, 508; Ferguson *v.* Laudram, 5 Bush, 230; Estey *v.* Westminster, 97 Mass., 324; Usher *v.* Colchester, 33 Conn., 567; Kelley *v.* Marshall, 69 Pa. St., 319; Perkins *v.* Milford, 59 Me., 315; Thompson *v.* Pittston 59 id., 545; Cover *v.* Baytown, 12 Minn., 124.

[5] Woodruff *v.* Fisher, 17 Barb., 224; Hartwell *v.* Armstrong, 19 id., 166; Anderson *v.* Kerns Draining Co., 14 Ind., 199, 202; Draining Company Case, 11 La. An., 338; Sessions *v.* Crunkilton, 20 Ohio, N. S., 347, 349.

Protection against calamities. Under the head of calamities against which the government should or might make provision for protection, may be mentioned fires, the overflow of the country by great freshets, the washing away of the shores of the sea, or the banks of rivers in populous districts, destruction of persons or property by wild beasts, and the like. If the danger is sufficiently great and extensive to make the threatened calamity a matter of general concern, the purpose is public; if not, it will not justify taxation.

Payment of the public debt. For whatever purposes taxes may be laid, government may contract debts. The converse of this is equally true, that for whatever purposes debts may be contracted, taxes may be laid. It follows that the payment of the public debt is always a public purpose, not only because of the importance of meeting the public engagements, but also because the debts themselves were contracted for public purposes. But an unlawful debt is no debt at all. If it has been contracted in violation of law or of the constitution, and for any other than a public purpose, it cannot be a public purpose to make provision for its payment. The purpose must be determined by the consideration for the debt, and not by the fact that public officials have unwarrantably assumed to contract it.[1]

Exclusiveness of public interest. The purposes to be accomplished by taxation need not be exclusively public in order to warrant an exercise of the power. There are sometimes cases in which the public have equally with private parties an interest, and in which, therefore, an apportionment of the burden between the public and such individuals might be appropriate. In such cases the public interest may properly invoke legislative action for the levy of a tax; and the legislative determination as to the just proportion to be borne by the public must be conclusive, so far at least as the public are concerned.[2] Cases in illustration might be suggested of a building for the common use of the public authorities and of private parties, and of a way for the use of the public, but in which individuals have such a peculiar and

[1] See Nougues *v.* Douglass, 7 Cal., 65, 75.

[2] See Eddy *v.* Wilson. 43 Vt., 362. Compare Greenbanks *v.* Boutwell, 43 id., 207.

special interest that the public authorities may decline to do more than to share with such parties the expense of the way. Taxation in these cases has relation to the public interest only, and the fact of private interest in the same object is an incidental circumstance of no legal importance.

CHAPTER V.

THE PURPOSE MUST PERTAIN TO THE DISTRICT TAXED.

The general rule. It has been seen that it is essential in taxation that the purpose for which contributions are demanded from the people shall be public in its nature. It is also equally essential that this shall be a purpose, one which in an especial manner pertains to the district within which it is proposed that the contribution shall be collected. The general idea has been expressed in the preceding chapter, but the subject seems to require a more particular consideration.

If a single township were to be required to levy upon its inhabitants and collect and pay over to the state whatever moneys were necessary to pay the salaries of the several state officers, it would be apparent "at first blush," that the enactment was not one which, either in its purpose or tendency, was calculated to make the taxpayers of that township contribute only their several proportions to the public purpose for which the tax was to be levied. If, on the other hand, for the purpose of purchasing and ornamenting a city park or any other improvement of mere local convenience, a tax should be imposed upon the whole state, it would be equally manifest that equality and justice were not the purpose of the imposition, but that, if carried into effect, the people of the state not residing in the city would be compelled to contribute to a purpose in which, in a legal sense, they had no interest whatever.[1] The cases supposed are extreme cases, but the principle which would govern them is universal, and the occasions

[1] "If the legislature should arbitrarily designate a certain class of persons on whom to impose a tax either for general purposes or for a local object of a public nature, without any reference to any rule of proportion whatever, having no regard to the share of public charges which each ought to pay relatively to that borne by all others, or to any supposed peculiar benefit or profit which would accrue to those made subject to the tax which would not enure to others, so that in effect the burden would fall on those who had been selected only for the reason that they might be made subject to the tax, we cannot doubt that the imposition of it would be an unlawful exercise of power, not warranted by the constitution, against the exercise of which a person aggrieved, might sue for protection." *Bigelow*, Ch. J., in Dorgan *v.* Boston, 12 Allen, 223,

for its application are not infrequent. Briefly stated, the principle is this: The burden of a tax must be made to rest upon the state at large, or upon any particular district of the state, according as the purpose for which it is levied is of general concern to the whole state, or, on the other hand, pertains only to the particular district. A state purpose must be accomplished by state taxation, a county purpose by county taxation, or a public purpose for any inferior district by taxation of such district. This is not only just, but it is essential. To any extent that one man is compelled to pay in order to relieve others of a public burden properly resting upon them, his property is taken for private purposes, as plainly and as palpably as it would be if appropriated to the payment of the debts or the discharge of obligations, which the person thus relieved by his payments might owe to private parties.[1] "By taxation," it is said in a leading case, "is meant a certain mode of raising revenue for a public purpose in which the community that pays it has an interest. An act of the legislature authorizing contributions to be levied for a mere private purpose, or for a purpose which, though it be public, is one in which the people from whom they are exacted have no interest, would not be a law, but a sentence commanding the periodical payment of certain sums by one portion or class of people to another."[2]

237. The following remarks are made by *Sharswood*, J., in Hammett *v.* Philadelphia, 65 Penn. St., 146, 151: "There is no case to be found in this state, nor, as I believe after a thorough research, in any other, with limitations in the constitution or without them, in which it has been held that the legislature, by virtue merely of its general powers, can levy or authorize a municipality to levy a local tax for general purposes. * * *

"It may be shown logically, and that without difficulty, that such a doctrine lands us in this absurd proposition: that the whole expenses of government, general and local, may be laid upon the shoulders of one man if one could be found able to bear such a burden. A conclusion so monstrous shows that the premises must be wrong. Such a measure would not be taxation but confiscation."

[1] Lexington *v.* McQuillan's Heirs, 9 Dana, 513; Howell *v.* Bristol, 8 Bush, 493, 497; Wells *v.* Weston, 22 Mo., 384; Gilman *v.* Sheboygan, 2 Black, 510; State *v.* Haben, 22 Wis., 660; Madison County *v.* People, 58 Ill., 456; Bright *v.* McCullough, 27 Ind., 223; Knowlton *v.* Rock County, 9 Wis., 410; Hale *v.* Kenosha, 29 id., 599; Sleight *v.* People, Sup. Ct. Ill., 1875; 7 Chicago Legal News, 292.

[2] *Black*, Ch. J., in Sharpless *v.* Philadelphia, 21 Pa. St., 147, 174: "It is of

This very forcible statement of the general doctrine has met with universal acceptance and approval, because it is as sound in morals as it is in law. "To tax occupations outside of the city," it is said in another case, "for the benefit of those living in the city, is in effect taking the property of the citizen for private use; that is, for the use of a particular community of which the outside citizen forms no part. Whether it be called a tax, or the appropriation of property, the result is precisely the same."[1]

Instances of violation of the rule. The cases in which so plain a rule is likely to be disregarded will naturally be those in which doubt might exist whether the circumstances were such as to warrant its application. Cases of highways afford some illustration. In the northern and western states, the cost of these is usually borne by the towns, and it is not surprising to find a general impression prevailing in some quarters, that the towns must always bear it. But there is probably no state that does not provide for highways of more general importance than the ordinary town ways; highways that are very properly called and treated as state or county roads, and which are made and kept in repair by an expenditure of state or county moneys. In such a case, the state or the county is the proper taxing district, and the town cannot tax itself for the purposes of the road, except as a part of the larger district to which it belongs.[2]

the essence of all taxation, that it should compel the discharge of the burden by those upon whom it rests; and if the state should attempt to compel any single county by taxation to pay the salaries of the state officers, or the expenses of the legislature, no one would for a moment doubt that while the act was arbitrary, unjust and tyrannical, it was also unconstitutional." Ryerson *v.* Utley, 16 Mich., 269, 276. See Washington Avenue, 69 Pa. St., 352; S. C. 8 Am. Rep., 255; Lexington *v.* McQuillan's Heirs, 9 Dana, 513, 516, per *Robertson*, Ch. J.; Weber *v.* Reinhard, 73 Pa. St., 370, 373, per *Sharswood*, J.; Sanborn *v.* Rice, 9 Minn., 273.

[1] *Adams*, J., in St. Charles *v.* Nolle, 51 Mo., 122; S. C. 11 Am. Rep., 440. Contrast with this the case of Falmouth *v.* Watson, 5 Bush, 661; in which license fees imposed by a town on those selling intoxicating drinks outside its limits but near it, were sustained as being imposed, partly at least, for police purposes. See also Langhorne *v.* Robinson, 20 Grat., 661.

[2] People *v.* Supervisors of Dutchess, 1 Hill, 50. In this case, the board of supervisors undertook to require two towns to raise town taxes for a bridge, which, under the law, was a charge upon the county. Parsons *v.* Goshen, 11 Pick., 396. This differs from the last in that here the town voluntarily as-

A case equally plain would be that of a single locality assuming to tax itself, or the state assuming to compel it to tax, for the construction of a state work, or the erection of a state public building. The right to impose an exceptional portion of the burden on the locality where such a work is to be constructed or building erected, on the ground that it receives special and peculiar benefits therefrom, will be considered elsewhere. It is not of that we speak in this place; but of the right of a town to assume, or of the state to compel it to assume, as a town charge, the burden of that which unquestionably should rest upon the state, and which in a legal sense concerns the state alone. It is manifest there can be no such right so long as taxation is laid on general rules, and not at the arbitrary caprice of legislative bodies.[1]

More difficult cases arise where the principle of assessments by benefits is resorted to for improvements which commonly are constructed by an expenditure of the ordinary taxes. In no part of the law of taxation has the practice of our state governments left the discretion of the legislature more entirely unfettered than in laying and apportioning such assessments, and the case must be

sumed to tax itself for the construction of a road, the expense of which was by law to be borne by the county. In neither of these cases was any question at issue regarding the power of the legislature to impose an exceptional portion of the expense upon towns specially benefited. The legislature made the burden wholly a county charge, and the county in the one case and the town in the other, assumed to set aside the legislation and substitute a rule of its own.

[1] See Ryerson *v.* Utley, 16 Mich., 269; State *v.* Haben, 22 Wis., 660. This latter case will be referred to more at length hereafter. It is supported by the case of Livingston County *v.* Wieder, recently decided by the supreme court of Illinois, and to be found in 64 Ill., 427. In Bergen *v.* Clarkson, 6 N. J., 352, the case was this: A city was partly in the two counties of Middlesex and Somerset. A city tax was voted to purchase of Middlesex county an interest in the court house for the purpose of accommodating the corporation with public buildings. *Kinsey*, Ch. J.: "The money thus raised and thus appropriated was not applied to the exigencies of the city; it was raised for a purpose which had no legal existence, and appropriated as a mere gift to the county. The effect therefore was to compel the inhabitants of the corporation residing on the Somerset side of the city, who had to build and maintain a court house of their own, to assist in defraying the expenses of the public buildings of another county." The tax was consequently illegal. The case of Sleight *v.* People, Sup. Co. Ill., 1875, 7 Chi. Leg. News, 292, presented a similar question, and was decided the same way.

most extraordinary and clearly exceptional to warrant any court in declaring that the discretion has been abused, and the legislative authority exceeded. In Pennsylvania, it has been decided that a case of clear abuse existed in an act imposing a special assessment upon the premises fronting on a county road, and others lying within a certain distance therefrom, for the purpose of constructing the road on a very costly plan, not, as the court found, for the local, but for the general public benefit. The act, consequently, was adjudged void.[1] It must be conceded that this legislative application of the law of special assessment was of very questionable propriety, and the conclusion of the court was doubtless just, notwithstanding it leaves us in great doubt touching the exact bounds of the legislative discretionary authority in this regard.[2]

Taxing districts in general. The cases which have been instanced show that the nature of the object to be accomplished will, in many cases, determine the district within which the tax must be levied and collected. But, in other cases, there may be questions of fact to be examined and considerations of equity to be weighed before the proper bounds of a taxing district can be fixed upon. When a local improvement is to be made or a local work constructed for the general public good, the general theory of taxation would seem to require that the cost should be collected from the state at large, or, in other words, from the whole public for whose benefit it is to be made. But, as has already been remarked of the common roads, it is not the custom of the country to provide for these improvements by general taxation. Instead of apportioning the cost of each through the state at

[1] In re Washington Avenue, 69 Penn. St., 352; S. C., 8 Am. Rep., 255. The case of People *v.* Springwells, 25 Mich., 153, in its main facts bears some resemblance to the foregoing. The legislature proposed to assess upon a township the expense of a costly road, which was to be constructed by state agents under state authority, and taken out of the control of the local officers. The act was adjudged invalid on the ground that by the constitution the state was forbidden to engage in internal improvements, and the towns were given control of these local works, and of the expenditure of their moneys therefor.

[2] People *v.* Flagg, 46 N. Y., 401, may usefully be compared with the case of Washington Avenue. It was a case of compulsory town taxation for a like expensive road. See also People *v.* Supervisors of Richmond, 20 N. Y., 252; Shaw *v.* Dennis, 5 Gilm., 405.

large, it has been found more satisfactory and more consistent with the general system of local government, that the works themselves should be apportioned for construction among the divisions of the state in which they respectively are to be constructed, and that each division should be left to bear the cost of that which falls within it. The advantages of this system are obvious. Presumptively the cost of these works is apportioned through the state as equally and justly in this mode as by spreading the cost of all among the whole people. Moreover, when each community is thus taxed for those works only which are constructed in the immediate vicinity, and the importance of which its members may be supposed to feel and appreciate, it is reasonable to expect that they will bear the cost more willingly and cheerfully than they would their proportion of a work at a distance, of the necessity of which they could know nothing except by report, and the construction of which they might attribute to local and personal considerations. These are not the only reasons for leaving highways and other public works of a similar nature to be constructed by the local divisions of the state only. Such a course has been found conducive to economy in expenditure, because the community upon whom the whole cost falls have the opportunity, and will be certain to have the disposition, to watch with reasonable jealousy in order to see that nothing is wasted and nothing is plundered. At the same time, as all local improvements tend to confer special and peculiar benefits upon the local community beyond what are received by the state at large, the people thus immediately and specially benefited may generally be relied upon to make liberal appropriations for the public works which are to add to the comforts, conveniences, and, perhaps, the adornment of their neighborhood, because the very moneys they thus vote appear to return to them in the increased value which the expenditure confers upon their estates. It is found to be a wise apportionment of the cost of public highways which leaves each separate division of the state, either town or county, to defray that which is to be expended within its limits.

There is a class of public works, however, which by general consent are not regarded as being general in their nature, though the use thereof may be open to the general public. As an illustration may be taken the case of the pavement of a city street. The street itself is a public highway, but the necessity for a heavy expenditure in paving arises from causes that are purely local. Moreover, in large cities, the pavement becomes absolutely essential, and must be made by the owners of adjoining property, if not provided for by the public. The ability to make profitable use of their property depends upon it, and they might, perhaps, be safely left to provide for it at their own expense, if all property was improved and occupied; and if, when individual action was relied upon, there was any method of insuring uniformity of action in the time, manner and expense of improving the streets. The necessity, however, for public supervision and direction is manifestly imperative, and the necessity for making the improvement a local burden is almost equally imperative, since it is not to be supposed that the state at large would understand and appreciate the absolute need of an improvement which was specially important to a few persons only.

Considered as a city work, the expense of paving a street may be levied upon the whole city, or a system of apportionment may be resorted to, analogous to that which is adopted in the construction and working of highways in general; that is to say, the cost of any such work may be assessed upon that part of the city which receives peculiar benefits from it. The latter method would require either a division of the city into taxing districts for the several local improvements within it, or the creation of a special taxing district for each improvement, setting apart for the purpose that portion of the city which was believed to receive the special benefits. These special taxing districts are most common, and they are either fixed after an examination of the circumstances of each particular case with a view to ascertaining how far the special benefits extend, and what property shares in them, or they are determined by some general rule which, though it may not be strictly just in any particular case, will, in the main, it is supposed, apportion all such expenses with reasonable equality and fairness.

Establishment of districts. When the nature of the case does not conclusively fix it, the power to determine what shall be the taxing district for any particular burden is purely a legislative power, and not to be interfered with or controlled, except as it may be limited or restrained by constitutional provisions. Reference to the cases cited in the margin will show that this is a principle which the courts assert with great unanimity and clearness.[1] "The judicial tribunals," it has justly been said, "cannot interfere with the legislative discretion, however onerous it may be."[2] And when it was objected that a certain construction of a statute would throw upon one locality the expense of constructing a road for state purposes, "the conclusive answer" was declared to be "that the state may impose such a burden where, in the wisdom of the legislature, it is considered that it ought to rest."[3] The right to

[1] People *v.* Brooklyn, 4 N. Y., 419, 425; Shaw *v.* Dennis, 5 Gilm., 405, 416, per *Caton*, J.; Philadelphia *v.* Field, 58 Penn. St., 320; Langhorne *v.* Robinson, 20 Grat., 661; Conwell *v.* Connersville, 8 Ind., 358; Malchus *v.* Highlands, 4 Bush, 547; Challis *v.* Parker, 11 Kansas, 394; Hingham, etc., Turnpike *v.* Norfolk County, 6 Allen, 353 and cases cited. In Howell *v.* Buffalo, 37 N. Y., 267, 273, *Parker*, J., speaking of the legislative power over special assessments, says: "The legislature was not bound to apportion the tax among the taxable persons within the city, but might, according to its own view of justice and right, apportion the whole tax among a part of such persons. It saw fit to apportion the tax upon the owners of the lands which had been benefited by the improvement, in proportion to the amount of such benefit. As it is impossible, under the doctrine adverted to, to say that it had not the constitutional power so to do, so it can scarcely be contended that, in so doing, it violated any principle of justice or right." Where lands constituting one parcel are situate in two townships or counties, they may under general legislation be made taxable in the one in which the owner or occupant has his domicile. Saunders *v.* Springstein, 4 Wend., 429; Hairston *v.* Stinson, 13 Ired., 479; Ellis *v.* Hall, 19 Penn. St., 292. But this mode of assessment cannot be claimed as a right by the owner. And assessment of the separate parts in the counties, etc., in which they lie, is not bad as to either for want of jurisdiction. Patton *v.* Long, 68 Penn. St., 260.

[2] *Ranney*, J., Scoville *v.* Cleveland, 1 Ohio, N. S., 126, 138. The same judge in Hill *v.* Higdon, 5 Ohio, N. S., 243, 245, after speaking of former decisions in the same state says: "It was there shown * * that the right to tax for such a purpose necessarily included the power to determine the extent, and upon what property the tax should be levied; and that its imposition upon the property particularly and specially benefited by the improvement, was but a lawful exercise of the discretion with which the legislative body was invested, in apportioning the tax." "We see," he says further on, "no reason to doubt the correctness of these conclusions." See also what is said by *Rapallo*, J., in Gordon *v.* Cornes, 47 N. Y., 608, 611. Also Allen *v.* Drew, 44 Vt., 174, 187; Alcorn *v.* Hamer, 38 Miss., 652, 761.

[3] *Johnson*, Ch. J., in People *v.* Supervisors of Richmond, 20 N. Y., 252, 255.

do this where the constitution has interposed no obstacles is declared to be not now open to controversy, if indeed it ever was.[1] The legislature judges finally and conclusively upon all questions of policy, as it may also upon all questions of fact which are involved in the determination of a taxing district.[2]

And having the authority to determine what shall be the taxing districts, the legislature must also be left to its own methods of reaching the conclusion. Most cases will be settled by general

See to the same effect, Shaw *v.* Dennis, 5 Gilm., 405. The case was one in which the legislature had required the levy of a special tax upon the taxable property of a single precinct for the purpose of repairing and maintaining a bridge over the Rock river at that place. The court declared the act valid, and that it was always in the power of the legislature to determine the district in which a tax shall be levied. See also Philadelphia *v.* Field, 58 Pa. St., 326; Waterville *v.* Kennebeck Co., 59 Me., 80.

[1]People *v.* Lawrence, 41 N. Y., 137, 141, per *Mason*, J. That the legislature may establish taxing districts independent of county or township, or boundaries of political subdivisions, see Malchus *v.* Highlands, 4 Bush, 547; Shelby Co. *v.* Railroad Co., 5 Bush, 225; Shaw *v.* Dennis, 5 Gilm., 405, 416; People *v.* Hawes, 34 Barb., 69. See also the next page.

[2] Litchfield *v.* Vernon, 41 N. Y., 123, 133. This was a very peculiar case of a special taxing district for a local improvement. *Grover*, J., states it thus: "An examination of the case shows that, at the time of the passage of the act, the Long Island Railroad Company had the right of way in a tunnel constructed in Atlantic street, Brooklyn, for a railroad operated by steam, and were operating their road thereon; that the legislature deemed it expedient to close the tunnel, grade the street, lay a track upon the surface to be operated by horse power, etc., and to authorize the making of a contract with the railroad company for doing the work and effecting the changes for a sum not exceeding $125,000. To carry into effect this design, the act in question was passed, authorizing the commissioners, whose appointment was provided for in the act, to make the contract, and to make an assessment for the payment of the contract price, together with the incidental expenses, upon the lands and premises situate in the district specified in the act. This local assessment for those purposes, it is apparent, was based upon the ground that the territory subjected thereto would be benefited by the work and change in question. Whether so benefited or not, and whether the assessment of the expense should for this, or any other reason, be made upon the district, the legislature was the exclusive judge." See also Hoyt *v.* East Saginaw, 19 Mich., 39, 43. In Kansas it is held that where several streets are to be improved, it is competent to make one district of them all, and apportion the expense by frontage along them all. Parker *v.* Challis, 9 Kansas, 155; Challis *v.* Parker, 11 id., 394. As to the assessment of railroad property in the same state, see *post*, p. 114, note.

law; but taxes for extraordinary purposes may require special legislation, or at least may justify it. In such cases it may be proper to enter upon such inquiries into the facts as cannot well be made directly by the legislative body of the state, whose duties are too multitudinous to admit of special investigations on a hearing of evidence or on personal examination by its members. Under such circumstances it may be proper and convenient to refer the whole subject to the local authorities; and this in the case of local works or improvements is the course usually adopted. The state does not determine whether a city shall be improved and a tax levied therefor, but, by provision in the city charter, or by special legislation, it refers the whole subject to the city common council, under such directions, regulations and instructions as it may be thought proper or prudent to give or impose. The state does not apportion the counties and towns into school districts, and order the construction of district school houses; but by general law submits the subject to the people specially concerned. This is the general course, and it has been found to be the satisfactory, and therefore the wise course. And if an apportionment is to be made on the basis of benefits to property, the local authorities may be and usually are empowered to refer the assessment of benefits to officers or commissioners chosen for the purpose, whose report, when under the provisions of the law it shall become final, will settle the limits of the special taxing district. These are only methods of giving effect to the legislative authority over this subject.[1]

Diversity of districts. Taxing districts may be as numerous as the purposes for which taxes are levied. The district for a single highway may not be the same as that for the school house located upon it. It is not essential that the political districts of the state shall be the same as the taxing districts,[2] but special districts may be established for special purposes, wholly ignoring

[1] People *v.* Brooklyn, 4 N. Y., 419, 430; Lexington *v.* McQuillan's Heirs, 9 Dana, 413; Williams *v.* Detroit, 2 Mich., 560; Dorgan *v.* Boston, 12 Allen, 223; Brewster *v.* Syracuse, 19 N. Y, 116; Hingham, etc., Turnpike Co. *v.* Norfolk County, 6 Allen, 353; Salem Turnpike, etc., Co. *v.* Essex County, 100 Mass., 282; Appeal of Powers, 29 Mich., 504.

[2] People *v.* Central R. R. Co., 43 Cal., 398, in which it was decided to be competent to divide a county into revenue districts. Malchus *v.* Highlands,

the political divisions. A school district may be created of territory taken from two or more townships or counties, and the benefits of a highway, a levee or a drain may be so peculiar that justice would require the cost to be levied either upon part of a township or county, or upon parts of several such subdivisions of the state.[1] The political divisions of the state are necessarily regarded in taxation only where the tax itself is for a purpose specially pertaining to one of them in its political capacity, so that, as already stated, the nature of the tax will determine the district.

Overlying districts. Even when the purpose for which a tax is demanded pertains to the state at large, or to one of its divisions, so that a general levy throughout the state or such division is essential, there may be peculiar reasons why a part of the general public who are concerned in the purpose should bear a proportion of the burden greater than that which should be borne by the others. A pertinent illustration might perhaps be the case of a tax for the construction of a state capitol. It would be clear, we should say, that such a tax should be spread over the state at large, because the purpose is a state purpose, and every individual

4 Bush, 547; S. C., 2 Withrow's Corp. Cas., 361, in which an act was sustained which created a special district near Newport, with authority to grade and pave or macadamize with rock or gravel, any public road passing through or into the same, on a favorable vote of two-thirds the owners of real estate, by or through which any such road may pass. See also County Judge *v.* Shelby R. R. Co., 5 Bush, 225. A strong illustration of legislative power in establishing districts is afforded when several streets are put into one district for the purposes of improvement, and the cost of improving all is assessed throughout the district; as in Challis *v.* Parker, 11 Kans., 394.

[1] County Judge *v.* Shelby R. R. Co., 5 Bush, 225. See also People *v.* Draper, 15 N. Y., 532; Buffalo, etc., R. R. Co. *v.* Supervisors of Erie, 48 id., 93; Litchfield *v.* McComber, 42 Barb., 288, 299; Sangamon, etc., R. R. Co. *v.* Jacksonville, 14 Ill., 163; Bakewell *v.* Police Jury, 20 La. An., 334; Malchus *v.* Highlands, 4 Bush, 547; Norwich *v.* County Commissioners, 13 Pick., 60; Brighton *v.* Wilkinson, 2 Allen, 27; Attorney Gen'l *v.* Cambridge, 16 Gray, 245; Salem Turnpike, etc., Co. *v.* Essex County, 100 Mass., 282. In Kansas a statute for an assessment of railroad property as a whole, and an apportionment to the different counties and townships, was sustained in Missouri River, etc., Co. *v* Morris, 7 Kans., 210; Same *v.* Blake, 9 id., 489; Smith *v.* Leavenworth Co., 9 id., 296. Several states assess railroad property in a similar manner. In Kentucky, railroads can only be taxed as an entirety and by the state. Applegate *v.* Ernst, 3 Bush, 648.

in the state is directly interested in its accomplishment. But it is also apparent that the people and the property at the place where the structure is proposed to be constructed would receive special and probably very great benefits in consequence of the construction, beyond what they would receive in common with all others. The fact is often recognized in the voluntary contributions which are made by the people to secure the location and construction of state buildings at the place where they reside or own property; and the question then arises whether these peculiar benefits may not constitute a basis for special taxation. To make them such, it would be necessary there should be two taxing districts: the one embracing the whole state, and the other embracing only the district which, in the opinion of the legislature, was so peculiarly benefited as to justify an exceptional burden upon its people and property. In such a case the people within the minor district, which is also embraced within the larger district, would contribute twice to the same burden; but this, though apparently a violation of the principles of taxation, is not so in fact, if the establishment of the minor district has only equality and justice in view, and if each taxpayer, though twice called upon, is by the two assessments only required to pay what, as between himself and the rest of the state, has been found to be his just proportion of a burden which, though general in its nature, distributes its benefits unequally.

This doctrine has been applied in Pennsylvania to the case of a county town, which, in addition to its proportion of the county levy, was specially assessed for the expense of constructing a court house and jail. "The advantages of a county town," it was said, "are too well appreciated, not to make every village use all its exertions to have a court house provided for its benefit and convenience, and as its inhabitants profited by, not only the disbursement of the tax among them, but a permanent increase of their business and an appreciation of their property, they were morally bound to contribute in proportion."[1] In the state of New York it has also been applied to a state work of public improvement, — a canal — which conferred or was likely to confer local

[1] *Gibson*, Ch. J., in Kirby *v.* Shaw, 19 Penn. St., 258, 261.

benefits on a locality specially taxed.[1] It has also been applied to the case of a building erected for the accommodation of a state educational institution. In one case where a local tax was provided for to meet a portion of the cost of erecting at that place a building for the state agricultural college, the principles which underlie such cases were so clearly stated that a quotation from the opinion will be more satisfactory than any synopsis that might be attempted, or any restatement in our own language.

"It may at first sight seem," it was said, "as if the establishment of a college and its endowment and support by the commonwealth for the education of all persons within the state, who might wish to receive instruction in certain branches of science or art, would stand on the same footing as the public schools, and that money raised for such an object ought to be apportioned and distributed in such manner as to bear on all persons and property equally, without resort to local taxation, which would operate partially, and in a certain sense disproportionately. We are not prepared to say that this proposition is in all respects incorrect. We doubt very much whether it would be competent for the legislature to impose the whole burden of supporting such an institution upon any particular municipality, section or district of the state. But we are clear in the opinion that there may exist a state of facts which would render it just and expedient, and strictly within the exercise of constitutional authority, for the legislature to enact that a portion of such a public burden should be borne by persons and estates situated within certain limits, and to authorize a special assessment on them for that purpose. If the establishment of a public institution of general utility or necessity in a particular locality would be productive of direct and appreciable benefit to persons or estates in the vicinity, either by increasing the value of property there situated, or by the opportunities which it would afford to those residing in the neighborhood to enjoy certain common advantages and privileges, with greater facility and at less cost than others having an equal right to participate in them, but who reside or own estates more remotely situated, or in distant parts of the state, we can see no reason

[1] Thomas *v.* Leland, 24 Wend., 65. See also Harbor Commissioners *v.* State, 45 Ala., 399.

why these special advantages or benefits should not be taken into consideration, in determining the mode in which the public burden of defraying the cost of the institution should be apportioned and distributed. While perfect equality in the raising of money for public charges is inattainable, it would certainly approximate more nearly to an equitable apportionment of them, to provide that such portion of the expenditure for a public object as will inure directly to the benefit or profit of a certain town or district, should be borne by the estates situated and persons resident therein, leaving only that sum to be treated as a public charge, and to constitute a general assessment on all persons and property in the commonwealth, which may reasonably be supposed to be expended for the equal and common benefit of all. Such distribution of a public burden would be reasonable, because it would tend to equality; and it would be proportional, because it would be borne in proportion to the benefits which each would receive."[1]

A like principle is sometimes applied to the construction and improvement of the streets. These, as has been said, constitute highways for the accommodation of the general public, but are calculated, by their improvement, to increase largely the value of all property fronting on, or lying in the immediate vicinity of them. Should the legislature determine that the cost of a street improvement should be borne in part by the whole city, and in part by an assessment made on the basis of benefits within a district to which the improvement was exceptionally valuable, we know of no valid objection that could be interposed. Whether the city shall bear the whole expense, the adjacent property the whole, or, on the other hand, the expense be apportioned between two districts, one of which includes the whole city, and the other the adjacent property only, must be deter-

[1] *Bigelow*, Ch. J., in Merrick *v.* Amherst, 12 Allen, 498, 504. See to the same effect, Marks *v.* Pardue University, 37 Ind., 155; Gordon *v.* Cornes, 47 N. Y., 608, 614. Every such special assessment must of course have express legislative authority. It could not be made under the general power conferred upon a municipality to levy taxes for corporate purposes. This was affirmed and explained in Livingston County *v.* Weider, 64 Ill., 427. See also Burr *v.* Carbondale, Sup. Ct. Ill., 1875, 6 Chicago Legal News, 350. Also Chap. XX.

mined by the legislature on a consideration of all the equities bearing on the case.[1] Other local city improvements may undoubtedly be provided for in the same way.

The legislature has sometimes applied the same doctrine to the case of general city taxation; constituting two districts, the one, consisting of the whole city, to be assessed equally, and the other consisting of the more compact portions of the city, which, because receiving a larger share of the benefits of city government, in the protection afforded by the police and fire departments and the like, was required to pay a greater proportionate share of the expense of such government. It is not perceived that such a case differs in principle from the other cases of overlying districts which have been mentioned. Nevertheless, in one case, the power of the legislature to discriminate in city taxation between what may be designated the *out* property, and that in the parts compactly built, has been denied, on the ground that the city constituted the taxing district for city purposes, and such a discrimination would give distinct rules of taxation within the same district, to the number of which there could be no limit except the legislative discretion; a doctrine wholly inconsistent, it was said, with the constitutional idea of taxation.[2] This conclusion seems to us to impose restraints on the constitutional power of the legislature to establish taxing districts, which can hardly be justified in reason, or by the decisions in analogous cases. Legislation, such as was condemned in the case, has not been uncommon in other states, and in some cases, has passed the test of judicial scrutiny.[3] Such

[1] See Municipality *v.* White, 9 La. An., 446; Municipality *v.* Dunn, 10 id., 57; Chicago *v.* Larned, 34 Ill., 203; Ottawa *v.* Spencer, 40 id., 211; Patton *v.* Springfield, 99 Mass., 627; S. C., 2 Withrow's Corp. Cas., 484.

[2] Knowlton *v.* Supervisors of Rock County, 9 Wis., 410, 421. Compare Zanesville *v.* Richards, 5 Ohio, N. S., 589.

[3] See Serrill *v.* Philadelphia, 38 Penn. St., 355, 358. In that case it appeared that the legislature had provided that land within the city of Philadelphia, which the assessors should mark "rural," should be taxed only two-thirds, and a part of it only one-half, what others were taxed for city purposes, they being released from the rest "because," as *Woodward*, J., says, "rural owners derived no benefit from lighting, paving and cleaning streets," etc. The act was enforced without question as to its validity. And see Gillette *v.* Hartford, 31 Conn., 351. The cases of Henderson *v.* Lambert, 8 Bush, 607; Benoist *v.* St Louis, 19 Mo., 179, and Lee *v.* Thomas, 49 id., 112, are all directly opposed to the case in Wisconsin.

legislation is sustained on the ground that it is only an equitable apportionment of the burdens of municipal government between those who receive a part of its benefits only, and those who participate in them all.[1]

A different case has been presented in some other states. City boundaries having been extended so as to embrace the lands of parties who insisted that their premises were agricultural lands merely, and would receive no benefit from the city government, such parties sought the protection of the courts, and prayed for injunction to restrain the imposition upon them of any tax in excess of what they would have been chargeable with had the boundaries not been extended to embrace them. It is to be observed of such cases that the legislature which has full and exclusive authority to determine the proper bounds of the municipal divisions of the state, and also to establish the taxing districts, had proceeded to do so, and in fixing the city boundaries without any provision for a discrimination in the taxation of property within them, had determined that no such discrimination should or ought to be made. The whole subject was one committed exclusively to the judgment and discretion of the legislature, whose members would make inquiry into the facts in their own way, and act upon their own reasons. No question could be made of the complete jurisdiction over the case, and if the action was unfair, and led to unequal and unjust consequences, it seems difficult to suggest any ground upon which it could be successfully assailed that would not warrant a judicial review of legislative action in every case in which parties complain of injustice and inequality. Nevertheless the courts have considered themselves warranted in inquiring into the facts, in order to determine whether the extension of municipal boundaries was fairly warranted, and having in some cases reached the conclusion that it was not, and that the extension was made for the purpose of subjecting to taxation adjacent property that would not receive the benefits of municipal government, and

[1] In Gillette *v.* Hartford, 31 Conn., 351, 357, *Butler*, J., delivering the opinion of the court, assumes as probable that the persons within the city limits whose lands have been brought in by an extension of city lines, had been so brought in on the application of the old corporation and against their own desire, and that the discrimination in taxation in their favor was only a just protection against inequality and unfairness.

was not in fact urban property, they have undertaken to protect the owners of property thus unfairly brought in, against the unequal taxation to which the legislation would expose them. In doing this they have not assumed to nullify the legislative action in extending the municipal limits, but they have undertaken to modify and relieve against its consequences, and to do this upon the express ground that the motive which has influenced the legislation was not legitimate.[1]

Some of these decisions are made by very able judges, whose opinions are always entitled to the highest respect, but it seems difficult to harmonize them with the conceded principles governing the law of taxation. For, 1. They do not question legislation as being in excess of legislative authority, as might be done where taxes are voted for a purpose not public; but they leave the legislation to stand, and only interfere to qualify its effect, on the ground that it has been adopted on improper grounds and will operate unequally; 2. This is done on an inquiry into the facts, and a substitution of the judicial conclusion for the legislative on a subject not at all judicial; a subject, too — the proper limits of city extension — upon which persons are certain to differ widely, and where an inquiry into the facts after the judicial method of an examination of witnesses is usually much less satisfactory than that personal knowledge and investigation which legislators are supposed to possess or to make.[2]

[1] Cheaney *v.* Hooser, 9 B. Monr., 330; Covington *v.* Southgate, 15 id., 491; Sharp's Ex'r *v.* Donavan, 17 id., 223; Arbegust *v.* Louisville, 2 Bush, 271; Morford *v.* Unger, 8 Iowa, 82; Langworthy *v.* Dubuque, 13 id., 86; Fulton *v.* Davenport, 17 id., 404; Buell *v.* Ball, 20 id., 282; Deeds *v.* Sanborn, 26 id., 419: Deiman *v.* Fort Madison, 30 id., 542; Bradshaw *v.* Omaha, 1 Neb., 16. The point is thus stated in a recent case in Kentucky: "As in ordinary cases of taxation, in which the reciprocal benefits are deemed commensurable, so the subjection of lands included in the town extension to the burden of a municipal tax is not considered an unlawful appropriation of private property to public use, unless the legitimate object of improving the town shall have been *palpably* perverted to the unauthorized purpose only of lessening the burden of taxation on the inhabitants, who will not be otherwise benefited by the extension." Swift *v.* Newport, 7 Bush, 37, 40, per *Robertson*, J.

[2] As to correcting the injustice of legislative action by the judiciary in matters of taxation, reference may be had to what is said by *Gibson*, Ch. J., in Kirby *v.* Shaw, 19 Penn. St., 258, 261.

Extra territorial taxation. Those cases in which it has been held incompetent for a state or municipality to levy taxes on persons or property not within its limits, have generally indicated the want of jurisdiction over the subject of the tax as the ground of invalidity. But such a burden would be inadmissible, also, for the further reason that, as to any property or person outside the district in which the tax was levied, the want of legal interest in the tax would preclude its being subjected to the burden. A state can no more subject to its power a single person or a single article of property whose residence or legal *situs* is in another state, than it can subject all the citizens or all the property of such other state to its power. The accidental circumstance that it may happen to have the means of reaching one and not the rest can make no difference; there must be an interest in the subject matter of the tax; there must be between the state and the tax payer a reciprocity of duty and obligation; and these in contemplation of law would be wholly wanting in the case supposed.[1] This is the general rule; whether it is subject to exceptions may be a question. In Missouri it has been held to be incompetent for the legislature to empower a city to tax for city purposes the land outside the city but adjacent to it, and therefore receiving, possibly, some of the benefits of the city

[1] State Tax on Foreign Held Bonds, 15 Wall., 300. Compare Jenkins *v.* Charleston, Sup. Ct., So. Car., 7 Chicago Legal News, 78. Where a town had for more than twenty years exercised jurisdiction over part of another with its acquiescence, a tax levied within this part by such first mentioned town was nevertheless held void. Ham *v.* Sawyer, 38 Me., 37, 39. And see Hughey's Lessee *v.* Horrell, 2 Ohio, 231. But where an act sets off one town from another, it may provide that taxes to pay existing liabilities shall be assessed and collected in both by the existing officers as if the act had not been passed. Winslow *v.* Morrill, 47 Me., 411. Towns cannot even by agreement establish the rule that each may tax lands of its residents lying in the other; there being no statute permitting it. Dillingham *v.* Snow, 5 Mass., 547. In some states it is provided by law that, where occupied lands lie partly in two townships, they may be taxed together in that in which is the mansion house, or in which the principal portion is situate. See Bausman *v.* Lancaster, 50 Penn. St., 208; Judkins *v.* Reed, 48 Me., 386; State *v.* Hay, 31 N. J., 275; State *v.* Hoffman, 30 id., 346; State *v.* Metz, 29 id., 122; Saunders *v.* Springstein, 4 Wend., 429. Assessments upon personalty as depending upon the residence of the owners will be considered in another chapter.

government and expenditures.[1] The contrary has been held in Virginia, where land for half a mile outside the corporate limits was made taxable to pay the interest of a debt contracted in aid of internal improvements.[2] And in Indiana an objection to similar legislation was put aside with very little consideration,[3] less, one would suppose, than its importance deserved. It is certainly difficult to understand how the taxation of a district can be defended whose people have no voice in voting it, in selecting the purposes, or in expending it. A city has sometimes been allowed to exact a license fee of those engaging in the sale of intoxicating drinks near its limits, but in such a case regulation is the principal object, and the city is the party chiefly concerned.[4]

[1] Wells *v.* Weston, 22 Mo., 384, 386, approved in St. Charles *v.* Nolle, 51 id., 122. And see Wilkey *v.* Pekin, 19 Ill., 160.

[2] Langhorne *v.* Robinson, 20 Grat., 661. In this case the city of Lynchburg was authorized to levy a tax "upon the lands, property and persons of all persons within the town proper and corporation, and for half a mile round about and beyond its present tax paying limits," for the purposes of aid to a railroad corporation. The act was sustained in reliance upon New York cases, and the broad assertion is made by the judge delivering the opinion, after referring to the undoubted right of the state to delegate the power of taxation to municipal authorities, "On principle I can imagine no reason why the power might not as well be delegated to any other persons in the discretion of the legislature." If we understand this opinion literally, it would sustain the legislature in a delegation to the city authorities of Lynchburg, or of any other favored town, of any indefinite power of taxation for any public purpose whatever, and upon any portion of the state; the town authorities in doing so, acting for and with the authority of the representatives of the people chosen to the legislature. But doubtless this was not intended. It is evident that the particular tax involved in that case was thought by the court to be just; had it been otherwise, perhaps the principle involved would have received further consideration.

[3] Conwell *v.* Connersville, 8 Ind., 358, 362. *Davison*, J., says: "The appellant, in his brief, propounds this inquiry: 'Can the appellees tax property lying outside of the corporate limits, and within two hundred yards?' No argument or authority is adduced in relation to the point involved in the interrogatory. Hence, we are inclined to answer briefly that the act of 1849 invests the president and trustees with full power to tax property within two hundred yards of the corporate line. And we do not advise that that act is in conflict with the constitution."

[4] Falmouth *v.* Watson, 5 Bush, 660. A town cannot give its ordinance such extra territorial effect without express authority by statute. Strauss *v.* Pontiac, 40 Ill., 301.

To give locality to a purpose in respect to which a public expenditure is to be made, it is obviously not essential that the expenditure should be within the district, nor that a public work created by means thereof should have its *situs* within the district. The district *interest* must be the true test whether an object is or is not a proper object of district taxation; and if the benefits are had by the district, the interest is manifest. The case of city waterworks located outside its limits is an illustration.[1]

[1] Goddin *v.* Crump, 8 Leigh, 120, 155, per *Tucker*, President; Denton *v.* Jackson, 2 Johns. Ch., 317, 336. But in general, specific authority would be required to enable a municipality to expend money outside its territorial limits for a purpose which presumptively is not local. Thus, a town under its general authority to vote taxes for township purposes cannot raise money to build or repair a bridge outside. Concord *v.* Boscawen, 17 N. H., 465. Compare North Hempstead *v.* Hempstead, Hopk. Ch., 288; Riley *v.* Rochester, 9 N. Y., 64. A city may be authorized to purchase and improve a public park outside its limits. M'Callie *v.* Chattanooga, 3 Head, 317.

CHAPTER VI.

EQUALITY AND UNIFORMITY IN TAXATION.

Requirement of equality. There is no imperative requirement that taxation shall be equal. If there were, the operations of government must come to a stop, from the absolute impossibility of fulfilling it. The most casual attention to the nature and operation of taxes will put this beyond question. No single tax can be apportioned so as to be exactly just, and any combination of taxes is likely in individual cases to increase instead of diminishing the inequality. Theoretically, tax laws should be framed with a view to apportioning the burdens of government so that each person enjoying government protection shall be required to contribute so much as is his reasonable proportion, and no more. The tax law that comes nearest to accomplishing this is, in theory, the most perfect. But to accomplish this it may not be requisite to require the tax-gatherer to call upon every individual, and collect from him in person this reasonable proportion. It may possibly be found that the most equal and just tax can be collected from the fewest persons.[1] A tax on an article of prime necessity, which few produce, but all use, may be collected of the producers alone without their feeling the burden beyond what others would feel it, because the tax in the natural course of business would be added to the price of the commodity, and would be collected by the producers from the whole community of consumers. Such a tax would be generally distributed, and would be wanting in equality only because of the fact that articles of prime necessity are not consumed by different members of the community in proportion to their means or income, and therefore the poorer classes would pay more than their just proportion. To collect all the revenues of government by a tax on breadstuffs exclusively, would consequently be to compel unequal con-

[1] Smith, Wealth of Nations, b. 5, ch. 2, pt. 2, art. 4. State taxes on property by valuation are collected from very few persons, five to eight per cent. of the whole population.

tributions to the support of the government, by means of the necessities of the poor. A tax on an article which is purely one of luxury would probably be more equal, and certainly less unjust, and would be diffused with some proportion to income; every man would tax himself, and would abstain or indulge as he felt the disposition and ability to pay. To collect the whole revenue of the state from an article of luxury like spirituous liquors, might be as little liable to objection as any other method if it were practicable, but to attempt the collection of all from one article would require a tax so heavy as to be difficult of enforcement, and which would probably defeat the purpose of the law by diminishing the consumption as the price increased. We have already seen that other kinds of taxes are open to serious objections on the score of equality and justice. A tax on property by valuation, which seems perhaps most fair of all, is subject, as has been shown, to difficulties which preclude its being laid, apportioned or collected with absolute justice. The objections need not be repeated here.

It being thus manifest that there are serious and often insurmountable difficulties in the way of equal taxation, it remains to be seen what is the rule of law where in the particular case the inequality can be pointed out and demonstrated. On this subject, certain points have already been covered. The legislature must decide when and how and for what public purposes a tax shall be levied, and must select the subjects of taxation. This is legislative, and the legislative conclusion in the premises must be accepted as proper and final. It follows that a tax cannot be attacked on averment and proof that some other tax for the same purpose would have been more just and more equal. An excise tax on one kind of business only is not illegal for the discrimination; it is always to be conclusively presumed that the legislature found good and controlling reasons impelling the action it has taken, and that, in view of all the circumstances which were known to its members, the tax which has been provided for is reasonable.[1]

Very strong language has been used by the courts in some

[1] See De Camp *v.* Eveland, 19 Barb., 81; Nor. Ind. R. R. Co. *v.* Connelly, 10 Ohio, N. S., 159, 165; People *v.* Brooklyn, 4 N. Y., 419; Lusher *v.* Scites, 4 W. Va., 11.

cases, and it may be useful to collect some of the expressions. The act in Pennsylvania by which the legislature allowed the county borough to levy a tax for the erection of a court-house and jail for the use of the county, was thought by some of its citizens to be void because unequal. The court thought otherwise. "As regards taxation," say the court, "there is no limitation of it. Equality of contribution is not enjoined in the bill of rights, and probably because it was known to be impracticable. Previous to the convention of 1838, we had double taxation of tracts of unseated lands lying foul of each other; of lands and mortgages of them; of grounds and rents issuing out of them; of bank charters and bank dividends under them, and perhaps of some other things. On the other hand, it was known that other descriptions of property had not been taxed at all. Since then, the exigencies of the state have brought to light many new sources of revenue, and more would have been discovered had more been wanted. No one imagined, however, that the inequality had made the previous taxation unconstitutional.

"If equality were practicable, in what branch of the government would power to enforce it reside? Not in the judiciary, unless it were competent to set aside a law free from collision with the constitution, because it seemed unjust. It could interpose only by overstepping the limits of its sphere, by arrogating to itself a power beyond its province; by producing intestine discord, and by setting an example which other organs of government might not be slow to follow. It is its peculiar duty to keep the first lines of the constitution clear, and not to stretch its power in order to correct legislative or executive abuses. Every branch of the government, the judiciary included, does injustice for which there is no remedy, because everything human is imperfect. The sum of the matter is, that the taxing power must be left to that part of the government which is to exercise it.

"But what if this power were so managed as to lay the public burthens on particular classes in ease of the rest? It is illogical to argue from an extreme case; or from the abuse of a power to a negation of it. Every authority, however indispensable, may be abused; and if it might not, it would be powerless for good."[1]

[1] *Gibson*, Ch. J., in Kirby *v.* Shaw, 19 Penn. St., 258, 260. "Equality of taxation,

"Perfect equality in the assessment of taxes," it is said in another case, "is unattainable. Approximation to it is all that can be had. Under any system of taxation, however wisely and carefully framed, a disproportionate share of the public burdens will be thrown on certain kinds of property, because they are visible and tangible, while others are of a nature to elude vigilance. It is only where statutes are passed which impose taxes on false and unjust principles, or operate to produce gross inequality, so that they cannot be deemed in any just sense proportional in their effect on those who are to bear the public charges, that courts can interpose and arrest the course of legislation by declaring such enactments void." [1]

"Perfectly equal taxation," it has again been said, "will remain an unattainable good as long as laws and government and man are imperfect." [2] "There is no provision in the constitution

as a maxim of taxation, means equality of sacrifice. It means apportioning the contributions of each person towards the expenses of government, so that he shall feel neither more nor less inconvenience from his share of the payment than every other person experiences from his. This standard, like other standards of perfection, cannot be completely realized." Mill., Pol. Econ., b. 5, ch., 2, § 2. There is a very elaborate examination of this general subject in Williams's Case, 3 Bland. Ch., 186, 220.

[1] *Bigelow*, Ch. J., in Commonwealth *v.* Savings Bank, 5 Allen, 428, 436. See Lowell *v.* Oliver, 8 Allen, 247; Ould *v* Richmond, 23 Grat., 464, 473; Howell *v.* Bristol, 8 Bush, 493. "Equality can never be but approximation." *Redfield*, J., in Allen *v.* Drew, 44 Vt., 174, 186.

[2] *Sharswood*, J., in Grim *v.* School District, 57 Penn. St., 433, 437. Compare Durach's Appeal, 62 Penn. St., 491; People *v.* Worthington, 21 Ill., 171; Commonwealth *v.* N. E. Slate & Tile Co., 13 Allen, 391; Youngblood *v.* Sexton, Sup. Ct. Mich., October term, 1875. In Coburn *v.* Richardson, 16 Mass., 213, 215, a tax on the lands of a nonresident for parish purposes was assailed. *Parker*, Ch. J. "Numerous are the inconveniences and great is the injustice which may flow from this statute. But it is for the legislature alone to determine whether these are or are not counterbalanced by any great public good which may be expected to be produced by it." In Conner *v.* Fulsom, 13 Minn., 219, 222, in which a town bounty tax was contested, on the ground that it benefited in part another town, as in fact it did, *Wilson*, Ch. J., holds this language. "It is generally true that a city, town or county, in expending money for the advancement of its own local interests, either directly or indirectly benefits some other subdivision of the state. If it builds a road or bridge, or aids in building a railroad, or in making any other public improvement, from which benefit to itself is expected to accrue, frequently some other subdivision of the state is directly and equally benefited; but it has not been considered that

that taxation shall be equal. Sound policy requires that it should be, so far as possible. But perfect equality is not possible. Indeed, if this was necessary there could be no taxation except such as would include every person and every thing; which would be manifestly impracticable and unjust."[1] These are strong expressions, but they do not go beyond the demands of strict accuracy.

But are there not cases which on their face are manifestly so unequal and unjust as to furnish conclusive evidence that equality has not been sought for but avoided; that oppression, not justice was desired, and confiscation, not taxation intended? Such cases it surely is possible to conceive, and if such has never been the intent of legislation, it is certain that it has sometimes been the result.

It has already been stated that inequality does not necessarily follow the restricting of a tax to a few subjects only, or to a single subject. A license tax cannot be deemed unequal because reaching one occupation only, if it is to reach all who follow that. Let it reach all of a class, either of persons or things, it matters not whether those included in it be one or many, or whether they reside in any particular locality or are scattered all over the state. It would be only when individuals of the class were singled out

this would be a legal objection to an appropriation or tax for such improvement. If our constitution required absolute or perfect equality in taxation, such objection would perhaps have to be admitted. But perfect equality is not required, nor is it possible. All taxes 'should be as nearly equal as may be,' in the language of the constitution. If the taxes imposed are distributed on just principles applicable alike to all for whose benefit the appropriation is made or intended, substantial equality is attained, and no constitutional right invaded." Compare People *v.* Whyler, 41 Cal., 351, 354, per *Rhodes*, J.

[1] *Sharswood*, J., in Weber *v.* Reinhardt, 73 Penn. St., 370, 373. See Opinions of Judges, 58 Me., 590; Loan Association *v.* Topeka, 20 Wall., 655, per *Miller*, J. "It was justly remarked by Judge Ellsworth in Savings Bank *v.* New London, 20 Conn., 117, and again in Carrington *v.* Farmington, 21 id., 65, 72; that taxes are at best arbitrary and unequal. Studied discriminations are made in all tax laws in favor of or against particular persons or subjects, or trades, or business, or institutions. The character of this kind of legislation, as arbitrary, partial, cumulative and capricious, is well exemplified in the recent acts of congress. From the nature of the case there can be no uniform rule of making the assessments." *McCurdy*, J., in Coite *v.* Society for Savings, 32 Conn., 173, 184.

for exemption, that the inequality would be manifest.[1] To tax all loans of money would be equal, and would enable all to adjust their rates of interest accordingly; but to tax all except those made by A., B. and C., or all but those of the inhabitants of a single city, would be unequal, and would create an invidious and unjust distinction in favor of the excepted persons, which would give them the advantage of higher net rates. The one would be taxation; the other would be lawless exaction. This, as a general principle, is undoubted.[2]

[1] Durach's Appeal, 62 Penn. St., 491, 494; Fletcher *v.* Oliver, 25 Ark., 289; State *v.* Parker, 32 N. J., 426, 435, per *Depue*, J.; Youngblood *v.* Sexton, Sup. Ct. Mich., Oct. Term, 1875. In the Franklin Insurance Co. *v.* State, 5 W. Va., 349, a tax of three per cent. on the premiums of insurance companies was held void; the constitution requiring taxation to be equal and uniform, and this tax law applying to no other class of subjects or corporations, or to individuals. The tax seems to have been regarded as a tax on *property.* Surely the requirement of uniformity cannot make it essential that all persons or subjects shall be taxed, nor that all corporations shall be taxed alike. Does it mean any more than that any particular tax shall be laid equally and uniformly upon the persons or subjects within the class taxed? Would not a tax of one per cent. on the net earnings of all railroad companies be equal and uniform? And if this is inadmissible, how can there be any equalization of taxation, as between, for instance, the insurance company and the saloon keeper, unless everything is brought to the standard of a property tax, in which case those who ought to pay most would sometimes pay least? To determine whether a tax on insurance companies alone would be unequal or unjust, it would be necessary to look to the result. The tax, we must suppose, would go to increase the premiums, and if the community generally insured, the tax would be generally distributed through the community, and would be paid in proportion to the protection received. See Slaughter *v.* Commonwealth, 13 Grat., 767; Carter *v.* Dow, 16 Wis., 298. In State *v.* Charleston, 12 Rich., 702, 732, *Dunkin*, Chancellor, says: "Essential characteristics of any system of taxation, properly so called, are certainty, equality, universality. All the persons or property within a state, district, city or other fraction of territory having a local sovereignty for the purpose of taxation, should, as a general rule, constitute the basis for taxation." Like language is made use of by *Tuck*, J., in O'Neal *v.* Bridge Co., 18 Md., 1, 23, and it is quite true and just where taxation by values is what the law provides for; but it has but limited application to the taxation of business in any form. That the legislature cannot designate one class of persons because of their race as special objects of taxation, see Lin Sing *v.* Washburn, 20 Cal., 534.

[2] A remarkable case of invidious exemption occurs in the legislation of Arkansas for 1871. A statute purporting to be passed in the interest of immigration and manufactures, exempts every species of manufacture and min-

Exemptions. There are some cases in which it has been customary for the legislature to make certain exemptions, either of persons or property, from the general rule which it has prescribed on the subject of taxation. Some of these, such as the exemptions of household furniture, tools of trade, etc., and the limited personal property which very poor persons may be possessed of, are to be looked upon rather as being in the nature of limitations of the general rule, than as exceptions from it; the taxation is only of all that is possessed over and beyond what has been left out as absolutely needful to the owner's support.[1] The same may be said of some kinds of property, such as church property, school property, burying grounds and the like, which are by many persons looked upon as fit objects for the public contributions.

Implied exemptions. Some things are always presumptively exempted from the operation of general tax laws, because it is reasonable to suppose they were not within the intent of the legislature in adopting them. A state may, if the legislature see

ing — the capital employed therein, the property used therefor, and the productions while in the ownership and possession of the original manufacturer or miner — from all taxation for a period of five years. Had the act stopped here, a question might possibly be made whether the exemption was unjust. It might be contended that releasing the manufacturer from taxation while leaving competition open would be likely to reduce prices in proportion as the cost of production was diminished by the exemption. But the legislation referred to went on to provide that no corporation or individual should have the benefit of the act whose productions should not average $900 per month. In other words, it exempted all the large manufacturers, but left the smaller ones not only taxed as before, but compellable also to share with the rest of the community in making up to the state what would be lost by not taxing the others. If anything could add to the injustice of an exemption of a portion only of those engaged in a particular business, it would be that the discrimination was made against the very class that the policy of the law is thought to favor; namely, the men of small means.

It was decided in Nashville *v.* Althorp, 5 Cold., 554, that where a merchant's privilege is taxed, discriminations can not be made: e. g., between those living within and those without a city. Compare Robinson *v.* Charleston, 2 Rich., 317.

[1] "I do not well perceive what definition can well be given to the words 'taxable property,' unless they be made to mean *all property not exempted by law from taxation.*" *Harper*, Ch. J., in City Council *v.* St. Philip's Church, 1 McMul. Eq., 139, 144. See Martin *v.* Charleston, 13 Rich. Eq., 50, 52; Levy *v.* Smith, 4 Fla., 154.

fit, tax all the property owned by its municipal divisions; but to do so, would render necessary new taxes to meet the demand of this tax, and thus the public would be taxing itself in order to raise money to pay over to itself, and no one would be benefited but the officers employed. It is always to be assumed that the general language of statutes is made use of with reference to taxable subjects, and the property of municipalities is not in any proper sense taxable. It is, therefore, by clear implication excluded.[1] It is not, like government agencies, excluded from the power of tax laws, but it is beyond the grasp of their intent.

[1] People *v.* Salomon, 51 Ill., 37; Directors of the Poor *v.* School Directors, 42 Penn. St., 21, 25 (case of poor house); State *v.* Gaffney, 34 N. J., 133 (case of city water works and land acquired therefor). And see People *v.* Doe, 36 Cal., 220; People *v.* Austin, 47 Cal., 353; Gibson *v.* Howe, 37 Iowa, 168; Trustees of Industrial University *v.* Champaign County, Sup. Ct. Ill., 1875, 7 Chicago Legal News, 160 (case of property conveyed to trustees in trust for a state educational institution). In Louisville *v.* Commonwealth, 1 Duvall, 295, 296, the following language is made use of by *Robertson*, J., the question being whether property belonging to the city of Louisville was taxable for state purposes: "A general law concerning persons may include artificial as well as natural persons, and every corporation is a legal person. Even the United States and every separate state, and every county in each state, are *quasi* corporations, and each of all such corporations is in law a person. And, consequently, a tax on the real estate of all persons would, without qualification or exception, literally include that of every corporation, municipal as well as private. But in this respect there is an obvious and essential distinction between municipal and private corporations. A private corporation, like a bank or railroad or turnpike, is, in technical language, altogether personal. But a municipal corporation, like a state, a county or the city of Louisville, is much more than a person. While nominally a person, it is vitally a political power, and each in its prescribed sphere is *imperium in imperio*. All are constituent demands of one total sovereignty. The city of Louisville, to the extent of the jurisdiction delegated to it by its charter, is but an effluence from the sovereignty of Kentucky; governs for Kentucky, and its authorized legislation and local administration of law are legislation and administration by Kentucky through the agency of that municipality. The tax law of Kentucky constructively applies to persons only, and not at all to political bodies exercising in different degrees the sovereignty of the state. Were this not true, then the statute literally embracing all persons, and the state being in one sense a person, her capital and penitentiary, and other public property, would, like the estate of a natural person, be subject to assessment for taxation; and so too would the court houses and jails and poor houses of all the counties of the state. But neither a state nor a county has ever been considered a person contemplated by any tax law ever enacted.

Express exemptions. Before referring to the express exemptions from general taxation, which it has been customary to make, it may be well to refer to certain constitutional provisions which have been adopted in different states with a view to secure uniformity in taxation. The provisions are various, and a reference to such as have come under judicial consideration will suffice for our purpose.

Arkansas. The constitution provided that "all property shall be taxed according to its value; the manner of ascertaining which to be as the general assembly shall direct, making the same equal and uniform throughout the state." Where the legislature, by a city charter, undertook to exempt the property of the inhabitants from taxation for the construction of roads in the county of which the city formed a part, this was held invalid as a violation of the rule of uniformity which the constitution had established.[1]

California. The constitution requires that "taxation shall be equal and uniform," and that "all property in the state shall be taxed in proportion to its value." Under this the following rulings have been made: 1. That "all property in the state" was to be understood as intending all *private* property only, and that it did not include the public property belonging to the United

And does not the only real reason for their constructive exclusion equally except the municipal property of Louisville, used for the convenience and facility of its local governments? We think so, and without elaborate argument we so adjudge." It was, nevertheless, held that such property as the corporation might own, not for carrying on its municipal government, but only for the convenience or profit of its citizens, individually or collectively, and which, therefore, it would own and use as a private corporation, would be subject to taxation under such general words of the statute as would embrace the like property owned by a private corporation. This private side to a public corporation has often been recognized in other than tax cases. Bailey *v.* New York, 3 Hill, 531; 2 Denio, 433; Lloyd *v.* New York, 5 N. Y., 369; Storrs *v.* Utica, 17 id., 104; Western Fund Savings Society *v.* Philadelphia, 31 Penn. St., 175; Commissioners *v.* Duckett, 20 Md., 468; Detroit *v.* Corey, 9 Mich., 165; *post.*, ch. XXI.

That the general power conferred upon a municipal corporation to tax, will not authorize the taxation of state or county property, see Nashville *v.* Bank of Tennessee, 1 Swan, 269; Piper *v.* Singer, 4 S. & R., 354.

[1] Fletcher *v.* Oliver, 25 Ark., 289. For other cases construing the constitutional provision, see Washington *v.* State, 13 Ark., 752; McGhee *v.* Mathis, 21 id., 40.

States or the state and its municipalities.[1] 2. That exemptions of private property would be inconsistent with the requirement of equality and uniformity, and consequently were forbidden.[2] 3. That special assessments for local improvements need not be levied by value,[3] but that whatever basis was adopted, exemptions of property falling within the class assessed were forbidden.[4] 4. That the requirement of uniformity in the taxation of property was not violated by a tax on business graduated by sales.[5] 5. That authority to a board of supervisors to remit a tax or a part of a tax in a specified district, would be inconsistent with the requirement of uniformity, and consequently invalid.[6] 6. That a state revenue law is not void for want of uniformity, because of the regulations of different counties as regards enforcing collection of delinquent taxes being different.[7]

Georgia. A provision that taxation on property shall be *ad valorem* only, will preclude the taxation of cattle by the head.[8] But the constitutional requirement of uniformity is not violated by taxes on business.[9]

Illinois. The constitution prescribed that the "general assembly shall provide for levying a tax by valuation, so that every person and corporation shall pay a tax in proportion to the value of his or her property." Also that "the corporate authorities of counties, townships, school districts, cities, towns and villages may be

[1] People *v.* McCreery, 34 Cal., 432. As to what is "equal and uniform" in taxation, see People *v.* Whyler, 41 Cal., 351, 355, per *Rhodes*, Ch. J.

[2] People *v.* McCreery, 34 Cal., 432; People *v.* Whartenby, 38 id., 461; People *v.* Eddy, 43 id., 331; S. C., 13 Am. Rep., 143; Lick *v.* Austin, 43 Cal., 590.

[3] Burnett *v.* Sacramento, 12 Cal., 76; Blanding *v.* Burr, 13 id., 343; Emery *v.* San Francisco Gas Co., 28 id., 345; Walsh *v.* Mathews, 29 id., 123; Crosby *v.* Lyon, 37 id., 242.

[4] People *v.* S. F. & A. R. R. Co., 35 Cal., 606.

[5] Sacramento *v.* Crocker, 16 Cal., 119.

[6] Wilson *v.* Supervisors of Sutter, 47 Cal., 91. (Case of a levee tax.)

[7] People *v.* Central Pacific R. R. Co., 43 Cal., 398. As to equality in taxation, see further, Beals *v.* Almador Co., 35 Cal., 624; Chambers *v.* Satterlee, 40 id., 497.

[8] Livingston *v.* Albany, 41 Geo., 21.

[9] Burch *v.* Savannah, 42 Geo., 596; Bohler *v.* Schneider, 49 id., 195; Home Ins. Co. *v.* Augusta, 50 id., 530.

vested with power to assess and collect taxes for corporate purposes, such taxes to be uniform in respect to persons and property within the jurisdiction of the body imposing the same." As to these provisions it has been decided that they "were manifestly inserted in the fundamental law for the purpose of insuring equality in the levy and collection of the taxes to support the government, whether levied for state, county or municipal purposes. The design was to impose an equal proportion of these burthens upon all persons within the limits of the district or body imposing them. Under these provisions the legislature has no power to exempt or release a person or community of persons from their proportionate share of these burthens. Not having such power themselves, they are unable to delegate such power to these inferior bodies."[1] These provisions preclude discrimination in favor of or against any classes of property or persons whatsoever;[2] they require the taxation of loans or any other credits, these being property as much as lands or chattels in possession;[3] they do not ad-

[1] *Walker*, J., in Hunsaker *v.* Wright, 30 Ill., 146, 148. See Trustees *v.* McConnell, 12 id., 138; O'Kane *v.* Treat, 25 id., 557, 561; Madison County *v.* People, 58 id., 456; Dunham *v.* Chicago, 55 id., 357.

[2] Primm *v.* Belleville, 59 Ill., 142; discrimination *in favor* of improvements and of personalty; Bureau County *v.* Chicago, etc., R. R. Co., 44 id., 229; Chicago, etc., R. R. Co. *v.* Boone County, 44 id., 240; discrimination *against* railroad property.

[3] Trustees *v.* McConnell, 12 Ill., 138. In People *v.* Worthington, 21 id., 171, 173, *Caton*, Ch. J., states the rule strongly and clearly: "The constitution means as it declares, that each shall pay a tax in proportion to the property which he has, whether that property consists of farms or mortgages; of visible substances or choses in action. It is not to be denied that this rule of taxation must in some, nay in many instances, operate unequally and even oppressively; and such may be the case of the defendant here. He sells a piece of land and gives a deed, and takes a note and a mortgage to secure the purchase money. He is taxed for the amount due on the mortgage, and the purchaser is taxed for the land, and if the purchaser neglects to pay these taxes, then the seller must do it himself or lose his security. This is a hardship no doubt, but like many other hardships which befall mankind, it results from the failure of another to perform his duty, and must be provided against by greater caution in selecting a purchaser, or in seeking satisfaction of him for the taxes paid on the land. It may be true in one sense to say that it is double taxation to tax the horse which is sold and also the note which is given for the purchase money; and so is it to tax the note which is given for one hundred dollars borrowed money, and also the money which is bor-

mit of residents in one part of a road district being exempted from taxes for the roads in another part;[1] nor of one class of counties being taxed a higher rate for state purposes than another class which happens to be more largely indebted for local purposes;[2]

rowed; and so we might go on throughout the whole system of human transactions which involves a credit for things tangible which are within the state and subject to taxation; and even so it is if they are beyond the state, for the presumption is that they are taxed wherever they may be. Whatever rights, credits or choses in action which may be taxed, are so much over and above the money and other physical objects within the state, and are in the same sense double taxation; for those very credits must ultimately be paid with those physical objects if they are ever paid. * * Although we might think that the provisions of the constitution on the subject of taxation are unjust and unequal, or even arbitrary and oppressive, neither the legislature nor the courts can, for any such reason, disregard them."

[1] O'Kane *v.* Treat, 25 Ill., 557. The exemption was of residents within a municipal corporation from being taxed for roads beyond its limits but within the same road district. Compare Pleasant *v.* Kost, 29 Ill., 490, 494; Madison County *v.* People, 58 id., 456.

[2] Ramsey *v.* Hœger, Sup. Ct. Ill., 1874; 6 Chicago Legal News, 318. The case was one of an attempt, indirectly, to saddle upon the state the local indebtedness incurred in the aid of railroads.

One important question under the provisions of the constitution of Illinois regarding taxation must be considered as still open. The constitution of 1870 declares that "the general assembly shall provide such revenue as may be needful by levying a tax by valuation so that every person and corporation shall pay a tax in proportion to his, her or its property, * * * but the general assembly shall have power to tax * * * persons or corporations owning or using franchises and privileges in such manner as it shall from time to time direct by general law, uniform as to the class upon which it operates." In assumed execution of this authority, the legislature of 1873 passed an act providing as follows: "The capital stock of all companies, now or hereafter created under the laws of this state shall be so valued by the state board of equalization as to ascertain and determine respectively the fair cash value of such capital stock, including the franchise, over and above the assessed value of the tangible property of such company or association. Said board shall adopt such rules and principles for ascertaining the fair cash value of such capital stock as to it may seem equitable and just, and such rules and principles, when so adopted, if not inconsistent with this act, shall be as binding and of the same effect as if contained in this act, subject, however, to such changes, alterations or amendments as may be found from time to time to be necessary by said board; provided, that in all cases where the tangible property or capital stock of any such company or association is assessed under this act, the shares of capital stock of any such company or association shall not be assessed in this state." Under this law the state board of equalization adopted the following resolution:

but they do not preclude taxes being laid on other subjects than property by some other standard than that of value, and conse-

"*Resolved*, That for the purposes of ascertaining the fair cash value of the capital stock including the franchises of all companies and associations, now or hereafter created under the laws of this state, or for the assessment of the same, or so much thereof as may be found to be in excess of the assessed or equalized value of the tangible property of such companies and associations, respectively, we, the state board of equalization, hereby adopt the following rules and principles, viz:

"1. The market or fair cash value of shares of capital stock, and the market or fair cash value of the debt, excluding indebtedness for current expenses, shall be combined or added together, and the aggregate amount so ascertained shall be taken and held to be the fair cash value of the capital stock, including the franchises, respectively, of such companies and associations.

"2. From the aggregate amount, ascertained as aforesaid, there shall be deducted the aggregate amount of the equalized or assessed valuation of all the tangible property, respectively, of such companies and associations; such equalized or assessed valuation being taken in each case, as the same may be determined by the equalization or assessment of property by the board, and the amount remaining in each case, if any, shall be taken and held to be the amount and fair cash value of the capital stock, including the franchise, which this board is required by law to assess, respectively, against companies and corporations now or hereafter created under the laws of this state."

The supreme court of the state sustained this assessment, not, however, passing upon the question of its fairness or justice, which they expressly disclaimed the right to do, but conceding to the state board of equalization the right to arrive at the valuation by any such rules as they should devise, which seemed to them calculated to reach the proper result. As the assessment made under these rules would be of the whole value of the franchise as if no indebtedness existed, there would manifestly be in the case what would be equivalent to double taxation; but as in valuing individual property under the laws of Illinois, debts are not deducted, this was no more than would exist in other cases, and the court attach importance to this fact as bearing upon the competency of the board to establish such rules. It is to be observed, however, that the law provided for assessing "the fair cash value of such capital stock including the franchise." A franchise may have a distinct value by itself irrespective of any debts that may be owing by the corporation or person possessing it, as a farm may have irrespective of the mortgage upon it; but there is certainly some difficulty in understanding how the capital stock of a corporation can be valued without taking into account its indebtedness, or how, if the corporation owes so much that its capital stock is absolutely worth nothing, and could be sold for nothing, it could have for any legal purpose a "fair cash value" given it by taking as the measure of its value that which renders it valueless. It may be that if, by enforcing the debt, the capital stock should become the property of the creditors, it would then have a value equal to the previous value of the debt; but this would be by the substitution of

quently, taxes on polls are not unconstitutional.[1] Neither do they take from the legislature the power to commute for taxes, receiving instead what they shall regard as an equivalent.[2]

Indiana. The constitution provides that "the general assembly shall provide by law for a uniform and equal rate of assessment and taxation, and shall prescribe such regulations as shall secure a just valuation for taxation of all property, both real and personal, excepting such only for municipal, educational, literary, scientific, religious or charitable purposes as may be specially exempted by law." It also provides that "the general assembly shall not pass local or special laws" "for the assessment and collection of taxes for state, county, township or road purposes." Of these provisions it has been said, they "do not prohibit local taxation for objects in themselves local. They require a general, uniform levy for state purposes, but they do not forbid local taxation under general laws. Nor do we think they prohibit indirect taxation by way of licenses upon particular pursuits, etc. Such indirect taxation may be made effectual as a police regulation. The taxing, which is a part of the legislative power of the state, is supreme, except where limitations are imposed. Indirect taxation, by way of tariffs, etc., has ever been regarded a legitimate exercise of the taxing power, and we do not think a provision in the constitution requiring the general levy of direct taxes for state purposes to be upon a uniform assessment, implies a prohibition of all other taxation. Such, at all events, is not the conventional force of its language."[3]

one thing of value for another. Before that time, certainly, the debt is no part of the capital stock. In these remarks no question is made of the correctness of the decision of the supreme court, which is certainly able and plausible. The opinion is given in full in 6 Chicago Legal News, 319. The federal circuit court for the same circuit held the assessment void, and it is believed the question is now in the United States Supreme Court.

[1] Sawyer *v.* Alton, 3 Scam., 127. This case arose under an earlier constitution, but the provisions were substantially the same.

[2] Illinois Central R. R. Co. *v.* McLean County, 17 Ill., 291, where an *ad valorem* tax was commuted for a percentage of gross receipts. And see State Bank *v.* People, 4 Scam., 303; Hunsaker *v.* Wright, 30 Ill., 146.

[3] *Perkins*, J., in Anderson *v.* Kerns Draining Co., 14 Ind., 199, citing La Fayette *v.* Jenners, 10 id., 70, 75; The Bank *v.* New Albany, 11 id., 139; Walk. Am. Law, 3d ed., p. 122; Aurora *v.* West., 9 Ind., 74. To the same effect is

Nor do these provisions require the rate of assessment to be equal for all purposes throughout the state, but only to be equal and uniform throughout the district for which the tax is levied.[1] Nor do they preclude the legislature making exemptions,[2] but they do preclude the levy of a specific tax on one species of property for any public purpose; for example, a specific tax by the acre on real estate for highway purposes.[3]

Iowa. The constitution provides that "the property of all corporations for pecuniary profit, now existing or hereafter created, shall be subject to taxation the same as that of individuals." This provision would preclude exemptions of corporate property from taxation, and consequently would require the court, in any doubtful case, to construe a revenue law as not intending such an exemption.[4]

Louisiana. A provision that "taxation shall be equal and uniform throughout the state" will not preclude the legislature authorizing the taxation of callings, trades and professions. The taxation will be equal and uniform if all persons in the same calling, trade or profession within the taxing district are taxed alike.[5] But it would preclude a discrimination as between those carrying on the same business,[6] and it would preclude a specific

Bright *v.* McCullough, 27 Ind., 223, in which the authorities are reviewed by *Elliott*, J.

[1] Adamson *v.* Auditor of Warren County, 9 Ind., 174; Conwell *v.* O'Brien, 11 id., 419; Covington Drawbridge Co. *v.* Auditor of Warren County, 14 id., 331; Bright v. McCulloch, 27 id., 223.

[2] Bank of the State *v.* New Albany, 11 Ind., 139. See Bank of Connersville *v.* State, 16 id., 105; King *v.* Madison, 17 id., 48.

[3] Bright *v.* McCullough, 27 Ind., 223.

[4] Iowa Homestead Co. *v.* Webster County, 21 Iowa, 221. If we understand correctly the case of Dubuque, etc., R. R. Co. *v.* Webster County, 21 id., 235, the provision above quoted would not prevent a taxation of corporations on their *gross receipts* in lieu of taxation on *property*.

[5] Municipality *v.* Dubois, 10 La. An., 56; New Orleans *v.* The Bank, id., 735; New Orleans *v.* Staiger, 11 id., 68; New Orleans *v.* South Bank, id., 41; New Orleans *v.* Turpin, 13 id., 56; Merriam *v.* New Orleans, 14 id., 318; State *v.* Volkman, 20 id., 585; Hodgson *v.* New Orleans, 21 id., 301. The doctrine applied to the case of license fees for theatrical and other exhibitions. Charity Hospital *v.* Stickney, 2 id., 550; Municipality *v.* Duncan, id., 182.

[6] New Orleans *v.* Home Ins. Co., 23 La. An. 449.

tax on any species of property, the value of which is not uniform, as, for example, a specific tax on cotton by the pound.[1]

Maryland. The constitution ordains that "the county commissioners shall exercise such powers and duties only as the legislature may from time to time prescribe; but such powers and duties, and the tenure of office shall be uniform throughout the state." Where the legislature made provision by law for the levy of a tax, by the county commissioners of a single county, for the support of public schools therein, the objection to this legislation, that it gave powers to and imposed duties on the commissioners of that county which were peculiar and exceptional, was held not to be well taken. It was not the purpose of the constitution that all local regulations should be the same in all parts of the state, or that every locality should levy taxes for the same objects and no others, or that the county commissioners should exercise their uniform powers on precisely the same subjects. And this legislation was not to be regarded as giving exceptional authority, but as requiring a special exercise, in one county, of the uniform power to tax which the commissioners possessed in all the counties.[2]

[1] Sims *v.* Jackson, 22 La. An., 440. See Livingston *v.* Albany, 41 Geo., 21, for the same principle. Also, State *v.* Endom, 23 La. An., 663, in which it was decided that a specific tax on drays, wagons, carriages, etc., in proportion to the number of animals drawing them, was forbidden as not being a uniform tax on the business which was taxed. A law which should make *no* discrimination in the taxation of business, we should say would in some cases, produce the grossest injustice and inequality; and it may be seriously questioned whether the requirement of uniformity in the taxation of business could be understood as forbidding the classification of those engaged in the business; for example, underwriters, by the business done or premiums received; merchants, by the capital invested or sales made, etc.; and the apportionment of taxes accordingly.

[2] *Bowie*, Ch. J., in Commissioners of Public Schools *v.* Commissioners of Allegany County, 20 Md., 449, 457, 458. As the decision is of very general application, we copy from it:

"It is said, there is no law conferring on the commissioners of the counties generally, power to make provision for public schools, and therefore the act of Allegany county is special, local, unequal, contrary to the letter and spirit of the constitution, which designed that all parts of the state should be subject to the same taxation for the same objects.

"When the organic law imposed this feature of uniformity upon county commissioners and other county officers, it cannot be supposed it was designed

Massachusetts. The constitutional provision that the legislature shall only impose proportional and reasonable taxes is not violated by permitting a town in which a state agricultural college is located, to levy a tax to pay an exceptional portion of the cost of erecting buildings for such college.[1]

Michigan. The provision that "the legislature shall provide a uniform rule of taxation, except on property paying specific taxes, and taxes shall be levied on such property as shall be pre-

to ignore the varieties of situation and condition of the people of the several counties, and the different institutions established among them. The levy courts for which the county commissioners were substituted, had exercised, from the organization of the state government, the power of levying taxes for every local purpose which the peculiar wants of each county might require, under the sanction of general or special acts of legislation.

"The legislation of the state exhibits various systems of internal regulation in respect to roads, schools, paupers and criminal trials, in the several counties, all of which ultimately involve the exercise of the power of taxation. Some of these systems, since the adoption of the new constitution, have been codified as part of the public local law of the state. If the position assumed in this case be correct, the laws requiring provision for the support of the poor, repairs of county roads, or the support of paupers, which are not uniform throughout the state, and require the levying of taxes for such purposes, are *ipso facto* void, because not within the powers legitimately granted by the constitution.

"Uniformity of power does not necessarily imply identity of purpose or object. The difference between power and object is, that the one is an attribute, faculty or means; the other an end or fact to be accomplished. Power is general, object is special. As in mechanics, the motive power may be applied to an almost infinite variety of uses; so in politics, the power of taxation, which is the great motor of government, may be exercised for the promotion of every object of society, among the chief and noblest of which is, the diffusion of knowledge and the education of the people.

"The 'power to levy all needful taxes, and to pay and discharge all claims on or against the county which have been expressly or impliedly authorized by law' (conferred by art. 28, § 3, Code of Maryland), conveys authority and imposes the duty of providing for any local object sanctioned by the legislature. * * In this instance, the commissioners of the county are not left to inference as to their duty and obligation to exercise the power of taxation, but are expressly enjoined to exert it for the most salutary public purposes. The power here called into requisition is uniformly vested in the commissioners of all the counties in the state, as is indicated in the public general laws. Its application to various specific objects is shown by the public local laws."

[1] Merrick *v.* Amherst, 12 Allen, 498.

scribed by law;" also that "all assessments hereafter authorized shall be on property at its cash value," do not preclude a taxation of business as such, although the property employed in the business is also taxed.[1]

Minnesota. The constitution provides that "all property on which taxes are to be levied shall have a cash valuation, and be equalized and uniform throughout the state." It is not competent where equality and uniformity are required to impose a tax exclusively upon one subdivision of the state to pay a claim or indebtedness which is not peculiarly the debt of such subdivision, or to raise money for any purpose not peculiarly beneficial to such subdivision.[2]

Missouri. A constitutional requirement that taxation shall be uniform, and shall be levied on property in proportion to its value, is not violated by the taxation of income and salaries. The purpose of it is to make the burdens of government rest on all property alike; to forbid favoritism and prevent inequality. Outside of this constitutional restriction, the legislature must be the sole judge of the propriety of taxation, and define the sources of revenue as the exigencies of the occasion may require.[3]

[1] Walcott *v.* People, 17 Mich., 68; Kitson *v.* Ann Arbor, 26 id., 325.

[2] Sanborn *v.* Rice, 9 Minn., 273. That the provision would preclude penalties for failure to list property for taxation, see McCormick *v.* Fitch, 14 id., 252.

[3] Glascow *v.* Rouse, 43 Mo., 479, 489. There is a summary of the doctrine of the courts in this case by *Wagner*, J., which is deserving of being copied at length:

"That taxes should be uniform, and levied in proportion to the value of the property to be taxed, is so manifestly just that it commends itself to universal assent. But, notwithstanding the constitutional provision, there are some kinds of taxes that are not usually assessed according to the value of property, and some which could not be thus assessed; and there is perhaps not a state in the Union, though many of them have in substance the same constitutional provision, which does not levy other taxes than those imposed on property.

"Every burden which the state imposes upon its citizens with a view to revenue, to carry on the operations of the state government, or for the support of municipal corporations, is a branch of the power of taxation, whether imposed under the name of a tax or some other designation. The license fees which are sometimes required of those who pursue particular employments are, when imposed for revenue, taxes. Lawyers and physicians may be compelled to pay a license for practicing their professions, for the purpose of revenue; and although not levied on property, it is still a tax. Stamp duties are

Ohio. The constitution provides that "laws shall be passed taxing by a uniform rule all moneys, credits, investments in bonds, stocks, joint stock companies or otherwise; and also all real and personal property according to its true value in money;

taxes. It is customary to require that corporations shall pay a certain sum annually, in proportion to their capital stock paid in, or by some other standard, which is generally fixed for mere convenience. It therefore seems plain that the constitutional requirement that 'taxation upon property shall be in proportion to its value,' does not include every species of taxation; nor, indeed, would it be possible to place such an interpretation upon it without doing the grossest injustice.

"A very large proportion of revenue is derived from other sources than a direct levy on property, and the doctrine contended for would release the former and throw the whole burden upon the latter. In cases of municipal corporations, a different construction has always prevailed. Assessments for the opening, making, improving, or repairing streets, the draining of swamps, the throwing up of levees, and the like local works, have been usually made upon property with some reference to benefits which it was supposed the property would receive.

"The requirement that property should be taxed in proportion to its value, applies as much to these local assessments as any other species of taxes. The local authorities have only such power as is delegated to them by the state, and the state can confer no power against the prohibitions of the constitution.

"There are three general classes of direct taxes: capitation, having effect solely upon persons; *ad valorem*, having effect solely upon property; and income, having a mixed effect upon persons and property.

"The argument of the plaintiff's counsel proceeds on the hypothesis that every species of tax comes within the constitutional prohibition. This is a mistake. The whole practice of the state has been different, and it has never been challenged, nor could it be, on legal principles. The statutes provide for a poll tax, which is in violation of the *ad valorem* rule, and is unequal, yet it is clearly within the constitution. A license is imposed upon shows, peddlers, auctioneers, dram shops and billiard tables, all of which taxes are in violation of the *ad valorem* principle, but not therefore unconstitutional. The taxes imposed are uniform as to the particular classes, but not in proportion to the taxes assessed on other property.

"The constitution enjoins a uniform rule as to the imposition of taxes on all property, but does not abridge the power of the legislature to provide for a revenue from other sources. It was intended to make the burdens of government rest on all property alike — to forbid favoritism and prevent inequality. Outside of the constitutional restriction, the legislature must be the sole judge of the propriety of taxation, and define the sources of revenue as the exigency of the occasion may require. The income tax was uniform and equal as to the classes upon which it operated; it did not come within the meaning of the term 'property,' as used and designated in the constitution, and I think it was not in conflict with any provision of that instrument."

but burying grounds, public school houses, houses used exclusively for public worship, institutions of purely public charity, public property used exclusively for any public purpose, and personal property to an amount not exceeding in value two hundred dollars for each individual, may, by general laws, be exempted from taxation," etc. This provision renders it imperative that all the property of which exemption is not permitted by it shall be taxed, and precludes any other exemptions than those indicated, as well when the tax is for a municipal purpose as when it is levied for a state purpose.[1]

It also precludes the debts of the tax payer being deducted from the value of his property; this being inconsistent with the requirement that *all* property shall be taxed.[2] But it does not preclude the taxation of business, as such, the licensing of stores, etc.[3]

Tennessee. A constitutional provision that "all property shall be taxed according to its value," and that "no one species of property from which a tax may be collected shall be taxed

[1] Zanesville *v.* Richards, 5 Ohio, N. S., 589. See Hill *v.* Higdon, 5 id., 243, 246. In the case first cited *Ranney*, Ch. J., says: "Before the adoption of the present constitution, the whole matter of taxation was committed to the discretion of the general assembly. It might be levied upon such property and in such proportion, as the body saw fit. The right to make exceptions and exemptions, was unquestionable. But this discretion no longer exists. The public burdens are made to rest upon the property of the state, and whenever money is to be raised by taxation, the positive injunction is, that 'laws shall be passed, taxing by an uniform rule, all moneys, credits, investments in bonds, stocks, joint stock companies, or otherwise; and also *all* real and personal property, according to its true value in money.' Without express authority of law, no tax, either for state, county, township or corporation purposes can be levied, and we see no reason to doubt that this section of the constitution is equally applicable to, and furnishes the governing principle for, all laws authorizing taxes to be levied for either purpose. The great object of the provision was to secure equality and uniformity in the imposition of these public burdens. The convention was very well aware that much the largest part would be required to answer the purposes of these local subdivisions; and equally well that it could only be levied as the general assembly should provide."

[2] Bank of Columbus *v.* Hines, 3 Ohio, N. S., 1. Obligations for the payment of money are to be taxed by *value*, and if of no value, are not taxable. *Id.*

[3] Baker *v.* Cincinnati, 11 Ohio, N. S., 534.

higher than any species of property of equal value," has no reference to the taxation of *privileges*, and such taxation is in the discretion of the legislature. It is therefore competent to authorize a town to levy license taxes on the various occupations carried on therein.[1]

Virginia. The requirement that taxation shall be equal and uniform does not preclude the state from authorizing a county to levy a tax on a county office,[2] nor does it require the license taxes on privileges or occupations to be equal or uniform.[3] On this last point the decision in West Virginia is to the contrary.[4]

Wisconsin. The constitutional provision that "the rule of taxation shall be uniform" extends to taxation by cities, towns and counties, as well as that levied by the state.[5] It does not preclude license taxes under the police power.[6] And the state having for a long period been in the practice of collecting specific taxes from corporations in lieu of the taxes on property levied generally, it was decided against the opinion of the judges, that such specific taxes were not in violation of the constitutional requirement of uniformity.[7]

The general right to make exemptions. It remains to see what is the rule regarding exemptions, where none is prescribed by the state constitution.

[1] Adams *v.* Somerville, 2 Head, 363; State *v.* Crawford, 2 id., 460.

[2] Gilkerson *v.* Frederick Justices, 13 Grat., 577. See also Gordon's Executors *v.* Baltimore, 5 Gill, 231. Compare Camden & Amboy R. R. Co. *v.* Hillegas, 18 N. J., 11; Same *v.* Commissioner of Appeals, 18 id., 71, and Gardner *v.* State, 21 id., 557, in which a provision in a charter that the corporation should pay a certain tax, "and no other tax or impost shall be levied or assessed" upon it, was held to apply to county and town taxes as well as those imposed for state purposes.

[3] Slaughter *v.* Commonwealth, 13 Grat., 767.

[4] Franklin Ins. Co. *v.* State, 5 W. Va., 349. This case is referred to, *ante*, p. 129.

[5] Knowlton *v.* Supervisors of Rock Co., 9 Wis., 410; Hale *v.* Kenosha, 29 id., 599; Gilman *v.* Sheboygan, 2 Black, 510.

[6] Carter *v.* Dow, 16 Wis., 298 (dog license); Tenney *v.* Lenz, id., 566; Fire Department *v.* Helfenstein, id., 136.

[7] Kneeland *v.* Milwaukee, 15 Wis., 454, overruling Attorney General *v.* Plankroad Co., 11 id., 35.

The exemptions commonly made by express statute are based upon reasons so forcible that they have seldom been contested. We refer now to the exemptions of tools of trade; of the limited personal property of very poor persons; the property of corporations or associations devoted exclusively to the work of public charity, or in other directions where what they accomplish operates in the relief of public burdens, and the like. Exemptions of the property of religious societies, and of persons or corporations engaged in instruction, have not passed unchallenged on the score of right and policy; but the power to make them is unquestioned. And upon the general subject of exemptions, the following rules are deduced from the authorities:

1. The general right to make exemptions is involved in the right to apportion taxes, and must be understood to exist wherever it is not forbidden.[1] The right is supposed to be exercised on reasons of state policy, and presumptively such exemptions contribute to the general public benefit.[2]

2. Exemptions thus granted on considerations of public policy, may be recalled whenever the legislative view of public policy shall have changed. To the individuals, corporations or associations benefited by them, they are to be regarded as favors or privileges merely, to continue during the pleasure of the sovereignty, and there can be no breach of faith — certainly no want of power — in terminating them at any time. Cases illustrative of this principle are cited on a previous page.[3]

[1] Butler's Appeal, 73 Penn. St., 448. See People *v.* Colman, 4 Cal., 46; State *v.* North, 27 Mo., 464; Hill *v.* Higdon, 5 Ohio, N. S., 243; State *v.* Parker, 33 N. J., 312; Indianapolis *v.* Sturdevant, 24 Ind., 391.

[2] The homestead is sometimes exempted, and when it is, if it is taxed with the tract of which it forms a part, the sale of the whole for taxes is void. Penn *v.* Clemans, 19 Iowa, 372, 374; Stewart *v.* Corbin, 25 id., 144. An exemption from taxation of all property employed in manufactures, was assumed to be valid in Gardiner C. & W. Factory Co. *v.* Gardiner, 5 Greenl., 133. New York once had a statute which exempted from taxation the buildings, machinery and manufactured articles in the hands of the manufacturer of every cotton, woolen or linen manufactory within the state. See Columbian Manf. Co. *v.* Vanderpool, 4 Cow., 556. Such exemptions are much less questionable and much less pernicious than would be an exemption of the property of a portion only of those engaged in a particular manufacture, leaving those with whom they would compete to pay taxes.

[3] *Ante*, p. 54. See in addition to cases there cited, Hospital *v.* Philadelphia,

3. The intention to exempt must in any case be expressed in clear and unambiguous terms; taxation is the rule, exemption is the exception.[1]

4. All exemptions are to be strictly construed. They embrace only what is within their terms. This general rule has many

24 Penn. St., 229; Commonwealth *v.* Fayette, etc., R. R. Co., 55 id., 452; Brewster *v.* Hough, 10 N. H., 138; St. Joseph *v.* Railroad Co., 39 Mo., 476; State *v.* Dulle, 48 id., 282; Tomlinson *v.* Jessup, 15 Wall., 454. When officers have power by law to make exemptions in special cases, if they refuse to make one, the party concerned is without remedy unless an appeal is given by law. Clinton School District's Appeal, 56 Penn. St., 315. Such a power is only admissible where an examination into facts is essential in order to determine whether the case is within the general rule of exemption which is prescribed by law. A general power to exempt property from taxation cannot be conferred by the legislature even upon a municipal corporation. Brewer Brick Co. *v.* Brewer, recently decided by the supreme court of Maine.

[1] See *ante*, pp. 52–56, and cases cited in the notes. "Taxation is an act of sovereignty to be performed, so far as it conveniently can be, with justice and equality to all. Exemptions, no matter how meritorious, are of grace, and must be strictly construed." This was said in a case where the court felt compelled to hold that a married woman was subject to a tax for the raising of bounty moneys, though her husband was actually in the military service. Crawford *v.* Burrell, 53 Penn. St., 219, 220. See also Lord Colchester *v.* Kewney, Law R., 1 Exch., 368; Platt *v.* Rice, 10 Watts, 352; Providence Bank *v.* Billings, 4 Pet., 514; Minot *v.* Philadelphia, etc., R. R. Co., or The Delaware Railroad Tax, 18 Wall., 206; Trask *v.* Maguire, id., 391; Gordon *v.* Baltimore, 5 Gill, 231; Howell *v.* Maryland, 3 id., 14; Baltimore *v.* State, 15 Md., 376; Hannibal, etc., R. R. Co. *v.* Shacklett, 30 Mo., 550; Washington University *v.* Rouse, 42 id., 308; Pacific R. R. Co. *v.* Cass County, 53 id., 17; Stewart *v.* Davis, 3 Murphy, 244; State *v.* Town Council, 12 Rich. Law, 339; Anderson *v.* State, 23 Miss., 459; B. & O. R. R. Co. *v.* Marshall County, 3 W. Va., 319; Same *v.* Wheeling, id., 372; State *v.* Bank of Smyrna, 2 Houston, 99; Municipality *v.* Railroad Co., 10 Rob. (La.), 187; Louis. Canal Co. *v.* Commonwealth, 7 B. Monr., 160; St. Peters Church *v.* Scott County, 12 Minn., 395; Portland, S. & P. R. R. Co. *v.* City of Saco, 60 Me., 196; State *v.* Parker, 32 N. J., 426; Hart *v.* Plum, 14 Cal., 148; People *v.* Whyler, 41 id., 351; Biscoe *v.* Coulter, 18 Ark., 423; Harvard College *v.* Boston, 104 Mass., 470, 475; Orr *v.* Baker, 4 Ind., 86; City of Indianapolis *v.* McLean, 8 id., 328; City of Madison *v.* Fitch, 18 id., 33; Methodist Church *v.* Ellis, 38 id., 3; Washburn College *v* Shawnee County, 8 Kans., 344; Vail *v.* Beach, 10 id., 214; St. Mary's College *v.* Crowl, 10 id., 442; Miami County *v.* Brackenridge, 12 id., 114; No. Mo. R. R. Co. *v.* Maguire, 20 Wall., 46. A general law on the subject of taxation, manifestly intended as a revision of all laws on the subject, operates to repeal the previous exemptions which it does not in terms renew. Columbian Manf. Co. *v.* Vanderpool, 4 Cow., 556; Fox's Adm'rs *v.* Commonwealth, 16 Grat., 1.

illustrations, one of the most striking of which is found in the case of exemption of church and school property. The general exemption of such property from taxation, it is held, will not exempt them from special assessment for local improvements, such as the paving and repair of the streets on which they stand, and the like. In the leading case, the words of the exemption were, that no church or place of public worship "should be taxed by any law of this state." Upon this the court remarked: "The word *taxes* means burdens, charges or impositions, put or set upon persons or property for public uses; and this is the definition which Lord Coke gives of the word *talliage*, 2 Inst., 232; and Lord Holt in Carth., 438, gives the same definition in substance of the word tax. The legislature intended by that exemption to relieve religious and literary institutions from these public burdens, and the same exemption was extended to the real estate of any minister not exceeding in value fifteen hundred dollars. But to pay for the opening of a street in the ratio of the benefit or advantage derived from it is no burden. It is no talliage or tax within the meaning of the exemption, and has no claim upon the public benevolence. Why should not the real estate of a minister as well as of other persons pay for such an improvement in proportion as it is benefited? There is no inconvenience or hardship in it, and the maxim of law, that *qui sentit commodum debet sentire onus*, is perfectly consistent with the interests of science and religion."[1] And yet these assessments are a legal exer-

[1] Matter of Mayor, etc., of New York, 11 Johns., 77; Bleecker *v.* Ballou, 3 Wend., 263; Chegaray *v.* Jenkins, 3 Sandf., 409; People *v.* Roper, 35 N. Y., 629; Buffalo City Cemetery *v.* Buffalo, 46 id., 506; Northern Liberties *v.* St. Johns Church, 13 Penn. St., 104; Crawford *v.* Burrell, 53 id., 219, 220; Second Universalist Society *v.* Providence, 6 R. I., 235; Matter of College St., 8 id., 474; Patterson *v.* Society, etc., 24 N. J., 385; State *v.* Robertson, id., 504; State *v.* Newark, 27 id., 185; State *v.* Mills, 34 id., 177; State *v.* Newark, 35 id., 157; S. C., 10 Am. Rep., 223; Broadway Baptist Church *v.* McAtee, 8 Bush, 508; S. C., 8 Am. Rep., 480; Alexander *v.* Baltimore, 5 Gill, 383, 396; Baltimore *v.* Cemetery Co., 7 Md., 517; Le Fevre *v.* Detroit, 2 Mich., 586; Kendrick *v.* Farquar, 8 Ohio, 189, 197; Armstrong *v.* Treasurer of Athens County, 10 id., 235; Cincinnati College *v.* State, 19 id., 110; Brewster *v.* Hough, 10 N. H., 138; Seymour *v.* Hartford, 21 Conn., 481; Bridgeport *v.* N. Y. & N. H. R. Co., 36 id., 255; First Presbyterian Church *v.* Fort Wayne, 36 Ind., 338; S. C., 10 Am. Rep., 35; Palmer *v.* Stumph, 29 Ind., 329; Trustees of Church *v.* Ellis, 38 id., 3; Bank of Republic *v.* Hamilton, 21 Ill., 53; Canal Trustees *v.* Chi-

cise of the taxing power, and can only be justified on that.

cago, 12 id., 403; Chicago *v.* Colby, 20 id., 614; McBride *v.* Chicago, 22 id., 574; Peoria *v.* Kidder, 26 id., 351; Pleasant *v.* Kost, 29 id., 490, 494; Paine *v.* Spratley, 5 Kans., 525; Orange & Alexandria R. R. Co. *v.* Alexandria, 17 Gratt., 176; Crowley *v.* Copeley, 2 La. An., 329; La Fayette *v.* Orphan Asylum, 4 id., 1; Rooney *v.* Brown, 21 id., 51; St. Louis Public Schools *v.* St. Louis, 26 Mo., 468; Sheehan *v.* Good Samaritan Hospital, 50 id., 155; S. C., 11 Am. Rep., 412; Lockwood *v.* St. Louis, 24 Mo., 20 (sewer tax); Emery *v.* Gas Co., 28 Cal. 345; Taylor *v.* Palmer, 31 id., 240; Hale *v.* Kenosha, 29 Wis., 599; Seamen's Friend Society *v.* Boston, 116 Mass., 181; Agricultural Society *v.* Worcester, id., 189. The real estate belonging to the board of public schools of the city of St. Louis, is liable to be assessed under and by virtue of the ordinances of the city of St. Louis, for the construction of sewers, paving of sidewalks, opening of streets, etc. St. Louis Public Schools *v.* City of St. Louis, 26 Mo., 468.

Some of the exemptions in these cases seem very strong and comprehensive, but they were generally applied only to the customary taxes. The following instances may be given: In Baltimore *v.* Cemetery Company, an exemption from "any tax or public imposition whatever" was held to apply only to "taxes or impositions levied or imposed for the purpose of revenue," and not to relieve the cemetery from "such charges as are inseparably incident to its location in regard to other property;" e. g., an assessment for paving the street in front. In Buffalo City Cemetery *v.* Buffalo, 46 N. Y., 506, where the cemetery was by law exempt from "all public taxes, rates and assessments," it was held not exempt from a paving assessment. *Folger*, J., says: "We think that the current of authorities in this and some of the sister states runs to this result: that public taxes, rates and assessments, are those which are levied and taken out of the property of the person assessed, for some public or general use or purpose, in which he has no direct, immediate and peculiar interest; being exactions from him towards the expense of carrying on the government, either directly and, in general, that of the whole commonwealth, or more mediately and particularly through the intervention of municipal corporations; and that those charges and impositions which are laid directly upon the property in a circumscribed locality, to effect some work of local convenience, which in its result is of peculiar advantage and importance to the property, especially assessed for the expense of it, are not public but are local and private so far as this statute is concerned." In Patterson *v.* Society, etc., 24 N. J., 385, the exemption was from "taxes, charges and impositions;" but it was held not to extend to an assessment for grading and paving a street. In State *v.* Newark, 27 N. J., 185, the exemption was from "charges and impositions," and the same ruling was had. In Bridgeport *v.* N. Y. & N. H. R. R. Co., 36 Conn., 255, the railroad company paid a tax which, by its charter, was to be "in lieu of all other taxes;" but the company was, nevertheless, held liable to a street assessment.

These cases show that the general inclination has been to confine the application of all such general language to the taxes imposed for ordinary revenue. But in Massachusetts it has been held that an assessment for altering a street

ground.[1] It is sometimes a matter of great nicety to determine how far a general or even a qualified exemption from taxation extends, in the case of a corporation which employs its means or some portion thereof in the purchase of property not required for

is a civil imposition within the meaning of a college charter exempting the college property from "all civil impositions, taxes and rates." Harvard College *v.* Boston, 104 Mass., 470.

[1] People *v.* Brooklyn, 4 N. Y., 419; Sharp *v.* Spier, 4 Hill, 76; Patterson *v.* Society, etc., 24 N. J., 385; State *v.* Fuller, 34 id., 227; State *v.* Newark, 35 id., 168, 171; Weeks *v.* Milwaukee, 10 Wis., 242; Motz *v.* Detroit, 18 Mich., 495; Baltimore *v.* Cemetery Co., 7 Md., 517; Glascow *v.* Rouse, 43 Mo., 479, 489; McComb *v.* Bell, 2 Minn., 295; Pray *v.* Northern Liberties, 31 Penn. St., 69; Walsh *v.* Mathews, 29 Cal., 123; Chambers *v.* Satterlee, 40 id., 497; Yeatman *v.* Crandall, 11 La. An., 220; Matter of Opening of Streets, 20 id., 497; Reeves *v.* Treasurer of Wood Co., 8 Ohio, N. S., 333; Hines *v.* Leavenworth, 3 Kans., 186.

An exemption from "all taxes and *assessments*," held to exempt from assessments for benefits, as well as from general taxes. State *v.* Newark, 36 N. J., 478; S. C., 13 Am. Rep., 464. Compare Patterson *v.* Society, etc., 24 N. J., 385; Oswald *v.* Gilfert, 11 Johns., 443; Codman *v.* Johnson, 104 Mass., 491. The following cases of exemptions may be specially mentioned: An exemption from a state tax will not preclude the levy of a tax by a city. Martin *v.* Charleston, 13 Rich. Eq., 50. An exemption of charitable societies from taxation, held to embrace the case of a masonic grand lodge, which for fifty years had not been taxed, this neglect to tax being regarded as having fixed the construction of the exemption. State *v.* Addison, 2 S. Car., N. S., 499. An exemption of universities, colleges, academies and school houses, held not to extend to an academy of fine arts, "as none can claim an exemption unless the exemption be so clearly expressed in the statute as to admit of no other construction." Academy of Fine Arts *v.* Philadelphia, 22 Penn. St., 496. The exemption from taxation of the property of soldiers in actual service will not exempt from a tax actually imposed before the soldier enlisted. Tobin *v.* Morgan, 70 id., 229. An exemption of "all houses of religious worship and the pews and furniture within the same," will exempt only that part of a building occupied for religious worship, and if other portions are leased for business purposes, they are taxable. Proprietors *v.* Lowell, 1 Met., 538. An exemption of such real estate of literary and scientific institutions "as shall be actually occupied by them, or by the officers of such institutions for the purposes for which they were incorporated," held not to extend to a house built on the real estate of Harvard College and leased by the corporation to one of the professors for a dwelling; the occupation of a lessee not being such an occupation as was intended by the statute. Pierce *v.* Cambridge, 2 Cush., 611. The same exemption held applicable to a farm and the farming stock owned by an educational institution, and by it worked solely to raise produce and do team work for a boarding house kept to supply students with board at cost. Wesleyan Academy *v.* Wilbraham, 99 Mass., 599. Compare

the purposes for which its corporate privileges were conferred, though capable, perhaps, of being made useful and profitable as an aid in its corporate business. The question is, in each instance, whether such property, in the manner in which it has been in-

State *v.* Ross, 24 N. J., 497. Under an exemption of school buildings, a building occupied in part for a school and in part for other purposes is not exempt. Wyman *v.* St. Louis, 17 Mo., 335. An exemption of every school house and every building erected for the use of a college, incorporated academy or other seminary of learning, held not to embrace a building used and occupied for a private boarding school. Chegaray *v.* New York, 13 N. Y., 220. To the same effect is State *v.* Ross, 24 N. J., 497. See a peculiar case, Mass. General Hospital *v.* Somerville, 101 Mass., 319. Bequests to colleges, etc., held to be taxable under the general statute taxing bequests, though after being received they would be exempt under a general provision exempting the property of such institutions. Barringer *v.* Cowan, 2 Jones' Eq., 436. Exemption from "taxation of every kind" does not exempt from an assessment for street improvements. Sheehan *v.* Good Samaritan Hospital, 50 Mo., 155. Compare Dunleith, etc., Bridge Co. *v.* Dubuque, 32 Ia., 427; Brightman *v.* Kirner, 22 Wis., 54. Exemption of the stock of a railway company from taxation held to include all property necessary and proper for the purpose of laying, building and sustaining the road. Ordinary of Bibb County *v.* Central R. R. Co., 40 Geo., 646. Where the shares of stock in a corporation were exempt from taxation, the *property* of the corporation was held to be exempt also. Baltimore *v.* B. & O. R. R. Co., 6 Gill, 288. See State *v.* Branin, 23 N. J., 484. A specific state tax on a railroad company held to preclude taxation of its property by valuation. Camden & Amboy R. R. Co. *v.* Commissioners, 18 id., 11. And see State *v.* Cook, 32 id., 338; Cook *v.* State, 33 id., 472; Douglass *v.* State, 34 id., 485. A branch road to procure gravel held liable to ordinary taxation. State *v.* Hancock, 33 id., 315. Compare State *v.* Hancock, 35 id., 537. A provision in a railroad charter was that "all machines, wagons, vehicles or carriages, belonging to the company, with all its works and all the property which may accrue from the same, shall be vested in the respective shareholders forever, in proportion to their respective shares, and shall be deemed personal estate, and exempt from any charge or tax whatever." This makes all the property of the company, owned and used for its purposes, personal estate and exempt. A city in which the company owns property cannot dispute this exemption on the ground of its lessening its power to pay its debts. Richmond *v.* Richmond & Danville R. R. Co., 21 Grat., 604. General exemption of the *property* of a corporation from taxation construed to include the *franchise*. Wilmington R. R. Co. *v.* Reid, 13 Wall., 264; Raleigh, etc., Railroad Co. *v.* Reid, 13 id., 269; State *v.* Berry, 17 N. J., 80; Camden & Amboy R. R. Co. *v.* Hillegas, 18 id., 11; Same *v.* Commissioners of Appeal, id., 71. An exemption of the "stock" of a corporation is an exemption of its gross income also, it being but an accessory to the stock. State *v.* Hood, 15 Rich. Law, 177.

Capital, it has been held, signifies the actual estate, whether in money or property, which is owned by an individual or corporation. In reference to a

vested, can be regarded as within the intent of the exemption? The general inclination of the courts has been to hold, that a charter which provides for a certain tax, and "that no other tax or impost shall be levied or assessed" upon the corporation, will exempt from taxation all the property held by it, necessary to effect the purpose of the incorporation, but not other property held by it which, though convenient and tending to increase the profits, is not necessary to the corporation and its business. But this is always a question of special construction and not of general law.[1]

corporation, it is the aggregate of the sum subscribed and paid in, or to be paid in, by the shareholders, with the addition of profits on the residue, after the deduction of losses. People *v.* Commissioners of Taxes, 23 N. Y., 192, 219. In Mechanics' etc. Bank *v.* Townsend, 5 Blatch., 315, *capital* was held not to include surplus earnings, though undivided.

A railroad company paid the state a specific tax under a law which provided that it should not "be assessed with any tax on its lands, buildings or equipments." Held not to preclude municipal taxation. Orange & Alexandria R. R. *v.* Alexandria, 17 Grat., 176. Compare this with Richmond *v.* Richmond & Danville R. R. Co., 21 id., 604, where an exemption from "any charge or tax whatsoever" was held to cover municipal as well as state taxes. See also Southern R. R. Co. *v.* Jackson, 38 Miss., 334; Neustadt *v.* Illinois Central R. R. Co., 31 Ill., 484; Gardner *v.* State, 21 N. J., 557.

Effect of *consolidation* of railways on a previous exemption of one of the roads. See Tomlinson *v.* Branch, 15 Wall., 460; Charleston *v.* Branch, id., 470. An exemption from taxation of "property necessarily used in operating the railroad," held to apply to an inn used exclusively by persons arriving and departing on the railroad. Milwaukee, etc., R. R. Co. *v.* Board, etc., of Crawford County, 29 Wis., 116. For other cases of special exemption, see State Bank *v.* Madison, 3 Ind., 43; Orr *v.* Baker, 4 id., 86; Lord *v.* Litchfield, 36 Conn., 116; State *v.* Haight, 35 N. J., 40. And see Rex *v.* Calder, 1 B. & Ald., 263; State *v.* Minton, 23 N. J., 529; Philadelphia, etc., R. R. Co. *v.* Bayless, 2 Gill, 355; State *v.* Norwich & Worcester R. R. Co., 30 Conn., 290; Armstrong *v.* Athens Co., 16 Pet., 281.

An exemption for the benefit of a religious society ceases on its making sale of the property. New Haven *v.* Sheffield, 30 Conn., 160. And as to strict construction in general, see Erie Railway *v.* Pennsylvania, 21 Wall., 492.

[1] Where a canal is exempt from taxation the toll house is not taxable. Schuylkill Nav. Co. *v.* Commissioners of Berks Co., 11 Penn. St., 202. Where a railroad is exempt, this will cover its water stations and depots, but not warehouses, coal lots, coal shutes, machine shops, wood yards etc., which are only necessary to the profits to be made by the company. Railroad *v.* Berks County, 6 id., 70. See Lehigh Co. *v.* Northampton, 8 W. & S., 334; Wayne Co. *v.* Delaware & Hudson Canal Co., 15 Penn. St., 351, 357, where the sub-

Invidious exemptions. An exemption, to be admissible, it would seem, ought to be either made on the basis of contract, in which case the public is supposed to receive a full equivalent

ject is considered at length; N. Y. & Erie R. R. Co. *v.* Sabin, 26 id., 242; West Chester Gas Co. *v.* Chester Co., 30 id., 232; Lackawana Iron Co. *v.* Luzerne Co., 42 id., 424; Milwaukee, etc., R. R. Co., *v.* Supervisors of Crawford, 29 Wis., 116; Milwaukee, etc., R. R. Co. *v.* Milwaukee, 34 id., 271; Orange, etc., R. R. Co. *v.* Alexandria, 17 Grat., 176, which does not allow the implied exemptions; Vermont Cent. R. R. Co. *v.* Burlington, 28 Vt., 193; Souhegan Nail, etc., Factory *v.* McConike, 7 N. H., 309; Gardiner *v.* State, 21 N. J., 557; State *v.* Mansfield, 23 id., 510; State *v.* Flavell, 24 id., 370; State *v.* Blundell, 24 id., 402; State *v.* Betts, 24 id., 555; State *v.* Newark, 25 id., 315; State *v.* The Collector of Newark, 26 id., 519; State Treasurer *v.* Somerville & Easton Railroad Co., 28 id., 21; State *v.* Elizabeth, 28 id., 103; State *v.* Lester, 29 id., 541; State *v.* Hancock, 33 id., 315; Hannibal & St. Joseph Railroad Co. *v.* Shacklett, 30 Mo., 550; State *v.* H. & St. Jo. R. R. Co., 37 id., 265; Boston & Me. R. R. Co. *v.* Cambridge, 8 Cush., 237; Wilmington R. R. Co. *v.* Reid, 13 Wall., 264, 268, per *Davis*, J.

An exemption to a railroad company of "all machines, wagons, vehicles or carriages belonging to the company, *with all their works*," etc., held to apply to their real estate as well as to their rolling stock. Richmond *v.* Richmond & Danville R. R. Co., 21 Grat., 604, citing Baltimore *v.* B. & O. R. R. Co., 6 Gill, 288. A provision that a certain tax on the capital and debts of railroad companies should "take the place of all other taxes on railroads and horse railroad property and franchises," held to exempt property whether used for railroad purposes or not. Osborn *v.* N. Y. & N. H. R. R. Co., 40 Conn., 491. And see in general, The Tax Cases, 12 G. &. J. 117.

A general exemption of railroad property from taxation has been said to be coëxtensive with the right of the railroad company to take property for its use by condemnation, and that the limit of such right is the limit of the exemption. State *v.* Hancock, 33 N. J., 315; Milwaukee, etc., R. R. Co. *v.* Milwaukee, 34 Wis., 271.

The act incorporating the Illinois Central Railroad Company provides as follows: "The * * * stock, property and assets belonging to said company shall be listed by the president, secretary, or other officer, with the auditor of state, and an annual tax for state purposes shall be assessed by the auditor upon all the property and assets of every name, kind and description belonging to said corporation. Whenever the taxes levied for state purposes shall exceed three-fourths of one per cent. per annum, such excess shall be deducted from the gross proceeds or income herein required to be paid by said corporation to the state, and the said corporation is hereby exempted from all taxation of every kind except as herein provided for." *Held*, that this exemption did not apply to a wharf boat and to a steamboat used principally in conveying the passengers and freight from the terminus of the road to the terminus of another railroad, thus making connections. Illinois Central R. R. *v.* Irvin, Sup. Court Ill., 1875, 7 Chicago Legal News, 286.

therefor, or it ought to be made on some ground of public policy, such as might justify a pension or a donation of the public funds on some general rule of which all who come within it may have the benefit.[1] It is difficult to conceive of an exemption law which selects single individuals or corporations, or single articles of property, and taking them out of the class to which they belong, makes them the subject of capricious legislative favor. Such favoritism could make no pretense to equality; it would lack the semblance of legitimate tax legislation. It is certain that municipal bodies or taxing officers have no authority to make such exemptions unless expressly empowered by legislation; and to make any would render invalid the whole tax roll on which the exempted property or person ought to have appeared. The motives of the exemption or the beneficial purposes expected to be accomplished by it can make no difference. No man is obliged to be more generous than the law requires; each may stand strictly on his legal rights, and refuse to submit to any exaction that purposely is made more burdensome to him than the rules of law permit.[2]

[1] "A common burden should be sustained by common contributions, regulated by some fixed general rule, and apportioned according to some uniform ratio of equality. Thus, if a capitation or personal tax be levied it must be imposed on all free citizens equally and alike, or if an ad valorem or specific tax be laid on property, it must be laid equally, according to value or kind, on all the property, or on each article of the same kind, owned by every citizen; and no citizen or class of citizens owning any property of the kind subject to taxation can be exempted constitutionally on any other ground than that of valuable and peculiar public services; for otherwise one man or set of men might be entitled to enjoy exclusive privileges, or legal exemptions which are substantially the same, without the only constitutional consideration of public services." *Robertson*, Ch. J., Sutton's Heirs *v.* Louisville, 5 Dana, 28, 31.

[2] Per *Paine*, J., in Weeks *v.* Milwaukee, 10 Wis., 242, 263. The case was one of an exemption of a block in the city of Milwaukee on which a hotel was about to be constructed; the common council directing it to be made "in view of the great public benefit which the construction of the hotel would be to the city." Compare Exchange Bank *v.* Hines, 3 Ohio, N. S., 1; Adams *v.* Beman, 10 Kansas, 37. In Henry *v.* Chester, 15 Vt., 460, a tax list was held void on two grounds: "1. The plain and obvious requisitions of the statute in regard to making up were disregarded, both by important and essential omissions, and by arbitrary additions without even the color of right or legal warrant. If this may be done and still the list be regarded as legal, so might it with equal

The legislature is equally powerless if the constitution has prescribed a rule of equality which forbids exemptions.[1] Such a rule, it has been seen, is prescribed by the constitutions of some of the states, which in terms or by necessary implication require all private property in the state to be taxed in proportion to its value.[2]

Accidental omissions from taxation. It has been decided in a number of cases that accidental omissions from taxation, of persons or property that should be taxed, occurring through the negligence or default of officers to whom the execution of the taxing

propriety if the entire real estate in town were omitted or inserted wholly at random, without even the form of an appraisal." See State *v.* Branin, 23 N. J., 484; Hersey *v.* Supervisors, etc., 16 Wis., 185; Crosby *v.* Lyon, 37 Cal., 242; Primm *v.* Belleville, 59 Ill., 142; Kneeland *v.* Milwaukee, 15 Wis., 454; Smith *v.* Smith, 19 id., 615; People *v.* McCreery, 34 Cal., 432. Including in the assessment persons who are not liable, and against whom a tax cannot be enforced, does not invalidate the tax against the rest. Inglee *v.* Bosworth, 5 Pick.. 498. See Dillingham *v.* Snow., 5 Mass., 547.

An illegal exemption by the common council of one man from a sewer tax will not authorize another to have his tax enjoined where it appears that his payment is not increased by the exemption. Page *v.* St. Louis, 20 Mo., 136. The principle is that no one is to be heard to complain of that which works no injury to him. See Sanford *v.* Dick, 15 Conn., 447; Case *v.* Dean, 16 Mich., 12.

[1] In Gilman *v.* Sheboygan, 2 Black, 510, it was held that under a constitutional provision requiring that "the rule of taxation shall be uniform, and taxes shall be levied upon such property as the legislature shall prescribe," it was not competent to provide that a tax for a special improvement should be laid exclusively on real estate. The cases of Weeks *v.* Milwaukee, 10 Wis., 242; Knowlton *v.* Supervisors of Rock Co., 9 id., 410; Lumsden *v.* Cross, 10 id., 282, and Attorney General *v.* Plankroad Co., 11 id., 35, 42, are referred to as having settled the construction of the constitution of the state which would forbid the sweeping exemption of personal property. It is to be observed that the general law of the state at that time required the taxation of "all property, real and personal, not expressly exempted therefrom." Compare Bright *v.* McCullough, 27 Ind., 223; Primm *v.* Belleville, 59 Ill., 142. In assessing by benefits the tax will be void if it appears that exemptions are made of property which should be taxed. Alexander *v.* Baltimore, 5 Gill, 383, 390. Compare Page *v.* St. Louis, 20 Mo., 136.

[2] See O'Kane *v.* Treat, 25 Ill., 557, 561 and other cases already cited. A constitutional provision that all real property shall be subject to taxation with certain enumerated exemptions, amounts to a prohibition of further exemptions. Fletcher *v.* Oliver, 25 Ark., 289.

laws is intrusted, would not have the effect to vitiate the whole tax. The reasons for this conclusion are summarized in one of the cases as follows: "The execution of these laws is necessarily intrusted to men, and men are fallible, liable to frequent mistakes of fact, and errors of judgment. If such errors on the part of those who are attempting in good faith to perform their duties should vitiate the whole tax, no tax could ever be collected. And therefore, though they sometimes increase improperly the burden of those paying taxes, the rule which holds the tax not thereby avoided is absolutely essential to the continuation of the government."[1] It seems difficult to resist the force of this rea-

[1] *Paine*, J., in Weeks *v.* Milwaukee, 10 Wis., 242, 262, where the following cases are cited and relied upon; Speer *v.* Braintree, 24 Vt., 414; State *v.* The Collector of Jersey City, 24 N. J., 108; Insurance Co. *v.* Yard, 17 Penn. St., 331; Williams *v.* School District, 21 Pick., 75. See also State *v.* Randolph, 25 N. J., 427, 431; Smith *v.* Smith, 19 Wis., 615; Schofield *v.* Watkins, 22 Ill., 66; Dunham *v.* Chicago, 55 id., 357, 361; People *v.* McCreery, 34 Cal., 432. In Watson *v.* Princeton, 4 Met., 599, 602, *Shaw*, Ch. J., says that the case of omission, through error of judgment or mistake of law, to tax property that should be taxed, can give no right of action to recover back any portion of the tax paid by another. "Various other remedies may be resorted to to secure just and legal taxation. The law is strict in requiring that the whole valuation shall be laid before the tax paying inhabitants, in order that any omission, mistake or irregularity may be corrected before the tax is collected. It is for the interest of the town, and of the inhabitants generally, that each inhabitant liable should be taxed, and to the extent of his liability; and therefore it must be presumed to be the inclination of assessors to impose rather than omit a tax, in case of doubt, leaving the individual aggrieved to raise the question if he shall think fit. And the final remedy, if the inhabitants believe that their assessors are acting upon erroneous principles, is to elect others in their places." See also George *v.* School District, 6 Met., 497; Dean *v.* Gleason, 16 Wis., 1. There has been some disposition in Illinois to hold that, even in the case of intentional omissions, the parties aggrieved should be left to their remedy against the assessor, and the tax roll sustained. Schofield *v.* Watkins, 22 Ill., 72; Merritt *v.* Farris, 22 id., 303, 311; Dunham *v.* Chicago, 55 id., 357, 361. But see Primm *v.* Belleville, 59 id., 142. In Muscatine *v.* Railroad Co., 1 Dill., 536, 542, Mr. Justice *Miller*, at the circuit, had occasion to consider the effect of omitting to tax certain property which, as it was claimed, the constitution expressly required should be taxed with all other. He said: "A statute of Iowa exempts railroad property from all other taxes except one per cent. per annum paid into the state treasury. The constitution of the state declares that all taxation shall be uniform. Whether this constitutional provision (the exact terms of which I have not attempted to state) renders the statute void, is a question upon which the supreme court of this state has twice, as I am

soning, and it applies to the case of a mistake of law with the same cogency as to the case of a mistake of fact. Indeed where the omission has occurred through no purpose to evade or disregard official duty, the occasion which produced it seems wholly immaterial.[1]

informed, been equally divided. If the question was presented to the circuit court by way of supervisory control over the officers, who, under its command, are collecting this tax, whether this railroad property should be assessed the same as other property, I confess I do not see how it could avoid deciding it. But, instead of an order to assess the property, I am asked to declare all other assessments void, because it is not assessed. This, it will be seen, is a very different question; and it is clear that I can only enjoin its collection on the ground that it is void. The case of Gilman *v.* Sheboygan, 2 Black, 510, is relied on as authority for the latter proposition. In that case, after the city of Sheboygan had issued bonds in aid of a railroad, the legislature of that state passed an act declaring that the tax to pay these bonds should be assessed exclusively on the real estate of the city. The constitution of Wisconsin has a provision similar to the one referred to in the constitution of Iowa, and the supreme court of the United States held this attempt to make a part only of the taxable property of the city responsible for this particular debt, was a violation of the constitution, which rendered the tax levied under that statute void.

"In the case before us there is no attempt to render any species of property liable to taxation for any specific debt, or class of debts, but an exemption of the railroad from all other burdens in consideration of a definite sum, which may be more or less than its share of such burden. Whether this exemption be forbidden by the constitution or not, I am quite clear that it does not render void the tax which is levied upon other property.

"The case of Gilman *v.* Sheboygan does not go so far as this, either in the facts on which it is grounded, or the reasons by which the judgment was sustained. There is a manifest difference between an attempt to impose the entire burden of a debt already incurred by a municipality, upon a particular species of property, and the attempt to exempt a species of property from all other taxation, in consideration of a sum supposed to be its just share of the general public burden. It is not inappropriate to look to the consequences of holding that this failure to assess the railroads renders all other tax void. It applies to the tax assessed for all other purposes as well as this tax. Every nonresident holder of property in the state could apply to me and insist on an injunction against the tax on his property. And if the state judges believe it to be void, they would be bound on the same principle to suspend the collection of all taxes throughout the entire state. A proposition which leads inevitably to such a result can not be sound. I cannot therefore grant an injunction on this ground, whether railroad property is liable to taxation or not."

[1] See People *v.* McCreery, 34 Cal., 432, where the mistake was one of law, but the omission was held not to be fatal.

Invidious assessments. A tax when assessed by valuation may be made unequal and oppressive by the unfairness with which the valuation is made. The remedies for an excessive valuation we have no purpose to consider in this place; they belong more properly to a subsequent part of the work. As a general rule, a tax cannot depend for its validity upon the ability to justify it to the satisfaction of a court or jury. Value is matter of opinion, and when the law has provided officers upon whom the duty is imposed to make it, it is the opinion of these officers to which the interests of the parties are referred. The court cannot sit in judgment upon their errors, nor substitute their own opinions for the conclusions the officers of the law have reached. It is possible, however, that there may be circumstances under which the action of these officers will not be conclusive. Suppose it admitted, or established beyond a peradventure, that a public officer who has been empowered by the law to apportion certain burdens among the citizens, as in his judgment shall be just, has been actuated by a fraudulent purpose, and instead of attempting to carry the law into effect, has wholly disregarded its mandate, declined to bring his judgment to bear upon the question submitted to him, and arbitrarily, with the intent and purpose to defeat the equity at which the law aims, has determined to impose an excessive burden upon a particular citizen. Suppose this to be unquestioned or unquestionable, can it be that the citizen has no remedy against the wrong intended?

Such a question, it would seem, could admit of but one answer. "A discretionary power cannot excuse an officer for refusal to exercise his discretion. His judgment is appealed to; not his resentments, his cupidity or his malice. He is the instrument of the law to accomplish a particular end, through specified means; and when he purposely steps aside from his duty to inflict a wanton injury, the confidence reposed in him has not disarmed the law of the means of prevention. His judgment may indeed be final if he shall exercise it, but an arbitrary and capricious exertion of official authority, being without law, and done to defeat the purpose of the law, must, like all other wrongs, be subject to the law's correction."[1] Assessors indeed are clothed with a power which

[1] Merrill v Humphrey, 24 Mich., 170. See Same Case, 11 Law Reg., N. S.,

is *quasi* judicial, but fraud vitiates even the most solemn judgments of courts, and the action of these *quasi* judicial bodies cannot stand on any higher ground. It may be that all presumptions should so far favor their action as to protect them against personal actions at the suit of parties aggrieved, but such presumptions cannot preclude inquiry when their action is questioned for fraud. The policy of the law may protect the person, but it would be defeated if legal effect should be given to such fraudulent levies.[1]

Duplicate taxation. It has been remarked on a preceding page[2] that when personal property is taxed, duplicate taxation is sometimes imposed. By this was meant that such property sometimes, after being subjected to one levy for the support of government for the current year, is by a change of circumstances subjected to taxation a second time for the support of government during the same period. Such a case would generally occur in consequence of the removal of the property, after the listing in

208, with note by Judge Redfield. See also Albany, etc., R. R. Co. *v.* Canaan, 16 Barb., 244; Buffalo, etc., R. R. Co. *v.* Erie County, 48 N. Y., 93; Western R. R. Co. *v.* Nolan, 48 id., 513; Fuller *v.* Gould, 20 Vt., 643, 644; Stearns *v.* Miller, 25 id., 20; Wilson *v.* Marsh, 34 id., 352; State *v.* Central Pacific R. R. Co., 7 Nev., 99. That neither a state nor a municipality has a right to discriminate in taxation between residents and nonresidents, see *ante*, p. 64; City Council of Charleston *ads.* State, 2 Speers L., 719; Nashville *v.* Althorp, 5 Cold., 554. Compare Jones *v.* Columbus, 25 Geo., 610, where it was held competent to discriminate between residents and nonresidents of a city in the taxation of slaves employed therein. But any such discrimination must be expressly authorized by law. Robinson *v.* Charleston, 2 Rich., 317.

The recent case of Adams *v.* Beaman, 10 Kansas, 37, should be considered in connection with the Michigan and Wisconsin cases referred to in this and the succeeding note.

[1] See Lefferts *v.* Supervisors of Calumet, 21 Wis., 688, where it was decided that the collection of a tax would be restrained where the taxing officers in their assessment had fraudulently discriminated against the complainant; Merrill *v.* Humphrey, 24 Mich., 17, a similar case with the same holding; Milwaukee Iron Co. *v.* Hubbard, 29 Wis., 51, approving and following the case first cited. See also Mason *v.* Lancaster, 4 Bush, 406, 408. Inequality in a legal sense is not produced by certain tax payers taking proceedings which vacate an assessment as to them, while others, who have lost the like right by delay, remain taxed, especially when the lands relieved are liable to reassessment. Matter of DeLancy, 52 N. Y., 80.

[2] *Ante*, p. 28.

one jurisdiction, into another where the time of listing was later. A system of indirect taxes, combined with a system of general taxation by value, must often have the effect to duplicate the burden upon some species of property or upon some persons, and the taxation of stockholders in a corporation, and also of the corporation itself must sometimes produce a like result. There is also sometimes what seems to be a double taxation of the same property to two individuals; as where the purchaser of property on credit is taxed on its full value, while the seller is taxed to the same amount on the debt.[1] How this would operate may be

[1] In California, whose constitution requires "all property" to be "taxed in proportion to its value," it is held not competent to exempt solvent debts from taxation to the creditor. People *v.* McCreery, 34 Cal., 432; People *v.* Yerke, 35 id., 677; People *v.* Black Diamond Co., 37 id., 54; People *v.* Whartenby, 38 id., 461. For a decision to the same purport in Illinois, see Trustees *v.* McConnell, 12 Ill., 138. The fact that the debt is secured by mortgage on property which is also taxed, can make no difference. People *v.* Eddy, 43 Cal., 331; compare Lick *v.* Austin, id., 590. But in Savings and Loan Society *v.* Austin, 46 id., 415, the majority of the court held that a debt *for money loaned*, which was secured by mortgage, could not be taxed to the creditor if the mortgaged property was also taxed. The reasoning of the court may be thus summarized: If the *debt* is taxed, the mortgagee will take this into account in making the loan, and it goes to increase the interest he demands. In effect, therefore, the tax on the debt will be paid by the mortgagor. But he also pays the tax on the property, and consequently duplicate taxation is imposed upon him. This reasoning, if applied universally to indirect taxation, would keep the boards very busy in correcting the inequalities of tax legislation. And why it should be limited to the case of a loan secured by mortgage, is not very apparent, since if all debts for property sold are taxed, it may with considerable plausibility be argued that the seller has anticipated the tax and added it to the price, so that the purchaser pays twice when he comes to pay the assessment on the property bought. But then, whether the tax does increase the interest demanded on the loan, must depend on circumstances. If all loans are taxed, it may be conceded that the interest will be increased; but if only a part of them are taxed, those making the taxed loans may not be able to add the tax to the interest. In a locality, for instance, in which nonresidents were loaning money freely, a resident might be compelled to submit to a loss of the tax in order to be able to make any loans at all. And then one who has borrowed money without security may be taxed on that, or on what he has bought with it, and if the lender is taxed on the loan, why is not this also a case of duplicate taxation? These are suggestions merely, but they may serve to indicate the labyrinth of difficulties into which the courts would be thrown if the effects of taxation were thus to be traced up for the purpose of correcting inequalities.

readily perceived by supposing the extreme case that *all* the property in a town is sold on credit, in which case, if the property is taxed to the purchasers, and the debts to sellers, it is manifest that the town taxes twice as much wealth as lies within its borders.

Now, whether there is injustice in the taxation in every instance in which it can be shown that an individual who has been *directly* taxed his due proportion is also compelled *indirectly* to contribute, is a question we have no occasion to discuss. It is sufficient for our purposes to show that the decisions are nearly, if not quite, unanimous in holding that taxation is not invalid because of any such unequal results.[1] It cannot be too distinctly borne in mind, that any possible system of tax legislation must inevitably produce unequal and unjust results in individual instances; and if inequality in result must defeat the general law, then taxation becomes impossible, and governments must fall back upon arbitrary exactions. But no such impracticable principle is recognized in revenue laws. While equality and justice

[1] It is no objection to a tax graduated by the amount of a merchant's sales, that a part of the goods sold had been purchased of another who had paid a tax thereon. Mayes *v.* Erwine, 8 Humph., 290.

The money of a depositor may be taxed to him, and the deposits of the bank, including this, may also be taxed to the bank. Yuba Co. *v.* Adams, 7 Cal., 35. And see other cases further on.

Income may be taxed though invested in real estate which is taxed the same year. Lott *v.* Hubbard, 44 Ala., 593.

Income, as used in a statute exempting incomes from taxation, held to mean the creation of capital, industry and skill. Wilcox *v.* Middlesex County, 103 Mass., 544. Income means that which comes in and is received from any business or investment of capital without reference to the outgoing expenditures. *Profits*, on the other hand, are understood to mean the net gain of any business or investment, taking into account both receipts and payments. Income, as applied to the affairs of individuals, expresses the same idea that *revenue* does when applied to the affairs of government. People *v.* Supervisors of Niagara, 4 Hill, 20, affirmed 7 Hill, 504. As to difference between "annual value" and "annnal income," see Troy Iron and Nail Factory *v.* Winslow, 45 Barb., 231. There is a case in Texas in which the indirect results of taxation were followed up somewhat sharply. The law subjected "all property, real and personal," with certain exceptions, to taxation. A planter was taxed on his corn and cotton, but contested the tax as duplicate, because he had already been taxed on his slaves and mules by which he produced the corn and cotton. The objection was found by the court to be insurmountable. State *v.* Jones, 5 Texas, 383.

are constantly to be aimed at, impossibilities are not demanded. Tax legislation must be practical.[1] It is one of the reasons for levying indirect taxes, and other taxes than those on property by value, that they tend to diminish the inequalities that would exist if a single species of taxation only were to be levied. The legislature must judge of the general result, and when the law has apportioned the tax, individual hardships must be regarded as among the inconveniences which are incident to regular government. The same necessity that justifies any taxation will justify and sustain any reasonable provisions for giving it effect. The necessity of the state and reasonable provisions for the security of the individual must be equally considered; the state is no more to be deprived of its revenue, because of individual hardship, resulting from general rules, than is the individual to be stripped of his property without law, because in its necessity the state finds it more convenient to take it thus than by regular proceedings. The incidental hardship or inconvenience must be submitted to in either case.

These general views have often been declared by able jurists. "Property," it is said in one case, "is liable in many cases to be taxed twice, when it would appear difficult or unsafe to make provision by law to prevent. Thus, stock in trade may be taxed to the owner, while he may be indebted for it to many persons, who may be taxed for those debts or the money loaned to purchase it. Real estate may be taxed to a mortgagor in possession while the mortgagee is taxed for the money secured by the mortgage. * * * So imperfect are all human institutions, that perfect equality in the imposition of burdens is not to be expected. These provisions for valuation are not considered to be in conflict with the general purpose to have all property subjected to taxation once, and only once at the same time."[2] "The power

[1] "There is nothing poetical about tax laws. Wherever they find property they claim a contribution for its protection, without any special respect to the owner or his occupation." *Lowrie*, Ch. J., in Finley *v.* Philadelphia, 32 Penn. St., 381.

[2] Augusta Bank *v.* Augusta, 36 Me., 255, 259, per *Shepley*, Ch. J. See People *v.* Worthington, 21 Ill., 171; Kirby *v.* Shaw, 19 Penn. St., 258; St. Louis Life Ins. Co. *v.* Assessors, 56 Mo., 503, per *Voris*, J. For cases of apparent double taxation by a tax on business, see Savannah *v.* Charlton, 36 Geo., 460; Burch

to tax twice," it is said in another case, "is as ample as to tax once."[1] We make out, therefore, no conclusive case against a

v. Savannah, 42 id., 596; Sacramento *v.* Crocker, 16 Cal., 119; Coulson *v.* Harris, 43 Miss., 728; Woolman *v.* State, 2 Swan, 353. As to the impossibility of avoiding inequalities in highway taxes, see Hingham, etc., Turnpike Co. *v.* Norfolk Co., 6 Allen, 353, 359, per *Bigelow*, Ch. J.

In Williams *v.* Cammack, 27 Miss., 209, 224, *Handy*, J., speaking of a special levee assessment, says: "Nor is it any objection to the constitutionality of the act that it operates injuriously upon the appellant. Every revenue bill, and every work of public improvement must, more or less, have such an effect. But they must be submitted to as the necessary action of the machinery of government, and as individual sacrifices to the general good, in order that the advantages of the social compact may be enjoyed. This principle rests on the very foundations of society, and is illustrated in every day's experience; the citizen yielding his natural rights, even of life, liberty or property, to the public good. But he can only claim immunity when it is secured to him by the principles of the constitution."

In People *v.* Whyler, 41 Cal., 351, 355, a levee tax was objected to as not equal, because not apportioned according to benefits. The court held that it was required to be apportioned by value, and *Rhodes*, Ch. J., says: "A tax is equal and uniform which reaches and bears with the like burden upon all the property within the given district, county, etc. It bears the like burden when the valuation of each parcel is ascertained in the same mode — the mode prescribed by law — and when it is subject to the same rate of taxation as other property within the district, county, etc. Absolute equality is unattainable, and the benefits derived or to be derived from the expenditure of the tax cannot be taken into account."

[1] West Chester Gas Co. *v.* Chester County, 30 Penn. St., 232, per *Porter*, J., cited with approval in Pittsburgh, etc., R. R. Co. *v.* Commonwealth, 66 Penn. St., 73, 77–8. See also Erie Railway Co. *v.* Commonwealth, id., 84. Congress having levied a tax upon an article, is not thereby precluded from levying another. U. S. *v.* Benson, 2 Cliff., 512. In Philadelphia Savings Fund *v.* Yard, 9 Penn. St., 359, 361, in referring to the case of The Carlisle Bank, 8 Watts, 291, the following remarks are made: "The horror of double taxation, manifested in that case, is unsuited to the times; for it has obtained, and must prevail in the exigencies of the commonwealth; moreover, it is expressly recognized and established by the 6th section of the act of 16th April, 1845. It exists in the case of ground rents, where the ground itself and the *reditum* issuing from it are taxed; in a tax upon a mortgage to the whole value of the land, and the land itself. And so, where A. borrows money on mortgage and loans it to C. on bond, and who loans a part of it to D., it is taxed in the current of each actual employment. In the complexity and involutions of business, a dollar is employed many times in a day, and in each actual employment represents the property, business, or the person of him who uses it. And in cases of this kind, it is the usufruct and not the actual or identical money, that is taxed." In Pittsburgh, etc., R. R. Co. *v.* Commonwealth, 66 Penn. St.

tax, when we show that it reaches twice the same property for the same purpose. This may have been intended, and in many cases at least, is admissible.[1]

77, the following remarks are made by the same court: "It [the case in judgment] resulted even in double taxation, that has never been considered unlawful in this state. On the contrary, it is of frequent occurrence. The real and personal property of a corporation may be taxed, although it pays a tax on the stock which purchased it. Lackawana Iron Co. *v.* Luzerne County, 42 Penn. St., 424, 431. See Carbon Iron Co. *v.* Carbon County, 39 Penn. St., 251; West Chester Gas Co. *v.* Chester County, 30 Penn. St., 332; Philadelphia Savings Fund *v.* Yard, 9 id., 361. The power of the legislature is as ample to tax twice as to tax once (30 id., 332); and it is done daily, as all experience shows. 9 id., 361. Equality of taxation is not required by the constitution. Kirby *v.* Shaw, 19 id., 258. The stock may be full taxed to the institution and also to the stockholders (Whitsell *v.* Northampton County, 49 id., 526, 529); and the stockholder in a corporation of another state is obliged to pay a tax to Pennsylvania on his stock, he being a resident here, although the whole profit and stock is subject to taxation in the state of its location." See also Toll-bridge Co. *v.* Osborn, 35 Conn., 7; St. Louis Life Ins. Co. *v.* Board of Assessors, 56 Mo., 503, per *Voris*, J. In Eyre *v.* Jacob, 14 Grat., 422, a tax on collateral inheritances was sustained against an objection that taxation of property was required to be uniform. *Lee*, J., points out that it is not a tax on property, but on the privilege of succeeding to the inheritance.

[1] The case of The Toll-bridge Co. *v.* Osborn, 35 Conn., 7, is a very strong one. A corporation was chartered to build and maintain a toll-bridge, with power, "for the purpose of carrying the resolve into effect," to purchase and hold lands not exceeding one hundred acres. The company built the bridge, and soon after purchased a large quantity of mud flats adjoining the bridge, and erected wharves upon it, which became of great value and were profitably rented. An act, passed in 1847, provided that the real estate of any private corporation, "above what was required and used for the transaction of its appropriate business," should be liable to be assessed and taxed to the same extent as if owned by individuals. *Held*, that the real estate thus used by the company for wharves, was liable to taxation under the statute.

The facts in this case were such, that the property was really taxed several times. By the decision of the court, the corporation was compelled to pay a tax upon this property; the shareholders paid a tax upon their shares of stock which represented this property; and the corporation also paid a tax upon its capital stock; and, furthermore, as a great part of the stock was owned by a railway company, they might be taxed as shareholders, and also upon their capital stock, of which these shares were a part, while the shareholders in the railway company might be required to pay a tax upon their shares also.

The court held, that it mattered not, so long as the legislative intent was clear. While it was the general policy of the law to avoid duplicate taxation, yet, where the meaning of the statutes is clear, the court cannot pronounce

There is a sense, however, in which duplicate taxation may be understood—and which we think is the proper sense—which would render it wholly inadmissible under any constitution requiring equality and uniformity in taxation. By duplicate taxation in this sense is understood *the requirement that one person or any one subject of taxation shall directly contribute twice to the same burden, while other subjects of taxation belonging to the same class are required to contribute but once.*

We do not see, for instance, how a tax on a merchant's stock by value could be supported, when by the same authority and for the same purpose the same stock was taxed by value as a part of his property. This is a very different thing from one tax upon property and another upon the business, though the latter may indirectly reach the property; here is no circumlocution, no question of ultimate effects; but a tax levied twice on the same subject only under a different name. The same may be said of a tax on the property of a corporation and also on the capital which is invested in the property; if the latter is taxed as property, this also is duplicate taxation, and as much unequal as would be the taxation of a farmer's stock by value, when on the same basis it is taxed as a part of his general property. When, for instance, the money paid in as capital of a manufacturing corporation has been invested in buildings and machinery, these are what then represent the capital, and to tax the capital as valuable property distinct from that which then represents it would be to tax a mere shadow;[1] it

them invalid because they admit of duplicate taxation. Compare Jones, etc., Manuf. Co. *v.* Commonwealth, 69 Penn. St., 137.

[1] That the capital of a corporation is represented by the property in which it has been invested, can hardly require the citation of authorities, but the following may be referred to. Gordon *v.* Baltimore, 5 Gill, 231; Baltimore *v.* Baltimore and Ohio R. R. Co., 6 id., 288; Tax Cases, 12 Gill and J., 117; Rome R. R. Co. *v.* Rome, 14 Geo., 275; Augusta *v.* Georgia R. R., etc., Co., 26 id., 651; Hannibal, etc., R. R. Co. *v.* Shacklett, 30 Mo., 550; Auditor, etc., *v.* New Albany, etc., R. R. Co., 11 Ind., 570; Conwell *v.* Connersville, 15 id., 150; Mutual Ins. Co. *v.* Supervisors of Erie, 4 N. Y., 442; Salem Iron Factory *v.* Danvers, 10 Mass., 515; Amesbury Woolen, etc., Co. *v.* Amesbury, 17 id., 461; Boston, etc., Glass Co. *v.* Boston, 4 Met., 181; Boston Water Power Co. *v.* Boston, 9 id., 199; Bangor & Piscataqua R. R. Co. *v.* Harris, 21 Me., 533; Cumberland Marine R. *v.* Portland, 37 Me., 444; Savings Bank *v.* New London, 20 Conn., 111, 117; Bridgeport *v.* Bishop, 33 id., 187; Toll Bridge Co. *v.* Osborn, 35 id., 7; New Haven *v.* City Bank, 31 id., 106; Bank of Cape Fear *v.* Edwards, 5

would be to make the shadow stand for the substance in order that it might be taxed, when the substance itself is taxed directly under its own proper designation. We do not speak here of a taxation of the property and also of the franchise; those being two things as will be seen further on.[1]

Presumption against duplicate taxation. It has very properly and justly been held that a construction of the laws was not to be adopted that would subject the same property to be twice charged for the same tax, unless it was required by the express words of the statute, or by necessary implication.[2] It is a fundamental maxim in taxation that the same property shall not be subject to a double tax payable by the same party, either directly or indirectly; and where it is once decided that any kind or class of property is liable to be taxed under one provision of the statutes, it has been held to follow as a legal conclusion, that the legislature could not have intended the same property should be subject to another tax, though there may be general words in the law which would seem to imply that it may be taxed a second time.[3] This

Ired., 516; Smith *v.* Exeter, 37 N. H., 556; Fitchburgh R. R. Co. *v.* Prescott, 47 N. H., 62. For the distinction between a tax on the franchise of a corporation, and a tax on its capital *as property*, see Bank of Commerce *v.* New York City, 2 Black, 620; Van Allen *v.* The Assessor, 3 Wall., 573; Bradley *v.* People, 4 id., 459. The law of these cases is that where the tax is on the capital by a valuation as property, it is invalid if the capital is invested in nontaxable securities.

[1] When the capital stock of a corporation is required to be assessed at its "actual value," this means above or below the par value according to the fact. Oswego Starch Factory *v.* Dolloway, 21 N .Y., 449.

[2] Salem Iron, etc., Co. *v.* Danvers, 10 Mass., 514; Amesbury Woolen, etc., Co. *v.* Amesbury, 17 id., 461; Water Power Co. *v.* Boston, 9 Met., 199, 202; Bank of Georgia *v.* Savannah, Dudley, 130; Gordon's Executors *v.* Baltimore, 5 Gill, 231; The Tax Cases, 12 Gill and J., 117; Savings Bank *v.* New London, 20 Conn., 111, 117; Toll Bridge Co. *v.* Osborn, 35 id., 7; Osborn *v.* N. Y. and N. H. R. R. Co., 40 id., 491; Smith *v.* Burley, 9 N. H, 423; Savings Bank *v.* Portsmouth, 52 N. H., 17.

[3] Savings Bank *v.* Nashua, 46 N. H., 389–398, citing Smith *v.* Burley, 9 N. H., 423 and other cases. And see Osborn *v.* N. Y. and N. H. R. R. Co., 40 Conn., 491, 494. In State *v.* Sterling, 20 Md., 502, a law taxed savings banks a certain percentage on all the deposits held by them on a certain day. *Held* to be void because not exempting the investments in securities otherwise taxed or not taxable at all.

is a sound and very just rule of construction, and it has been applied in many cases where, at first reading of the law, a double taxation might seem to have been intended. [1]

Application of the presumption. A few instances in which this rule of presumption has been applied will show what taxation has been held to be in effect duplicate taxation, and for that reason excluded from the general language made use of in tax laws.

Under a statute in Massachusetts, shares in any incorporated company possessing taxable property were taxable to the owners in the towns of their residence respectively. While this was in force, a manufacturing corporation was assessed under the general law for the taxation of property to its owners, for all its real and personal estate in the town where its business was carried on. It was held that this taxation of shares was by implication to be regarded as standing in the place of a taxation of the personal estate to the corporation itself, since, if both were taxed, it would in effect be duplicate taxation. As to the real estate, however, the conclusion was different. The taxes upon that had always, in that state, been paid exclusively to the town in which it was situated. In all successive valuations made in pursuance of the laws for that purpose, each town had been charged with the value of all the real estate within it, in the apportionment of the tax among the several towns. It would therefore be unjust if the real estate which was included in estimating the amount of taxes charged on a town, by being assessed as represented by the shares of stockholders elsewhere, should be exempted from contributing to the discharge of such taxes. The policy of all the tax laws had been that the land should contribute to the local taxes irrespective of the residence of the owner, and the implication that this was intended in the case of corporate real estate was so strong

[1] Bank of Georgia *v.* Savannah, Dudley, 132; Factory Co. *v.* Gardiner, 5 Greenl., 133; Glass Co. *v.* Boston, 4 Met., 181; Savings Bank *v.* Worcester, 10 Cush., 128; American Bank *v.* Mumford, 4 R. I., 478, 482; Savings Bank *v.* Gardiner, 4 id., 484; Smith *v.* Exeter, 37 N. H., 556; Toll Bridge Co. *v.* Osborn, 35 Conn., 7; State *v.* Hannibal, etc., R. R. Co., 37 Mo., 265. In the case of Kimball *v.* Milford just decided by the supreme court of New Hampshire (2 Am. Law Times' Reports, 504), stock in a foreign corporation, which by its charter pays a specific tax in lieu of all others, was held not taxable in New Hampshire, under its statutes.

that the counteracting presumption against an intent to impose duplicate taxation must yield to it.[1]

So in Georgia it has been held under a city charter empowering the corporation in general terms to levy taxes on real and personal estate, that while the city might tax the stockholders of a bank upon their shares, this taxation would by implication exclude the taxation of the bank on its capital stock.[2] In Pennsylvania it has been decided that a tax on the discount business of a bank is in a degree a tax upon the capital of the bank. Where therefore it was provided by its charter that the bank should not be subject to taxation on its capital stock, for any other than state purposes, the tax on its discount business would be inadmissible but for the fact that the charter was granted under and subject to a provision in the state constitution which made it at all times subject to legislative alteration or repeal.[3]

So in Massachusetts it is held that a bank which pays a specific tax on its capital stock is not taxable on collaterals deposited with

[1] Salem Iron Factory *v.* Danvers, 10 Mass., 514. This case was followed after some change in the statute, in Amesbury Woolen, etc., Co. *v.* Amesbury, 17 id., 461. And see as to the real estate, Amesbury Nail Factory Co. *v.* Weed, 17 id., 53; Tremont Bank *v.* Boston, 1 Cush., 142; Boston Water Power Co. *v.* Boston, 9 Met., 199. In Middlesex R. R. Co. *v.* Charleston, 8 Allen, 330, where shareholders in a street railway were taxable on their shares in the towns where they resided, it was held not competent to tax the personal property of the corporation used in and necessary for the prosecution of its business. "The value of the personal property owned by the corporation is included as a subject of taxation in the value of the shares; as in the case of banks, insurance companies, manufacturing corporations and other railroads." *Hoar*, J., p. 333. Compare The Tax Cases, 12 G. & J., 117. To tax a bank on its property and also the stockholders on their shares was regarded as duplicate taxation, and not allowable under the Maryland laws, in Gordon's Ex'rs *v.* Baltimore, 5 Gill, 231, and Baltimore *v.* B. & O. R. R. Co., 6 Gill, 288. And see in Rhode Island, American Bank *v.* Mumford, 4 R. I., 478; Providence Institution *v.* Gardiner, 4 id., 484.

[2] Bank of Georgia *v.* Savannah, Dudley, 132, citing with approval the Massachusetts cases. So where a bank was exempt from any tax, except one of twenty-five cents on every share of its stock owned by individuals, it was decided that stockholders were not taxable on their shares. Bank of Cape Fear *v.* Edwards, 5 Ired., 516. See also Johnson *v.* Commonwealth, 7 Dana, 338; State *v.* Tunis, 23 N. J., 546.

[3] Iron City Bank *v.* Pittsburgh, 37 Penn. St., 340.

it as security for loans.[1] So if it appear that a corporation is by its charter exempt from taxation; the shares in the hands of the shareholders are to be understood as exempt also.[2]

On the other hand a tax on the market value of the capital stock of a corporation, over and above the value of its real and personal property, is not duplicate taxation by reason of the tangible property being also taxed, but is a tax upon the franchise.[3] So a tax on the deposits of savings societies has been held a tax on the franchise and not a tax on property.[4] And where by statute "no income shall be taxed which is derived from property subject to taxation;" a merchant may nevertheless be taxed on his income under the general law taxing income from a profession, trade, or employment, this income being the "net result of many combined influences; the use of the capital invested; the personal labor and services; * * the skill and ability with which they lay in or from time to time renew their stock; the carefulness and good judgment with which they sell and give credit; and the

[1] Waltham Bank *v.* Waltham, 10 Met., 334; Tremont Bank *v.* Boston, 1 Cush., 142; and see Salem Iron Factory *v.* Danvers, 10 Mass., 514.

[2] State *v.* Branin, 23 N. J., 484, citing Johnson *v.* Commonwealth, 7 Dana, 342; Tax Cases, 12 G. & J., 117; Gordon's Ex'rs *v.* Baltimore, 5 Gill, 231; Smith *v.* Burley, 9 N. H., 423. See also State *v.* Bentley, 23 N. J., 532; State *v.* Powers, 24 id., 400; Bank of Cape Fear *v.* Edwards, 5 Ired., 516. And compare Wilmington, etc., R. R. Co. *v.* Reid, 13 Wall., 264.

[3] So held in Hamilton County *v.* Massachusetts, 6 Wall., 632, in reliance upon a settled course of decisions in Massachusetts. See Commonwealth *v.* Hamilton Man'f. Co., 12 Allen, 298, 306. Shares of stock in a foreign corporation may be taxed in full to resident owners, irrespective of the taxation of its property where it is located. Dwight *v.* Boston, 12 Allen, 316. A state may tax the franchise or the capital of a corporation by such rule as it may prescribe, even though it be arbitrary. And if the corporation be a railroad company owning a road in two states, one state may tax the corporation on a proportional part of its stock, measured by the length of the road in that state. Minot *v.* Philadelphia, etc., R. R. Co., 18 Wall., 206.

[4] Society of Savings *v.* Coite, 6 Wall., 594; Provident Institution *v.* Massachusetts, id., 611. See Portland Bank *v.* Apthorp, 12 Mass, 252; Com'th *v.* Savings Bank, 5 Allen, 428; People *v.* Supervisors of Niagara, 4 Hill, 20; Farmers' Loan & Trust Co. *v.* New York, 7 id., 261; Bank of Utica *v.* Utica, 4 Paige, 399; Coite *v.* Society for Savings, 32 Conn., 173; Coite *v.* Conn. Mu. Life Ins. Co., 36 id., 512; Illinois Mu. Ins. Co. *v.* Peoria, 29 Ill., 180; Oliver *v.* Washington Mills, 11 Allen, 268; Commonwealth *v.* Cary Improving Co., 98 Mass., 19; Attorney General *v.* Mining Co., 99 id., 148.

foresight and address with which they hold themselves prepared for the fluctuations and contingencies affecting the general commerce and business of the country. To express it in a more summary and comprehensive form, it is the creation of capital, industry and skill."[1] So it is competent to tax brokers upon their annual receipts, notwithstanding they pay a license tax for the privilege of carrying on that business.[2] So a tax upon the amount of the nominal capital of a bank, without regard to loss or depreciation, has been likened to "one annexed to the franchise as a royalty for the grant."[3] A tax on the interest paid by a corporation on its indebtedness, though collected from the corporation, is still a tax on the creditor; the corporation being only made use of as a convenient means of collecting the tax.[4] So a tax on the shares of stockholders in a corporation is a different thing from a tax on the corporation itself or its stock, and may be laid irrespective of any taxation of the corporation when no contract relations forbid.[5] So it has been held that a corporation which was required to pay

[1] Wilcox *v.* Commissioners of Middlesex, 103 Mass., 544, per *Ames*, J.

[2] Drexel *v.* Commonwealth, 46 Penn. St., 31. In this case the tax law was objected to as retrospective because, in order to arrive at the proper measure of taxation, it required a return of the receipts for the preceding year, and made that the basis of taxation, but the court justly held there was nothing to this.

[3] Bank of Commerce *v.* New York, 2 Black, 620, 629, per *Nelson*, J.

[4] Haight *v.* Railroad Co., 6 Wall., 15; Railroad Co. *v.* Jackson, 7 id., 262; United States *v.* Railroad Co., 17 id., 322. In the second of these cases a state tax on the interest on bonds issued by a railroad company and secured by mortgage on a line lying partly in another state was held to be void, on the ground that to the extent of the road out of the state she was "taxing property and interests beyond her jurisdiction." It is to be said of this case that the plaintiff was a nonresident, and for that reason not taxable in the state on his bonds, under the subsequent decision of the same court. State Tax on Foreign Held Bonds, 15 Wall., 300, 323. Railroad bonds are taxable to the owners notwithstanding the company pays a tax on "the market value of their stock and their funded and floating debt, in lieu of all other taxes on railroad property and franchises." Bridgeport *v.* Bishop, 33 Conn., 187.

[5] Tremont Bank *v.* Boston, 1 Cush., 142; State *v.* Petway, 2 Jones Eq., 396; State *v.* Thomas, 26 N. J., 181; Lycoming County *v.* Gamble, 47 Penn. St., 106; Whitsell *v.* Northampton County, 49 id., 526; Union Bank *v.* State, 9 Yerg., 490; Oswego Starch Factory *v.* Dollaway, 21 N. Y., 449; People *v.* Bradley, 39 Ill., 130, 141; Conwell *v.* Connersville, 15 Ind., 150; Van Allen *v.* Assessors, 3 Wall., 573, 584; State Tax on Foreign Held Bonds, 15 id., 300, 323; Cumberland Marine Railway *v.* Portland, 37 Me., 444.

a bonus on its capital in lieu of a tax on dividends, might nevertheless be taxed on its "net earnings or income;" this not being the same thing as dividends.[1] So in case of a corporation which pays a specific tax, an exemption "from any other or further tax or imposition," will not prevent any real estate it may own, and which is not needed for corporate purposes, from being taxed. "The power granted to a corporation to hold land is limited to the purposes for which the power was conferred. This is the general rule, and governs in the construction of the exempting clause. The tax levied may so far operate as a double tax, the property being already taxed in the shape of capital; but if the company choose to invest capital in property not necessary for their business, such as the legislature did not contemplate in their grant, they cannot complain that it is twice taxed. Double taxation is not unconstitutional."[2]

It has often been decided that a tax on the franchise of a corporation, and also on its capital or property, was not duplicate taxation.[3] The franchise, nevertheless, has a property value, and as a question of construction, it may sometimes be necessary to

[1] Jones, etc., Manf'g Co. *v.* Commonwealth, 69 Penn. St., 137. That stock divided among stockholders as profits are dividends, see Lehigh Crane Iron Co, *v.* Commonwealth, 55 Penn. St., 448; State *v.* Farmer's Bank, 11 Ohio, 94; Sun Mu. Ins. Co. *v.* New York, 8 N. Y., 241, 250.

[2] *Potts*, J., in State *v.* Newark, 25 N. J., 315, 317, citing Tatem *v.* Wright, 23 id., 429. See also Railroad Co. *v.* Reid, 13 Wall., 264, 268, per *Davis*, J., Illinois Central R. R. Co. *v.* Irwin, Sup. Ct. Ill., 1875, 7 Chicago Legal News, 286.

[3] Carbon Iron Co. *v.* Carbon County, 39 Penn. St., 251; Lackawana Iron Co *v.* Luzerne County, 42 id., 424; Tremont Bank *v.* Boston, 1 Cush., 142; Commonwealth *v.* Lowell Gas Light Co., 12 Allen, 75; Commonwealth *v.* Hamilton Manf. Co., id., 298; Wilmington, etc., R. R. Co. *v.* Reid, 64 N. C., 226; Mason *v.* Lancaster, 4 Bush, 406; Monroe Savings Bank *v.* Rochester, 37 N. Y., 365; Bank of Commerce *v.* New York, 2 Black, 620, 629; Minot *v.* Railroad Co., 18 Wall., 206. In Commonwealth *v.* N. E. Slate & Tile Co., 13 Allen, 391, 393, *Wells*, J., says: "The fact that the defendant corporation held property which was the subject of taxation in other ways, does not render this tax upon its franchise illegal. In the practical operation of the powers of taxation, which are given in several forms, it is inevitable that double taxation shall occur in some cases. The legislature may relieve against it by allowing deductions if it sees fit to do so; but the court can only apply the law as it stands." If the capital is invested in nontaxable securities, the franchise may still be taxed. Monroe Savings Bank *v.* Rochester, 37 N. Y., 365. And see

hold that an exemption of the property of a corporation from taxation is an exemption of the franchise also. It has been so held in the case of a railroad corporation whose charter provided that "the property of said company and the shares therein shall be exempt from any public charge or tax whatever."[1] The intent in such a case, when reasonably apparent on the face of the legislation, must control. It has been held that a tax on the capital stock measured by dividends was not a tax on dividends, and the corporation paying it was therefore liable to a tax on net earnings under a statute which provides that corporations not paying a tax on dividends shall be taxed on net earnings.[2] A tax on "the capital stock actually paid in or secured to be paid in," is a tax on the capital at its nominal amount, and is not to be increased or diminished by accumulations or losses.[3] These cases will perhaps illustrate sufficiently the power of the legislature to impose taxation that in its result duplicates the burden, as well as the force of the presumption that the legislature, in its desire to lay all burdens of government justly, has never intended duplicate taxation unless plain language expressive of that intent has been employed.

So far, the subject has been considered as the questions of equality and justice in taxation arise on the tax laws themselves. Of the steps necessary or proper to be taken in order to secure equality under such laws, it will be necessary to speak further on.

Society for Savings *v.* Coite, 6 Wall., 594; Provident Inst. *v.* Massachusetts, 6 id., 611; Hamilton Co. *v.* Massachusetts, id., 632.

[1] Wilmington Railroad Co. *v.* Reid, 13 Wall., 264; Raleigh, etc., Railroad Co. *v.* Reid, id., 269. In New Jersey where a corporation by its charter was to pay a certain tax on its capital stock paid in, and it was declared that "no further or other tax or impost shall be levied or assessed upon said company," this was held to exempt not the franchises merely, but the property also. State *v.* Berry, 17 N. J., 80; Camden & Amboy R. R. Co. *v.* Commissioner of Appeals, 18 id., 71. So it has been held that a tax on the gross income of a corporation cannot be laid when the stock is exempt. State *v.* Hood, 15 Rich., 117.

[2] Phœnix Iron Co *v.* Commonwealth, 59 Penn. St., 104. A tax on capital invested in shipping is not duplicate taxation as applied to vessels upon which the harbor master's fees have been paid. State *v.* Charleston, 4 Rich., 286.

[3] Farmers' Loan & Trust Co. *v.* New York, 7 Hill, 261, citing Bank of Utica *v.* Utica, 4 Paige, 390; People *v.* Supervisors of Niagara, 4 Hill, 20. See Gordon *v.* New Brunswick Bank, 6 N. J., 100; Rudderow *v.* State, 31 id., 512.

Commuting taxes. Tax laws sometimes provide for commutation; that is to say, for the substitution of something else for the tax that is levied. Thus, road taxes are sometimes levied in labor, with permission to commute by the payment of what is deemed an equivalent in money. Many of the special exemptions we have referred to were in the nature of commutations; the state has received something as an equivalent for the ordinary taxation which was released.[1] Such commutations are competent when not forbidden by the constitution, and are supposed to produce no inequality.[2] But a commutation must not be invidious; if, as between individuals it selects one class for favor, and excludes others, it is void.[3]

Diversity of taxation in different districts. Reference has been made to cases which recognize the right to establish different rules of taxation in different districts, even when by the state constitution uniformity and equality in taxation are required. Such general rules are made in view of the universal custom to consult the circumstances of different districts, and the wishes of their people regarding the taxes to be levied therein as district taxes; and all presumptions are against any purpose to set aside that custom. Local taxes may be levied on a different system in the different municipal districts, and for different purposes;

[1] See Gardiner *v.* State, 21 N. J., 557; Daughdrill *v.* Ins. Co., 31 Ala., 91. Where a railroad company pays a tax on its annual income in lieu of a tax on its property, the tax so paid is supposed to be a full equivalent for the property tax, and therefore there is no room for applying the rule of strict construction against the company, as if the substitution of one tax for the other was a privilege. Milwaukee, etc., R. R. Co. *v.* Supervisors of Crawford, 29 Wis., 116.

[2] State Bank *v.* People, 4 Scam., 303; Illinois Central Railroad *v.* McLean County, 17 Ill., 291. It was one of the stipulations in the charter of the Baltimore & Ohio R. R. Co., that the corporation should pay to the state one-fifth of the passenger fares received for passage on its branch road between Washington and Baltimore. A stipulation of this nature violates no provision of the federal constitution. B. & O. R. R. Co. *v.* Maryland, 21 Wall., 456. The same decision had previously been made by the state courts, and the position affirmed that the stipulation did not violate the state constitution. Waters *v.* State, 1 Gill, 302, 308.

[3] So held of a commutation in labor for a highway tax; the permission to commute being extended only to male tax payers between the ages of 21 and 50. Cooper *v.* Ash, Sup. Ct. Ill., 1875, 7 Chi. Leg. News, 393.

and this, not only when they are laid to supply mere local works and conveniences, but also when they are for purposes — like the highways, for instance — which, though paid for locally, are for the benefit of the whole state and the use of all its people.[1]

Monopolies. It seems scarcely necessary to say, that the rule of equality in taxation will forbid the power being employed for the purpose of building up monopolies. That it is capable of being so employed needs no demonstration; and that it sometimes has been so employed, especially in the arrangement of the customs duties, is unquestionable; always, of course, under the pretense of an apportionment of taxes for the public good. Taxation of business and the license taxes are peculiarly liable to abuse in this direction,[2] especially if they undertake to limit the number to whom permits shall be granted; and if the state can exempt the large manufacturer from taxation while taxing his feeble competitor, as has been done in one state at least, it may take in this way a long stride in the direction of establishing a monopoly. The spirit of a free constitution, if not its letter, forbids such legislation, and sound public policy forbids it also. One reason why taxation for private purposes is inadmissible, is that its tendency is to the building up of monopolies at the expense of the public who would suffer from them;[3] it begins in a pretense for the public good, and it ends in crippling the general industry while it excites the general discontent.[4]

[1] See in general, People *v.* Central Pacific R. R. Co., 43 Cal., 398; Bright *v.* McCullough, 27 Ind., 223; Commissioners of Schools *v.* Alleghany County, 20 Md., 439, 457; Merrick *v.* Amherst, 12 Allen, 500.

[2] See Judge *Nott's* article on Monopolies in the International Review, Vol. 1, p. 370. Charles I. was able to exact large sums of money by enforcing a royal proclamation forbidding the erection of buildings in extension of London, and granting special permits on the payment of large sums for the privilege. Green's England, ch. 8, sec. 5.

[3] See Philadelphia Association *v.* Wood, 39 Penn. St., 73, 82, per *Lowrie*, Ch. J.

[4] The right of a city to levy a tax for the construction of a patented pavement has been denied in some states, on the express ground, that the patent was a monopoly, and there could be no competition in bidding for the contract to construct it. Nicholson Pavement Co. *v.* Fay, 35 Cal., 695; Same *v.* Painter, id., 699; Dean *v.* Charlton, 23 Wis., 590; Burgess *v.* Jefferson, 21

Permanence in legislation. It should be added, that in order that tax laws may not be oppressive, they should not be subject to frequent changes. Tariff laws frequently changed become a serious impediment to the business of the country, from the impossibility on the part of business men to calculate upon the future. To all the other contingencies of business is added this one, which is, perhaps, greatest of all: that the federal legislature may so change the customs laws as to detract considerably from the market value of merchandise on hand, or increase largely the cost of something employed in manufacture, or in some other way to change greatly the outlook for any particular trade. The excise laws are seldom changed without serious injury to individuals; and if others, perhaps, make fortunes by the change, the possibility of such prosperity leads to speculations in possible changes, and even to endeavors to procure alterations for speculative purposes. Changes in other tax laws are not so injurious, but they are always liable to be oppressive, in individual cases, and for this reason are not to be made except to cure positive evils. Mere inconveniences, to which the people have become accustomed, or even impolitic or unequal taxation to which trade and business have adapted themselves, are usually less harmful than considerable changes in the law with a view to their correction. This is a consideration of policy, with which the courts have no concern, but it seems sufficiently important to justify mention in this connection.

La. An,, 143. *Contra*, Hobart *v.* Detroit, 17 Mich., 246; *In re* Eager, 46 N. Y, 100; *In re* Dugro, 50 id., 513.

CHAPTER VII.

THE APPORTIONMENT OF TAXES.

The distinction between an exercise of the eminent domain, and one of the power to tax, consists mainly in this: that the one is an exceptional exaction for the public benefit, while the other is an exaction based upon the idea that it is only an equal and fair contribution to the public wants.[1] In order to make it equal and fair, apportionment is a necessary element in all taxation.

The apportionment of a tax consists in a selection of the subjects to be taxed, and in laying down the rule by which to measure the contribution which each of those subjects shall make to the tax.[2] Apportionment is therefore a matter of legislation. "The power of taxing and the power of apportioning taxation are identical and inseparable. Taxes cannot be laid without apportionment, and the power of apportionment is, therefore, unlimited, unless it be restrained as a part of the power of taxation."[3]

The methods of apportionment are diverse and numerous, but all taxes may possibly be arranged under the three heads of specific taxes, *ad valorem* taxes, and taxes apportioned by special benefits.

Specific Taxes. Under this head may be ranged those which impose a specific sum by the head or number, or by some standard of weight or measurement, and which require no assessment beyond a listing and classification of the subjects to be taxed. License taxes and other taxes on business or occupations, stamp taxes, taxes on franchises and privileges, are usually specific, as are also many excise and customs taxes.

[1] Blackwell on Tax Titles, 1; People *v.* Brooklyn, 4 N. Y., 419; *post*, Ch. XX.

[2] "The power to tax necessarily involves the right to designate the property on which it is to be levied; in other words, to apportion the tax." *Ranney*, J., in Scoville *v.* Cleveland, 1 Ohio, N. S., 126, 123, citing Cincinnati *v.* Gwynne, 10 Ohio., 192; Bonsall *v.* Lebanon, 19 id., 418.

[3] *Ruggles*, J., in People *v.* Brooklyn, 4 N. Y., 419, 426-7. See Glascow *v.* Rouse, 43 Mo., 479, 489.

As regards all such taxes, the law by which they are laid is of itself a complete apportionment. Ministerial officers have nothing to do but to list the subjects of taxation; classify them where that is necessary; ascertain the number, weight, measurement, etc., and collect the sum which the law has definitely fixed. If the taxes are stamp or license taxes, even the listing may not be required, but the individual who is to pay them will purchase his stamp or his license, by voluntary payment, as he may have occasion.

Ad Valorem Taxes. A large proportion of the duties on imports are of this description, and so, sometimes, are many of the taxes which make up the internal revenue. The statute laying them prescribes the rule, but requires the action of appraisers in apportioning them between individuals. By far the larger proportion of all state taxation is also upon property by a valuation, and effect can only be given to it by means of assessors, who value the property and apportion the tax by their estimate.

Taxes Apportioned by Benefits. As between *districts*, where an object for which taxes are to be levied pertains to two or more, the legislature sometimes makes the apportionment by its own action directly, with reference to the supposed interest of each in such object, or to the benefit each is likely to derive therefrom. It may also provide for the apportionment by commissioners appointed for the purpose.[1] This often becomes necessary in the case of roads and bridges lying partly in two or more districts, and also on the division of towns, counties, etc.[2]

[1] See Salem Turnpike, etc., Corp. *v.* Essex County, 100 Mass., 282, and cases cited. The case was one of the appropriation of a turnpike road under the eminent domain, and an apportionment of the cost among the counties, cities and towns which it accommodated. See also Shaw *v.* Dennis, 5 Gilm., 405.

[2] On the division of a county or town and the setting off of territory for a new one, the old county, unless it is otherwise provided by statute, will retain the property and remain liable for the debts. North Hempstead *v.* Hempstead, 2 Wend., 109, 135; Hartford Bridge Co. *v.* East Hartford, 16 Conn., 149, 171; Windham *v.* Portland, 4 Mass., 384–390; Hampshire *v.* Franklin, 16 id., 76, 85; Medford *v.* Pratt, 4 Pick., 222; Montpelier *v.* East Montpelier, 29 Vt., 12, 20; Milwaukee *v.* Milwaukee, 12 Wis., 93. It will also retain the right to proceed in the collection of the taxes previously voted, and they will belong to it though collected in part from territory now set off. Devor *v.* McClintock, 9 W. & S., 80; Waldron *v.* Lee, 5 Pick., 323; Harman *v.* New Marlborough, 9 Cush., 525; Moss *v.* Shear, 25 Cal., 38; Morgan County *v.* Hendricks County,

Elsewhere the constitutional provisions of a number of the states are referred to, which require state taxation of property to be by value. The judicial decisions are also cited, which hold that the local levies, commonly known under the head of assessments, though laid under the taxing power, are not taxes as the term is employed in the constitutions, and consequently may be laid by some other standard than that of value, if the legislature shall so prescribe. The standard more often established than any other is one which seeks to put upon each item of property a tax proportioned to the special benefit it is to receive from the expenditure. There are different methods of making the apportionment between individuals: 1. Assessors or commissioners may be empowered to examine the district and apportion the tax according as they shall find that benefits will be received. 2. The legislature may determine that the benefits will be in proportion to value, area or frontage, and direct an apportionment accordingly. In another place it is shown that either course is admissible.[1]

General principles of apportionment. The principles by which the legislative apportionment of taxes is to be tested have been so admirably stated in a Kentucky case, that we give at length the language of the court in preference to any attempt at stating them in our own language: "When shall a tax be levied? To what amount? Shall it be a capitation or property tax? Direct or indirect? *Ad valorem* or specific? And what classes of property are the fittest subjects of taxation? are all questions wisely confided by our constitution to the discretion of the legislative department, subject to no other limitation than that of the moral influence of public virtue or responsibility to

32 Ind., 234. See Alvis *v.* Whitney, 43 id., 83. But it is competent for the legislature to make apportionment of debts and property in such a case, or to provide for its being done, and to compel the necessary taxation to do what may be just in the premises. Bristol *v.* New Chester, 3 N. H., 524; Londonderry *v.* Derry, 8 id., 320; Willimantic *v.* Windham, 14 Conn., 457; Hartford Bridge Co. *v.* East Hartford, 16 id., 149–172; Granby *v.* Thurston, 23 id., 416; Montpelier *v.* East Montpelier, 29 Vt., 12–20; Milwaukee *v.* Milwaukee, 12 Wis., 93; State *v.* Rice, 35 id., 178; Bowdoinham *v.* Richmond, 6 Greenl., 112; Marshall County Court *v.* Calloway County Court, 2 Bush, 93; Richland County *v.* Lawrence County, 12 Ill., 1; Borough of Dunmore's Appeal, 52 Pa. St., 374.

[1] See Chapter XX.

public opinion. But in some other respects, and so far as the power of taxation may be effectual without being thus limited, it is in our opinion limited by some of the declared ends and principles of the fundamental laws. Among these political ends and principles, *equality*, as far as practicable, and security of property against irresponsible power, are eminently conspicuous in our state constitution. An exact equalization of the burdens of taxation is unattainable and utopian. But still there are well defined limits within which the practical equality of the constitution may be preserved, and which, therefore, should be deemed impassable barriers to legislative power. Taxation may not be universal, but it must be general and uniform. Hence, if a capitation tax be laid, none of the class of persons thus taxed can be constitutionally exempt upon any other ground than that of public service; and if a tax be laid on land, no appropriation land within the limits of the state can be constitutionally exempted, unless the owner be entitled to such immunity on the ground of public service. The legislature, in the plenitude of the taxing power, cannot have constitutional authority to exact from one citizen, or even from one county, the entire revenue for the whole commonwealth. Such an exaction by whatever name the legislature might choose to call it, would not be a tax, but would be, undoubtedly, the taking of private property for public use, and which could not be done constitutionally without the consent of the owner or owners, or without retribution of the value in money.

"The distinction between constitutional taxation and the taking of private property for public use by legislative will, may not be definable with perfect precision. But we are clearly of the opinion, that whenever the property of a citizen shall be taken from him by the sovereign will, and appropriated without his consent to the benefit of the public, the exaction should not be considered as a tax unless similar contributions be made by that public itself, or shall be exacted rather by the same public will, from such constituent members of the same community generally, as own the same kind of property.

"Taxation and representation go together. And representative responsibility is one of the chief conservative principles in our form of government. When taxes are levied, therefore, they must be imposed on the public in whose name and for whose benefit they are required, and to whom those who impose them are responsible. And although there may be a discrimination in the subjects of taxation, still persons in the same class, and property of the same kind, must generally be subjected alike to the same common burden. This alone is taxation according to our notion of constitutional taxation in Kentucky. And this idea, fortified by the spirit of our constitution, is, in our judgment, confirmed by so much of the twelfth section of the tenth article as declares, 'Nor shall any man's property be taken or applied to public use without the consent of his representatives, and without just compensation being previously made to him.'"[1]

Apportionment presumptively just. Whatever the rule of apportionment that is thus established by legislation, it is presumptively as just and equal in the opinion of the legislature as the circumstances would permit. It is not to be questioned for impolicy, and cannot be overthrown by showing that in particular instances it operates unjustly.[2]

[1] *Robertson*, Ch. J., in Lexington *v.* McQuillan's Heirs, 9 Dana, 513, 516. See also Youngblood *v.* Sexton, Sup. Ct., Mich., Oct. term, 1875.

[2] As to diversity in apportionment, see Anderson *v.* Kerns Draining Co., 14 Ind., 199; Layton *v.* New Orleans, 12 La. An. 515; Wallace *v.* Shelton, 14 id., 498. Taxation of merchants by sales is not unequal. Sacramento *v.* Crocker, 16 Cal., 119. That the courts can afford no relief for what is merely an unwise apportionment, see Tallman *v.* Butler County, 12 Iowa, 531.

That a license tax may be apportioned in reference to the size of the town in which the privilege is to be exercised, see State *v.* Schlier, 3 Heiskell, 281. A singular case of apportionment was that in Ould *v.* Richmond, 23 Grat., 464. The tax was a license tax on lawyers, who were classified in six classes by the finance committee of the common council, and the tax was different in the several classes. The tax was sustained against an objection to its inequality. The classification seems to have had in view the value of the privilege the license gave, the extent of the business, the income, etc.

In Berney *v.* The Tax Collector, 2 Bailey 654, 681, *O'Niell*, J., in speaking to objections which were made to a tax on bank dividends, says: "It may be that the tax on the dividends may operate unequally in that it is virtually a tax on money at interest, which is not generally subjected to taxation. This objection, however, is not addressed to the proper *forum;* it belongs to the legislature, not to the judiciary, to decide on its propriety and force. The legislature may select any property they please, to be taxed. If the tax is to operate generally on every citizen, who may own the property declared liable to it, it would be constitutional. If an act purports to exempt one class of

Apportionment imperative. But the requirement of apportionment is imperative.[1] And whenever the tax is a direct levy on property, there must be a taxing district. Given a tax and a district, then the sum demanded of any one person, or laid upon any one parcel of property, must have fixed relation to the whole tax, as well as to that demanded of every other person or laid upon every other piece of property. Without this the exactions of money for the public are mere forced contributions, and taxation will differ from the eminent domain only in this, that the latter demands the property of the citizen when necessity requires it, and on making compensation, while the former exacts it at discretion and without compensation.[2]

Of apportionment in general the following rules may perhaps safely be predicated:

1. Though the districts are established at the discretion of the legislature, the basis of apportionment which is fixed upon must be applied throughout the district.[3] There cannot be two rules of apportionment for the same tax in the same district; if there could be, there might be any number, and in effect there would be none at all, and every man might be assessed arbitrarily.[4]

citizens, owning property upon which it imposes a tax in the hands of others, it might be a discriminating tax, and unconstitutional." In Youngblood *v.* Sexton, Sup. Ct., Mich., Oct. term, 1875, a tax on business was objected to because the sum levied was uniform and did not discriminate according to the business done; but the court say, this is clearly within the power of the legislature, who must determine conclusively whether this method is or is not more just and politic than any other.

[1] Henry *v.* Chester, 15 Vt., 460; Tide Water Co., *v.* Coster, 18 N. J. Eq., 518, per *Beasley*, Ch. J.

[2] *Christiancy*, J., in Woodbridge *v.* Detroit, 8 Mich., 274, 309, following and approving Lexington *v.* McQuillan's Heirs, 9 Dana, 513. Compare State *v.* Portage, 12 Wis., 562; Weeks *v.* Milwaukee, 10 id., 242, 258; Chicago *v.* Larned, 34 Ill., 203; Creote *v.* Chicago, 56 id., 422; Weller *v.* St. Paul, 5 Minn., 95; Wilson *v.* Supervisors of Sutter, 47 Cal., 91.

[3] O'Kane *v.* Treat, 25 Ill., 557, 561; Fletcher *v.* Oliver, 25 Ark., 289.

[4] Tide Water Co. *v.* Coster, 18 N. J. Eq., 518. In Wilson *v.* Supervisors of Sutter, 47 Cal., 91, it was held incompetent to authorize the supervisors to remit a levee tax on part of the district. And yet it would have been competent originally to so bound the district as to exclude the part on which it was proposed to remit the tax.

That the basis of the apportionment is not necessarily the same for general

2. Though the apportionment must be general, a diversity in the methods of collection violates no rule of right, and is as much admissible as a diversity in police regulations. Indeed, this may, under some circumstances, be an absolute necessity. Thus, before the civil war had been brought to a termination, the taxes under internal revenue laws were laid by general rules, but special regulations were required for their enforcement in insurrectionary districts. So a land tax might be assumed by one state, while in another it might be necessary to have elaborate provisions for the salê of the property taxed.

3. It is no objection to a tax that the rule of apportionment which has been provided for it fails in some instances, or even in many instances, of enforcement. Evasions of duty are liable to

and local taxes, even when value is the standard, is illustrated by the case of Insurance Co. *v.* Baltimore, 23 Md., 296. It appears from that case that for the purposes of an apportionment of state taxation among the municipal divisions, the nominal capital of private coporations was assumed to be the value. But in imposing the tax on the corporations themselves, or their members, the actual value was ascertained. This method would be likely to lead to some inequalities in the distribution of state taxation between districts, but they could not be serious.

In this connection may be mentioned several cases in which classes of taxable property were attempted to be relieved from the apportionment. In one of these, the personal property was not to be taxed for the payment of a city debt, for the reason, probably, that the purpose for which the debt was contracted was supposed to have benefited specially the real estate. Gilman *v.* Sheboygan, 2 Black, 510.

Others were where in assessing the real estate for municipal taxes, the value of improvements was required to be excluded. In all these cases, the discrimination has been held to be beyond the constitutional power of the legislature. If the tax is to be assessed for a corporate purpose, it must be uniform as to persons and property. The burden must be imposed upon all the property within the limits to be taxed. Any other rule would utterly destroy the equality and uniformity contemplated by the constitution. If personal property or improvements may be exempted, with the same propriety and justice the law might compel one half the real estate within this district to sustain the whole burden. *Thornton*, J., in Primm *v.* Bellville, 59 Ill., 142, 144; Hale *v.* Kenosha, 29 Wis., 599. The tax in the Wisconsin case was for a railroad debt; in the other for a sewer. In Baltimore *v.* Hughes, 1 G. & J., 480, where a city council had authority to levy a tax for a public improvement on the district benefited thereby, it was held that if the ordinance providing for the tax showed the improvement to be for the general benefit of the city, and not of the particular district in which the tax was ordered, the tax was void.

occur under all laws; but an evasion by one individual cannot give another a legal right to be excused. If the law establishes a uniform rule, its validity cannot depend upon the certainty or uniformity of its enforcement.[1]

4. The apportionment of the tax is not to be extended to embrace persons or property outside the district. This is a matter of jurisdiction, and if there are any exceptions to the rule they must stand on very special and peculiar reasons.[2]

5. Although exemptions may be made, as has been previously shown, special and invidious discriminations against individuals are illegal.[3] This, so far as we know, is not disputed; and there is plausible ground for at least a question, whether the principle may not apply in some cases to the establishment of small districts for the construction of important public works; districts, the establishment of which, in view of the purpose for which the tax is to be laid, is equivalent to the singling out of a few persons for invidious discrimination. It has been held in one case that a statute was void which, as to certain portions of a city street, empowered the common council to cause it to be improved in a manner exceptionally expensive, at the cost of the abutting owners, and against their will, when as to all the other streets of the city the owners of the larger proportion of the frontage must petition for such an improvement before it could be ordered.[4] The statute was looked upon as an abuse of the legislative power to apportion tax-

[1] In United States *v.* Riley, 5 Blatch., 204, 209, *Shipman*, J., speaking of the internal revenue law, says: "The law is uniform, and thereby conforms to the constitution. Its validity does not depend on the celerity or uniformity with which it can be executed in some disturbed districts of the country. Tax laws, both state and national, are required to be uniform. This is an elementary principle of legislation, resting upon the solid foundation of justice. But it is a novel doctrine that a law, uniform in its provisions, can be annulled by the refusal of a portion of those on whom it is designed to operate to comply with its provisions. If this notion were to prevail, civil commotion or foreign invasion within a small district of the country would paralyze the government and repeal the fundamental law upon which its existence depends."

[2] See *ante*, pp. 14, 42.

[3] The rule of uniformity applies to wharf and dockage charges laid on the commerce of a city. People *v.* S. Fr., etc., Railroad Co., 35 Cal., 606.

[4] Howell *v.* Bristol, 8 Bush, 493, 497. Compare Covington *v.* Casey, 3 id., 698; Washington Avenue, 69 Penn. St., 352.

es; as perhaps it was. But the case must be very clear to warrant the court in holding that the legislature, in acting upon a subject within its admitted authority, has deprived itself of power by abusing it.[1]

[1] In Arbegust *v.* Louisville, 2 Bush, 271, 275, *Williams*, J., has the following remarks regarding the change of taxing districts by extension of city boundaries: "When, in the judgment of the legislature, the interest of a suburban population demands local regulations, and the peace, tranquillity and order of the public indicates that such is necessary, we cannot doubt its constitutional power to so enact, nor question its power to tax, for such purposes, the real as well as the personal estate of the people, nor the large as well as the small lots included therein; for it is more consonant with the entire genius, equality and justice of our constitution and laws, that each should bear the burdens of that government which protects his person and property according to the worth of his estate, than to discriminate against the small in favor of the large property holders. But whatever may be said of the intrinsic justice of such a measure, there is no power in the courts to control this, when the taxing power is conferred in good faith to uphold local government and give police regulations to the population, and not merely to embrace taxable property for revenue purposes in order to lighten the burdens of others."

CHAPTER VIII.

OFFICIAL ACTION IN MATTERS OF TAXATION.

Necessity for official action. Taxation is an act of government. Government can only perform its functions by means of officers, and must make all its demands upon its citizens through the medium of official action. However just it may be, that an individual, in any condition or under any specified circumstances, should contribute a part of his means to government revenues, there is no lawful method of compelling him to do so, except through the compulsion of official process. No individual as such, or by virtue of his citizenship, can compel another to perform his duty to the state. He must come clothed with the authority of the state for the purpose, or, in contemplation of law, he comes as a trespasser, whose lawless intrusion may rightfully be resisted and repelled.

Officers, who are. An office is defined to be a public charge or employment, and he who performs the duties of that office is an officer.[1] There are legislative, executive and judicial officers, with duties pertaining to their respective departments of the government, and there are also inferior officers, commonly designated ministerial, whose duty it is to execute mandates lawfully directed to them by superiors, whether of one department or of another.[2] The proceedings in tax cases are entrusted by the law in part to officers who perform mere ministerial duties, and in part are confided to those who, though not belonging to the judicial department, have functions which in a certain sense are judicial.

Officers de facto. It is sometimes found that the person who is performing the duties of an office is not the one to whom the

[1] *Marshall*, Ch. J., United States *v.* Maurice, 2 Brock., 96, 102. Bouvier's definition of an officer is "one who is lawfully invested with an office;" which seems to exclude what are known as officers *de facto*.

[2] Bouvier Dic., Tit., Officers; People *v.* The Governor, 29 Mich., 320.

law, if properly followed, would have confided it. This may happen from an uncertainty regarding the method by which the officer should be chosen, a dispute of fact concerning the result of the election which has been held, or from many other causes. If in any such case, a person claiming to be chosén solves the doubt in his own favor, and takes possession of the office, and if the public acquiesce in his assumption, he then performs the duties of the office, and comes within the definition which has been given of an officer. But while he is an officer in fact, if he is not rightfully such, he may at any time be ousted of his position by judicial proceedings, instituted in behalf of the state, at the instance of the public prosecutor. Perhaps also the law of the state will allow the person rightfully entitled, and who, by the wrongful possession, is excluded from the office, to institute a proceeding for the purpose on his own behalf. From what has been said, it will be seen that there may therefore be officers *de jure* and officers *de facto.* An officer *de jure* is one who not only is invested with the office, but who has been lawfully appointed or chosen, and therefore has a right to retain the office and receive its perquisites and emoluments. An officer *de facto* is defined to be one who has the reputation of being the officer he assumes to be, and yet is not a good officer in point of law.[1] He comes in by claim and color of right, or he exercises the office with such circumstances of acquiescence on the part of the public, as at least afford a strong presumption of right, but by reason of some defect in his title, or of some informality, omission or want of qualification, or by reason of the expiration of his term of service, he is unable to maintain his possession, when called upon by the government to show by what title he holds it.[2] It is immaterial in what the defect consists, or whether the claim is in good faith or merely colorable. The public acquiescence and reputation attach certain important consequences

[1] Parker *v.* Kett, 1 Ld. Raym., 658, per *Holt*, Ch. J.; King *v.* Corp. of Bedford Level, 6 East, 356, 368, per *Ellenborough*, Ch. J.; Tucker *v.* Aiken, 7 N. H., 113, 140; Davis *v.* Police Jury, 1 La. An., 288; Ray *v.* Murdock, 36 Miss., 692. "An officer *de facto* is one who exercises the duties of an office under color of appointment or election to that office." *Storrs*, J., in Plymouth *v.* Painter, 17 Conn., 585, 588. To the same effect is Brown *v.* Lunt, 37 Me.. 423, 438; Strang ex parte, 21 Ohio, N. S., 610.

[2] Blackwell on Tax Titles, 92-3; Wilcox *v.* Smith, 5 Wend., 231.

to his occupation of the office, which the interest of the state does not permit to depend upon his own motives or the degree of plausibility which attaches to his claim.[1]

Usurpers. It is possible also that one may attempt to per-

[1] In several recent cases, where persons have been performing official functions under assumed legislative authority which proved to be unconstitutional, the position has been taken, that one who acts as an officer under legislation of this nature, could not be an officer *de facto*, because the legislation was no law and consequently could give no color of right. It has also been insisted, that an officer *de facto* always is one who comes in by color of appointment or election by the authority having competent power to appoint or elect; so that, if any office is elective, it matters not that the governor claims and exercises the right to appoint, and that the appointee is enabled by public acquiescence to act: the appointment being without authority of law, the appointee is a mere usurper. The subject is very carefully considered in State *v.* Carroll, 38 Conn., 449, 471; S. C., 9 Am. Rep., 409, where the authorities are reviewed at length. The conclusions are summarized by *Butler*, Ch. J., as follows: "An officer *de facto* is one whose acts, though not those of a lawful officer, the law upon principles of policy and justice will hold valid, so far as they involve the interests of the public and of third persons, where the duties of the office were exercised: 1. Without a known appointment or election, but under such circumstances of reputation or acquiescence, as were calculated to induce people, without inquiry, to submit to or invoke his action, supposing him to be the officer he assumed to be. 2. Under color of a known and valid appointment or election, but where the officer has failed to conform to some precedent requirement or condition, as to take an oath, give a bond, or the like. 3. Under color of a known election or appointment, void because the officer was not elegible, or because there was a want of power in the electing or appointing body, or by reason of some defect or irregularity in its exercise; such ineligibility, want of power or defect being unknown to the public. 4. Under color of an election or appointment by or pursuant to a public unconstitutional law, before the same is adjudged to be such." In Commonwealth *v.* McCombs, 56 Penn. St., 436, substantially the same conclusion was reached. So it was also in Ex parte Strang, 21 Ohio, N. S., 610, where the legislature, in disregard of a requirement of the constitution, had made an appointment. The following cases, the most of which are referred to in State *v.* Carroll, support the same views; O'Brian *v.* Knivan, Cro. Jac., 552; Harris *v.* Jays, Cro. Eliz., 699; Parker *v.* Kett, 1 Ld. Raym., 658; Fowler *v.* Beebe, 9 Mass., 231; Taylor *v.* Skrine, 3 Brev., 516; Wilcox *v.* Smith, 5 Wend., 231; Parker *v.* Baker, 8 Paige, 428; People *v.* Kane, 23 Wend., 414; People *v.* White, 24 id., 520; Burke *v.* Elliott, 4 Ired., 355; Gilliam *v.* Reddick, 4 id., 368; Brown *v.* Lunt, 37 Me., 423, 428; State *v.* Bloom, 17 Wis., 521; People *v.* Bangs, 24 Ill., 184; Clark *v.* Commonwealth, 29 Penn. St., 129; Mallett *v.* Uncle Sam Co., 1 Nev., 188; Kimball *v.* Alcorn, 45 Miss., 151; Cocke *v.* Halsey, 16 Pet., 71; Gibb *v.* Washington, 1 McAll., 430; Vaccari *v.* Maxwell, 3 Blatch., 368.

form the duties of an office, who is neither chosen to do so, pursuant to law, nor is supported by the public acquiescence. Such a person cannot acquire the reputation of being the officer he assumes to be; he is a mere usurper, and his acts are wholly void for all purposes. No one is under obligation to recognize his claim to the office, and whoever does so must take upon himself the consequences. It is of high importance that the encouragement of such claims should not be allowed to bring disorder and insecurity into public affairs.[1]

Questioning title of officer de facto. The case of an officer *de facto* is different. To deny validity to his acts would lead to insecurity in both public and private affairs. It would compel those having occasion to transact business with a public officer, before they could put faith in his official acts, to go into a careful examination of all the evidences of his title, and of the provisions of law bearing upon them, in order to determine whether the assumption of official character is warranted by law, and is supported by a compliance with the necessary formalities. "It would constitute every citizen a judge of official titles. He must look to the constitution to see that the officer was eligible to an election or appointment; to the statute to ascertain when, where and how the election or appointment is required to be made, and to the poll books and archives of the state for the purpose of ascertaining the facts; and then determine at his peril the mixed question of law and fact involved in the ascertainment of official character."[2] The mere statement of the case is sufficient to show that such a requirement would in the highest degree be unjust to the private citizen, and detrimental to public interests. But to treat the official acts of a *de facto* incumbent as void would be equally

[1] See Plymouth *v.* Painter, 17 Conn., 585, 593; Peck *v.* Holcombe, 3 Port., 329; Keeler *v.* Newbern, 1 Phil., N. C., 505; Munson *v.* Minor, 53 Ill., 594. In Birch *v.* Fisher, 13 S. & R., 208, an assessment made by persons not shown to have been either elected or sworn, held to be by "mere intruders who came in without color of authority." An officer who holds over in good faith, though without warrant of law, is not a usurper. Kreidler *v.* State, 24 Ohio, N. S., 22. Compare State *v.* McFarland, 25 La. An., 547. To support oue's acts as those of an officer *de facto*, they must have been done under color of an office whose duties have been discharged by him. Bailey *v.* Fisher, 38 Iowa, 229.

[2] Blackwell on Tax Titles, 94.

unjust to him. When the controversy should arise collaterally, as commonly it must, the officer himself would not be a party to the record, and would have no opportunity and no privilege of meeting the issue raised, although the decision might as effectually determine his right to act, as if he had been proceeded against directly by the appropriate process of *quo warranto*. "This would be judging a man unheard, contrary to the principles of natural justice and the policy of the law." Until he is removed by proceedings directly instituted for the purpose, and in which he is permitted to be heard, "he holds the office by the sufferance of the state, and the silence of the government is construed by the courts as a ratification of his acts, which is equivalent to a precedent authority. When the government acquiesce in the acts of such an officer, third persons ought not to be permitted to question them."[1] When, however, the officer himself attempts to build up a right in his own favor, it is not unreasonable to require him to defend his right, as he would be compelled to do if he should assert title to any article of property as against the true owner. His suit for the legal fees may therefore be successfully resisted, as may any attempt by him to enforce official process by the aid of the law. These are cases in which he is a party, and is properly called upon to demonstrate his title. Besides, if citizens were not permitted to resist his official claims in such proceedings, their acquiescence in them, until the state itself should be able to bring to a conclusion the formal proceedings to try the title, would be only an enforced acquiescence, and could not justly support a title to an office by reputation. The most that public policy could require in such cases would be that his *de facto* incumbency should be evidence of a right *prima facie* in his favor, but leaving the actual right subject to be disproved.[2] And if he is sued for

[1] Blackwell on Tax Titles, 94; Bucknam *v.* Ruggles, 15 Mass., 180. See People *v.* Lothrop, 24 Mich., 235. Proceedings of a common council in levying a tax cannot be contested on the ground that by a change in the charter a portion of the seats were vacated, if the members continued *de facto* to act. Scoville *v.* Cleveland, 1 Ohio, N. S., 126.

[2] Kent *v.* Atlantic Delaine Co., 8 R. I., 305, where it was held that one who sues as collector to recover a tax gives sufficient *prima facie* evidence of his authority if he shows he has acted as such officer in regard to that tax; but that this *prima facie* case is open to rebuttal. See also Colton *v.* Beardsley 38 Barb., 29; Auditors of Wayne *v.* Benoit, 20 Mich., 176; Pejepscott Propri-

any act which he can only justify as an officer, he is put to the proof that he was duly elected or appointed, and that any conditions precedent have been complied with.[1]

Validity of acts of officers de facto. On the other hand, the public, by whose acquiescence the *de facto* officer has been permitted to act, and individuals who have transacted official business with him, have a right to rely upon the validity of that which has been done by him, to the same extent precisely as if the same acts had been performed in the same way by an *officer de jure.* When such acts come collaterally in question, neither the public, that has thus acquiesced, nor individual citizens, are permitted to question them. They are as valid, to all intents and purposes, as if the title to the office had been unquestionable. This is the general rule, as it has been settled on grounds of public policy from the time of the year books.[2]

etors *v.* Ransom, 14 Mass., 145. It was decided in Universalist Society *v.* Leach, 35 Vt., 108, that if an ineligible person is chosen sole prudential committee of a school district, his assessment of a tax voted by the district is void.

[1] Lightly *v.* Clouston, 1 Taunt., 113; Riddle *v.* Bedford, 7 S. & R., 386, 392; Fetterman *v.* Hopkins, 5 Watts, 539; Pike *v.* Hanson, 9 N. H., 491; Colburn *v.* Ellis, 5 Mass., 427; Fowler *v.* Beebe, 9 id., 231, 234; Sprague *v.* Bailey, 19 Pick., 436; Patterson *v.* Miller, 2 Met., Ky., 493; People *v.* Hopson, 1 Denio, 574, 579; Greene *v.* Burke, 23 Wend., 488, 492; Schlencker *v.* Risley, 3 Scam., 483; Blake *v.* Sturtevant, 12 N. H., 567; Cummings *v.* Clark, 15 Vt., 653; Olney *v.* Pearce, 1 R. I., 292; Samis *v.* King, 40 Conn., 298, 310; Venable *v.* Curd, 2 Head, 582. In First Parish in Sherbourne *v.* Fiske, it is said that if parish assessors fail to take the oath of office, a tax assessed by them would be illegal and might be recovered back. 8 Cush., 264. But a tax which has been paid cannot be recovered back on the ground that the collector *de facto* had never been legally elected and sworn. Williams *v.* School District 21 Pick., 75. It is not intended to assert here that in every case in which the state might oust an officer by *quo warranto* an individual could also take advantage of a defect in his title. The inquiry on behalf of the state may and does go beyond that which individuals may institute. A *prima facie* right is sufficient as against individuals, but only an indefeasible right as against the state. As an illustration of what is meant, the case of one holding a legal certificate of election may be taken: if a lawful election was held, the certificate may conclude private parties, but the government would be at liberty to go beyond it and show that the election was accomplished by illegal votes, or that for any other reason the *prima facie* case was defective. See the discussion in Auditors of Wayne *v.* Benoit, 20 Mich., 176.

[2] "The law favors the acts of one in a reputed authority, and the inferior

Officers de facto in tax cases. It remains to be seen whether these general principles are applicable in tax cases. It has sometimes been urged that in tax proceedings there was no proper room for the application of the doctrine, which is applied in other cases in support of action by officers *de facto*; that the proceedings are summary and for the most part *ex parte*; that they may deprive the owner of his freehold by means of process which usually and perhaps necessarily is somewhat arbitrary, and that he is therefore entitled of right to have all the security, which the law has intended he should have; in the character and standing of an officer duly and properly chosen for the particular duty; in

shall never inquire if his authority is lawful." Vin. Abr., tit. "Officer," G., 3. See Bac. Abr., "Offices and Officers," B.; People *v.* Collins, 7 Johns., 549, 551; McInstry *v.* Tanner, 9 id., 135; People *v.* Dean, 3 Wend., 438; Wilcox *v.* Smith, 5 id., 231, 234; Parker *v.* Baker, 8 Paige, 429; People *v.* Kane, 23 Wend., 414; People *v.* White, 24 id., 520; Fowler *v.* Beebe, 9 Mass., 231; Commonwealth *v.* Fowler, 10 id., 290; Nason *v.* Dillingham, 15 id., 170; Bucknam *v.* Ruggles, id., 180; Gilmore *v.* Holt, 4 Pick., 257; Williams *v.* School District, 21 id., 75; Blackstone *v.* Taft, 4 Gray, 250; Burke *v.* Elliott, 4 Ired., 355; Gilliam *v.* Reddick, id., 368; Farmers & Merchants' Bank *v.* Chester, 6 Humph., 458; Beard *v.* Cameron, 3 Murph., 181; Brush *v.* Cook, Brayt., 89; Taylor *v.* Skrine, 3 Brev., 516; Plymouth *v.* Painter, 17 Conn., 585; Douglass *v.* Wickwire, 19 id., 489; State *v.* Carroll, 38 id., 449; Samis *v.* King, 40 id., 298; McGregor *v.* Balch, 14 Vt., 428; Downer *v.* Woodbury, 19 id., 329; Lyon *v.* State Bank, 1 Stew., 442; Barret *v.* Reed, 2 Ohio, 409; Johnson *v.* Steadman, 3 id., 94, 96; Eldred *v.* Sexton, 5 id., 216; Ex parte Strang, 21 Ohio, N. S., 610; Justices of Jefferson *v.* Clark, 1 T. B. Monr., 82, 86; Rice *v.* Commonwealth, 3 Bush, 14; Prickett *v.* People, 1 Gilm., 525, 529; Keyser *v.* McKissam, 2 Rawle, 139; Riddle *v.* Bedford County, 7 S. & R., 386, 392; Baird *v.* Bank of Washington, 11 id., 411; Neal *v.* Overseers, 5 Watts, 538; McKim *v.* Somers, 1 Penrose & Watts, 297; Commonwealth *v.* McCombs, 56 Penn. St., 436; Gregg *v.* Jamison, 55 id., 468; Cooper *v.* Moore, 4 Miss., 386; Kimball *v.* Alcorn, 45 id., 145; Cabot *v.* Given, 45 Me., 144; Jones *v.* Gibson, 1 N. H., 266; Moore *v.* Graves, 3 id., 408; Morse *v.* Calley, 5 id., 222; State *v.* Tolan, 33 N. J., 195; Leach *v.* Cassidy, 23 Ind., 449; McCormick *v.* Fitch, 14 Minn., 252; Auditors of Wayne County *v.* Benoit, 20 Mich., 176; Ex parte Bollman, 4 Cranch, 75; Sawyer *v.* Steele, 3 Wash. C. C., 464; Willink *v.* Miles, Pet. C. C., 188; Ronkendorf *v.* Taylor, 4 Pet., 349; Lawrence *v.* Sherman, 2 McLean, 488; United States *v.* Bachelder, 2 Gall., 15.

There is a discussion in McNutt *v.* Lancaster, 9 S. & M., 570, of the question whether, where the statute declared that the acts of one who should presume to execute the duties of an office, before taking the official oath, should be "absolutely void," could have any validity as those of an officer *de facto*. No decision was reached.

the official oath of such officer, when one is required by law; in the official bond if one is made necessary; and indeed such security as would be afforded by a strict compliance with every provision which has been made by the revenue laws for the protection of taxpayers.[1] The reasons are plausible, but they are not very conclusive. Indeed if official action of officers *de facto* in judicial positions can be sustained, as it often has been,[2] though not only property but also liberty may depend upon it, it is difficult to suggest any distinguishing reason to remove tax cases from the application of the same principle. The clear and very strong preponderance of authority is, that the general policy of the law requires the acts of officers *de facto* to be sustained in tax cases, under the same circumstances and on the same imperative reasons that sustain them in others.[3]

Estoppel against intruders who have acted. The rule which supports official action, may perhaps in some cases be carried with propriety even farther than is above stated. If one has assumed to act as an officer under revenue laws, and has made collections, as such, he cannot be permitted, when the government calls upon him for an accounting, to turn about and say that he was

[1] Cardigan *v.* Page, 6 N. H., 182; Payson *v.* Hall, 30 Me., 319; Coite *v.* Wells, 2 Vt., 318; Isaacs *v.* Wiley, 12 id., 674; People *v.* Hastings, 29 Cal., 449. Some of the cases which may seem to support this view are properly to be referred to some other principle. They turn often upon the question, whether the statute is mandatory in requiring that something should be done, which has been omitted, or whether the person who has assumed to act as officer held *de facto* the particular office to which the duty pertained; or some other question foreign to the precise point now under discussion.

[2] Lord Dacre's Case, 1 Leon., 288; Margate Pier *v.* Hannam, 3 B. & Ald., 266; Wilcox *v.* Smith, 5 Wend., 231; People *v.* Kane, 23 id., 414; People *v.* White, 24 id., 520; Brown *v.* Lunt, 37 Me., 423; Taylor *v.* Skrines, 3 Brev., 516; Mallett *v.* Uncle Sam Co., 1 Nev., 188; Clark *v.* Commonwealth, 29 Penn. St., 129; Laver *v.* McGlachlin, 28 Wis., 364; In re Griffin, 2 Am. Law Times, 93.

[3] Tucker *v.* Aiken, 7 N. H., 113; Smith *v.* Messer, 17 id., 420; Hall *v.* Cushing, 2 Greenl., 218; Adams *v.* Jackson, 2 Aiken, 145; Spear *v.* Ditty, 8 Vt., 419; Downer *v.* Woodbury, 19 id., 329; Sheldon *v.* Coates, 10 Ohio, 278; Washington *v.* Miller, 14 Iowa, 584; Allen *v.* Armstrong, 16 id., 515; Scott *v.* Watkins, 22 Ark., 556; Twombly *v.* Kimbrough, 24 id., 459, 474; Ronkendorf *v.* Taylor, 4 Pet., 349; Ray *v.* Murdock, 36 Miss., 692; Jones *v.* Scanland, 6 Humph., 195.

never elected or appointed, but has acted as a mere usurper without right, and that the proper remedy of the government was to have resisted his intrusion, or caused his ouster. On every principle of right and justice he is precluded from denying his official character under such circumstances.[1] Such a person has a right at any time to refuse to proceed farther in official action, and he cannot be held responsible as for a neglect of duty in such refusal; but it is doubtful if one under any circumstances, even though he be a mere usurper, who has collected revenue for the government under claim of right, can be permitted to protect himself against an accounting, by showing that he was an intruder without any just pretense to the place. To the extent that he has acted, the government may properly adopt his agency, and require him to give to taxpayers, who have recognized his authority, the benefit of their payments.[2]

[1] Johnston *v.* Wilson, 2 N. H., 202, 206; Horn *v.* Whittaker, 6 id., 88; Sandwich *v.* Fish, 2 Gray, 298, 301; Barrington *v.* Austin, 8 id., 444; Wendell *v.* Fleming, id., 613; Cheshire *v.* Howland, 13 id., 321; Williamstown *v.* Willis, 15 id., 427; Borden *v.* Houston, 2 Texas, 594; Billingsley *v.* State, 14 Md., 369. In Jones *v.* Scanland, 6 Humph., 195, it appeared that a defaulter had been chosen sheriff. By law such a choice was absolutely void. He nevertheless gave bond and acted in the collection of taxes. On motion, judgment was entered on his official bond for failure to pay over. *Reese*, J.: "The election of sheriff was void, and he did not thereby become sheriff *de jure;* but thus intruding himself into office, and assuming its duties, he became sheriff *de facto*, and those who voluntarily bound themselves for the faithful performance of his duties cannot absolve themselves from their obligation, by insisting that he was no sheriff. They will be held to their undertaking, till the proper public authority has produced his amotion from the office which he in point of fact fills."

[2] See United States *v.* Maurice, 2 Brock., 96; Bell *v.* Railroad Co., 4 Wall., 598; State *v.* Cunningham, 8 Blackf., 339; Church *v.* Sterling, 16 Conn., 387; Commonwealth *v.* Philadelphia, 27 Penn. St., 497; Wentworth *v.* Gove, 45 N. H., 160; Trescott *v.* Moan, 50 Me., 347. A Sheriff who has collected taxes without having the proper list is nevertheless liable to account. The Governor *v.* Montgomery, 2 Swan, 613. Cases of sale of the office of collector and the effect thereof are found in Meredith *v.* Ladd, 2 N. H., 517; Carleton *v.* Whitcher, 5 id., 196; Tucker *v.* Aiken, 7 id., 113; Alvord *v.* Collin, 20 Pick., 418; Howard *v.* Proctor, 7 Gray, 128; Spencer *v.* Jones, 6 id., 502. Where the fact of an official oath is in question it may be shown by parol that the oath was taken, though the law requires a record. Briggs *v.* Murdock, 13 Pick., 305; Pease *v.* Smith, 24 id., 122; Hall *v.* Cushing, 2 Greenl., 218; and see

Joint official action. In some cases, under the tax laws, official action is required to be taken by a board composed of several persons. It may then appear that there has been an impossibility to secure concurrence, or that, through neglect or inadvertence, less than the whole board has acted; and it becomes necessary to determine whether, in any such case, the action can be supported. The rules of law on this subject are well settled. The law contemplates, that all the members of a board, who are to exercise a joint public authority, shall meet to consider the subject of their authority, and that the whole board shall have the benefit of the judgment and advice of each of the members. In revenue cases, especially, and in others in which the official action may eventuate in divesting the citizen of his estate, it is to be supposed the law intended that this joint deliberation and action should be for the benefit of the citizen also. If, therefore, no such meeting is held, and no opportunity had for joint consultation and action, the joint authority is not well executed, even though all acting separately may have signed such a document as would have been sufficient, were it the result of a proper meeting. Such action is not the action of the board, but of individuals. It is always presumable that it might have been different had there been a meeting and comparison of views, such as the law contemplated. At any rate, there can be no conclusive or satisfactory evidence of what would have been the joint judgment, when it has never been exercised; and the members of the board have no discretion to substitute individual action when the law has required the action of the organized body.[1] No custom of the locality, or long continued practice can legalize the putting aside of this rule of law. The members of the board are officers of law, and must obey the rules that presumably for beneficial

Scott *v.* Watkins, 22 Ark., 566. And as to the right of a collector to contest the validity of a tax he has collected, see People *v.* Brown, 55 N. Y., 180.

[1] See Downing *v.* Rugar, 21 Wend., 178, 182, per *Cowen*, J.; Lee *v.* Parry, 4 Denio, 125; Powell *v.* Tuttle, 3 N. Y., 396; People *v.* Supervisors of Chenango, 11 id., 563; Fuller *v.* Gould, 20 Vt., 643.

If only two of a board of three qualify and act, there is no board, and the action is void. Schenck *v.* Peay, 1 Dill., 267; S. C., 1 Woolw., 175. So, if only two of the three are chosen, the two cannot act. Williamsburg *v.* Lord, 51 Me. 599. And see Downing *v.* Rugar, 21 Wend., 178, 182.

purposes, have been prescribed for them.[1] But the law does not require impossibility, and it may be found impossible for the members to agree in joint action. In such a case, it is to be presumed the intent was, that the law should not fail of execution, but that the action of the majority should be sufficient. And, where a majority have acted, the legal intendment in favor of the correctness of official action, requires us to conclude that such action is the result of due meeting and consultation, or at least of a meeting duly called, at which all had the opportunity to attend, and a majority did attend. It is therefore *prima facie* valid, though the legal presumption in its favor may be overcome by evidence that no such meeting was called or had.[2]

[1] In Middleton *v.* Berlin, 18 Conn., 189, a tax list was signed by one only of a board of five assessors. An attempt was made to support it by showing a usage of the town to divide the town into districts, in each of which one of the assessors acted separately; but the court said "assessors are the officers of the law, and must obey the law, and no direction of the town, or long continued usage can justify a departure from the law." See People *v.* Supervisors of Chenango, 11 N. Y., 563. In Kinney *v.* Doe, 8 Blackf., 350, the list was made by the official lister, but it was not shown that two householders acted with him as the law required, and it was held void.

[2] In support of the general principle, that the action of a majority is sufficient, see Wadham College, Cowp., 377; Grindley *v.* Barker, 1 B. & P., 236; The King *v.* Beeston, 3 T. R., 592; Withnell *v.* Gartham, 6 id., 388; Cooley *v.* O'Conner, 12 Wall., 391, 398; Commonwealth *v.* Canal Commissioners, 9 Watts, 466, 471; Jewett *v.* Alton, 7 N. H., 253; Babcock *v.* Lamb, 1 Cow., 238; Rogers, ex parte, 7 id., 526; McCoy *v.* Curtice, 9 Wend., 17, 19; Downing *v.* Rugar, 21 id., 178; Crocker *v.* Crane, id., 211, 218; Doughty *v.* Hope, 3 Denio, 594; Bank of Chenango *v.* Brown, 26 N. Y., 467; Caldwell *v.* Harrison, 11 Ala., 755; Soens *v.* Racine, 10 Wis., 271; Sprague *v.* Bailey, 19 Pick., 436; Williams *v.* School District, 21 id., 75; Fire District *v.* County Commissioners, 108 Mass., 142; People *v.* Coghill, 47 Cal., 361; Johnson *v.* Goodridge, 15 Me., 29; Bangor *v.* Lancey, 21 id., 472; Lowe *v.* Weld, 52 id., 588.

This is on the ground that all are presumed to have met and consulted, a presumption that may be overcome by proof. Doughty *v.* Hope, 3 Denio, 594, 598, per *Bronson*, J.; Ex parte Baltimore Turnpike Co., 5 Binn., 481; Blackwell on Tax Titles, 111. Under the decisions which are above cited, it is difficult to understand how a case like Howard *v.* Proctor, 7 Gray, 128, can be supported. There, one who was selectman and also assessor, was chosen collector, and it was decided that the choice was valid, though his bond was to be approved by the selectmen, and the assessors, in certain cases, had authority to remove him. The decision was put on the ground that these boards might act by majorities; but the very nature of the action was such as to preclude one member of the board from consultation and action with the

Official returns and certificates. It is generally held that the returns and certificates required of an officer in the performance of official duty are to be taken, in the proceeding in which they are made, as of unquestionable verity. They are not to be attacked, and proof entered into in a collateral proceeding, to which the officer is not a party, to show that they are false.[1]

rest, or if he could act, made him interested adversely to the public. See also Fox *v.* Fox, 24 Ohio (N. S.), 335. Kinyon *v.* Duchene, 21 Mich., 498, is *contra.*

Where a drainage law provided that the commissioners shall jointly view and assess, etc., this requires the presence of all, both in viewing and assessing. People *v.* Coghill, 47 Cal., 361. Compare Palmer *v.* Doney, 2 Johns. Cas., 346.

[1] Com. Dig. Return, G.; Flud *v.* Pennington, Cro. Eliz., 872; Harrington *v.* Taylor, 17 East, 378; Rex *v.* Elkins, 4 Burr., 2129; Andrews *v.* Linton, 1 Salk., 265; Wheeler *v.* Lampman, 14 Johns., 481, 482; Putnam *v.* Man, 3 Wend., 202, Case *v.* Redfield, 7 id., 398; Boomer *v.* Laine, 10 id., 525; Baker *v.* McDuffie, 23 id., 289; Sperling *v.* Levy, 1 Daly, 95, 98; McArthur *v.* Pease, 46 Barb., 423; Livermore *v.* Bagley, 3 Mass., 487, 512; Slayton *v.* Chester, 4 id., 478; Gardner *v.* Hosmer, 6 id., 324, 327; Bott *v.* Burnell, 9 id., 96; Estabrook *v.* Hapgood, 10 id., 313, 314; Bott *v.* Burnell, 11 id., 163; Saxton *v.* Nimms, 14 id., 313, 320; Bean *v.* Parker, 17 id., 591, 601; Lawrence *v.* Pond, id., 433; Thayer *v.* Stearns, 1 Pick., 109, 112; Whittaker *v.* Sumner, 7 id., 551, 555; Boynton *v.* Willard, 10 id., 165, 169; Bruce *v.* Holden, 21 id., 187, 189: Pullen *v.* Haynes, 11 Gray, 379; Campbell *v.* Webster, 15 Gray, 28; McGough *v.* Wellington, 6 Allen, 505; Hathaway *v.* Phelps, 2 Aiken, 84; Stevens *v.* Brown, 3 Vt., 420; Eastman *v.* Curtis, 4 id., 616; Barret *v.* Copeland, 18 id., 67, 69; White River Bank *v.* Downer, 29 id., 332; Lewis *v.* Blair, 1 N. H., 68; Whiting *v.* Bradley, 2 id., 79, 81; Sias *v.* Badger, 6 id., 393; Brown *v.* Davis, 9 id., 76; Angier *v.* Ash, 26 id., 99; Clough *v.* Monroe, 34 id., 381; Ladd *v.* Wiggins, 35 id., 421; Bolles *v.* Bowen, 45 id., 124; Morse *v.* Smith, 47 id., 474; Phillips *v.* Elwell, 14 Ohio St., 240; Eastman *v.* Bennett, 6 Wis., 232; Carr *v.* Commercial Bank, 16 id., 50; Castner *v.* Symonds, 1 Minn., 427; Tullis *v.* Brawley, 3 id., 277; Folsom *v.* Carli, 5 id., 333; Delenger *v.* Higgins, 26 Mo., 180; McDonald *v.* Leewright, 31 id., 29; Reeves *v.* Reeves, 33 id., 28; Stewart *v.* Stringer, 44 id., 400; Washington, etc., Co. *v.* Kinnear, 1 Wash. Ter., 110; Tillman *v.* Davis, 28 Ga., 494; Brown *v.* Way, 28 id., 531; Allender *v.* Riston, 2 Gill. & J., 86; Tribble *v.* Frame, 3 Monr., 51; Caldwells *v.* Harlan, 3 id., 349, 351; McConnel *v.* Bowdry's Heirs, 4 id., 392; Smith *v.* Hornback, 3 A K. Marsh, 378, 392, 393; Small *v.* Hagden, 1 Litt., 16, 17; Trigg *v.* Lewis' Ex'rs, 3 id., 129, 132; Hunter *v.* Kirk, 4 Hawks, 277; Stinson *v.* Snow, 1 Fairf., 263; Wilson *v.* Hurst's Ex'rs, 1 Pet. (C. C.), 441; Hawks *v.* Baldwin, Brayt., 85; Welsh *v.* Bell, 32 Penn. St., 12; Paxon's Appeal, 49 id., 195; Hill *v.* Grant, 49 id., 200; Rice *v.* Groff, 58 id., 116; Ayres *v.* Duprey, 27 Texas, 593; Angell *v.* Bowler, 3 R. I., 77; Castner *v.* Styer, 23 N. J., 236; State *v.* Clerk of Bergen, 25 id., 209; Martin *v.* Barney, 20 Ala., 369; Crow *v.* Hudson, 21 id., 560; Hinckley *v.* Buchanan, 5 Cal., 53.

If the party is injured by a false return, he has his remedy by action against the officer.[1]

In general it is believed that these rules have been held to be applicable in tax cases.[2]

[1] Wheeler *v.* Lampman, 14 Johns., 481; Putnam *v.* Man, 3 Wend., 202; Case *v.* Redfield, 7 id., 398; Baker *v.* McDuffie, 23 id., 289; McArthur *v.* Pease, 46 Barb., 423; Livermore *v.* Bagley, 3 Mass., 487, 512; Slayton *v.* Chester, 4 id., 478; Gardner *v.* Hosmer, 6 id., 324, 327; Whitaker *v.* Sumner, 7 Pick., 551; Boynton *v.* Willard, 10 id., 165, 169; Bruce *v.* Holden, 21 id., 187, 189; Pullen *v.* Haynes, 11 Gray, 379; Campbell *v.* Webster, 15 id., 28; McGough *v.* Wellington, 6 Allen, 505; Clough *v.* Monroe, 34 N. H., 381; Lewis *v.* Blair, 1 id., 68; Sias *v.* Badger, 6 id., 393; Angier *v.* Ash, 26 id., 99; Bolles *v.* Bowen, 45 id., 124; Tomlinson *v.* Long, 8 Jones L. 469; Albright *v.* Tapscott, 8 id., 473; McBee *v.* State, 1 Meigs, 122; Castner *v.* Symonds, 1 Minn., 427; Folsom *v.* Carli, 5 id., 333; Goodal *v.* Stuart, 2 Hen. & Munf., 105, 112; Trigg *v.* Lewis' Ex'rs, 3 Litt., 129, 132; Hunter *v.* Kirk, 4 Hawks, 277; Stinson *v.* Snow, 1 Fairf., 263; Philips *v.* Ewell, 14 Ohio St., 240; McDonald *v.* Leewright 31 Mo., 29; Stewart *v.* Stringer, 41 id., 400; State *v.* Clerk of Bergen, 25 N. J., 209; Mentz *v.* Hamman, 5 Whart., 150; Paxon's Appeal, 49 Penn. St. 195; Eastman *v.* Bennett, 6 Wis., 232.

[2] There are cases which hold official returns of ministerial officers to be only *prima facie* evidence of facts recited: Cockrell *v.* Smith, 1 La. An., 1; Waddell *v.* Judson, 12 id., 13; Leverich *v.* Adams, 15 id., 310; Wallis *v.* Bourg, 16 id., 176; Newton *v.* Prather, 1 Duv., 100; Fleece *v.* Goodrum, 1 id., 306; Kingsbury *v.* Buchanan, 11 Iowa, 387; Pomeroy *v.* Parmelee, 9 id., 140, 150; Owens *v.* Ranstead, 22 Ill., 161, 167; Rivard *v.* Gardner, 39 id., 125, 129; Gregg *v.* Strange, 3 Ind., 366; Doe *v.* Attica, 7 id., 641; Butler *v.* State, 20 id., 169; Tucker *v.* Bond, 23 Ark., 268; Ingraham *v.* McGraw, 3 Kans., 521.

In Lothrop *v.* Ide, 13 Gray, 93, a collector sued for arresting a person on a tax warrant, relied upon his return as showing that the party had no goods on which to levy. The plaintiff was allowed to give evidence that he offered to turn out goods in satisfaction of the tax. On exceptions the following opinion was given by *Dewey*, J:

"The questions in the present case concern the admission and effect of the evidence offered by the plaintiff, that prior to the actual arrest of the plaintiff for the nonpayment of his tax, he tendered to the defendant sufficient personal property, that might have been levied upon to satisfy the same. The objection to its admission is that it contravenes the return of a sworn officer. The officer does not in the present instance directly aver that there were not sufficient goods of the plaintiff that might have been found to levy upon, but merely says, 'not finding sufficient goods upon which it may be levied,' he arrested the body. There is no allegation that he made search for the goods, or that the same might not have been found with proper diligence. Without deciding the more general question of directly contradicting a return of a collector of taxes, and whether, in a suit brought against such collector for an illegal arrest, his return is to be considered *prima facie* evidence merely, and

CHAPTER IX.

THE CONSTRUCTION OF TAX LAWS.

One of the most serious of the difficulties which are encountered in the administration of the revenue laws, is that of ascertaining the intent of the legislature in the enactment of particular provisions, and in giving that intent the proper application and effect.

Rules of construction in general. Artificial rules of construction have probably found more favor with the courts than they have ever deserved. The application of them has oftentimes been pushed to an extreme which has defeated the plain and manifest purpose in enacting the laws. Penal laws have

presumed to be correct until the contrary be shown, it might perhaps be sufficient in the present case to say that no such direct averment is made here.

"But the court are of the opinion that, in case of an action instituted against a collector of taxes for an illegal arrest, the certificate of the collector is not conclusive evidence in his own favor. In cases of certificates of field-drivers, they have been treated as *prima facie* evidence of their doings rather than conclusive. In the somewhat loose language, formerly used, they were said to change the burden of proof, by which language we understand, when used in reference to this class of cases, not a change of the technical burden of proof upon the issue, but that they are to avail until controlled by a greater weight of evidence overpowering them. In Pickard *v.* Howe, 12 Met., 207, it was considered as *prima facie* evidence, and also in the case of Bruce *v.* Holden, 21 Pick., 187. In the case of Barnard *v.* Graves, 13 Met., 19, it was said that the certificate of a collector of taxes, of his doings on a levy of his warrant, is to be deemed *prima facie* evidence as to all matters upon which they are by law to make returns. We have not felt that the decision in Livermore *v.* Bagley, 3 Mass., 513 should require us to come to a different result in the present case from that stated in Barnard *v.* Graves.

"The evidence being admissible, we think it is such as would have warranted the jury in returning a verdict for the plaintiff. The authority to arrest the body, which is given by Rev. Stat., ch. 8, § 11, arises only where the collector cannot find sufficient goods upon which to levy. This provision continues in force at all times previous to an act of arrest."

In Bowen *v.* Donovan, 32 Ind., 379, it was held competent to defeat a tax sale of lands by showing that the tax-payer had personal property from which the tax might have been collected. And see Scales *v.* Alvis, 12 Ala., 617.

been construed out of all meaning, and in remedial laws remedies have sometimes been found which the legislature never gave. Something of this fate has befallen the revenue laws. In some of the earlier cases they seem to have been regarded as things which, like the obligations entered into with a usurer, were to be confined to the very letter of the bond, if enforced at all; and every intendment was made against them and the proceedings under them. The legislature has endeavored to remedy the evil by going to the opposite extreme. It has passed statutes from time to time in the supposed exercise of a control over rules of evidence which, if literally construed and enforced, are in the nature of judicial decrees, determining conclusively against the person whose property has been seized for taxes, all such questions of law or right as he might raise in support of his inheritance. It is difficult to determine which is more unreasonable, the old strictness of some of the courts against tax proceedings, or the new strictness of some legislation against those who have the misfortune to be confronted with a tax deed.

The intent to govern. The underlying principle of all construction is that which seeks the intent of the legislature in the words employed to express it. Beyond the words we are not to look, where the meaning is plain and intelligible.[1] If the law is plain and unambiguous, the legislature must be intended to mean what has been plainly expressed, and nothing remains but to give the intent effect.[2] When doubts arise on the meaning

[1] The construction of a statute is to be gathered only from the words used where they are plain and intelligible. Therefore, where a statute providing for the summary arrest of a defaulting collector, authorized him to be released on giving bond after he had been committed to prison after his arrest, it was held that a bond taken without committing him to prison was unauthorized. Daggett *v.* Everett, 19 Me., 373.

[2] United States *v.* Fisher, 2 Cranch, 358, 399; Sturgis *v.* Crowninshield, 4 Wheat., 122, 202; People *v.* Purdy, 2 Hill, 31, 35; S. C., 4 id., 384; Newell *v.* People, 7 N. Y., 9, 83; McClusky *v.* Cromwell, 11 id., 593; People *v.* N. Y. Central R. R. Co., 24 id., 485, 492; Alexander *v.* Worthington, 5 Md., 471; Cantwell *v.* Owens, 14 id., 215; Case *v.* Wildridge, 4 Ind., 51; Spencer *v.* State, 5 id., 41, 49; Ludlow's Heirs *v.* Johnson, 3 Ohio, 553; Ezekiel *v.* Dixon, Kelly, 146; *In re* Murphy, 23 N. J., 180; State *v.* Blasdel, 4 Nev., 241; Patterson *v.* Yuba, 13 Cal., 175; District Township *v.* Dubuque, 7 Iowa, 262; Bidwell *v.* Whittaker, 1 Mich., 479; Bartlett *v.* Morris, 9 Port., 266; McAdoo *v.* Benbow, 63 N. C., 461, 464.

of the words, the antecedent law, the evil to be remedied, the circumstances under which the law has been enacted, and to some extent the contemporaneous or even the subsequent practical construction may be resorted to, for any light they may possibly throw upon the meaning. And here rules of interpretation come in which are discussed with more or less fullness in various elementary treatises.[1] But rules of interpretation are only in the nature of suggestions, by means of which we may be enabled to reach an intent which has been doubtfully expressed. If the intent is plain without them, they are useless, and may introduce doubts where none existed; but if the words are capable of several constructions, they may serve to indicate, with reasonable certainty, the one which was in the mind of the legislature.

Construction of revenue laws. In the construction of the revenue laws,[2] special consideration is of course to be had of the purpose for which they are enacted. That purpose is to supply the government with a revenue. But in the proceedings to obtain this it is also intended that no unnecessary injury shall be inflicted upon the individual taxed. While this is secondary to the main object — the impelling occasion of the law — it is none the less a sacred duty. Care is taken in constitutions to insert provisions to secure the citizen against injustice in taxation,

[1] See especially Blackstone's Commentaries; the Treatises of Sedgwick & Smith; Dwarris on Statutes, with Potter's additions; Bishop on Statutory Crimes; Story on the Constitution; Cooley Const. Lim., Chapter IV.

[2] It may be noted here, that while under the federal government the term most usually applied to the laws by which taxes are laid and collected is *revenue laws*, in a number of the states that term is seldom made use of as applying to the laws of the state for the corresponding purpose. There is no substantial difference, however, in the meaning of the two terms, tax laws and revenue laws. In Peyton *v.* Bliss, 1 Woolw., 170, 173, Mr. *Justice Miller* says: 'Any law which provides for the assessment and collection of a tax to defray the expenses of the government is a revenue law. Such legislation is commonly referred to under the general term "revenue measures," and those measures include all the laws by which the government provides means for meeting its expenditures. I can imagine no definition of a government revenue which would not include all the money raised by any form of taxation." But an act imposing a penalty which goes to the government is not for that reason merely a revenue law. Revenue laws are those laws only whose principal object is the raising of revenue, and not those under which revenue may incidentally arise. The Nashville, 4 Biss., 188.

and all legislative action is entitled to the presumption that this has been intended. We are therefore at liberty to suppose that the two main objects had in view in framing the provisions of any tax law, were *first*, the providing a public revenue, and *second*, the securing of individuals against extortion and plunder under the cover of the proceedings to collect the revenue. The provisions for these purposes are the important provisions of the law. Other provisions may be made for subordinate purposes; to encourage order, regularity and promptitude in the proceedings, and to give to the government a security against losses and frauds beyond what might be had in the integrity of officers.

The question regarding the revenue laws has generally been, whether or not they should be construed strictly. The general rules of interpretation require this in the case of statutes which may divest one of his freehold by proceedings not in the ordinary sense judicial, and to which he is only an enforced party. It is thought to be only reasonable to intend that the legislature, in making provision for such proceedings, would take unusual care to make use of terms which would plainly express its meaning, in order that ministerial officers might not be left in doubt in the exercise of unusual powers, and that the citizen might know exactly what were his duties and liabilities. A strict construction in such cases is reasonable, because presumptively the legislature has given in plain terms all the power it has intended should be exercised. It has been very generally supposed that the like strict construction was reasonable in the case of tax laws. Mr. Dwarris in his Treatise on Statutes has the following remarks:

"Statutes made for the advancement of trade and commerce, and to regulate the conduct of merchants, ought to be perfectly clear and intelligible to persons of their description. By the use of ambiguous clauses in laws of that sort, the legislature would be laying a snare for the subject, and a construction which conveys such an imputation ought never to be adopted. Judges, therefore, where clauses are obscure, will lean against forfeitures, leaving it to the legislature to correct the evil, if there be any. With this view, the ship registry acts, so far as they apply to defeat titles and to create forfeitures, are to be construed strictly, as penal, and not liberally, as remedial laws. In like manner in the revenue laws, where clauses inflicting pains and penalties are ambiguously or obscurely worded, the interpretation is ever in favor of the subject; 'for this plain reason,' said *Heath*, J., in Hubbard *v.* Johnstone, 'that the legislature is ever at hand to explain its own meaning, and to express more clearly what has been obscurely expressed.'" The same author on another page says: "It is a well settled rule of law, that every charge upon the subject must be imposed by clear and unambiguous language. Acts of parliament which impose a duty upon the public will be critically construed with reference to the particular language in which they are expressed. When there is any ambiguity found, the construction must be in favor of the public; because it is a general rule, that when the public are to be charged with a burden, the intention of the legislature to impose that burden must be explicitly and distinctly shown."[1] This statement of the general rule expresses the view which it is believed has always prevailed in England.[2] It is also that which

[1] Dwarris on Statutes, 742, 749.

[2] Quotations from a few cases may be here given. In Warrington *v.* Furbor, 8 East, 242, 245 (case of a stamp tax), Lord *Ellenborough*, Ch. J., says: "Where the subject is to be charged with a duty, the cases in which it is to attach ought to be fairly marked out, and we should give a liberal construction to words of exception confining the operation of the duty." In Williams *v.* Sangar, 10 East, 66, 69 (case of turnpike tolls), Lord *Ellenborough* says: "In the construction of these tax acts we must look at the strict words, however we may sometimes lament the generality of the expression used in them; but we must construe those words according to their plain meaning with reference to the subject matter." In Denn *v.* Diamond, 4 B. & C., 244 (case of an *ad valorem* duty on sales), *Bayley*, J., says: "It is a well settled rule of law that every charge upon the subject must be imposed by clear and unambiguous language." It was therefore held that a conveyance in consideration of natural love and affection was not taxable as a "sale." In Tompkins *v.* Ashby, 6 B. & C., 541, 543 (case of a stamp duty), Lord *Tenterden*, Ch. J., says: "Acts of parliament imposing duties are so to be construed as not to make any instruments liable to them unless manifestly within the intention of the legislature." In Doe *v.* Snaith, 8 Bing., 147, 152 (case of a stamp duty), *Tindal*, Ch. J., says: "As all stamp acts, being a burden on the subject, must be clearly expressed, wherever they impose the burden, I should say that even if there were doubt, we should take the smaller sum." In Wroughton *v.* Turtle, 11 Mees. & W., 561, 567, *Park*, B., says: "It is a well settled rule of law that every charge on the subject must be imposed by clear and unambiguous words." In Marquis of Chandos *v.* Commissioners of Inland Revenue, 6 Exch., 464, 479, *Pollock*, C. B., says: "It is a well established rule in the construction of revenue acts that a duty cannot be imposed on the subject except

has been adopted in the several states.[1] Like views have been frequently expressed by the federal courts. Thus, Mr. Justice Story in giving reasons for holding that the revenue act of 1841 did not intend to levy a certain permanent duty on indigo, says: "My reasons for this conclusion are these: In the first place, it is, as I conceive, a general rule in the interpretation of all statutes, levying taxes or duties, upon subjects or citizens, not to extend their provisions, by implication, beyond the clear import of the language used, or to enlarge their operation so as to embrace matters not specifically pointed out, although standing upon a close analogy. In every case, therefore of doubt, such statutes are construed most strongly against the government, and in favor of the subjects or citizens, because burdens are not to be imposed nor presumed to be imposed, beyond what the statutes expressly and clearly import. Revenue statutes are in no just sense remedial laws, or laws founded upon any permanent public policy, and therefore, are not to be liberally construed. Hence, in the present case, if it be a matter of real doubt, whether the intention of the act of 1841 was to levy a permanent duty on indigo, that doubt will absolve the importer from paying the duty, beyond the period when it would otherwise be free."[2] Duties it is said by Mr. Justice *Nelson* "are never imposed upon the citizen upon vague or doubtful interpretations."[3]

by clear words. The meaning of the legislature must be distinctly made out from the terms of the statute." In Gurr *v.* Scudds, 11 Exch., 190, 192, *Pollock*, C. B., says: "If there is any doubt as to the meaning of the stamp act, it ought to be construed in favor of the subject, because a tax cannot be imposed without clear and express words for that purpose."

[1] "Statutes which impose restrictions upon trade or common occupations, or which levy an excise or tax upon them, must be construed strictly." *Parker*, Ch. J., in Sewell *v.* Jones, 9 Pick., 412, 414. "A statute conferring authority to impose taxes must be construed strictly." *Anderson*, Ch. J., in Moseley *v.* Tift, 4 Fla., 402, 403. "A strict construction of the [tax] law is fully authorized by the nature and consequences of the proceeding." *Stuart*, J., in Barnes *v.* Doe, 4 Ind., 132, 133, quoting Williams *v.* State, 6 Blackf., 36. "It is a well settled rule that every charge under a stamp act must be imposed by clear and unambiguous words." *Ray*, J., in Smith *v.* Waters, 25 Ind., 397, 399. See Savannah *v.* Hartridge, 8 Ga., 23; Williamsburg *v.* Lord, 51 Me., 599; Boyd *v.* Hood, 57 Penn. St., 98.

[2] United States *v.* Wigglesworth, 2 Story, 369, 373.

[3] Powers *v.* Barney, 5 Blatch., 202, 203.

"The revenue laws," it is said in another case are not to be so construed as to extend their meaning beyond the clear import of the words used."[1] In another case remarks are made by an able circuit judge, which apply with great force to nearly all the federal revenue laws. "In construing a severe statute, declaring a heavy forfeiture (and according to one construction claimed, for small offenses), it is just to say, that those who are called upon to conduct their business affairs in view of all its provisions, ought to be fairly apprised of its requirements, and its penalties of whatever kind. They are bound to know the law, but law makers owe to them the duty to make the law intelligible; and those whose business it is to construe or expound a law which is of doubtful or double meaning, should not incline to the harshest possible meaning, when it is obvious that those to whom it is to be applied may well have been led to trust in another, which is less severe, but equally satisfying its terms. This is not saying that laws of the kind in question are to be strictly construed in favor of the subject and against the state, but only, that they should be construed with reasonable fairness to the citizen."[2] There are some cases, however, from which, if the expressions made use of in the opinions are taken literally, a different rule might be deduced. Thus it is said in one case: "A revenue law is not to be strictly construed, but *rather the contrary*, so as to attain the ends for which it was enacted."[3] In other cases it is said that, "the penalties annexed to violations of general revenue laws do not make them penal, in the sense which requires them to be construed strictly."[4] And in the decision of a recent case in the United States supreme court, a similar view seems to be taken. "Revenue statutes," it is said, "are not to be regarded as penal, and therefore to be construed strictly. *They are remedial in their character* and to be construed *liberally*, to carry out the purposes of their enactment."[5]

[1] United States *v.* Watts, 1 Bond, 580, 583, per *Leavitt*, J.

[2] *Woodruff*, J., in United States *v.* Distilled Spirits, 10 Blatch., 428, 433.

[3] *Deady*, J., in United States *v.* Olney, 1 Abb., U. S., 275, 282. See Twenty-eight Cases, 2 Ben., 63.

[4] United States *v.* Barrels of Spirits, 2 Abb., U. S., 305, 314, per *Dillon*, J. And see United States *v.* Cases of Cloth, Crabbe, 356.

[5] United States *v.* Hodson, 10 Wall., 395, 406, citing Cliquot's Champagne, 3 Wall., 114, 115.

It seems highly probable that the word *remedial* has been employed by the learned judge delivering the opinion in this case, in a sense differing from that in which it is commonly used in the law. A remedial law, as the term is generally employed, is something quite different from the revenue laws. An author of accepted authority expresses the ordinary understanding, when he defines a remedial statute to be "one which supplies such defects and abridges such superfluities of the common law as may have been discovered[1]; such as may arise either from the imperfection of all human laws, from change of time and circumstances, from mistakes and unadvised determinations of unlearned (or even learned) judges, or from any other cause whatever; and this being done either by enlarging the common law where it was too narrow and circumscribed, or by restraining it where it was too lax and luxuriant, has occasioned another subordinate division of remedial acts into *enlarging* and *restraining* statutes. So it seems that a remedial statute may also have its application to, and effect upon other existing statutes, and give the party injured a remedy; and for a more general definition, 'it is a statute giving a party a mode of remedy for a wrong where he had none or a different one before.'"[2]

Mr. Justice Blackstone speaks of statutes against frauds as remedial, but the context shows he is speaking of statutes giving parties a remedy against frauds; and he adds: "when the statute acts upon the offender and inflicts a penalty, as the pillory or a fine, it is then to be taken strictly, but when the statute acts upon the offense by setting aside the fraudulent transaction, here it is to be construed liberally."[3] Another author in pointing out the distinction between penal and remedial laws remarks that "the remedy for breach of a remedial statute is by an action for damages, sustained from such a breach, at the suit of the party grieved; that for breach of a penal statute, by an action of debt for the penalty, or, in more concise terms, the legal distinction between remedial and penal statutes is, that the former gives relief

[1] 1 Bl. Com., 86.

[2] Potter's Dwarris on Statutes, 73, citing, Chitty's note to 1 Bl. Com., 86. The definition in Bouvier's Law Dictionary is the same.

[3] 1 Bl. Com., 88.

to the party grieved; the latter imposes penalties for offenses committed."[1] These considerations would seem to justify the conclusion that the learned judge, in applying the word remedial to tax laws, has used it in some political or special, rather than in the strict legal sense, and that it was not the intention of the court to overrule the opinion of Mr. Justice Story in Wigglesworth's case.[2]

There may and doubtless should be a distinction taken in the construction of those provisions of revenue laws which point out the subjects to be taxed, and indicate the time, circumstances and manner of assessment and collection, and those which impose penalties for obstructions and evasions. There is no reason for peculiar strictness in construing the former. Neither is there reason for liberality. The difference in some cases is exceedingly important. The one method squeezes everything out of the statute which the unyielding words do not perforce retain; the other reaches out by intendment, and brings within the statute whatever can fairly be held embraced in its beneficent purpose. The one narrows the statute as it is studied; the other expands it. Every lawyer knows how much easier it is to find a remedy in a statute than an offense. There must surely be a just and safe medium between a view of the revenue laws which treats them as harsh enactments to be circumvented and defeated if possible, and a view under which they acquire an expansive quality in the hands of the court, and may be made to reach out and bring within their grasp, and under the discipline of their severe provis-

[1] 13 Pet. Abr., 297, note. And see Cummings *v.* Frye, Dudley, 182; Carey *v.* Giles, 9 Geo., 253. Also the instance of remedial statutes in Potter's Dwarris on Stat., 231, 245.

[2] The opinion in U. S. *v.* Hodson, 10 Wall., 395, refers to Cliquot's Champagne, 4 Wall., 114, which in turn refers to Taylor *v.* United States, 3 How., 193. The opinion in this last case was given by Mr. Justice Story, and the language made use of, which consists largely in a quotation from the opinion given in the lower court, does not express his own views so clearly as was customary with that learned judge. What is manifest in his opinion is, that the point was not regarded as of importance in that case, the meaning of the statute being plain; and while the distinction pointed out by the lower court between penal and remedial laws is approved and shown to be in accordance with the authorities, it is not clear that the general remarks of the judge were intended to go further. It would have been a remarkable circumstanee if Mr. Justice Story had overruled his own opinion, delivered so recently that, at that time, his son (and reporter) had not issued the volume containing it.

ions, subjects and cases, which it is only conjectured may have been within their intent. Revenue laws are not to be construed from the standpoint of the tax payer alone, nor of the government alone. Construction is not to assume either that the tax payer, who raises the legal question of his liability under the laws, is necessarily seeking to avoid a duty to the state which protects him, nor, on the other hand that the government, in demanding its dues is a tyrant, who, while too powerful to be resisted, may justifiably be obstructed and defeated by any subtle device or ingenious sophism whatsoever. There is no legal presumption either that the citizen will, if possible, evade his duties, or, on the other hand, that the government will exact unjustly or beyond its needs. All construction, therefore, which assumes either the one or the other, is likely to be mischievous, and to take onesided views, not only of the laws, but of personal and official conduct. The government in its tax legislation is not assuming a hostile position towards the citizen, but, as we have elsewhere said, is apportioning for and as the agent of all, a duty among them; and the citizen, it is to be presumed, will perform that duty when it is clearly made known to him, and when the time of performance has arrived. Unjust exactions, if such are made, must be attributed to human imperfection, not to intent; and frauds and evasions are to be supposed exceptional. A recent decision of the supreme court of Connecticut lays down a rule, which, as applied to those provisions of the revenue laws which apportion the taxes and give ordinary remedies for their collection, seems not objectionable, though more liberal than is recognized by the authorities generally. The case was a revenue case, and the question was whether a statute for imposing a personal tax on "persons who are residents" of the taxing districts, could be applied to the personalty belonging to the estate of a deceased person. In support of such a construction it is said: "The greatest, and perhaps the only, objection that can be urged against this rule is, that we cannot say in strictness that the deceased or his estate is a resident of the district. This objection assumes that the statute is to be strictly construed. But we do not think that the doctrine of strict construction should apply to it. Statutes relating to taxes are not penal statutes, nor are they in derogation of natural rights. Although taxes are regarded by many as burdens, and many look upon them even as money arbitrarily and unjustly extorted from them by government, and hence justify themselves and quiet their consciences in resorting to questionable means for the purpose of avoiding taxation, yet, in point of fact, no money paid returns so good and valuable a consideration as money paid for taxes laid for legitimate purposes. They are just as essential and important as government itself; for without them, in some form, government could not exist. The small pittance we thus pay is the price we pay for the preservation of all our property, and the protection of all our rights. But there is not only a necessity for taxation, but it is eminently just and equitable that it should be as nearly equal as possible. Hence it is the policy of the law to require all property, except such as is specially exempted, to bear its proportion of the public burdens. Not only so, but the law manifestly contemplates that property rated in the list shall be liable for all taxes, town and school district taxes alike. This is evident from the provision that district taxes shall be laid on the town list, with special provision for certain changes rendered necessary in order to tax all the real estate situated within the district, and none situated without, and also to assess the tax in each instance upon the right person. In construing statutes relating to taxes, therefore, we ought, where the language will permit, so to construe them as to give effect to the obvious intention and meaning of the legislature, rather than to defeat that intention by a too strict adherence to the letter."[1]

[1] Cornwall *v.* Todd, 38 Conn., 443, 447, per *Carpenter*, J. So it is said in Hubbard *v.* Brainard, 35 id., 563, 568, by *Butler*, J.: "A law imposing a tax is not to be construed strictly because it takes money or property *in invitum* (although its provisions are for that reason to be strictly executed), for it is taken as a share of a necessary public burden; nor liberally, like laws intended to effect directly some great public object, but fairly for the government and justly for the citizen; so as to carry out the intention of the legislature, gathered from the language used, read in connection with the general purpose of the law, and the nature of the property on which the tax is imposed, and the legal relation of the tax payer to it." And in Rein *v.* Lane, Law R., 2 Q. B., 144, 150, *Blackburn*, J., says: "We must construe the words of the statute imposing the duty according to the intention which those words express when used in such a statute for such a purpose." And in Lord Foley *v.* Commissioners of Revenue, Law R., 3 Exch., 263, 268, *Kelley*, C. B., justly remarks that "it is better for the subjects and the state that the ordinary rules of construction should be applied." Prof. Parsons in his Treatise on Con-

If there should be any leaning in such cases it would seem that it should be in the direction of the presumption that every thing is expressed in the tax laws which was intended to be expressed. The laws are framed by the government for its own needs, and if imperfections are found to exist, the legislature, in the language of Mr. Dwarris, "is at hand to explain its own meaning, and to express more clearly what has been obscurely expressed." But there can be no propriety in construing such a law either with exceptional strictness amounting to hostility, or with exceptional favor beyond that accorded to other general laws. It is as unreasonable to sound a charge upon it as an enemy to individual and popular rights, as it is to seek for sophistical reasons for grasping and holding by its authority every subject of taxation which the drag net of the official force has brought within its supposed compass. The construction, without bias or prejudice, should seek the real intent of the law; and if the leaning is to strictness, it is only because it is fairly and justly presumable that the legislature, which was unrestrained in its authority over the subject, has so shaped the law as, without ambiguity or doubt, to bring within it everything it was meant should be embraced.

In the state revenue laws the penal provisions are few and by no means severe. In the federal revenue laws, some of them are of a severity very seldom to be met with in penal statutes, and only to be justified by the supposed impossibility of collecting the revenue without them. In illustration of what is here said, reference need only be made to the case of forfeiture of property for the mere indulgence of a fraudulent intent never carried into effect; a forfeiture too, which may be visited upon a purchaser who has bought in good faith, and without suspicion of the intended fraud.[1] If such provisions are to be construed with liberality, there is no reason why any other penal provisions whatsoever should not be.

tracts, vol. 3, p. 287, states the proper rule very clearly and concisely: "It is a well settled principle that every charge upon the subject must be imposed by clear and unambiguous words. * * But it is equally certain that no interpretation will be adopted which must defeat the purpose of the law, provided the language of the statute admit fairly and rationally of an interpretation which sustains that purpose."

[1] Henderson's Distilled Spirits, 14 Wall., 44.

Construction of local powers to tax. In the construction of any grant of the power to tax made by the state to one of its municipalities, the rule which is accepted by all the authorities is, that it should be with strictness. The reasonable presumption is held to be, that the state has granted in clear and unmistakable terms, all it has intended to grant at all; and whatsoever authority the municipal officers assume to exercise, they must be able to show the warrant for in the words of the grant. There is no inherent power in the municipalities to levy taxes; they can tax only as the state in its wisdom has thought proper to permit, and if the state has erred in the direction of strictness, the legislature alone can correct the evil.[1]

[1] See the following cases which have laid down and will serve to illustrate this rule of strictness: Sharp *v.* Spier, 4 Hill, 76; Doughty *v.* Hope, 3 Denio, 574; Tallman *v.* White, 2 N. Y., 66; Manice *v.* id., 8 id., 120; Cruger *v.* Dougherty, 43 id., 107; Litchfield *v.* Vernon, 41 id., 123; Mays *v.* Cincinnati, 1 Ohio, N. S., 268; Cincinnati *v.* Bryson, 15 id., 625; Reed *v.* Toledo, 18 id., 161; Jonas *v.* Cincinnati, 18 id., 318; Savannah *v.* Hartridge, 8 Geo., 23; Augusta *v.* Walton, 37 id., 620; Sanders *v.* Butler, 30 id., 679; Vanover *v.* The Justices, 27 id., 354; Richmond *v.* Daniel, 14 Grat., 385; Orange & Alexandria R. R. Co., *v.* Alexandria, 17 id., 176; Holland *v.* Baltimore, 11 Md., 186; Bouldin *v.* Baltimore, 15 id., 18; Harmony *v.* Osborne, 9 Ind., 458; Kyle *v.* Malin, 8 id., 34; Indianapolis *v.* Mansur, 15 id., 112; Carron *v.* Den, 26 N. J., 594; Leavenworth *v.* Norton, 1 Kan., 432; Snyder *v.* North Lawrence, 8 id., 82; Shawnee County *v.* Carter, 2 id., 115; Chicago *v.* Chicago, etc., R. R. Co., 20 Ill., 286; Drake *v.* Phillips, 40 id., 388; Douglass *v.* Placerville, 18 Cal., 643; Hewes *v.* Reis, 40 id., 255; Kniper *v.* Louisville, 7 Bush, 599; Campbell County Court *v.* Taylor, 8 id., 206; Broadway Baptist Church *v.* McAtee, 8 id., 508; Bullock *v.* Curry, 2 Met., Ky., 171; Boston *v.* Schaffer, 9 Pick., 415; Nichol *v.* Nashville, 9 Humph., 252; Philadelphia *v.* Tryon, 35 Penn. St., 401; Bennett *v.* Birmingham, 31 id., 15; St. Louis *v.* Laughlin, 49 Mo., 559; St. Charles *v.* Nolle, 51 id., 122; Lott *v.* Ross, 38 Ala., 156; Montgomery *v.* State, 38 id., 162; Henry *v.* Chester, 15 Vt., 460; Municipality *v.* Pance, 6 La. An., 515; Asheville *v.* Means, 7 Ired., 406; Dean *v.* Charlton, 27 Wis., 522; Clark *v.* Davenport, 14 Iowa, 494; Fairfield *v.* Ratcliffe, 20 id., 396; Oregon Steam, etc. Co.. *v.* Portland, 2 Ore., 81; United States *v.* Burlington, 2 Am. L. Reg., N. S., 394; Leonard *v.* Canton, 35 Miss., 189; Dillon, Mun. Corp., § 605; Cooley's Const. Lim., 195.

"The power to tax is a high governmental power, but fortunately for the people it cannot be exercised by the legislative authority without limit, and when the legislature grants that high power to another tribunal, it can only be exercised in strict conformity to the terms in which the power is granted, and a departure in any material part will be fatal to the attempt to exercise it." *Peters*, J. in Campbell County Court *v.* Taylor, 8 Bush, 206, 208. It was held in this case that authority to the voters of a county to vote a specified tax was

This rule confines the municipalities, in the levy of taxes, strictly to the ordinary purposes for which such municipalities are accustomed to make levies. The customary grant does not go a step beyond this, and unusual purposes cannot be brought within the scope of their taxing power without an express grant which clearly indicates the special object.[1] This is not only in accordance with the general rule that construes sovereign grants with strictness, but it is also obviously wise. The mischief of a strict construction is easily obviated by the legislature; but the mischief of a liberal construction may be irremediable before it can be reached.[2] It is in accordance with this rule, that the authority conferred upon a county to levy a tax "for county purposes" was held, in Georgia, not to warrant a tax for the construction of public buildings; county purposes, as understood in that state, being the support of the poor, public education, and the like.[3] In Maine, it was held that a general power in a town to tax for corporate purposes would not include the right to tax in order to make a toll bridge free.[4] Whatever doubt might be

not exercised by a vote of the county excluding a city therein. See for a similar principle, Attorney General *v.* Supervisors of St. Clair, 11 Mich., 63. Authority to levy a tax on taxable property will not authorize a specific tax on an insurance company (not on their capital). Augusta *v.* Walton, 37 Geo., 620. It will authorize a tax on the shares in a bank without their being specially mentioned. Frederick *v.* Augusta, 5 id., 561; Pearce *v.* Augusta, 37 id., 597; Augusta *v.* National Bank, 47 id., 562. A statute authorizing a tax on dividends over a certain per cent. on capital, means capital actually paid in, and not merely authorized capital. Street Railway Co. *v.* Philadelphia, 51 Penn. St., 465; Philadelphia *v.* Ferry Railway Co., 52 id., 177. A power to tax all personal property within a city, held not to reach shares in a railroad owned by a resident. Richmond *v.* Daniel, 14 Grat., 385. An interpretation of a statute for the assessment of a special tax which will interfere with the general tax law, is not to be adopted unless there is the clearest language to justify it. State *v.* Douglass, 33 N. J., 363.

[1] Stetson *v.* Kempton, 13 Mass., 272; Alley *v.* Edgecomb, 53 Me., 446.

[2] Where a city has authority to levy taxes only to a certain percentage on the assessment, the power to levy more is not to be implied from the fact that, by the charter, it is made the duty of the city to erect hospitals, poor houses, etc., and more would be needed for those purposes. Leavenworth *v.* Norton, 1 Kansas, 432.

[3] Vanover *v.* The Justices, 27 Geo., 354. As to what are "county purposes" in Minnesota, see McCormic *v.* Fitch, 14 Minn., 252.

[4] Bussy *v.* Gilmore, 3 Greenl., 191.

raised as to this last decision, there can be none, we should suppose, of the correctness of those which have held that a power to tax for necessary town charges would not warrant a tax to raise military forces or to pay military bounties. This is clearly no part of the corporate duty of a town, and could not be supposed within the intent of the legislature in providing for necessary town charges.[1] Similar rulings have been made in a great variety of cases, in which particular powers have been claimed; but the reader must be referred to works on the special subject of municipal law, for a reference to these decisions.[2]

[1] The leading case on this point is Stetson *v.* Kempton, 13 Mass., 272, 278, in which *Parker*, Ch. J., gives his idea of what constitutes town charges, as follows: "The phrase *necessary charges* is indeed general; but the very generality of the expression shows that it must have a reasonable limitation. For none will suppose that, under this form of expression, every tax would be legal which the town should choose to sanction. The proper construction of the terms must be that, in addition to the money to be raised for the poor, schools, etc., towns might raise such sums as should be necessary to meet the ordinary expenses of the year; such as the payment of such municipal officers as they should be obliged to employ, the support and defense of such actions as they might be parties to, and the expenses they would incur in performing such duties as the laws imposed, as the erection of powder houses, providing ammunition, making and repairing highways and town roads, and other things of a like nature: which are necessary charges, because the effect of a legal discharge of their corporate duty. The erection of public buildings for the accommodation of the inhabitants, such as town houses to assemble in, and market houses for the sale of provisions, may also be a proper town charge, and may come within the fair meaning of the term *necessary;* for these may be essential to the comfort and convenience of the citizens. But it cannot be supposed that the building of a theater, a circus or any other place of mere amusement, at the expense of the town, could be justified under the term *necessary town charges.* Nor could the inhabitants be lawfully taxed for the purpose of raising a statue or monument, these being matters of taste and not of necessity, unless, in populous and wealthy towns, they should be thought suitable ornaments to buildings or squares, the raising and maintenance of which are within the duty and care of the governors or officers of such towns." See Alley *v.* Edgecomb, 53 Me., 446. Compare Lisbon *v.* Bath, 21 N. H., 319; Bangs *v.* Snow, 1 Mass., 181; Cruckshanks *v.* Charleston, 1 McCord, 360; State *v.* Charleston, 2 Speers, 623; Simmons *v.* Wilson, 66 N. C., 336.

[2] Dillon on Municipal Corporations is specially referred to. Mention of the following cases may, perhaps, be useful in this connection: A vote at a township meeting to raise "all the law will allow for school purposes," held good, though informal. State *v.* Sickles, 24 N. J., 125. The authority that may vote a tax cannot refer it to a committee or to officers with power. State *v.*

Liability of power to abuse. The liability of the taxing power to abuse is often assigned as a reason why, in particular cases, it should be held not to have been conferred. But this is illogical and unreasonable. "Every authority, however indispensable, may be abused, and if it might not, it would be powerless for good."[1] The point is forcibly put by the supreme court of Ohio. "It has been strongly urged that this power is peculiarly liable to abuse. It is liable to be abused; perhaps peculiarly so. But so is all government, and all governmental powers. Yet government is nevertheless a necessity among men. It is a very bad government indeed which is not better than the inevitable anarchy and outrage which follow the absence of all government. And the fact that a power is liable to be abused, affords no conclusive argument against it."[2] It is only a reason for caution in construction, in order to be certain that the power is intended to be given, and for holding the donee of the power to a strict execution of the authority.

Directory and mandatory provisions. Much use is made in the law of taxation of the words *directory* and *mandatory*, as words of classification of the various provisions of tax laws, as regards the imperative nature of the obligation they impose on the revenue officers to obey them strictly. All the provisions of a statute not on their face merely permissory or discretionary, are intended to be obeyed, or they would not be enacted at all; and therefore they come to the several officers who are to act under them, as

Sickles, *supra;* Robinson *v.* Dodge, 18 Johns., 351; Trumbull *v.* White, 5 Hill, 46; Mercer County Court *v.* Navigation Co., 8 Bush, 300. A tax, purporting to be levied by the authorities of two districts, meeting and acting jointly, is void. State *v.* Reeves, 28 N. J., 520. Authority to a county to levy a *tax* for county buildings, will not authorize the issue of bonds for the purpose. Shawnee County *v.* Carter, 2 Kansas, 115. The power to impose license fees is not contained in a grant of general local legislation. Sanders *v.* Butler, 30 Geo., 679. A city charter, conferring power to tax in general terms, is to be understood, in speaking of "property within the city," to mean visible property within the city, and would not include debts owing to a citizen by people residing abroad. Johnson *v.* Lexington, 14 B. Monr., 648. Followed in Covington *v.* Powell, 2 Met. (Ky.), 226; Louisville *v.* Henning, 1 Bush, 381.

[1] *Gibson*, Ch. J., in Kirby *v.* Shaw, 19 Penn. St., 258, 260.

[2] *Brinkerhoof*, J., in Reeves *v.* Treasurer of Wood County, 8 Ohio, N. S., 333, 343. See Breevort *v.* Detroit, 24 Mich., 322, 325; Bridgeport *v.* Nichols, 23 Conn., 189, 203.

commands. But the negligence of officers, their mistakes of fact or of law, and many other causes will often prevent a strict obedience, and when the provisions which have been disregarded constitute parts of an important and perhaps complicated system, it becomes of the highest importance to ascertain the effect the failure to obey them shall have on the other proceedings with which they were associated in the law. The form the question most commonly assumes is this: Some official act which the law provides for, and which constitutes one step to be followed by others in reaching a specified result, having failed to be taken, Does the authority to proceed toward the intended result, terminate when that particular step has been neglected, or may the proceeding go on to a conclusion treating the neglect as immaterial? If the proceeding fails at that point, the requirement of the official act which has been neglected is said to be mandatory, but if it may still proceed, the requirement is directory only; that is to say, the law directs that particular act to be performed, but does not imperatively command it as a condition precedent to anything further.

In some cases the question assumes a different form. The municipalities, it has been seen, levy and collect taxes not only for their own purposes, but also under state apportionment for the state at large. The power to levy taxes is usually conferred upon them in merely permissory terms; terms implying a discretion to levy them or not at the will of the local majority or the local board. These may sometimes raise the question whether they are intended to confer a discretionary authority merely, or, on the other hand, whether they were not meant to impose a duty and put the municipality under an imperative obligation.

A solution of this question will commonly depend upon the purpose of the tax for which authority is given. If the tax is for purely local purposes, the permission to levy it can seldom be regarded as anything more than an enabling statute, of which advantage may be taken or not, at discretion; but if it is for general purposes, the law must be regarded as imposing a duty. In whatever terms the authority is conferred upon a county to levy its proportion of the state tax, the levy is imperative; and permissory words in the statute may be construed as commands, and a reluctant local authority may be coerced into a performance of the duty. The rule is the same where what is authorized is for the purpose of meeting some legal obligation of the municipality; "for where a statute directs the doing of a thing for the sake of justice or the public good, the word *may* is the same as the word shall," and imports a duty equally imperative.[1] In most cases, however, the question whether any particular provision of a tax law is mandatory or not, will arise between the government and its officers, or some one claiming under their proceedings on the one side, and the person taxed on the other; and the form it will take will be, whether the person taxed is entitled to defeat any proceeding which is being taken adversely to him, by reason of the failure on the part of the officers to observe some direction of the statute under which they derive their authority. If he may, it is because the direction was mandatory, and obedience to it a condition precedent to any further adverse proceedings.

The phraseology of the statute may sometimes settle this question very conclusively. If by the use of negative words it requires a particular proceeding to be taken in a particular time or manner, and makes it void if not so done,[2] or gives it effect, provided it is so done,[3] or declares that, unless it is taken, subsequent proceedings shall not be had,[4] or prohibits its being done except at the time the statute prescribes,[5] or if any terms plainly imperative are employed, the intent is clear, and no discretion can be permitted in construction. It is not often, however, that these or similar words are met with in the statutes which define official duties under the revenue laws, and the construction of particular provisions must be left for determination in such light as the obvious purpose they were intended to accomplish may afford. And that purpose, it would seem, ought generally to be conclusive.

[1] Rex *v.* Barlow, 2 Salk., 609. See Rex *v.* Inhab. of Derby, Skinner, 370; Virginia *v.* The Justices, 2 Virg. Cas., 9; Justices of Clark County *v.* Railroad Co., 11 B. Monr., 143; Coy *v.* Lyons City, 17 Iowa, 1; State *v.* Harris, 17 Ohio, N. S., 608; Baltimore *v.* Marriott, 9 Md., 160, 174; New York *v.* Furz, 3 Hill, 612; Minor *v.* Mechanics' Bank 1 Pet., 46; Mason *v.* Fearson, 9 How., 248; Supervisors *v.* United States, 4 Wall., 435; Galena *v.* Amy, 5 id., 705.

[2] The King *v.* Hepswell, 8 B. & C., 466.

[3] The King *v.* Inhab. of St. Gregory, 2 Ad. *v.* El., 99.

[4] Stayton *v.* Hulings, 7 Ind., 144.

[5] *In re* Douglass, 46 N. Y., 42.

No one should be at liberty to plant himself upon the nonfeasances or misfeasances of officers, under the revenue laws, which in no way concern himself, and make them the excuse for a failure on his part to perform his own duty. On the other hand he ought always to be at liberty to insist that directions which the law has given to its officers for his benefit shall be observed. Many eminent judges have endeavored to lay down a general rule on this subject, by which the difficulties in tax cases may in general be solved. In one of the most recent cases in which this has been attempted, the general doctrine is stated as follows: "There are undoubtedly many statutory requisitions intended for the guide of officers in the conduct of business devolved upon them, which do not limit their power, or render its exercise in disregard of the requisitions ineffectual. Such generally are regulations designed to secure order, system, and dispatch in proceedings, and by a disregard of which the rights of parties interested cannot be injuriously affected. Provisions of this character are not usually regarded as mandatory, unless accompanied by negative words, importing that the act required shall not be done in any other manner or time than that designated. But when the requisitions prescribed are intended for the protection of the citizen, and to prevent a sacrifice of his property, and by a disregard of which his rights might be and generally would be injuriously affected, they are not directory but mandatory. They must be followed, or the acts done will be invalid. The power of the officer in all such cases is limited by the measure and conditions prescribed for its exercise."[1]

The same rule in nearly the same terms has been laid down in other cases,[2] and it seems a sound and just rule, and may reasonably be believed to be in accord with the legislative will in the

[1] *Field*, J., in French *v.* Edwards, 13 Wall., 506, 511.

[2] See especially Torrey *v.* Milbury, 21 Pick., 64, per *Shaw*, Ch. J., approved and followed in State *v.* Jersey City, 35 N. J., 381, 386; Clark *v.* Crane, 5 Mich., 151, 154, per *Manning*, J.; O'Neal *v.* Va. & Md. Bridge Co., 18 Md., 1, per *Tuck*, J.; McDonough *v.* Gravier, 9 La. An., 546; Spear *v.* Ditty, 8 Vt., 419; Shawnee County *v.* Carter, 2 Kansas, 115; Wheeler *v.* Chicago, 24 Ill., 105, 108; Walker *v.* Chapman, 22 Ala., 116; Kelly *v.* Craig, 5 Ired., 129; Magee *v.* Commonwealth, 46 Penn. St., 358. All acts required by the statute in order to make the tax chargeable are conditions precedent and must be strictly complied with, or the tax cannot be collected. Hewes *v.* Reis, 40 Cal., 255.

cases to which it is applicable. All legislation must be supposed to take into account the possible, if not probable mistakes and irregularities of officers in executing the provisions of the law, and it is hardly reasonable to infer an intent, on the part of a legislative body, that a failure of administrative officers to comply with any provision made for the benefit of the state exclusively, or merely as a guide in orderly proceedings, should deprive the state of all benefit to be derived from a compliance with other provisions that embody the main purpose and object of the law. Nor, on the other hand, is it to be supposed the legislature intended its own securities for the protection of individual rights and property should be disregarded with impunity.[1]

Instances of mandatory provisions. What, then, are the provisions of tax laws which are made for the benefit and protection of the individual tax payer? In many cases this question, as applied to particular provisions, is easily solved; in others there is more difficulty. That the tax payer shall be entitled to such protection as the official responsibility of officers can give him; that the tax shall be voted by the competent authority and under any conditions which the law has prescribed; that there shall be official warrant for any compulsory proceedings;[2] all

[1] See Corbett *v.* Bradley, 7 Nev., 106, 108, per *Lewis*, Ch. J.; Briggs *v.* Georgia, 15 Vt, 61, 72, per *Hubbard*, J.; Dryfuss *v.* Bridges, 45 Miss., 247; State *v.* Lean, 9 Wis., 279, 292. In Sandwich *v.* Fish, 2 Gray, 298, 301, *Shaw*, Ch. J., in answering an objection made on behalf of a defaulting collector, that certain provisions regarding the authority to collect had not been complied with, says: "The provisions of the statutes as to the form of warrants and tax lists, and the place where the lists shall be deposited, are intended for the benefit of the taxpayers. As to all other persons they are directory merely, and not conditions precedent. Defects in the warrant or tax list might be a good excuse for not executing the warrant. But to say that a collector who has collected the money without objection by the tax payers, is not liable to account therefor would be as contrary to the rules of law as to justice. He can only avail himself of such defects as have prevented his performance of his duty."

[2] Where the statute provided that a tax voted at an annual town meeting in March should be assessed on the tax list of the May following, it was held mandatory and the town incompetent by vote to authorize the selectmen to assess it on the list of the previous year. Alger *v.* Curry, 38 Vt., 382. Where the statute requires the tax list to be verified by an oath "made and subscribed," this means an oath duly certified in writing, and the absence of it is fatal to the proceedings. "Applying to the case the rules which have governed the courts in passing upon this class of titles, the objection must be held

these are manifestly conditions precedent to any lawful demand whatever upon the citizen. They are of the highest importance, because it is only by means of the requirement of official action in an orderly manner and at periodical times, that he can be protected against arbitrary and capricious action. Moreover, they go to make up the power which the law gives to its agents over the property and persons of the people; and without the power to act, all attempted action is a trespass upon individual rights.[1] There must be a voting of the tax by the proper authority; there must be an assessment and an apportionment. So far all is clear.[2] So

fatal. The assessor acts under a special and limited authority, conferred by the law and not by the owner of the estate. He is the mere instrument to pass the title. The proceeding is construed strictly, and the power must be strictly pursued in every particular. The law requires that every prerequisite to the exercise of the power to sell the estate must precede its exercise. The agent must pursue the power or his act will not be sustained by it. These principles have been recognized by this court in their application to tax titles in repeated decisions. Yenda *v.* Wheeler, 9 Texas, 408; Robson *v* Osborn, 13 id., 298; Wafford *v.* McKinna, 23 id., 36." *Wheeler*, Ch. J., in Davis *v.* Farnes, 26 id., 296, 297.

[1] See Chapter VIII. Where an act providing for local improvements required the certificate of the commissioners of public works, as to the amount of expense paid or actually incurred by the city, as the basis of the assessment, it was held that nothing could be the substitute for this. The affidavit of the surveyor will not be received. Petition of Cameron, 50 N. Y., 502.

[2] "Many of the provisions of our statute regulating the imposition of taxes, must be considered directory merely. Some are doubtless conditions; such as those which are intended to secure an equality of taxation or burdens among the citizens, that is, that the citizen may know for what he is taxed, know his valuation, and have notice of the time and place of appeal." *Coulter*, J., in Insurance Co. *v.* Yard, 17 Penn. St., 331, 338. In O'Neal *v.* Va. & Md. Bridge Co., 18 Md., 1, 23, *Tuck*, J., explains the distinction between directory and mandatory provisions in tax laws, and refers to Youngs *v.* State, 7 G. & J., 253, and other Maryland cases. Where the statute required the county judge in case of default of a tax collector to collect and pay over, on his own knowledge or on complaint of the treasurer, to hold a court within 20 days to try such delinquent collector, this was held to be in point of time directory merely, the time not being prescribed for the benefit of the collector, "but rather to quicken the diligence of the judge, so that justice may be promptly administered and the greater certainty of collections insured." Stickney *v.* Huggins, 10 Ala., 106. A requirement that taxation shall be by value is mandatory. Life Association *v.* Board of Assessors, 49 Mo., 512. Where a lot omitted from the assessment of the preceding year is to be placed upon the roll with the valuation of the last year when it was assessed, if the lot was

all provisions designed to give him the opportunity of a review of the assessment, whether by the assessors themselves or on an appeal from their conclusions, are exclusively in his interest. Every notice which the statute provides for to that end, whether by publication or otherwise, must be given with scrupulous observance of all its requisites. The notice cannot be shortened a single day without rendering it ineffectual; the presumption being that the law has made it as short as was deemed consistent with due protection.[1] A published notice cannot be received as the substitute for a notice to be personally delivered to the party concerned.[2]

The same rules apply to any notice required of subsequent proceedings: if required to be given within a certain time, or in any prescribed mode,[3] it must be so given. A statute declaring that

never on the roll, it cannot be put on under the provision. People *v.* Goff, 52 N. Y., 434. *Hall*, J., in Chandler *v.* Spear, 22 Vt., 388, 398, says, " when the statute under which the sale is made directs a thing to be done, or prescribes the form, time and manner of doing anything, such thing must be done, and in the form, time and manner prescribed, or the title is invalid; and in this respect the statute must strictly, if not literally, be complied with. Spear *v.* Ditty, 9 Vt., 282; Bellows *v.* Elliott, 12 id., 569, 574; Sumner *v.* Sherman, 13 id., 909, 612; Carpenter *v.* Sawyer, 17 id., 122, 124. But in determining what is required to be done, the statute must receive a reasonable construction; and when no particular form or manner of doing a thing is pointed out, any mode which effects the object with reasonable certainty is sufficient; and in judging of these matters the court is to be governed by such rational rules of construction, as direct them in other cases. Spear *v.* Ditty, 8 Vt., 419, 421; Bellows *v.* Elliott, 12 id., 569, 574; Isaacs *v.* Shattuck, 12 id., 668."

[1] See cases cited in Chapter XV.

[2] Moulton *v.* Blaisdell, 24 Me., 283; Lovejoy *v.* Lunt, 48 id., 377. And see Lagroue *v.* Rains, 48 Mo., 536. Where the notice is to be given personally and also by publication, a failure in either is fatal. Appeal of Powers, 29 Mich., 504.

[3] The statute required the sheriff at the next term of the county court preceding a tax sale, to return a list of the lands on which taxes were unpaid, with the names of the owners if known, and other particulars, and this was to be read aloud, recorded in the minutes, and posted in the room. *Held* to be mandatory. Kelly *v.* Craig, 5 Ired., 129. In Sprague *v.* Bailey, 19 Pick., 436, a provision that notice of abatement to those who should pay their taxes promptly, should be posted in public places, was regarded directory merely. The point was not reasoned. All provisions regarding notice of sale and the place of sale are mandatory. State *v.* Rollins, 29 Mo., 267; Rubey *v.* Huntsman, 32 id., 501; McNair *v.* Jenson, 33 id., 312. A tax was assessed to the owner of the equity of redemption and lands sold therefor. The statute then in force pro-

all resolutions, etc., involving an appropriation of money, or taxation, shall be published "in all the newspapers employed by the corporation," and not be passed until after notice has been published at least two days, is plainly intended to be imperative.[1] Whatever tends to make the right to redeem more valuable to him must be observed; and here time may be of the very highest importance; and at no stage of the proceedings should the requisites of notice be more strictly observed. These are illustrations of mandatory requirements. Many others are noticed in other chapters.[2]

Instances of directory provisions. On the other hand, the requirement of an official bond or oath from an officer is for the protection of the public, and not of the tax payer.[3]

So in general the fixing of an exact time for the doing of an act is only directory, where it is not fixed for the purpose of giving the party a hearing, or for any other purpose important to him.[4] So the requirement of a warrant to the town assessors requiring them to assess the state tax, is directory, as this becomes

vided that no sale of real estate for taxes should affect the rights of any person not taxable therefor, unless a written demand was first made upon said person by the collector for the payment of said taxes. No demand in this case was made upon the mortgagee before the sale. *Held*, that a repeal of this statute did not leave him liable for the tax. Tinslar *v.* Davis, 12 Allen, 79.

1 Petition of Douglass, 46 N. Y., 42; Petition of Smith, 52 id., 526.

2 See in general, in addition to the cases already cited regarding mandatory provisions, Hoffman *v.* Bell, 61 Penn. St., 444; Kniper *v.* Louisville, 7 Bush, 599; First Presb. Ch. *v.* Fort Wayne, 36 Ind., 338; Sibley *v.* Smith, 2 Mich., 486; Rayner *v.* Lee, 20 id., 384; People *v.* Clark, 47 Cal., 456; Richardson *v.* Heydenfeldt, 46 id., 68; Culver *v.* Hayden, 1 Vt., 359; Richardson *v.* Dorr, 5 id., 9; Brown *v.* Wright, 17 id., 97; Judevine *v.* Jackson, 18 id., 470; Taylor *v.* French, 19 id., 49; Langdon *v.* Poor, 20 id., 13; Lane *v.* James, 25 id., 481; see also *post*, Chapter XV.

3 See Hale *v.* Cushing, 2 Greenl., 28; Scarborough *v.* Parker, 53 Me. 252; *ante*, Chapter VIII. In Vermont the decisions are that if the collector appointed to collect any tax assessed on lands for roads and bridges shall fail to give the required bond, any sale made by him is void. See Oatman *v.* Barney, 46 Vt., 594, and cases cited.

4 Hart *v.* Plum, 14 Cal., 148. As where an assessment was to be filed within twenty days, but this was only to make it a lien. Magee *v.* Commonwealth, 46 Penn. St., 358.

of no moment if they act without it.[1] A provision that the true value and the equalized value of lands shall appear in distinct columns on the roll is directory only, as the failure to obey it in no way affects the person taxed.[2] So putting a special tax in a column by itself on the roll when it should be put with the town tax is equally harmless, and therefore cannot affect the proceedings.[3] And manifestly the tax payer has nothing to do with any accounting by the officer, or with any report or document to be made by him for the security of the public or for the information of superiors only, and which is not to be warrant for, or to affect in any manner subsequent proceedings for enforcing the tax.[4] In the margin many other cases are referred to in which statutory provisions have been decided to be merely directory.[5]

[1] Alvord *v.* Collin, 20 Pick., 418. In this case it was decided that a levy which was excessive as to the school tax, but not excessive in the aggregate was valid.

[2] Torrey *v.* Milbury, 21 Pick., 64. The failure of the clerk to enter the word *sold* in the book opposite the description of the land as required by the statute, does not defeat the sale. Playter *v.* Cockran, 37 Iowa, 258.

[3] Wall *v.* Trumbull, 16 Mich., 228. Compare Case *v.* Dean, 16 id., 12. A statute required that a school district tax should be assessed within thirty days after the clerk of the district should certify to the assessors the sum to be raised. This is only directory. Pond *v.* Negus, 3 Mass., 230; Williams *v.* School District, 21 Pick, 75; similar ruling in Gale *v.* Mead, 2 Denio, 160; Gearhart *v.* Dixon, 1 Penn. St., 224; Smith *v.* Crittenden, 16 Mich., 152; Harrison Co. Commissioners *v.* McCarty, 27 Ind., 475. For somewhat similar provisions held to be mandatory, see Mix *v.* People, Sup. Ct., Ill., June term, 1874, 7 Chicago Legal News, 2; Cowgill *v.* Long, 15 Ill., 202. Compare Eames *v.* Johnson, 4 Allen, 382.

[4] Tweed *v.* Metcalf, 4 Mich., 578. The clause in the tax warrant, "and you are hereby directed to settle with the selectmen by the 20th day of September next," is merely directory, and does not limit the collector's power to that time. Picket *v.* Allen, 10 Conn., 145.

[5] Craig *v.* Bradford, 3 Wheat., 594; U. S. *v.* Kirkpatrick, 9 id., 720; U. S. *v.* Dandridge, 12 id., 64; Hale *v.* Cushing, 2 Greenl., 218; Muzzy *v.* White, 3 id., 290; Scarborough *v.* Parker, 53 Me., 252; Holland *v.* Osgood, 8 Vt., 276, 280; Cortiss *v.* Corbiss, 8 id., 373, 390; Allen *v.* Parish, 3 Ohio, 187; Fry *v.* Booth, 19 Ohio, N. S., 25; Vance *v.* Schuyler, 1 Gilm., 160; Webster *v.* French, 12 Ill., 302; State *v.* McGinly, 4 Ind., 7; Stayton *v.* Hulings, 7 id., 144; Noland *v.* Busby, 28 id., 154; New Orleans *v.* St. Romes, 9 La. An., 573; Edwards *v.* James, 13 Texas, 52; Lawrence *v.* Speed, 2 Bibb, 401; Hayden *v.* Dunlap, 3 id., 216; People *v.* Allen, 6 Wend., 486; *Ex parte* Heath, 3 Hill, 43; Jackson *v.* Young, 5 Cow., 269; People *v.* Holley, 12 Wend., 481; Striker *v.*

Retrospective taxation. The basis of an apportionment of taxes may as lawfully be retrospective as the reverse; that is to say, it may as well have regard to benefits theretofore received as to those which may be received thereafter. Where taxes are levied for a series of years upon the same valuation of property, they are necessarily retrospective, and one may be taxed upon property which he has long ceased to own when the tax is levied. But there is commonly a presumption that any new tax law was not intended to reach back and take for its standard of apportionment a state of things that may no longer be in existence. "New burdens," it is very justly said, "ought always to be prospective,"[1] and it is reasonable to suppose the legislature has intended that they should be. Such a supposition is in harmony with the general rule of law which requires the courts to "always construe statutes as prospective and not retrospective, unless constrained to the contrary course by the rigor of the phraseology."[2] This is

Kelley, 7 Hill, 9; Gale *v.* Mead, 2 Denio, 160; People *v.* Peck, 11 Wend., 604; Doughty *v.* Hope, 3 Denio, 252; Elmendorf *v.* New York, 25 Wend., 693, 696; People *v.* Cook, 8 N. Y., 67; Pond *v.* Negus, 3 Mass., 230; Lowell *v.* Hadley, 8 Met., 180; People *v.* Doe., 1 Mich., 451; Parks *v.* Goodwin, 1 Doug., Mich., 56; Hickey *v.* Hinsdale, 8 Mich., 267; People *v.* Hartwell, 12 id., 508; State *v.* Click, 2 Ala., 25, 26; Savage *v.* Walsh, 26 id., 620; McKune *v.* Weller, 11 Cal., 49; State *v.* County Commissioners, 29 Md., 516; Hucy *v.* Van Wie, 23 Wis., 613; Adams v. Seymour, 30 Conn., 402. The omission of the collector to enter upon his warrant the true day and year when he received it does not invalidate his proceedings under it. Goodwin *v.* Perkins, 39 Vt., 598. The right of the commonwealth to levy a tax on the market value of the capital stock of a corporation is not defeated by the neglect of the city assessors to make return of the corporation to the treasurer of the commonwealth as required by statute. Commonwealth *v.* New England Slate & Tile Co., 13 Allen, 391.

[1] Commonwealth *v.* Pennsylvania Ins. Co., 13 Penn. St., 165. In that case it was decided that a tax measured by dividends "from and after January 1, 1841" would not apply to a dividend declared by the proper committee December 30, 1840, but not passed upon by the directors until January 4, 1841.

[2] *Woodward*, J., in Price *v.* Molt, 52 Penn. St., 315, 316. And see Philadelphia *v.* Ferry Railway Co., 52 id., 177; Marsh *v.* Chestnut, 14 Ill., 223; Thames Manuf. Co. *v.* Lathrop, 7 Conn., 550; Warren R. R. Co. *v.* Belvidere, 35 N. J., 584; Clark *v.* Hall, 19 Mich., 356; Potter's Dwarris on Statutes, 163, 166; Cooley's Const. Lim., 370, and cases cited. A law declaring that certain defenses shall not be made to tax deeds until the redemption money is paid will not apply to prior sales. Conway *v.* Cable, 37 Ill., 82. Where taxes are levied under a law which is repealed by a subsequent act, unless it appears clearly that the legislature intended the repeal to work retrospectively, it will be as-

the rule not only as a construction of the grant of power, but also as to all the incidents;[1] though a remedial provision may well be presumed to have been intended to reach back for the purposes of justice.[2] And in cases where a tax is levied to meet expenses previously incurred, or to pay the cost of something of which the persons to be taxed have already had the benefit, any presumption against an intent to give the law retroactive operation may be overcome by the apparent justice of such a construction.

sumed that it intended the taxes to be collected according to the law in force when they were levied. Oakland *v.* Whipple, 44 Cal., 303. In Allen *v.* Drew, 44 Vt., 174, an act was construed so as to govern the proceedings by one subsequently approved, the two having been pending together, and the one first approved expressly in terms referring to the other. A statute making mortgagees personally liable for taxes on the land after taking possession, held applicable to mortgages given before but under which the mortgagees took possession after the statute was passed. Andrews *v.* Worcester, etc., Ins. Co., 5 Allen, 65.

[1] In Gerry *v.* Stoneham, 1 Allen, 319, a statute providing that where a party was assessed more than his due and legal proportion, the tax and assessment should be void only for the excess, and a recovery by suit should be limited to the excess, was held not applicable to pending actions.

[2] When the Michigan tax laws have been revised, it has been held that stringent provisions therein designed to favor tax titles must be understood to apply to cases originating under the revision. Clark *v.* Hall, 19 Mich., 356; Smith *v.* Auditor General, 20 id., 398. That revision, however, contained a section which required every person redeeming from the tax sale to pay, not only the redemption money with heavy interest to the purchaser, but also a penalty of twenty-five per cent. to the state. Now there was no more reason and no more justice in the state exacting a penalty for the privilege to one party to redeem from the tax purchase of another, than there would be for demanding a like penalty for the privilege of redeeming from an execution sale, or for voluntarily paying an honest debt; the exaction, if legal — which may well be questioned — was unjust and impolitic, for it tended to bring about the forfeiture of estates, and every state is interested that this shall not happen to its citizens. It was, therefore, held to be a reasonable presumption, when this provision was repealed, that the state intended the repeal to apply to past as well as to future sales. People *v.* Auditor General, Sup. Ct. Mich., at June term, 1875, not yet reported. Compare Tinslar *v.* Davis, 12 Allen, 79, which was a strong case for the application of the opposite presumption. The repeal of a tax law which makes deeds on tax sales *prima facie* evidence of title, where it is done by a new tax law which contains a similar provision, will not prevent deeds given under the repealed law being *prima facie* evidence of title; the fair presumption being that the legislature intended that rule to be continuous. Blackwell *v.* Van Vleet, 30 Mich., 118.

CHAPTER X.

CURING DEFECTS IN TAX PROCEEDINGS.

A subject intimately connected with that of the construction of tax laws, is that of the power of the legislature by other legislation to dispense with obedience to those regulations which have been prescribed by itself for the protection of those who are taxed. It is a subject which presents, perhaps, more intrinsic difficulties than the other.

An act of dispensation may assume any one of several forms:

1. It may assume the form of a rule of conclusive evidence, which should preclude a departure from the law being shown.

2. It may take the form of a mandate to officers, commanding them to give effect to proceedings that have been taken, disregarding any defects.

3. It may be a special curative statute to heal defects in certain specified proceedings which have been taken.

4. It may be a general curative statute to heal irregularities or defects in any proceedings whatsoever previously taken.

5. It may be a general statute for future cases, which, while marking out a course for the officers to pursue, shall at the same time declare that irregularities shall not vitiate any proceedings had under the statute.

6. Besides these, there may be either a special or a general law for reassessing the tax, when the proceedings for its collection have proved ineffectual.

Legislation coming under each of these heads is to be met with in the statutes of the several states, and is entitled to some consideration.

1. *Conclusive Rules of Evidence.* A legislative act which should declare a tax conveyance conclusive evidence that the title of the former owner was divested, and was passed by the deed to the purchaser, could only be supported under the sovereign legislative power to frame and change at its will the rules of evidence. That power is confessedly great, but it is not unlimited. It is a

power to shape and mould, for the purposes of justice, the rules under which parties are to make a showing of their rights, and not a power to preclude their showing them. "The most formal conveyance may be a fraud or a forgery; public officers may connive with rogues to rob the citizen of his property; witnesses may testify or officers certify falsely, and records may be collusively manufactured for dishonest purposes; and that legislation which would preclude the fraud or wrong being shown, and deprive the party wronged of all remedy, has no justification in the principles of natural justice or of constitutional law. A statute, therefore, which should make a tax deed conclusive evidence of a complete title, and preclude the owner of the original title from showing its invalidity, would be void, because not a law regulating evidence, but an unconstitutional confiscation of property."[1] In this connection, it is hardly necessary to say that no reference is had to cases under statutes of limitation, nor to cases resting on principles of equitable estoppel.

2. *Legislative Mandates.* A mandate to officers commanding them to give effect to invalid proceedings would be ineffectual for reasons equally conclusive. If such an act proceeds without an inquiry into the facts, it is a naked attempt to transfer one man's property to another by mere legislation, and this is not an authority which belongs to any legitimate government.[2] If it

[1] McCready *v.* Sexton, 29 Iowa, 356. And see Groesbeck *v.* Seeley, 13 Mich., 329; Case *v.* Dean, 16 id., 12; White *v.* Flynn, 23 Ind., 46; Corbin *v.* Hill, 21 Iowa, 70; Abbott *v.* Lindenbower, 42 Mo., 162; S. C., 46 id., 291; Wright *v.* Cradlebaugh, 3 Nev., 341, 349; Young *v.* Beardsley, 11 Paige, 93; East Kingston *v.* Towle, 48 N. H., 57; S. C., 2 Am. Rep., 174; Taylor *v.* Miles, 5 Kans., 498; S. C., 7 Am. Rep., 558; Powers *v.* Fuller, 30 Iowa, 476. The case of Smith *v.* Cleveland, 17 Wis., 556, contains some very general and unqualified language on this subject. That a deed may be made conclusive that the mere *sale* was according to law has been held in Iowa. McCready *v.* Sexton, 29 Iowa, 356; Ware *v.* Little, 35 id., 234; Jeffrey *v.* Brokaw, id., 505. Under a provision that, before issuing a warrant for collection of a local assessment, the assessment shall be examined and certified as correct by street commissioners, and the attorney and counselor of the city, which certificate shall be conclusive evidence of regularity of the proceedings, it has been decided that the certificate would only cover the formal proceedings. It does not determine the fact that the assessment is made against the proper persons. Newell *v.* Wheeler, 48 N. Y., 486.

[2] Bowman *v.* Middleton, 1 Bay, 252; Wilkinson *v.* Leland, 2 Pet., 627, 657;

assumes to proceed upon evidence, then it is usurpation of authority, and for that reason void.[1] The legislature must prescribe rules, but when questions arise between parties whether rules have been complied with, the judiciary is the appointed arbiter.

3. *Special Curative Acts.* A special act to cure defects in tax proceedings may undoubtedly be passed in some cases. In the margin a number of cases are mentioned where the power to cure defects in legal proceedings has been distinctly affirmed, and they are in point here.[2]

There are some limitations of the power, and there is some embarrassment in considering them, because, though often alluded to, they have never been very fully examined in the judi-

Terrett *v.* Taylor, 9 Cranch, 43; Ervine's Appeal, 16 Penn. St., 256, 266; Lambertson *v.* Hogan, 2 id., 22, 24.

[1] An act requiring the board of supervisors of a county to proceed to the apportionment and assessment of drain taxes, some portion of which had already been adjudged void, and the others palpably were so, was adjudged void on this ground in Butler *v.* Supervisors of Saginaw, 26 Mich., 22. The cases of Lewis *v.* Webb, 3 Greenl., 326; Lane *v.* Dorman, 3 Scam., 238, 242; Campbell *v.* Union Bank, 6 How., Miss., 625, 661; Ervine's Appeal, 16 Penn. St., 256, 266; Cash, appellant, 6 Mich., 193; McDaniel *v.* Correll, 19 Ill., 226; Denny *v.* Mattoon, 2 Allen, 361; Budd *v.* State, 3 Humph, 483; Wally's Heirs *v.* Kennedy, 2 Yerg., 554, and Piquet, appellant, 5 Pick., 64, are referred to as illustrating under different circumstances the distinction between legislative and judicial authority. See also Lambertson *v.* Hogan, 2 Penn. St., 22; Greenough *v.* Greenough, 11 id., 489, 494; Haley *v.* Philadelphia, 68 id., 45; S. C., 8 Am. Rep., 153, 155; Calhoun *v.* McLendon, 42 Geo., 405; Trustees *v* Bailey, 10 Fla., 238; People *v.* Frisbie, 26 Cal., 135; Sydnor *v.* Palmer, 32 Wis., 406, 409.

[2] Kearney *v.* Taylor, 15 How., 494; Strauch *v.* Shoemaker, 1 W. & S., 166, 175; McCoy *v.* Michew, 7 id., 386; Williston *v.* Colkett, 9 Penn. St., 38; Montgomery *v.* Meredith, 17 id., 42; Dunden *v.* Snodgrass, 18 id., 151; Schenley *v.* Commonwealth, 36 id., 29; State *v.* Union, 33 N. J., 350; State *v.* Newark, 34 N. J., 236; Walter *v.* Bacon, 8 Mass., 468, 472; Patterson *v.* Philbrook, 9 id., 151, 153; Locke *v.* Dane, 9 id., 360; Trustees *v.* McCaughey, 2 Ohio, N. S., 152; Butler *v.* Toledo, 5 id., 225; Cowgill *v.* Long, 15 Ill., 202; Mitchell *v.* Deeds, 49 id., 416; Boardman *v.* Beckwith, 18 Iowa, 292; Allen *v.* Archer, 49 Me., 346; People *v.* Seymour, 16 Cal., 332; People *v.* Todd, 23 id., 181; Boyce *v.* Sinclair, 3 Bush, 261; Davis *v.* State Bank, 7 Ind., 316; Lucas *v.* Tucker, 17 id., 41; Musselman *v.* Logansport, 29 id., 533; Brevoort *v.* Detroit, 24 Mich., 322; Pillsbury *v.* Auditor General, 26 id., 245; Tucker *v.* Justices, etc., 34 Geo., 370; Bellows *v.* Weeks, 41 Vt., 590. The legislature may validate a city ordinance so as to save the lien of a tax levied under it. Schenley *v.* Commonwealth 36 Penn. St., 29.

cial decisions, or even enumerated. Some of the restrictions that should attend the exercise of the power rest in policy only, and therefore address themselves to the legislative judgment and sense of right, but do not constitute limitations upon legislative power. One of these concerns the retroactive character of such legislation; there being a special liability to abuse in retrospective legislation. The people in some states have felt this so strongly, that by their constitutions, retrospective laws have been expressly forbidden;[1] but in the absence of any such express restriction, there is nothing in the fact that curative statutes operate retrospectively which can preclude their passage.[2] Another objection to such laws is, that they may be invidious and inspired by favoritism, as they select for confirmation certain proceedings — those of a single district, for instance — leaving all others untouched. But the defects may be in a single district only, and the need of legislation exclusively confined to it. Moreover, in different districts different regulations may have been politic originally, and if so, there can be no very conclusive reason why they may not in effect be made by a retrospective sanction of the regulations actually applied. Cities always have rules of taxation differing in some particulars from those which prevail in towns; and, as in the case of police regulations, such rules must be allowed to vary, because in some cases there may be the most conclusive reasons why they should. But we should think the very limit of such legislation would be reached, when a particular assessment and the proceedings under it, in their operation throughout the district, were confirmed. To discriminate in such proceedings, and say they shall be valid as to a particular purchaser, or against a particular person or estate taxed, would not be legislation, because it would establish no rule. Its purpose would be, while leaving in force the rule which defeats the

[1] Provisions of this nature will be found in the constitutions of Louisiana New Hampshire, Missouri, Tennessee and Texas. In North Carolina retrospective taxation of sales, purchases and other acts done, is forbidden.

[2] State *v.* Newark, 27 N. J., 185; People *v.* Supervisors of Ingham, 20 Mich., 95. A statute which is but a mode of continuing or reviving a tax which might be supposed to have expired, and is in this sense retrospective, but which does not give a judicial construction to a former statute, is not unconstitutional. Stockdale *v.* The Insurance Co., 20 Wall., 323.

assessment, to exempt from its operation the case of a favored party. No department of the government possesses this authority. And all special confirmations of assessments and other proceedings are forbidden in some states by the constitutional requirement that all laws shall be general.

One very precise limit to the power to cure these proceedings is this: They cannot be cured when there was a lack of jurisdiction to take them. This is a rule applicable to every species of legal proceedings. Curative laws may heal irregularities in action, but they cannot cure a want of authority to act at all.[1] What constitutes a want of jurisdiction is the difficult question in these cases. And in this regard the rules which apply to retrospective and to prospective healing acts are the same.

It is certain that whatever the legislature could not have authorized originally it cannot confirm. The unauthorized acts of individuals cannot confer upon the state a power it did not before possess.[2] Therefore no unconstitutional taxation can be confirmed, and none that entirely wants any essential element of taxation. Taxation without an assessment must consequently be incapable of confirmation, because apportionment is indispensable.[3] And if

[1] Denny *v.* Mattoon, 2 Allen, 361; Nelson *v.* Rountree, 23 Wis., 367; Daniel *v.* McCorrell, 19 Ill., 226, 228; Richards *v.* Rote, 68 Penn. St., 248; State *v.* Doherty, 60 Me., 504; Griffin's Ex'r *v.* Cunningham, 20 Grat., 31, 109, per *Joynes*, J.; Atchison, etc., R. R. Co. *v.* McQuilkin, 12 Kans., 301; People *v.* Goldtree, 44 Cal., 323; Abbott *v.* Lindenbower, 42 Mo., 162.

[2] National Bank of Cleveland *v.* Iola, 9 Kans., 689, 696, per *Dillon*, J.

[3] The Pennsylvania statute of 1815 declared that "no inequality in the assessment or in the process or otherwise, shall be construed or taken to affect the title of the purchaser, but the same shall be declared to be good and legal." Also that only "when the owner or owners of lands sold for taxes shall have paid the taxes due on them previously to the sale, or within two years thereafter shall have tendered the amount of the taxes and costs with twenty-five per centum additional, and the tender has been refused, shall he or they be entitled to recover the lands by due course of law, and that in no other case and on no other plea shall an action be sustained." Notwithstanding this act it was decided that if an unseated lot was put on the seated list, and then transferred to the unseated without notice to the owner, a sale on this assessment would be void. Millikin *v.* Benedict, 8 Penn. St., 169, reviewing and approving Lorimer *v.* McCall, 4 W. & S., 133; and Harper *v.* Mechanics' Bank, 7 W. & S., 214. In Commercial Bank *v.* Woodside, 14 Penn. St., 404, 409, *Bell*, J., says: "It is essential to the validity of every tax sale of lands that the subject of it should be assessed and returned, by some competent authority,

the party has been illegally deprived of the opportunity to be heard in opposition to the assessment, the defect is jurisdictional.[1] And it is clear that a tax for an illegal purpose cannot be affirmed; the inability to authorize such a tax being perpetual.[2]

A tax discriminating against an individual could not be affirmed; but a merely excessive levy for lawful purposes, apportioned through the district, might be. It has often been decided that, where the only defect in a tax was the want of previous legislation, this might be supplied retrospectively.[3] But a tax

as unseated, or, where it has been rated as a *seated* tract or lot, that it be transferred to the unseated list, by the commissioners of the county, or their authorized agents, with notice to the owner, if that be possible. This is the doctrine of all the cases in which the subject has been treated. They settle indisputably, that an omission, in this particular, is uncured by the act of 1815, which applies only to irregularities in the proceeding. It is the assessment says Lorrimer *v.* McCall, 4 W., 351; S. C., 4 W. & Serg., 133, which confers the power to sell in the same manner as a judgment on which an execution is issued. Without this, there is no authority to divest the title of the owner, and if a tract be returned as seated it cannot be sold for taxes. To the same effect are the other adjudications, down to Milliken *v.* Benedict, 8 Barr, 169." To the same effect is Stewart *v.* Trevor, 56 Penn. St., 374. That the want of an assessment is not an irregularity capable of being thus cured, see Steward *v.* Shoenfelt, 13 S. & R., 360; Bratton *v.* Mitchell, 1 W. & S., 310; Miller *v.* Hale, 26 Penn. St., 432: McReynolds *v.* Longenberger, 57 id., 13. That the want of a notice required by the constitution is an incurable defect, see Wilson *v.* McKenna, 52 Ill., 43. An assessment so defective as to be totally void cannot be cured by legislation. People *v.* Holliday, 25 Cal., 300. So with a want of valuation: People *v.* Savings Union, 31 id., 132. The confirmation by a city council of a void assessment cannot make it good. Doughty *v.* Hope, 3 Denio, 594.

[1] See Thames Manufacturing Co. *v.* Lothrop, 7 Conn., 550, which however is not an adjudication upon the point. Marsh *v.* Chestnut, 14 Ill., 223; Billings *v.* Detton, 15 id., 218, are decisions which support the text. If one man's land is taxed to another and sold, the sale is void and cannot be made otherwise by legislation. Abbott *v.* Lindenbower, 42 Mo., 162. And see Hume *v.* Wainscott, 46 id., 145. If land is taxed by a city which is not within it, the tax cannot be validated though it is afterwards brought in. Atchison, etc., R. R. Co., *v.* McQuilkin, 12 Kans., 301.

[2] Conway *v.* Cable, 37 Ill., 82; Hart *v.* Henderson, 17 Mich., 218; Dean *v.* Borchsenius, 30 Wis., 235.

[3] In Grim *v.* School District, 57 Penn. St., 433, *Sharswood*, J., speaking of a bounty tax, says: "It has not been pretended, and could not be, that the legislature had not the power antecedent to authorize it. If so, they could cure any irregularity or want of authority in levying it by a retroactive law, even

sale that was made after a tax had been paid, would be void and incapable of confirmation, the officer losing all jurisdiction to proceed when payment has been made.[1]

The general rule has often been declared, that the legislature may validate, retrospectively, the proceedings which they might have authorized in advance. Therefore, if any directions of the statute fail of observance, which are not so far of the essence of the thing to be done that they must be provided for in any statute on the subject, the legislature may retrospectively cure the defect. But there are probably some exceptions to this general rule. If the law has afforded the party an opportunity to be heard, when it might have been dispensed with, he has a right to rely upon this for his protection, and we should doubt the right of the legislature to take it away by retroactive law. There are some cases which, we think, recognize this right to a hearing which the law has given, as constituting an exception to the general right of the legislature to cure defects. And the reason of the exception will apply to all cases in which notice to the party, by publication or otherwise, has been provided for his protection. If this can be dispensed with by a healing act, the very provision for a notice for the party's protection becomes a trap for his destruction.[2]

though thereby a right of action, which had been vested in an individual, should be divested. It is within the principle of all the decisions of admitted authority." And see Booth *v.* Woodbury, 32 Conn., 118; Crowell *v.* Hopkinson, 45 N. H., 9; Lowell *v.* Oliver, 8 Allen, 247; Comer *v.* Folsom, 13 Minn., 219; State *v.* Demorest, 32 N. J., 528; Barbour *v.* Camden, 51 Me., 608; Board of Commissioners *v.* Bearss, 25 Ind., 110; Taylor *v.* Thompson, 42 Ill., 9; Tucker *v.* Justices, 34 Geo., 370.

[1] Reading *v.* Finney, 73 Penn. St., 467.

[2] In Miller *v.* Hale, 26 Penn. St., 432, in which it was decided that a sale of unseated lands, made before the expiration of a year from the time when the tax was due and unpaid, could not be validated by the statute curing irregularities, the following remarks are made by *Woodward*, J.: "If it be granted that this was a regular assessment, or that its irregularities were such as the curative provisions of the act of 1815 would remedy, it cannot be claimed that the taxes were 'due and unpaid for the space of one year before' the sale — a condition on which the jurisdiction of the treasurer is expressly limited by the first section of the act of 1815. It was said with great truth, by Judge Huston, in McCall *v.* Lorimer, 4 Watts, 351, 352, that taxes cannot be

4 and 5. *Prospective Curative Laws.* As already observed, a general healing statute is subject to the same rules as a special act for the like purpose, and requires no separate consideration. A statute providing that in proceedings thereafter to be taken, errors and irregularities shall not vitiate, comes also under the same restrictions upon legislative authority,[1] though possibly it

due unless they have been assessed. It is, indeed, the assessment that makes the tax. It is the duty of all owners of unseated lands to return them for taxation, and to pay the taxes when assessed; but how is he to pay before they are assessed? It is not for him to fix the valuation or the rate, but for the county commissioners; and, until they have performed their duty, he has no duty to perform. But, when the assessment has been made and the tax ascertained, there is no authority for proceeding to sell the land until the tax shall have remained unpaid a year. A sale short of that period is simply void. It is like a sale where there has been no assessment, which has often been declared insufficient to pass the title. Nor does the curative provision of the fourth section of the act of 1815 apply to such a sale, for that was intended to remedy irregularities in proceedings where jurisdiction had attached, not to confer jurisdiction in cases that were beyond the purview of the act. A system was provided by the legislature for enforcing the payment of taxes upon unseated lands, but until a tract has been assessed and the tax remained due and unpaid a year, it is not within the system nor subject to any of its provisions. If such were not the rule of decision, titles could be divested, without notice to the owner, whenever it suited the interest or caprice of the county officers to expose them to sale. A law, intending to promote public objects without a wanton sacrifice of private rights, would thus become an instrument of intolerable mischief, and the doubts of its constitutionality, which, with all its checks and balances, attended its enactment and early history, would grow into a conviction that would sweep it from the statute book."

The cases of Milliken *v.* Benedict, 8 Penn. St., 169, and Commercial Bank *v.* Woodside, 14 id., 404, turn upon a failure to give a notice which, in advance, might have been dispensed with. See also Prindle *v.* Campbell, 9 Minn., 212; Dubuque *v.* Wooten, 28 Iowa, 571. But see People *v.* Seymour, 16 Cal., 332.

[1] A Minnesota tax law came under review in Prindle *v.* Campbell, 9 Minn., 212. Among other things it provided, that "all the instructions and directions herein given for the assessing of lands and personal property, and the levying and collecting of taxes and assessments, shall be deemed only directory, and no error or informality in the proceedings of any of the officers entrusted with the same, not affecting the substantial justice of the tax itself, shall vitiate, or in any wise affect the validity of the tax or assessment, or of the title conveyed under the sale for taxes under this chapter." *Held*, that this does not embrace such errors and informalities as go to the jurisdiction of the

may go farther in some particulars, as the parties concerned would be apprised in advance that they were not to rely upon an exact compliance with the law, and would be under greater obligation to watch the proceedings. It is not an objection to a curative statute that it is passed while suits are pending, and was designed to defeat the proceedings cured. The court must apply the statute

officers charged with the performance of the duties imposed by the chapter, or the validity of their acts, but only such as do not substantially affect the material steps in the proceedings. *Held*, further, that a defective notice of sale was not cured by the act. An assessment in which the lands of two persons were assessed together under one aggregate assessment was in Hamilton *v.* Fond du Lac, 25 Wis., 490, 495, held void, and the defect not corrected by a statute that an assessment shall be valid, "notwithstanding any omission, defect or irregularity" in the proceedings. *Paine* J., says "it would be clearly going beyond the scope and intent of this act to say that it made valid an assessment against one person of a tax upon another person's lots. That is something more than a mere omission, defect or irregularity in the proceedings."

Under the Pennsylvania statute the following irregularites held to be cured: A failure of the assessor to sign his roll. Townsen *v.* Wilson, 9 Penn. St., 270. A sale of seated land with unseated; the sale being good as to the proportion of the tax for which the unseated was chargeable, and the title passing after redemption expired. Mitchell *v.* Bratton, 5 W. & S., 451; Campbell *v.* Wilson, 1 Watts, 503; Harper *v.* McKeehan, 3 W. & S., 238; McCord *v.* Bergautz, 7 Watts, 487; Dietrick *v.* Mason, 57 Penn. St., 40. Paying over surplus moneys instead of giving a surplus bond. Rogers *v.* Johnson, 67 id., 43, citing and relying upon Ash *v.* Ashton, 3 W. & S., 510, and Iddings *v.* Cairns, 2 Grant's Cas., 88. The statute does not cure the want of a deed. Hoffman *v.* Bell, 61 Penn. St., 444. As to curing irregularities in general, see Laird *v.* Heister, 24 id., 452; Cuttle *v.* Brockway, 24 id., 145; Heft *v.* Gephart, 65 id., 510, 518; Witherspoon *v.* Duncan, 4 Wall., 210, 217. A Massachusetts statute provided, that "if in the assessors' list, or their warrant and list committed to the collector, there shall be any error in the name of any person taxed, the tax assessed to him may, notwithstanding such error, be collected of the person intended to be taxed; provided he is taxable, and can be identified by the assessors." This applied to the case of one taxed by his surname only. Tyler *v.* Hardwick, 6 Met., 470. See Sargeant *v.* Bean, 7 Gray, 125, where this statute was further considered. And for cases under a law for like purpose in Ohio, see Welker *v.* Potter, 18 Ohio, N. S., 85; Upington *v.* Oviatt, 24 id., 232. The cases under the Iowa statute go farther, we think, than any others, in sanctioning broad powers in the legislature to cure defects. The following are referred to: Eldridge *v.* Kuehl, 27 Iowa, 160; McCready *v.* Sexton, 29 id., 356; Hurley *v.* Rowel, 31 id., 64; Rima *v.* Cowan, 31 id., 461; Thomas *v.* Stickle, 32 id., 71; Henderson *v.* Oliver, 32 id., 512; Bulkley *v.* Callanan, 32 id., 461; Ware *v.* Little, 35 id., 234; Jeffrey *v.* Brokaw, 35 id., 505; Genther *v.* Fuller, 36 id., 604.

in the pending suits.[1] But such a statute cannot affect cases already passed into judgment.[2]

6. *Reassessments.* The method of curing defects by reassessment of the tax is less open to abuse than any that has hitherto been mentioned. Whether this is done by general law, which provides for all cases in which tax proceedings prove invalid, and authorizes the same tax to be imposed on the persons or property that should be charged therewith, by proceedings begun *de novo*, or assumes the form of a special law providing for the like reassessment in any particular case, it is scarcely possible that it should cause serious injustice beyond what is incident to all tax legislation. In the new proceedings the party concerned has all the opportunity to watch the various steps, and to be heard in review of them, that he has in any case, and he is precluded by nothing that has taken place in the proceedings which proved abortive. The assessment is for the purpose merely of enforcing against him a duty which he was likely to evade, by reason of the nonfeasances or misfeasances of the officers whose duty it was to enforce it; and as the new proceeding gives him the same opportunity of being heard that is given in other cases, and is conducted on principles that operate generally, he has no reasonable ground of complaint.[3] The only cases in which hardship is likely

[1] See Cowgill *v.* Long, 15 Ill., 202; Miller *v.* Graham, 17 Ohio, N. S., 1; State *v.* Squiers, 26 Iowa, 340; State *v.* Norwood, 12 Md., 195; Hepburn *v.* Curts, 7 Watts, 300; Grim *v.* School District, 51 Penn. St., 433. *Certiorari* dismissed where a defect in the assessment was cured by special act after it was sued out. State *v.* Apgar, 31 N. J., 358. And see Newark *v.* State, 32 id., 453; Bristol *v.* Supervisors of Ingham, 20 Mich., 95; Ex parte McCardle, 7 Wall., 506; U. S. *v.* Tyner, 11 id., 88.

[2] Lambertson *v.* Hogan, 2 Penn. St., 22; People *v.* Supervisors of Saginaw, 26 Mich., 22. The legislature has no authority to reverse judgments directly or indirectly, and a legislative act legalizing a tax roll and healing defects therein will be so construed as not to affect an existing judgment for tresspass against the collector for seizing and selling property to satisfy the illegal tax. Moser *v.* White, 29 Mich., 59.

[3] A statute which, in case of an invalid or irregular tax, provides that it may be assessed by the assessors for the time being, "to the just amount to which, and upon the estate or to the person to whom such tax ought at first to have been assessed," may be used to correct an error which extends to the entire list. Goodrich *v.* Lunenburg, 9 Gray, 38. It justifies a reassessment to the wife, of a tax wrongfully put to the husband and abated the preceding

to be inflicted by such legislation, are those in which a tax is reassessed upon an estate which has changed hands since the tax should have been collected from it; but a proper examination of the records will, in most cases, lead the purchaser to a discovery of the liability, and enable him to provide against it.[1] Where the tax itself was originally void by reason of having been levied for an illegal purpose, it is obviously impossible to breathe vitality into it by new proceedings.[2] If it was void because of want of legislation justifying it, it may be reassessed after proper legislation has been had.[3] If it was void because of a disregard of apportionment, or for any reason affecting a part of the list only, it may be reassessed with the proper corrections, where corrections are practicable.[4] And here it may be observed that a judicial decision against the first proceedings, if based upon errors and defects merely, and not upon the vicious nature of the tax itself, is not a bar to a reassessment. Such a decision merely points out the error, and the reassessment may be of all others the most proper and effectual way of correcting it.[5]

Judicial corrections. Still another method of curing defects may be noticed. It is that which is sometimes provided by statutes allowing the parties concerned to have a judicial review of the proceedings on a proper application.[6] We do not refer

year. Hubbard *v.* Garfield, 102 Mass., 72: and see Overing *v.* Foote, 43 N. Y., 290.

[1] That the tax may be reassessed, notwithstanding such a change of title, see Tallman *v.* Janesville, 17 Wis., 71; Cross *v.* Milwaukee, 19 id., 509. That local assessments may be reassessed as well as general taxes, May *v.* Holdridge, 23 id., 93; Brevoort *v.* Detroit, 24 Mich., 322. And as to such laws in general, see further, Tweed *v.* Metcalf, 4 id., 579, 590; State *v.* Newark, 34 N. J., 236; *In re* Van Antwerp, 56 N. Y., 261. A failure to require the payment of a tax, or the decision of the auditor general that it is not payable, or the receipt of taxes for subsequent years, works no estoppel as against the state. Delaware Division Canal Co. *v.* Commonwealth, 50 Penn. St., 399.

[2] Dean *v.* Charlton, 23 Wis., 590; Dean *v.* Borchsenius, 30 id., 236.

[3] Mills v. Charlton, 29 Wis., 400. See *In re* Van Antwerp, 56 N. Y., 261.

[4] See Dean *v.* Charlton, 27 Wis., 522; Cook *v.* Ipswich Local Board of Health, L. R., 6 Q. B, 451; Brevoort *v.* Detroit, 24 Mich., 322.

[5] Dean *v.* Charlton, 23 Wis., 590: compare Butler *v.* Supervisors of Saginaw, 26 Mich., 22.

[6] For cases of this nature, see State *v.* Jersey City, 35 N. J., 381; Miller *v.*

now to those cases in which proceedings are, under general laws, referred to a court at some stage for confirmation, but to those in which the proceedings are attacked after their conclusion, and they are subjected to a judicial examination with a view to the correction of any errors, if correction shall be found practicable.

Corrections by amendment. Of the errors that creep into the records of tax proceedings very many are merely clerical, or occur in consequence of a failure to put in proper form the evidence of transactions in themselves correct. Tax proceedings must stand by the record; and a failure to make the proper record may be as fatal as a failure to take the proceeding of which the record should have been made.

If, however, the defect in a record is obviously clerical and nothing more; that is to say, if the record on its face sufficiently shows that the proper steps have in fact been taken, but there is some error on the part of the recording officer in putting the evidence upon the record in precise conformity to the law; some omission of a word, or the accidental employment of one word for another, or any similar error which cannot mislead; the mistake may be overlooked, and the court, when the record becomes the subject of judicial investigation, may by intendment supply what is omitted, and correct what is erroneous, and then sustain the record as though the proper corrections had been made by the recording officer himself.[1] But corrections cannot be made by intendment unless the necessary facts appear, either in the record

Graham, 17 Ohio, N. S., 1. The statute in each case is quite peculiar. That of New Jersey forbade any collateral questioning of the proceedings in the case of certain assessments for local objects, but permitted them to be reviewed *at any time* on *certiorari*, or other proper proceeding in the supreme or circuit court.

[1] Mr. Blackwell, speaking of Atkins *v.* Hinman, 2 Gilm., 437, 451, says: "Where in a collateral action, amendments of the tax record were permitted in the circuit court, the supreme court sustained them upon the ground that they were only corrections of clerical mistakes, and could prejudice no person's rights; that they brought no new matter in the case, and gave no additional efficacy to the proceedings, but simply put them in stricter conformity to the provisions of the statute. And it must be remembered that these amendments were of the judgment and precept under the Illinois statute of 1839, and the anterior proceeding on the files of the court, furnished the facts whereon the amendments were based." Blackwell on Tax Titles, 399.

as actually made, or in the official documents on file from which the record should have been drawn up; the courts cannot imply the existence of facts which are not recited any where in the official proceedings.

Where the proceedings are conducted under the supervision of a court of record, or must go before such a court for confirmation, the facts which do not appear of record may be supplied by leave of the court, on a proper showing by affidavit.[1] The authority of the court to permit such amendments, in order to make the record correspond to the facts, is probably not different from what it is to permit amendments in the exercise of its ordinary jurisdiction.

If the facts to be supplied are such as affect individual cases on the roll, and may prejudice the parties, it would seem to be a matter of right that the persons to be affected should have notice of an application to amend, and an opportunity to meet the showing. This should certainly be so if the application is made at a stage of the proceedings when the party, if the correction is made, will have no opportunity subsequently to raise any questions regarding the propriety or justice of the amendment. As an illustration, the case may be instanced of a judgment which is erroneous by reason of some defect which it is desired to supply by an amendment; in such case clearly the party against whom the judgment is to be validated should be allowed the privilege to contest the truth of that which it is proposed to put upon the record, and by which it is expected to bind him.[2] And the application ought to be a distinct proceeding for the purpose, and not be made in a suit brought to recover lands which have been sold under the judgment.[3] On such an application counter affidavits would be ad-

[1] Young *v.* Thompson, 14 Ill., 380, 381.

[2] See Dunham *v.* Chicago, 55 Ill., 357.

[3] In an action of ejectment, to recover possession of land by virtue of a tax title, motion was made to amend the precept. *Treat*, Ch. J., says: "If such an amendment is allowable, it should only be made upon a distinct application to the court for that purpose. The application should have no connection with any other case. A contrary course would introduce much confusion and inconvenience into judicial proceedings. A court engaged in the trial of a case ought not to be delayed and embarassed, by a motion to amend the record of another proceeding, which is but collaterally in question before it. Such an application might involve the necessity of bringing in other parties

missible, and the court ought to insist upon a very clear showing of the facts, before giving its sanction to the introduction of any changes in a record not originally made under its supervision. There is a manifest difference between such a case and the correction of errors in the record of proceedings which have been taken in the court itself, and of which the judges themselves may be presumed to have some recollection.

There are undoubtedly cases in which ministerial officers may correct errors without judicial permission; and there are also some cases in which it would be apparent they could have no such power. Still other cases may be open to reasonable doubt.

Where the defect consists merely in the failure to copy into a book of records the official document which evidences some legal transaction, the proper recording officer may correct it at any time, by making the required record. This may be done by the officer who should have done it in the first place, or it may be done by his successor in office. But where the document which should go upon record is defective, a case of more difficulty is presented. Many cases involving the right to make amendments have been considered in the state of New Hampshire, and it may be useful to notice them.

In a very early case the validity of a town vote to raise money was in question, and the court, while the cause was on trial, permitted the record to be amended so as to show that the proper vote had been had. The amendment was made by the person who was town clerk at the time the meeting was held; and the case does not show that he was still in office. The authority to make the amendment was not much considered; the judge contenting himself with saying that, "On this point we think that great care must be taken that amendments be made only accord-

and different interests before the court." Pitkin *v.* Yaw, 13 Ill., 251, 253. In another case the same judge, in speaking of a defective judgment on a delinquent tax list, says: "It may be that the circuit court, upon a proper application, will allow the record to be so amended as to show when the judgment was rendered. But until the record is thus perfected, no title can be asserted under the proceedings." Young *v.* Thompson, 14 Ill., 380, 381. Where the certificate of publication of the collector's notice of his intended application for judgment for taxes is deficient, it may be amended by order of the court, upon notice being given to the opposite party, even after judgment. Dunham *v.* Chicago, 55 Ill., 357, citing Coughran *v.* Gutchens, 18 Ill., 390.

ing to the fact; but we have no doubt that a record may be amended to conform to the truth."[1]

In the next case in which a like question was raised, the point was more fully considered. It was admitted that there were defects in the record of town proceedings, which would be fatal to a tax title then under consideration in a case on trial, unless they could be cured. The defects are summed up by the court, and the case disposed of as follows: "The return of the posting up of the warrant for the town meeting is insufficient. It does not state when it was posted up. Nor does it show that it was posted at a public place. It does not appear that Thirston, who was chosen collector, took the oath of office prescribed by law. And there are defects in the return of the collector, to which exceptions have been taken.

"The tenants move that these proceedings may be amended. It has been already settled that the records of towns may be amended to conform to the truth of the fact.[2] The amendment must be made by the person who was in office at the time.[3]

"It seems probable that in the prior cases where amendments have been allowed, the officers who were permitted to make them were not in office at the time; if they were, it must have been under subsequent election; and the right to have the amendment made cannot depend upon the question whether the officer has again been elected. The form in which such amendments are to be made, has never yet been settled. It would be very dangerous to sanction alterations of the books themselves, by erasures and interlineations. And we are of opinion that they should be made only upon evidence showing the truth of the facts, and then by drawing out in form the amendment which the facts authorize. The amendment, with the order under which it is made, may then be annexed to the books where the original is recorded, so that the whole matter will appear; and in furnishing copies the original and amendment should both be furnished.

"But it is objected, on the part of the demandant, that no

[1] Bishop *v.* Cone, 3 N. H., 513, 516, per *Richardson*, Ch. J., who cites, as authority, Welles *v.* Battelle, 11 Mass., 477, and Taylor *v.* Henry, 2 Pick., 397.

[2] Citing Bishop *v.* Cone, 3 N. H., 513; Welles *v.* Battelle, 11 Mass., 477; Cardigan *v.* Page, 6 N. H., 182.

[3] Taylor *v.* Henry, 2 Pick., 397.

amendment ought to be made to her prejudice. That when she purchased, these defects in the vendue title were apparent, and that she must be presumed to have purchased with knowledge that the title was defective.

"The general rule is that amendments of records are made with saving of the rights of third persons acquired since the existence of the defect. Chamberlain *v.* Crane, 4 N. H. 116; Bowman *v.* Stark, 6 id., 459.

"To apply this rule, however, to all cases of defects in sales of lands for taxes, would, in effect, be very nearly denying a right to amend; as the owner of the land sold would attempt to defeat any amendment, by conveying to some friend, who would bring a suit in his behalf. It would, at least, be necessary to confine the application of the principle to cases where the land had been actually conveyed *bona fide.*

"But instances might exist, when the purchaser, although he might not have found upon the records all that was necessary to make a formal and valid record, might have been well assured, from what he did find, that all that was necessary had in fact been done.

"For instance, in relation to the two first defects in the records in this case — in the return of the warning of the meeting, and in the record of the oath of the collector — although these records are not sufficient in point of law, they lead the mind of any one to the belief that what was requisite was probably done. And in such cases, where the fact appears to be stated, but not in a formal manner, there is no reason why he who purchases should not be subjected to the same liability to have the amendment made, and the record put in form, that his grantor would have been, had he attempted to recover the land.

"There are cases where, although all that is required may not appear of record, it may be left to the jury to presume that all that was required was done. As in Bishop *v.* Cone — although the application of the principle in that case may, perhaps, have been questionable, on account of the transactions having been so recent, that, if the truth would have warranted it, an amendment might have been made. Whether that principle could be applied against a subsequent purchaser, it is not necessary to determine. But where what is necessary, is, although not formally stated, so far set down as to lead to a belief that a correct record might have been made, there seems to be no reason why a purchaser, who has access to the records, should not take it subject to a right to have the record put in form, if the truth will warrant it.

"When, on the other hand, nothing appears upon the record in relation to any particular fact necessary to make out a title, nor is any thing set down from which it is naturally to be inferred that the fact existed, a subsequent *bona fide* purchaser ought not to have his title defeated by supplying a record instead of amending a record."[1]

The subsequent cases in New Hampshire are in accord with these, and fully sustain them in their conclusions.[2] It is said that "it has never been held that such amendments could be allowed by any other tribunal than one of the superior courts."[3] And yet unless some statute confers upon them the authority, it is not

[1] Gibson *v.* Bailey, 9 N. H., 168, 176, per *Parker*, Ch. J. The judge thereupon proceeds to say that "upon these principles, if the facts will warrant it" the various defects which he points out in detail may be amended. But he adds, "we must first have evidence to show that these amendments may be made with truth."

[2] On the trial of Bean *v.* Thompson, 19 N. H., 290, involving the validity of a tax voted at a town meeting, it appearing that there was no return upon the warrant calling the meeting, the selectmen who were in office when it was held were permitted, on motion, to make the proper return. *Woods*, J., says: "Leave is often granted to officers, whose returns of their doings, or records of public transactions, are, by law, made evidence, to correct errors or to supply omissions, to conform to the truth. The interest which the public have in the correctness and fullness of the record, and the responsibility of the officer himself for the accuracy of his own doings, are primarily a good cause for granting such indulgences tending to the promotion of reasonable objects. And it has never been deemed an objection to the amendment of a return or record, that proceedings were pending which might be affected by it, except that where rights or claims *bona fide* have intervened, amendments that would entirely defeat them have been in some instances denied." And he refers to Gibson *v.* Bailey, *supra*, as laying down the proper rule on the subject. In Scammon *v.* Scammon, 28 N. H., 419, 429, Bishop *v.* Cone and Gibson *v.* Bailey, are again referred to with approval. In Cass *v.* Bellows, 31 id., 501, they also are approved, but the proper person to make the corrections then necessary was dead, and consequently they could not be made. See further Prescott *v.* Hawkins, 12 id., 19; Pearce *v.* Richardson, 37 id., 306, 309; Jaquith *v.* Putney, 48 id., 138.

[3] Pierce *v.* Richardson, 37 N. H., 306, 311, per *Bell*, J.

very clear whence they derive it, nor how a township officer, or one who has been such, can, in this collateral way, have authority conferred upon him to do anything which, without such authorization, would be an illegal act.

An early case in Massachusetts, often quoted in New Hampshire, involved the validity of a correction by a town clerk, of his own motion, to cure a defect in an entry made by himself. The amendment was sustained; the court expressing the opinion that the clerk might have made it at any time while he held the office, even though under a subsequent election.[1] But it is held in the same state that the successor of the clerk can have no authority to make corrections in records of transactions which were had before he came into office.[2]

In Vermont it has been said that "the practice of amending and altering the records, when a controversy has arisen, to meet a particular case, or in consequence of a decision of the court, cannot be defended."[3] In a later case the right to amend, under proper restrictions, was asserted. "While it is obvious," say the court "some limits must be fixed to such amendments, we do not fee prepared to say, as matter of law, that they are never allowable. If the officer making the record were out of office, or were a party to the suit, as in Hadley *v.* Chamberlin, 11 Vt., 618, and in many other cases, it might be improper. * * But we think in general it must be regarded as the right of the clerk of a town, or other municipal corporation, while having the custody of the records, to make any record according to the facts. And we do not perceive that his having been out of office and restored again, could deprive him of that right. But even the officer could not alter or amend a record upon the testimony of third persons ordinarily, and ought not to do it upon his own recollection, unless in very obvious cases of omission or error, of which the present might fairly be regarded as one probably. Such amendments

[1] Welles *v.* Battelle, 11 Mass., 477, 481, per *Parker*, Ch. J.

[2] Taylor *v.* Henry, 2 Pick., 397. The defect consisted in the failure to record the adjournment of the town meeting at which the new clerk was chosen.

[3] *Williams*, Ch. J., in Hadley *v.* Chamberlin, 11 Vt., 618. The amendment was made in open court on the trial of a cause involving the sufficiency of the record. One peculiarity of the case was that the officer making the amendment was a party to the suit, and made it for his own protection.

should ordinarily be made by the original documents or minutes."[1]

It is observable of this case that the amendment, which consisted in the signing of the record of warning of a school district meeting, was made by the clerk on the trial of a cause, where the record was in question, and without the permission of the court. From the case it appears that "the court decided that they had no power over the clerk, and could give him no directions, but said that in the opinion of the court the clerk had a right, if he chose to do so, to amend the record in that particular, if such amendment would be according to the truth; but that the clerk must judge for himself whether he would or should make such amendment, and the court added that if such amendment was made, the record, in the opinion of the court, would be admissible." This remark distinguishes the case broadly from those in New Hampshire, and leaves the responsibility of all amendments with the officer himself.

In New York, in a case in which the affidavit of the assessors, attached to the assessment roll, was found to be defective, the opinion was expressed that it would be competent for the board of supervisors, when in session for the purposes of a review of the rolls, "to send for the assessors of any one town to come before them, and supply omissions, and make the necessary affidavits, where the omission occurred through accident or mistake."[2] This opinion appears entirely reasonable; and it would seem that the officer who, through any carelessness or error, has executed, or even delivered, a defective process or return, ought to be at liberty to correct it at any time afterwards, before any decisive action has been taken, under the process or document amended, and while, therefore, there is no possibility that the error can have prejudiced any one.

Of course the amendment could not be made by one who was no longer in office, as under such circumstances it would not be an official act.[3] Neither could it be made under circumstances

[1] *Redfield*, Ch. J., in Mott *v.* Reynolds, 27 Vt., 206, 208.

[2] Parish *v.* Golden, 35 N. Y., 462, 465, per *Morgan*, J.

[3] *Shaw*, Ch. J., in Hartwell *v.* Littleton, 13 Pick., 229, 232. "The first question is whether the town clerk of a former year, who does not now hold that

where it could operate unjustly upon the rights of parties. Thus, it has been held in Vermont, that if a tax sale is fatally defective by reason of the failure of the town clerk to certify in his record that the advertisements were published as required by law, the clerk cannot make it good by amending his record after the time for redeeming from the sale has expired. The reason is, that the owner, relying upon the record, may have omitted to redeem, inasmuch as his land has not been legally sold.[1] But until the rights of third parties have intervened, or conclusive action has been taken in reliance upon the records or documents, as representing in their imperfect state the actual facts, it is not perceived why a mistake once made should be crystalized and preserved as an instrument for the destruction of all that shall follow, instead of being corrected, that legal proceedings may be supported upon it. The question to some extent is one of public policy; and while undoubtedly it is wise to hold strictly to the rule, that records shall not be tampered with to the injury of parties concerned, there is no principle or reason of public policy which should preclude the correction of errors before rights have become fixed, but many considerations which support it.

No amendment can make valid a tax sale that was void for want of a proper description of the land in the assessment and subsequent proceedings.[2] And if fatal errors occur in tax con-

office, can be allowed to come in and amend the record of a former year, made whilst he was in that office; and the court are of opinion that he cannot. It has been held in Welles *v.* Battelle, 11 Mass., 477, that where a clerk continues in office several years, by repeated annual elections, he may amend the record of a former year, notwithstanding an election has intervened, and though he does not hold the office under the same appointment. But we think there is an obvious distinction in principle between the two cases. In the latter the clerk not only knows the fact, in relation to which the amendment is to be made, which is a circumstance common to both, but he still enjoys the confidence of the town, is by their vote entrusted with the custody of their records, and is held responsible for their purity and correctness under the sanction of his official oath, and all such other guards as the law has thought it necessary to prescribe in the case of a clerk actually in office. The intervening election is substantially a continuance of the clerk in the same office." And see School District *v.* Atherton, 12 Met., 112.

[1] Judevine *v.* Jackson, 18 Vt., 470, approved and followed in Langdon *v.* Poor, 20 id., 13. Compare Jaquith *v.* Putney, 48 N. H., 138.

[2] Roberts *v.* Chan Lin Pen, 23 Cal., 259.

veyances, they can neither be amended by the officer, nor corrected by motion in a court of law. The proper tribunal for that purpose is a court of equity. A court of law, where the defective conveyance was in question, might order the case continued to give opportunity for relief in equity, but could not do more.[1]

An officer to whom return has been made by another, has no authority to amend such return,[2] but a correction in an immaterial point can give no one a ground of complaint.[3]

[1] Annan *v.* Baker, 49 N. H., 161, 171, per *Nesmith*, J., citing Prescott *v.* Hawkins, 12 id., 19.

[2] Blight *v.* Banks, 6 T. B. Monr., 192, 206; Blight *v.* Atwell, 7 id., 264, 268. See Bellows *v.* Weeks, 41 Vt., 590, 600; Jones *v.* Tiffin, 24 Iowa, 190.

[3] Case *v.* Dean, 16 Mich., 12. As to amendments permitted by statute in Iowa, see Jones *v.* Tiffin, 24 Iowa, 190; Conway *v.* Younkin, 28 id., 298.

CHAPTER XI.

THE VOTING OF THE TAX.

Necessity for legislative authority. There must be distinct legislative authority for every tax that is levied. This is a principle that admits of no exception whatever,[1] unless one is made by the constitution of the state, operating to that extent as a restriction upon what would otherwise be the soverign legislative power over this subject. And in the several states the principle applies to every tax, whether state or municipal.

But while the legislature must originate the power to tax, and prescribe the rules under which taxes are to be levied, the determination of the amount, even of a state tax, may be referred to some other authority. When a state auditing board is provided for by the constitution of the state, the allowances of the board will perhaps be made conclusive, and be required to go into the general tax levy for the year.[2] And in any case there seems to be no objection in principle to legislation under which the salaries of state officers, the general expenses of state government, and other demands against the state, which are audited in accordance with general legislation, shall be provided for by a levy made under general rules, without the necessity of a special act prescribing the amount of the particular tax. No legislative power is delegated by such an arrangement.

The amount of the local taxes is determined in various ways: 1. In some cases they are fixed by the legislature or under its direction; as will be shown in a subsequent chapter. 2. In some

[1] See Norris *v.* Russel, 5 Cal., 249; Litchfield *v.* Vernon, 41 N. Y., 123; Allen *v.* Peoria, etc. R. R. Co., 44 Ill., 85; Bangs *v.* Snow, 1 Mass., 181; Stetson *v* Kempton, 13 id., 272; Lisbon *v.* Bath, 21 N. H., 319; Daily *v.* Swope, 47 Miss., 367; Columbia *v.* Guest, 3 Head, 413; Cruikshanks *v.* Charleston, 1 McCord, 360; State *v.* Charleston, 2 Speers, 623; Simmons *v.* Wilson, 66 N. C., 336; Vanover *v.* Justices, 27 Geo., 354; Lott *v.* Ross, 38 Ala., 156; Richmond *v* Daniel, 14 Grat., 385; Bullock *v.* Curry, 2 Met., Ky., 171; Bright *v.* McCullough, 27 Ind., 223.

[2] See People *v.* Supervisors of Queens, 1 Hill, 195.

cases they are determined by local boards, which exercise a *quasi* legislative authority; such as the boards of supervisors of many states, the county courts or boards of justices of others, the common councils of cities and boroughs, the village boards of villages, the township boards or selectmen of towns, and the corresponding boards in other corporate bodies. 3. Many taxes are required to be voted by popular assemblages composed of all the voters of the municipality to be taxed, or, in some instances, of certain classes of the voters, supposed to be specially interested in the tax. It is consistent with the practice of early days that this method shall be adopted in all districts whose population is not too great to render it impracticable; and we find it general in school districts, and to a large extent also in towns, villages and even some small cities. But in the larger districts like counties, as well as in the cities generally, the authority is of necessity confided to representatives of the people, who are usually chosen by popular ballot.

Voting taxes in popular assemblages. A popular assemblage for any legal purpose must be regularly convened in such manner as the law may have prescribed. The coming together of a majority of the people of a municipality, or even of all the people, at a time and in a manner not provided for by law, and the voting upon the levy of a tax, will have no legal force or validity whatever. In levying taxes, or in exercising any other function of government, the local community are wielding a part of the sovereign power of the state, but only with the state's permission, and under such conditions, restrictions and regulations as the state has prescribed. One of these invariably is, that the power shall be exercised in an orderly manner, at a meeting assembled after due notice, and conducted according to legal forms, in order that there may be full opportunity for reflection, consultation and deliberation upon the important work to be done. Nothing short of this will insure deliberative meetings, or prevent popular gatherings degenerating into mobs, and thereby defeating the purposes for which they are authorized.

Corporate meetings may be appointed by general statute which names a certain day in the year on which they are to be held. In this manner provision is usually made for annual town meetings and school district meetings. Of such statutes every citizen takes notice at his peril, and a meeting assembled at the time and place appointed is a lawful meeting. This is probably the rule even where the notice of the meeting, which some statutes require to be given by publication, has been omitted; the notice by publication being only additional to the notice by statute, and being provided for by way of additional precaution, to remind the people of the statutory provision which they are nevertheless bound to take notice of, whether the publication takes place or not. The right to hold the meeting comes from the statute, not from the published notice.[1] The same statute will commonly specify the subjects which may be considered at such meetings, and will limit any power to levy taxes which is permitted to be exercised.[2]

All special meetings must be regularly called as the statute may have prescribed. The following are customary regulations: That the meeting shall be called by the officers of the municipality, either on their own motion or on the application of a certain number of the voters or freeholders; that it shall be notified either by a warning[3] delivered or its contents stated to the several voters, or by notice published or posted in a manner particularly indicated by the statute; and that the subjects to be considered at the meeting shall be specified in the warning or notice. With all these provisions there must be careful compliance, and the meeting when held must confine itself strictly to the subjects indicated in the notice or warning.[4]

[1] People *v.* Cowles, 13 N. Y., 350; People *v.* Brenham, 3 Cal., 477; State *v.* Jones, 19 Ind., 356; People *v.* Hartwell, 12 Mich., 508; Dishon *v.* Smith, 10 Iowa, 212; State *v.* Orvis, 20 Wis., 235; State *v.* Gætze, 22 id., 363. See Marchant *v.* Langworthy, 6 Hill, 646..

[2] As to the necessity of a vote of the electors before a school tax can be levied in Arkansas, see County Court *v.* Robinson, 27 Ark., 116. And in California, see People *v.* Castro, 39 Cal., 65.

[3] Difference between "calling" a meeting and "warning" it: see Stone *v.* School District, 8 Cush., 592; Rideout *v.* School District, 1 Allen, 232. And see as to the call, George *v.* School District, 6 Met., 497.

[4] That a tax can only be voted at a meeting legally warned, see Bowen *v.* King, 34 Vt., 156. As to what is a sufficient warning, see Allen *v.* Burlington, 45 id., 202. Where the warrant for a meeting specified as the object "to adopt such measures in relation to their ministerial concerns as may then and there seem expedient, and to act thereon as they see cause," *held* sufficient to sup-

In voting taxes all the local bodies act in a political capacity, and their action is to be favorably construed, and not to be overruled or set aside by judicial or any other authority, so long as they keep within the limits of the power bestowed upon them. But their action in voting taxes should always appear of record. "Every essential proceeding in the course of a levy of taxes," it is said in one case, "must appear in some written and permanent form in the record of the bodies authorized to act upon them. Such a thing as a parol levy of taxes is not legally possible under

port a vote of money in fulfillment of a contract between the minister and a committee, under which he was to discontinue the pastoral relation. Blackburn *v.* Walpole, 9 Pick., 97. A warrant "To choose a district committee and to act on other business that may be thought necessary," does not authorize prescribing a method for calling subsequent meetings by the clerk, and therefore a subsequent meeting called by the clerk cannot legally vote taxes. Little *v.* Merrill, 10 Pick., 543. A warning for a school meeting which stated the object to be "to take into consideration the expediency of raising for the use of schooling for the year ensuing," held sufficient. A vote was taken "to raise one cent and five mills on the dollar" on the list for the year, without naming any time of payment. *Held* to be sufficiently definite, and the tax would be payable on demand, or within a reasonable time. Bartlett *v.* Kinsley, 15 Conn., 327. As to the effect of custom on the construction of votes of town meetings, see Freeland *v.* Hastings, 10 Allen, 570, 578–9. An article in the warning of a school meeting, to see whether the district will have a school the ensuing winter, and to see what method the district will take to pay the expenses of said school, is sufficient to authorize the district to vote a tax upon the grand list to defray the expenses of the school. Chandler *v.* Bradish, 23 Vt., 416. A warning to see if a town will vote a tax for the purpose of paying a bounty does not authorize a vote to borrow money for that purpose. Atwood *v.* Lincoln, 44 Vt., 332. A school district tax voted at a meeting not legally called is void. Haines *v.* School District, 41 Me., 246; Rideout *v.* School District, 1 Allen, 232; People *v.* Castro, 39 Cal., 65. A tax voted for a purpose not specified in the notice of special meeting is void. Holt's Appeal 5 R. I., 603. Construction of particular notices; Williams *v.* Larkin, 3 Denio, 114; Torrey *v.* Milbury, 21 Pick., 64. A tax voted at a meeting warned without naming the hour of the meeting in the warrant is void, and it will not justify the collector in an action of trespass against him for taking property to satisfy the tax. Sherwin *v.* Bugbee, 16 Vt., 439. The return of a freeholder upon a warrant from the selectmen for warning a meeting of the inhabitants of a school district, that he had warned them according to law, was held to be conclusive in an action by one of the inhabitants against the assessors for assessing a tax on him which had been voted at such a meeting. Saxton *v.* Nimms, 14 Mass., 314. Under a statute which provided that "every town meeting shall be held in pursuance of a warrant under the hands of the selectmen," a warrant signed by one only was held void, and a tax voted at a meeting held pursuant thereto

the laws."[1] And in another, in which the action of a convention of town delegates in voting a county tax was in question, "a record of the doings of such a convention is the only evidence to show a county tax duly granted."[2] But if the record is lost, the

was invalid, and one who had paid it might recover back of the town. Reynolds v. New Salem, 6 Met., 340. As to the effect of fraudulent neglect to give notice or giving misleading notice, see People v. Allen, 6 Wend., 486; People v. Peck, 11 id., 604; Marchant v. Langworthy, 6 Hill, 646; Randall v. Smith, 1 Denio, 214. That in proving notice of a meeting it is not sufficent to state in the affidavit or return that the notice was given "in accordance with the act," but it should state the facts, see State v. Hardcastle, 26 N. J., 143; Hardcastle v. State, 27 id., 551; Cardigan v. Page, 6 N. H., 182; Tuttle v. Cary, 7 Greenl., 426: compare People v. Highway Commissioners, 14 Mich., 528. But see Briggs v. Murdock, 13 Pick., 305; Houghton v. Davenport, 23 id., 235; Bucksport v. Spofford, 12 Me., 487. Where the defendants in an action of trespass justified as assessors, and showed by the records of the town that they were duly elected at a town meeting legally warned, they were held not bound to go behind the records to show that the proceedings of the warning officer had been regular. Thayer v. Stearns, 1 Pick., 109. In a vote of a school district laying a tax for its purposes, it is not essential to its validity that the particular object for which it was laid should be specified. West School District v. Merrils, 12 Conn., 436. A school house having been erected under invalid votes, the district may lawfully vote a tax to pay for it. Greenbanks v. Boutwell, 43 Vt., 207. As to such meetings in general, their regularity and powers, see Blackburn v. Walpole, 9 Pick., 97; Perry v. Dover, 12 id., 206; Little v. Merril, 10 id., 543; Williams v. School District, 21 id., 75; School District v. Atherton, 12 Met., 105; Cardigan v. Page, 6 N. H., 182; Nelson v. Pierce, id.., 194; Brewster v. Hyde, 7 id., 206; Lisbon v. Bath, 21 id., 319; Schoff v. Gould, 52 id., 512; Hunt v. School District, 14 Vt., 300; Pratt v. Swanton, 15 id., 147; Sherwin v. Bugbee, 17 id., 337; Wyley v. Nelson, 44 id., 404; Greenbanks v. Boutwell, 43 id., 207; Allen v. Burlington, 45 id., 202; Lander v. School District, 33 Me., 239; Jordan v. School District, 38 id., 164; Belfast, etc., R. R. Co. v. Brooks, 60 id., 568; State v. Hardcastle, 26 N. J., 143; Hardcastle v. State, 27 id., 551. The officers or the inhabitants merely treating the proceedings of an invalid meeting as valid does not make them so. Pratt v. Swanton, 15 Vt., 147.

[1] *Campbell*, J., in Moser v. White, 29 Mich., 59, 60. See also appeal of Powers, 29 id., 504: Doe v. McQuilkin, 8 Blackf., 335.

[2] *Richardson*, J., in Cardigan v. Page, 6 N. H., 182, 191. See Farrar v. Fessenden, 39 id., 268, 277. *Fowler*, J., says: "The records of taxes were properly received to prove the taxation which, being matter of record, could be proved in no other way, unless the loss of the records were first shown." In Gearhart v. Dixon, 1 Penn. St., 224, 228, it is said of the record of a school tax, that, "where it was defective, it might be explained or supplied by parol testimony. * * The law does not require school directors to keep a record of their proceedings, although it is better that they should do so." Compare Moor v. Newfield, 4 Greenl., 44.

contents are subject to parol proof as in other cases.[1] And any informalities are to be overlooked and disregarded if the substantial requisites of a vote appear.[2] It is always to be assumed that all these inferior municipalities have decided wisely and well upon the matters of discretion submitted to them, and it is incompetent anywhere to attack the validity of their action, upon the ground that the facts and circumstances which were laid before, and which surrounded them, did not call for the conclusion which they reached. From this broad statement the only exception that need be made, is that which rests upon the power of legislative supervision and control, when they refuse or neglect to perform a duty to the state, or when they vote local taxes which seem to the legislature impolitic and oppressive.

A learned and able court has spoken very clearly and pointedly concerning the absence of power in the judicial tribunals to entertain appeals from the municipal bodies, in the exercise of their discretionary power to tax. The case was one in which the attempt was made to enjoin school directors from the levy of a tax regularly voted. "No such appeal lies, for none is given by law. Most of our tax laws entitle the citizen to a hearing before he is obliged to pay; not to a judicial hearing, indeed, but to an

[1] Farrar *v.* Fessenden, 39 N. H., 268; Quinby *v.* North American, etc., Co., 2 Heiskell, 596; Irwin *v.* Miller, 23 Ill., 401.

[2] As to what is a sufficient vote in raising a town tax, see Blodgett *v.* Holbrook, 39 Vt., 336, 339. As to the particularity required in specifying the purpose of the tax, *Peck*, J., says, in that case "all that is necessary in this respect is that a vote of a town raising money should indicate, in general terms, the purpose or object for which the money is raised; and if that purpose or object is such as comes within the scope of the powers of the town, it is sufficient. It is not necessary to the validity of the vote that it should state the particular facts which show the present necessity of the town for the use of the money. The object specified being within the powers of the town, it is to be intended that the town has judged properly as to the occasion and necessity for the exercise of the power in the particular instance." See, also, as to the sufficiency of a vote for a school tax, Adams *v.* Hyde, 27 Vt., 221; West *v.* Whittaker, 37 Iowa, 598. A failure of the officers to sign the record of the board of supervisors, does not vitiate a tax levied by it. Lacey *v.* Davis, 4 Mich, 140; People *v.* Eureka, etc., Co., 48 Cal., 143; Martin *v.* Cole, 38 Iowa, 141. The record cannot be attacked collaterally, and its recitals shown to be false. Taylor *v.* Henry, 2 Pick., 397; Manning *v.* Fifth Parish in Gloucester, 6 id., 6; Hartwell *v.* Littleton, 13 id., 229; Edd *v.* Wilson, 43 Vt., 362; Bissel *v.* Jeffersonville, 24 How., 287.

appeal to some special tribunal, generally the county commissioners; but the school law gives no such appeal. This is the reason why the ear of the courts should be open to well founded complaints on the part of the citizen; but where he has no irregularity, no neglect of duty, no excess of authority to complain of, nothing, indeed, but an indiscreet use of clearly granted discretion, he will vex the judicial ear in vain, for the judicial arm can redress no such wrong. The power of taxation, altogether legislative, and in no degree judicial, is committed by the legislature, in the matter of schools, to the directors of school districts. If the directors refuse to perform their duties, the court can compel them. If they transcend their powers, the court can restrain them. If they misjudge their power, the court can correct them. But if they exercise their unquestionable powers unwisely, there is no judicial remedy."[1] This is a clear and strong statement of a wise and salutary general principle.

Restrictions upon municipal taxation. Upon the power of municipal corporations to tax, there are a number of restrictions which may be stated as follows:

1. Those imposed by the constitution of the United States. No state can confer upon its municipalities a power to tax, which

[1] *Woodward*, J., in Wharton *v.* School Directors, 42 Penn. St., 358, 364. See, to the same effect, Williams *v.* School District, 21 Pick., 75, 82; Petition of Powers, 52 Mo., 218. In each of these cases it was held, that after a school district had properly decided upon the erection of a school house, the determination was final, and that no inquiry could be entered upon regarding the necessity for the building. So in Jenkins *v.* Andover, 103 Mass., 94, 104, where the attempt was to enjoin a town from purchasing ground for a cemetery, on the ground that it was unnecessary, and that the expense would be disproportionate and unreasonable, *Chapman*, C. J., after showing that the language of the statute, authorizing towns to provide burial grounds, is very broad, and leaves them to judge what sum shall be raised, what quantity of land shall be appropriated for the purpose, and how it shall be fenced, laid out, arranged and managed, without any specified restriction, denies the jurisdiction of the court to control their discretion in these particulars, and declares that "the exercise of their discretion extends to matters of taste," in the matter of making the burial grounds beautiful and attractive, instead of unsightly and repulsive. That courts cannot restrict or restrain a power conferred to grant licenses for revenue, see Kemper *v.* Louisville, 7 Bush, 599; citing Mason *v.* Lancaster, 4 id., 406. As to the conclusiveness of a school district vote, see Eddy *v.* Wilson, 43 Vt., 362.

by the charter of general government is forbidden to itself. The limitations imposed upon state authority are imposed with equal emphasis upon every subordinate instrument of the state machinery.[1]

2. Those imposed by the constitution of the state. And here it is not a matter of course, that restrictions imposed on the state are restrictions on its corporations also. Some restrictions are sometimes imposed on the state itself as a corporation, which are not intended to apply to its municipal creations, while others declare a general policy, and are limitations upon the state power to tax either generally or by delegation. It is clearly within the province of the people, when they agree upon a constitution, to limit the state as they think proper, and to give, in some particulars, a larger liberty to the municipal corporations if that shall be thought wise. The question upon these limitations is one of construction merely.[2] But except as these express restrictions limit the state power specially, the state can delegate to none of the subordinate bodies an authority which, if no such body existed, it could not itself exercise.

3. Those which inhere in the nature of taxation itself. These have been sufficiently dwelt upon in another place.[3]

4. Those which inhere in local taxation specially, and confine it to purposes and objects which are local.

5. Those which the state attaches, as conditions or regulations, to the exercise of the authority it gives.

One of the most important purposes to be subserved by formal

[1] Stuyvesant *v.* New York, 7 Cow., 588; Illinois Conference Female College *v.* Cooper, 25 Ill., 148; Haywood *v.* Savannah, 12 Geo., 404; O'Donnell *v.* Bailey, 24 Miss., 386.

[2] See Slack *v.* Railroad Co., 13 B. Monr., 1, 16; Dubuque County *v.* Railroad Co., 4 Greene (Iowa), 1; Clapp *v.* Cedar County, 5 Iowa, 15; State *v.* Wapello County, 13 Iowa, 388; Clark *v.* Janesville, 10 Wis., 136; Bushnell *v.* Beloit, 10 id., 195; Prettyman *v.* Supervisors, 19 Ill., 406; Robertson *v.* Rockford, 21 id., 451; Johnson *v.* Stark County, 24 id., 75; Perkins *v.* Lewis, 24 id., 208; Butler *v.* Dunham, 27 id., 474; People *v.* Chicago, 51 id., 17, 34; Richmond *v.* Scott, 48 Ind., 568; People *v.* Supervisor, etc., 16 Mich., 254; Bay City *v.* State Treasurer, 23 id., 449, 504. An exemption from "public taxes," held not to be an exemption from taxation for municipal purposes Morgan *v.* Cree, 46 Vt., 773; S. C., 14 Am. Rep., 640.

[3] See Chapter III.

written constitutions is the protection of minorities against oppressive action on the part of majorities. Such oppressive action in the case of the local bodies might consist in the levy of enormous taxes, or the incurring of enormous debts, under the influence of temporary excitements and passions, for purposes which cooler reflection would condemn. By some state constitutions it is expressly made the duty of the legislature, in conferring local powers of taxation, to impose restrictions on the power in order to prevent its abuse. Such a provision is addressed to the discretion of the legislature, who will impose such and such only as are deemed advisable.[1] In the absence of such provisions in conferring the power to tax, it is restricted only as is above shown.[2] But in thus authorizing local taxation, the state does not deprive itself of the general power to control. There is nothing in the nature of a contract in such a delegation,[3] and what the state gives it may at any time take away. It may attach new con-

[1] People *v.* Mahaney, 13 Mich., 481, 487. In this case it was decided, that the power of a police board, to determine what sums should be raised for their purposes, was limited; the statute confining the power to the necessary police expenses. And see Paine *v.* Spratley, 5 Kans., 525; Bank of Rome *v.* Rome, 18 N. Y., 38; Hill *v.* Higdon, 5 Ohio, N. S., 243, 248; Northern Ind. R. R. Co. *v.* Connelly, 10 id., 159, 165; Maloy *v.* Marietta, 11 id., 636. A provision requiring the legislature to restrict the power of municipal taxation is complied with, in an act for a special street assessment, by limiting it to an assessment to the middle of the block upon adjacent property. Hines *v.* Leavenworth, 3 Kans., 186.

[2] The state may give complete power to tax all the subjects of taxation within the municipality. Wingate *v.* Sluder, 6 Jones L., 552; Durach's Appeal, 62 Penn. St., 491; Cheaney *v.* Hooser, 9 B. Monr., 330, 339; Augusta *v.* National Bank, 47 Geo., 562. Authority to assess "all taxable property" embraces all taxable at the time the authority is given, and all made taxable by subsequent legislation. Buffalo *v.* La Couteulx, 15 N. Y., 451. A limitation of taxes to a certain percentage of the assessed valuation is enlarged by implication when the legislature authorize the creation of any particular debt, to the extent that may be necessary to meet the demand. Commonwealth *v.* Commissioners of Alleghany County, 40 Penn. St., 348. Compare United States *v.* Burlington, 2 Am. Law Reg., N. S., 374.

[3] Where a state has no power to lay a certain tax, or to contract a certain debt, but it nevertheless assumes to do so, such a law is void, and cannot be treated as a contract between the state and those who have claims for which the law undertakes to provide payment. Ramsey *v.* Hœger, Sup. Ct., Ill., 1874, 6 Chicago Legal News, 318.

ditions, it may impose new restrictions or make new regulations.[1] These are matters of legislative discretion. Even after a tax had been collected, if, in the opinion of the legislature, the purpose was unwise and impolitic, it would doubtless have power to interpose and forbid the money being appropriated to it. This would seem to be a legitimate exercise of the general power of control and supervision which the legislature retains over all the inferior entities which have been created by it for political purposes. But the most efficient restriction of all, for practical purposes, is that rule of law which requires all municipal organizations or boards to show their grant of any authority they may assume to exercise. Towns, it has been said — and the remark applies to all such organizations — are corporations of limited powers; they cannot vote and assess money upon the inhabitants for all purposes indiscriminately, but must be confined to the established powers of towns, as settled by positive enactment or by well defined and ancient usage.[2] They cannot, therefore, tax

[1] A general authority given by a city charter to tax property for its purposes does not preclude the state making exemptions within the city afterwards. Richmond *v.* Richmond and Danville R. R. Co., 21 Grat., 604. If city boundaries are extended after the time for the annual assessment has passed, it is competent to provide for an assessment for the current year of the property newly added. Swift *v.* Newport, 7 Bush, 37. Compare Waldron *v.* Lee, 5 Pick., 323 ; Jackman *v.* School District, 5 Gray, 413. The right to tax may be taken away by the legislature even after the tax has been levied. Augusta *v.* North, 57 Me., 392.

[2] *Shaw*, Ch. J., in Cushing *v.* Newburyport, 10 Met., 508, 510. There is a very valuable statement in this case of the power of towns in respect to schools, and its history. For a history of the legislation of Michigan territory and state on the same subject, and the powers of the districts, see Stuart *v.* School District, 30 Mich., 69.

As to the right to establish free schools in a particular district of a state by a statute which leaves the final decision to the voters of the district, see Bull *v.* Read, 13 Grat., 78. The right to refer such questions to the voters of the locality was also affirmed in Slack *v.* Railroad, 13. B. Monr., 1, 9, 28; Stein *v.* Mobile, 24 Ala., 591, and numerous other cases. The legislature may, in its discretion, create independent school districts without the assent of the residents, and authorize a board chosen by its voters to make an annual levy for the erection of buildings and the support of schools therein. (The most plausible objections to the act seemed to be, that it took from the towns authority which properly pertained to them, and that the district was composed of parts of two townships, and the constitution required township officers to be chosen by " the voters thereof.") Kuhn *v.* Board of Education,

except for the very purpose allowed by law, and in the manner and under the conditions prescribed by law.[1]

Conditions precedent. In particular cases taxes have been authorized to be levied only after they have been petitioned for by a certain number of taxpayers. This is a condition precedent to any tax.[2] In Iowa it has been decided that if the township trustees have passed upon the sufficiency of such a petition, and declared it sufficient and levied the tax, this is conclusive in all collateral inquiries; the decision being on a matter within their jurisdiction.[3] But in New York the decisions were otherwise.[4]

4 W. Va., 499. On the creation of a new district by the union of two, the property of both becomes its property. It has no power to bargain and pay over to the old district the value of its school house, or to levy a tax for the purpose. Bacon *v.* School District, 97 Mass., 421. Where a district is divided after a tax is assessed, the inhabitants set off remain liable for its portion of the tax. Waldron *v.* Lee, 5 Pick., 323. That a school district tax is not within a statute which limits the amount of a tax for town and county purposes, see Taft *v.* Wood, 14 Pick., 362; Goodrich *v.* Lunenburg, 9 Gray, 38, 40; Blickensderfer *v.* School Directors, 20 Penn. St., 38.

[1] A tax voted to build a school house on a site not legally designated is invalid; that being a condition precedent. Marble *v.* McKenney, 60 Me., 332. Where the statute required assessors, before assessing any school district tax, to determine in which district the lands of persons residing out of the town should be taxed, and to certify their determination to the town clerk, who was to record the same: *Held*, that an assessment without complying with this requirement was invalid, and an inhabitant of the district might avail himself of the defect. The determination, it will be seen, was really as to what should be the limits of the district. Taft *v.* Wood, 14 Pick., 362. See also Rawson *v.* School District, 100 Mass., 134. By statute a town was not to be redistricted oftener than once in ten years, "so as to change the taxation of lands of proprietors." A tax levied in a new district established in violation of this provision, is void. Gustin *v.* School District, 10 Gray, 85. See Holmes *v.* Baker, 16 id., 259.

[2] Where an extraordinary tax was authorized on the recommendation of two-thirds of the grand jury, *held*, that this was a condition precedent, and the adjournment of the grand jury without action upon it would not justify the tax. Cooper *v.* Rowe, 42 Geo., 229.

[3] Ryan *v.* Varga, 37 Iowa, 78; West *v.* Whitaker, id., 598.

[4] Starin *v.* Genoa, 23 N. Y., 439; People *v.* Mead, 24 id., 114; Same *v.* Same, 36 id., 224. In the subsequent case of People *v.* Brown, 55 N. Y., 180, the same point was somewhat considered, but it became unnecessary to decide it, as the collector, who was defending a proceeding to compel him to pay over moneys he had collected, was held incompetent to raise the question. See *post*, chapter XX.

In some cases taxes are allowed to be voted by taxpayers only, while taxes in general are voted by the whole body of the electors. Such legislation is admissible, and the submission must conform to it.[1] When taxes are voted by a city council or other local body, a common and very useful provision is one that the yeas and nays shall be entered on the journal, so that no member shall escape his proper share of responsibility for the vote.[2] Without such a provision, it would be necessary only that the record should show a quorum present and a resolution adopted.[3]

Repeal or modification of local powers. The power to vote local taxes is at all times subject to the legislative modification and control.[4] The general law may modify their powers even when they were conferred by special charter, if the terms of the general law are sufficiently comprehensive for the purpose.[5] But

[1] In such cases, if the question is submitted to the whole body of the voters, the vote is void. Bullock *v.* Curry, 2 Met., Ky., 171. It has been decided in North Carolina that the legislature may authorize less than a majority to vote taxes. State *v.* Woodside, 9 Ired., 496; Same *v.* Same, 8 id., 104, 106. As to what is a majority vote, see Stanford *v.* Prentice, 28 Wis., 358.

[2] Such a provision is mandatory. Dillon's Mun. Corp., § 229, and cases cited. Compare Tobin *v.* Morgan, 70 Penn. St., 229, and Steckert *v.* East Saginaw, 22 Mich., 104.

[3] Where the record stated that A., B., C., and others, justices of the county court, were present, *held* not enough, as it did not affirmatively appear that a majority was present. Dudley's Ex'rs *v.* Oliver, 5 Ired., 227. Compare State *v.* McIntosh, 7 id., 68; Insurance Co. *v.* Sortwell, 8 Allen, 217; Lacey *v.* Davis, 4 Mich., 140.

[4] Richmond *v.* Richmond, etc., R. R. Co., 21 Grat., 604; Tucker *v.* The Justices, 34 Ga., 370. A repeal of a law by which a corporation was authorized on vote of its electors to levy a tax in aid of a public work, takes away the power, even though a favorable vote has already been had. Covington, etc., R. R. Co., *v.* Kenton Co. Court, 12 B. Monr., 144, 150. (The vote was in favor of levying the tax, but the *rate* had not been determined upon at the time of the repeal, and as this was a condition precedent, and had not been followed, the county court had no power to levy the tax, at least none before determining the rate.)

[5] A provision in a village charter that the village taxes shall be assessed upon the freeholders and inhabitants "according to law," means, unless otherwise explained, according to the general law of the state. Ontario Bank *v.* Bunnell, 10 Wend., 186, 194, per *Nelson*, Ch. J. Whenever a tax is authorized by law, and no special provision is made as to the source from which the revenue is to be derived, the law implies that the tax shall be levied upon all

where the power to tax is conferred by special charters, it is not usual to modify them in this manner, and in doubtful cases we should say the presumption was against an intent to do so.[1]

Exhausting authority. The taxing power once conferred is presumptively continuous, and to be exercised again and again as often as may be required by the exigencies of government and as often as may be consistent with the act of delegation.[2] But custom has much to do with the construction of such powers, and sometimes a single exercise must be deemed to exhaust the power for the time being, when the custom is to tax but once within a certain period of time; as for instance, within the year. And this is the general custom in the case of local taxes.[3] But an abortive attempt to make an assessment does not exhaust the power, and if no other obstacle exists, the officers may disregard the futile action and proceed anew.[4]

property subject to general taxation, and collected as other taxes. Hale *v.* Kenosha, 29 Wis., 599; State *v.* Bremond, 38 Tex., 116. As to the effect of general legislation upon special charters, see House *v.* State, 41 Miss., 737; S. C., 2 Withrow's Corp. Cas., 563.

[1] In Ohio it was decided that special acts, giving authority to municipal corporations to levy special taxes in aid of railroads, were not repealed by a constitutional provision forbidding such legislation. Cass *v.* Dillon, 2 Ohio, N. S., 607; Fosdick *v.* Perrysburg, 14 id., 472. In Iowa it was held that where a special law limits the power of a municipal corporation to levy taxes, a subsequent general law will not give power beyond the prior limitation. Clarke *v.* Davenport, 14 Iowa, 494. *Contra*, Butz *v.* Muscatine, 8 Wall., 575. See United States *v.* Burlington, 2 Am. Law Reg., N. S., 394. A grant of power to a municipal corporation to lay a tax for a particular purpose is a repeal, *pro tanto*, of all prior statutory restrictions on the power of taxation. Commonwealth *v.* Common Council of Pittsburgh, 34 Penn. St., 496.

[2] See Municipality *v.* Dunn, 10 La. An., 57; Williams *v.* Detroit, 2 Mich., 560.

[3] A school board having power to levy a tax not exceeding one per cent. in one year, held that when they ordered a tax, though below the maximum, they had exhausted their power for the year. Oliver *v.* Carsner, 39 Texas, 396. So in Oregon it has been decided that after one assessment of all the taxable property has been made and returned, and the tax levied thereon, there is no power to make a new assessment in order to reach property which has been brought within the district since the regular assessment. Oregon Steam Nav. Co. *v.* Portland, 2 Ore., 81. But an omission of the county court to exact license taxes when making the general levy does not preclude requiring them afterwards. State *v.* Maguire, 52 Mo., 420.

[4] Himmelman *v.* Cofran, 36 Cal., 411, citing Pond *v.* Negus, 3 Mass., 230;

Strict execution of authority. It is also a familiar rule that in the execution of the power to tax, the municipalities must confine themselves closely within the power conferred.[1] Many illustrations of this rule will be given further on, as the successive steps, which are to be taken to render taxation effectual, are enumerated and explained.

Libby *v.* Burnham, 15 Mass., 144; Bangor *v.* Lancy, 21 Me., 472. On the general subject see also Woodruff *v.* Fisher, 17 Barb., 224; Howell *v.* Buffalo, 15 N. Y., 512; People *v.* Haines, 49 id., 587; Lappin *v.* Nemaha County, 6 Kans., 403.

[1] That the provisions of the statute must be strictly pursued, see Henderson *v.* Baltimore, 8 Md., 352; Sharp *v.* Johnson, 4 Hill, 92; State *v.* Davenport, 12 Iowa, 335; *In re* Trufler, 44 Barb., 46; Howell *v.* Buffalo, 15 N. Y., 512; Bennett *v.* Buffalo, 17 id., 383; Smith *v.* Davis, 30 Cal., 536; Taylor *v.* Downer, 31 id., 480; Smith *v.* Cofran, 34 id., 310; Montgomery *v.* State, 38 Ala., 162; St. Joseph *v.* Anthony, 30 Mo., 537; McComb *v.* Bell, 2 Minn., 295; State *v.* Jersey City, 26 N. J., 444; Municipality No. 1 *v.* Millandon, 12 La. An., 769; Kyle *v.* Malin, 8 Ind., 34; Chicago *v.* Wright, 32 Ill., 192; Scammon *v.* Chicago, 40 id., 146; Doughty *v.* Hope, 3 Denio, 594; Tallman *v.* White, 2 N. Y., 66; Cruger *v.* Dougherty, 43 id., 107.

CHAPTER XII.

THE ASSESSMENT OF PROPERTY FOR TAXATION.

When taxes have been properly decided upon, an assessment may become an indispensable proceeding in the establishment of any individual charge against either person or property. This is always requisite when the taxes are to be levied in proportion to an estimate, either of values, of benefits or the results of business. It is of an assessment by the value of property that we shall speak in this place.

It is proper to remark, that it is usual to provide by law that one assessment shall be made use of for the levy of both state and local taxes, for the year or other period for which assessments are made, instead of directing a separate assessment for each description of tax. This is a matter as well of economy as of convenience, as one assessment answers all purposes. Independent assessments are sometimes provided for in the case of school taxes and some others, but they raise no peculiar questions, and require no special consideration.

An assessment, strictly speaking, is an official estimate of the sums which are to constitute the basis of an apportionment of a tax between the individual subjects of taxation within the district. As the word is more commonly employed, an assessment consists in the two processes of *listing* the persons, property, etc., to be taxed, and of *estimating* the sums which are to be the guide in an apportionment of the tax between them. When this listing and estimate are completed in such form as the law may have prescribed, nothing remains to be done in order to determine the individual liability, but the mere arithmetical process of dividing the sum to be raised among the several subjects of taxation, in proportion to the amounts which they are respectively assessed. Sometimes the word assessment is used as implying the completed tax list; that is to say, the list of persons or property to be taxed, with the estimates with which they are chargeable, and the tax duly apportioned and extended upon it; but this employment of the word is unusual except in the cases in which the levy is apportioned by benefits; and in those cases the act of determining the amount of the benefits is of itself, under most statutes, a determination of the individual liability, and its entry upon the roll is an extension of the tax.[1]

Necessity for an assessment. Of the necessity of an assessment, no question can be made. Taxes by valuation cannot be apportioned without it. Moreover, it is the first step in the proceedings against individual subjects of taxation, and is the foundation of all which follow it. Without an assessment they have no support, and are nullities.[2] It is, therefore, not only indispens-

[1] In Pennsylvania it is said "by the terms of the law the taxable or his property is assessed when the assessor has returned his list of property and valuation thereupon, and the commissioners have apportioned the rate per cent. upon the several townships." Wells *v.* Smyth, 55 Penn. St., 159, 162.

[2] A tax levied without any list and valuation is void. Thurston *v.* Little, 3 Mass., 429; Thayer *v.* Stearns, 1 Pick., 482; McCall *v.* Lorimer, 4 Watts, 351; Miller *v.* Hale, 26 Penn. St., 432; Matter of Nichols, 54 N. Y., 62. A statute which cures irregularities cannot cure this defect of jurisdiction. McReynolds *v.* Longenberger, 57 Penn. St., 13. See Brady *v.* Offutt, 19 La. An., 184; McCready *v.* Sexton, 29 Iowa, 356. In California a tax, in order to be valid, must rest upon an assessment duly made by an assessor chosen by the people of the district assessed. People *v.* Hastings, 29 Cal., 449. See Ferris *v.* Coover, 10 id., 589. A school or other township assessment by county assessors is void. People *v.* Hastings, 29 Cal., 449; People *v.* Sargeant, 44 id., 430; Williams *v.* Corcoran, 46 id., 553; Reiley *v.* Lancaster, 39 id., 354. See Granger *v.* Parsons, 2 Pick., 392. But in Massachusetts, school district taxes may be on the town valuation, the statute providing for no other. Waldron *v.* Lee, 5 Pick., 323. In Weber *v.* Reinhard, 73 Penn. St., 370, 375, the act under consideration provided "that in addition to the taxes collectible under existing laws, the owner or owners of ore beds, situated in Upper Saucon township, Lehigh county, shall, from and and after the passage of this act, pay to the supervisors of the roads in said township, one and a half cents for each and every ton of ore mined and carried away with teams over the public road, in said township, which said payments shall be made at the end of every six months after the passage of this act; and in default of payment, the same to be collected as debts of like amount are collectible by law; provided, that the said supervisors shall appropriate to the same purpose, and render an account in the same manner for the funds coming in their hands under this act, as they are required by law with respect to other funds coming to their hands by virtue of their office." *Agnew*, J., was of opinion that the act was void, because it provided for no assessment; but the other judges sustained the law. *Sharswood*, J., says of the tax payer: "He can save himself from the costs of a suit by a tender, in time, of the amount actually due. It is not a case where a val-

able, but in making it, the provisions of the statute under which it is to be made, must be observed with particularity. If this were not compulsory, if the officers were to be at liberty to disregard important provisions of the statute in this initiatory step, the chief protection which the law has intended for individuals in tax cases would be removed. For if the proceedings which the law has prescribed to insure uniformity and equality in the contributions which are demanded for the public service can be set aside with impunity, it is difficult to suggest any reason why all others may not be set aside with like impunity; and the distinction between regular taxation and arbitrary exaction will then wholly disappear. It is the prescribed course of law for the one, and the absence of it in the case of the other, which distinguishes the two, and the prescribed course is only a course suggested but not required, if it remains upon the statute book, but need not be followed. But as the course unquestionably is prescribed in order that it shall be followed, and as without it the citizen is substantially without protection from unequal and unjust demands, the necessity for a strict compliance with all important requirements is manifest.[1]

Date of the assessment. Assessments are made periodically, and in many of the states every year. The customary regulation is that the assessment shall be made or completed on a certain day, or that it shall be made as of a certain day. This fixes the liability of persons and property to taxation for the year. There are some inconveniences and inequalities resulting from this, but some regulation of the kind is indispensable. A force of tax officers cannot be kept employed for the year in watching the transfers of property, the movements of persons, and vicissitudes of business, in

uation of property is required. It is a fixed rate upon the number of tons; and that the owner may be presumed to know, or to have the means of ascertaining, whether he is a landlord or himself the actual occupant. It is not, indeed, expressly provided that the supervisors shall ascertain and assess the amount. But they must do so in order to maintain their suit and recover a judgment; and they must do more; they must prove it by competent evidence."

[1] Where the law provides for an annual assessment, copying the roll of a former year does not make one. Nason *v.* Whitney, 1 Pick., 140; People *v.* Hastings, 29 Cal., 449. See Greenough *v.* Fulton Coal Co., 74 Penn. St., 486.

order to equalize the charges upon them; periodical assessments, if they produce injustice in one case, may correct them in the next, and on the whole are likely to be fair. At any rate, they constitute the best regulation the law can establish. "In the imposition of taxes, exact and critical justice and equality are absolutely unattainable. If we attempt it, we might have to divide one year's tax upon a given article of property among a dozen different individuals who owned it at different times during the year, and then be almost as far from the desired end as when we started. The proposition is utopian. The legislature must adopt some practicable system;"[1] and this practicable system is found to be the one which has been indicated. Every person is therefore to be taxed for the year upon his personalty, estimated as of the time of the assessment, and every parcel of land according to its value at that time. Subsequent changes cannot be noticed until another assessment.[2]

Tax payers' lists. It has been deemed advisable in some of the states to provide by law that persons resident within the several taxing districts shall, by a specified time, deliver to the assessor a written exhibit of their property or business for the purpose of taxation. In some cases the list has been required to be made

[1] Shaw *v.* Dennis, 5 Gilm., 505, 518. A mortgage not in existence at the time fixed by law for the making of the assessment cannot be taxed, though the assessment is made later. People *v.* Kohl, 40 Cal., 127.

[2] State *v.* Hardin, 34 N. J., 79. One is to be taxed where he resides, on the day fixed by statute for taking the assessment, though set off into another town before it is completed. Harmon *v.* New Marlborough, 9 Cush., 525. But if he moves out of the town before the day fixed for its completion, he cannot be taxed for his personalty in it. People *v.* Supervisors of Chenango, 11 N. Y., 563; Ware *v.* First Parish, etc., 8 Cush., 267. In Vermont, a person resident in a school district at the time of listing, and properly listed there, remains liable on the list while it continues in force, notwithstanding he has subsequently removed from the district. Woodward *v.* French, 31 Vt., 337; Walker *v.* Miner, 32 id., 769; Ovitt *v.* Chase, 37 id., 196. Where plaintiff had a place of business in Boston every year from 1st of December to 1st of March, but none on 1st of May when assessment was to be made, *held*, that he was not taxable in Boston. Field *v.* Boston, 10 Cush., 65. The fact that a debt is contracted while one is an inhabitant, does not justify a personal tax upon him in respect of it, after he has ceased to be such. Dow *v.* First Parish in Sudbury, 5 Met., 73. An illustration of the resorts to avoid taxation will be found in Mitchell *v.* Leavenworth County, 9 Kans., 344.

under oath. The failure to hand it in is made to subject the person to some specified liability; sometimes to the doubling for taxation such estimate as the assessor shall make of his property; sometimes to a definite penalty; sometimes to deprivation of any right to appeal against what he may regard as an unjust assessment. The right to discriminate in some manner against those who fail to hand in lists has been often recognized.[1] When the discrimination consists merely in submitting the party to the "doom" of the assessor, and depriving him of any appeal, it would seem that there could be no valid objection to it.[2] But where it goes further and subjects the party to penalties of any kind, to be inflicted by a ministerial officer without a hearing, for a neglect that may have been unintentional and perfectly excusable, it is not so clear on what principle it can be defended.[3] It is certainly not consistent with the genius of the common law that penalties for neglect of duty should be inflicted without judicial investigation.[4]

It has been decided in Kentucky that penal provisions of this character must be strictly construed;[5] a decision that is in har-

[1] See State *v.* Bell, 1 Phil. (N. C.), 76; Winnimisset Co. *v.* Chelsea, 6 Cush., 477; Donovan *v.* Insurance Co., 30 Md., 155; State *v.* Welch, 28 Mo., 600; State *v.* Leavell, 3 Blackf., 117; State *v.* Hamilton, 5 Ind., 310; Louisville, etc., R. R. Co. *v.* State, 25 id., 177.

[2] See Porter *v.* County Commissioners, 5 Gray, 365; Otis Company *v.* Ware, 8 id., 509; State *v.* Apgar, 31 N. J., 358; State *v.* Board of Equalization, 7 Nev., 83.

[3] In Minnesota it has been decided that where the constitution requires all taxation to be by value, it is incompetent to provide by law for increasing the assessed valuation by a sum to be added as a penalty for not handing in a list. McCormick *v.* Fitch, 14 Minn., 252. And see State *v.* Allen, 2 McCord, 55. A contrary ruling in Indiana was made in the case of Boyer *v.* Jones, 14 Ind., 354, where a party had refused to list property which he claimed was not taxable, and was subjected to a penalty of fifty per cent. on the valuation, for the refusal.

[4] Some statutes make provision for enforcing by suit the penalties for neglect to hand in lists. See Drexel *v.* Commonwealth, 46 Penn. St., 31.

[5] Alexander *v.* Commonwealth, 1 Bibb, 515; McCall *v.* The Justices, 1 id., 516; Olds *v.* Commonwealth, 3 A. K. Marsh., 465; Chiles *v.* Commonwealth, 4 J. J. Marsh., 577. The point was made in Drexel *v.* Commonwealth, 46 Penn. St., 31, but not decided, In Connecticut it is held that a list sufficient as to the personal estate cannot be rejected as to that because not sufficient as to the realty. New Canaan *v.* Hoyt, 23 Conn., 148. In Alabama a statute requiring

mony with the general rules of construction. But when the construction is clear, they are generally enforced. The Massachusetts statute (1835) took away all right to abatement of an excessive assessment on appeal to the county commissioners, when the appellant had failed to bring in a list of his estate to the assessors, unless he could show good cause for the failure; and also when he had failed to make oath to the truth of the list if required by the assessors to do so. Under this statute it was held that the assessors could not waive the bringing in of the list; that corporations as well as natural persons must comply with it; that an exhibition to the assessors of a plan of the tax payer's real estate, or referring them to the list of a preceding year, would not be a compliance with the statute;[1] that the list must be handed in before the tax is actually assessed,[2] and that if not handed in, the taxpayer submits himself to the "doom" of the assessors.[3]

It has also been held on a construction of the statute, that no abatement would be made before a list was brought in, though a sufficient excuse for not bringing it in at the proper time was shown.[4] Handing in a list which, by mistake of the lister's rights,

every person in the state "who is liable to pay taxes" to render "a list of his taxable property" to the assessors, and providing that if he does not, they may call at his residence for a list of his taxables or for the amount of taxes due from him, held applicable to one liable only to a poll tax. Carter *v.* Mercer, 9 Ala., 556. As to what is a sufficient listing in Vermont, see Blodgett *v.* Holbrook, 39 Vt., 336.

[1] Winnimisset Co., *v.* Chelsea, 6 Cush., 477. And see Otis Co. *v.* Ware, 8 Gray, 509. The statute required the assessors to notify the inhabitants, at the town meeting or otherwise, to bring in lists. It was held in the first of these cases that if a failure to give notice was relied upon, it devolved on the tax payer to show it. Corporations may be required to furnish for taxation lists of their stockholders to all the local authorities where they severally reside. Donovan *v.* Insurance Co., 30 Md., 155.

[2] Porter *v.* County Commissioners, 5 Gray, 365; Otis Co. *v.* Ware, 8 id., 809.

[3] Lincoln *v.* Worcester, 8 Cush., 55, 63. But where a list was not brought in until after the time limited for it had expired, but the delay was chargeable to the assesors themselves, who expressly told the party's agent nothing should be lost by the delay, it was held that the right to apply for an abatement was not lost. Lowell *v.* County Commissioners, 3 Allen, 546.

[4] Charlestown *v.* County Commissioners, 101 Mass., 87. In abating a tax which has been paid, the county commissioners have no right to allow interest; the statute not providing for it. Lowell *v.* County Commissioners, 3 Allen, 550. Nor costs, for the same reason. Same *v.* Same, id, 556. Successors of asses-

is made to embrace property not liable to taxation, will not estop him from claiming an abatement as to such exempt property; there being no reason of justice or public policy why it should.[1] But while this is true, it is also true that the tax payer cannot complain of any mere irregularity in the action of the assessors into which they have been led by an error or imperfection in his own list, not affecting his substantial rights.[2] These references will perhaps sufficiently indicate the views which have been taken by the courts of statutes of this nature.[3]

sors who have levied a tax may abate it if application therefor is made within the statutory time. Hibbard *v.* Garfield, 102 Mass., 72; Carleton *v.* Ashburnham, 102 id., 348. One who has handed in no list and is overtaxed, cannot pay his tax, and then recover back on showing a mistake in the assessors: a mistake not rendering the tax illegal. Lott *v.* Hubbard, 44 Ala., 593.

[1] Charlestown *v.* County Commissioners, 109 Mass., 270, citing Dunnell Manuf. Co. *v.* Pawtucket, 7 Gray, 277, where the point was substantially the same. In Illinois it has been decided that if one voluntarily lists for taxation corporate stocks which are not taxable, and they are taxed accordingly, he cannot complain, as it is his own fault. Republic Life Ins. Co. *v.* Pollak, 7 Chicago Legal News, 357, Sup. Ct. Ill., 1875.

[2] As where, the party's agent being called upon for a list, he furnished it, but omitted one parcel of land which was taxed as nonresident in consequence. Kinsworthy *v.* Mitchell, 21 Ark., 145. To the same effect is Nelson *v.* Pierce, 6 N. H., 194. The tax payer giving an erroneous description of his lands to the assessor is estopped from complaining of it. Hubbard *v.* Windsor, 15 Mich., 146.

[3] Where a list is required to be given in under oath, a refusal to swear to a list is a refusal to give it in. Lee *v.* Commonwealth, 6 Dana, 311. The person from whom a list is required under a penalty cannot excuse himself by showing as to an article he should have listed (a billiard table), that another person had listed it. Olds *v.* Commonwealth, 3 A. K. Marsh., 465. Where one excused himself from making a list, saying it was unnecessary, held to be a refusal. State *v.* Parker, 33 N. J., 192. See State *v.* Bishop, 34 id., 45; State *v.* Parker, 34 id., 49; State *v.* McChesney, 34 id., 63. The list is not conclusive on the assessors. Thompson *v.* Tinkcom, 15 Minn., 295. But it has been said they ought to adopt the valuation of the lister in the absence of any evidence of its incorrectness. People *v.* Reddy, 43 Barb., 539; People *v.* Assessors of Albany, 40 N. Y., 154: though they are not liable for any bona fide exercise of of their power in this regard. Vose *v.* Willard, 47 Barb., 320; Bell *v.* Pierce, 48 id., 51; Stearns *v.* Miller, 25 Vt., 20; Wilson *v.* Marsh, 34 id., 352. But for a failure to perform ministerial duties to the lister's prejudice the officers may be liable. Kellogg *v.* Higgins, 11 id., 240; Fairbanks *v.* Kittredge, 24 id., 9.

In Nevada, a tax payer who fails to hand in his list, is allowed no standing before the board of equalization. State *v.* Board of Equalization, 7 Nev., 83. In New Jersey he loses his right to appeal. State *v.* Apgar, 31 N. J., 358. An

Right to a hearing. The summary nature of tax proceedings has been remarked upon. Every inhabitant of the state is liable to have a demand established against him on the judgment of others regarding the sum which he should justly and equitably contribute to the public revenues. Every property owner in the state, whether an inhabitant or not, is liable to have a lien in like manner established against his property. Moreover, the persons who make the assessment lighten the burden upon themselves in proportion as they increase it upon others. In such proceedings, therefore, it must be a matter of the utmost importance to the person assessed that he should have some opportunity to be heard before the charge is fully established against him; and it would seem to be a dictate of strict justice that the law should make reasonable provision to secure him as far as may be against partiality, malice or oppression.

The obligation to make provision for this purpose is recognized by the statutes of the several states. By some the person assessed is allowed to reduce what he claims to be an excessive assessment by his own oath; by others he is allowed an appeal to some board of review, and in all, perhaps, some method is provided by which he may have a hearing before the assessment becomes fixed and final against him. Thus the statutes have taken precautions against oppression and injustice, and perhaps made all the provision that is needful, if their directions are fully observed.

It is too often the case, however, that statutory provisions are not strictly observed, and that either the public or individuals must suffer in consequence. The question presented may then be, whether the provisions which have not been obeyed are mandatory to the officers, or it may arise on the provisions of some curative statute which proposes to heal the defects. In substance the question will be, whether the right to be heard in tax cases is a right which is indefeasible.

early statute in South Carolina provided that a "tax of ten thousand dollars" should be imposed upon every person keeping open an office for the sale of lottery tickets, and that "it shall be the duty of the tax collector in the district where such lottery offices are opened, in default of the person or persons keeping such offices to return the same and pay the tax imposed by this law, to issue his execution as in other cases of defaulters." The court held this, though called a tax, to be really a penalty, which it was not competent to authorize the collector to impose. State v. Allen, 2 McCord, 55,

We should say that notice of proceedings in such cases, and an opportunity for a hearing of some description, were matters of constitutional right.[1] It has been customary to provide for them as a part of what is "due process of law" for these cases; and it is not to be assumed that constitutional provisions, carefully framed for the protection of property, were intended or could be construed to sanction legislation under which officers might secretly assess one for any amount in their discretion, without giving him an opportunity to contest the justice of the assessment. It has often been very pointedly and emphatically declared that it is contrary to the first principles of justice that one should be condemned unheard; and it has also been justly observed of taxing officers, that "it would be a dangerous precedent to hold that any absolute power resides in them to tax as they may choose without giving any notice to the owner. It is a power liable to great abuse," and it might safely have been added, it is a power that under such circumstances would be certain to be abused. "The general principles of law applicable to such tribunals oppose the exercise of any such power."[2] This being the case, it is not to be supposed that the legislature in any doubtful language has undertaken to confer it. All reasonable presumptions in construction should favor justice and right.

It is not customary to provide that the tax payer shall be heard before the assessment is made, but a hearing is given afterwards, either before the assessors themselves, or before some court or board of review. And of the meeting of that court or board the tax payer must in some manner be informed; either by personal notice, or by some general notice which is reasonably certain to reach him, or, — which is equivalent — by some general law which fixes the time and place of meeting, and of which he must take notice. The last is a common method of enabling him to be heard.[3]

[1] "Notice," it is said by *Agnew, J.*, in Philadelphia *v.* Miller, 49 Penn. St., 440, 448, "or at least the means of knowledge, is an essential element of every just proceeding which affects rights of persons or property." And see Darling *v.* Gunn, 50 Ill., 424; State *v.* Drake, 33 N. J., 194; Butler *v.* Supervisors of Saginaw, 26 Mich., 22.

[2] *Baldwin*, J., in Patten *v.* Green, 13 Cal., 325, 329. See also Cleghorn *v.* Postlewaite, 43 Ill., 428.

[3] There being no jurisdiction to assess a personal tax upon a nonresident,

All these provisions, being of vital importance to the tax payer, must be regarded as compulsory, and a compliance with them as conditions precedent to any further step to charge him with a tax.[1]

When they fix a certain time for the meeting of a board of review, and the board fails to meet; or a certain time for the return and filing of the assessment for inspection before the meeting of the board, and it is not filed, whereby opportunity for inspection is lost; the tax proceedings must be regarded as having failed to become effectual, because of the failure of the officers properly to follow them up as required by law. No argument can be admissible in such a case which proposes the acceptance of something else as a substitute for the securities the statute has provided. To substitute anything would require legislation; and even legislation for the purpose would be of doubtful validity if it failed to provide what would fully accomplish the same purpose. Such regulations for the protection of individual rights are reasonable, and they are demanded by justice and general convenience. On general principles they must be regarded as mandatory,[2] and a strict observance of their provisions held to be essential.[3]

he is not chargeable with constructive notice of the action of assessors, and is under no obligation to appear before them. St. Paul *v.* Merritt, 7 Minn., 258. The determination of the tax to be paid by a corporation is not void because of being made without notice, where the statute provides for a subsequent notice — which was duly given — and an appeal. Commonwealth *v.* Runk, 26 Penn. St., 235.

[1] Thames Manuf. Co. *v.* Lathrop, 7 Conn., 550, 555; Lowell *v.* Wentworth, 6 Cush., 221; Kansas Pacific R. R. Co. *v.* Russell, 8 Kans., 558.

[2] Thames Manuf. Co. *v.* Lathrop, 7 Conn., 550, 555; Marsh *v.* Chestnut, 14 Ill., 223; Cleghorn *v.* Postlewait, 43 id., 428; Nashville *v.* Weiser, 54 id., 245; Mix *v.* People, Sup. Court, Ill., June term, 1874; Philips *v.* Stevens Point, 29 Wis., 594; Walker *v.* Chapman, 22 Ala., 116; Insurance Co. *v.* Yard, 17 Penn. St., 331, 338; French *v.* Edwards, 13 Wall., 506, 511. In the case in 7 Conn., 550, the assessment was held void because an abstract thereof which the law required should be filed by the first of December, was actually not filed till the 20th, though this was ten days before the meeting of the board of review. That the tax payer must take notice of the general law fixing the time and place of hearing, see Methodist Pr. Church *v.* Baltimore, 6 Gill, 391; O'Neal *v.* Bridge Co., 18 Md., 1, 26.

[3] When one has by city charter the right to appear "and be heard" before the common council, it is not competent for the council to limit the objections to such as may be made in writing. State *v.* Jersey City, 25 N. J., 309. But

The courts have been particularly careful to see that revisory tax tribunals[1] did not change assessments to the prejudice of tax-payers who, under the circumstances, had no reason to look for or anticipate any such change. If the tax-payer himself does not appeal, he has a right to suppose that the assessment against him will be allowed to stand as made. If authority is conferred upon the board of review to change assessments under any specified circumstances, the existence of those circumstances is a condition precedent to their action. An illustration is afforded by a case in New York. A city council had authority to correct descriptions of lands returned for nonpayment of taxes or assessments; but this, it was held, gave them no right to put to a description of land a new name, as that of the owner, when the effect, if valid, would be to make the tax a personal charge against him. Such a change in the assessment, if it could be supported, would deprive the person assessed of the statutory right to notice, and of the opportunity to apply for correction secured to those named in the original roll.[2] And in several states it has been decided that after the assessment has been completed, no increase in valuation can legally be made, without notice to the tax-payer, either express or implied, with the opportunity for hearing.[3]

neither one who has made objection to the assessment in writing, nor those who do not appear at all, can object. State *v.* Jersey City, 28 id., 500. And as to the right to be heard in general the following cases may also be referred to. Lorimer *v.* McCall, 4 W. & S., 133; Stewart *v.* Trevor, 56 Penn. St., 374. And that there must be opportunity afforded for it at the time and place fixed by law, see Sioux City, etc., R. R. Co. *v.* Washington County, 3 Neb., 30.

[1] Courts, in reviewing assessments, exercise a special and limited jurisdiction. *Hand*, J., in Woodruff *v.* Fisher, 17 Barb., 224, 232.

[2] Bennett *v.* Buffalo, 17 N. Y., 383. Compare Overing *v.* Foote, 43 N. Y., 290, 294, where this is said to be a "close case." Where the revisory board orders a change made in the assessment, the assessor, it seems, may be compelled to make it in a *certiorari* proceeding. Keck *v.* Keokuk County, 37 Iowa, 547.

[3] Philips *v.* Stevens Point, 25 Wis., 594; Matherson *v.* Mazomanie, 20 id., 191; Cleghorn *v.* Postlewaite, 43 Ill., 428; Darling *v.* Gunn, 50 id., 424; Griswold *v.* School District, 24 Mich., 262; Patten *v.* Green, 13 Cal., 325; Sioux City, etc., R. R. Co. *v.* Washington County, 3 Neb., 30; Leavenworth County *v.* Lang, 8 Kans., 284; Kansas Pacific R. R. Co. *v.* Russell, 8 id., 558. Where a party liable to taxation makes out and delivers to the assessor a list of his taxable property, which is accepted by the assessor without question, the latter has no power afterwards, of his own motion, to alter it, without giving

Personal assessments. Little need be said of poll taxes, as they are seldom levied, and when they are, the case is not likely to raise any other question than that of the jurisdiction of the assessors in the particular case. And this will generally be a question only of whether the person taxed has his domicile within the district. Such a question is usually one more of fact than of law.[1]

A tax assessed against the person for personal estate is to be

notice to the party. McConkey *v.* Smith, Sup. Ct. Ill., 1875, 7 Chicago Legal News, 210. Where, on appeal from assessment, the appellate board has power to increase valuations on giving ten days' notice to the tax-payer, notice to his tenant is not sufficient. State *v.* Drake, 33 N. J., 194. Where, after valuation by assessors, the party taxed is permitted by law to make affidavit of the actual value of his property, this is only evidence to be considered, and not conclusive, unless made so by statute. People *v.* Barker, 48 N. Y., 70. In Oregon, the decisions of the assessors and county clerk, constituting a board of review, are made reviewable in the supreme court. Rhea *v.* Umatilla County, 2 Ore., 298, 300; Shumway *v.* Baker County, 3 id., 246.

[1] A poll tax can only be assessed on residents. Herriman *v.* Stowers, 43 Me., 497. On the question, what constitutes residence, the following cases will throw light. Harvard College *v.* Gore, 5 Pick., 369, 373; Sears *v.* Boston, 1 Met., 250; Thorndike *v.* Boston, id., 242, 245; Lyman *v.* Fiske, 17 Pick., 231, 234; Otis *v.* Boston, 12 Cush., 44; Cabot *v.* Boston, id., 52; Lee *v.* Boston, 2 Gray, 484; Bulkley *v.* Williamstown, 3 id., 493; Carnoe *v.* Freetown, 9 id., 357; Briggs *v.* Rochester, 16 id., 337; Warren *v.* Thomaston, 43 Me., 406, 412; Parson *v.* Bangor, 61 id., 457; Foster *v.* Hall, 4 Humph., 346, 348; State *v* Ross, 23 N. J., 517; Daniel *v.* Sullivan, 46 Geo., 277; Bell *v.* Pierce, 51 N. Y., 12; Matter of Nichols, 54 id., 62; Fry's Election Case, 71 Penn. St., 302; S. C., 10 Am. Rep., 698; Arnold *v.* Davis, 8 R. I., 341; Tripp *v.* Brown, 9 id., 240. One living on lands, subject to the exclusive jurisdiction of the United States, is not subject to taxation on polls. Opinions of Judges, 1 Met., 580. One who has left the town of his residence, without the intention of returning, is nevertheless taxable there while he remains in the commonwealth, until he has acquired another residence. Bulkley *v.* Williamstown, 3 Gray, 493. Residence is presumed to continue where it has been until a change is affirmatively shown, or at least until there is satisfactory evidence of abandonment. Matter of Nichols, 54 N. Y., 62. If a line runs through one's house, he must be taxed in the town which includes the most necessary and indispensable portion. He cannot be taxed in both. Judkins *v.* Reed, 48 Me., 386; Chenery *v.* Waltham, 8 Cush., 327. If he is assessed in two towns, his election to pay in one rather than the other is not conclusive, but he is liable in the one of his actual inhabitancy. Lyman *v.* Fiske, 17 Pick., 231; Chenery *v.* Waltham, 8 Cush., 327. See also Hardy *v.* Yarmouth, 6 Allen, 277, 284. His being taxed in one is not evidence that his residence and proper place of taxation is not in another. Mead *v.* Roxborough, 11 Cush., 362.

assessed to him at the place of his residence, because in contemplation of law his movable property accompanies him wherever he goes. This is the general rule, though, as has been shown elsewhere, tangible personal property may be taxed where it is, irrespective of ownership, if the statute shall so provide.[1] Property

[1] *Ante*, p. 14. A vessel registered in New York, plying between Panama and San Francisco, held not taxable in California. Hays *v.* Pacific Mail Steamship Co., 17 How., 596. See also, State *v.* Haight, 30 N. J., 428; People *v.* Commissioners of Taxes, N. Y. Ct. of Appeals (1875), 11 Albany Law Journal, 401. Ferry boats running to a city, but owned in an other state, are not taxable to the city as property "within" it. St. Louis *v.* Ferry Co., 11 Wall., 423. See also Morgan *v.* Parham, 16 id., 471. So under a statute for the taxation of "all lands and personal estates within this state," one cannot be assessed on capital invested in business in another state, or on chattels upon a farm in another state. People *v.* Commissioners of Taxes, 23 N. Y., 224. A bond is to be taxed where the owner resides, though the obligor resides elsewhere. Hayne *v.* Deliesseline, 3 McCord, 374; Augusta *v.* Dunbar, 50 Geo., 387. But perhaps if both obligor and obligee reside within the state, it would be competent to provide by statute for collecting the tax from the former. See Harper *v.* Commissioners, 23 Geo., 566; Bridges *v.* Griffin, 33 id., 113. See what is said of this last case in Augusta *v.* Dunbar, 50 id., 387. The personalty owned by a citizen out of the state is taxable where he resides. Commonwealth *v.* Hays, 8 B. Monr., 1, 2. So are stocks he may hold in a foreign corporation. McKeen *v.* Northampton Co., 49 Penn. St., 519; Whitsell *v.* Same, id., 526. The statute provided that nonresidents "doing business" in the state should be taxed on sums invested "in said business." *Held* not to apply to a manufactured article merely sent into the state for sale by an agent, who sold and remitted the price. Parker Mills *v.* Commissioners of Taxes, 23 N. Y., 242. That money due on a land contract in the hands of an agent of a nonresident is taxable, see People *v.* Ogdensburg, 48 id., 390. Compare Supervisors *v.* Davenport, 40 Ill., 197. That nonresidents of a state or district may be taxed therein in respect to property there situate or business there carried on, see Corfield *v.* Coryell, 4 Wash. C. C, 371, 380; State *v.* City Council, 2 Speers, 623; Harrison *v.* Vicksburg, 3 S. & M., 581; Worth *v.* Fayetteville, Winston's L. & Eq., 70; Padleford *v.* Mayor, 14 Geo., 438; Peace *v.* Augusta, 37 id., 597; Shirver *v.* Pittsburg, 66 Penn. St., 446: compare Bennett *v.* Birmingham, 31 id., 15. Personalty received by a distributee in the state from the estate of one abroad is liable to taxation in the state under a statute taxing property distributed "to or among the next of kin" of an intestate. Alvany *v.* Powell, 2 Jones Eq., 51. The personal property belonging to the estate of a deceased person is held in Connecticut to be taxable at his last domicile; the representatives of the estate not being trustees in the sense of the statute which makes personal property in the hands of a trustee taxable in the town where the trustee resides. Cornwall *v.* Todd, 38 Conn., 443. A town which taxes a man as a resident takes the burden of showing that he is such, if the right is questioned. Hurlburt *v.* Green, 41 Vt., 490; Same *v.* Same, 42

held in trust should be assessed to the trustee where he resides,[1] except where the trust is under the direction of a court, in which case it would be taxable in the jurisdiction having control of it.[2] A partnership being only a business association of individuals. the members are severally taxable for their interests where they reside,[3] unless the statute lays down a different rule.[4] But a private banker living in one place, and having a bank in another, is for the purposes of taxation to be regarded as resident where the bank is located.[5]

The principles upon which personal assessments are made are different under different statutes. The most common method is to assess the owner a sum which is supposed to represent the value

id., 316. Consent by a person to be taxed where he does not reside does not give jurisdiction and would not bind him. Blood *v.* Sayre, 17 id., 609.

[1] State *v.* Mathews, 10 Ohio St., 431, 437; Hardy *v.* Yarmouth, 6 Allen, 277, 285; Catlin *v.* Hull, 21 Vt., 152; Baltimore *v.* Stirling, 29 Md., 48; Carlisle *v.* Marshall, 36 Penn. St., 397; People *v.* Assessors of Albany, 40 N. Y., 154. If there are two trustees, one half may be assessed to each. State *v.* Mathews, *supra*; Baltimore *v.* Stirling, 29 Md., 48. Residence of *cestui que trust* immaterial. People *v.* Assessors of Albany, *supra.*

[2] Lewis *v.* Chester County, 60 Penn. St., 325. But it is said in this case that if the trustee invests money on mortgage in another state, he may be taxed upon it at the place of investment. And see Supervisors *v.* Davenport, 40 Ill., 197. An executor may be assessed personally for taxes against the estate, and have them collected from his own property. Williams *v.* Holden, 4 Wend., 223. So it is competent by statute to make the tax on a minor's estate a personal charge against his guardian. Payson *v.* Tufts, 13 Mass., 493.

[3] Bemis *v.* Boston, 14 Allen, 366, citing Dwight *v.* Boston, 12 id, 316; Peabody *v.* County Commissioners, 10 Grey, 97. To the same effect is Fairbanks *v.* Kittredge, 24 Vt., 9.

[4] Hoadley *v.* County Commissioners, 105 Mass., 519.

[5] Miner *v.* Fredonia, 27 N. Y., 155. And see Gardiner, etc. Co. *v.* Gardiner, 5 Greenl., 133; Bates *v.* Mobile, 46 Ala., 158. But it has been held that the furniture of an inn is only taxable to the innkeeper at the place of his residence. Charlestown *v.* County Commissioners, 109 Mass., 270. An army officer held taxable on his furniture where he was temporarily stationed in the service. Finley *v.* Philadelphia, 32 Penn. St., 381. Under a statute in California, personal property is to be assessed and taxed in the county where it is situated, except money and gold dust, which may, at the option of the owner, be taxed at the place of his domicile. But to authorize the assessment of any property in another county from the one in which he resides, it must appear that the property is kept and maintained there, and is not there temporarily or *in transitu*. People *v.* Niles, 35 Cal., 282; City of Oakland *v.* Whipple, 39 id., 112.

of his personal property in bulk; though an enumeration of certain articles is sometimes provided for.[1] The statute may or may not designate what shall be included by the assessors in their estimate; but the taxable property will be indicated in some form, either by an enumeration of what shall be considered taxable property, or by some general provision that all property shall be taxed except what is specifically exempt.[2]

[1] Compare Falkner *v.* Hunt, 16 Cal., 167, and People *v.* Sneath, 28 id., 612. Every article specified in an assessment list must on the face of the list be so described as to appear to be taxable. Adam *v.* Litchfield, 10 Conn., 127; Whittlesey *v.* Clinton, 14 id., 72.

[2] Taxable property does not necessarily include all subjects of taxation: e. g. polls may be taxable, gross sales by merchants, etc. "When the words 'taxable property' occur in an independent act, it would seem that they should be understood in the sense of things taxed which are susceptible of ownership or possession, unless there is something in the context which affixes to them a different meaning, or unless the plain object of the law will be defeated if they are not held to cover subjects of taxation which are not property in the ordinary sense." *R. W. Walker*, J. in Lott *v.* Ross, 38 Ala., 156, 160, citing Mosely *v.* Tift, 4 Fla., 402; De Witt *v.* Hays, 2 Cal., 468. "Property" in a statute authorizing the imposition of taxes, without further explanation, would not include a mere right to wharfage fees, though that as a franchise has property value. De Witt *v.* Hays, 2 Cal., 468. It will include solvent debts. Savings and Loan Association *v.* Austin, 46 id., 415. See People *v.* Park, 23 id., 138; Catlin *v.* Hull, 21 Vt., 152.

Damages to which a land owner is entitled for the taking of his land for a highway are not taxable as a "debt" before they have become fixed and receivable. (A suit was pending.) Lowell *v.* Boston, 106 Mass., 540. As to what is included in taxable property, see further, Louisville *v.* Henning, 1 Bush, 381. Where "*certificates of deposit*" are taxable, an entry on a pass book is held to be one. Oulton *v.* Savings Institution, 17 Wall., 109; S. C., 1 Sawyer, 695.

The word *machinery* held to include gas pipes laid under the streets, and gas meters. Commonwealth *v.* Lowell Gas Light Co., 12 Allen, 75. See Providence Gas Co. *v.* Thurber, 2 R. I., 15.

As to meaning of "*income*" when that is taxable, see People *v.* Supervisors of New York, 18 Wend., 605; Matter of Western Railway, 5 Met., 596; Commonwealth *v.* Ocean Oil Co., 59 Penn. St., 61. Where *dividends* are taxed, the tax may be laid though the dividends are declared in stock. Commonwealth *v.* Cleveland, etc., R. R. Co., 29 Penn. St., 370. If dividends are applied to increase capital, they are taxable the same as if paid over. State *v.* Farmers' Bank, 11 Ohio, 94; Lehigh Crane Iron Co. *v.* Commonwealth, 55 Penn. St., 448 As to tax on dividends in general, see State *v.* Charleston, 5 Rich., 561; Haight *v.* Railroad Co., 6 Wall., 15; Railroad Co. *v.* Jackson, 7 id., 262; United States *v.* Railroad Co., 17 id., 322; Chicago, etc., R. R. Co. *v.* Page, 1 Bissell, 461; Phœnix Iron Co. *v.* Commonwealth, 59 Penn. St., 104.

Assessment of corporations. As regards corporations, special rules are generally made. It has been decided, that corporations are to be regarded as inhabitants, under a statute which makes the personalty of inhabitants taxable.[1] But this is matter of construction, and must depend on the intent to be gathered from the context.[2] All corporations are taxable when the state has not expressly relinquished the right to tax by a stipulation in the charter,[3] and the method of taxation, and what shall be taken as the measure of the tax, are in the discretion of the legislature. It has been shown elsewhere, that sometimes the franchise is specifically taxed, sometimes the capital, or capital stock,[4] sometimes the tangible property, and so on. Where railroad property is taxed as other property is, the personalty should be assessed to the company at the place of its business office; that being the legal *situs* of its personalty,[5] and for the purposes

[1] Baldwin *v.* Trustees, etc., 37 Me., 369. The word "persons" in the tax law includes corporations. Louisville, etc., R. R. Co. *v.* Commonwealth, 1 Bush, 250.

[2] The word held not to include corporations. Hartford Fire Ins. Co. *v* Hartford, 3 Conn., 15; Cherokee, etc., Ins. Co. *v.* The Justices, 28 Geo., 121. Compare British Commercial Life Ins. Co. *v.* Com'rs of Taxes, 1 Keyes, 303.

[3] Bank of Pennsylvania *v.* Commonwealth, 19 Penn. St., 144; Portland Bank *v.* Apthorp, 12 Mass., 252. And see *ante*, pp. 15, 25.

[4] Where a mutual insurance company was authorized to accumulate from its profits a fund to continue liable for its losses during the term of its existence, held that this accumulation was *capital*, and liable to taxation as such. Sun Mut. Ins. Co., *v.* New York, 8 N. Y., 241; People *v.* Supervisors of New York, 16 id., 424. For a peculiar question on taxation of capital see Commonwealth *v.* Penn Gas Coal Co., 62 Penn. St., 241.

[5] Portland, etc., R. R. Co. *v.* Saco, 60 Me., 196; State *v.* Person, 32 N. J., 134; Pacific R. R. Co. *v.* Cass County, 53 Mo., 17; Orange and Alexandria R. R. Co. *v.* Alexandria, 17 Grat., 176. It is so held of the rolling stock of a railroad, though it has also been held competent to distribute the taxation of rolling stock through the various counties where the road runs. Kansas City, etc., R. R. Co. *v.* Severance, 55 Mo., 378. But on the point, whether the rolling stock of a railroad is to be regarded as real or personal estate, there is great diversity in decisions. See Randall *v.* Elwell, 52 N. Y., 521. Other corporations are also to be taxed on personalty at the place of their principal office. Western Transportation Co. *v.* Scheu, 19 N. Y., 408. Where a manufacturing corporation is required to be assessed in the town "where the operations of the company are to be carried on," this means the manufactory, and not the place of financial operations. Oswego Starch Factory *v.* Dolloway, 21 N. Y., 449. As to assessment of railroad beds, see *ante*, 114.

of taxation, it is sometimes provided that all railroad property shall be considered personal and taxable accordingly; a provision which the legislature is supposed to be entirely competent to make.[1] The corporation is, of course, taxable on corporate property only; the individual corporators, if taxed on their shares of stock, are to be taxed where they respectively reside,[2] though they may be, and sometimes are taxed at the place where the corporate business is carried on, and the corporation made the collector. In some states railroad companies are taxed upon the road and property as a unit;[3] in others the line in each county is separately assessed,[4] and in still others the whole is assessed, and then the assessment apportioned between the several counties and towns. A railroad track, it is held, cannot be assessed as "nonresident" lands; that term being applied to property not occupied and used.[5] The track of a local railway company may be assessed as real estate, though laid down in a highway where the company has no title.[6]

[1] *Held*, under such a provision, that it was not competent to tax it as real. Bangor and Piscataqua R. R. Co. *v.* Harris, 21 Me., 533. See Cumberland Marine R'y. *v.* Portland, 37 id., 444, where it is said that a statute which would have required a different decision was overlooked in the previous case. The right to treat the rolling stock of a railroad as personal estate for the purposes of taxation affirmed. Louisville, etc., R. R. Co. *v.* State, 25 Ind., 177. See Maus *v.* Logansport, etc., R. R. Co., 27 Ill., 77; Sangamon, etc., R. R. Co. *v.* Morgan County, 14 id., 163.

[2] Cornwell *v.* Connersville, 15 Ind., 150; Madison *v.* Whitney, 21 id., 261. Compare Whitney *v.* Madison, 23 Ind., 331; Cumberland Marine R'y *v.* Portland, 37 Me., 444. The word "stock" in a statute authorizing the taxation of stock in corporations, means not only the stock subscriptions, but the actual tangible property of the corporation. State *v.* Hamilton, 5 Ind., 310; Auditor of Floyd County *v.* New Albany and Salem R. R., 11 id., 570; Mich. Cent. R. R. Co. *v.* Porter, 17 id., 380; Whitsell *v.* Northampton County, 49 Penn. St., 526; McKeen *v.* Same, 49 id., 519; State *v.* Branin, 23 N. J., 484.

[3] See Toledo and Wabash R. R. Co. *v.* Lafayette, 22 Ind., 262.

[4] See Albany, etc., R. R. Co. *v.* Osborn, 12 Barb., 223; Albany, etc., R. R. Co *v.* Canaan, 16 id., 244; The Tax Cases, 12 Gill & J., 117; State *v.* Ill. Cent. R. R. Co., 27 Ill., 64; Sangamon, etc., R. R. Co. *v.* Morgan County, 14 id., 163; Providence, etc., R. R. Co. *v.* Wright, 2 R. I., 459.

[5] People *v.* Barker, 48 N. Y., 70; Buffalo and State Line R. R. Co. *v.* Supervisors of Erie, 48 N. Y., 93.

[6] People *v.* Cassity, 46 N. Y., 46; New Haven *v.* Fair Haven, etc., R. R. Co., 38 Conn., 422.

Taxes on real property. In regard to the assessment of real estate it is customary, and is certainly extremely proper, to give very careful and specific directions by statute.[1] These directions for the most part have in view the protection of persons taxed. Very simple proceedings might be all that would be requisite to enable the state to collect its revenues if its interests alone were to be regarded; but so many circumstances are liable to leave the owner of property in ignorance that proceedings are being taken for that purpose, and possibly in ignorance or forgetfulness that any duty on his part remains undischarged, that a government careful of the interests of its individual citizens will not fail to make such provisions as will be reasonably certain to notify him of any default, and give him ample opportunity to protect his property from sacrifice or forfeiture. And this is seen to be specially important in tax cases when it is remembered that property sold for taxes, — particularly real estate — seldom brings more than a small fraction of its value.

Seated and unseated lands. Among the most useful of these provisions for the protection of persons taxed is one that unoccupied lands, unseated lands, or nonresident lands shall be assessed on a different list from the occupied or seated lands; or if not on a different list, then on a different part of the same list. The purpose is that the two distinct classes of land shall be assessed separately, so that the owner of any parcel, knowing its character, shall know exactly where to look for his, and shall thus be more certain to discover any claim made upon him by reason of its ownership, and be enabled to discharge it before any thing shall be lost to him in consequence of a default.[2]

[1] That a possession of and claim to public lands is taxable to the claimant, see People *v.* Shearer, 30 Cal., 656; People *v.* Frisbie, 31 id., 146; People *v.* Cohen, id., 210; People *v.* Mining Co., 37 id., 54. That in Massachussetts, a house built by one man on the land of another and owned by a nonresident is not taxable as personalty in the town where it is, nor as realty, separate from the land, see Flanders *v.* Cross, 10 Cush., 514. As to assessment of Indian lands after the Indian title is extinguished by treaty, see Fellows *v.* Denniston, 23 N. Y., 420. It has been decided in Connecticut that in the assessment of "mills," the machinery contained therein should be included, even though it was personalty, and the owner a nonresident. Sprague *v.* Lisbon, 30 Conn., 18.

[2] See Burd *v.* Ramsey, 9 S. & R., 109.

The terms "seated," "resident," and "occupied" lands may not convey precisely the same idea as they are employed in the several state statutes, and probably do not.[1] They will in general, however, be found sufficiently explained in the several statutes. The general idea of the statutes classifying lands for taxation is, that those which are cultivated or occupied, so that some one within the taxing district is personally liable for taxation in respect to them, shall be taxed in a list by themselves. There are very essential distinctions, however, to be observed in considering the several statutes. The custom in most of the states is that, when the periodical assessments are made, the lands are examined or their condition inquired into, and they are classed irrespective of any former assessment; while in Pennsylvania the rule is that lands once seated are presumed to continue so, and nothing but an unequivocal abandonment by the occupier, without the intention of returning, will warrant their being changed to the unseated list.[2] And the abandonment of part of an entire tract while the occupation of the remainder continues will not prevent the

[1] As to what are to be regarded as "seated" lands in Pennsylvania, see Wilson *v.* Waterson, 4 Penn. St., 214, in which it is held that lands having a house upon them and some improvements, though not occupied, are not to be regarded as unseated without unequivocal marks of the abandonment of the improvement, and its permissive return to its natural state. The improvement of part of a tract makes the whole seated, though divided by a county line. Ellis *v.* Hall, 19 Penn. St., 292. Where a number of unoccupied tracts are to be used in the supplying a mill with timber to cut, this does not make them seated. Heft *v.* Gephart, 65 id., 510. Lands are seated when occupied, even though the occupant is an intruder. Campbell *v.* Wilson, 1 Watts, 503; Lorimer *v.* McCall, 4 W. & S., 183. And the occupation and cultivation of part of a warrant fixes the character of the whole. Biddle *v.* Noble, 68 Penn. St., 279. Residence without cultivation, or cultivation without residence, will preclude land being sold as unseated. George *v.* Messenger, 73 id., 418. As to what will constitute seated lands in general, see Campbell *v.* Wilson, 1 Watts, 503; Sheafer *v.* McCabe, 2 id., 421; Fish *v.* Brown, 5 id., 441; Kennedy *v.* Dailey, 6 id., 269; Wallace *v.* Scott, 7 W. & S., 247; Lorimer *v.* McCall, 4 id., 133; Michell *v.* Bratton, 5 id., 451; Millikin *v.* Benedict, 8 Penn. St., 169; Jackson *v.* Sassaman, 29 id., 106; Hathaway *v.* Ellsbree, 54 id., 498; Lackawana Iron, etc., Co. *v.* Fales, 55 id., 90; Stewart *v.* Trevor, 56 id., 374; Green *v.* Watson, 34 id., 332; Hoffman *v.* Bell, 61 id., 444; George *v.* Messenger, 73 id., 418.

[2] Harbeson *v.* Jack, 2 Watts, 124; Millikin *v.* Benedict, 8 Penn. St., 169; Negley *v.* Breading, 32 id., 325; Arthurs *v.* Smathers, 38 id., 40, 44; Stewart *v.* Trevor, 56 id., 374.

whole being regarded as seated.[1] So again, the general rule is that while the owner or occupant is taxed personally for the land he owns or occupies, the tax is also made a lien upon the land, and the land will be sold for its satisfaction in case it is not collected of the person. In Pennsylvania, on the other hand, while the tax on seated lands is a personal charge, that on the unseated lands alone has until recently been made a lien to be enforced by sale. And even since the recent law which makes seated lands liable to sale for taxes, the proceedings are different; personal notice to the owner being required.[2]

Under all the statutes, however, the requirement of a classification of lands as seated and unseated, resident or nonresident, etc., is probably to be considered imperative.[3] It has been so held in Maine,[4] Massachusetts,[5] New York,[6] Pennsylvania,[7] and in so many other states that any question that might once have been an open one must now be regarded as finally settled.[8]

[1] Patterson *v.* Blackmore, 9 Watts, 104. See Ellis *v.* Hall, 19 Penn. St., 292.

[2] See Broughton *v.* Journeay, 51 Penn. St., 31; Lovejoy *v.* Lunt, 48 Me., 377.

[3] Possibly Connecticut is an exception. See Adams *v.* Seymour, 30 Conn., 402.

[4] The law required improved lands to be assessed to the owner. *Held*, that an assessment to person unknown was void. Brown *v.* Veazie, 25 Me., 359; Barker *v.* Hesseltine, 27 id., 354. To same effect are Carmichael *v.* Aiken, 13 La. An., 205; Bidleman *v.* Brooks, 28 Cal., 72. An assessment of a whole lot to a person, and a sale of the whole is void if a part was never owned or possessed by him. Barker *v.* Blake, 36 Me., 433. For a case of resident land assessed as nonresident, see Lunt *v.* Wormell, 19 Me., 100.

[5] Rising *v.* Granger, 1 Mass., 48.

[6] Whitney *v.* Thomas, 23 N. Y., 281; Crooke *v.* Andrews, 40 id., 547; Newell *v.* Wheeler, 48 id., 486.

[7] Milliken *v.* Benedict, 8 Penn. St., 169. As to effect of consent to land being assessed in the wrong list, see Lorimer *v.* McCall, 4 W. & S., 133; Milliken *v.* Benedict, *supra;* Negley *v.* Breading, 32 Penn. St., 325; Hathaway *v.* Ellsbree, 54 id., 498. And as to erroneous listing in general, see Commercial Bank *v.* Woodside, 14 Penn. St., 404; Stewart *v.* Trevor, 56 id., 374. Lands assessed as seated cannot be transferred to the unseated list without notice to the owner where practicable. Lorimer *v.* McCall, 4 W. & S., 133; Milliken *v.* Benedict, 8 Penn. St., 169; Commercial Bank, *v.* Woodside, 14 id., 404; Stewart *v.* Trevor, 56 id., 374; Bechdle *v.* Lingle, 66 id., 38. But if a parcel has been on no list for several years, the owner has no such right. Bechdle *v.* Lingle, *supra*. Nor generally, it seems, in case of abandonment. Laird *v.* Hiester, 24 Penn. St., 452.

[8] See Messenger *v.* Germain, 1 Gilm., 631; Green *v.* Craft, 28 Miss., 70; Ray-

Assessment of resident lands. There has been the same strictness of ruling under statutes which require the assessment of resident or seated property to be made to the owner personally, or to the occupant.[1] Such an assessment is intended to establish a personal liability, and it is very manifest that assessors can have no power to charge one class of persons, when the statute specifies a different class for the purpose. Thus if the statute says the *owners* shall be assessed, the assessors cannot lawfully charge *occupants* who are not owners,[2] though if the statute only requires the

nor *v.* Lee, 20 Mich., 384; Milwaukee Iron Co. *v.* Hubbard, 29 Wis., 51, 56; Washington *v.* Pratt, 8 Wheat., 681. Where the law requires the land to be assessed to the patentee when the owner is unknown, any other assessment is invalid. Yenda *v.* Wheeler, 9 Texas, 408.

Putting to an assessment of nonresident lands the name of a former owner, held immaterial. Alvord *v.* Collin, 20 Pick., 418. See Miller *v.* Hale, 26 Penn. St., 432; Philadelphia *v.* Miller, 49 id., 440; O'Grady *v.* Barnhisel, 23 Cal., 287; O'Neal *v.* Virginia, etc., Co., 18 Md., 1. If one is owner when proceedings are commenced, an assessment to him is not rendered invalid by a change in ownership, before they are confirmed, of which the assessors have no notice. Morange *v.* Mix, 44 N. Y., 315.

[1] It need not be so assessed unless the statute requires it. Thompson *v.* Carroll's Lessee, 22 How., 422; Witherspoon *v.* Duncan, 4 Wall., 210, 219. The rule has been applied with great strictness in Wisconsin in holding that an assessment of the wife's separate estate to the husband, he living with her upon it, was void under a statute requiring lands to be assessed to the owner or occupant. Hamilton *v.* Fond du Lac, 25 Wis., 496. Listing of land belonging to an estate to "widow and heirs," of the deceased person, held sufficient. Wheeler *v.* Anthony, 10 Wend., 346. But a listing to the widow alone was held void in Yancey *v.* Hopkins, 1 Munf., 419. A listing to "estate of J. B. Coles," held good. State *v.* Jersey City, 24 N. J., 108. Compare Cruger *v.* Dougherty, 43 N. Y., 107.

They have a statute in Arkansas that "no sale of any lands or town lots for the payment of taxes shall be considered invalid on account of its having been charged on the tax book in any other name than that of the rightful owner, if such land be in other respects sufficiently described in the tax book, and the taxes for which the same is sold be due and unpaid at the time of such sale." This statute enforced in Merrick *v.* Hutt, 15 Ark., 331. And see Kinsworthy *v.* Mitchell, 21 id., 145; Garabaldi *v.* Jenkins, 27 id., 453, 456. Compare the Missouri cases of Abbott *v.* Lindenbower, 42 Mo., 162; S. C., 46 id., 291; Hume *v.* Wainscott, 46 id., 145. Mistakes in names, not calculated to mislead will not vitiate. Van Voorhis *v.* Budd, 39 Barb., 479; Pierce *v.* Richardson, 37 N. H., 306.

[2] Mansfield *v.* Martin, 3 Mass., 419. But the assessment of the lands of a company to one member who was in possession as agent was held sufficient, and the addition of "agent" to his name treated as surplusage. Wells *v.* Bat-

assessors to list in the names of the owners respectively, *if known*, if they omit the name in the list, or set down the lands as belonging to persons unknown, the presumption that they performed their duty in endeavoring to ascertain the owner may support the assessment, until evidence that the officers did know the owner overcomes this presumption.[1]

Separate tracts to be separately assessed. It is also generally made a requirement that separate and distinct parcels of land shall be assessed separately. This is certainly essential where the lands are resident or seated, and owned by different persons, each of whom has a right to know exactly what demand the government makes upon him.[2] And a failure to do this is not a mere "omission, defect or irregularity," which can be overlooked, under a statute which provides that assessments for taxation shall be valid "notwithstanding any omission, defect or irregularity" in

telle, 11 Mass., 477. See further, Coombs *v.* Warren, 34 Me., 89; Knox *v.* Huidekoper, 21 Wis., 527; Cardigan *v.* Page, 6 N. H., 182; Ainsworth *v.* Dean, 21 id., 400; Kelsey *v.* Abbott, 13 Cal., 609; Abbott *v.* Lindenbower, 42 Mo., 162; S. C., 46 id., 291; Hume *v.* Wainscott, 46 id., 145; Johnson *v.* McIntire, 1 Bibb, 295.

[1] Blackwell on Tax Titles, 145, citing Cardigan *v.* Page, 6 N. H., 182; Smith *v.* Messer, 17 id., 420; Nelson *v.* Pierce, 6 id., 194; Ainsworth *v.* Dean, 21 id., 400; Brown *v.* Veazie, 25 Me., 359; Merritt *v.* Thompson, 13 Ill., 716; Shimmin *v.* Inman, 26 Me., 228; Jaquith *v.* Putney, 48 N. H., 138.

The statute provided that the assessment should show "the owner of each lot or portion of a lot (if known to the superintendent), if unknown, the word 'unknown' shall be written opposite the number of the lot," etc. *Held*, that when the assessment was returned with the word "unknown" thus placed, "it amounted to an official certificate, by the proper officer, that in point of fact the owner of the particular lot designated was unknown to him," and this was conclusive of the fact certified, and could not be collaterally called in question in an action brought to recover the tax. Chambers *v.* Satterlee, 40 Cal., 497, 518, per *Wallace*, J.

The assessment to S. M. Whipple of property belonging to S. B. Whipple, held void. People *v.* Whipple, 47 Cal., 591. That where land required to be assessed to the owner is assessed to another, the proceedings are void, see Dunn *v.* Winston, 31 Miss., 135; Abbott *v.* Lindenbower, 42 Mo., 162; Hume *v.* Wainscott, 46 id., 145; People *v.* Castro, 39 Cal., 65; Himmelman *v.* Steiner, 38 id., 175; Bidleman *v.* Brooks, 28 id., 72; Kelsey *v.* Abbott, 13 id., 609; Yenda *v.* Wheeler, 9 Texas, 408.

[2] Barker *v.* Blake, 36 Me., 433; State *v.* Williston, 20 Wis., 228; Roby *v.* Chicago, 48 Ill., 130; People *v.* Shimmins, 42 Cal., 121; Boardman *v.* Bourne, 20 Iowa, 135; Ware *v.* Thompson, 29 id., 65.

the proceedings.[1] The like separate assessment is also essential in other cases if the statute requires it. The reasons are sufficiently manifest. If separate parcels of land belonging to different individuals, and presumably of different values, can be assessed together, neither of the owners has any means of determining the amount of tax which is properly chargeable to his property, and consequently no means of discharging his own land from the lien, and of protecting his title, except by paying the whole of a demand some undefined and undefinable portion of which is neither in equity nor in law a proper charge against him.[2] Nay, when the two parcels are owned by the same person, if the statute requires a separate assessment, obedience to the requirement is essential to the validity of the proceedings. It cannot be held in any case that it is unimportant to the tax payer whether this requirement is complied with or not. Indeed it is made solely for his benefit; it being wholly immaterial, so far as the interest of the state is concerned, whether separate estates are or are not separately assessed. And where a requirement has for its sole object the benefit of the tax payer, the necessity for a compliance with it cannot be made to depend upon the circumstances of a particular case, and the opinion of a court or jury regarding the importance of obedience to it in that instance. That method of construing statutes would abolish all certainty.[3]

[1] Hamilton *v.* Fond du Lac, 25 Wis., 490. Compare Stewart *v.* Shoenfelt, 13 S. & R., 360; Bratton *v.* Mitchell, 1 W. & S., 310; Mitchell *v.* Bratton, 5 id., 451; Russell *v.* Werntz, 24 Penn. St., 337; Miller *v.* Hale, 26 id., 432; McReynolds *v.* Longenberger, 57 id., 13; Dietrich *v.* Mason, id., 40; Rogers *v.* Johnson, 67 id., 43; Sargeant *v.* Bean, 7 Gray, 125.

[2] See Shimmin *v.* Inman, 26 Me., 228; Baker *v.* Blake, 36 id., 433; Hayden *v.* Foster, 13 Pick., 492; Jennings *v.* Collins, 99 Mass., 29; Crane *v.* Janesville, 20 Wis., 305; Orton *v.* Noonan, 25 id., 672, 677; Siegel *v.* Outagamie Co., 26 id., 70; Willey *v.* Scoville's Lessee, 9 Ohio, 44; Douglass *v.* Dangerfield, 10 id., 152, 156; Cooley *v.* Waterman, 16 Mich., 466; Hanscom *v.* Hinman, 30 id., 419; McLaughlin *v.* Kain, 45 Penn. St., 113; Dunn *v.* Winston, 31 Miss., 135; Terrill *v.* Groves, 18 Cal., 149.

[3] See Ins. Co. *v.* Yard, 17 Penn. St., 331, 338; French *v.* Edwards, 13 Wall., 506, 511; Walker *v.* Chapman, 22 Ala., 116; Martin *v.* Cole, 38 Iowa, 141, 153; Sandwich *v.* Fish, 2 Gray, 298, 301. But the grouping of two or more parcels owned by the same person was held in Russell *v.* Werntz, 24 Penn. St., 337, to be only an irregularity, and therefore cured under a statute which provided that "no irregularity in the assessment, or in the process or otherwise, shall

What are separate parcels. Assessors are sometimes embarrassed by the necessity for determining what is to be regarded a separate parcel for the purposes of taxation. "A dwelling house with the land and appurtenances occupied with it, a warehouse so occupied, a farm or other parcel of real estate let to the same tenant by one and the same lease, parcels detached from each other, and used and occupied for different purposes, may respectively be regarded as separate and distinct estates. When this can be done, they must be deemed to be separate and distinct estates, to be distinctly valued and assessed."[1] But in the case of unimproved lands, the general understanding appears to be, that an assessment as one parcel of that which was purchased by the owner as such is sufficient, though by the government survey it was subdivided, for the purpose of being offered for sale, into several parcels, each of which might have been sold separately. Thus, an assessment of the whole south half of a section has been held good, though it contained four distinct eighty acre lots.[2] This is on the assumption that the whole is still owned as one parcel,[3] or at least that it is not known to the assessors to have

be construed or taken to affect the title of the purchaser, but the same shall be declared to be good and legal." But this would not validate the assessment of unseated land on the seated list, and then transferring it to the unseated without notice. Milliken *v.* Benedict, 8 Penn. St., 169.

[1] *Shaw*, Ch. J., Hayden *v.* Foster, 13 Pick., 492, 497.

[2] Atkins *v.* Hinman, 2 Gilm., 437, 443. And see Spellman *v.* Curtenius, 12 Ill., 409, where the two halves of a half section were separately described, but assessed together. The assessment and sale of a whole section together was sustained in Martin *v.* Cole, 38 Iowa, 141. There is a good deal of discussion in this case as to what is to be regarded as a separate parcel for the purposes of assessment and sale.

[3] In Jennings *v.* Collins, 99 Mass., 29, 31, several lots were assessed together to one Packard, who was owner of a part of them only. *Wells*, J., says "If the lots had all been the property of Packard at the time the tax was laid, the mere fact that he had divided the land into small lots for the purposes of sale, would not require the assessors to make a separate valuation of each lot. But where lands are separated, either by the use or purpose to which they are devoted, or by the mode of their occupation, or are disconnected in location, a tax laid generally upon an entire valuation cannot be made a lien upon each separate parcel, even when they are all owned and occupied by the same person." In California the decisions are that blocks of land in a city may be assessed by blocks when assessed to the owner, even if they have been subdivided into lots. People *v.* Culverwell, 44 Cal., 620; People *v.* Morse, 43 id., 534.

been divided by sale.[1] But an assessment which divides such a parcel into the lowest legal subdivisions can not prejudice the owner where the land is unoccupied and unimproved,[2] and would seem to be unobjectionable. Unimproved water power, it has been held, cannot be taxed independently of the land on which the power is obtained,[3] and the authorities in general are imperative in holding that an unauthorized division of a tract in the assessment, which tract has no known legal subdivisions, is as fatal as an unauthorized grouping of distinct parcels would be.[4]

Description. In listing the land, it must be described with particularity sufficient to afford the owner the means of identification, and not to mislead him.[5] A description that would be suffi-

It is proper to assess partnership lands to the partnership, instead of the individual partners. Hubbard *v.* Winsor, 15 Mich., 146.

[1] It is usual to provide by statute for the case of lands where different persons claim distinct interests in different portions; allowing each to pay the tax on any portion he will distinctly define; the amount being ascertained by the proportion in quantity which that tax bears to the whole.

[2] See Jennings *v.* Collins, 99 Mass., 29, 31. If two town lots are occupied and used as one lot, the buildings thereon being partly on each, they may be sold for taxes together as one lot, their use and nature determining that they are to be regarded as one lot. Weaver *v.* Grant, Sup. Ct. Iowa, 8 Western Jurist, 587.

[3] Boston Manuf. Co. *v.* Newton, 22 Pick., 22. It was held in Stein *v.* Mobile, 17 Ala., 234, that where one holds real estate within a city, and in connection therewith an exclusive right to supply the city with water, this intangible right is subject to valuation and taxation like tangible property.

[4] Reading *v.* Finney, 73 Penn. St., 467. In Brown *v.* Hays, 66 id., 229, it appeared that warrant No. 4023 containing 1026 acres, all but 16 of which was in Polk township, was assessed in Polk by the number, and the taxes paid for several years. Afterwards it was assessed by number in Polk as 726 acres, and the remaining 300 acres in the other township. The owner paid the taxes in Polk, and the remainder was sold. *Held*, that the payment by the number of the warrant was payment in full, and the sale of the 300 acres was wholly void. The assessor had no right to divide the tract in Polk into two parcels when not divided by the owner; and the assessment with a wrong specification of quantity would not be notice to the owner that the remainder was assessed elsewhere. And see Williston *v.* Colkett, 9 Penn. St., 38, where an assessment of a tract as 200 acres was held good, though it contained 600; the remainder of the description sufficiently identifying it.

[5] Mr. Blackwell, in his Treatise on Tax Titles, p. 124, says: "A description sufficiently certain to convey land between man and man which, if contained in an agreement to convey, would authorize a court of equity to decree a specific execution, will not answer in the proceedings to enforce collection of a

cient in a conveyance between individuals would generally be sufficient here. It is, nevertheless, possible for cases to arise in which such a criterion would be an unsafe one to apply. In a deed which one executes for the purpose of conveying a particular description of land, if errors of description occur, they may well be rejected and the deed sustained if, after rejecting them, a sufficient description remains to identify the land intended; because the erroneous circumstances which were added could not have misled the party conveying, who, all the time, had in mind a particular parcel which the erroneous particulars did not fit. But the same errors in a description prepared by another, might very likely

tax. In the case of private transactions, the courts, in construing the document, endeavor to collect the intention of the parties, and give that intention effect. If a latent ambiguity exists in the description, parol evidence is resorted to for the purpose of explaining it, and giving to the intention of the parties complete operation; and where the estate to be conveyed is sufficiently described in the deed, or other writing, the addition of a circumstance, false or mistaken, will be rejected as surplusage, in order to carry that intention into effect. In tax proceedings the owner of the estate has nothing to do — he intends nothing; the government is acting, through its agents, in hostility to him, and with a view of enforcing the collection of a tax from him. If the officers undertake to list for him lands lying in one place for those which lie in another, or have no existence at all, they intend to do what the law, under which they profess to act, does not permit. The rule is laid down that a listing is fatally defective and void, if it contain such a falsity in the designation or description of the land listed as might probably mislead the owner, and prevent him from ascertaining by the notices that his land is to be sold or redeemed. Such a mistake or falsity defeats one of the obvious and just purposes of the law;— that of giving the owner an opportunity of preventing the sale by paying the tax." With deference it may be suggested that quite too much importance is sometimes attached to the idea that "the government, through its agents, is acting in hostility to" the tax payer, "and with a view to enforcing the collection of a tax from him." The proceedings in the assessment of a tax, are not, in any proper sense, hostile to the citizen; they are, on the other hand, proceedings necessary and indispensable to the determination of the exact share which each resident, or property owner, ought to take, and may and ought to be supposed desirous of taking in meeting the public necessity for a revenue;— proceedings which the willingness of the tax payer cannot dispense with, and which only become hostile when the duty to pay, once fixed, fails to be performed by payment. Then, and then only, do the steps taken by the government assume a compulsory form; until then the reasonable presumption is that government and taxpayer will act together in harmony, and that the latter will meet his obligation to pay as soon as the former has performed its duty in determining the share to be paid.

mislead the owner who would be informed of no error, and who must, from the description alone, discover what land was intended. The same may be said of any imperfection in the description; the owner, if it has been prepared by himself, will read it in connection with his own knowledge of those surrounding circumstances, in the light of which he has framed it; but an equally imperfect description, prepared by another and unaccompanied by any such circumstances, would fail to convey to his mind any idea that his own land was intended. It certainly would be much less likely to do so than where he had prepared it himself.

The purposes in describing the land are, *first*, that the owner may have information of the claim made upon him or his property; *second*, that the public, in case the tax is not paid, may be notified what land is to be offered for sale for the nonpayment; and *third*, that the purchaser may be enabled to obtain a sufficient conveyance. If the description is sufficient for the first purpose, it will ordinarily be sufficient for the others also. Several attempts have been made to lay down some general rule as to what is sufficient, and what not, for a description in the listing. "Notice," it is well said, "or at least the means of knowledge, is an essential element of every just proceeding which affects rights of persons or of property. But how can the duty of the payment of taxes be performed without the identity of the subject matter of the duty being made known to him who is to perform it, by name or description? A thing, whether land or chattel, to be the subject of legal action, must be proceeded against by name or by description, but a name is descriptive only because it has become associated with the person or thing named. A name, therefore, which has never become connected in any manner with any title or possession of land, clearly infers no means of its identification. So the mathematical contents expressed in figures is not a mark of identity peculiar to the land; but like a common noun, has no immediate or cognate relation to a particular tract. * * Identity is said to be a matter for the jury. Certainly this is so; but from its very nature, the fact of identity is dependent on circumstances which attach themselves to the land. It is because the thing described answers to the circumstances of description, we are able to identify it. The evidence of identity is the record which contains the description and fixes the duty. Assessment is, from its legal requirement, and the necessity of preserving its evidence, a written entry, and must depend upon the records of the commissioner's office, and not upon parol testimony, or the private duplicate of the assessor."[1] And after an examination of cases decided, it is added: "The result of the whole is, that where the assessment wholly fails to lead to identification, so that neither the owner nor the officer can tell that his land is taxed, the duty of payment cannot be performed, and the assessment is void."[2] The rule thus given is quite as liberal in support of imperfect or inaccurate descriptions as would be applied to conveyances *inter partes.* In another case in the same state, it is said a sale "will pass the title, although assessed in a wrong name or by a wrong number, if otherwise designated and capable of identification. The reason for this is the recognized principle, that it is the land, and not the owner, which is chargeable, and to be charged with the tax. It must, however, be susceptible of identification as the land assessed, otherwise the sale would be void."[3] But identification may possibly be made out to the satisfaction of a jury by a description that would be extremely likely to mislead the owner himself; the jury having their attention called to the errors or defects which exist, and the owner not

[1] Philadelphia *v.* Miller, 49 Penn. St., 440, 448, per *Agnew*, J., citing and commenting upon McCall *v.* Lorrimer, 4 Watts, 351, 355; S. C., 4 W. & S., 133; Dunn *v.* Relyea, 6 W. & S., 475; Stewart *v.* Shoenfelt, 13 S. & R., 360; Luffborough *v.* Parker, 16 id., 351; Morton *v.* Harris, 9 Watts, 319, 325; Hubley *v.* Keyser, 2 P. & Watts, 496; Strauch *v.* Shoemaker, 1 W. & S., 166: Burns *v.* Lyon, 4 Watts, 363; Harper *v.* McKeehan, 3 W. & S., 238; Russel *v.* Werntz, 24 Penn. St., 337; Laird *v.* Heister, id., 452; Miller *v.* Hale, 26 id., 432; Cooper *v.* Brockway, 8 Watts, 162, 165; Thompson *v.* Fisher, 6 W. & S., 520; Dunden *v.* Snodgrass, 18 Penn. St., 151; Woodside *v.* Wilson, 32 id., 52. These cases pass upon a great variety of descriptions, some of which are held sufficient, and some are not.

[2] Philadelphia *v.* Miller, 49 Penn. St., 440, 455; Harris *v.* Tyson, 24 id., 347. See also Glass *v.* Gilbert, 58 id., 266. It is the return of the tract by the assessors which fixes its identity and liability to taxation. Brown *v.* Hayes, 66 Penn. St., 229. In some states, however, provision is made by law for a correction of the descriptions by the county board.

[3] *Thompson*, J., in Woodside *v.* Wilson, 32 Penn. St., 52, 54. This statement would, of course, be inapplicable to the case of an assessment of resident land. When the law requires it to be assessed to the owner, it must be so assessed, as preceding cases show.

being aware that there are any, but having a right to assume, until notified to the contrary, that all descriptions in the list have accurate application to some particular pieces of property, and fit some others when not appearing to fit his. A more satisfactory rule would seem to be that "the designation of the land will be sufficient if it afford the means of identification, and do not positively mislead the owner,"[1] or be calculated to mislead him.[2] It is thus expressed in a New York case: "An assessment of nonresident land is fatally defective and void if it contain such a falsity in the designation or description of the parcel assessed, as might probably mislead the owner and prevent him from ascertaining by the notices that his land was to be sold or redeemed. Such a mistake or falsity defeats one of the obvious and just purposes of the statute — that of giving to the owner an opportunity of preventing the sale by paying the tax."[3] Under this rule each case must depend so much upon its own special facts that little service could be done by giving the decided cases in detail here. Several are given in the note, and others are referred to.[4]

[1] *Thompson*, J., in Woodside *v.* Wilson, 32 Penn. St., 52, 55.

[2] See Curtis *v.* Supervisors of Brown County, 22 Wis., 167, in which it is denied that a description sufficient as between parties will be sufficient always in an assessment, or that particulars in it which are erroneous can be rejected as surplusage. To the same point is Dike *v.* Lewis, 4 Denio, 237; see also Orton *v.* Noonan, 23 Wis., 102, in which it is said words cannot be supplied by intendment. It is to be observed of this case, however, that the words it was proposed to supply would have wholly changed the apparent meaning.

[3] *Ruggles*, J., in Tallman *v.* White, 2 N. Y., 66, 71. See also Lafferty *v.* Byers, 5 Ohio, 458; Turney *v.* Yeoman, 16 id., 24; Farnum *v.* Buffum, 4 Cush., 260: Amberg *v.* Rogers, 9 Mich., 332; Green *v.* Lunt, 58 Me., 15; State *v.* Union, 36 N. J., 309. In Hill *v.* Mowry, 6 Gray, 551, the rule is laid down that a tax deed, taking effect only as the execution of a statute power, should be construed with some strictness, so as to enable the grantee to identify the land, and to enable the owner to redeem it. And it was held that a deed which bounds the land correctly on two sides, bounds it on the third by land on which in fact it is bounded in part only, and on the fourth by land from which it is separated by the land of a third person, is void for uncertainty.

[4] Where the only description was "William Bush's heirs, 2560 acres," held insufficient. Bush *v.* Williams, Cooke (Tenn.), 274. So where the description was "Moses Buffum, house and land," Buffum not being the occupant. Farnum *v.* Buffum, 4 Cush., 260. Compare Coombs *v.* Warren, 34 Me., 89. So where the description is *part* of a lot without showing how much, or giv-

Valuation. Where the grouping of lands for assessment is inadmissible, the valuation of several parcels in gross is equally so. No valuable purpose could be subserved by separate descriptions if the parcels, though separately described, were to be grouped in valuation.[1]

ing boundaries. Detroit Young Men's Society *v.* Detroit, 3 Mich., 172; Massie *v.* Long, 2 Ohio, 287, 289; Green *v.* Lunt, 58 Me., 518. But a description, as "that part of private claim 61, lying east of the north branch of the river Ecorse," in a township named, is sufficient. Gilman *v.* Riopelle, 18 Mich., 145. Error in stating the quantity of the land, however great, will not vitiate. Brown *v.* Hays, 66 Penn. St., 229; Williston *v.* Colkett, 9 id., 38; Gilman *v.* Riopelle, 18 Mich., 145. Omission of the number of a town lot, or the name of the owner, is fatal where the law requires them to be given. Thacher *ex parte*, 3 Sneed, 344. Description in the notice of tax sale, as "Tract No. 8, S. D., advertised, 4197," held wholly insufficient. Griffin *v.* Crippen, 60 Me., 270. Compare Glass *v.* Gilbert, 58 Penn. St., 266, 290. An assessment as definite as the grant under which the land is held, is sufficient. People *v.* Crockett, 33 Cal., 150. A description, "one hundred varas square," with definite boundaries on three sides, is sufficient. Garwood *v.* Hastings, 38 Cal., 216. An assessment of a large tract of land, which describes it by metes and bounds, and then excepts from the tract parcels of the same which have been previously conveyed, but does not describe the excepted portions by metes and bounds, nor in any manner but by a reference to recorded deeds, is *void* on its face. People *v.* Cone, 48 Cal., 427; People *v.* Hyde, id., 431; see also People *v.* Hancock, id., 631. A description of the land by well understood abbreviations is sufficient, thus: "E. ½, s. w. ¼, sec. 24, town 3 south, of range 7 west," etc. Sibley *v.* Smith, 2 Mich., 486, 503; see also Long *v.* Long, 2 Blackf., 293; Jordan, etc., Association, etc., *v.* Wagoner, 33 Ind., 50; Atkins *v.* Hinman, 2 Gilm., 437; Olcott *v.* State, 5 id., 481; Blakely *v.* Bestor, 13 Ill., 714; Stevens *v.* Hollister, 18 Vt., 294; Goodell *v.* Harrison, 2 Mo., 124. Further, as to what is a sufficient description, the following cases are instructive. Ronkendorf *v.* Taylor, 4 Pet., 349; Lafferty's Lessee *v.* Byers, 5 Ohio, 458; Trevor *v.* Emerick, 6 id., 391; Larrabee *v.* Hodgkins, 58 Me., 412; Griffin *v.* Crippin, 60 id., 270; Orono *v.* Veazie, 61 id., 431; Currie *v.* Fowler, 5 J. J. Marsh, 145; Le Fever *v.* Detroit, 2 Mich., 586; Wright *v.* Dunham, 13 id., 414; Atwell *v.* Zeluff, 26 id., 118, 121; Jaques *v.* Kopman, 6 La. An., 542; Woolfolk *v.* Fonbene, 15 id., 15; Latchman *v.* Clark, 14 Cal., 131; High *v.* Shoemaker, 22 id., 363; Bosworth *v.* Danzien, 25 id., 296; People *v.* Flint, 39 id., 670; Ainsworth *v.* Dean, 21 N. H., 400; Bidwell *v.* Webb, 10 Minn., 59; Bidwell *v.* Coleman, 11 id., 78; St. Peters Church *v.* Scott County, 12 id., 395; Shaw *v.* Orr, 30 Iowa, 355. A falsity in the description which might mislead, runs through and invalidates all the subsequent proceedings. Yenda *v.* Wheeler, 9 Texas, 408.

[1] People *v.* Mining Co., 39 Cal., 511; People *v.* Hollister, 47 id., 408. In this last case there was a separate valuation of each parcel in the column with the descriptions, but not carried into the appropriate column. "Value," it is

It is elsewhere shown[1] that valuation is in its nature a judicial act, and the assessors in making it are entitled to the customary protection which the law accords to officers exercising corresponding judicial functions. The party injured by their errors, committed without fraud or malice, has in general only such remedy as the statute may afford him. And in no proceeding is one to be heard who complains of a valuation which, however erroneous, charges him only with a just proportion of the tax. If his own assessment is not out of proportion, as compared with valuations generally on the same roll, it is immaterial that some one neighbor is assessed too little and another too much.[2]

The legislature cannot make the valuations of property for taxation.[3] The nearest approach to the exercise of such an authority by the legislature is where it definitely fixes the basis for a local assessment, by the acre, by frontage, etc. But in such cases the considerations which affect benefits are matters of notoriety, and may well be taken notice of by the legislative body when prescribing a rule which, at least in the particular case, is to operate generally and with uniformity. In a majority of the states the rule prescribed by the statutes is that lands and other real estate shall be valued *as such*, irrespective of the separate estates that individuals may have in them. Under such a practice, he who, for the time being, enjoys the possession of the real estate, and the pernancy of the profits may be charged with the tax.[4] The practice, however, has not been universal; in some states, and partic-

said, "can only be determined by the ordinary selling and buying prices, for cash, at the time." *Caruthers*, J., in Brown *v.* Greer, 3 Head, 695, 697. This is a criterion which, it is safe to say, is very seldom applied.

[1] See Chapter XXIV.

[2] Chicopee *v.* County Commissioners, 16 Gray, 38. As to actual value, and how it is to be got at, see State *v.* Ferris, 23 N. J., 546; State *v.* Randolph, 25 id., 427; Oswego Starch Factory *v.* Dolloway, 21 N. Y., 449; People *v.* Dolan, 36 id., 59, 62; People *v.* Ferguson, 38 id., 89; People *v.* Barker, 48 id., 70.

[3] People *v.* Hastings, 29 Cal., 449. Of course the assessment is fatally defective if it lacks the valuation. Garwood *v.* Hastings, 38 id., 216. As to the valuation of railroad property, see State *v.* Illinois Central R. R. Co., 27 Ill., 64.

[4] Turner *v.* Smith, 14 Wall., 553; Atkins *v.* Hinman, 2 Gilm., 437, 449; Parker *v.* Braxton, 2 Gray, 185; Willard *v.* Blount, 11 Ired., 624; Brown *v.* Austin, 41 Vt., 262; Merrick *v.* Hutt, 15 Ark., 331; Briscoe *v.* Coulter, 18 Ark., 423; Blackwell on Tax Titles, ch. 38 and notes.

ularly in some special proceedings, the statutes have required separate interests to be separately assessed.[1] When the whole is assessed as an entirety, provision is usually made under which the respective owners may pay their proportions of the tax, and have their respective interests discharged of the lien.[2]

Authentication of the assessment. The result of the action of the assessors is embodied in an assessment roll or list. The statutes provide how this shall be authenticated, and compliance with their provisions is essential.[3] The methods are different in the different states, and are sometimes changed in the same state. But the rule of law is clear. Where the law required the roll to

[1] Separate interests in Pennsylvania assessed and sold separately. See McLaughlin *v.* Kain, 45 Penn. St., 113. As to Mississippi, see Dunn *v.* Winston, 31 Miss., 135. As to Kentucky, see Oldhams *v.* Jones, 5 B. Monr., 464. In the case of special assessments it has been more usual to assess distinct interests separately, sometimes, however, providing for a sale of the fee. See Jackson *v.* Babcock, 16 N. Y., 246; Matter of De Graw St., 18 Wend., 568. And see further Williams *v.* Brace, 5 Conn., 190. The case of Jackson *v.* Babcock, 16 N. Y., 246, was this: The statute provided for proceedings in court under which, in street opening cases, where there were distinct interests in lands which were subject to a lien for the assessment, one owner of an interest might proceed in the supreme court against all the others, including unknown owners, for an equitable apportionment of the assessment, and after advertising for the appearance of the unknown owners, obtain an order for an absolute sale of the fee; the proceeds to be applied, so far as necessary, to the discharge of the assessment. This statute was held to be valid, and effectual to cut off all contingent as well as vested rights.

[2] There are some cases in which it has been held that the omission of the dollar mark as a prefix to the figures which represent the value of the property in the assessment roll will render the assessment nugatory; there being nothing in its absence by which to determine what the figures indicate. Braley *v.* Seaman, 30 Cal., 610; People *v.* Savings Union, 31 id., 132. And see People *v.* Empire, etc. Co., 33 id., 171. The contrary has been held in New Hampshire. Cahoon *v.* Coe, 52 N. H., 518, 524. And see State *v.* Eureka, etc., Co., 8 Nev., 15; Chickering *v.* Faile, 38 Ill., 342; Elston *v.* Kennicott, 46 id., 187, 202. In Illinois it is decided that a judgment for taxes in which the sums are expressed in figures without a dollar mark prefixed, is void for want of certainty. Lawrence *v.* Fast, 20 Ill., 338; Lane *v.* Bommelmann, 21 id., 143; Epinger *v.* Kirby, 23 id., 521, 523; Dukes *v.* Rowley, 24 id., 210; Chickering *v.* Faile, 38 id., 342; Cook *v.* Norton, 43 id., 391; Potwin *v.* Oades, 45 id., 366; Elston *v.* Kennicott, 46 id., 187; Pittsburg, etc., R. R. Co. *v.* Chicago, 53 id., 80. These decisions were followed in Woods *v.* Freeman, 1 Wall., 398; and Randolph *v.* Metcalf, 6 Cold., 400, 408.

[3] Warner *v.* Grand Haven, 30 Mich., 24.

be signed, and a certificate to be attached, the signing of the certificate was held not to dispense with a signing of the roll, and if that was not signed, no proceedings could be taken upon it.[1] Where the statute required the assessors to certify that they had assessed the property at its true value, according to the best of their knowledge and belief, a certificate that they had assessed it "according to the usual way of assessing" was declared void.[2] The same was held of a certificate that the assessors had estimated the real estate "at a sum which, for the purposes of the assessment, we believe to be the true value thereof."[3] In these cases the assessors had endeavored to make the certificates correspond to the fact, it being notorious that whatever they may certify, they are not in the practice of estimating property at its true value. A failure, however, to comply literally with a statutory form will not vitiate if there is a substantial compliance.[4]

Equalization. In some states, when assessment rolls are completed and signed, they are subject to review by a higher authority, for the purpose of an equalization, in case the assessment of one district is found to be relatively higher or lower than that of

[1] Sibley *v.* Smith, 2 Mich., 486. The statute was afterwards changed. See Lacy *v.* Davis, 4 Mich., 140. See further Colby *v.* Russel, 3 Greenl., 227; Foxcroft *v.* Nevens, 4 id., 72; Kelley *v.* Craig, 5 Ired., 129; Johnson *v.* Elwood, 53 N. Y., 431, 435. A similar defect held a mere irregularity and cured as such by a statute that no irregularity should defeat the tax title. Townsen *v.* Wilson, 9 Penn. St., 270.

[2] Van Rensselaer *v.* Whitbeck, 7 N. Y., 517: compare Parish *v.* Golden, 35 id., 462.

[3] Clark *v.* Crane, 5 Mich., 151. See also Colby *v.* Russell, 3 Greenl., 227; Foxcroft *v.* Nevens, 4 id., 72; Johnson *v* Goodridge, 15 Me., 29; Kelar *v.* Savage, 20 id., 199.

[4] Parish *v.* Golden, 35 N. Y., 462; Buffalo, etc., R. R. Co. *v.* Supervisors of Erie, 48 N. Y., 93; Bradford *v.* Randall, 5 Pick., 496; People *v.* Mining Co., 39 Cal., 511. See Bangor *v.* Lancey, 21 Me., 472. In this case it appeared that the statute required the list to have the official sanction of a majority of the assessors, evidenced by their signatures. The original list was not signed, but a supplementary list referring to it as containing the assessment for the year was duly signed. *Held* sufficient. As to what irregularities will defeat an assessment the following cases may be consulted. Willey *v.* Scoville's Lessees, 9 Ohio, 44; Shimmin *v.* Inman, 26 Me., 228; Smith *v.* Davis, 30 Cal., 536, cited in Huntingdon *v.* Central Pacific R. R. Co., 2 Sawyer, 503. What will not avoid: Gulf R. R. Co. *v.* Morris, 7 Kansas, 210; Smith *v.* Leavenworth Co., 9 id., 296.

another; so that, if the general taxes were to be assessed upon it, the district would pay more or less than its due proportion.[1] Thus, town assessment rolls are equalized by county boards of supervisors or commissioners, and the aggregate of the county assessments by a state board, established for the purpose. This is not done by changing individual assessments, but by fixing the aggregate sums for the several districts at what, in the opinion of the board, they should be, so that general taxes may be levied according to this determination, instead of on the assessor's footings. These boards act judicially in equalizing, and their decision is conclusive. The boards are composed of popular representatives, and they act upon their own judgment of what is equal and just.[2] But such a board has a special and limited jurisdiction, and any unauthorized action is void.[3] And their powers, like those of all similar boards, are to be strictly construed.[4] They cannot release a tax, or its lien, when not expressly empowered to do so.[5]

[1] As to the equalization and the necessity therefor, see County Commissioners *v.* Parker, 7 Minn., 267; Tweed *v.* Metcalf, 4 Mich., 579; Tallmadge *v.* Supervisors of Rensselaer, 21 Barb., 611; State *v.* Allen, 43 Ill., 456; People *v.* Nichols, 49 id., 517. The members of a state board of equalization are really assessors, and, where all assessors are required to be elected by the people, this board cannot be created by appointment. Houghton *v.* Austin, 47 Cal., 646; People *v.* Raymond, 37 N. Y., 428.

[2] See Tweed *v.* Metcalf, 4 Mich., 579; Case *v.* Dean, 16 id., 12; Bellinger *v.* Gray, 51 N. Y., 610.

[3] See State *v.* Allen, 43 Ill., 456; People *v.* Nichols, 49 id., 517; Darling *v.* Gunn, 50 id., 424; McKee *v.* Supervisors of Champaign, 53 id., 477. That the valuation of assessors is conclusive on the county board, except when the statute otherwise provides, see Respublica *v.* Deaves, 3 Yeates, 465. In raising or reducing the assessment of a district, it is sufficient if the board designate the percentage increase or reduction. Hubbard *v.* Winsor, 15 Mich., 146.

[4] Sioux City, etc., R. R. Co. *v.* Washington County, 3 Neb., 30.

[5] State *v.* Central Pacific R. R. Co., 9 Nev., 79. Where the board has authority to equalize, and also to discharge assessments, they do not exhaust their authority by a hearing and decision on equalization. State *v.* Ormsby County Com'rs, 7 Nev., 392.

A board, having authority to equalize assessments as between townships, cannot, of their own motion, increase an individual assessment above that returned by the assessor. McConkey *v.* Smith, Sup. Ct. Ill., 7 Chicago Legal News, 210.

CHAPTER XIII.

THE COLLECTOR'S WARRANT.

Before the collector is authorized to proceed in the collection of the taxes, he must have his warrant for the purpose, in due form of law. This, in different states, may be the assessment roll or list, with the tax extended upon it, or it may be a duplicate of the list with a like extension, or it may be either of these, with a formal warrant attached, particularly indicating what are his duties under it, and commanding their performance.[1] Whatever the statute provides for, in this regard, the collector must have, and he is a trespasser if he proceeds to compulsory action without it.[2] Upon this point the decisions are numerous and uniform. In a case arising under a statute which required that a warrant should be attached to the tax duplicate, the following remarks have been made: "The authority of a collector of taxes to collect is his warrant. The duplicate is but a memorandum of the amount he is to collect from the parties therein named respectively. Without a warrant, the collector becomes a trespasser as soon as he intermeddles with the property of the tax payer. There must also be a law authorizing the issue of a warrant, and some person appointed to issue it, and it must conform to the law authorizing it, and be issued by the proper person designated by law, or it is no protection to a collector."[3] No question is made anywhere of the correctness of this doctrine.

Whatever may be the requisites of the warrant under the statute, care must be taken that they be observed. One of the most im-

[1] The tax roll is void if made out before the tax is voted. Gale *v.* Mead, 4 Hill, 109.

[2] Blackwell on Tax Titles, 168, and cases cited.

[3] Hilbish *v.* Horner, 58 Penn. St., 93, citing Pearce *v.* Torrence, 2 Grant's Cases, 82; Stephens *v.* Wilkins, 6 Penn. St., 260. And see Chalker *v.* Ives, 55 id., 81. The same doctrine is declared under a different law, in Slade *v.* Governor, 3 Dev., 365; Kelly *v.* Craig, 5 Ired., 129. And see Brown *v.* Wright, 17 Vt., 97.

portant of these is the direction. If it is directed to one officer when under the statute it should be to another, the process is fatally defective.[1] It has been decided in Maine, under a statute which gives a form to be followed "in substance," that the omission of that part of the form which directs the treasurer to levy distress in default of payment renders the warrant nugatory, and the treasurer may refuse to execute it.[2] But variances in immaterial matters will not vitiate the warrant. Thus under the Maine statute it is held that the omission in the warrant, "In the name of the state of Maine," which is a part of the form, is immaterial.[3]

In Vermont the question is made whether the date is an indispensable part of the warrant, but if it is, it is held that an error in the date will not avoid it.[4] The decisions in the same state are very liberal in holding that other accidental errors and defects shall not vitiate the process.[5] In Massachusetts where the statute provides that "the assessors shall commit the tax list, with the warrant under their hands, to the collector for collection," a failure to attach them, if both are delivered to the collector, is immaterial.[6] And in the same state an error in the command of the warrant, by which the collector was directed to arrest the person taxed within twelve days, instead of fourteen, as it should have been, after demand of the tax, if the same should not be paid, etc., will not vitiate the warrant, nor become material, unless the direction to arrest is acted upon.[7] In New York a warrant issued and

[1] Stephens v. Wilkins, 6 Penn. St., 260; Cannell v. Crawford County, 59 id., 196.

[2] Bachelder v. Thompson, 41 Me., 539. In Wilson v. Seavey, 38 Vt., 221, it was held that naming the collector's predecessor in the address of the warrant, instead of naming him, did not invalidate it.

[3] Mussey v. White, 3 Greenl., 290. A constitutional provision that all process shall run "in the name of the people," etc., held not applicable to a collector's warrant. Tweed v. Metcalf, 4 Mich., 579; Wisner v. Davenport, 5 id., 501; Curry v. Hinman, 11 Ill., 420; Scarritt v. Chapman, 11 id., 443; State v. Birchard, 1 Wis., 457.

[4] Bellows v. Weeks, 41 Vt., 590.

[5] Goodwin v. Perkins, 39 Vt., 598. See Spear v. Braintree, 24 id., 414; Chandler v. Spear, 22 id., 388.

[6] Barnard v. Graves, 13 Met., 85.

[7] Barnard v. Graves, 13 Met., 85, citing King v. Whitcomb, 1 id., 328. In Connecticut it is held that if the warrant is not attached to the list, and the of-

signed by the supervisors as required by law, is good, though they fail to add to their signatures the official title.[1] An error in the direction to the collector by which he is commanded to account to the wrong officer is immaterial; this being a matter that does not concern the tax payers.[2] The same is true of a failure to limit by the warrant the time within which the treasurer shall collect the tax.[3]

Different rolls for different taxes. It is not always the practice to have one assessment and tax roll for the state taxes and another for the local taxes. On the contrary, for what may be called the *general* taxes of the municipality, it is customary to provide that, when voted, they shall be certified to such state or county officer or board as is authorized to issue the tax warrant for state or county taxes, and by such officer or board shall be spread upon the same roll or list, though in a separate column, and be collected by authority of the same warrant. The regulation may be the opposite of this; that the state taxes shall be certified to county or town officers, and by them spread upon the roll. Such provisions do not give the state or county functionaries any power to review, revise or set aside, the local action, but they must levy what has been voted, and may be compelled to do so.[4]

ficer is commanded by his warrant "to collect of the persons named in the annexed list," etc., there is nothing to which these words can apply; the command in the warrant is nugatory, and he can take the property of no individual. Picket *v.* Allen, 10 Conn., 145.

[1] Sheldon *v.* Van Buskirk, 2 N. Y., 473.

[2] Clemons *v.* Lewis, 36 Vt., 673. Compare Tweed *v.* Metcalf, 4 Mich., 579.

[3] Walker *v.* Miner, 32 Vt., 769. Such a warrant may be defective as between the collector and the public he acts for, but the defect does not invalidate any action taken to collect the tax under it. *Id.* In Iowa it seems that the authority to sell lands comes from the statute and not from a tax warrant. See Parker *v.* Sexton, 29 Iowa, 421; Rhodes *v.* Sexton, 33 id., 540.

[4] Where the law gives a city full authority to vote money for the support of the poor, etc., and requires the supervisors to "cause the same to be raised, assessed and collected," the supervisors have no discretion to refuse on the ground that funds for the like purposes have previously been misapplied. *Ex parte* Common Council of Albany, 3 Cow., 358. Compare Williams *v.* School District, 21 Pick., 75. Sometimes the auditing of accounts is made by law equivalent to the vote of a tax. See People *v.* Supervisors of Queens, 1 Hill, 195.

Delivery of the warrant. A provision of statute that the officer or board making out the warrant shall deliver it to the collector by a day named is only directory.[1] But any such delay as would leave the collector insufficient time for compulsory proceedings under the statute, would of course preclude their being taken.

Exhausting authority. The issue of a void tax warrant would not exhaust the authority to issue a valid one. In some states by statute, or by a customary course of procedure, when one valid process does not result in the collection of all the tax, another may issue.[2] For personal taxes which remain uncollected suits are sometimes provided for, especially where the failure to collect is in consequence of a removal of the party taxed from the treasurer's jurisdiction.

Blending taxes. A very common provision of statute, where several taxes are to be spread upon the same roll is, that they shall be kept separate and placed in distinct columns on the roll. This advises the tax payer of the nature of the several demands that are made upon him, and enables him to pay or tender the amount of any one the justice and legality of which he concedes, and to decline to pay any other if he considers it unwarranted. Such provision is mandatory, and if not obeyed, the taxes cannot be enforced.[3] A custom to blend them cannot make the roll valid.[4] But separating the taxes when the statute does not require it will not affect the roll; as this deprives no one of any right whatever.[5]

Excessive taxes. All statutes are mandatory which expressly or by implication limit the amount of taxes which may be levied. When these are exceeded by a sum which is spread upon the whole roll, the whole levy is void. The levy is in excess of the jurisdiction of the officers, and will be as deficient in the legal

[1] Alvord *v.* Collins, 20 Pick., 418; Hubbard *v.* Winsor, 15 Mich., 146; Smith *v.* Crittenden, 16 id., 152. The case of Cardigan *v.* Page, 6 N. H., 182, is *contra*.

[2] See Eddy *v.* Wilson, 43 Vt., 362. The warrant is sometimes extended or renewed, under statutes providing therefor. See Griswold *v.* School District, 24 Mich., 262.

[3] Thayer *v.* Stearns, 1 Pick., 482; Case *v.* Dean, 16 Mich., 12.

[4] State *v.* Falkinburge, 15 N. J., 320; Camden & Amboy R. R. Co. *v.* Hillegas, 18 id., 11.

[5] Wall *v.* Trumbull, 16 Mich., 228: compare Torrey *v.* Milbury, 21 Pick., 64.

competency to make out a valid charge, as if made without any authority whatever. This would not defeat a separate tax placed in a separate column on the roll, but it would invalidate whatever is blended with the excessive levy, and incapable of being separated.

Excess in a levy may happen from a sum which has been voted for an unauthorized purpose being included with others that are authorized, or from imposing more than is permitted for lawful purposes, or from the addition of unauthorized charges, or from errors of the officers, by which either the aggregate is made too large, or individuals are charged more than their proportion. In the latter case the individual taxes which were unjustly increased would alone be void; in the others the whole levy.[1] Some disposition has been manifested to save the taxes when the excess was comparatively insignificant, on the maxim, *de minimis lex*

[1] "The authority to impose taxes, while it is an inherent and essential power of government, which is fully recognized in our constitution and conferred on the legislature in clear and comprehensive terms, is nevertheless a delicate trust, nearly affecting the rights and interests of the citizens, and to be exercised carefully, and within the exact limits which are prescribed by that clause in the frame of government which creates the power and defines the extent to which the legislature may go in its exercise. If they have exceeded it, if the constitutional boundary has been overstepped, there can be no doubt of the right of the citizens to resist such unauthorized exercise of power, and of the duty of this court to declare such legislative action void, and to protect all persons against its unlawful exactions." *Bigelow*, Ch. J., Commonwealth *v.* Savings Bank, 5 Allen, 428, 430. See Stetson *v.* Kempton, 13 Mass., 272; Libby *v.* Burnham, 15 Mass., 144. In Joyner *v.* School District, 3 Cush., 567, 572, where an excessive school tax was levied, *Dewey*, J., says: "Each member of a school district has a right to insist that no more than his proportional amount be demanded of him, to pay the debts of the school district, that the assessments shall be in a legal form, and in a form that will also compel the other members of the district to pay their proportionate share of the corporate debts." See also School District *v.* Merrills, 12 Conn., 437; Hubbard *v.* Brainard, 35 id., 563; First Ecclesiastical Society *v.* Hartford, 38 id., 274; Elwell *v.* Shaw, 1 Greenl., 339; Huse *v.* Merriam, 2 id., 375; Lacy *v.* Davis, 4 Mich., 140; Gerry *v.* Stoneham, 1 Allen, 319; Goodrich *v.* Lunenburg, 9 Gray, 38, 41; Stone *v.* Bean, 15 id., 42; Kemper *v.* McClelland, 19 Ohio, 308 324; Mason *v.* Roe, 5 Blackf., 98; Hutchins *v.* Doe, 3 Ind., 528; Drew *v.* Davis, 10 Vt., 506; Johnson *v.* Colburn, 36 id., 693; Wells *v.* Burbank, 17 N H., 393; Kinsworthy *v.* Mitchell, 21 Ark., 145; Bucknall *v.* Story, 36 Cal., 67, 72; Tucker *v.* The Justices, 34 Geo., 370. As to levy of excessive fees, see Mosher *v.* Robie, 11 Me., 135; Stetson *v.* Kempton, 13 Mass., 272; Buell *v.* Irwin, 24 Mich., 245; Prindle *v.* Campbell, 9 Minn., 212.

non curat. Of this maxim it has been said in a case where a tax was but slightly in excess of authority: "The maxim is so vague in itself as to form a very unsafe ground of proceeding or judging; and it may be almost as difficult to apply it as a rule in pecuniary concerns as to the interest which a witness has in the event of a cause; and in such case it cannot apply. Any interest excludes him. The assessment was therefore unauthorized and void. If the line which the legislature has established be once passed, we know of no boundary to the discretion of the assessors."[1] The like rule has been adopted in another case, which has held that any addition perceptibly increasing an individual tax avoids it.[2]

[1] *Mellen*, Ch. J., in Huse *v.* Merriam, 2 Greenl., 375, 376.

[2] Case *v.* Dean, 16 Mich., 12. But an unintentional error may not have this effect. Kelley *v.* Corson, 8 Wis., 182; O'Grady *v.* Barnhisel, 23 Cal., 287, 296. See State *v.* Newark, 25 N. J., 399. In Iowa there is a statute that a tax sale shall be upheld if any portion of the tax for which the sale was made was legal. See Parker *v.* Sexton, 29 Iowa, 421. Where part is legal and part is illegal the former will be sustained if they are capable of being distinguished. See O'Kane *v.* Treat, 25 Ill., 557; Briscoe *v.* Allison, 43 id., 291; State *v.* Allen, 43 id., 456; Allen *v.* Peoria, etc., R. R. Co., 44 id., 85; People *v.* Nichols, 49 id., 517; Mix *v.* People, Sup. Ct. Ill. (1875), 7 Chicago Legal News, p. 2; State *v.* Plainfield, Sup. Ct. N. J. (1875), 12 Albany Law Journal, p. 172. And as to sale on judgment for taxes, see Reeve *v.* Kennedy, 43 Cal., 643. An excess inserted to cover possible contingencies in collecting, held not to render assessors liable in trespass where they had acted in good faith, and only erred in judgment. Colman *v.* Anderson, 10 Mass., 105, 117, 120.

CHAPTER XIV.

THE COLLECTION OF THE TAX.

Summary remedies necessary. Very summary remedies have been allowed, in every age and country, for the collection by the government of its revenues. They have been considered a matter of state necessity. Without them it might be possible for defeated and dissatisfied parties to cripple and, possibly, to break up the government, by depriving it of the resources for continuing its existence until they could be gathered in by the slow processes which are available to private parties. It has been shown in the preceding chapters, that the invaluable principles of the common law are not supposed to be violated by a resort to summary proceedings in these cases. Summary processes are not necessarily unjust. They would be so if they deprived the party of a hearing, or if they precluded the opportunity for a patient and deliberate examination of the questions upon which his rights depend, before such rights could be finally concluded and cut off. But this it is not the design of legitimate tax legislation to accomplish in any case. It may reverse somewhat the course of ordinary proceedings to enforce rights at the common law, but it can never finally and conclusively condemn without a hearing.

When a tax is duly and properly levied[1] it is to be collected after some method prescribed by law. The several methods may be classified as *direct*, when the taxes are demanded from the parties taxed in person, or enforced against the property on which they are laid; and *indirect* when, for convenience, they are collected of others than the persons upon whom the burden is in the end to rest. All such taxation as comes in this second class, seems to require no special mention. But provision is sometimes made by law under which other taxes are, for the convenience of the government, indirectly collected. A government which taxes

[1] "*Levy*," as applied to a tax, "imports the ascertainment of the amount to be raised, and the performance of such acts as would authorize the tax collector to proceed to collect." *Handy*, J., in Moore *v.* Foote, 32 Miss., 469, 479.

the salaries of its officers might be its own collector; first deducting the tax and then paying over the remainder; and the like might be provided for in any case where moneys were to be paid over by the government itself.[1] So a convenient method of collecting taxes on the dividends or other receipts of shareholders from the profits of corporations, or on payments to creditors, may be to make the corporation itself the collector, and require it to deduct the tax, and pay it to the government before paying over to the parties thus taxed.[2]

The methods of collecting taxes which have been provided for under various statutes are:[3]

1. By suit.
2. By the arrest of the person taxed.
3. By distress of goods and chattels.
4. By taking possession of goods and chattels and retaining them until the taxes are paid, or selling them for the payment.
5. By the sale of lands.
6. By imposing penalties for nonpayment.
7. By forfeiting to the government the property upon or in respect to which the tax is payable.
8. By making the payment a condition to the exercise of some lawful right.

[2] So a court, where a fund is in its charge, may order the taxes paid out of it before the fund is paid over.

[3] Maltby *v.* Reading R. R. Co., 52 Penn. St., 140; Haight *v.* Railroad Co., 6 Wall., 15; National Bank *v.* Commonwealth, 9 id., 353; United States *v.* Railroad Co., 17 id., 322; Minot *v.* Railroad Co., 18 id., 206, 230.

[4] An important principle of the common law may also be called an assistant in the collection of taxes. It is this: That all contracts and arrangements made for the defeat or evasion of the revenue laws of a country are illegal, and the courts will give the parties no remedy in respect to them. Clugas *v.* Penaluna, 4 T. R., 466; Waymell *v.* Reed, 5 id., 599; Cope *v.* Rowlands, 2 M. & W., 149; Smith *v.* Mawhood, 14 id., 452; Favor *v.* Philbrick, 7 N. H., 326, 340; Harris v. Runnels, 12 How., 79. See, also, Bancroft *v.* Dumas, 21 Vt., 456; Alexander *v.* O'Donnell, 12 Kan., 608; Howard *v.* First Independent Church, 18 Md., 451. It is necessary, perhaps, that both parties should have knowledge of the intent to violate the law; for if one be innocent there is no reason why the guilty intent of the other shall cause him to suffer. See Briggs *v.* Lawrence, 3 T. R., 454; Lightfoot *v.* Tenant, 1 B. & P., 551, 556; Clugas *v.* Penaluna, 4 T. R., 466; Kreiss *v.* Seligman, 8 Barb., 439; Ritchie *v.* Smith, 6 M., G. & Scott, 462; Pellecat *v.* Angell, 2 Cromp. M. & R.,

These will be briefly considered in their order.[1]

1. Collection by suit. It has been shown that taxes are not debts in the ordinary acceptation of that term, and that the statutory measures are to be resorted to for their collection. Generally no others are admissible.[2] But the remedy by suit may be given by statute either directly or by implication. If no specific remedy is expressly given, or only an imperfect or inadequate one, the presumption that a remedy by suit was intended is but reasonable.[3] Nothing need be said regarding the proceedings in such suits beyond this: that they would take the ordinary course prescribed by law for the collection of money demands, except as the statute may have otherwise provided.[4]

311; Foster *v.* Thurston, 11 Cush., 322; Webster *v.* Munger, 8 Gray, 584; Cambioso *v.* Maffitt, 2 Wash. C. C., 98; Armstrong *v.* Toler, 11 Wheat., 258. The principle does not apply to contracts made in evasion of the laws of a foreign country, but it does apply to all contracts made abroad to be performed here. See cases above cited. Also Holman *v.* Johnson, 1 Cowp., 341. And compare Dater *v.* Earl, 3 Gray, 482, with Cambioso *v.* Maffitt, 2 Wash. C. C., 98.

[1] *Farming out the revenue* for collection, has been a favorite method in some countries. It consists in putting the collection into the hands of contractors, who are to return to the treasury a certain net result, having the remainder for their own compensation. Such a system, by making it the personal interest of those who are to administer the tax laws to render them as productive as possible, might increase the public revenues both by inducing a more vigilant search for subjects of taxation, and by ensuring more strict enforcement of collections; and Bentham has defended it on these grounds. Works, Edinb. ed., Vol. 2, p. 241–251. But it is so much liable to abuse and oppression as to be generally condemned. Before the Revolution in France it was estimated that of the taxes extorted from the people, not more than one fifth was paid into the public treasury! The farming of the revenue would not be even proposed in America; much less tolerated.

[2] *Ante*, page 13. It is no defense to a suit to collect a tax that the relative valuations between individuals are unequal. "If an assessment can be set aside and the right to collect taxes defeated by proof of this kind, there never was and there never will be a valid assessment in the state, for it is impossible to find two persons who will concur in all respects in their estimate of a particular piece of property, and of its value compared to another piece." *Richardson*, J., in Potosi *v.* Casey, 27 Mo., 372, 373. A fraud in the valuation, may, however, constitute a defense. State *v.* Central Pacific R. R. Co., 7 Nev., 99; Western R. R. Co. *v.* Nolan, 48 N. Y., 513.

[3] Dillon Mun. Corp., § 653. See Territory *v.* Reyburn, McCahon, 134; State *v.* Williams, 8 Texas, 384; Houston, etc., R. R. Co. *v.* State, 39 id, 148.

[4] Where action is given for taxes, interest is not recoverable, unless the statute

2. By the arrest of the person taxed. We refer here to arrest as the ordinary proceeding, and not in the course of prosecution for a penalty or forfeiture. The early state laws authorized process against the body of the person taxed, as an ordinary process for all personal taxes.[1] They have generally been repealed. It is only needful to say of such proceedings, that the officer must be sure of his process and follow its command. What is said under the next subdivision regarding process is applicable here.

3. By distress. To authorize distress, the collector must have

gives it. Danforth *v.* Williams, 9 Mass., 324. Tax assessed against a person by name after his death. This is no debt against the administrator on which suit can be brought. The assessment should have been against the heirs or whoever else was in possession. Cook *v.* Leland, 5 Pick., 236. The statute gave a suit for taxes against anyone who should *remove* out of the precinct after assessment. This applied to the case of one who left, but with the intention of returning after six months. Houghton *v.* Davenport, 23 Pick., 235. Where by statute the personalty of an estate was to be assessed to the executor or administrator, if it is taxed to "the estate" of the deceased, a suit will not lie against the administrator for the tax. Wood *v.* Torrey, 97 Mass., 321. One cannot be made liable for a tax assessed after he has removed from the municipality, even though the vote granting the money was had while he was a resident. Wade *v.* First Parish, 8 Cush., 267. A collector who pays over a tax without having collected it, may recover by suit of the taxpayer. McCracken *v.* Elder, 34 Penn. St., 239. Compare Wallace's Estate, 59 id., 401. That taxes must be demanded before suit can be brought, see Thompson *v.* Gardner, 10 Johns., 404; St. Anthony, etc., Co. *v.* Greely, 11 Minn., 321, 325. It may be otherwise under a statute of Arkansas. Kinsworthy *v.* Mitchell, 21 Ark., 145; Garbaldi *v.* Jenkins, 27 id., 456. The words "ordinary process of law," in the Missouri tax laws, do not mean an ordinary judgment and execution, but such process as is adapted to enforce a lien or specific charge upon the property assessed. Neenan *v.* Smith, 50 Mo., 525. Contractors for municipal improvements are under some statutes allowed to bring suit in their own names for the collection of the assessments made to cover the cost of such improvements. The case last cited was one of this kind.

[1] Arrest is allowed usually only after a failure to find property. Lothrop *v.* Ide, 13 Gray, 93; Hall *v.* Hall, 3 Allen, 5. Arrest after return day sustained. Bassett *v.* Porter, 4 Cush., 487. As to relief from arrest, see Aldrich *v.* Aldrich, 8 Met., 102. It is competent to provide for enforcing license taxes, by imprisonment of the delinquent. Commonwealth *v.* Byrne, 20 Grat., 165 (citing Barrett *v.* Porter, 4 Cush., 487; Daggett *v.* Everett, 19 Me., 373; Rising *v.* Granger, 1 Mass., 47; Appleton *v.* Hopkins, 5 Gray, 530; Kingman *v.* Glover, 3 Rich., 27). And see *post*, Chapter XIX.

the proper legal warrant.[1] Of this, sufficient has been said in the preceding chapter.

Collection by distress has been objected to, as a process which condemned the party before he had been heard, and proceeded to execution without trial. In a very important sense, the objection states the case with accuracy. The process, in the nature of an execution, does issue, at least under some tax laws, before the liability of the party has been finally and conclusively determined. But, as has already been said, this does not deprive a party aggrieved of his remedy. It only makes his remedy wait the superior urgency of government necessities. It has been well said of collection by distress: "This method of collecting taxes is as well established by custom and usage as any principle of the common law. A similar practice prevailed in all the colonies from the first dawn of their existence; it has been continued by all the states since their independence, and had existed in England from time immemorial. Indeed, it is necessary to the existence of every government, and is based upon the principle of self preservation. * * * I think, therefore, that any legal process that was founded on necessity, has been consecrated by time, and approved and acquiesced in by universal consent, must be an exception to the right of trial by jury, and is embraced in the alternative — the law of the land. Such I consider to be the summary proceedings allowed in the collection of taxes."[2] No judge, and no writer ever presented the point with more terseness, more precision or more accuracy.

But it has sometimes been deemed necessary, after giving the ordinary remedy by distress, to go further. That remedy will not justify any invasion of the rights or any interference with the property of others than the very persons upon whom the tax is imposed. If the property of another is distrained, the officer may be sued in trespass, or the property may be taken from him on writ of replevin.[3] Under pretense of this right, it has been found

[1] A municipal corporation cannot provide for such a warrant by ordinance, without statutory authority for the purpose. Bergen *v.* Clarkson, 6 N. J., 352.

[2] *Nott*, J., in State *v.* Allen, 2 McCord, 55, 60. See also Harris *v.* Wood, 6 T. B. Monr., 641, 643; McCarrol *v.* Weeks, 5 Hayw., 246; Willis *v.* Wetherbee, 4 N. H. 118; New Orleans *v.* Cannon, 10 La. An., 764.

[3] A chattel belonging to A. cannot be taken for a tax against B., even

possible seriously to embarrass the officer in the performance of his duties, by means of unfounded claims, or those the officer believes to be such. To preclude this, statutes have, in some cases, been passed, taking away the ordinary remedies against the collector, and leaving the claimant to some other remedy. Some of these statutes, which merely prohibit replevin being brought against the officer, are referred to elsewhere. The New York revised statutes authorized the collector to seize and sell not only goods and chattels of the party taxed, but any goods and chattels in his possession, and declared that "no claim of property made by any other person shall be available to prevent a sale." This statute was enforced without question of its validity.[1] A similar statute in Michigan was strongly contested as not being due process of law, and was upheld by a divided court.[2] In Pennsylvania a statute has been enforced which empowered the collector to distrain the property of an occupier of land wherever found, for the satisfaction of a tax assessed in respect to the land against the owner.[3] So it has been held competent by law to make a purchaser of land, who enters into possession, chargeable personally with the tax previously assessed.[4] These are illustrations of the stringent rules which are sometimes applied in cases of taxation.

though it formerly belonged to B., and is still in his possession. Daniels *v.* Nelson, 41 Vt., 161.

[1] Sheldon *v.* Van Buskirk, 2 N. Y., 473. No point was made of the constitutional competency of such legislation.

[2] Sears *v.* Cottrell, 5 Mich., 251.

[3] McGregor *v.* Montgomery, 4 Penn. St., 237. The warrant is no lien upon personalty until actual seizure. Moore *v.* Marsh, 60 Penn. St., 46.

[4] Henry *v.* Horstick, 9 Watts, 412. See also Smeich *v.* York County, 68 Penn. St., 439. But an express statute would be requisite to create such a liability. Atlantic, etc., R. R. Co. *v.* Cleino, 2 Dillon, 175. Where property, after alienation is allowed by the vendor to remain on the tax books of the county, and he fails to avail himself of the means provided by law to have the assessment corrected, he is liable for such taxes, and they may be recovered by suit. County Commissioners *v.* Clagett, 31 Md., 210. Where, on a tax warrant issued by assessors having jurisdiction, and fair on its face, bank shares are sold, the cashier of the bank is justified in issuing new certificates to the purchaser, who, thereby, becomes entitled to the dividends, whether the tax was rightfully assessed or not. Smith *v.* Northhampton Bank, 4 Cush., 1.

It is very proper that a demand of the tax should be made a prerequisite to the levy by distress;[1] and it is not often that statutes are passed which are so little regardful of the rights of the citizen, as to authorize distress without the persons taxed being at least called upon, and given the opportunity to pay without the expense and annoyance of a levy. A requirement by statute of demand or personal notification is imperative, and distress without it would be illegal.[2] Statutes regarding notice, and limiting the time within which sale of the distrained property shall be made, are also imperative, and the officer becomes a trespasser *ab initio*, if he proceeds to a sale in disregard of them.[3]

[1] Such a demand is not essential before levy of distress unless the statute requires it. Ives *v.* Lynn, 7 Conn., 504.

[2] Cones *v.* Wilson, 14 Ind., 465, 466. The collector's authority must be strictly pursued. Bishop *v.* Lovan, 4 B. Monr., 116. Where the sheriff was to distrain for taxes, if on presenting an account of the taxes and offering a receipt they were not paid, a distress without these was illegal. Hoozer *v.* Buckner, 11 B. Monr., 183, 184. See to the same point Johnson *v.* McIntire, 1 Bibb, 295; Atkinson *v.* Amick, 25 Mo., 404; Thompson *v.* Rogers, 4 La., 9; Burd *v.* Ramsey, 9 S. & R., 109; St. Anthony, etc., Co. *v.* Greely, 11 Minn., 321; Bonnell *v.* Roane, 20 Ark., 114; Moulton *v.* Blaisdell, 24 Me., 283; Ives *v.* Lynn, 7 Conn., 504; Harrington *v.* Worcester, 6 Allen, 576. A demand at the last and usual place of abode of a nonresident in the town, if he has no agent there, is sufficient to justify a subsequent seizure and sale of his goods under the statute which requires that "the collector shall, before distraining the goods of any person for his tax, demand payment thereof of such person, if to be found within his precinct." King *v.* Whitcomb, 1 Met., 328. Where the law required supervisors, before issuing duplicate and warrant for the collection of road taxes, to give notice to all persons rated for such taxes, by advertisement or otherwise, to attend at such times and places as such supervisors may direct, so as to give such persons full opportunity to work out their respective taxes; *held* to be mandatory and a condition precedent. Miller *v.* Gorman, 38 Penn. St., 309.

[3] The statute required property seized for taxes to be sold within four days. Keeping it longer held to make the officer a trespasser *ab initio*. Brackett *v.* Vining, 49 Me., 356. Sale void which is made after the time thus limited. Pierce *v.* Benjamin, 14 Pick., 356; Noyes *v.* Haverhill, 11 Cush., 338. As to defects in a notice of sale that do not avoid it, see Barnard *v.* Graves, 13 Met., 85; Scott *v.* Watkins, 22 Ark., 556. Where the statute provides for notice, the party cannot be in default until he has received it. Smith *v.* State, 43 Ala., 344. A premature levy by a collector without sufficient cause, renders him liable in trespass. Veit *v.* Graff, 37 Ind., 53. Where the collector is required to appoint a time and place to receive payment of the tax, if the tax payer when called upon expresses a purpose not to pay at all, the collector need not

4. By the detention of goods and chattels. We refer here, not to the proceedings in which goods are distrained or seized for forfeitures or penalties, but to those under which goods, in respect to which the tax is demanded, are required to pass through the hands of government officers, who are to exact the tax before the owner or consignee is entitled to their custody. Cases of this nature arise under the laws for the collection of customs duties, but do not require special mention.

5. By sale of lands. Taxes are not commonly a lien upon lands, unless made so by express legislative authority.[1] It is competent by legislation to declare that they shall constitute a lien, and as such take precedence of all other liens and claims whatever.[2] And where the tax is assessed upon the land itself — not upon any particular interest in it — and when all the legal remedies, if any, for collection of the tax without resort to the land are exhausted, leaving the land liable to sale, the assessment acquires the full force of a lien, overriding all other claims,[3] since a sale

name time and place for the purpose, but may levy at once. Downer *v.* Woodbury, 19 Vt., 329; Wheelock *v.* Archer, 26 id., 380; Hurlburt *v.* Green, 42 id., 316. In Vermont it is decided that provisions in a statute requiring the collector to keep a distress four days before advertising, and to advertise six days, do not restrict him to this exact time, though he may not sell in less. Clemons *v.* Lewis, 36 Vt., 673. That a levy on personalty is *prima facie* a satisfaction of a tax, see Henry *v.* Gregory, 29 Mich., 68. In Indiana there seems to be a lien for taxes on personalty from the time when the duplicate comes to the collector's hands. Barber *v.* Morton, 19 Ind., 146. And this would not be divested in favor of an execution subsequently issued. Evans *v.* Bradford, 35 Ind., 527; McNeil *v.* Farneman, 37 id., 203.

[1] Hine *v.* Levee Commissioners, 19 Wall., 655. In Kansas under the ordinary tax warrant, lands cannot be sold. Kirkwood *v.* Magill, 6 Kansas, 540. That is the general rule throughout the country.

[2] Wallace's Estate, 59 Penn. St., 401, 404; Durgan's Appeal, 68 id., 204. A provision that a tax shall be preferred to all judgments, executions, incumbrances and liens of any description whatsoever, and shall be a lien on the real estate, does not make it a lien on the personal estate also. Anderson *v.* State, 23 Miss., 459; Bailey *v.* Fuqua, 24 id., 497. In Indiana, lands are liable for the poll tax, and tax on personal property assessed against the owner, notwithstanding his title is afterwards extinguished by the foreclosure of a mortgage of older date than his purchase. Isaac *v.* Decker, 41 Ind., 410.

[3] See Hutchins *v.* Moody, 30 Vt., 655; Same *v.* Same, 34 id.. 433; Post *v.* Leet, 8 Paige, 337; Kern *v.* Towsley, 45 Barb, 150; Dowdney *v.* New York, 54 N. Y., 186; Cochran *v.* Guild, 106 Mass , 29. Compare Holmes *v.* Taber, 9 Allen, 246.

of the lands, unless the tax is voluntarily paid, must take place in the ordinary course of law, and extinguish other liens and incumbrances.[1] A change in the ownership would not affect such a lien, the law taking no notice of such change.[2] Where, as is often the case with the lien for special assessments, provision is made for its enforcement by judicial proceedings, mere delay in taking steps for the purpose will not extinguish it.[3] Sometimes by statute a particular day is named, from which a tax shall be deemed a lien upon lands, and this, it is held, will determine, as between vendor and vendee, which should pay the tax in the absence of any stipulation on the subject.[4]

In California a lien for taxes relates to the time of the assessment. Reeve *v.* Kennedy, 43 Cal., 643.

[1] Parker *v.* Baxter, 2 Gray, 185. See Dale *v.* McEvers, 2 Cow., 118; Briscoe *v.* Coulter, 18 Ark., 423. Where separate interests are taxed, previous liens would not be reached by the tax unless the statute should so declare. See Appeal of Pittsburgh, 40 Penn. St., 455; Alleghany City's Appeal, 41 id., 60; Cadmus *v.* Jackson, 52 id., 295.

[2] Oldham *v.* Jones, 5 B. Monr., 458, 465; Covington *v.* Boyle, 6 Bush, 204.

[3] Swan *v.* Knoxville, 11 Humph., 130, 132. An act of congress made a tax a lien on land for two years. *Held* that this did not preclude the land being sold for the tax after the two years had expired, the title not having changed. Holden *v.* Eaton, 7 Pick., 15. Where by law taxes are a lien on land, but subject to be divested by a subsequent judicial sale, except as to any sum which the proceeds of the sale should be insufficient to pay, a sale sufficient *prima facie* to pay all taxes, and the bringing the money into court, divests the tax lien, though the money is not applied to the satisfaction of the taxes. Smith *v.* Simpson, 60 Penn. St., 168. A personal action brought for a tax does not divest the lien. Eschbach *v.* Pitts, 6 Md., 71. If a time is limited by statute for proceedings to enforce a lien, it is sufficient if they are begun within the time, and they may proceed to judgment afterwards. Randolph *v.* Bayne, 44 Cal., 366; Dougherty *v.* Henarie, 47 id., 9; Himmelman *v.* Carpenter, 47 id., 42. That a statute giving a lien is to be strictly construed, see Creighton *v.* Manson, 27 id., 613.

[4] Harrington *v.* Hilliard, 27 Mich., 271. See Rundell *v.* Lakey, 40 N. Y., 513; Gromley's Appeal, 27 Penn. St., 49; Densmore *v.* Haggarty, 59 id., 189. As to the liability as between tenant for life, and remainder man, see Plympton *v.* Boston Dispensary, 106 Mass., 544.

The following are decisions as to the liability to taxes under special agreements: A clause in a mortgage that the mortgage moneys should be paid "without any deduction, defalcation or abatement to be made of any thing for or in respect to any taxes," *held* to refer to taxes on the land and not on mortgage security. Clopton *v.* Phila., etc., R. R. Co., 54 Penn. St., 356. A covenant to pay "all assessments for which the premises shall be liable," will

Municipal corporations, of course, have no authority to create liens, by ordinance or otherwise, when none has been expressly conferred upon them.[1]

Return of "No Goods," etc. Where a tax against lands is assessed to a resident, and is a personal charge against him, the statutes, with almost unvarying uniformity, have made the personal property of the person taxed the primary fund for the payment, and have given a remedy for enforcing payment from it. Until that remedy has been exhausted, no authority exists to go further. It is also customary to allow a certain time after the levy of a tax on nonresident or unseated lands, before any proceedings are taken against the land. To authorize further proceedings in either case, there must be the proper official evidence that in the one case the remedy against the personalty is exhausted, and in both that the taxes are still unpaid.[2] This evidence will consist of such official return, affidavit, or other document by the collector, as the statute may indicate. This document will be void if made prematurely;[3] and it will be void, also, if it fails to

embrace an assessment only authorized by a law passed after the covenant. Post *v.* Kearney, 2 N. Y., 394. One who conveys by warranty after an assessment is completed, is liable on his covenant for a tax laid in pursuance of this assessment. *Held*, therefore, the vendee who had paid it might recover the amount of the vendor on an agreement of the latter to repay "in case he was legally liable to pay it." Rundell *v.* Lakey, 40 N. Y., 513.

[1] Philadelphia *v.* Greble, 38 Penn. St., 339. As to what will give the power, see Eschbach *v.* Pitts, 6 Md., 71. The lien cannot exist where the statutory steps have not been taken, and a simple allegation in a proceeding to enforce a lien that the taxes are due and unpaid, is not sufficient to show a lien. Louisville *v.* Bank of Kentucky, 3 Met., Ky., 148. As to the liability of land for personal assessments in Indiana, see Bodertha *v.* Spencer, 40 Ind., 353.

[2] See Thatcher *v.* Powell, 6 Wheat., 119; Jones *v.* McLain, 23 Ark., 429; Scales *v.* Alvis, 12 Ala., 617; Francis *v.* Russell, 5 Hayw., 294; Schæffer *v.* People, 60 Ill., 179; St. Anthony, etc., Co. *v.* Greely, 11 Minn., 321; Kelley *v.* Craig, 5 Ired., 129; Harrington *v.* Worcester, 6 Allen, 576; Huntington *v.* Brantley, 33 Miss., 451; Sharp *v.* Johnson, 4 Hill, 92; Ring *v.* Ewing, 47 Ind., 246. No title can be made to lands on a sale for taxes if personalty is not sought for. Catterlin *v.* Douglass, 17 Ind., 213.

[3] Ronkendorff *v.* Taylor's Lessee, 4 Pet., 349. Where the law gave a nonresident owner nine months to pay taxes in, before they were to be returned by the collector as delinquent, a return one day before the nine months were fully completed, was held to make void the proceedings. Flint *v.* Sawyer, 30 Me., 226. A similar ruling was made in Hobbs *v.* Clements, 32 id., 67. A

set forth all the facts that the statute requires shall be shown by it. If the collector is required to demand the tax, his return, it would seem, should show that he has done so; if he is required to make collection by distress and sale of goods, if any can be found to levy upon, there should be such a showing of diligent search for goods, and failure to find them, as would be required of officers to whom executions are committed for service. In other words, the return should show full and complete compliance with all the conditions which, under the statute, are to precede a resort to the land.[1] Such is unquestionably the general rule;[2] though doubtless if the statute should prescribe the form of a return, it would be sufficient for the officer to follow that.[3] But the decisions are justly very rigid in requiring conformity to the statute in the substantial matters of the return.[4] The return, if in conformity to the law, is not only a support to subsequent proceedings, but is evidence, also, in favor of the officer himself.[5]

sale of land is not to be made where the taxpayer is not in default. Therefore, if he tenders the tax, his land is not subject to sale, even though at the time, the collection of the tax is enjoined in a suit to which the taxpayer is not a party. Jones *v.* Burford, 26 Miss., 194. For a decision that, under the statute in question, resort might be had, either to the land or to chattels, see Den *v.* Carron, 26 N. J., 228.

[1] A recital in a collector's return that, "not knowing of any goods or chattels, etc.," is not equivalent to a return that none could be found. Jones *v.* McLain, 23 Ark., 429. But it is sufficient to throw the burden of proof on the taxpayer, to show that there was enough of personalty to satisfy the tax.

[2] Where the statute provided that "when the delinquent has no goods and chattels within the county, then the lands and tenements of said delinquent may be sold," etc., *held*, that if the delinquent were shown to have such goods and chattels it was fatal to a sale of the lands. The delinquent's knowledge of the sale, and assent to it do not bind him. Scales *v.* Alvis, 12 Ala., 617; citing Jackson *v.* Sheppard, 7 Cow., 88.

[3] Such has been the ruling of the supreme court of Illinois. Taylor *v.* People, 2 Gilm., 349; Job *v.* Tibbetts, 5 id., 376, 382. Judge *Pope*, the federal district judge, held otherwise. Mayhew *v.* Davis, 4 McLean, 213.

[4] See Harmon *v.* Stockwell, 9 Ohio, 93; Harrington *v.* Worcester, 6 Allen, 576; Sharp *v.* Johnson, 4 Hill, 92; Spellman *v.* Curtenius, 12 Ill., 409; Homer *v.* Cilley, 14 N. H., 85; Hannell *v.* Smith, 15 Ohio, 134; Tallman *v.* White, 2 N. Y., 66. A return not made in the time prescribed by statute, held not to support subsequent proceedings to forfeit the land. Hopkins *v.* Sandidge, 31 Miss., 668, 676.

[5] Bruce *v.* Holden, 21 Pick., 187; Brainerd *v.* Graves, 13 Met, 85. See cases cited, *ante*, p. 185, 186.

Under some tax laws the same officer who collects the taxes is empowered to make sale of the lands of delinquents. In such cases no return is required, though the filing of some official document showing the delinquency is sometimes provided for. Such a document takes the place of a collector's return, and will be governed by the rules above laid down. If none is required by law, the collector is allowed to proceed and sell lands on his own knowledge of the delinquency. How far his proceedings will be open to question afterwards, must depend, to some extent at least, on the force given by statute to such report or certificate of sale as he is subsequently required to make, or to the official conveyance.

The proceedings in making sale of lands for taxes, the privilege of redemption, and the conveyance when redemption is not made, require, and will receive, separate consideration.

6. By the imposition of penalties. In tax laws penalties are imposed for mere delinquencies, in order to hasten payment, and they are also imposed as a punishment for frauds, evasions, and neglect of duty. In some cases, also, special inducements are held out to prompt performance of duty, by making deductions in case of early payment.[1]

Great use is made of penalties in the federal tax laws, especially under the internal revenue laws, and the laws for the collection of customs duties. The justification for this is the supposed necessity of the case, and the absolute impossibility of securing a collection of the revenues without resort to these extreme measures.[2]

[1] Sprague *v.* Bailey, 19 Pick., 436.

[2] A charge by District Judge *Benedict*, of the southern district of New York, to the grand jury, and given in an appendix to 6 Blatchford's Reports, is deserving of being copied here, for the reasons it gives for stringent measures in revenue cases:

"The war, which decided the question whether a government framed like ours had the ability to quell by force of arms a great rebellion, raised another question, which is now in process of solution, namely, whether such a government can surely provide for the payment of the interest upon a great debt. The interest upon the public debt must be obtained by taxation, and this taxation, under the most favorable circumstances, must be heavy. It will become odious and intolerable, if it is to be borne by the honest and well disposed classes alone, and avoided by those willing to grow rich at the expense of their fellow citizens, through fraudulent evasions of the law. This latter

In some cases they are imposed by the taxing officers, in others they are recovered by suit, or indictment. Under the state laws

class, numerous and powerful, both socially and politically, has, from the beginning, confronted the government in its efforts to collect the revenue. At first, the government attempted to compel their obedience by seizure of their property, and large quantities of merchandise detected in the act of escaping taxation was forfeited and sold. But the attempt was a failure; the frauds increased both in number and in magnitude, and the government was compelled to turn to its last resort — the criminal jurisdiction of its courts. It is now, therefore, here and elsewhere, engaged in the effort to check these frauds by means of criminal prosecutions — the indictment, trial, conviction and imprisonment of defrauders of the revenue. Inasmuch then, as no man can be tried until accused by a grand jury, the government and the community, of which the government is but the representative, now turns to the grand juries of the land, and asks the indictment of every man, whether high or low, rich or poor, who is found to be engaged in fraudulent evasions of legal taxes. Time would fail me to describe to you the various forms which these frauds assume; but it is my duty to put you in possession of what I have understood to be the facts in regard to some transactions which must come before you, and to allude in general terms to others which your own inquiries will expose.

"I begin with what have been designated the drawback cases. These cases have been the subject of examination in the adjoining district, and are transferred to this district because most of the transactions took place here. They are frauds perpetrated under cover of the provisions of law which enable a person who has paid taxes upon manufactures which he afterwards exports, to receive back the taxes which he has paid, upon proving actual exportation of the goods. To obtain this drawback, a set of papers is necessary in every case, consisting first of an internal revenue collector's certificate, that the tax on the goods has been paid; second, a certificate of the collector of customs, that such goods appear on a ship's manifest, on file in the custom house, as actually exported; third, an affidavit by the shipper as to the identity of the goods upon the manifest and the goods upon the tax receipt; fourth, a certificate of an internal revenue collector, that a proper bond to secure the government against any relanding of the goods has been filed with him. These papers must be certified to at the custom house, and then go to the department at Washington, to be examined there. If found correct, a check for the amount of tax, drawn to the order of the shipper, upon the treasury, is returned. Numerous sets of such papers, representing sums of from $300 to $7,000 each, all false, no such goods having been exported, there being no such shipper, and no such manifest on file, the bonds being fraudulent, the signatures forgeries, and the affidavits perjuries, have, within a space of six months time, passed through the custom house here and been certified; have then passed through the department at Washington and been there approved, and corresponding checks have been drawn and paid, every one, or nearly every one, upon a forged indorsement, until the total probably exceeds the sum of $700,000. The fraud, which I am thus enabled to describe because

they are not so common. Where lists or statements are required to be furnished as a basis for taxation, the privilege of being

it has already been the subject of examination in the adjoining district, is not disputed, and the money is gone. It will be your duty to say who shall be accused before this court as criminally responsible for the transaction. Some of the parties supposed to have been engaged in this affair are already under bail. One has been brought from Florida; for the arm of the government is long. Others have escaped beyond the seas. It will be your duty, however, to indict all who appear to have been connected in the design, whether present or absent. In your examination of this case, you will have occasion to see with what looseness the public business is sometimes conducted, for it will appear that great numbers of bonds required by law have been accepted as good, without any identification of signatures or of persons, and without any inquiry as to the sufficiency or even existence of the sureties, the greater part being, in fact, executed in fictitious names, or by persons entirely worthless. It will also appear that the genuine seal of an internal revenue collector can constantly appear upon certificates now claimed to be forged, and that part of the files of the collector's office, being bonds required by law, can be removed and taken to a neighboring city by persons having no connection whatever with the government, there to be dealt with as unknown parties may desire, and then be returned without objection or remark. I have explained the features of this case to you fully, because you will be called on to act in regard to it, and not because it is to any very great extent exceptional.

"If you extend your inquiries into other departments of the custom house, you will find that similar frauds have been there committed. You will find that in the warehouse department, it has been possible for certain parties to withdraw dutiable goods without payment of any duty, until the loss from a single warehouse has equalled $400,000, according to the estimate of an official. The parties who committed this fraud walk the streets to-day, well known, but unprosecuted and unpunished, unless the repayment of a part of their great gains is to be called punishment. Nor is the case to which I am now alluding, and which you will find fully disclosed upon the files of this court, the only one of this class which has occurred, and with a similar result, if I am correctly informed. You may think proper to inquire into them all. Frauds like these are, of course, not to be accomplished without connivance on the part of officials; and you will have occasion, no doubt, to consider what persons shall be accused before this court, for giving or accepting bribes.

"There is also an abuse at the custom house, proper to be spoken of in this connection, which I notice, by the public prints, is now attracting some attention, and of the evil effects of which the drawback cases will give you painful proof. I refer to the custom of giving and taking gratuities for the performance of official duties. Strengthen the hands of the collector, gentlemen, in any effort to stop this steady flow. The law lies at your hands, and it reads thus (*Act of March* 3, 1863, § 4, 12 U. S. Stat. at Large, 793): 'If any officer of the revenue * * * shall knowingly accept, from any person engaged in the importation of goods, wares or merchandise into the United States, or

heard in abatement of the tax is sometimes taken away as a penalty upon the tax payer for not furnishing it. Perhaps it would

interested, as principal clerk or agent, in any such importation or in the entry of any goods, wares, or merchandise, any fee, gratuity or emolument whatever, such officer shall, on conviction thereof, be removed from office and shall be fined in any sum not exceeding five thousand dollars, or be imprisoned not exceeding two years at the discretion of the court.' The 6th section of the same act is as follows: 'If any person who shall be engaged in the importation of goods, wares or merchandise, into the United States, or shall be interested, as principal, clerk or agent, in the entry of any goods, wares or merchandise, shall at any time make, or offer to make, to any officer of the revenue any gratuity or present of any money or other thing of value, such person shall, on conviction thereof, be fined in any sum not exceeding five thousand dollars, or be imprisoned not exceeding two years, at the discretion of the court.'

"The market price of whisky is still less than the first cost of manufacture, with taxes added. From the tobacco trade, honest dealers are fast being driven out. Much of the income tax remains uncollected. The fraudulent bond-maker still plies his busy trade. Men known to have grown rich by illegal means have escaped even the accusation of fraud, and flaunt their wealth before the public eye. Honest officials have been compelled to leave the service for want of due support in the performance of their duty, while other officers of the revenue who have remained and dared to endeavor to protect the government have found the very government they sought to serve turned against them and used with effect to accomplish their destruction and disgrace. In view of a demoralization such as these facts disclose, do you wonder that some men query whether the proper enforcement of revenue laws is possible for such a government as ours, with such a civil service as it has hitherto had? These remarks will have failed of their intended effect, if they have not served to deepen your sense of the responsibility which rests on you, and to strengthen your determination to discharge yourselves of that responsibility in such a manner as to satisfy the proper demands of the community in which you live. To enable you to do this, great powers are given you. No matter within the jurisdiction of the court is exempt from your scrutiny. No man, of whatever degree, can refuse to obey your summons or decline to answer your proper interrogatories. No compromise of a department can have effect to stay your hand. Within your extended sphere you are supreme. Use, then, these great powers freely, examine diligently and inquire widely, but accuse with all due care, mindful always, that the mere examination of a transaction in open court, is often of great public benefit, but, also, mindful that such an examination is often, of itself, a great punishment. It is not your province to try the cases which you may consider. That duty devolves upon the petit jury and the court; but you are diligently to inquire and true presentment make of every offense arising under the laws of the United States which shall be made to appear by reasonable *prima facie* proof. This duty I charge you to perform, and if to its performance you shall bring that patience, that intelligence and that good courage which the occasion demands,

be more proper to say that his right to be heard is made to depend upon this, not unreasonable condition.[1] A more common provision is one that adds a penalty to the assessed taxes for neglect to pay them in due season.

There are some cases in which the right to impose any penalty except on a judicial investigation by a competent court has been denied, as being the imposition of punishment without a trial.[2]

you will render an important service to your fellow citizens, as well as to the government which protects you and under which it is your good fortune to live."

[1] See Winnisimmet Co. *v.* Chelsea, 6 Cush., 477; Otis Co. *v.* Ware, 8 Gray, 509; Lincoln *v.* Worcester, 8 Cush., 55; Porter *v.* County Commissioners, 5 Gray, 365; Lott *v.* Hubbard, 44 Ala., 593: State *v.* Apgar, 31 N. J., 358; Young *v.* Parker, 33 id., 192. Compare McCormick *v.* Fitch, 14 Minn., 252.

[2] In Scammon *v.* Chicago, 44 Ill., 269, 278, the court held a provision of a statute imposing a penalty of five per centum for delay in making payment of an assessment beyond a certain day to be void. On application for a rehearing on this point, the following opinion was given by *Breese*, J.: "On this application for a rehearing, we are referred to the case of Bristol *v.* The City of Chicago, 22 Ill., 587, as controlling the question of imposing five per cent. on the amount of taxes not paid on or before the 1st day of January in each year. In that case the law authorized the collection of ten per cent. on the amount of the special assessment, in case the owner refused to pay it before the collector filed the delinquent list, on an application for an order of sale, as additional costs. That the legislature may provide for the recovery of reasonable costs, either by a percentage on the amount of the recovery, or by fixing specific sums in a bill of items, there can be no doubt. In that case the law was sustained, as it gave that per cent. as additional cost, which was manifestly designed to cover the expense of making and advertising the delinquent list, together with other expenses and outlays incurred by the application.

"The per cent. imposed in that case was upon a special assessment levied for the improvement of a wharf in the city. In such cases, after the levy has been made, labor is performed and expenses incurred by the city in completing the improvement, on the faith of the collection of the assessment to meet the outlay; and it is therefore but reasonable, that the person failing or refusing to pay his assessment, should contribute to the payment of interest which may have accumulated, by delay in paying for labor and material procured by the city for the construction of the improvement. One of the objects in giving costs is to cover expenses incurred in prosecuting a suit for the recovery of the demand. Hence it is reasonable that the delinquent tax payer should in some mode be required to meet the expense incurred in prosecuting a suit for the recovery of the amount which remains delinquent, and the same is equally true of unpaid special assessments.

"That the legislature may authorize the court to impose and render a judg-

But when the penalty is imposed in the course of the proceedings to assess, and by officers who, for that purpose, exercise a *quasi* judicial authority, and where the party is given the opportunity to be heard and to contest his delinquency, either before the assessing officer, or in some form of appeal, the imposition of

ment for such a penalty, we have no doubt; but we do not believe that such a power can be conferred upon a mere ministerial officer, without any opportunity to be heard by the taxpayer. It will be observed that in Bristol's case the law did not authorize the collector to impose the additional per cent. until he filed his report on the application for the order of sale of the property, and it was then adjudicated upon by the court; while in this case the officer was authorized to impose it long before the term of the court at which he is required to file his report of the delinquent list, which is at the term at which he applies for judgment. Had the ordinance in this case only provided for the imposition of this five per cent. at the time of passing the order for the sale of the lands, thus affording the taxpayer an opportunity until that time to pay his tax, and to be heard in the court whether he was liable to the forfeiture, this case would then have come within the principle of Bristol's.

"The facts in this case afford an illustration of the hardship that is liable to occur, from accident or otherwise, by imposing a penalty at a previous time. It appears that there was a mistake of a large amount in the case of the Chamber of Commerce, and before it could be corrected, the first of January had arrived and the penalty was claimed and attempted to be imposed without any fault on their part. To impose such a penalty under these circumstances, would be, to say the least, a hardship and a wrong. If, however, the penalty should not be imposed until after the collector's report is filed on the application for the judgment, then all have a fair opportunity to pay their taxes or to be heard against a forfeiture. We are aware of no case where a forfeiture may be imposed and enforced except by a judgment of a court of competent jurisdiction. If the collector may impose this per cent., he can enforce it by distress and sale of property, without the taxpayer having been legally adjudicated to have incurred a penalty. When a per cent. is imposed for taking an appeal for delay, or for failing to pay a note due to the school fund, the penalty is imposed by the judgment of the court and not by the creditor or a ministerial officer. It is believed to be a general rule, without an exception, that forfeiture cannot be enforced except through the judgment of a court of competent jurisdiction, and this is true whether it be called costs, damages, or a penalty. A judgment must be first had before satisfaction can be enforced.

"We do not, therefore, regard Bristol's case as governing this, as it is materially different both in the facts and principles involved." See also Clayton *v.* Chicago, 44 Ill., 286; Burger *v.* Caster, 1 McMullen L., 410, 420; Blackwell on Tax Titles, 30. In Wauwatosa *v.* Gunyon, 25 Wis., 271, 276, Judge *Dixon*, referring to an objection that a provision authorizing the clerk of the board of supervisors to impose a penalty of fifty per cent. of the assessment for the refusal of the person assessed to swear, was void because, "being a

a penalty does not seem to be out of harmony with the general spirit or general course of tax proceedings, and perhaps may be sustained on the same principles that support tax laws in general. But we should doubt the right to make any finding by any such tribunal conclusive; and there may be reason to question whether, for delay in the payment of a tax, it is competent for the government to authorize any merely ministerial officer to impose a penalty, though a reasonable interest, and the expenses and costs occasioned by the delay, might doubtless be demanded and collected.[1] The point is not left in a very satisfactory state on the authorities.

7. By forfeiture of property taxed. It is provided by law in some states, that if the taxes assessed against lands shall not

punishment for the violation of public law, it cannot, under our constitution, be legally imposed except by prosecution in the courts of justice," says: "this proposition is not without some well considered authorities in its favor, and none that we are aware of against it;" and on rehearing, he says (p. 282): "We think that the fifty per centum mentioned is a penalty which can be imposed only in the due course of judicial prosecution, and consequently that the clerk had no lawful or constitutional authority to add it to the value of the property returned." In Lacey *v.* Davis, 4 Mich., 140, a penalty of ten per centum added to taxes remaining unpaid after a certain day, was sustained as not being unreasonable; and in Scott *v.* Watkins, 22 Ark., 556, a penalty of twenty-five per centum on nonresidents who should fail to pay their taxes in due season, was sustained against the objection which was deemed insuperable in Illinois and Wisconsin. See also Craig *v.* Flanagin, 21 Ark., 319; Pope *v.* Macon, 23 id., 644; High *v.* Shoemaker, 22 Cal., 363; People *v.* Todd, 23 id., 181; Mulligan *v.* Hintrager, 18 Iowa, 171. In Butler *v.* Bailey, 2 Bay, 244, it was held competent to impose double taxes as a penalty for failure to make due return of property to be taxed.

[1] Bristol *v.* Chicago, 22 Ill., 587. For cases of penalties imposed in Pennsylvania by the taxing officers, under laws which gave an appeal to the courts, reference may be made to Drexel *v.* Commonwealth, 46 Penn. St., 37; Commonwealth *v.* Wyoming Valley Canal Co., 50 id., 410. As to penalties collected by prosecution, see State *v.* Welch, 28 Mo., 600; Olds *v.* Commonwealth, 3 A. K. Marsh., 465; Lee *v.* Commonwealth, 6 Dana, 311; Alexander *v.* Commonwealth, 1 Bibb, 515; McCall *v.* Justices, id., 516; Chiles *v.* Commonwealth, 4 J. J. Marsh., 578; State *v.* Manz, 6 Coldwell, 557; Elam *v.* State, 25 Ala., 53; Smith *v.* State, 43 id., 344. These cases, as well as that of Delaware Division Canal Co. *v.* Commonwealth, 50 Penn. St., 399, recognize the rule that all statutes of this nature must be construed strictly. A municipal corporation cannot impose a penalty for neglect to pay taxes promptly, unless expressly authorized by law to do so. Augusta *v.* Dunbar, 50 Geo., 387.

be paid by a certain time, and, after some prescribed notice, the land shall be forfeited to the state. The Virginia statute of 1790 may be taken as an illustration. After making provision for the taxation of lands; that the sheriff should make to the auditor of public accounts a return, under oath, of all those, the taxes upon which he could find no effects for the satisfaction of; that certain prescribed steps should be taken for collection the following year, and, if these failed, there should be published in the Virginia Gazette, for three weeks, the names of delinquents, the quantity of land, the situation thereof and the taxes due thereon, and that in case the tax on any part should not be paid for the space of three years, "the right to such lands shall be lost, forfeited and vested in the commonwealth," etc. This was a more liberal statute, in the time it allowed for payment, than those usually are which provide for such a forfeiture, but the general characteristics of all are alike.

Serious question has been made of the right of the government to take to itself title to lands, under a forfeiture based on a personal default, without a judicial finding that such a default exists. The question was made in the early cases arising under these statutes, and has continued to be made ever since, without having yet reached conclusive settlement. One of the most learned and able of the early Virginia judges declared his opinion, under the act of 1790, that the forfeiture could not be perfected so as to divest the title of the former owner without inquest of office.[1] This view was accepted in Kentucky,[2] and has recently been assented to in an elaborate opinion by the supreme court of Mississippi.[3] But the settled doctrine in Virginia is now the other way,[4] and the decisions are supported by those of Maine.[5]

[1] *Tucker*, J., in Kinney *v.* Beverley, 2 H. & M., 318. The other judges gave no opinion on this point.

[2] Barbour *v.* Nelson, 1 Litt., 60; Robinson *v.* Huff, 3 id., 38. And see Currie *v.* Fowler, 5 J. J. Marsh., 145; Harlan's Heirs *v.* Seaton's Heirs, 18 B. Monr., 312. The decisions in Minnesota favor the same doctrine. See St. Anthony Co. *v.* Greely, 11 Minn., 321; Baker *v.* Kelley, id., 480; Hill *v.* Lund, 13 id., 451.

[3] Griffin *v.* Mixon, 38 Miss., 414. There is an able dissenting opinion in this case by *Handy*, J.

[4] Wild's Lessee *v.* Serpell, 10 Grat., 405; Hale *v.* Branscum, id., 418; Flanagan *v.* Grimmet, id., 421; Usher *v.* Pride, 15 id., 190.

[5] Hodgdon *v.* Wight, 36 Me., 326; Adams *v.* Larrabee, 46 id., 516, 519.

Some ground we may safely occupy here without liability to controversy. It is conceded on all sides that an intent to transfer title to the government by forfeiture will not be inferred in any case from language capable of any milder construction.[1] The courts of Ohio acted upon this view when they held that a statute which declared, that after due record of the default, the land "shall be considered as forfeited to the state of Ohio, and be subject to be disposed of in such manner as any future legislature may direct," did not work an absolute forfeiture, and the owner might redeem afterwards. But this was partly, at least, on the ground that the legislature had never treated this forfeiture as vesting a title in the state for any other purpose than as security for taxes due and owing.[2] That statutes of forfeiture are strictly construed, is an elementary principle,[3] and there are no cases in which the rule requiring a substantial compliance with all the important provisions of the statute will more rigidly be insisted upon.[4]

Where the power of legislation *ipso facto* to work a forfeiture is in question, it is important that there be a clear and precise understanding of what is intended in the use of this word forfeiture. The usual method of enforcing the payment of taxes upon property is by putting the property up to a public sale. No one questions the right to do this, and no one doubts that the sale, if fair and made in compliance with the law, and after all the necessary preliminary steps have been taken, vests a perfect

[1] Fairfax's Devisee *v.* Hunter's Lessee, 7 Cranch, 603, 625; Schenck *v.* Peay, 1 Dillon, 267; Bennett *v.* Hunter, 18 Grat., 100; S. C. in error, 9 Wall., 326, 336.

[2] Thevenin *v.* Slocum's Lessee, 16 Ohio, 519, 532. This case is cited and relied upon in St. Anthony, etc., Co. *v.* Greely, 11 Minn., 321.

[3] See Schenck *v.* Peay, 1 Dill. C. C., 267; Lohrs *v.* Miller's Lesssee, 12 Grat., 452; Twiggs *v.* Chevallie, 4 W. Va., 463. A subsequent taxing of lands by the state, and the receipt thereof from the former owner, was held in Hodgdon *v* Wight, 36 Me., 326, to be no waiver of the forfeiture. The same decision was made in Crane *v.* Reeder, 25 Mich., 303, which was a case of escheat. In that case *Campbell*, J., discusses at length the question of necessity of inquest of office, and concludes that it is not necessary.

[4] See Hopkins *v.* Sandige, 31 Miss., 668, 676, in which the delay of a few days after the time fixed by statute for the return of the list was held to defeat the forfeiture. See also Kinney *v.* Beverley, 2 H. & M., 318, 331; Dentler *v.* State, 4 Blackf., 258; Williams *v.* State, 6 id., 36.

title in the purchaser to the full extent that the statute shall declare. No judicial proceedings are required to perfect the title, and if the purchaser have need of a resort to them, in order to obtain possession, it is only what might occur to any owner of property under any undisputed title. In what important particular does this differ from the case of forfeitures, except that to the proceedings which are to work the forfeiture there is added the one requirement of a public sale? But there are in the sale no elements of an adjudication; it does not stand in the place of one; its purpose is only to bring to the public treasury the tax for which the sale is made. Incidentally in the proceedings a purpose is kept in view, not to sacrifice any farther than shall be necessary the interests of the owner; and to this end notice of the sale is required with a view to invite competition among bidders. But we are not aware of any constitutional principle that entitles a party to have his duty coerced by a public sale of property, rather than by a forfeiture of it. A sale by a ministerial officer which, as the closing step in administrative action, is to divest the owner of his title, is as much obnoxious to the charge that it deprives him of his freehold without a hearing, as is the legislative forfeiture. Whatever there is of the nature of judicial inquiry lies back of these proceedings in the action of the assessing officers, and, as has already been stated, is the same in both cases. If the owner is condemned without a hearing in the one case, he is in the other.

It may be that a public sale would be most advantageous to the person taxed, because it might leave to him some portion of his property after the tax was satisfied. In the vast majority of cases, however, the sale is of the whole land, and the possible benefit is not had. But there is no imperative principle of government which requires the legislature in prescribing rules of administration, to fix upon those which would be most for the advantage of a negligent or defaulting citizen. We suppose, on the other hand, that the legislature has very ample discretion to determine the rule on its own view of public policy. If it deems a sale more advantageous to the state than a forfeiture, it will provide for it; otherwise not.

But if by forfeiture is understood the vesting in the state a title which shall be absolute and beyond dispute, the question presented is different. It is impossible that there can be any right to declare such a forfeiture, except as the result of an adjudication to which the owner was a party, which has determined that the default, upon which the forfeiture was based, existed in fact, and that the requisite steps which were to precede the forfeiture have actually been taken. In some judicial tribunal, the party whose freehold is seized has a right to a hearing on these questions: a constitutional right, if constitutional protections to property are of any avail. But if by forfeiture is understood only that without sale there shall pass to the state such title as a purchaser would acquire if a sale were to take place, the declaration of forfeiture can, of itself, work no absolute deprivation of right. If the default existed and the tax proceedings are regular, the state has the title; if not, it remains in the person taxed. And in the absence of any statute changing the burden of proof, it would devolve on the state to prove the regularity of the proceedings, precisely as it would on the purchaser when demanding the land under a purchase.[1]

8. By conditions on the exercise of a right. In some instances statutes have attached to the privilege of exercising the elective franchise, the condition that taxes should have been paid for the current year, or within some short period preceding. In some states this is a matter of constitutional requirement. If one evades his duty to the government, he may reasonably be denied the privilege of participating in the direction of its affairs; and these constitutional provisions appear to assume that he, who, in his own business, acquires nothing upon which he can be taxed, must lack the wisdom and discretion to take part in the business of the state.[2] In some instances the payment of a tax

[1] See Kinney *v.* Beverly, 2 H. & M., 318, 331; Hopkins *v.* Sandige, 31 Miss., 668, 676. See, also, *post*, Chapter XVII.

The proceedings for forfeiture, where a judicial prosecution is required, it seems unnecessary to consider. An intent to defraud is made a ground of forfeiture under some of the federal revenue laws. See United States *v.* Hogsheads of Tobacco, 2 Bond, 137; United States *v.* Caddies of Tobacco, 2 id., 305; Henderson's Spirits, 14 Wall., 44. The statute imposing the penalty of forfeiture of land and buildings employed in violation of a revenue law, sustained as constitutional. United States *v.* McKinley, 4 Brewster, 246. See United States *v.* Spreckens, 1 Sawyer 84; Quantity of Tobacco, 5 Ben., 407.

[2] Constitutional provisions of the kind exist in Deleware, Georgia, Massa-

assessed against one in respect to a chose in action owned by him has been made a condition to the maintenance of a suit upon it.[1] In some instances the right to maintain a suit to recover property, which the party claims has illegally been taken from him, has been subjected to the condition that he should first pay the tax for which the property was sold, and perhaps all subsequent taxes; but this, we think, has been pushed beyond the constitutional power of the legislature, as we shall endeavor to show hereafter.[2]

Stamp taxes are collected by requiring them to be affixed to some commodity before it can be sold, some written instrument before it can be made use of, and the like. An early law of congress provided for such taxes, and they were imposed again during and since the rebellion. No reasonable objection in principle can be opposed to such taxes, and except where they were so made use of as to invade the province of state authority, their validity was not seriously questioned.[3]

chusetts and Pennsylvania. As to liability of assessors for depriving one of his right to vote by not assessing him, see Griffin *v.* Rising, 11 Met., 339: And see *Re* Duffy, 4 Brewster, 531; Batterson *v.* Barlow, 60 Penn. St., 54.

[1] See Lott *v.* Dysart, 45 Geo., 355; Redwine *v.* Hancock, id., 364; Scruggs *v.* Gibson, id., 509; Green *v.* Lowrey, 46 id., 55; and many other cases in the subsequent Georgia reports.

[2] See Taylor *v.* Burdett, 11 Leigh, 334, in which it was decided to be competent to require evidence of the payment of the taxes as a condition precedent to maintaining a suit for the recovery of the lands taxed. See, also, Tharp *v.* Hart, 2 Sneed, 569. But such a provision is to be strictly construed, and will not be applied to the case of special assessments, unless made applicable in terms. Glass *v.* White, 5 Sneed, 475. See Williamsburg *v.* Lord, 51 Me., 599. In Maine, in a contest between the original owner of land and a tax purchaser, it is held that the former is not required to tender taxes until the latter has made out a *prima facie* case. Orono *v.* Veazie, 57 Me., 517; S. C., 61 id., 431. Nor need he make a tender where several parcels have been sold together, so that it cannot be determined how much he should pay. Phillipps *v.* Sherman, 61 Me., 548, 551. In Weller *v.* St. Paul, 5 Minn., 95, the right to enact such laws was denied as being inconsistent with the constitutional right of every citizen to "obtain justice freely and without purchase." Similar rulings have been made in Illinois. Wilson *v.* McKenna, 52 Ill., 43; Reed *v.* Tyler, 56 id., 288. A requirement that no person shall be permitted to question a tax title, without showing payment of all taxes due upon the land will only be applied to plaintiffs, and not to parties in possession defending against a tax deed. Curry *v.* Hinman, 11 Ill., 420. Power denied to make it applicable. Conway *v.* Cable, 37 id., 82.

[3] For cases under the Virginia Stamp Act of 1812, Mumford's Reports may be referred to. The cases, however, are not very important.

It is competent in the case of such taxes on business as cannot be collected in advance, to require security for their payment before the business is entered upon.[1]

Collection as between the state and its municipalities. Where state levies are collected through the agency of county, city or township officers, it is competent for the state to make the county or other district liable as principal debtor for the quota of the state tax assessed within it.[2] Provisions to this effect are common in the statutes. And where the county treasurer is required to give bond to the state for the state taxes to be received by him, the failure to give a sufficient bond will not excuse the county. The state is not to suffer from the laches of its agents in such matters.[3]

[1] Mason *v.* Rollins, 2 Biss., 99; United States *v.* Mathoit, 1 Sawyer, 142.

[2] Schuylkill County *v.* Commonwealth, 36 Penn. St., 524; People *v.* Supervisors of St. Clair, 31 Mich. When the state treasurer charges over to a county its proportion of the state tax, the county becomes debtor, and cannot burden the state with any drawback of percentage. Multnomah Co. *v.* State, 1 Oregon, 358.

[3] See cases cited in the preceding note. A county is liable to towns for money collected by a defaulting county treasurer. Potter County *v.* Oswayo, 47 Penn. St., 162. But it is not liable to the town for its quota until the amount has been actually collected. Guittard *v.* Marshall County, 4 Kans., 388.

CHAPTER XV.

THE SALE OF LANDS FOR UNPAID TAXES.

When made. Lands are sold by the government for taxes, either because the assessments made upon them are not paid within the time allowed by law for their voluntary satisfaction by the owner, or because a personal assessment against the owner remains uncollected by the ordinary process. Whether the sale is to be made for the one reason or for the other, the same principles will govern it, though in some particulars the proceedings will differ.

The land must be liable. As government has no inherent right to deprive the citizen of his property except in pursuance of regular and lawful proceedings, and for a lawful demand, a sale of lands will be void if they were not liable for the tax. If by law they were exempt from taxation, a sale will be void though for a tax actually assessed;[1] and so it will be if made for a tax legally assessed but which in some lawful manner has been discharged.

Payment of the tax by the owner, or by any one entitled to make it, is an absolute defeat and termination of any statutory power to sell.[2] The persons who, besides the owner, are entitled to make payment, are those who are assessed for the tax, and any others whose interests would be injuriously affected by a sale, either because of liens they may have, or of contract relations;[3] and any one having the right may depute another to make it for him. Whether any third person may make payment is not so clear; but

[1] Hobson *v.* Dutton, 9 Kans., 477.

[2] Dougherty *v.* Dickey, 4 W. & S., 146; Hunter *v.* Cochran, 3 Penn. St., 105; Montgomery *v.* Meredith, 17 id., 42; Ankeny *v.* Albright, 20 id., 157; Laird *v.* Heister, 24 id., 452; Jackson *v.* Morse, 18 Johns., 441; Den *v.* Terrell, 3 Hawks, 283; Rowland *v.* Doty, Har. Ch., 3; Johnson *v.* Scott, 11 Mich., 232; Rayner *v.* Lee, 20 id., 384; Curry *v.* Hinman, 11 Ill., 420; Morrison *v.* Kelley, 22 Ill., 610; Walton *v.* Gray, 29 Iowa, 440; Sprague *v.* Coenan, 30 Wis., 209; Wallace *v.* Brown, 22 Ark., 118; Bennett *v.* Hunter, 9 Wall., 326.

[3] See Bennett *v.* Hunter, 18 Grat., 100; Same case in error, 9 Wall., 326; Tacey *v.* Irwin, 18 id., 549.

as the state is only interested in obtaining the revenue it has called for, it would seem that, before any sale, and consequently before any rights of third parties have intervened, any mere volunteer may pay the tax if he chooses;[1] and certainly if the proper officer should receive payment, any question concerning the right to make it would be precluded. Payment is an act *in pais*, which may be proved not only by the record, but by the original receipt;[2] and it may also be made out by any other evidence which satisfies a jury of the fact.[3] But payment cannot be shown in opposition to a judicial finding; at least as between the parties thereto and their privies.[4]

Tender of the tax by any one who has a right to make payment, is effectual to prevent a sale, whether the tender is accepted or not.[5] But a tender, in order to be effectual, must be of the full amount of the tax; it can not be of any thing less, unless the statute makes provision for payment of a part by itself, as it does sometimes for the benefit of tenants in common or owners of distinct portions of the premises taxed.[6]

Necessity for regular proceedings. To the validity of any sale of lands for taxes, it is imperatively necessary that there shall

[1] See Reading *v.* Finney, 73 Penn. St., 467; Martin *v.* Snowden, 18 Grat., 100; Kinsworthy *v.* Austin, 23 Ark., 375.

[2] Johnstone *v.* Scott, 11 Mich., 232; McReynolds *v.* Longenberger, 57 Penn. St., 13; Deen *v.* Wills, 21 Texas, 642.

[3] Dennett *v.* Crocker, 8 Greenl., 239; Hammond *v.* Hannin, 21 Mich., 374; Rand *v.* Schofield, 43 Ill., 167; Cook *v.* Norton, 61 id., 285; Adams *v.* Beale, 19 Iowa, 61.

[4] Gaylord *v.* Scarff, 6 Iowa, 179; Cadmus *v.* Jackson, 52 Penn. St., 295; Wallace *v.* Brown, 22 Ark., 118. In this last case it is strongly intimated that if the collector, after the tax has been paid to him, proceeds to a sale of the land, and then obtains a judicial confirmation of the sale under a statute providing therefor, and which makes the confirmation "a complete bar against any and all persons who may thereafter claim said land in consequence of informality or illegality in the proceedings," the sale might and ought, in a direct proceeding for the purpose, to be set aside for fraud, though it could not be attacked collaterally.

[5] Schenck *v.* Peay, 1 Dill. C. C., 269; Loomis *v.* Pingree, 43 Me., 299; Kinsworthy *v.* Austin, 23 Ark., 375; Tacey *v.* Irwin, 18 Wall., 549.

[6] Hunt *v.* McFadgen, 20 Ark., 277; Heft *v.* Gebhart, 65 Penn. St., 510; Crum *v.* Burke, 25 id., 377.

have been a substantial compliance with the law in all the official proceedings which have led to it.[1]

Tax sales are made exclusively under a statutory power. The officer who makes them sells something he does not own, and which he can have no authority to sell except as he is made the agent of the law for the purpose. But he is made such agent only by certain steps which are to precede his action, and which under the law are conditions to his authority. If these fail, the power is never created. If one of them fails, it is as fatal as if all failed. Defects in the conditions to a statutory authority cannot be aided by the courts; if they have not been observed, the courts cannot dispense with them, and thus bring into existence a power which the statute only permits when the conditions have been fully complied with. Neither, as a general rule, can the courts aid the defective execution of a statutory power; they may do this when the power has been created by the owner himself, and when such action would presumptively be in furtherance of his purpose in creating it; but a statutory power must be executed according to the statutory directions, and presumptively any other execution is opposed to the legislative will, instead of in furtherance of it. It is therefore accepted as an axiom when tax sales are under consideration, that a fundamental condition to their validity is that there should have been a substantial compliance with the law in all the proceedings of which the sale was the culmination. This would be the general rule in all cases in which a man is to be divested of his freehold by adversary proceedings; but special reasons make it peculiarly applicable to the case of tax sales. These reasons are thus summarized by the supreme court of Maine: "Sales of real estate for the nonpayment of taxes must be regarded in a great measure as an *ex parte* proceeding. The owner is to be deprived of his land thereby; and a series of acts preliminary to the sale are to be performed to authorize it on the part of the assessors and collector, to which his attention may never have been particularly called; and experience and observation render it notorious that the amount paid by

[1] There must be express statutory authority for selling lands for taxes. A power to tax does not include the power to cause lands to be sold for nonpayment of the taxes. See McInery *v.* Reed, 23 Iowa, 410; Sibley *v.* Smith, 2 Mich., 486; Sharp *v.* Spier, 4 Hill, 76.

purchasers at such sales is uniformly trifling, in comparison with the value of the property sold. It has therefore been held, with great propriety, that to make out a valid title under such sales, great strictness is to be required; and it must appear that the provisions of law preparatory to and authorizing such sales, have been punctiliously complied with."[1]

In Virginia, somewhat stronger language has been employed. "These sales and purchases," it is said, "founded on forfeitures, deserve no indulgence from the court. It is therefore the well settled law that he who claims under a forfeiture, must show that the law has been exactly complied with."[2] This language, if strictly taken, is unquestionably more exacting in its requirements than the authorities generally will justify. It is not necessary, we apprehend, in any proceedings so complicated as those in which lands are sold for taxes, that there should be shown an exact and punctilious compliance with all the provisions of law before they can be supported. With many of these provisions, as we have endeavored to show in a preceding chapter, the party interested in defeating such a sale could have no concern whatever. They are not made for his protection or benefit, and whether observed or not, they do not affect his interest. A failure to observe them, can, therefore, furnish no ground of complaint on his behalf; and it is not perceived that it can constitute for him any just or equitable protection against the demands of the state for its lawful revenues. It is sufficient for his case if the provisions which do concern him have been observed; and if others which are made in the interest of the public are overlooked or disregarded, the public, through its proper authorities, must be the proper

[1] *Whitman*, Ch. J., in Brown *v.* Veazie, 25 Me., 359, 362. See also Keene *v.* Houghton, 19 id., 368; Smith *v.* Bodfish, 27 id., 289; Flint *v.* Sawyer, 30 id., 226; Payson *v.* Hall, 30 id., 319; Matthews *v.* Light, 32 id., 305; Howe *v.* Russel, 36 id., 115; Stevens *v.* McNamara, 36 id., 176; Loomis *v.* Pingree, 43 Me., 299; Lovejoy *v.* Lunt, 48 id., 377; Williamsburg *v.* Lord, 51 id., 599; French *v* Patterson, 61 id., 203.

[2] *Carr*, J., in Wilson *v.* Bell., 7 Leigh, 22, 24. And see Yancey *v.* Hopkins, 1 Munf., 419; Christy *v.* Minor, 4 id., 431; Nalle *v.* Fenwick, 4 Rand., 585; Allen *v.* Smith, 1 Leigh, 231, 254; Chapman *v.* Doe, 2 id., 329, 357; Jesse *v.* Preston, 5 Grat., 120; Martin *v.* Snowden, 18 id., 100. In California it has been said that the proceedings in these cases are *strictissimi juris*. Ferris *v* Coover, 10 Cal., 589, 632; Kelsey *v.* Abbott, 13 id., 609.

party to complain. This is reasonable, and this is the rule that is laid down by the authorities.

Onus of proof. At the common law it was necessary that one who claimed to have obtained title to property of another, under proceedings based upon a neglect of public duty, should take upon himself the burden of showing that the law had been complied with by those who had had the proceedings in charge. Especially if the proceedings would operate with severity, and be in their effects something in the nature of a forfeiture, the law was strict in its requirement that his evidence should exhibit the proceedings from step to step, and show that each of the safeguards with which the statute had surrounded the delinquent for his protection in this very emergency, had been duly observed. And this tenderness for his interests appeared but reasonable. Of what service could it be that safeguards were provided, if observance was not essential; if a careless or incompetent officer might overlook or disregard them with impunity, and deal with the property of the citizen as if his position as an officer of the government vested him with a dispensing authority over legislation, and authorized him to make, in his discretion, a law for the case as he proceeded?

This rule of the common law has not been modified by decisions, and is still recognized and enforced, where statutes have not changed it. It may consequently be said to be the general rule, that the party claiming lands under a sale for taxes, must show affirmatively that the law under which the sale was made, has been substantially complied with, not only in the sale itself, but in all the anterior proceedings.[1] But although the authorities

[1] Stead's Ex'rs *v.* Course, 4 Cranch, 402; Parker *v.* Rule's Lessee, 9 id., 64; Williams *v.* Peyton's Lessee, 4 Wheat., 77; McClung *v.* Ross, 5 id., 116; Thatcher *v.* Powell, 6 id., 119; Games *v.* Stiles, 14 Pet., 332; Pillow *v.* Roberts, 13 How., 472; Moore *v.* Brown, 11 id., 414; Early *v.* Doe, 16 id., 610; Parker *v.* Overman, 18 id., 142; Little *v.* Herndon, 10 Wall., 26; Hughey's Lessee *v.* Horrell, 2 Ohio, 233; Holt's Heirs *v.* Hemphill's Heirs, 3 id., 232; Lafferty's Lessee *v.* Byers, 5 id., 458; Thomson's Heirs *v.* Gotham, 9 id., 170; Kellogg *v.* McLaughlin, 8 id., 114; Polk *v.* Rose, 25 Md., 153; Pope *v.* Headen, 5 Ala., 433; Elliott *v.* Eddins, 24 id., 508; Garrett *v.* Wiggins, 1 Scam., 335; Fitch *v.* Pinckard, 4 id., 69; Doe *v.* Leonard, 4 id., 140; Wiley *v.* Bean, 1 Gilm., 302; Irving *v.* Brownell, 11 Ill., 402; Spellman *v.* Curtenius, 12 id., 409; Marsh *v.* Chestnut, 14 id., 224; Gœwey *v.* Urig, 18 id., 242; Lane *v.* Bommelmann, 21 id., 143; Charles

concur in this rule with great unanimity, they are not so entirely in accord when the question regards the strictness required in the showing that shall be made. On this point some of the cases, particularly those which were decided at a very early day, have used language importing a strictness greater than in most cases would be possible, and greater than is demanded by any considerations of policy or of justice to the party whose estate is in question. The later cases lay down a more just and reasonable rule, and warrant us in saying, that the requirement of a compliance with the law, when the question arises as one of title, is satisfied by obedience to those provisions of the law which are in the nature of conditions to the power to sell, and are not merely *directory* under the rules laid down in another chapter.[1] To require more than this would be needless for any beneficial purpose, and would greatly embarrass, and in innumerable cases, defeat the collection of the revenue.

The requirement that the claimant under a tax sale should show the proceedings to have been regular, was entirely according to the natural order of evidence. The original owner would show a *prima facie* right by producing the documents and evidence which demonstrated his original ownership. To overcome this, there must be evidence of a title overriding or extinguishing it; and such a title would not appear in the tax purchaser until the successive steps, taken in compliance with the tax law, and ending in a sale and conveyance, had been shown. To prove merely a sale, would be futile, unless the power to make the sale was established; and to prove merely an instrument purporting to be a conveyance, would be even more idle.

v. Waugh, 35 id., 315; Norris *v.* Russell, 5 Cal., 250; Keane *v.* Cannovan, 21 id., 291; O'Brien *v.* Coulter, 2 Blackf., 421; Williams *v.* State, 6 id., 36; Wiggins *v.* Holley, 11 Ind., 2; Gavin *v.* Sherman, 23 id., 32; Ellis *v.* Kenyon, 25 id., 134; Jackson *v.* Shepard, 7 Cow., 88; Atkins *v.* Kinman, 20 Wend., 241; Sharp *v.* Spier, 4 Hill, 76; Sharp *v.* Johnson, 4 id., 92; Newell *v.* Wheeler, 48 N. Y., 486; Westfall *v.* Preston, 49 id., 349; Hall *v.* Collins, 4 Vt., 316; Bellows *v.* Elliott, 12 id., 569; Brown *v.* Wright, 17 id., 97; Waldron *v.* Tuttle, 3 N. H., 340; Cass *v.* Bellows, 31 id., 501; Hawley *v.* Mitchell, 31 id., 575; Annan *v.* Baker, 49 id., 161; Scott *v.* Young Men's Society, 1 Doug. Mich., 119; Latimer *v.* Lovett, 2 id., 204; Scott *v.* Babcock, 3 Green, Iowa, 133; Gaylord *v.* Scarff, 6 Iowa, 179; McGahen *v.* Carr, 6 Iowa, 331; Morton *v.* Reads, 6 Mo., 64; S. C. 9 id., 878; Nelson *v.* Grebel, 17 id., 161; Kelly *v.* Medlin, 26 Texas, 38

[1] Chapter IX.

Nor was there any special injustice or hardship in the rule of the law, which required the tax purchaser to prove the regularity of the proceedings under which he claimed. Whether the interest of the state might not be best subserved by casting the *onus* of showing defects in the title on the adverse claimant, and whether, therefore, on grounds of public policy it might not be advisable to change the rule accordingly, are questions that stand quite apart from any which concern the claims or rights of the purchaser; but regarding his position only, there was no hardship in calling upon him to give proof of his title by showing a sale made with due authority. A tax sale is the culmination of proceedings which are matters of record; and it is a reasonable presumption of law that, where one acquires rights which depend upon matters of record, he first makes search of the record in order to ascertain whether anything shown thereby would diminish the value of such rights, or tend in any contingency to defeat them.[1] A tax purchaser consequently cannot be, in any strict technical sense, a *bona fide* purchaser, as that term is under-

[1] That the proceedings on which tax sales depend are to be proved by the records, or by the originals from which the records should be made up; the following cases are authority, if indeed any is necessary: Job *v.* Tebbetts, 5 Gilm., 376, 380; Graves *v.* Bruen, 11 Ill., 431, 442; Schuyler *v.* Hull, 11 id., 462, 465; Boston *v.* Weymouth, 4 Cush., 538; Bucksport *v.* Spofford, 12 Me., 487; Adams *v.* Mack, 3 N. H., 493, 499; Blake *v.* Sturtevant, 12 id., 567; Pittsfield *v.* Barnstead, 40 id., 477 493; McCrory *v.* Manes, 47 Geo., 90; Sheldon, Lessee *v.* Coats, 10 Ohio, 278; Thevenin *v.* Slocum, 16 id., 519, 531; Blodgett *v.* Holbrook, 39 Vt., 336; Iverslie *v.* Spaulding, 32 Wis., 394; Gearhart *v.* Dixon, 1 Penn. St., 224; Diamond Coal Co. *v.* Fisher, 19 id., 267; Miner *v.* McLean, 4 McLean, 138; Games *v.* Stiles, 14 Pet., 322. But such records do not import absolute verity like those of courts, and it may be shown in contradiction to their recitals that the facts were otherwise than as there stated. Diamond Coal Co., *v.* Fisher, 19 Penn. St., 267, 273; Boston *v.* Weymouth, 4 Cush., 538, 541; Blake *v.* Sturtevant, 12 N. H., 567; Graves *v.* Bruen, 11 Ill., 431, 443; Tebbetts *v.* Job, 11 id., 453; Schuyler *v.* Hull, 11 id., 462 465. In Kellogg *v.* McLaughlin, 8 Ohio, 114, 116, the record of tax proceedings was held to be conclusive against the party claiming under a tax sale, but not against the party contesting it. In Miner *v.* McLean, 4 McLean, 138, 140, it is said that "parol evidence is not admissible to supply a defect in the record. This well established rule can admit of no exception." In Coit *v.* Wells, 2 Vt., 318, it was decided that the records of the advertisements in the case of road taxes were not evidence at all unless they contained all the particulars required by the statute. These cases, however, are not inconsistent with a resort to parol evidence as secondary to that of record when the latter is lost or destroyed.

stood in the law; because a *bona fide* purchaser is one who buys an apparently good title without notice of anything calculated to impair or affect it; but the tax purchaser is always deemed to have such notice when the record shows defects. He cannot shut his eyes to what has been recorded for the information of all concerned, and relying implicitly on the action of the officers, assume what they have done is legal because they have done it. It is indeed a presumption of law that official duty is performed; and this presumption stands for evidence in many cases; but the law never assumes the existence of jurisdictional facts; and throughout the tax proceedings the general rule is, that the taking of any one important step is a jurisdictional prerequisite to the next; and it cannot therefore be assumed, because one is shown to have been taken, that the officer performed his duty in taking that which should have preceded it.[1]

Presumptions of regularity. But while the tax purchaser is making his showing, the strictness required in the proof may reasonably be made to depend, to some extent, upon the circumstances. Presumptions are indulged in every class of proceedings; and in some cases presumptions may give an efficient support to evidence which, without them, would be insufficient to establish the necessary facts. Indeed, in some cases, presumptions may supply links which appear to be missing in the testimony. It was once said by an eminent judge in a tax case, that "full evidence of every minute circumstance ought not, especially at a distant day, to be required. From the establishment of some facts it is possible that others may be presumed, and less than positive testimony may establish facts."[2] Nothing, under some

[1] A tax purchaser comes strictly within the rule *caveat emptor*. If his title fails because the collector failed to give notice of sale, he has no remedy against the collector. Hamilton *v.* Valiant, 30 Md., 139. Neither has he for any error or irregularity which defeats his title a remedy against the town. Lynde *v.* Melrose, 10 Allen, 49. And see Jenks *v.* Wright, 61 Penn. St., 410, 414. In Michigan the Auditor General is authorized to refund the bids to purchasers in some cases in which titles prove defective; but his right to do so is limited strictly to the cases enumerated in the statute; the state taking no responsibility for the action of officers where the purchaser has the same opportunity for knowing the facts that the state officers have. People *v.* Auditor General, 30 Mich., 12.

[2] *Marshall*, Ch. J., in Stead's Executors *v.* Course, 4 Cranch, 413. See, to the same effect, Freeman *v.* Thayer, 33 Me., 76.

circumstances, could be more just or reasonable. But when that "distant day" arrives, when presumptions are relied upon, it will be found necessary to observe, with some circumspection, what has been the position of the parties, relative to the property claimed, from the time the sale was made. That position may sometimes very reasonably have a controlling influence. If the tax purchaser has made no claim under his title, and has left the original owner to treat the property as his own, it is difficult to understand on what ground any presumption can be built up in aid of the tax title, deriving its force from the lapse of time. "The older it is without any claim being made under it, the weaker it is, and the weaker are all presumptions in its favor."[1] If, on the other hand, he has made claim in practical and effective form by taking possession, and especially if, after the possession was taken, the other party, with full knowledge thereof, has neglected, for any considerable period, to assert his own rights, it must be conceded that the claim of the tax purchaser will come before the courts under circumstances entitling it to much greater indulgence.

The reasons for this are manifest. If one who claims to have title to property shall lie by for a long term of years without asserting it, while another is in the enjoyment of that which, if the title is valid, should be enjoyed by himself, it is not a very violent presumption that his supineness is due to his being aware of some defect which would defeat his claim if he were to assert it in legal proceedings. The longer he delays the stronger this presumption becomes; and if the time could ever arrive when, because the claim is old, it could be presumed without defects, it is obvious that it could only be on an indulgence of presumptions that are opposed to reason. That he may lie by because of defects, until the time can arrive when, because of his lying by, it will be presumed that no defects exist, and then be put by the law in possession of that which it is inferable he did not venture to demand before, is an absurdity so manifest that time need not be wasted in the attempt to make it more so.

[1] Alexander *v.* Bush, 46 Penn. St., 62. See, to the same effect, Read *v.* Goodyear, 17 S. & R., 350; Hole *v.* Rittenhouse, 19 Penn. St., 305; Worthing *v.* Webster, 45 Me., 270; Richardson *v.* Dorr, 5 Vt., 9; Townsend *v.* Downer, 32 id., 183.

It is different when the tax purchaser has been in possession.[1] That fact is some evidence that he at least believes his title to have validity; and if those who might dispute it neglect to do so, the inferences will be more or less strong, according to the circumstances, that their action is attributable to the belief that a contest must be ineffectual. It is doubted if in any case, on common law principles, a tax title could be presumed valid before the full period allowed by the statute of limitations for bringing suit had expired. The court of appeals of Virginia decided at an early day that it could not be,[2] and no satisfactory reason has been suggested in any quarter to cast a doubt upon the correctness of this conclusion. Still, presumptions may be very forcible in some cases, where, on the evidence, it is left in doubt whether the tax proceedings have or have not been conducted in conformity to law. If possession has been held under them for a considerable period, though it may not have been for a length of time sufficient to bar suits for the recovery of lands, there may reasonably spring from such possession an inference in favor of its legality, of sufficient force to turn the scales on any point left in doubt on the proofs, and to justify a jury, to whom the case is submitted, in drawing the conclusion which supports the possession. The longer the possession has continued, the stronger should be the intendments in favor of the title under which it is held; and although these cannot make valid that which in itself is void, they may, and should, be allowed their weight when a case is to be determined which the evidence has left in doubt. What their weight should be must depend on the circumstances; there can

[1] Possession, recovery against the grantor of defendant in trespass, and payment of taxes, are evidence in favor of a tax deed thirty years old that a surplus bond, the cost of which is receipted in the deed, was given. Lackawana Iron Co. *v.* Failes, 55 Penn. St., 90. As to the force of recitals in deeds generally, where there has been possession under them, see Worthing *v.* Webster, 45 Me., 270.

[2] Allen *v.* South, 1 Leigh, 231, 255. The validity of a tax sale is not to be presumed from the mere deed of the collector, unaccompanied by extrinsic evidence that the prior proceedings were regular. Nor, in an action of ejectment, will any presumptions be made in favor of the validity of the deed, merely because the party claiming it proves a possession adverse to the title of another party, but for a period short of that prescribed by the statute of limitations. Townsend *v.* Downer, 32 Vt., 183.

be no definite rule of law on the subject which can be applied in all cases.[1]

Presumptions could in no case supply the want of a record when the law requires one, and it has never been made; neither can they help out a record which is so defective as not to answer the requirements of the law.[2] But when it has been once made to appear that a record has existed which is now lost or destroyed, presumptions may justly be allowed great weight in support of the secondary evidence, in proof of the contents of the record, and that it was in compliance with the law.[3]

[1] Five years' possession does not warrant a finding in favor of the regularity of proceedings, when their correctness is not shown by the evidence. Phillips *v.* Sherman, 61 Me., 548. See Pejepscut Proprietors *v.* Ransom, 14 Mass., 145. As to what will be overlooked in Pennsylvania, under their statute, which declares that no irregularities in the assessment, process, or otherwise, shall be allowed to affect the title of the purchaser, see Laird *v.* Hiester, 24 Penn. St., 452. As to the force of the presumption in favor of the correctness of official action under that statute, see Cuttle *v.* Brockway, 24 Penn. St., 145; Heft *v.* Gephart, 65 id., 518. In Schoff *v.* Gould, 52 N. H., 512, the tax proceedings depended on the vote of a meeting, and the question was made upon proof of the warrant for holding it. The court say: "The meeting was held in March, 1841 — more than thirty years ago — and officers were chosen who acted as such, and the jury might have presumed that the warrant remained posted the requisite time. Bishop *v.* Cone, 3 N. H., 513; Northwood *v.* Barrington, 9 id., 373; Petersborough *v.* Lancaster, 14 id., 372; School District *v.* Bragdon, 23 id., 514. In Cavis *v.* Robertson, 9 N. H., 524, it was held that this rule did not apply where the facts were recent, and the records might be amended, but would apply where, from the lapse of time, it may be presumed that the officers who made the records are no longer living, or have no recollection of the facts. It does not appear that the officers who made the record are dead, but it is a fair presumption that they have lost recollection of the fact that the notice remained posted."

The following cases are important, as showing what, under their varying circumstances, was held sufficient evidence of an assessment: Bratton *v.* Mitchell, 7 W. & S., 259; Crum *v.* Burke, 25 Penn. St., 377, 381; Heft *v.* Gephart, 65 id., 510; McDermott *v.* Hoffman, 70 id., 31; McReynolds *v.* Longenberger, 57 id., 13; Pittsfield *v.* Barnstead, 40 N. H., 477. The sale book does not prove an assessment. Bratton *v.* Mitchell, 1 W. & S., 310. Neither do the recitals in the tax warrant. Hoffer *v.* Matteson's Ex'rs, 16 N. J. Eq., 382.

[2] Coit *v.* Wells, 2 Vt., 318; Capron *v.* Raistrick, 44 id., 515; Kellogg *v.* McLaughlin, 8 Ohio, 114; Porter *v.* Byrne, 10 Ind., 146; Iverslie *v.* Spaulding, 32 Wis., 394; Moser *v.* White, 29 Mich., 59.

[3] Where a record is not found in the proper office, and it is not shown that one was ever in existence, there is no presumption that one was made. Hall *v.* Kellogg, 16 Mich., 139. In Cass *v.* Bellows, 31 N. H., 501, 510, *Eastman*, J.,

Special authority to sell. The various proceedings which usually are required to precede a sale of the lands have been successively mentioned. Whether, when these have been taken, the officer will require any special warrant or process as his authority for proceeding to a sale, must depend upon whether something of that nature is provided for by law. In some of the states a list of delinquent lands is made out and properly certified by the state auditor, or some other designated officer of state, to whom the returns of delinquent taxes have been made, and this list is transmitted to the county or township official who by law is entrusted with the duty of making sales, and constitutes his warrant for doing so. In other states, the statutes make other special provisions for the purpose. Whatever list, certificate or warrant is prescribed by the statute, it is to be looked upon as in the nature of process, and it is indispensible that the officer should have it before taking any steps towards making a sale.[1] And in all his action he must keep within the command of his warrant and of the law; for his authority will fail to support him when he fails to observe it.[2]

uses the following language: "In Cavis *v.* Robertson, 9 N. H., 524, it was held that there are cases in which it may be submitted to a jury to presume, from a defective record of the election of a town officer, and from his having acted under the appointment, that the meeting was duly held, the proceedings of the town regular and the officer duly sworn; but that this cannot be done where the proceedings are recent, and no cause is shown why the defective record cannot be amended if the truth will warrant it." And, after commenting upon Gibson *v.* Bailey, 9 N. H., 168, he adds: "In the case before us, the town clerk had deceased before the suit was brought. The record was defective, but showed that the collector was evidently sworn in some way. Nearly forty years had elapsed from the making of the record to the commencement of the suit, and, from the authority of the cases cited, and the principles therein stated, we think the evidence was competent to be submitted to a jury, as tending to show the collector to have been duly elected and duly sworn. It can make no difference whether the demandant was the proprietor of the lot at the time it was sold, or a subsequent purchaser. The record that the collector 'was sworn into office' was open to all; and, if he purchased with that before him, he took the title, subject to the same rights in regard to the record, as had existed with respect to former owners."

[1] See Horner *v.* Cilley, 14 N. H., 85; Hannel *v.* Smith, 15 Ohio, 134; Kelley *v.* Craig, 5 Ired., 129; Gossett *v.* Kent, 19 Ark., 602; Miner *v.* McLean, 4 McLean, 138.

[2] Where the statute requires the sale to be made within two years from the date of the warrant, a sale at a later day is void. Usher *v.* Taft, 33 Me., 199.

Notice of sale. The first proceeding usually required of the officer who is to make sale is, that he shall give public notice of his intention to do so. Under different statutes notices in various forms are required, as may be thought most suitable to the case. If the statute fails to specify the character of the notice, doubtless one in writing must be intended;[1] but a provision so indefinite will not often be met with. Unusual care is required in obeying the directions of the statute regarding notice, as no one who is entitled to notice can be bound by a sale which has been made without it. There is no constitutional provision entitling one to notice in a particular mode: what the statute has made sufficient must be deemed so. In the case of residents, personal notice is sometimes required;[2] but for nonresidents, a notice published in a newspaper is generally all that is provided for.[3] Sometimes the published notice is all that is made requisite even in the case of residents; while other statutes direct that the tax list shall be kept posted in some public place or places for a certain period. Whatever the provision is, it must be complied with

See, for the same principle, Avery *v.* Rose, 4 Dev., 549; Doe *v.* Allen, 67 N. C., 346. A sale preceding the day is of course void. Conrad *v.* Darden, 4 Yerg., 307. See Orr *v.* Travacier, 21 Iowa, 68.

It has been decided that where, by the statute, the proceedings are different in the case of nonresidents from what they are in the case of residents, the subsequent proceedings will be invalid unless they follow the assessment. Merrick *v.* Hutt, 15 Ark., 331; Kinsworthy *v.* Mitchell, 21 id., 145; McDermott *v.* Skully, 27 id., 226; Garabaldi *v.* Jenkins, id., 453.

[1] Pearson *v.* Lovejoy, 53 Barb., 407.

[2] Where the statute required notice to be given to the occupant, if the land was occupied, it was held that one having a paper title to a lot of 169 acres, and who, though not on it, cultivated a small piece of it, was entitled to notice, and a sale made without giving it was void. Leland *v.* Bennett, 5 Hill, 286, citing Comstock *v.* Beardsley, 15 Wend., 348; Bush *v.* Davison, 16 Wend., 550. In North Carolina it seems that the mortgagee is regarded as the owner of land mortgaged, so as to be entitled to the notice required to be given to the owner. Whitehurst *v.* Gaskill, 69 N. C., 449; S. C., 12 Am. Rep., 655.

[3] The owner of unseated lands is only entitled to such notice as the statute shall provide for, and he must take notice of the tax proceedings at his peril. Cuttle *v.* Brockway, 32 Penn. St., 45. It is said in Louisiana that it is in the power of the legislature to determine what shall be sufficient to bring parties into court in tax cases, and if a published notice is provided for and given, that is sufficient. New Orleans *v.* Cordeviolle, 10 La. An., 732; Draining Co. Case, 11 id., 338.

strictly. This is one of the most important of all the safeguards which has been deemed necessary to protect the interests of parties taxed; and nothing can be a substitute for it or excuse the failure to give it.[1] The notice being a prerequisite to the officer's authority, the fact that in the particular case it can be shown that the party concerned was fully aware of the proceedings, will be of no avail in supporting them. He is under no obligation to take notice of the proceedings unless duly notified. Mere informalities or unimportant variances in an attempt to comply with the law may not be fatal, but variance in substance cannot be overlooked.

It may be useful to notice some of the cases on the subject. Where the statute required the notice to contain a particular statement of the taxes on each lot, a notice not containing it was held void.[2] So where the notice was for less than the statutory time, though but for a single day, the proceeding was held to be as fatally defective as if no notice at all had been given.[3] So where the notice was required to be published for a certain time in the paper of the state printer, and the publication was duly begun, but before completion the paper ceased to be that of the state printer, it was held insufficient.[4] So a notice is defective if

[1] Washington *v.* Pratt, 8 Wheat., 681; Early *v.* Doe, 16 How., 610; Moulton *v.* Blaisdell, 24 Me., 283; Flint *v.* Sawyer, 30 id., 226; Hill *v.* Mason, 38 id., 461; Bush *v.* Davison, 16 Wend., 550; Alexander *v.* Pitts, 7 Cush., 503; Blalock *v.* Gaddes, 33 Miss., 452; Reed *v.* Morton, 9 Mo., 878; Prindle *v.* Campbell, 9 Minn., 212; Jenks *v.* Wright, 61 Penn. St., 410. A written notice will not answer where a printed notice is required by statute. Lagrone *v.* Rains, 48 Mo., 536. Nor can posting the list be omitted when required by statute. Yenda *v.* Wheeler, 9 Texas, 408: see Pitts *v.* Booth, 15 id., 453.

[2] Washington *v.* Pratt, 8 Wheat., 681: see Jenks *v.* Wright, 61 Penn. St., 410.

[3] State *v.* Newark, 36 N. J., 288. A similar ruling was made in Pope *v.* Headon, 5 Ala., 433. And see Elliott *v.* Eddins, 24 id., 508; Flint *v.* Sawyer, 30 Me., 226; Hobbs *v.* Clements, 32 Me., 67. Twelve weeks' notice of sale requires eighty-four full days. Early v. Doe, 16 How., 610. Where notice is required to be for ten days, Sundays excepted, and it is omitted two days, not Sundays, it is void. Haskell *v.* Bartlett, 34 Cal., 281. See further as to time of publication, Kellogg *v.* McLaughlin, 8 Ohio, 114; Cass *v.* Bellows, 31 N. H., 501; Moore *v.* Brown, 4 McLean, 211; S. C., in error, 11 How., 414; Westbrook *v.* Wiley, 47 N. Y., 457; Dubuque *v.* Wooton, 28 Iowa, 571.

[4] Bussey *v.* Leavitt, 12 Me., 378. Compare Pope *v.* Headon, 5 Ala., 433; Lyon *v.* Hunt, 11 id., 295; Sharp *v.* Johnson, 4 Hill, 92; Cambridge *v.* Chan-

the collector in appending his name fails to add his name of office, so that it does not appear to be official;[1] or if given before the person has in fact been sworn into office;[2] or if delayed after the time prescribed by law for its publication.[3] And the notice is bad if it differs from the assessment in giving the name of the person to whom the land is taxed;[4] or if it fails to give the name of the person taxed when the statute requires it;[5] or if the description of the land is insufficient.[6] As regards all such cases, the law is well summed up in a case in which the statute required the notice to state the "amount of taxes assessed," and the notice given was incorrect in this particular. "The advertisement did not state the amount of the tax assessed on the land, but stated a wholly different amount, and for all legal purposes might as well have contained no statement whatever of the amount of the tax. To comply with the statute the exact amount must be given. A deviation, however small, must be fatal, because a rule of law cannot be made to fluctuate according to the degree or extent of its violation."[7]

The most important of the usual requisites of notice of sale, are that it shall give a proper description of the land to be sold, and a statement of the time and place when and where the sale

dler, 6 N. H., 271. A change in the name of the paper in which the notice is required to be published will not affect the notice. Isaac *v.* Shattuck, 12 Vt., 668. Where a city common council is required to give notice in a paper to be designated, the designation must be made by the council. Appeal of Powers, 29 Mich., 504.

[1] Spear *v.* Ditty, 9 Vt., 282. See Broughton *v.* Journeay, 51 Penn. St., 31.

[2] Langdon *v.* Poor, 20 Vt., 13. See Hannell *v.* Smith, 15 Ohio, 134.

[3] Hill *v.* Mason, 38 Me., 461. Compare Brackett *v.* Vining, 49 Me., 356; Kelly *v.* Craig, 5 Ired., 129; Magee *v.* Commonwealth, 46 Penn. St., 358; Pierce *v.* Benjamin, 14 Pick., 356; Noyes *v.* Haverhill, 11 Cush., 338.

[4] Bettison *v.* Rudd, 21 Ark., 578, citing Wait *v.* Gilmore, 2 Yeates, 330; Shimmin *v.* Inman, 26 Me., 232. And see Alvord *v.* Collin, 20 Pick., 418.

[5] Sargeant *v.* Bean, 7 Gray, 125.

[6] Such a defect could not be aided by any information imparted by the auctioneer to the bidders at the sale. Ronkendorf *v.* Taylor, 4 Pet., 349.

[7] *Bigelow*, J., in Alexander *v.* Pitts, 7 Cush., 503. The amount of the tax was $3.30; that stated in the notice was $4.12. Compare Clarke *v.* Strickland, 2 Curt. C. C., 439. That an immaterial variation in the notice from that required by the statute may be overlooked, see Ogden *v.* Harrington, 6 McLean, 418; Scott *v.* Watkins, 22 Ark., 556.

will be made. The requisites for a description in the assessment roll have been heretofore given. In the notice as in the assessment, there is precisely the same necessity that the description shall be sufficiently definite to identify the land, in order that the owner may be apprised of the peril to which his interests are exposed.[1] What has been said regarding the description under the head of assessment, is consequently applicable here. The cases referred to in the margin discuss other defects, or alleged defects, in notices of sale, and may be useful for reference.[2] Consent of the owner of land to a defective publication of notice, it has been held, would not bind him, as he cannot, in that manner, confer an authority upon an officer of the law, nor can he pass a title to his freehold by mere waiver.[3] Proof of giving the notice should be duly made of record, and it ought to show what the facts are, so that any one inspecting the record may know that the statute has been complied with. An affidavit, or a return, which undertakes to state merely the legal conclusion, that "due notice" was given, or "legal notice," or "notice as required by the statute," or to make any other general allegation of a similar nature, ought not to be received as sufficient evidence that the law has been complied with. It is, in fact, evidence only of the officer's opinion that he has performed his duty.[4]

[1] See Farnum *v.* Buffum, 4 Cush., 260; Eastman *v.* Little, 5 N. H., 290; Williams *v.* Harris, 4 Sneed, 332; Bidwell *v.* Webb, 10 Minn., 59; Bidwell *v.* Coleman, 11 id., 78.

[2] Porter *v.* Whitney, 1 Greenl., 306; Shimmin *v.* Inman, 26 Me., 228; Hobbs *v.* Clements, 32 id., 67; Greene *v.* Lunt, 58 id., 518; Smith *v.* Messer, 17 N. H., 420; Pierce *v.* Richardson, 37 id., 306, 314; Langdon *v.* Poor, 20 Vt., 13; Hughey *v.* Horrell, 2 Ohio, 231; Styles *v.* Weir, 26 Miss., 187; Sutton *v.* Calhoun, 14 La. An., 209. If the statute gives a form for a notice, it is sufficient to follow it, even though it does not specially name the place of sale; that being otherwise fixed. Clark *v.* Mowyer, 5 Mich., 562. Mr. Blackwell says: "Where the form is prescribed by the statute, that form must be strictly and literally followed; the court will not admit the substitution of a different one." Blackw. on Tax Titles, 223. True, if it is different in substance; but to say that the statute form must be *literally* followed, is stating a more strict rule of compliance than we can find authorities to justify. The publication of notice, not in the regular issue of a paper, but in extra sheets, is insufficient, unless these are sent to all the subscribers. Davis *v.* Simms, 4 Bibb, 465.

[3] Scales *v.* Alvis, 12 Ala., 617.

[4] Gilbert *v.* Turnpike Co., 3 Johns. Cas., 107; Cheatham *v.* Howell, 6 Yerg.,

Time and place of sale. The sale must be made at the very time and place provided by law for that purpose. In this regard, the utmost strictness is required, since otherwise the whole purpose of the notice, both as regards information to the public and protection to the owner of the land, will be defeated. A sale inside a building, when the law requires it to be at the outer door, has been held to be void.[1] So a sale either before or after the time which has been named for the purpose, is wholly without warrant of law, and cannot be sustained.[2] If, however, an adjournment from day to day is authorized, in order to complete a sale after it has been begun, perhaps a reasonable presumption that the sale was begun in season, and adjourned as thus provided, should uphold a sale appearing to have been made afterwards, in the absence of any showing to the contrary.[3]

311; Gwin *v.* Van Zant, 7 id., 143; Nelson *v.* Pierce, 6 N. H., 194; Wells *v.* Burbank, 17 id., 393; Lovejoy *v.* Lent, 48 Me., 377; Briggs *v.* Whipple, 7 Vt., 18; Farnum *v.* Buffum, 4 Cush., 260; People *v.* Highway Commissioners, 14 Mich., 528; Games *v.* Stiles, 14 Pt., 322. As to the strictness of proof required in showing notice, see County Commissioners *v.* Clarke, 36 Md., 206; Jarvis *v.* Silliman, 21 Wis., 607; Iverslie *v.* Spaulding, 32 id., 394; Pierce *v.* Sweetzer, 2 Ind., 649. Evidence of the officer, in general terms, that a sale was made in exact pursuance of the statute, is not sufficient without specifying what was done. Jesse *v.* Preston, 5 Grat., 120.

[1] Ruby *v.* Huntsman, 32 Mo., 501; Vassar *v.* George, 47 Miss., 713, 721. See State *v.* Rollins, 29 Mo., 267; McNair *v.* Jenson, 33 Mo., 312.

[2] Wilkins' Heirs *v.* Huse, 10 Ohio, 139; Hope *v.* Sawyer, 14 Ill., 254. The sheriff has no general power to sell for taxes, but only to sell at the time and place fixed by law. Hogins *v.* Brashears, 13 Ark., 242; Merrick *v.* Hutt, 15 id., 331; Bonnell *v.* Roane, 20 id., 114. Where the regular time for sale is the first Monday of March, but a sale at another time may be ordered by the county court, a deed reciting a sale at another time, but reciting no order, is void on its face. McDermott *v.* Skully, 27 Ark., 226. A sale not begun on the day fixed by law, is void on its face. Prindle *v.* Campbell, 9 Minn., 212; Park *v.* Tinkham, 9 Kan., 615; Entrekin *v.* Chambers, 11 id., 368.

[3] See Burns *v.* Lyon, 4 Watts, 363; Bestor *v.* Powell, 2 Gilm., 197; Lacy *v.* Davis, 4 Mich., 140; Harley *v.* Street, 29 Iowa, 429; Love *v.* Welch, 33 id., 192. Where a collector's sale was advertised at a particular time and place, and the collector's return states it to have been held in the town and on the day designated, it will be presumed, in absence of proof to the contrary, that it was held at the precise time and place specified. Spear *v.* Ditty, 8 Vt., 419. In Connecticut, it seems, a tax collector need not specify in his return the day on which the sale was made. Picket *v.* Allen, 10 Conn., 146. In Iowa a tax deed showing that the land was sold at an adjourned sale, without reciting

Competition at the sale. The sale must be a public sale, with opportunity for open competition.[1] This is a universal requirement; and it may seriously be questioned whether the legislature possesses the power to provide for the extinguishment of the owner's title by a secret or private sale. The sale itself is a proceeding to perfect a statutory forfeiture. The legislature has probably authority to declare a forfeiture of property taxed, for delinquency in making payment; but in such an act the sovereign power of the state is pushed to the very limit, and it is believed that a statute which comes short of such a declaration, and leaves the title still in the owner, could not provide for divesting him of it by means of administrative proceedings secretly taken, and of which neither actual nor constructive notice was to be given him. A public sale is the usual and proper course; and this, in order to constitute any protection to the owner, must be so made as to invite competition. And, as having an important influence on this subject, the courts have been compelled to take notice of fraudulent practices, which are almost as common as tax sales themselves. "I am aware," says one learned judge, "that there is much management and fraudulent perversion of the law about purchasing at treasurer's sales. It is our duty to discountenance it."[2] "Over a sale of this description," says another, "the owner has no control; he cannot refuse a bid, or adjourn the sale, or fix a sum below which the property shall not be struck down. The sale is managed by the agent of the state. The owner is not consulted. The highest bidder becomes the purchaser, although the sum bid be less than a hundredth part of the value of the property."[3] Acres for cents is the rule; the purchasers who congregate at the sale are usually speculators anticipating enormous profits on their investments; and competition in purchases is usually the last thing they desire. The persons in default will, in many cases, be poor and friendless; at any rate they will not be present; and the officer will commonly be found sufficiently dis-

the causes justifying it, is at least *prima facie* evidence that the sale was properly held, and that a proper cause for adjournment existed. Lorain *v.* Smith, 37 Iowa, 67.

[1] Jenks *v.* Wright, 61 Penn. St., 410.

[2] *Burnside*, J., in Donnel *v.* Bellas, 11 Penn. St., 341, 351.

[3] Dudley *v.* Little, 2 Ohio, 504.

posed to be complaisant to the interests of those who are at hand. It is not surprising, therefore, if in some instances it is discovered that he has accommodated them to an extent that practically excludes all competition.[1] It is still more common, perhaps, that purchasers in a friendly way arrange among themselves, that no competition shall take place, and that the harvest shall be equitably apportioned between them. All such arrangements are a fraud upon the law, and upon those whose protection is had in view when a public sale is provided for. "It is essential to the validity of tax sales, not merely that they should be conducted in conformity with the requirements of the law, but that they should be conducted with entire fairness. Perfect freedom from all influences likely to prevent competition in the sale should be in all cases strictly exacted. The owner is seldom present, and is generally ignorant of the proceeding until too late to prevent it. The tax usually bears a very slight proportion to the value of the property; and thus a great temptation is presented to parties to exclude competition at the sale, and to prevent the owner from redeeming when the sale is made. The proceeding, therefore, should be closely scrutinized, and whenever it has been characterized by fraud or unfairness, should be set aside, or the purchaser be required to hold the title in trust for the owner." Such is the language of the supreme court of the Union, in a case in which the purchaser of land at a tax sale had contrived to prevent competition, by the representation that the owner would defeat the sale by redemption. The court, very properly and justly, held the sale to be void as a fraud,[2] following in this regard an early case in Ohio, where a combination between bidders to preclude competition was also held fatal to the sale.[3]

[1] As in Brown *v.* Hogle, 30 Ill., 119, where the treasurer in proceeding to make sale, permitted favored persons to go through his list and select out in advance the lands they would purchase.

[2] *Field*, J., in Slater *v.* Maxwell, 6 Wall., 268, 276. See also Kerwer *v*, Allen, 31 Iowa, 578.

[3] Dudley *v.* Little, 2 Ohio, 504. In Case *v.* Dean, 16 Mich., 12, it was decided that such a combination between bidders would not defeat the title of a purchaser who was nor a party to, nor shown to be aware of it. See also Martin *v.* Cole, 38 Iowa, 141. In Reeve *v.* Kennedy, 43 Cal., 643, it is held that a sale cannot be attacked collaterally for fraud in obtaining it.

Officer not to buy. In order that there may be free competition, it is essential that the officer who makes the sale should act as salesman only, and not become interested in the purchases. He cannot be allowed to occupy the inconsistent positions of purchaser and seller, in which his cupidity would draw him in one direction and his duty in another. The law cannot safely intrust the securities provided for private parties to the care of those who are interested to prevent their accomplishing the purpose for which the securities are provided. No provision of law, it is assumed, would ever be made which would subject official integrity to the trial of such conflicts between interest and duty, as would be sure to arise if the officer were allowed to bid at a sale where his duty would be to obtain the highest practicable bid in the interest of another. To put himself in that position is regarded as a fraud in the officer upon the law; and on general principles of public policy, the sale which he makes to himself is void.[1] On no other principle can integrity and good faith be secured in proceedings of this *ex parte* character.

Sale in separate parcels. The sale should also be made of the parcels of land as they appear in the list. This is the general rule. Exceptions are made by statutes for various reasons. Where a tract is capable of subdivision, the statute may authorize the owner of a part to relieve such part from liability by paying a proportionate part of the tax.[2] Under some statutes, any one who will distinctly define any portion of an unimproved tract of land, may pay the tax upon that portion. So statutes permit the owner or claimant of an undivided interest to pay upon that by itself.[3] In any of these cases the part of the land,

[1] Pierce *v.* Benjamin, 14 Pick., 356; Clute *v.* Barron, 2 Mich., 192; Payson *v.* Hall, 30 Me., 319; Taylor *v.* Stringer, 1 Grat., 158; Chandler *v.* Moulton, 33 Vt., 245. In Fox *v.* Cash, 11 Penn. St., 207, it is decided that this principle will not preclude a clerk in the treasurer's office from becoming a purchaser. To the same effect is Wells *v.* Jackson Manuf. Co., 47 N. H., 235. The officer selling cannot act as agent for others in buying; though if he does so, and the purchase is afterwards set aside on that ground, the owner must refund to the purchaser what he has paid. Everett *v.* Bebe, 37 Iowa, 452.

[2] See Fellows *v.* Denniston, 23 N. Y., 420.

[3] Without express statutory authority, undivided interests cannot be sold separately when the tract is assessed as an entirety. Roberts *v.* Chan Tin Pen, 23 Cal., 259. In Vermont, it appears that a collector's deed of land sold for

or the interest in the land, upon which the tax is not paid, remains subject to sale and may be sold by itself. But in other respects the listing is to be followed in the sale.[1] To group lands in the sale which are assessed as separate interests, is incompetent, even though they be owned by the same person.[2] Each parcel is chargeable with its own taxes, and is to be redeemed by paying them; but such a joint sale charges it with the tax upon the other also, and is like issuing one execution upon several judgments, and selling jointly the lands which are charged with separate liens.[3] It may or may not be important to the owner

taxes, which describes the land simply as so many acres of a large lot, passes an undivided interest in such lot equal to the proportion which the number of acres sold bears to the whole number of acres in the lot. Sheafe *v.* Wait, 30 Vt., 735.

[1] Ballance *v.* Forsyth, 13 How., 18; Walker *v.* Moore, 2 Dill. C. C., 256; Morton *v.* Harris, 9 Watts, 319; Woodburn *v.* Wireman, 27 Penn. St., 18; Hayden *v.* Foster, 13 Pick., 492; Willey *v.* Scoville, 9 Ohio, 43; Atkins *v.* Hinman, 2 Gilm., 437; Spellman *v.* Curtenius, 12 Ill., 409; Pitkin *v.* Yaw, 13 id., 251; Penn *v.* Clemans, 19 Iowa, 372; Ware *v* Thompson, 29 id., 65; Martin *v.* Cole, 38 id., 141; Moulton *v.* Blaisdell, 24 Me., 283; Wallingford *v.* Fiske, id., 386; Andrews *v.* Senter, 32 id., 394; State *v.* Richardson, 21 Mo., 420; Baskins *v.* Winston, 24 Miss., 431. Though a sale together of several lots which really constitute one tract may be good, yet this can only be so when they were assessed together, or when they constitute a definite portion or fraction of what was assessed, so that, by mere division or subtraction, the amount of tax chargeable on the property sold can be determined from the assessment roll. McQuesten *v.* Swope, 12 Kans., 32. In Pennsylvania, the sale of seated lands with unseated is void for want of jurisdiction. Dietrick *v.* Mason, 57 Penn. St., 40. Unseated lands are sold without regard to ownership. Reading *v.* Finney, 73 Penn. St., 467. See Cuttle *v.* Brockway, 32 id., 45. In New York, it is held competent, where distinct interests are held subject to a lien for taxes, to provide by statute for a judicial sale of the whole fee, on the application of one party, after publication of notice to unknown owners. Jackson *v.* Babcock, 16 N. Y., 246.

[2] Andrews *v.* Senter, 32 Me., 394; Woodburn *v.* Wireman, 27 Penn. St., 18; Hayden *v.* Foster, 13 Pick., 492. In Minnesota, when an assessment is of a whole block, the treasurer cannot sell in parcels. Moulton *v.* Doran, 10 Minn., 67.

[3] To sell one's "right, title and interest" in land is not equivalent to a sale of the land itself. Clarke *v.* Strickland, 2 Curt. C. C., 439. Where the sale was of an undivided interest when all was assessed together, the sale was held void. Roberts *v.* Chan Tin Pen, 23 Cal., 259. It would be otherwise if the statute provided for the sale of undivided interests after the tax on other interests had been paid.

that he have the opportunity of a separate redemption, but the fact that it possibly may be so is sufficient reason why the law should protect the right.

Surplus bond. Various methods are adopted in different states to save something to the owner, if that shall be possible, when his land is sold. One of these is, to have the land put up for sale for what it will bring, and if the bid exceed the tax, with interest and expenses, require the surplus to be deposited in the state or county treasury for the benefit of the party who shall show his right. Another is to require a bond to be given by the purchaser to account for the excess over the taxes and charges, which bond shall be a lien on the land.[1] Still another is to require so much of the land to be sold as may be requisite to satisfy the tax and charges, either prescribing a general rule as to where the parcel sold shall be taken off, or allowing a discretion to the officer in that regard.

Excessive sale. It has been said that in the absence of any statute limiting the officer's right to sell, to so much as would be requisite to pay the tax and charges, a restriction to this extent would be intended by the law.[2] Whether this is so or not is perhaps not very material, as it is not for a moment to be supposed that any statute would be adopted without this or some equivalent provision for the owner's benefit. And such a provision must be strictly obeyed. A sale of the whole when less would pay the tax is void,[3] and a sale of the remainder after the tax had been

[1] Peters *v.* Heasley, 10 Watts, 208; Loud *v.* Penninan, 19 Pick., 539; People *v.* Hammond, 1 Doug., Mich., 276. The giving of the surplus bond is a condition precedent to the passing of the title to the purchaser at the tax sale. Sutton *v.* Nelson, 10 S. & R., 238; McDonald *v.* Maus, 8 Watts, 364; Donnel *v.* Bellas, 10 Penn. St., 341; Cuttle *v.* Brockway, 24 id., 145. As to suit upon it, see Crawford *v.* Stewart, 38 Penn. St., 34. That there is no presumption such a bond was given, where the tax purchaser does not take possession or pay taxes, see Alexander *v.* Bush, 46 Penn. St., 62.

[2] O'Brien *v.* Coulter, 2 Blackf., 421. The power to provide by law that the whole should be sold, when not necessary to pay the tax, was denied in Martin *v.* Snowden, 18 Grat., 100; Downey *v.* Nutt, 19 id., 59.

[3] Loomis *v.* Pingree, 43 Me., 299; Lovejoy *v.* Lunt, 48 id., 377; French *v.* Patterson, id., 203, 210; Ainsworth *v.* Dean, 21 N. H., 400; Lyford *v.* Dunn, 32 id., 81; Jaquith *v.* Putney, 48 id., 138; Avery *v.* Rose, 4 Dev., 554; Love *v.* Welbourn, 5 Ired., 347; Baskins *v.* Winston, 24 Miss., 431; Crowell *v.* Good-

satisfied by the sale of a part would also be void, for the very plain reason that the power to sell would be exhausted the moment the tax was collected.[1]

It has been shown in a preceding chapter that an excessive levy is void, whether it is made excessive by including with lawful taxes those which are unlawful, or in any other manner. If the levy would be void, there would of course be nothing to uphold a sale. And if a valid levy were to be increased afterwards by unlawful additions, the sale would be equally bad. A sale for anything more than is lawfully chargeable is a sale without jurisdiction, and therefore void.[2]

Sale to highest bidder and for cash. The sale must be to the highest bidder, or, which is equivalent, when that method is prescribed, to the person who offers to pay the tax and charges for the smallest parcel of land.[3] And as the conveyance must be in execution of a sale actually made, if the sale is made to one man, and by arrangement the deed is made to another, such deed can convey no title whatever.[4] The sale must be for *cash*. The officer can give no credit where the statute provides for none.[5]

win, 3 Allen, 535; Stead's Executors *v.* Course, 4 Cranch, 403; Mason *v.* Fearson, 9 How.. 248; French *v.* Edwards, 13 Wall., 506. Under the Massachusetts statute providing that if an estate is capable of division the collector may sell so much thereof as would be sufficient to discharge the taxes and intervening charges, it must appear by the collector's deed or otherwise, that the land was so divided that no greater portion was sold than was necessary to satisfy the tax and charges, or that it could not be conveniently divided to that extent. Crowell *v.* Goodwin, 3 Allen, 535.

[1] See Washington *v.* Pratt, 8 Wheat., 681; Mason *v.* Fearson, 9 How., 248. When the land as assessed consists of several distinct parcels constituting one tract, if the several parcels are offered separately and no bids obtained, the whole may then be offered together. State *v.* Maxwell, 6 Wall., 268. Where a quarter section contained several village lots, it was held incompetent to sell off an acre from one side for the tax on the whole. Ballance *v.* Forsyth, 13 How., 18.

[2] McQuilkin *v.* Doe, 8 Blackf., 581; Hutchens *v.* Doe, 3 Ind., 528; Hardenburgh *v.* Kidd, 10 Cal., 402; McQuesten *v.* Swope, 12 Kans., 32. Sale void where an illegal percentage is added. Bucknall *v.* Story, 36 Cal., 67. And see *ante* pp. 295–297.

[3] See Cardigan *v.* Page, 6 N. H., 182; Bean *v.* Thompson, 19 id., 290.

[4] Keene *v.* Houghton, 19 Me., 368.

[5] Cushing *v.* Longfellow, 26 Me., 306. In Longfellow *v.* Quimby, 29 id.,

It must not be for more than is due, as this would be a plain excess of jurisdiction.[1] Observing the statutory directions and precautions, and the principles of the common law and of public policy, to which reference has been made, the officer may transfer to the purchaser the full interest in the land which has been assessed, and may convey a complete and perfect title, if such is the provision of law on the subject.[2] And inadequacy of price does not defeat such a sale; if it did, the power to collect revenue by this method would be futile.[3]

Who may acquire tax titles. Some persons, from their relation to the land or to the tax, are precluded from becoming purchasers. The title to be transferred on such a sale is one based on the default of the person who owes to the government the duty to pay the tax. But one person may owe this duty to the government, and another may owe it to the owner of the land. Such a case may exist where the land is occupied by a tenant, who, by his lease, has obligated himself to pay taxes. Where this is the relation of the parties to the land, it would cause a shock to the moral sense if the law were to permit this tenant to neglect his duty and cut off his lessor's title by buying in the land at a tax sale. So the mortgagor, remaining in possession of the land, owes it to the mortgagee to keep down the taxes; and

196 it was decided, that where the sale was for cash, the giving of credit to the purchaser afterwards would not defeat it. In Donnel *v.* Bellas, 34 Penn. St., 157, the treasurer took a note from the purchaser instead of cash. The sale was held void, and incapable of being affirmed by the treasurer by receiving payment after leaving office. See the same case, 10 Penn. St., 341; 11 id., 341.

[1] Peters *v.* Heasely, 10 Watts, 208; Loud *v.* Penniman, 19 Pick., 539. A sale for the taxes of several years, one of which has been paid, is void. Kinsworthy *v.* Mitchell, 21 Ark., 145. And see Douglass *v.* Short, 3 Dev., 432. Sale of lands for the tax of the wrong party is void. Gardner *v.* Brown, Meigs, 354. Sale for two taxes, one of which is illegal, also void. Elwell *v.* Shaw, 1 Greenl., 339; Hardenburgh *v.* Kidd, 10 Cal., 402.

[2] It has already been stated, that the separate interests of different owners are, under some laws, assessed separately. In such a case, a sale of the land for a tax assessed against one does not cut off the interests of others. Irwin *v.* Bank of United States, 1 Penn. St., 349. Where the whole title is sold, it cuts off back taxes, unless other provision is made. Trego *v.* Huzzard, 19 Penn. St., 441; Irwin *v.* Trego, 22 id., 368; Same *v.* Same, 35 id., 9.

[3] See State *v.* Maxwell, 6 Wall., 268.

the law would justly be chargeable with connivance at fraud and dishonesty, if a mortgagor might allow the taxes to become delinquent, and then discharge them by a purchase which would at the same time cut off his mortgage. There is a general principle applicable to such cases; that a purchase made by one whose duty it was to pay the taxes shall operate as payment only; he shall acquire no rights as against a third party, by a neglect of the duty which he owed to such party. This principle is universal, and is so entirely reasonable as scarcely to need the support of authority. Show the existence of the duty, and the disqualification is made out in every instance.[1]

The cases to which attention is called in the margin, and many others to which they refer, will show the application of the rule under a great variety of circumstances. It has been applied to cases where the default was only in part that of the purchaser; as where he was tenant in common with others,[2] or where his own land was taxed as one parcel with that of another, and the

[1] Varney *v.* Stevens, 22 Me., 331; Gardiner *v.* Gerrish, 23 id., 46; Fuller *v.* Hodgdon, 25 id., 243; Mathews *v.* Light, 32 id., 305; Coombs *v.* Warren, 34 id., 89; Williams *v.* Hilton, 35 id., 547; Haskell *v.* Putnam, 42 id., 244; Coxe *v.* Wolcott, 27 Penn. St., 154; Coxe *v.* Gibson, id., 160; Oldhams *v.* Jones, 5 B. Monr., 458, 467; Blake *v.* Howe, 1 Aikens, 306; Willard *v.* Strong, 14 Vt., 532; Lacey *v.* Davis, 4 Mich., 140; Taylor *v.* Snyder, Wal. Ch., 492; Frye *v.* Bank of Illinois, 11 Ill., 367; Prettyman *v.* Walston, 34 id., 175; Higgins *v.* Crosby, 40 id., 260; Smith *v.* Lewis, 20 Wis., 369; Avery *v.* Judd, 21 id., 262; Barrett *v.* Welch, 22 id., 175; Phelan *v.* Boylan, 25 id., 679; Edgarton *v.* Schneider, 26 id., 385; Brown *v.* Simons, 44 N. H., 475; McLaughlin *v.* Green, 48 Miss., 175, 207; Carithers *v.* Weaver, 7 Kans., 110; Krutz *v.* Fisher, 8 id., 90; Kelsey *v.* Abbott, 13 Cal., 609; Barrett *v.* Amerein, 36 id., 322; McMinn *v.* Whelan, 27 id., 300; Coffinger *v.* Rice, 33 id., 408; Garwood *v.* Hastings, 38 id., 216; Savings and Loan Society *v.* Ordway, 38 id., 679.

[2] Lloyd *v.* Lynch, 28 Penn. St., 419; Maul *v.* Rider, 51 id., 377; Piatt *v.* St. Clair's Heirs, 6 Ohio, 227; Page *v.* Webster, 8 Mich., 263; Butler *v.* Porter, 13 id., 262; Dubois *v.* Campau, 24 id., 360; Choteau *v.* Jones, 11 Ill., 300, 322; Brown *v.* Hogle, 30 id., 119; Chickering *v.* Faile, 38 id., 342; State *v.* Williston, 20 Wis., 240; Phelan *v.* Boylan, 25 id., 679; Baker *v.* Whiting, 3 Sum., 475, Downer's Adm'r *v.* Smith, 38 Vt., 464. That payment by one tenant in common enures to the benefit of all, see Chickering *v.* Faile, 38 Ill., 342; McConnel *v.* Konepel, 46 id., 519. As to what right one might have to buy the interest of his cotenant after paying his own tax, there is some discussion in Butler *v.* Porter, 13 Mich., 262. As to the right of one tenant in common to buy in a matured tax title, see Kirkpatrick *v.* Mathiot, 4 W. & S., 251; Reinboth *v.* Zerbe Run Co., 29 Penn. St., 139; Frentz *v.* Klotsch, 28 Wis., 312.

whole was sold together;[1] and to a case where an agent to pay taxes made a purchase of his principal's lands, assuming to justify himself on the ground that his principal had neglected to supply him with the means of making payment.[2] In all such cases, and all to which the like reasons apply, the purchase, as between the parties, is in law a payment only; or, if made at second hand, from another who was purchaser at the public sale, it is allowed to operate, for the purposes of justice, only as a redemption,[3] and the party making it may have a remedy over for the money paid, or for any portion thereof, if in equity any other person who is benefited by the purchase ought to have paid it; otherwise not.

Some other cases are not so plain, because the duty as between the parties is not so definitely determined by their contract, or by their legal relation. While a mortgagor in general cannot be allowed to cut off his mortgage, by buying in the land at tax sale, yet if the mortgagee were in possession, receiving the issues and profits, and bound to pay the taxes himself, it might not be so clear that the mortgagor should be precluded from taking advantage of the mortgagee's neglect. If it were to be so held, there would seem to be reason for holding that the mortgagee also, by reason of his relation to the title, was precluded from becoming purchaser of the mortgagor's interest at a tax sale, and that his remedy would be confined to a payment for the protection of his lien, with a remedy over for the amount paid. It cannot be said in such a case, that either mortgagor or mortgagee is under no obligation to the government to pay the tax. On

[1] Cooley *v.* Waterman, 16 Mich., 366.

[2] McMahon *v.* McGraw, 26 Wis., 614. As to the disqualification of the agent to purchase his principal's land at tax sale, see further Oldhams *v.* Jones, 5 B. Monr., 458; Bartholomew *v.* Leach, 7 Watts, 472; Matthews *v.* Light, 32 Me., 305; Lindsley *v.* Sinclair, 24 Mich., 380; Krutz *v.* Fisher, 8 Kans., 90; Schedda *v.* Sawyer, 4 McLean, 181; Kelsey *v.* Abbott, 13 Cal., 609; Bernal *v.* Lynch, 36 id., 135, 146; Barton *v.* Moss, 32 Ill., 50. One who has bargained for the land, and is in possession under an agreement to purchase, occupies a similar position. Haskell *v.* Putnam, 42 Me., 244; Voris *v.* Thomas, 12 Ill., 442; Oliver *v.* Croswell, 42 id., 41. See Coxe *v.* Wolcott, 27 Penn. St., 154; Quin *v.* Quin, 27 Wis., 168.

[3] See Shepardson *v.* Elmore, 19 Wis., 424; Coxe *v.* Wolcott, 27 Penn. St., 154; Carithers *v.* Weaver, 7 Kan., 110; Bernal *v.* Lynch, 36 Cal., 135, 146.

the contrary, the tax being one that purposely is made to override the lien of the one as well as the title of the other, it might well, as it seems to us, be held that neither mortgagor nor mortgagee was at liberty to neglect the payment, as one step in bettering his condition at the expense of the other, but that the presumption of law should be that the party purchasing did so for the protection of his own interest merely. And so are some of the authorities.[1]

Whether one should be precluded by the naked fact that he claims title to the land, or that he has possession of it, from making a purchase in extinguishment of the right of another with whom he stands in no contract or fiduciary relations, is a question often touched by the discussions of courts without having as yet been very fully or comprehensively examined. So far as the cases hold that one who ought, as between himself and some third person, to pay the taxes, shall not build up a title on his own default, the principle is clear and well founded in equity. But when one owes no duty to any other in respect to the land, it is not so clear upon what principle of equity or of estoppel such other is to set up, as against him, his neglect to perform in due season his duty to the government.

There are some cases in which it has been distinctly held that possession, when the tax was assessed, fixed upon the possessor

[1] Fisk *v.* Brunette, 30 Wis., 102. In this case the mortgagee held the legal title, and he is spoken of in the opinion as being, in a certain sense, a trustee. *Dixon*, Ch. J., delivering the opinion, makes no mention of the earlier case of Sturdevant *v.* Mather, 20 Wis., 576, 585, in which he had referred to the same question, and to the decision in Williams *v.* Townsend, 31 N. Y., 411, 415, in a manner understood by the reporter to imply an approval. In the same connection he also referred "to Walthall *v.* Rives, 34 Ala., 91, and Harrison *v.* Roberts, 6 Fla., 711, in which it was held that a mortgagee may purchase and hold a paramount title under older judgment liens, and to Chapman *v.* Mull, 7 Ired. Eq., 292, and the observations of Sir Thomas Plummer, M. R., in Cholmondely *v.* Clinton, 2 Jac. & Wal., 181, et seq., upon the general question how far the principles applicable to dealings between trustee and *cestui que trust* apply to the case of mortgagor and mortgagee." The Illinois cases are very emphatic, that a mortgagee, like a trustee, cannot affect the rights of the mortgagor by purchasing the property at a sale for delinquent taxes accruing on the premises. Chickering *v.* Faile, 26 Ill., 507; Moore *v.* Titman, 44 id., 367. In Brown *v.* Simons, 4 N. H., 475, is a like decision, in a case in which the mortgagee was in possession. It is not very clear how far Williams *v.* Townsend, *supra*, was designed to lay down a contrary doctrine.

the duty to pay, and precluded his becoming a purchaser at a sale for the taxes when they became delinquent. In the leading case the occupant had gone into possession under an invalid tax title, and by the decision he was precluded from relying upon a second title which accerued while he was in the occupancy of the land.[1] The subject is dismissed with very brief mention, the court appearing to regard the claim as inequitable and unjust, but for what reason is not very clearly explained. Other cases treat the point as equally plain.[2] But it seems to us that it is deserving of more

[1] Douglas *v.* Dangerfield, 10 Ohio, 152.

[2] Choteau *v.* Jones, 11 Ill., 300, 322, per *Treat*, Ch. J. "The purchase of a portion of the land by George W. Jones, at a sale for taxes, did not stregthen his title. That purchase was made prior to the sale by the administrator. He was then one of the owners of the land, and as such bound to pay the taxes assessed upon it. The purchase was but a mode of paying the taxes legally chargeable against him." "He admits in his answer that he suffered the land to be sold, and bid it in for the purpose of defeating an older tax title, and not with a view of acquiring any new title." This doctrine is affirmed in Lacey *v.* Davis, 4 Mich., 140, 152, where it is said by *Martin*, J., to be of no importance whether a party claiming title to land is assessed personally for the tax or not. "It is the possession which creates the disability in the purchaser." The case holds that if one acquires the possession while the tax is a lien on the land, he is bound to discharge the lien, and cannot buy at tax sale. But see Lybrand *v.* Haney, 31 Wis., 230; Blackwood *v.* Van Vleet, 30 Mich., 118. In Tweed *v.* Metcalf, 4 id., 579, it was decided that one who had bought at a tax sale might buy the same land at a subsequent sale made at any time before redemption from the first had expired. The doctrine of Choteau *v.* Jones, *supra*, was affirmed in Voris *v.* Thomas, 12 Ill., 442, and the same general doctrine is asserted in Smith *v.* Lewis, 20 Wis., 350, 354, though there the case was between mortgagee and the assignee of the mortgage, and the relation of the parties precluded a purchase. The same remark may be made of Dubois *v.* Campau, 24 Mich., 368. Bassett *v.* Welch, 22 Wis., 175, goes the full length of deciding that the mere fact of possession when the taxes are assessed is a disqualification to buy. Jones *v.* Davis, 24 Wis., 229, was a case where one in possession of land had endeavored to cut off a judgment lien by a purchase at tax sale, corresponding to the case of purchase by a mortgagor. Whitney *v.* Gunderson, 31 Wis., 359, 379, asserts the broad doctrine that if one was in possession when the tax was assessed, "it then became his duty to pay the taxes, and he could not permit the lands to be sold for such taxes, and obtain a tax deed for the purpose of destroying an outstanding title." And see McMinn *v.* Whelan, 27 Cal., 300; Burrett *v.* Amerein, 36 Cal., 322. In Blakely *v.* Bestor, 13 Ill., 708, 714, *Trumbull*, J., apparently puts the case on the ground of an obligation or duty as between parties. "It is insisted," he says, "that the defendant is not in a position to avail himself of an outstanding tax title, be it ever so regular, for the reason that he is shown by the record to have been in the posses-

consideration whether, where parties stand to each other in the position of adverse claimants to land, either of them can insist that the other shall discharge a duty to the government for his protection. There being nothing in the relation of the parties to each other upon which an estoppel can be raised, it is necessary to look elsewhere for the disqualification insisted upon; and this can only be found in some general rule of public policy. It is certainly an imperative requirement of public policy that the revenues of the state shall be collected, and that no one shall be allowed to defraud the treasury of his due proportion; but in the case where a tax sale has been made there is no fraud, and the revenue chargeable upon the land has been received. No wrong has consequently been done to the state. There has been delay in payment, but it is one for which the state makes ample provision, and for which it charges the party concerned with all costs, and an interest sufficient fully to compensate for any public inconvenience. It is not perceived that the state can then have any complaint to make, as the duty owing to it, though performed tardily, has been performed at last. The state, then, not being wronged in the purchase, it would seem that whatever individual objects to it ought to be able to point out how and in what particular it wrongs him.

It is difficult to dispute the truth of what is said by the supreme court of Pennsylvania, that "there is nothing in reason or law to

sion of the premises at the time the taxes accrued and the sale took place, wherefore it is said that it was his duty to have paid the taxes, and that he ought not to be permitted to avail himself of a tax title acquired through his default. This may or may not be so. It does not necessarily follow that because a person is in possession of premises he is bound to pay the taxes assessed upon them; he may occupy them as a tenant under an agreement that his landlord shall pay the taxes, and in such case there would be no obligation on the tenant to pay them, particularly if, in pursuance of the agreement, they were listed for taxation in the landlord's name." In Swift *v.* Agnes, 33 Wis., 228, it is decided that where one owning land, and bound to pay taxes thereon, permits them to be sold and deeded for such taxes, and then purchases the tax title, and causes it to be conveyed to a third person for his benefit, he cannot set up such title as a defense in ejectment against one who has purchased at a sale on execution against him since the execution of the tax deed. There is nothing in the fact that the owner of land has become the purchaser at tax sale which can estop him from claiming the surplus moneys. Russell *v.* Reed, 27 Penn. St., 166.

prevent a man who holds a defective title from purchasing a better at a treasurer's sale for taxes."[1] As between himself and any adverse claimant it is an unimportant consideration whether the one or the other was in possession. If the state, in taxing land, takes any notice of ownership, it is either for the convenience of the officers in making collections, or for information to parties concerned. The tax is upon every possible interest in the land; and all parties having interests are equally under obligation to the state to make payment. The penalty for failure is a forfeiture or sale which will cut them all off; and while, without doubt, any one may defeat such a sale who can give satisfactory reasons for an assertion that it would be unjust to him for the purchaser to be allowed to rely upon it, it is not perceived that any other person can well insist upon a right to do so. This, of course, is aside from any question of irregularities or defects; in general, any person may rely upon those when the tax title is made use of against him; as they go, or may go, to the power of the officer to sell at all.[2]

Bids by the state or county. It is not an uncommon provision that, if no bidders offer to take the land and pay the tax, it shall be bid in for the state or for the county. A purchase on such a bid would give the state or county the usual rights of a

[1] *Woodward*, J., in Coxe *v.* Gibson, 27 Penn. St., 160, 165. And see Blackwood *v.* Van Vleet, 30 Mich., 118.

[2] It is held in California that one in possession of lands, if under no legal or moral obligation to pay the tax, may buy in the lands at tax sale. Moss *v.* Shear, 25 Cal., 38. The same ruling is made in Kansas. Bowman *v.* Cockrill, 6 Kans., 311, 332. In Blackwood *v.* Van Vleet, 30 Mich., 118, it is said that "to preclude any person from making and relying upon a purchase of lands at tax sale, there must be something in the circumstances of the case which imposes upon him a duty to the state to pay the tax, or something which renders it inequitable, as between himself and the holder of the existing title, that he should make the purchase." And it is denied that the mere fact, that one is in possession of the land when the tax is levied, should preclude his becoming purchaser when the land is not assessed to him, and he is bound by no contract relations to pay the tax. The person taxed cannot get a title at tax sale. Garwood *v.* Hastings, 38 Cal., 216; McMinn *v.* Whelan, 27 id., 300. A collusive purchase, made to cut off a mortgage, may be set aside. Savings and Loan Society *v.* Ordway, 38 Cal., 679; Stears *v.* Hollenbeck, 38 Iowa, 550.

purchaser, and no more. Whether a deed would be requisite to carry into effect such a purchase must depend upon the statute.[1]

Different sales at the same time. Where the taxes of several years are delinquent at the same time, sales are sometimes permitted to be made separately for each year's tax. Such sales might raise serious questions as between purchasers, if two or more should severally buy the land at sales bearing the same date, and subject to the same redemption. In Iowa it seems that such separate sales are unauthorized.[2] Such questions might and should be settled by statute.

Certificate of sale. The sale is usually accompanied or followed by the issue to the purchaser of a certificate, which recites the fact of sale, and states the time when the purchaser will become entitled to a conveyance.[3] No title passes until the time

[1] Commissioners authorized to bid the amount of the tax on behalf of the county, if they bid more, may have the land left on their hands unless the county see fit to take it. The bid cuts off the prior title. Russell *v.* Reed, 27 Penn. St., 166. And see Cuttle *v.* Brockway, 32 id., 45. Commissioners *authorized* to bid off land for the United States, unless some person will bid two-thirds the appraised value, are not *compelled* to do so, and a sale to another bidder for less is not invalid. Turner *v.* Smith, 14 Wall., 553, 562. Where lands are bid in by a county at a tax sale, and the law provides for their being subsequently sold after a specified notice, a private sale without the notice is void. The provision for such a sale is to be regarded as a proceeding to collect taxes, and must be followed. Jenks *v.* Wright, 61 Penn. St., 410.

In Kansas, the county treasurer holds a certificate of sale to the county until it can be sold to an individual, and then assigns the certificate. The county commissioners cannot control his action in this regard. State *v.* Magill, 4 Kan., 415.

[2] Preston *v.* Van Gorder, 31 Iowa, 250; Shoemaker *v.* Lacey, 38 id., 277. In Iowa, where the treasurer, on the same day, made different sales of the same land for the taxes of different years, and the owner, being aware of but one sale, had redeemed therefrom in good faith, he was held entitled to redeem from the other after the statutory time, by paying the amount for which the land was sold, with legal interest and penalty. Shoemaker *v.* Lacey, 38 Iowa, 277, citing Noble *v.* Bullis, 23 id., 559. In California, it is held that a sale for a city tax of one year will not cut off the tax for the preceding year. Cowell *v.* Washburn, 22 Cal., 519.

[3] The certificate is evidence of the sale, but the record of sale is better evidence. McCready *v.* Sexton, 29 Iowa, 356; Henderson *v.* Oliver, 32 id., 512; Clark *v.* Thompson, 37 id., 536.

allowed for redemption, if any, has expired,[1] nor until the proper conveyance has been executed. Until then the purchaser has an inchoate right, which he might perhaps protect as a purchaser on execution might;[2] but he has no title.[3]

The deed. The requirements of a deed are not uniform in the different states. In general it should recite enough to show an authority to sell, but it need not set out all the prior proceedings.[4]

The tax deed as evidence. It has been shown that, according to the principles of the common law, the purchaser at a tax sale when he attempts to enforce rights under his purchase, is under the necessity of taking upon himself the burden of showing that the purchase was made pursuant to law. To do this he must show the substantial regularity of all the proceedings. The deed of

[1] In Kansas it seems to be held that title passes at the sale, subject to be defeated by redemption. Stebbins *v.* Guthrie, 4 Kans., 353.

[2] See Ferguson *v.* Miles, 3 Gilm., 358; Stout *v.* Keyes, 2 Doug., Mich., 184. Under the Missouri statute it has been held that the tax deed does not relate back to the sale, where redemption was allowed afterwards. Donohoe *v.* Veal, 19 Mo., 331.

[3] Tilson *v.* Thompson, 10 Pick., 359; Hightown *v.* Freedle, 5 Sneed, 312; Alexander *v.* Bush, 46 Penn. St., 62; Stephens *v.* Holmes, 26 Ark., 48. A deed executed after the officer's term has expired is void. Hoffman *v.* Bell, 61 Penn. St., 444. But it is no objection that it was executed after the taxpayer's death. Curry *v.* Fowler, 3 A. K. Marsh., 504.

[4] See Little *v.* Herndon, 10 Wall., 26; Sibley *v.* Smith, 2 Mich., 486; Elston *v.* Kennicott, 46 Ill., 187; Wetherbee *v.* Dunn, 32 Cal., 106; Large *v.* Fisher, 49 Mo., 307. Where a statute authorized a sale of real estate after fourteen days demand of payment, but required the deed to "state the cause of sa le," etc. and also the particulars of the proceedings preparatory to a sale: *Held*, that a deed was void which did not state that the taxes were not paid within fourteen days after demand. Harrington *v.* Worcester, 6 Allen, 576. Where notice is required by law to be given to the owner before a deed is made, the requirement must be strictly complied with. Denike *v.* Rourke, 3 Biss., 39. A tax deed is not void for slight irregularities or variances from the statutory form Bowman *v.* Cockrill, 6 Kans., 311; Haynes *v.* Heller, 12 id., 381. The recitals in a tax deed are in Kansas *prima facie* evidence of the facts recited. Hobson *v.* Dutton, 9 Kans., 477. The deed shows no title without acknowledgment. Tilson *v.* Thompson, 10 Pick., 359; Stierlin *v.* Daley, 37 Mo., 483; Dalton *v.* Fenn, 40 id., 109. In New York it seems that if the deed purports to be given on a sale of the lands as nonresident, when in fact they were assessed to a former owner, it is void. Ratler *v.* Worth, N. Y. Court of Appeals, 11 Albany Law Journal, 401.

conveyance would not stand for this evidence. It would prove its own execution; nothing more. The power to execute it must be shown before the deed itself could have any force; for no officer can make out his own jurisdiction to act by the mere fact of acting. In all administrative proceedings the facts upon which jurisdiction depends must always be shown by him who claims anything under its exercise. This principle is undisputed. It leads us inevitably to this conclusion; that whoever claims lands under a sale for delinquent taxes, must take upon himself the burden of proving that taxes were duly assessed, which were a charge upon the land, and that the successive steps were taken which led to a lawful sale therefor, at which he or some one under whom he claims became the purchaser.[1]

The difficulty of making the complete showing in these cases has been thought to be so great as to render some modification of the rule reasonable, and statutes have from time to time been made in that direction. The early statutes were probably not as comprehensive in their terms as their authors intended; at least,

[1] Stead's Lessee *v.* Course, 4 Cranch, 403; Williams *v.* Peyton, 4 Wheat., 77; McClung *v.* Ross, 5 id., 116; Thatcher *v.* Powell, 6 id., 119; Rondendorff *v.* Taylor, 4 Pet., 349; Clarke *v.* Strickland, 2 Curt. C. C., 439; Minor *v.* McLean, 4 McLean, 138; Moore *v.* Brown, 4 id., 211; same case in error, 11 How., 414; Mahew *v.* Davis, 4 McLean, 213; Parker *v.* Overman, 18 How., 137; Brown *v.* Veazie, 25 Me., 359; Payson *v.* Hall, 30 id., 319; Loomis *v.* Pingree, 43 id., 299; Lovejoy *v.* Lunt, 48 id., 377; Williamsburgh *v.* Lord, 51 id., 599; French *v.* Patterson, 61 id,. 203; Doe *v.* Roe, 2 Hawks, 17; Avery *v.* Rose, 4 Dev., 549; Love *v.* Gates, 4 Dev. & Bat., 353; Garrett *v* White, 3 Ired. Eq., 131; Jordan *v.* Rouse, 1 Jones, L., 119; Yancey *v.* Hopkins, 1 Munf., 419; Christy *v.* Minor, 4 id., 431; Nalle *v.* Fenwick, 4 Rand., 585; Allen *v.* Smith, 1 Leigh, 231; Chapman *v.* Doe, 2 id., 329; Polk *v.* Rose, 25 Md., 153; Beatty *v.* Mason, 30 id., 409; Dyer *v.* Boswell, 39 id., 465; Doe *v* .Insurance Co., 8 S. & M., 197; Natchez *v.* Minor, 10 id., 246; Rule *v.* Parker, Cooke, 278; Hamilton *v.* Burum, 3 Yerg., 355; Pope *v.* Headen, 5 Ala., 433; Lyons *v.* Hunt, 11 id., 295; Blakeney *v.* Ferguson, 8 Ark., 272; Shearer *v.* Woodburn, 10 Penn St., 511; McReynolds *v.* Longenberger, 57 id., 13; Bucknall *v.* Story, 36 Cal., 67; Richardson *v.* Dorr, 5 Vt., 9; Fitch *v.* Casey, 2 Greene, Iowa, 300; Kellog *v.* McLaughlin, 8 Ohio, 114; McMillan *v.* Robbins, 5 id., 31; Williams *v.* State, 6 Blackf., 36; Doe *v.* Flagler, 1 Ind., 542; Doe *v.* Sweetzer, 2 id., 649; Barnes *v.* Doe, 4 id., 132; Kyle *v.* Malin, 8 id., 34; Atkins *v.* Kinman, 20 Wend., 241; Doughty *v.* Hope, 3 Denio, 595; Waldron *v.* McComb, 1 Hill, 107; Sharp *v.* Spier, 4 id., 76; Tallman *v.* White, 2 N. Y., 66; Bennett *v.* Buffalo, 17 id., 383; Cruger *v.* Dougherty, 43 id., 107; Chicago *v.* Wright, 32 Ill., 192; Scammon *v.* Chicago, 40 id., 146.

as construed by the courts, they did not change to any considerable extent the former rule. Thus, a statute which declared that the deed should be evidence of the regularity of the sale, was held to prove *only* the regularity of the proceedings at the sale, leaving the purchaser still under the necessity of showing the regularity of the prior proceedings.[1]

Where the statute makes the deed *prima facie* evidence that the requirements of the sale have been complied with, it is necessary first that the holder of the tax title should prove the performance by the assessor and collector of the several acts which are conditions precedent to the power to sell; and then the contestant is put to proof that the requirements of the law, as to time and manner of sale, were not complied with.[2] So a statute which makes the deed evidence of a title in fee simple in the owner, is held to be evidence only of such a title after the right to give the deed has been shown by the proof of anterior proceedings that support it.[3] In later statutes language has been chosen with more care, and the tax deed, given by a competent officer, has been declared *prima facie* evidence not only of the regularity of the sale, but of all prior proceedings, and of title in the purchaser. This, it will be seen, changes wholly the burden of proof, which before rested upon the purchaser, and casts it upon the party who would contest the sale. The purchaser is no longer under the necessity to show the correctness of the proceedings, but the contestant must show in what particular he claims them to be incorrect. The power to enact such laws has been denied in argument, but the decisions sustain them.[4] These decisions are that the statutes

[1] Tallman *v.* White, 2 N. Y., 66; Striker *v.* Kelly, 2 Denio, 323; Doughty *v.* Hope, 3 id., 594; Beekman *v.* Bigham, 5 N. Y., 366; Westbrook *v.* Willey, 47 id., 457; Rowland *v.* Doty, Har. Ch., 3; Scott *v.* Young Men's Society, 1 Doug., Mich., 119; Latimer *v.* Lovett, 2 id., 204; Ives *v.* Kimball, 1 Mich., 308; Yenda *v.* Wheeler, 9 Texas, 408; Wilson *v.* Lemon, 23 Ind., 433.

[2] Robson *v.* Osborn, 13 Texas, 298.

[3] See cases above cited. Also Merrick *v.* Hutt, 15 Ark., 331. A declaration in a tax law that the tax deed should be "good and effectual both at law and in equity," gives no special sanction to the conveyance beyond that derived from the general principles of law. The purchaser must show that all prerequisites were complied with. Hadley *v.* Tankersley, 8 Texas, 12.

[4] Pillow *v.* Roberts, 13 How., 472; Williams *v.* Kirtland, 13 Wall., 306, 310; Freeman *v.* Thayer, 33 Me., 76; Orono *v.* Veazie, 57 Me., 517; Hand *v.* Ballou,

take away no substantial rights; they only regulate the order of proceeding in the legal tribunals, in exhibiting the evidence of substantial rights; and they rest on the solid foundation of the supreme authority of the legislature over the whole subject of evidence; an authority, however, which has this very plain limit; that it cannot deprive one of his property by making his adversary's claim to it, whatever that claim may be, conclusive of its own validity. It cannot, therefore, make the tax deed conclusive evidence of the holder's title to the land.[1]

Statutes giving a peculiar effect to conveyances on sales made for taxes, unless in express terms declared applicable to the case

12 N. Y., 541; Forbes *v.* Halsey, 26 id., 52; Johnson *v.* Elwood, 53 id., 435; Steedman *v.* Planter's Bank, 7 Ark., 424; Briscoe *v.* Coulter, 18 Ark., 423; Butts *v.* Francis, 4 Conn., 424; Ray *v.* Murdock, 36 Miss., 692; Belcher *v.* Mhoon, 47 id., 613; Abbott *v.* Lindenbower, 42 Mo., 162; S. C., 46 id., 291; Cook *v.* Hackleman, 45 id., 317; Hoffman *v.* Bell, 61 Penn. St., 444; Delaplaine *v.* Cook, 7 Wis., 44; Stewart *v.* McSweeney, 14 id., 468; Whitney *v.* Marshall, 17 id., 174; Smith *v.* Cleveland, 17 id., 556; Lumsden *v.* Cross, 10 id., 282; Allen *v.* Armstrong, 16 Iowa, 508; Adams *v.* Beale, 19 id., 61; Eldridge *v.* Kurhl, 27 id., 160; Clark *v.* Connor, 28 id., 311, 315; Hurley *v.* Woodruff, 30 id., 260; Genther *v.* Fuller, 36 id., 604; Sprague *v.* Pitt, McCahon, 212; Sibley *v.* Smith, 2 Mich., 486; Lacey *v.* Davis, 4 id., 140; Amberg *v.* Rogers, 9 id., 332; Wright *v.* Dunham, 13 id., 414; Groesbeck *v.* Seeley, id., 329; Stanbery *v.* Sillon, 13 Ohio (N. S.), 571; Turney *v.* Yeoman, 14 Ohio, 207; Smith *v.* Chapman, 10 Grat., 445. It is competent to make certificate of city engineer *prima facie* evidence of the validity of a charge against owners of property for special assessment. St. Louis *v.* Coons, 37 Mo., 44; St. Louis *v.* Armstrong, 38 id., 29.

[1] In Iowa statutes are sustained which make tax deeds conclusive evidence that the property was regularly listed and assessed, and that it was regularly advertised and sold. Allen *v.* Armstrong 16 Iowa, 508; McCready *v.* Sexton, 29 id., 356; Rima *v.* Cowan, 31 id., 125; Clark *v.* Thompson, 37 id., 536; Madison *v.* Sexton, id., 562; Smith *v.* Easton, id., 584; Easton *v.* Perry, id., 681. The original owner may still contest the liability of the land to any tax; and it is said in general terms by the court that on all *jurisdictional* questions the deed cannot be made conclusive. See Martin *v.* Cole, 38 Iowa, 141. It is manifest, however, that this word *jurisdictional* is not employed in the same sense here as it often is in tax cases; a sense that makes each necessary step a jurisdictional requisite to the next; for in Iowa some of the most important steps in the proceedings are held to be conclusively established by the deed. On the question what shall be sufficient to rebut the *prima facie* case made for the tax purchaser by his deed, and cast upon him the *onus* of showing regular proceedings, the following cases are instructive: Bidleman *v.* Brooks, 28 Cal., 72; Rayburn *v.* Kuhl, 10 Iowa, 92; Lacey *v.* Davis, 4 Mich., 140; Wright *v.* Dunham, 13 id., 414; Case *v.* Dean, 16 id., 12; Hall *v.* Kellogg, id., 130.

of local and special assessments, such as those for paving streets, etc, do not apply to them at all, and the purchaser under proceedings of that nature will be compelled to rely upon the common law rule, and prove regularity.[1]

Judicial sales for taxes. In some of the states it has been deemed advisable to provide that, before sales shall be made of lands for the satisfaction of delinquent taxes, a judicial determination of the delinquency shall be had.[2] A judicial hearing in such a case may fairly be understood to have in view, *first*, the protection of the parties taxed, by giving them the opportunity to inspect the proceedings and make their objections before the final steps are taken which might conclude their rights forever; and, *second*, the greater security of purchasers at the sales, which may reasonably be supposed to follow a judicial determination that the proceedings are such as, under the law, will justify a sale being made. It has not been deemed advisable, in a work so general in its plan as the present, to enter at large into an examination of the proceedings for which provision is made under statutes of different states. The same general principles apply to them all. In some cases — usually cases of street or other special assessments — the judicial proceedings begin when the assessors have completed their work, and the assessment is examined and confirmed before process for collection is issued; or, if the assessment is found to be defective, or is believed to be unjust, it is set aside at that stage, and the case sent back to the assessors for new action; or the proceedings are simply quashed, leaving the authorities to begin anew if they shall think it advisable to do so.[3] The local statutes differ so much in the authority

[1] Sharp *v.* Spier, 4 Hill, 76; Bucknall *v.* Story, 36 Cal., 67; Kelly *v.* Medlin, 26 Tex., 48; Stierlin *v.* Daley, 37 Mo., 483; Glass *v.* White, 5 Sneed, 475.

[2] The present constitution of Illinois requires the legislature to provide, in all cases where it is necessary to sell real estate for the nonpayment of taxes or assessments, for state, county or municipal purposes, that a return shall be made to some general officer of the county having authority to receive state and county taxes; and such officer alone, upon the order or judgment of some court of record, is to have the power to sell. Hills *v.* Chicago, 60 Ill., 86; Otis *v.* Chicago, 62 id., 299; Webster *v.* Chicago, 62 id., 302.

[3] The following are cases of confirmation of special assessments under New York statutes: Matter of Harman Street, 16 Johns., 231; Matter of Dover Street, 1 Cow., 74; Matter of Fourth Avenue, 3 Wend., 452; Matter of Twenty-

they confer upon the courts, that the decisions made in one state are commonly of little service as affording a guide to the action of courts in other states. Under some statutes the action of the assessing boards is allowed to be reviewed on the facts as well as on the law; under others, only questions of the regularity and legality of the proceedings are submitted to the court. More generally the court takes up the case at the point were the collector has demonstrated his inability to collect the tax from residents by distress and sale of goods and chattels, and when the tax upon nonresident or unseated lands has remained unpaid, for the period allowed by law for making voluntary payment, before compulsory proceedings are suffered to be resorted to.

In any judicial proceeding the court which assumes to act must have that authority of law for the purpose which is called jurisdiction. This consists in *first*, authority over the subject matter, and *second*, authority over the parties concerned. The first comes from the statutory law, which designates the particular proceeding as one of which the court may take cognizance when the parties are properly before it; the second comes from the proper institution of proceedings, and the service of process upon the parties concerned, or something which is equivalent to such service. Concerning jurisdiction of the subject matter, it is only necessary to observe that it must come wholly from the constitution or statutes of the state; the common law giving to the courts no authority in such cases. Moreover that which is conferred is a special and limited jurisdiction. The importance of this fact appears in that familiar principle that nothing is taken by intendment in fav-

Sixth Street, 12 id., 203; Matter of Furman Street, 17 id., 649; Matter of Livingston Street, 18 id., 556; Matter of De Graw Street, 18 id., 568; Matter of Pearl Street, 19 id., 651; Matter of John and Cherry Streets, 19 id., 659; Matter of William and Anthony Streets, 19 id., 678; Matter of South Seventh Street, 48 Barb., 12; Matter of Bushwick Avenue, 48 id., 9; Matter of Central Park, 51 id., 277, 303; *In re* Sharp, 56 N. Y., 257; *In re* Van Antwerp, 56 id., 261; Striker *v.* Kelley, 7 Hill, 9; S. C., 2 Denio, 323; Embury *v.* Connor, 3 N. Y., 511, 523; Matter of Canal and Walker Streets, 12 id., 406; King *v.* Mayor, etc., of New York., 36 id., 182; Matter of Broadway, 49 id., 150. That the court in passing upon the assessment cannot review political action, such as the determination of the necessity or propriety of opening the street, or the proper limits of an assessment district, see Matter of Albany Street, 11 Wend., 149; Matter of William and Anthony Streets, 19 id., 676; Matter of John and Cherry Streets, 19 id., 659; Matter of Livingston Street, 18 id., 556.

or of the action of a court of special and limited jurisdiction, but it must appear, by the recitals of the record itself, that the facts existed which authorized the court to act, and that in acting the court has kept within the limits of its lawful authority. And this principle is applicable to the case of a court of general jurisdiction, which in the particular case is exercising a special and limited authority, as well as to the case of special courts created for such special and limited authority only.[1]

Taking up the case after a failure to make collection is supposed to have occurred, the first step commonly required to be taken is, the making by the collector or some proper officer, of a report to the court showing that the supposed delinquency actually exists. This being the document that calls into activity an authority of the court before latent, it must conform to the law in every substantial requirement, or it will fail entirely to have any efficiency for the purpose.[2]

The next step will perhaps be, the giving of notice which shall stand in the place of the process which in ordinary cases brings the parties before the court.

Proceedings of this nature are not usually proceedings against

[1] McClung *v.* Ross, 5 Wheat., 116; Thatcher *v.* Powell, 6 id., 119; Francis' Lessee *v.* Washburn, 5 Hayw., 294; Tift *v.* Griffin, 5 Geo., 185; Dakin *v.* Hudson, 6 Cow., 221; Deming *v.* Corwin, 11 Wend., 647; Sheldon *v.* Wright, 5 N. Y., 497; Bridge *v.* Ford, 4 Mass., 641; Smith *v.* Rice, 11 id., 511; Barrett *v.* Crane, 16 Vt., 246; Jennings *v.* Stafford, 1 Ired., 404; Harshaw *v.* Taylor, 3 Jones (N. C.), 513; Perrine *v.* Farr, 22 N. J., 356; Platt *v.* Stewart, 10 Mich., 260. Proceedings in these cases are governed by the same principles which govern other judicial sales. Jones *v.* Gillis, 45 Cal., 541; Eitel *v.* Foote, 39 Cal., 439. Certain lands were sold for taxes. In all the proceedings, including the order of sale, the lands were described as in A. county. In point of fact two-thirds thereof were in B. county. *Held*, that as to these at least the sale was void. Williams *v.* Harris, 4 Sneed, 332. The confirmation of an assessment by the court fixes the character of the property as resident or nonresident, and if a resident becomes nonresident afterwards, the collector will still proceed as against a resident. Gossett *v.* Kent, 19 Ark., 601.

[2] See Marsh *v.* Chestnut, 14 Ill., 223; Charles *v.* Waugh, 35 id., 315; Morrill *v.* Swartz, 39 id., 108; Fox *v.* Turtle, 55 id., 377; People *v.* Olin, Sup. Ct. Ill., (1875); 7 Chicago Legal News, 323. The collector's report is only *prima facie* evidence of delinquency, and is subject to be disproved. Andrews *v.* Rumsey, Sup. Ct. Ill. (1875), 7 Chicago Legal News, 322. See Denham *v.* People, 67 Ill., 414.

parties,[1] nor, in the case of lands or interests in lands belonging to persons unknown, can they be. They are proceedings which have regard to the land itself rather than to the owners of the land, and if the owners are named in the proceedings, and personal notice is provided for, it is rather from tenderness to their interests, and in order to make sure that the opportunity for a hearing shall not be lost to them, than from any necessity that the case shall assume that form. As in all other cases of proceedings *in rem*. if the law makes provision for publication of notice in a form and manner reasonably calculated to bring the proceedings to the knowledge of the parties who exercise ordinary diligence in looking after their interests in the lands, it is all that can be required.

We refer to a few cases as illustrative of the general principles on which the judicial action must be supported. In a leading case in the federal supreme court, it appeared that the statute under which the proceeding was had, required the sheriff, in the event of nonpayment of taxes by a specified time, to levy the same by distress and sale of the goods and chattels of the person in default. Failing thus to collect, he was to report the failure to the county court, whose duty it then was to direct its clerk to make out a certificate of the lands liable for the taxes, together with the amount of the taxes and charges due thereon, and to publish the same, and if the taxes and charges were not then paid within thirty days, judgment was to be entered for the amount due, and execution to issue upon which the land might be sold and conveyed. The sheriff made no such report as the statute provided for, and for want of this it was held that the court never obtained jurisdiction to proceed in the case.[2] Moreover the clerk never made publication of the list, and this failure would have

[1] Parks *v.* Miller, 48 Ill., 360; Schaeffer *v.* People, 60 id., 179. Where a sale is to be confirmed by a court, no one is to be heard to oppose it who is not adversely interested. One describing himself simply as "tenant in possession" shows no right to be heard. Black *v.* Percifield, 1 Ark., 472.

[2] Thatcher *v.* Powell, 6 Wheat., 119, following with approval Francis' Lessee *v.* Washburn, 5 Hayw., 294. To the same effect is McClung *v.* Ross, 5 Wheat., 116. And see Thacher *ex parte*, 3 Sneed, 344; Spellman *v.* Curtenius, 12 Ill., 409; Morrill *v.* Swartz, 39 id., 108; Fox *v.* Turtle, 55 id., 377; Fortman *v.* Ruggles, 58 id., 207; Schæffer *v.* People, 60 id., 79; Mayo *v.* Ah Loy, 32 Cal., 477.

been fatal to the proceedings if the proper report had been made.[1] In other cases the following errors and imperfections have been held to render the judicial proceedings void: Proceeding to judgment before the time limited for voluntary payment of the taxes had expired;[2] rendering the judgment in a proceeding not taken against "all owners and claimants," and by service on the land, as the statute required;[3] rendering judgment upon a collector's report which failed to show, as the statute required, whether the delinquent taxes were state taxes or county taxes;[4] applying for and obtaining judgment at a different term from that at which the statute required the application to be made.[5] And a judgment is void which is given in figures merely, with neither words nor signs to indicate that money is intended, or if it is, what denomination of money the figures stand for.[6]

The defects which were held fatal in the cases referred to, it will be seen, were with one exception in which the judgment was meaningless, all defects which went to the power of the court to act at all. The proceeding to judgment and sale is an ulterior proceeding which, under the law, must have for its antecedents the proper showing that an attempt to collect has proved ineffectual,[7] and that the case has been brought before the court by proper notice and at a proper time. But when those facts ap-

[1] Thatcher v. Powell, 6 Wheat., 119. See also Spellman v. Curtenius, 12 Ill., 409; Charles v. Waugh, 35 id., 315; McKee v. Champaign County, 53 id., 477; Fortman v. Ruggles, 58 id., 207; Abbott v. Lindenbower, 42 Mo., 162; McGahen v. Case, 6 Iowa, 331.

[2] Williams v. Gleason, 5 Iowa, 284. For the same principle, see Pickett v. Hartsock, 15 Ill., 279.

[3] Mayo v. Ah Loy, 32 Cal., 477.

[4] Morrill v. Swartz, 39 Ill., 108. See also Pickett v. Hartsock, 15 id., 279.

[5] Brown v. Hogle, 30 Ill., 119.

[6] Lawrence v. Fast, 20 Ill., 338; Lane v. Bommelmann, 21 id., 143; Eppinger v. Kirby, 23 id., 521; Dukes v. Rowley, 24 id., 210; Bailey v. Doolittle, 24 id., 577; Woods v. Freeman, 1 Wall., 398.

[7] It can be no objection to a judgment against the land for taxes, that the collector did not make the tax out of the personalty, when the collector did distrain the personalty, and the objector replevied the same out of the collector's hands. Deerham v. People, 67 Ill., 414. It is no objection to an application for judgment against lands that the valuation is excessive. Spencer v. People, Sup. Ct. Ill. (1874), 6 Chicago Legal News, 215.

pear by the record of the court, and the judgment has been rendered, all questions of regularity in the prior proceedings are foreclosed..[1] And not only that, but irregular action of the court itself will not render its judgment invalid, though it might authorize a reversal in an appellate court if a review is allowed by statute. It is a principle of general application, that while a judgment which has been rendered without competent jurisdiction may be treated as a mere nullity everywhere, yet that for mere irregularities it can be assailed only in a direct proceeding for that purpose; that is to say, by motion or petition in the same case, or by some proceeding in the nature of a review in error.[2]

In the proceedings subsequent to judgment the rules which govern ordinary judicial sales are applicable.[3] The deed given by the officer who sells by virtue of such a judgment should show, by its recitals, an authority presumptively sufficient to authorize it, and indeed this is usually required by the statute, which prescribes a form reciting the judgment and sale.[4] The deed cannot be evidence of the regularity of the proceedings unless made so by statute.[5]

[1] See Mayo *v.* Foley, 40 Cal., 281; Reeve *v.* Kennedy, 43 id., 643; Jones *v.* Gillis, 45 id., 541.

[2] Chestnut *v.* Marsh, 12 Ill., 173, is a leading case in tax matters illustrative of this principle. See also Atkins *v.* Hinman, 2 Gilm., 437; Merritt *v.* Thompson, 14 id., 716; Wilkins' Lessee *v.* Husc, 9 Ohio, 154; Eitel *v.* Foote, 39 Cal., 439; *Ex parte* Kellogg, 6 Vt., 509; Edgarton *v.* Hart, 8 id., 207; Wall *v.* Trumbull, 16 Mich., 228; Daily *v.* Newman, 14 La. An., 580; Cadmus *v.* Jackson, 52 Penn. St., 295; Wallace *v.* Brown, 22 Ark., 118; Carter *v.* Walker, 2 Ohio (N. S.), 339. As to the recitals necessary in such cases see Atkins *v.* Hinman, 2 Gilm., 437; Young *v.* Thompson, 14 Ill., 380; Dukes *v.* Rowley, 24 id., 210; Bailey *v.* Doolittle, 24 id., 577; Dentler *v.* State, 4 Blackf., 258; Williams *v.* State, 6 id., 36. In Cadmus *v.* Jackson, 52 Penn. St., 295; it was held that a tax sale under a judgment could not be defeated by showing that the tax was paid before judgment. This showing is sometimes permitted under statutes. See Curry *v.* Hinman, 11 Ill., 420; Conway *v.* Cable, 37 id., 82.

[3] Jones *v.* Gillis, 45 Cal., 541.

[4] As to the necessary recitals in the deeds, see McDermott *v.* Scully, 27 Ark., 226; Brown *v.* Hogle, 30 Ill., 119; Wetherbee *v.* Dunn, 32 Cal., 106.

[5] See Elston *v.* Kennicott, 46 Ill., 187; Little *v.* Herndon, 10 Wall., 26. In California where lands are assessed as an entirety to several, a part of whom pay portions of the tax, the court in rendering judgment should ascertain what interests are delinquent, and exonerate the rest. People *v.* Shimmins, 42 Cal., 121.

CHAPTER XVI.

REDEMPTION OF LANDS FROM TAX SALES.

It is not the policy of the law that any man should forfeit his estate because from inability, or even from negligence, he has failed to meet his engagements or to perform his duties by some exact day which has been prescribed by statute. On the contrary, it is for the welfare of every community, that the law should favor the citizen in all reasonable measures for the preservation of his estate, against losses which might result from his misfortunes or his faults, extending to him all the liberality that is consistent with justice to others and a proper regard to the interest of the state. The principle is recognized in the liberality shown to those desirous to redeem from the forfeiture of mortgages, and in the provisions made for redemption from judicial sales. It is also recognized in the laws providing for redemption from tax sales.

The statutes on this subject have little uniformity, but certain general rules govern the right to redeem under them all; and it may be sufficient for our purposes to refer to these.

1. The statutes which give the right are to be regarded favorably and construed with liberality. Abundant reason for this is assigned in the cases which recognize the rule. It has been justly remarked that the right of the government to sell lands for taxes, as it is accustomed to do, can only be maintained on "the absolute sovereignty of the state in the exercise of its taxing power. But it is a severe exercise of power. To divest ownership, without personal notice and without direct compensation, is the instance in which a constitutional government approaches most near to an unrestrained tyranny. Whatever tends to modify this right is favorable to the citizen, and ought to be liberally construed, on the principle that remedial statutes are to be beneficially expounded. Redemption is the last chance of the citizen to recover his right of property."[1]

[1] *Woodward*, J., in Gault's Appeal, 33 Penn. St., 94, 97. See also Dubois *v.* Hepburn, 10 Pet., 1; Corbett *v.* Nutt, 18 Grat., 674, and 10 Wall., 464; Patter-

2. But while the statutes are to be favorably regarded, it is at the same time to be borne in mind that the right to redeem comes from the statute exclusively, and is to be asserted only in the cases and under the circumstances which are there prescribed. The courts can grant no extension of the statutory time; they can make no exceptions from general provisions of the statutes to meet the circumstances of hard cases; and if the statutes fail to provide for the cases of disability, like those of infancy, coverture or absence from the country, the courts are without authority to do so.[1] The statutes of some states make special provisions for the cases of infants, and sometimes for other classes, permitting redemption by them after the time allowed to owners generally has expired; but such statutes are far from general.[2] And where

son *v.* Brindle, 9 Watts, 98; Masterson *v.* Beasley, 3 Ohio, 301; Jones *v.* Collins, 16 Wis., 594; Winchester *v.* Cain, 1 Rob., La., 421; Rice *v.* Nelson, 27 Iowa, 148; Schenck *v.* Peay, 1 Dillon, 267. Where the deed was required to lie twelve months in the town clerk's office, during which the party might redeem, it was held that it should be deposited with all convenient speed. Four years after the sale was too late. Ives *v.* Lyon, 7 Conn., 504. Statutes have sometimes provided for judicial proceedings to *foreclose* or cut off the right to redeem, not only in cases where lands were to be forfeited for delinquent taxes, but also in case of sales. In the latter case the proceedings will be taken by the purchaser, who will be held to great strictness in complying with the statute. See Dentler *v.* State, 4 Blackf., 258; Gaylord *v.* Scarff, 6 Iowa, 179; Abell *v.* Cross, 17 id., 171. Such proceedings are not applicable to sales for municipal taxes unless expressly made so. Grimmer *v.* Sumner, 21 Wis., 179.

[1] McCormack *v.* Russell, 25 Penn. St., 185; Smith *v.* Macon, 20 Ark., 17; Heard *v.* Walton, 39 Miss., 388. Redemption cannot be had in equity. Mitchell *v.* Green, 10 Met., 101. Except as it may be permitted by statute, and then it must be under such conditions as the statute may attach. Craig *v.* Flanagin, 21 Ark., 319. Where the owner neglected to pay taxes or to redeem his lands after sale, under a belief that the taxes had been paid, the mistake does not entitle him to relief against the consequences of the omission. Playter *v.* Cochran, 37 Iowa, 258. A purchaser of lands which had been sold for taxes prior to his purchase is not entitled to redeem because of having, after the purchase, inquired of the treasurer if there were unpaid taxes, and been told there were not; at the same time making no inquiry for tax sales. Moore *v.* Hamlin, 38 Iowa, 482. Compare Van Benthuysen *v.* Sawyer, 36 N. Y., 150. The pendency of the civil war, and the fact that the owner resided in a state in rebellion, cannot enlarge his statutory right to redeem. Finley *v.* Brown, 22 Iowa, 638.

[2] An infant who has a right to redeem may sell it with the land. Stout *v.* Merrill, 35 Iowa, 47. As to redemption by infants and married women under

the statute makes no provision for the redemption of an undivided interest, the party owning such an interest can only redeem by paying the whole redemption money.[1]

3. Whatever the statute may make provision for, subsequent to the sale, in order to the protection of the interest of the parties having the right to redeem, must be strictly performed. The reasons which require this are the same that render imperative a strict compliance with all those provisions which are to be observed in the interest of the tax payer before the sale is made. Perhaps the most usual requirement is, the publication of a notice to the tax payer, with sometimes a personal service upon the owner in case he is known, and is a resident. All provisions of this nature must be strictly complied with. Nothing can be substituted for it by the officers;[2] the right to it cannot be waived by one who chances to be in possession of the land but who has no interest in it,[3] and the owner may rely on his right to it, and

statutes making exceptions in their favor, see Jones *v.* Collins, 16 Wis., 594; Lynch *v.* Brudie, 63 Penn. St., 206.

[1] Quinn *v.* Kenney, 47 Cal, 147; People *v.* McEwen, 23 id., 54; Curl *v.* Watson, 25 Iowa, 35. Where the statute permits redemption of an undivided interest, the right may be enforced by *mandamus*. People *v.* Treasurer of Detroit, 8 Mich., 14. That rents and profits received by the tax purchaser cannot be applied by way of equitable redemption, see Spengin *v.* Forry, 37 Iowa, 242. As to the right of one tenant in common who redeems for all to retain the land until the others repay their share, see Watkins *v.* Eaton, 30 Me., 529.

[2] Where a leasehold interest was sold and was to be conveyed at the expiration of two years from the sale, but the statute required the corporation, at least six months before the expiration of two years from the sale, to cause an advertisement to be published at least twice in each week, for six weeks successively, that unless the lands were redeemed by a certain day they would be conveyed, *held*, that this was imperative, and that the six weeks must be completed six months before the expiration of two years. Doughty *v.* Hope, 3 Denio, 594. See Jackson *v.* Estey, 7 Wend., 148; Comstock *v.* Beardsley, 15 id., 348; Westbrook *v.* Willey, 47 N. Y., 457; Jenks *v.* Wright, 61 Penn. St., 410; Wilson *v.* McKenna, 52 Ill., 43. And compare Wright *v.* Sperry, 21 Wis., 331. If lands are improperly grouped and sold, this does not affect the right to redeem in parcels. Penn *v.* Clemans, 19 Iowa, 372.

[3] So held under the New York statute. The statute required notice to be given to the party in possession if any; but it was held that an occupant who had no interest in it could not waive the right to the notice. Jackson *v.* Estey, 7 Wend., 148. As to who is to be deemed in possession, see Comstock *v.* Beardsley, 15 Wend., 348; Bush *v.* Davison, 16 id., 550. The occupation intended by the statute is that at the time notice is given. Hand *v.* Ballou, 12 N. Y., 541.

wait until he receives it before taking proceedings to redeem.[1] Notice, when to be given by an officer, is an official act, and should be put in writing; but whether in writing or not, must be distinct and full, and the evidence of giving it should be preserved in the proper office.[2]

4. As to the persons who may redeem, something may depend upon the phraseology of the statute. The general rule is, that any one may redeem who has in the land an interest which would be affected by the tax conveyance.[3] A statute giving the right to redeem to the "owner," will be construed to embrace the case of the original owner, notwithstanding there is an outstanding tax title.[4] It may also embrace any one who has a substantial interest in the premises; even a wife having a homestead right in her husband's lands,[5] or a lien creditor.[6] A purchaser at sheriff's sale of the right of one in possession, may redeem, though he shows no title in the occupant.[7] And so may a husband who claims in right of his wife;[8] or a dowress;[9] or the assignee of a mortgage;[10]

[1] Arthurs *v.* Smathers, 38 Penn. St., 40; Doughty *v.* Hope, 3 Denio, 594; Dentler *v.* State, 4 Blackf., 258. In Illinois it has been decided that where by law notice to redeem was required to be served on the person who was assessed, and the notice was not given, the tax deed was void even though the person assessed had no interest in the land, and though the purchaser had published notice in a newspaper three months before the time to redeem had expired, describing the land, stating his purchase, and also when the redemption would expire. Barnard *v.* Hoyt, 63 Ill., 341. In Missouri the statute required the certificate of purchase to be recorded, and gave the owner two years after the sale in which to redeem. It was held that recording the certificate was essential. Morton *v.* Reeds, 9 Mo., 878.

[2] Broughton *v.* Journeay, 51 Penn. St., 31.

[3] Dubois *v.* Hepburn, 10 Pet., 1; Schenck *v.* Peay, 1 Dillon, 261; McBride *v.* Hoey, 2 Watts, 436.

[4] Lancaster *v.* County Auditor, 2 Dillon, 478.

[5] Adams *v.* Beale, 19 Iowa, 61.

[6] Schenck *v.* Peay, 1 Dillon, 269. And see as lessees, etc., Byington *v.* Rider, 9 Iowa, 566.

[7] Shearer *v.* Woodburn, 10 Penn. St., 511.

[8] Dubois *v.* Hepburn, 10 Pet. 1.

[9] Rice *v.* Nelson, 27 Iowa, 148.

[10] Faxon *v.* Wallace, 101 Mass., 444. The statute gave the right to the "mortgagee," and it was held the assignee was included. The redemption is for

or a party claiming the land by executory contract.[1] And one interested in lands sold *in solido* may redeem for all.[2] Probably none of the statutes are so restricted in the terms in which they grant the right to redeem as to fail in protecting all interests like those which have been mentioned, and all others of a beneficial character.

5. A stranger to the title cannot defeat a tax purchase by redemption. The purchaser has acquired a title which is subject only to the right of those interested to redeem; and no payment of the amount by a stranger, and no acceptance of it by any official from a stranger, can affect this right.[3] Probably the acceptance of the redemption money by the purchaser himself would preclude his afterwards claiming rights under his purchase; but nothing short of his own recognition of the unauthorized act of one who, if he had no interest, would be a mere intermeddler, could conclude him in such a case.[4]

6. Although redemption is a statutory right, yet a party attempting in good faith to make it may be relieved against the mistakes or frauds of the officer or of the purchaser. If he has attempted to redeem, and done all he was required to do by those entitled to receive the money, the sale is discharged even though, in consequence of the mistake of the officer, he has paid less than the proper amount.[5] But where one claims to have discharged

the benefit of the owner as well as the holder of the mortgage. Duncan *v.* Smith, 31 N. J., 325.

[1] One who has bought the land by executory contract may compel the purchaser for taxes to assign to him on receipt of the redemption money. Rogers *v.* Rutter, 11 Gray, 410.

[2] Loomis *v.* Pingree, 42 Me., 299. It appears to be the rule in Iowa that one must redeem all he has a right to redeem, and cannot compel the purchaser to accept less. Curl *v.* Watson, 25 Iowa, 135; Jacobs *v.* Porter, 34 id., 342, 345. See People *v.* McEwen, 23 Cal., 54.

[3] See Eaton *v.* North, 25 Wis., 514; Cousins *v.* Allen, 28 id., 232.

[4] Byington *v.* Bookwalter, 7 Iowa, 512; Penn *v.* Clemens, 19 id., 372. The officer to whom redemption is made need have no proof that the person offering to make it is authorized to do so, unless the statute requires this. Chapin *v.* Curtenius, 15 Ill., 427.

[5] Thus, in Budd, *v.* Tompkins, 47 Penn, St., 359, it was decided that the redemption was effectual, though by mistake of the county treasurer all of the taxes were not included which should have been. And see Price *v.* Mott, 52 Penn. St., 315; Dietrick *v.* Mason, 57 id, 40; Noble *v.* Bullis, 23 Iowa, 559.

lands from a tax sale, by the payment of all taxes demanded of him, which was less than the whole, it must appear that no responsibility for the error rests upon him. If when he applied to the treasurer to redeem, that officer was left to understand that only a certain sale was inquired for, and received the money upon that alone, this will not discharge any other sale.[1]

7. The purchaser may waive strict compliance with the statutes. This he will do if he receives payment after the day.[2] But such a transaction is to be regarded purely as a redemption, and not as a purchase;[3] as would be also an assignment made by the purchaser to the original owner, on a claim being made by the latter of a right to redeem.[4]

8. Redemption gives no new title; it simply relieves the land from the sale which had been made. And this is true whether redemption is made before the statutory time had expired, or by consent of the purchaser afterwards.[5] If the purchaser had any other title or interest in the land besides that redeemed from, it remains entirely unaffected; his acceptance of the redemption money cannot estop him from setting it up and relying upon it.[6]

9. The purchaser has no title to the land until the time for redemption has expired. He has consequently no constructive pos-

[1] Lamb *v.* Irwin, 69 Penn. St., 436. If redemption is prevented by the officer refusing to give a statement and receive the amount, the title is not cut off. Van Benthuysen *v.* Sawyer, 36 N. Y., 150.

[2] Coxe *v.* Wolcott, 27 Penn. St., 154; Philadelphia *v.* Miller, 40 id., 440.

[3] Coxe *v.* Wolcott, 27 Penn. St., 154. In Rogers *v.* Johnson, 70 id., 224, a written agreement given by the purchaser to the owner, agreeing to convey on being paid the amount of the bid with twenty-five per cent. additional, was regarded as a good redemption. So is a tender to the purchaser sufficient, though, under the law redemption is to be made to the treasurer. Broughton *v.* Journeay, 51 Penn. St., 31. And see Price *v.* Mott, 52 id., 315. In Massachusetts one entitled to redeem should make tender to the purchaser, notwithstanding he has while disseized made conveyance to another. Faxon *v.* Wallace, 98 Mass., 44. See Same *v.* Same, 101 id., 444. A tender, accepted or not, is equivalent to redemption. Sperry *v.* Gibson, 3 W. Va., 522; Brooks *v.* Hardwick, 5 La. An., 675.

[4] Coxe *v.* Sartell, 21 Penn. St., 480. See Steiner *v.* Coxe, 4 id., 13.

[5] Coxe *v.* Wolcott, 27 Penn. St., 154. For the general rule, see Phillips *v.* Improvement Co., 25 id., 56; Cuttle *v.* Brockway, 32 id., 45; Jenks *v.* Wright, 61 id., 410; Gray *v.* Coan, 30 Iowa, 536.

[6] Cooper *v.* Bushley, 72 Penn. St., 252.

session of the premises, and no more right to go upon and make use of them than any stranger to the title would have. His entry upon the premises would be a trespass upon the possession, actual or constructive, of the owner, who might recover against him for any injury committed.[1]

10. Neither the purchaser nor the officer can add conditions to the right to redeem. A direct attempt to do this would so manifestly be an attempt to legislate to the prejudice of the owner, that nothing could be said in justification of it. But peculiar cases, which would amount to this in legal effect, sometimes require to be tested by the general principle. Thus, where the land of one person was irregularly sold with that of others, but the infirmity in the sale was afterwards cured by a healing act, it was *held*, that the owner could not be required, as a condition to redemption, to pay any more than the proportion of the bid that was fairly chargeable to his land; this being all that he could have been charged with had the sale been regular.[2] So if the purchaser has paid taxes, subsequently assessed upon the land, he cannot demand these as a condition to redemption, unless this is the provision of the statute.[3] And, if a resident's lands have been assessed and sold as nonresident, their character has been fixed for all the purposes of that proceeding, and the owner cannot be required to redeem on any different terms from a nonresident.[4]

11. In the matter of tax sales, it is important to understand what authority the legislature retains over them, especially in view of the very frequent and radical changes which are made in the law, and which in terms if not in intent apply to inchoate transactions previously had, as well as to those which are to take place under the new law. The question, for instance, whether a statute extending the right to redeem can be applied to pre-

[1] Shalemiller *v.* McCarty, 55 Penn. St., 186. See Gault's Appeal, 33 Penn. St., 94; Lightner *v.* Mooney, 10 Watts, 407. This may possibly be otherwise under some statutes, but there can be no question that the general rule is stated in the text.

[2] Dietrich *v.* Mason, 57 Penn. St., 40. As to the right to redeem from the counties in Kansas, see Farr *v.* Haughey, 5 Kan., 625.

[3] Stephens *v.* Holmes, 26 Ark., 48.

[4] Garabaldi *v.* Jenkins, 27 Ark., 453.

vious sales, is one constantly liable to arise, and which, in fact, has arisen in several cases.

If the time to redeem has already expired before the passage of the statute, it is manifest the statute can have no effect upon the sale. The title has now become absolute, and the legislature can no more create rights in the land in favor of the former owner than in favor of any other person. But if the time has not expired, and redemption is still open to the owners, the want of power is not so entirely beyond dispute.

In one case it has been decided that the time for redemption might lawfully be extended from one year to two, after the sale had taken place. The decision is reasoned on the liberal construction which should be put upon redemption laws; and the conclusion was just, if no other considerations need be taken into the account.[1] Other cases have held the contrary, and, as we believe, on reasons that are conclusive. They plant themselves upon the principle that the obligation of contracts is inviolable. Now the purchase at a tax sale is clearly a contract. It is made under the law as it then exists, and upon the terms prescribed by the law. No subsequent statute can import new terms into the contract, or add to those before expressed. If it could be changed in one particular, it could be in all; if subject to legislative control at all, it is wholly at its mercy.[2] The same rule ought in morals to apply to a statute shortening the time to redeem; as it is equally unjust to legislate against the owner of the land in such circumstances as in his favor. But with him there is no contract when the sale is made, and perhaps the remedy by redemption which the statute gives him, like remedies in general, is subject to legislative discretion.[3]

[1] Gault's Appeal, 33 Penn. St., 94.

[2] Robinson *v.* Howe, 13 Wis., 341; Dikeman *v.* Dikeman, 11 Paige, 484; Goenen *v.* Schroeder, 8 Minn., 387. And see Cargill *v.* Power, 1 Mich., 369.

[3] It was so intimated in Robinson *v.* Howe, 13 Wis., 341, and Smith *v.* Packard, 12 id., 371. The right to shorten the time to redeem from a mortgage sale was affirmed in Butler *v.* Palmer, 1 Hill, 324, but denied in Cargill *v.* Power, 1 Mich., 369, on the ground that the right pertained to the contract itself which the parties had made; that is to say, to the mortgage. And see State *v.* Commissioners of School, etc., Lands, 4 Wis., 414.

CHAPTER XVII.

PROCEEDINGS AT LAW TO RECOVER LANDS SOLD FOR TAXES.

Where lands have been sold and conveyed in satisfaction of delinquent taxes, the purchaser, if he finds the land occupied, may bring ejectment in the common law courts to obtain possession. If, on the other hand, he finds the land unoccupied and takes possession without suit, the original owner may have the like remedy against him.

It has in some cases been thought proper, with a view to a speedy settlement of all questions concerning the validity of tax titles, to establish, by statute, some special rules regarding the proceedings to contest them. These rules are to be classed under two heads: Those which make it a condition to any recovery by the original owner of lands sold for taxes, that he should do equity in the premises; and those which require him to bring his suit in a very short time, specially limited for the purpose.

1. Under the first head may be ranged those provisions which require, as a condition to maintaining any suit, that the owner of the title adverse to the tax title shall pay the taxes for which the land was sold, and those which, in the event of his establishing his title to the land, require him to pay for any betterments that have been made by the tax purchaser or his assignees in reliance upon the purchase.

The requirement, that the party recovering in ejectment, shall pay the fair value of betterments which an adverse claimant has made in good faith upon the land, and which the party making them must now lose, is one that, under ordinary circumstances, is eminently just and proper. No serious question of the right of the legislature to make such requirements can well arise, and if it could, it must now be considered as conclusively settled by the decisions in its favor.[1] There is more difficulty with the requirement of payment of taxes.

[1] Brown *v.* Storm, 4 Vt., 37; Whitney *v.* Richardson, 31 id., 300, 306; Armstrong *v.* Jackson, 1 Blackf., 375; Fowler *v.* Halbert, 4 Bibb, 52, 54; Brackett

It has been decided in one state that an act which provided that "no person shall be permitted to institute any proceedings to set aside any assessment or special tax, hereafter levied or assessed upon any lot or tract of land, or to set aside any deed executed in consequence of nonpayment of such taxes, and the sale of the premises therefor, unless such person shall first pay or tender to the proper party, or deposit for his use with the treas-

v. Norcross, 1 Greenl., 89, 92; Withington *v.* Corey, 2 N. H., 115; Hunt's Lessee *v.* McMahan, 5 Ohio, 133; Longworth *v.* Worthington, 6 id., 9, 10; Bacon *v.* Callender, 6 Mass., 303; Jones *v.* Carter, 12 id., 314; Scott *v.* Mather, 14 Texas, 235; Saunders *v.* Wilson, 19 id., 194; Childs *v.* Shower, 18 Iowa, 261; Pacquette *v.* Pickness, 19 Wis., 219; Coney *v.* Owen, 6 Watts, 435; Steele *v.* Spinance, 22 Penn. St., 256; Lynch *v.* Brudie, 63 id., 206; Dothage *v.* Stuart, 35 Mo., 251; Fenwick *v.* Gill, 38 id., 510; Craig *v.* Flanagin, 21 Ark., 319; Pope *v.* Macon, 23 id., 644; Marlow *v.* Adams, 24 id., 109; King *v.* Harrington, 18 Mich., 213; Howard *v.* Zeyer, 18 La. An., 407; Love *v.* Shartzer, 31 Cal., 487; Stebbins *v* Guthrie, 4 Kans., 353. Some of the statutes give the value of the improvements to those only who have been in possession, claiming title in good faith. In Texas it has been held, that the tax purchaser is not a possessor in good faith, and, consequently, not entitled to compensation for improvements, if his deed was void for want of authority in the officer to sell, and by proper diligence he might have known the fact. Robson *v.* Osborn, 13 Texas, 298, 307. In Indiana the claimant must have had at least color of title. Cain *v.* Hunt, 41 Ind., 466. But in Pennsylvania, and, perhaps, in most of the states, the owner, recovering his lands, may have judgment against him for improvements, though the tax proceedings were wholly void. Gilmore *v.* Thompson, 3 Watts, 106, (where the tax had been paid before sale); Coney *v.* Owen, 6 id., 435, (where the land was exempt from taxation); Lynch *v.* Brudie, 63 Penn. St., 206. But it would be otherwise if the lands were seated so that the sale would be void, not because of defective proceedings, but because of the absence of jurisdiction to proceed at all. See Lambertson *v.* Hogan, 2 Penn. St., 22, and cases cited. In Rogers *v.* Johnson, 67 id., 43, 47, *Agnew*, J., gives the explanation of the difference: "The distinction between a sale absolutely void, from want of jurisdiction to sell, and one merely void because of a fatal defect in the proceedings, is palpable. Thus in McKee *v.* Lamberton, 2 W. & S., 107, 114, and Cramer *v.* Hall, 4 id., 36, where the land was seated and the treasurer had no authority to sell, it was held, that the purchaser was not entitled to be compensated for his improvements: while in Coney *v.* Owen, 6 Watts, 435, and Gilmore *v.* Thompson, 3 id., 106, where the lands were unseated and the treasurer had general jurisdiction, but the sales were void because, in the first place, of exemption from taxation, and in the second, because of a prior payment of the taxes, the purchaser was held to be entitled to his improvements. There are other cases, even where the irregularity has deprived the owner of his surplus bond, where the sales have been sustained. Thus, the sales were supported in Gibson *v.* Robbins, 9 Watts, 156, where the treasurer charged too much costs, and appropriated the whole bid, where

urer, the amount of all state, county and city taxes that may remain unpaid upon such lot or tract, together with the interest and charges thereon," was void as being inconsistent with that clause in the constitution that declares that every person "ought to obtain justice freely, and without purchase."[1] If this statute were confined to the requirement of a payment or tender of legal taxes and costs for which the sale may have been made, the soundness of the conclusion might well be made a question. No one is denied a remedy in the courts, when he is merely required to submit to a condition which, under the circumstances, is reasonable. Conditions to the assertion of a right in court are imposed in many cases, none of which are supposed to work to the detriment of justice. The requirement of security from a plaintiff in replevin or attachment is an instance, and the payment of taxes upon the legal process or upon the entry of the suit is another.[2] Courts of equity on general principles of right are in the frequent habit of imposing conditions where one seeks in equity to restrain a tax, only a part of which is illegal. The authority of the legislature over the whole subject of legal remedies is very ample, and it is not to be supposed that any general declaration of the right of the

a surplus would have existed for which a bond should have been taken; and in Peters *v.* Heasley, 10 Watts, 208, and Russell *v.* Reed, 27 Penn. St., 166, where the commissioners of the county bid more than the taxes and costs, and the owner was thereby deprived of his security for the surplus. So also the sale was supported in Frick *v.* Sterrett (4 W. & S., 269), where the treasurer, by mistake, took the bond for less than the true surplus. To these cases may be added Bayard *v.* Inglis (5 W. & S., 465), and Burd *v.* Patterson (22 Penn. St., 219), where no bonds were given when the sale was made and deed delivered. In the former the bond was not given until nearly two years afterwards, and it was never filed."

[1] See *ante*, p. 320, note 2.

[2] The validity of a tax on the unsuccessful party to a lawsuit was questioned in Harrison *v.* Willis, 7 Heis., 35, as "the imposition of a burthen upon the right of the citizen to go into the courts to have his wrongs redressed, and his rights vindicated," and as an infraction of that section of the bill of rights which declares that "all courts shall be open, and every man for an injury done him in his lands, goods, person or reputation, shall have remedy by due course of law, and right and justice administered without sale, denial, or delay." The court sustained the law, remarking that such laws had long existed, and this clause, taken from magna charta, was not to be understood as prohibiting such a tax, but to be interpreted in the light of the history of the times when adopted.

citizen to his day in court was intended to preclude the legislature from exercising its authority to require him to do equity when he did come. Other cases have distinctly affirmed the right to require payment of the taxes, as a condition precedent to a recovery of the land from the tax purchaser, when it was proposed to do so on the ground of the invalidity of the tax proceedings.[1]

These decisions, if limited in their application to cases in which taxes were justly and equitably a charge upon the land, and only failed to become a legal charge by reason of the negligence or mistakes of officers in the discharge of their duties under the tax law, may fairly be said to rest upon sound grounds of broad equity, and to be supported on the same reasons which support remedial laws in general. If the tax purchaser has, by his purchase, paid a charge which the state might fairly and justly make a legal one upon the land, and which the owner of the land ought himself to have paid to the state, there is no reason why the state should not give to the purchaser, when he loses the expected benefit of the purchase, a remedy to recover the amount of the tax from the party who ought to have paid it. This is the province of remedial laws; to give new remedies where none at all or only inadequate remedies existed before. And so favorably are such laws regarded that they always receive at the hands of the courts a benign and favorable construction.

[1] Tharp *v.* Hart, 2 Sneed, 569; Glass *v.* White, 5 id., 475; Craig *v.* Flanagin, 21 Ark., 319; Pope *v.* Macon, 23 Ark., 644. Compare Wakely *v.* Nichols, 16 Wis., 558. In Henderson *v.* Staritt, 4 Sneed, 470, it was decided that the plaintiff in ejectment to recover land sold for taxes may show that any necessary proceeding subsequent to the judgment and order of sale, such as the advertisement of the sale itself, was irregular and void, without first being required to show that the taxes had been paid anterior to such judgment and order of sale. A constitutional provision that "appeals and writs of error shall be allowed from the final determination of county courts as may be provided by law," is not violated by a statute which, in tax cases, requires the appellant to deposit with the county treasury the amount of the judgment. Andrews *v.* Rumsay, Sup. Ct. Ill. (1875), 7 Chicago Legal News, 321; citing People *v.* Wallace, in same court, same term. A statute precluding the owner from contesting a tax sale, unless he has paid or tendered the taxes, cannot be extended by contstruction to embrace the case of lands forfeited to the state. Williamsburg *v.* Lord, 51 Me., 599.

A decree settling the title to land in the original holder, as against a tax purchaser, does not bar an action to recover for taxes paid by the latter in good faith upon the land in controversy. Stewart *v.* Corbin, 38 Iowa, 571.

But if the tax itself were vicious; if it were laid for a private, and not a public purpose; if it were a special and arbitrary exaction from one person while the rest of community equally interested was not taxed at all, or if for any similar reason the charge was not just and equitable as against the owner of the land or the land itself, so that the legislature could not have validated it retrospectively by a direct enactment, it is not perceived on what grounds an authority to validate it by this indirect and circuitous method can be supported. The legislature can have no more authority to compel the land owner to pay a lawless exaction to a third person than it has to compel a like payment to the state directly. The one as much as the other would be robbery. If the land owner performs all his duty to the state, nothing which the tax officers can do without his consent, and in the direction of depriving him of his freehold, can raise against him any equity requiring him to do more. The rule *caveat emptor* applies to the purchaser. He takes all the risks of his purchase, and if he finds in any case that he has secured neither the title he bid for nor any equitable claim against the owner, the state may, if it see fit, make reparation itself, but it has no more authority to compel the owner of the land to do so than to exercise the like compulsion against any other person.[1]

[1] This is the substance of the decision in Hart *v.* Henderson, 17 Mich., 218. How far it may be just, and therefore competent, to compel the land owner, in cases where the tax was just but the proceedings to make it a charge on person or property void, to pay the cost of such void proceedings, is a question that will be very likely at some time to come up for determination. It is certainly difficult to perceive how any equitable claim can exist against any one for the cost of void proceedings. The Illinois statute of 1839 provided that "no person shall be permitted to question the title acquired by a sheriff's deed without first showing that he or she, or the person under whom he or she claims title, had title to the land at the time of the sale, or that the title was obtained from the United States or this state after the sale, and that all taxes due upon the land have been paid by such person or the person under whom he claims title aforesaid." It has been decided that notwitstanding this statute, the party defendant may contest the tax title, if the taxes due to the state have been paid, no matter by whom. Curry *v.* Hinman, 11 Ill., 420. See Conway *v.* Cable, 37 id., 82. Also that if one was in possession of the land claiming title when the sale was made, that is sufficient evidence of title. Lusk *v.* Harber, 3 Gilm., 158; Curry *v.* Hinman, 11 Ill., 420. The following cases throw light on the construction of this statute: Hinman *v.* Pope, 1 Gilm., 131, 138; Bestor *v.* Powell, 2 id., 119; Atkins *v.* Hinman, 2 id., 437, 453; Spellman *v.* Curtenius,

2. The statutes limiting a short time within which the owner of the original title shall contest the tax claim, are supposed to be enacted in pursuance of a sovereign authority in the legislature to fix a reasonable time within which a party shall be allowed to assert his rights by suit, or be debarred. The policy of such laws is unquestionable, and the power to enact them is undisputed. But like all other powers in government, this has its limits, and it is probable that some of the statutes to which we have referred, if literally construed, would be found to be unwarranted.

The most common limitation of actions for the recovery of lands is twenty years after the right of action accrued. But whenever the legislative wisdom shall determine that a shorter limitation for all cases or for any class of cases would be wise, it is unouestionably competent to prescribe it. Advantage has been taken of this power in some instances, by parties interested in tax titles, and laws have been secured which, in tax cases, limit the time to five years, or to three years. But in some of these laws another peculiarity will be found besides the short period that is prescribed for contesting the tax claim. They do not on their face purport to be statutes which limit the time in which a party may bring suit against one in possession, claiming by tax title, but they fix a time after which the tax title shall not be questioned. The short period of limitation it is entirely competent for the legislature to prescribe,[1] but it may be questioned whether an act which merely limits a time within which a bad title may ripen into a good one is, either in spirit, purpose or effect, an act in the nature of an act of limitations.

Three different classes of cases may be affected by such statutes: 1. Those in which the owner of the original title remains in possession after the tax sale. 2. Those in which the land is then and remains afterward unoccupied. 3. Those in which the tax purchaser enters and holds possession claiming title.

In the third class of cases there can be no sufficient reason why

12 Ill., 409; Hope *v.* Sawyer, 14 id., 254; Billings *v.* Detten, 15 id., 218: Polk *v.* Hill, 15 id., 130; Chapin *v.* Curtenius, 15 id., 427, 432. And see *ante*, p. 227, *et seq.*

[1] Thomas *v.* Stickle, 32 Iowa, 71 (citing Henderson *v.* Oliver, 28 id., 20; Eldridge *v.* Kuehl, 27 id., 160); Shiek *v.* McElroy, 20 Penn. St., 25; Edgerton *v.* Bird, 6 Wis., 527, 532; Sprecker *v.* Wakely, 11 id., 432.

the holder of the original title should not be required to bring suit in a time less than twenty years. By the adverse possession he is excluded from the enjoyment of any right he may claim, and public policy no less than justice to the tax purchaser requires that he should bring his suit within a reasonable time, in order that all contested questions may be put at rest while the facts are recent and presumably susceptible of proof. In the first class of cases it would be manifest and most gross injustice to make lapse of time alone extinguish the owner's title. He is in full possession of his rights, and it is the adverse claimant and not himself who is negligent in not bringing suit. And it seems to us very clear that, under such circumstances, it is not competent to limit a period at the expiration of which the tax title shall become a perfect title and not open to controversy or dispute.[1]

In the second class of cases the proper rule is not so clear. If no provision is made by statute under which ejectment can be brought in the case of a vacant possession, it would seem that neither claimant could be considered in law negligent, so as to render his claim the proper subject of a statute of repose, until possession was taken by his adversary; but if ejectment is allowed in such cases, then it may possibly be within the power of the legislature to declare that the title of that one of the parties who, constructively, is to be regarded as in possession, shall become absolute if not questioned by suit within the time by the statute limited for that purpose.

The Pennsylvania statute of 1804 declared that no action for the recovery of lands sold under the act should lie, unless brought within five years after the sale. But this the courts refused to apply literally, because, in the case of a vacant possession, it would cut off the original owner without giving him the right to contest the title; there being no statute permitting ejectment in such cases. They consequently held that the statute began to run, not from the sale, but from the time of posession taken under it.[2] Subsequently, when the right to maintain ejectment for an unoccupied tenement had been conferred by the stat-

[1] Groesbeck *v.* Seeley, 13 Mich., 329. See Conway *v.* Cable, 37 Ill., 82; Case *v.* Dean, 16 Mich., 12; Waln *v.* Shearman, 8 S. & R., 357.

[2] Waln *v.* Shearman, 8 S. & R., 357; Cranmer *v.* Hall, 4 W. & S., 36. See also Baker *v.* Kelly, 11 Minn., 480.

ute, it was held that the statute began to run in favor of the tax purchaser at the time the sale was perfected by deed, he being constructively in possession of the unoccupied premises from that time.[1] These decisions have perhaps given effect to the statute as near as was possible, consistent with fundamental rules of right.[2]

The Wisconsin statute provides that "any suit or proceeding for the recovery of land sold for taxes, except in cases where the taxes have been paid or the lands redeemed as provided by law, shall be commenced within three years from the time of recording the tax deed of sale, and not thereafter." That this statute is valid does not seem to have been very seriously questioned.[3] That it ap-

[1] "It was argued that the limitation in the act of 1804 does not apply to a case where the owner is in possession. That is true, as was determined in Bigler *v.* Karnes, 4 W. & S., 137, and Shearer *v.* Woodburn, 10 Penn. St., 511. But that is where the possession is *actual*, and the owner is thus daily and hourly challenging the validity of the tax title. It is not so, however, in any other case, and it is settled that in all other cases the limitation runs from the time of the sale, and not from the time when possession is taken by the purchaser. Parish *v.* Stevens, 3 S. & R., 298, the first case decided under the act of 1804, on this point, was overruled by Waln *v.* Shearman, 8 S. & R., 357, on the ground that an ejectment would not lie against a vacant possession. But the act of 29th March, 1824, having provided a remedy for the owner in the case of a vacant possession, this court returned to the doctrine of Parish *v.* Stevens, and it is now held that the limitation runs from the time of the sale, and not of possession. Robb *v.* Bowen, 9 Penn. St., 71; Sheik *v.* McElroy, 20 id., 25; Burd *v.* Patterson, 22 id., 219; Stewart *v.* Trevor, 56 id., 385. In the last case, Justice Strong summing up the cases, says: "Since the act of 29th March, 1824, the limitation is perfect at the end of five years from the delivery of the deed to the purchaser, without regard to possession." *Agnew*, J., in Rogers *v.* Johnson, 67 Penn. St., 48. See also to same effect, Johnston *v.* Jackson, 70 id., 164.

[2] A statute providing that no action for the recovery of land sold for taxes shall lie, "unless brought within five years after the sale thereof for taxes, as aforesaid," will not benefit the holder of the tax title when suing as plaintiff; and if he sues after five years he must show a valid title. Bigler *v.* Karnes, 4 W. & S., 137; Shearer *v.* Woodburn, 10 Penn. St., 511; Hole *v.* Rittenhouse, 19 id., 305; McReynolds *v.* Longenberger, 57 id., 13. It has been decided in Pennsylvania that as against a mere intruder, the tax deed, with evidence of title out of commonwealth, is sufficient. Crum *v.* Burke, 25 Penn. St., 371, 381, citing Foust *v.* Ross, 1 W. & S., 501; Foster *v.* McDivitt, 9 Watts, 341, 344; Dikeman *v.* Parrish, 6 Penn. St., 210. And see Shearer *v.* Woodburn, 10 Penn. St., 512; Troutman *v.* May, 33 id., 455; Wheeler *v.* Winn, 53 id., 122; Hess *v.* Herrington, 73 id., 438.

[3] For decisions sustaining like statutes where the tax purchaser has been in

plies against the holder of the tax title as well as in his favor has been the conclusion of the courts, and it therefore cuts off either the original owner or the tax purchaser, if the adverse claimant has been in the occupation of the land for the period named.[1] It is also decided that, when the land is unoccupied, the holder of the tax title has constructive possession, and if the owner of the original title does not bring ejectment (which the statute permits in such case) within the three years, he is barred,[2] but that if the tax deed is void on its face, the grantee in it has no constructive possession, and in such case the statute does not run in his favor,[3] though it would do so, even under a void deed, if his possession were actual, open and notorious.[4]

possession, see Pillow *v.* Roberts, 13 How., 472; Vancleave *v.* Milliken, 13 Ind., 105; Doe *v.* Hearick, 14 id., 241, 245; Cofer *v.* Brooks, 20 Ark., 542; Sprague *v.* Pitt, McCahon, 212; Bowman *v.* Cockrill, 6 Kans., 311. See DeGraw *v.* Taylor, 37 Mo., 310; Pease *v.* Lawson, 33 id., 35; McNamara *v.* Estes, 22 Iowa, 246; Eldredge *v.* Kuehl, 27 id., 160; Henderson *v.* Oliver, 28 id., 20; Case of Albee, 28 id., 277; McCready *v.* Sexton, 29 id., 356; Henley *v.* Street, 29 id., 429; Thomas *v.* Stickle, 32 id., 71; Douglass *v.* Tullock, 34 id., 262; Jeffrey *v.* Brokaw, 35 id., 505.

[1] Edgarton *v.* Bird, 6 Wis., 527; Sprecker *v.* Wakeley, 11 id., 432; Knox *v.* Cleveland, 13 id., 245; Jones *v.* Collins, 16 id., 594; Parish *v.* Eager, 15 id., 552; Whitney *v.* Marshall, 17 id., 174. These decisions held applicable to the Iowa statute. Brown *v.* Painter, 38 Iowa., 456.

[2] Gunnison *v.* Hœhn, 18 Wis., 268; Lawrence *v.* Kenney, 32 id., 281. See Hill *v.* Kricke, 11 id., 442; Dean *v.* Early, 15 id., 100.

[3] Lain *v.* Shepardson, 18 Wis., 59. To the same effect are Taylor *v.* Miles, 5 Kans., 498; Shoat *v.* Walker, 6 id., 65. See Leffingwell *v.* Warren, 2 Black, 599.

[4] Lindsay *v.* Fay, 25 Wis., 460. On this point, see also Cofer *v.* Brooks, 20 Ark., 542; Hoffman *v.* Harrington, 28 Mich., 90; Washburn *v.* Cutter, 17 Minn., 361. The statute does not apply to a tax title fraudulently obtained, as for example, by an agent who bought in his principal's land when he should have paid the tax. McMahon *v.* McGraw, 26 Wis., 614. And see Carithers *v.* Weaver, 7 Kans., 110. The Michigan statute has been held not to apply in favor of one who was in possession under another claim at the time of acquiring the tax title. Gilman *v.* Riopelle, 18 Mich., 143, 163. Neither the fact that one is assessed for the land, or that he has paid taxes for a series of years thereon is sufficient proof that he is in the adverse possession of it. McDermott *v.* Hoffman, 70 Penn. St., 31, 54; Chapman *v.* Templeton, 53 Mo., 463. And merely cutting timber without actual possession, cultivation or inclosure, is not adverse possession, but a mere trespass on the constructive possession of the owner. Washburn *v.* Cutter, 17 Minn., 361; Safford *v.* Basto, 4 Mich., 406; Rivers *v.* Thompson, 46 Ala., 335.

There is serious objection in point of policy to making the tax deed give constructive possession of the land, with the consequences that have been made to follow, whether there are, or are not, any in point of law. The principal hardships perhaps under any system of tax sales spring from the fact that, in a considerable portion of the cases in which valuable lands are lost to the owners from delinquency, it is not so much in consequence of culpable neglect of the owners themselves, as through the negligence of agents, or through circumstances which have cast the ownership upon children, or other persons unaccustomed to business, who are found to be in default before they have fully become possessed of a knowledge of either their rights or their duties. In all these cases the tax purchaser knows that he has bought a title which, if legal, is to dispossess some title previously valid; while the adverse claimant frequently does not know or suspect that he or his land has been proceeded against for delinquency, and he may, for a series of years thereafter, continue to pay taxes without any suspicion that he is paying upon the land of another. No man thinks of making periodical visits to the records, in order to see that his land is clear of liens, when he is not conscious of any default; and to allow the tax purchaser to lie by under such circumstances, without asserting a claim by entry or notice, until, by the lapse of a few years, his deed shall ripen into an indisputable title, is to encourage him to commit what, in morals at least, is a fraud upon the original owner. And the fraud is still more gross and palpable if, in point of fact, the original owner was not at all in default, and his land has been sold and conveyed in consequence of the carelessness, incompetency or fraud of public officers.

There is another difficulty with those cases which bar a right by constructive adverse possession of the tax claimant. If they proceed upon the statute alone, which bars an action unless brought within a certain number of years after it accrued, then it would seem they might have held the tax purchaser barred with the same propriety as to make the like holding against the original owner; since either might have brought the suit, and, therefore, the one is as much within the words of the statute as the other.[1] If, on the other hand, they attach importance to adverse

[1] The Wisconsin statute authorizes an action for the recovery of lands to be

possession as by implication limiting the application of the statute to one only of the two classes of persons, who equally might have brought suit, then they import new principles into the law; for the law, unless by the force of these decisions, has no knowledge or recognition of such a thing as an adverse possession that is merely constructive.

Possession of a vacant tenement is and must be purely a matter of fiction. Constructive possession is recognized for some purposes, because, under our peculiar forms of action, it is found necessary in order to the protection of the rights of the owner against trespassers. The fiction is accepted, as all fictions in the law are, for the sake of justice; never to do injustice.[1] But if one's freehold has been illegally sold under adverse proceedings, there is no justice in resorting to a fiction of law in order to sustain the sale. What equity could exist in such a case, if one has honestly paid all that was demanded of him, or all that he has any reason to believe he owed?[2]

brought, when the premises are unoccupied, against "some person exercising acts of ownership on the premises claimed, or claiming title thereto, or some interest therein, at the commencement of the action." R. S., 1858, p. 838. This would seem to apply as well to the tax claimant as to the original owner, and if both are liable to suit, the obligation to sue would seem to be fairly divided between them.

[1] Truett *v.* The Justices, 20 Geo., 104; Low *v.* Little, 17 Johns., 346; Johnson *v.* Ballou, 28 Mich., 379, 396. In Taylor *v.* Miles, 5 Kans., 498, in which it is held that the recording of a void tax deed cannot be made the date from which the statute of limitations shall run, *Valentine*, J. says (p. 515): "*First.* A statute of limitations can only be applied where one person has received or suffered some injury from another person, either in contract or tort. It must operate to bar a *cause of action*, for it seems absurd to say that a cause of action can be barred, if no cause of action has ever accrued. *Second.* Every statute of limitation must give the injured party a reasonable time in which to commence his action, or the statute itself is void, tending to disturb vested rights. *Third.* When the statute has run its full time, the effect is to leave the parties in possession of just what they had before, nothing more and nothing less; and neither party has a right of action against the other; the injured party has lost his remedy." Compare Bowman *v.* Cockrill, 6 Kans., 311.

[2] We employ here the language of *Agnew*, J., in Brown *v.* Hays, 66 Penn. St., 229, 236. The case was one in which a single warrant of 1026 acres had been assessed as two of 726 and 300, respectively, and the owner had paid the assessment on the warrant by the number. *Held*, that the assessment of the warrant at 726 acres was not, by implication, notice to him that the 300 acres were assessed separately.

In the very worst light in which his equities may be viewed, they are at the least equal to those of the purchaser; and to make a fiction the instrument by which he is to be debarred of his rights is a very severe, if not excessive, exercise of authority, where the legislature had already put him quite sufficiently at disadvantage. Rules of evidence are subject to legislative control; and therefore the legislature may make the tax deed evidence of title. Rules of limitation are also subject to its control, and therefore the statute may quiet an open and public exercise of a right which remains unchallenged; but a purely nominal and fictitious exercise of a right by means of the record of a paper, or even without that, if the legislature shall think proper to dispense with it, is a very unsubstantial basis for a conclusive muniment of title to land. Constructive possession in any case it would seem should be in the party having the legal title; and this would leave questions of title open so long as actual possession was had by no one.[1]

Peculiar questions arise under some statutes regarding the nature of the claim under which possession is held. The Illinois statute of 1839 declared the person in possession of land "under claim and color of title," who should continue in possession for seven years, and pay all taxes, should be held and adjudged the legal owner, "to the extent and according to the purport of his or her paper title." Here was a distinct requirement of a paper title of some kind, and of one also that should give "color" of title. Where the tax deed is made *prima facie* evidence of title, it is plain that it gives color of title; and the decisions have been that the seven years possession under the circumstances required by the statute was sufficient with such a conveyance.[2] The same decisions hold, however, that the deed

[1] Possession and cultivation of a few acres cannot be constructive possession of a whole township. Chandler *v.* Spear, 22 Vt., 388.

[2] Dawley *v.* Van Court, 21 Ill., 460; Fell *v.* Cessford, 26 id., 522, 525; Halloway *v.* Clark, 27 id., 483; Bride *v.* Watt, 23 id., 507; Webster *v.* Webster, 55 id., 325; Worthy *v.* Bowman, 47 id., 17; Morrison *v.* Norman, 47 id., 477; Dickerson *v.* Breeden, 30 id., 279, 325; Hardin *v.* Crate, 60 id., 215. To constitute color of title it is only necessary that the deed purports to convey title, and has been received in good faith. Winstanlay *v.* Meacham, 58 Ill., 97. See Halloway *v.* Clark, 27 id., 483, 486, per *Walker*, J.; Dalton *v.* Lucas, 63 id., 337. But where he goes into possession and continues to hold the land and

must be one, not by reason of defects, or of its recitals, void on its face.[1] In Iowa the statutes are different, and protect the occupant who has been in possession under "claim" of title for the requisite period; and this may be with or without a deed or other documentary evidence giving color of right to the claim.[2] It is a principle of the law that where the statute of limitations has run in favor of any party, this perfects his right, and he may make it the ground of affirmative proceedings thereafter. This principle applies in favor of the tax title, and dispenses with any necessity for proof of the proceedings when the title is subsequently brought in question, and precludes its being attacked.[3]

pay taxes for seven years, he will be protected, although the deed is void on its face; and good faith will be presumed, but the contrary may be shown. Dalton *v.* Lucas, 63 Ill., 337. An instrument which merely purports to contain an agreement to convey title at a future time, cannot constitute color of title. Osterman *v.* Baldwin, 6 Wall., 116. "What is meant by *color* of *title?* It may be defined to be a *writing*, upon its face professing to pass title, but which does not do it, either from want of title in the person making it, or from the defective conveyance that is used — a title that is imperfect, but not so obviously that it would be apparent to one not skilled in the law:" per *Lumpkin*, J., in Beverly *v.* Burke, 9 Geo., 440, 443.

[1] See besides the Illinois cases above referred to, Shoat *v.* Walker, 6 Kansas, 65; Carithers *v.* Weaver, 7 id., 110; Sapp *v.* Morrill, 8 id., 677; Wofford *v.* McKenna, 23 Texas, 36; Kilpatrick *v.* Sisneras, id., 114; Cain *v.* Hunt, 41 Ind., 466. A tax deed which does not show that the land it purports to convey was sold for delinquent taxes, is void on its face; and where the holder of such deed has not been in actual possession of the property, the statute of limitations will not run so as to bar the right to bring an action in two years, to have the deed declared void. Hubbard *v.* Johnson, 9 Kans., 632.

[2] Hamilton *v.* Wright, 30 Iowa, 485. And see Taylor *v.* Buckner, 2 A. K. Marsh., 18; McCall *v.* Neeley, 3 Watts, 69, 72. That a tax deed in due form is color of title, see also Dillingham *v.* Brown, 38 Ala., 311; Rives *v.* Thompson, 43 id., 633, 641; Cofer *v.* Brooks, 20 Ark., 542; Pleasants *v.* Scott, 21 id., 370, 374; Chapman *v.* Templeton, 53 Mo., 463; King *v.* Harrington, 18 Mich., 213. See further, Moore *v.* Brown, 4 McLean, 21; S. C. in error, 11 How., 414; Willow *v.* Roberts, 13 id., 472.

[3] Sprecker *v.* Wakeley, 11 Wis., 432; Knox *v.* Cleveland, 13 id., 245, 249; Pleasants *v.* Rohrer, 17 id., 557; Lawrence *v.* Kenney, 32 id., 281; Morton *v.* Sharkey, McCahon, 113; McKenney *v.* Springer, 8 Blackf., 606; Slipp *v.* Brown, 2 Ind., 647; Lewis *v.* Webb, 3 Greenl., 326; Atkinson *v.* Dunlap, 50 Me., 111; Thompson *v.* Caldwell, 3 Lit., 137; Couch *v.* McKee, 1 Eng. (Ark.), 484, 495; Girdner *v.* Stephens, 1 Heisk., 280; S. C., 2 Am. Rep., 700; Bradford *v.* Shine's Adm'r, 13 Fla., 393; S. C., 7 Am. Rep., 239; Holden *v.* James, 11 Mass., 596; Wright *v.* Oakley, 5 Met., 400; Woart *v.* Winnick, 3 N. H., 473;

CHAPTER XVIII.

TAXATION OF BUSINESS.

The general right. It has been seen that government may, in the discretion of its legislature, levy a tax on every species of property within its jurisdiction, or, on the other hand, that it may select any particular species of property, and tax that only. The same is true of occupations; government may tax one, or it may tax all. There is no restriction upon its power in this regard unless one is expressly imposed by the constitution.[1]

Federal taxation. The government of the United States has general power to levy taxes on all the subjects of taxation within the several states and territories, and in the District of Columbia.[2] The exceptions to this general power have been mentioned in preceding pages [3] and need not be repeated. But although it has this general power, its exercise is commonly limited to comparatively few subjects, and the government revenues are collected in the main from taxes levied in various forms upon business.

Customs duties are levied exclusively by the United States, but internal taxes on business may be laid by the United States and the states as well; and what is said in this chapter is as applicable to taxation by the one as by the other, where the contrary is not indicated.

The methods in which business shall be taxed are also in the legislative discretion. The taxes which are most customary are: 1. On the privilege of carrying on the business. 2. On the amount of business done. 3. On the gross profits of the bus-

Martin *v.* Martin, 35 Ala., 560; Briggs *v.* Hubbard, 19 Vt., 86; Wires *v.* Farr, 25 id., 41; Davis *v.* Minor, 1 How. (Miss.), 183; Moore *v.* Luce, 29 Penn. St., 262; Hinchman *v.* Whetstone, 23 Ill., 185; Chiles *v.* Davis, 58 id., 411.

[1] Butler's Appeal, 73 Penn. St., 448, 451, per *Mercur*, J., citing Durach's Appeal, 62 Penn. St., 491. As to equality in such taxation, see Dillon, Mun. Corp., § 593 et seq.

[2] Loughborough *v.* Blake, 5 Wheat., 317.

[3] See Index, tit. United States.

iness. 4. On the net profits or profits divided. But the tax may be measured by other standards prescribed for the purpose as well as by these.

It has been seen that it is no conclusive objection to any such tax that it duplicates the burden to the person who pays it. To tax a merchant upon his stock as property, and also upon his gross sales, may seem burdensome, but it is not unconstitutional when not expressly forbidden by the constitution.[1] The two taxes are not identical, and though they may operate unjustly in particular cases, they are supposed to be imposed because the general result is equal and just.

Taxes on privileges. A tax on the privilege of following any particular employment, is usually confined to those which in some particular are exceptional, either because supposed to be specially profitable, or because they require special regulations, or because the privilege is in the nature of a franchise, or because they supply a general demand, so that the burden imposed will be generally distributed.[2] But no employment is absolutely exempt from the liability to be taxed. The necessities of the government may require that the lowest employment as well as the most lucrative shall contribute to its support, and if any is exempted, motives of policy will govern the discrimination.

When the tax takes the form of a tax on the privilege of following an employment, convenience in collection will commonly dictate the requirement of a license, and the person taxed will be compelled to pay the tax as a condition to the right to carry on the business at all.[3] In such a case the business carried on without a license will be illegal, and no recovery can be had upon contracts made in the course of it.[4] This distinguishes such a case from one of neglect to pay taxes in general; for except

[1] See Washington *v.* State, 13 Ark., 752; Straub *v.* Gordon, 27 id., 625; Mabry *v.* Tarver, 1 Humph., 94; Lewellen *v.* Lockharts, 21 Grat., 570.

[2] The following of an ordinary employment, e. g., that of keeping a livery stable, is not to be regarded as a "privilege" unless made so by statute. Columbia *v.* Guest, 3 Head, 413.

[3] License Tax Cases, 5 Wall., 472. As to the nature of licenses as taxes, see Lucas *v.* Lottery Commissioners, 11 Gill. & J., 490.

[4] Bancroft *v.* Dumas, 21 Vt., 456; Alexander *v.* O'Donnell, 12 Kans., 608. See Page *v.* State, 11 Ala., 849.

where payment is thus made a condition to the right to transact business, a default therein cannot affect the validity of business transactions.[1] But license and tax do not necessarily go together; a license may be required when no tax is imposed, and an unconditional license does not exempt the licensee from being taxed upon the privilege it gives him. In this particular all valuable privileges stand upon the same footing; they are all liable to taxation at the will of the state, unless the state has bargained to exempt them. As is said in one case, "There is a clear distinction recognized between a license granted or required as a condition precedent, before a certain thing can be done, and a tax assessed on the business which that license may authorize one to engage in. A license is a right granted by some competent authority to do an act which, without such authority, would be illegal. A tax is a rate or sum of money assessed upon the person, property, etc., of the citizen."[2] The privilege obtained by the license may therefore be taxed in consideration of the property value it possesses,[3] and this not only by the state directly, but by the county and town also, if proper authority has been conferred upon them for the purpose.[4]

[1] Larned *v.* Andrews, 106 Mass., 435, citing Smith *v.* Mawhood, 14 M. &. W. 452.

[2] *Trippe*, J., in Home Ins. Co. *v.* Augusta, 50 Geo., 530, 537. And see Savannah *v.* Charlton, 36 id., 460; Burch *v.* Savannah, 42 id., 596; Robinson *v.* The Mayor, etc., of Franklin, 1 Humph., 156; Ould *v.* Richmond, 23 Grat., 464; Drexel *v.* Commonwealth, 46 Penn. St., 31; Reed *v.* Beall, 42 Miss., 472.

[3] See authorities cited in last note. Also Coulson *v.* Harris, 43 Miss., 728, in which a license for which a large sum was paid was held taxable as property. Also Drysdale *v.* Pradat, 45 id., 445.

[4] Where one is licensed by the state to carry on any particular business, a county, city, or town cannot compel him to take out a further license as a condition of doing business within it. Durham *v.* Rochester, 5 Cow., 462; Ould *v.* Richmond, 23 Grat, 464; Napier *v.* Hoge, 31 Texas, 287; Floyd *v.* Edenton, 14 Geo., 354: Cuthbert *v.* Conly, 32 id., 211; Savannah *v.* Charlton, 36 id., 460; Burch *v.* Savannah, 42 id., 596; Ordinary *v.* Retailers of Liquors, 42 id., 325; Home Ins. Co. *v.* Augusta, 50 id., 530. So a town cannot defeat a county license by requiring a town license in addition. Dunham *v.* Rochester, *supra;* Rome *v.* Lumpkin, 5 Geo., 447. But these several cases recognize the right of the state to give to the municipalities the authority to tax occupations licensed by the state. In Heise *v.* Columbia, 6 Rich., 404, it was decided that a license granted by the state could not be forfeited by a municipal corporation for breach of condition, any more than could any other thing of value.

Construction of municipal powers. The general rule that the powers of a municipal corporation are to be construed with strictness, is peculiarly applicable to the case of taxes on occupations. It is presumed the legislature has granted in plain terms all it has intended to grant at all. If it is not manifest that there has been a purpose by the legislature to give authority for collecting a revenue by taxes on specified occupations, any exaction for that purpose will be illegal.[1] If a minimum tax is prescribed by statute, one measured by the business, and which may exceed the sum named, is unauthorized and void;[2] but where a discretionary power is conferred, its exercise will not be interfered with, unless it clearly appears to have been abused.[3]

Kinds of business taxed. If taxes were levied on any well matured or intelligible system, it might be practicable to classify those which are levied upon business, with reference to the special reasons which have induced the selection of particular branches of business for taxation, and the exemption of others. But this is wholly impracticable. Many impolitic taxes are laid, and many unjust taxes, without any purpose to do what is not for the public interest, or what is unfair and unequal. A vast number

[1] See Kip *v.* Patterson, 26 N. J., 298, in which the requirement of a fee of five cents from every person selling hay or other produce within the city was held unauthorized, the power to tax in that manner not having been conferred, and the requirement not appearing to be made as a police regulation. For the general principle, see Robinson *v.* Franklin, 1 Humph., 156; St. Louis *v.* Laughlin, 49 Mo., 559; Dubuque *v.* Life Ins. Co., 29 Iowa, 9.

[2] Kniper *v.* Louisville, 7 Bush, 599. On the principle of a strict construction of powers, it was held in Butler's Appeal, 73 Penn. St., 448, that the authority to impose a license fee did not carry with it authority to punish the failure to pay the fee by fine and imprisonment.

[3] Burlington *v.* Putnam Ins. Co., 31 Iowa, 102; Kniper *v.* Louisville, 7 Bush, 599; citing Mason *v.* Lancaster, 4 id., 406. It was decided in the case first named, that the city might graduate the rate of licenses when not restricted in that regard. And see East St. Louis *v.* Wehrung, 46 Ill., 392. Authority "to make such assessment on the inhabitants of Augusta, or those who hold taxable property within the same, as may seem expedient," will warrant a tax on a foreign insurance company doing business within the city. Home Ins. Co. *v.* Augusta, 50 Geo., 530. See Commonwealth *v.* Milton, 12 B. Monr., 212. That special powers conferred upon towns to charge license fees are valid, though the like licenses are not allowed by the general laws of the state, see Woodward *v.* Turnbull, 3 Scam., 1; Ottawa *v.* La Salle, 12 Ill., 339; Byers *v.* Olney, 16 id., 35

of subjects are sometimes selected for taxation, because it is supposed justice requires it, when, had the same burden been laid upon a few, it would have been quite as just, quite as equally distributed, and the tax collected with greater economy. Classification will, therefore, not be attempted, but some reference may be made to those occupations which are most often selected for taxation.

Bankers. There are various methods of taxing the business of bankers. When it is carried on under corporate powers, the franchise is sometimes subjected to a specific tax; but taxes are also imposed which are measured by the business done, the deposits received, the profits made, etc. Brokers are taxed after similar standards.[1]

Carriers of Goods and Persons. While railway corporations are generally taxed upon their property, they are also sometimes taxed in other modes. In some states they are taxed a specific rate on their capital, in others the franchise is taxed, in others the business or profits.[2] The vehicle, by means of which the business is carried on may also be taxed, when the tax does not amount to a regulation of inter-state commerce.[3]

Practitioners of Law and Medicine. These are frequently taxed a specific sum upon the privilege of pursuing their calling for a year or other specified time. Such a tax is not a poll tax, and may therefore be levied when poll taxes are forbidden.[4]

[1] As to definitions of bankers and brokers under the federal revenue laws, see Northrup *v.* Shook, 10 Blatch., 243; U. S. *v.* Cutting, 3 Wall., 441; U. S. *v.* Fisk, id., 445. Of cattle brokers, see U. S. *v.* Kenton, 2 Bond, 97. Of brokers, State *v.* Field, 49 Mo., 270. A statute of Tennessee required those buying notes at a greater shave than six per cent. to take out a license, make a statement of the amount employed in the business the preceding year, and pay thereon a tax of five cents on each $100. The penalty for a failure to comply with it was $500. This act enforced. Young *v.* The Governor, 11 Humph., 147. Bankers whose whole capital is invested in government securities are not taxable as such. Chicago *v.* Lunt, 52 Ill., 414.

[2] See State Tax on Gross Receipts, 15 Wall., 284.

[3] See *ante*, pp. 61–64. A wharfage tax may be levied by a city as a tax on all vessels touching at its wharves. Marshall *v.* Vicksburgh, 15 Wall., 146. As to duties on tonage, see *ante*, p. 61.

[4] Egan *v.* County Court, 3 H. & McH., 169. Authority to tax "trades, occupations and professions," does not authorize a tax on notaries public. New Orleans *v.* Bienvenu, 23 La. An., 710.

Sometimes the tax is graduated by the supposed value of the privilege.[1]

Auctioneers and Commission Dealers. These are commonly taxed either a specific sum periodically, or a sum measured by the extent of their dealings.[2] It has been held that a tax "on the gross amount of auction sales made in and during the tax year" is to be assessed against and paid by the auctioneer, and not by the owner of property sold.[3] This is doubtless correct, though in the end such a tax is paid by the employer.

Merchants. This class of persons is often selected for taxation.[4] The fact that they pay taxes on their stock in trade as property, does not preclude their occupation being specially taxed.[5]

[1] See Simmons *v.* State, 12 Mo., 268; Ould *v.* Richmond, 23 Grat., 464. A tax on the "privilege" of a lawyer may be enforced (under proper legislation), by levy on the body. Stewart *v.* Potts, 49 Miss., 749. See Jones *v.* Page, 44 Ala., 657. Where the charter of a city enumerated certain classes that should be compelled to take out a license before exercising their vocation in the city, and then followed with these words: "and all other business, trades, avocations, or professions whatever," it was held that if the profession of "law" was not specifically enumerated in the section, that the city had no power to lay a license tax on lawyers. The rule is, where general words follow particular ones, to construe them as applicable only to persons or things of the same general character or class. City of St. Louis *v.* Laughlin, 49 Mo., 559. Clergymen are sometimes subjected to an occupation tax. See Miller *v.* Kirkpatrick, 29 Penn. St., 226. So are college professors. See Union County *v.* James, 21 id., 525.

[2] Moseley *v.* Tift, 4 Fla., 402; Paddleford *v* Savannah, 14 Geo., 438. In Pearce *v.* Augusta, 37 id., 597, it was decided that a general authority to levy taxes on *taxable property* would support a tax on the amount of gross sales and on the commissions received. In Lott *v.* Ross, 38 Ala., 156, it was held that a tax on "the gross amount of sales of merchandise" is not a property tax, but an occupation or privilege tax, the amount being regulated by the extent to which the privilege has been enjoyed. (Citing Moseley *v.* Tift, 4 Fla., 402; State *v.* Stephens, 4 Texas, 137; State *v.* Bock, 9 id., 369; De Witt *v.* Hays, 2 Cal., 468; Nathan *v.* Louisiana, 8 How., 80). Such a tax would therefore not be leviable under a power to levy a tax "not exceeding twenty cents upon each hundred dollars of taxable property" within the county. Id.

[3] State *v.* Lee, 38 Ala., 222.

[4] As to what constitutes a "merchant," see State *v.* Whittaker, 33 Mo., 457; State *v.* West, 34 id., 424. What a "dealer in tobacco," Carter *v.* State, 44 Ala., 29.

[5] Woolman *v.* State, 2 Swan, 353; State *v.* Stephens, 4 Texas, 137; State *v.* Bock, 9 id., 369. As to such taxes in general, see Wilmington *v.* Roby, 8

Other dealers are taxed under proper designations. But where a municipal corporation is empowered to tax a particular occupation, it cannot, by definition, bring persons within the power who do not in fact follow the occupation.[1] But a merchant, paying a tax as such, if he adds to that occupation another though kindred business which is separately taxed, is not by his license as a merchant excused from paying the tax on such other occupation.[2]

Peddlers and transient dealers are commonly taxed a specific sum by the year, because they are likely to escape any other.[3]

Manufacturers and Dealers in Liquors. This is a class of dealers commonly selected for exceptional taxation. Their occupation is sometimes taxed for federal, state and municipal purposes, though their stocks are taxed as property, and whatever has been imported has paid a heavy duty. The right to levy these several taxes has almost ceased to be contested.[4] Regulation is generally had in view in such taxes, and they will be referred to again

Ired., 250; Commissioners *v.* Patterson, 8 Jones' L., 182; Cousins *v.* Commonwealth, 19 Grat., 807; French *v.* Barber, 4 Sneed, 193. A statute required a license to be obtained by every person selling goods by sample who was not a "resident merchant." *Held*, that, as a man may be a resident citizen and not a resident merchant, and the reverse, there was no discrimination in favor of citizens of the state, and therefore the statute was constitutional. Such a statute is not a regulation of commerce between the states. Speer *v.* Commonwealth, 23 Grat., 935; S. C., 14 Am. Rep., 164.

[1] Mays *v.* Cincinnati, 1 Ohio, N. S, 268. Case of a tax on "hucksters."

[2] Hirsh *v.* Commonwealth, 21 Grat., 785. Case of a merchant taxed as junk dealer also.

[3] For definition of "peddler," see State *v.* Hodgdon, 41 Vt., 139. The following are cases of such taxes: Wyne *v.* Wright, 1 Dev. & Bat., 19; Cowles *v.* Brittain, 2 Hawks, 204; Wilmington *v.* Roby, 8 Ired., 250; Whitfield *v.* Longest, 6 id., 268; Plymouth *v.* Pettijohn, 4 Dev., 591; State *v.* City Council, 10 Rich., 240; State *v.* Pinckney, 10 id., 474; City Council *v.* Ahrens, 4 Strob., 241; Keller *v.* State, 11 Md., 525. For case of a tax on those canvassing to buy or actually buying means of subsistance, see Sledd *v.* Commonwealth, 19 Grat., 813.

[4] See Durach's Appeal, 62 Penn. St., 491; Aulanier *v.* The Governor, 1 Texas, 653; Baker *v.* Panola County, 30 id., 86; Kitson *v.* Ann Arbor, 26 Mich., 325; Block *v.* Jacksonville, 36 Ill., 301. Such taxes when laid by municipalities are not void because of their discriminating as between different localities therein. East St. Louis *v.* Wehrung, 46 Ill., 392. As to tne difference between a manufacturer and a dealer, see State *v.* Campbell, 33 Penn. St., 380.

in the next chapter. Some of the cases which have considered taxes of this nature are referred to in the note.[1]

Theatrical Exhibitions and Shows. These are a very proper subject for special taxation, and are commonly charged either a specific tax by the year or for single representations. Such taxes call for no special remark.[2]

Hackmen, Draymen, etc. While these classes of persons are usually required to take out a license for purposes of regulation, they are also sometimes charged a substantial sum for revenue purposes. A few cases are referred to in which the license fee was construed to be a tax.[3]

Taxes on Manufactures. These are generally excise taxes. For a time, during the civil war, nearly all manufactures were taxed by the federal government, but only a few kinds are now taxed, either by the nation or by the states. Any or all may be taxed by both.[4]

Taxes on Offices. The United States may tax the salaries or compensation of its officers, and the states may tax those of the

[1] It was once a question whether license to keep a tavern included authority to sell liquors, and the following cases have considered it, or points bearing upon it. Hirn *v.* State, 1 Ohio, N. S., 15; Page *v.* State, 11 Ala., 849; Commissioners, etc., *v.* Jordan, 18 Pick., 228. Compare State *v.* Chamblyss, 1 Cheves, 220; Commissioners of Roads *v.* Dennis, id., 229. As to tavern licenses, see further, State *v.* Prettyman, 3 Harr., 570; Bonner *v.* Welborn, 7 Geo., 296; Hannibal *v.* Guyott, 18 Mo., 515; St. Louis *v.* Siegrist, 46 id., 593; Commonwealth *v.* Thayer, 5 Met., 246; Overseers of Crown Point *v.* Warner, 3 Hill, 150. That under the power to "tax" and also to "restrain" the liquor traffic, a town may license it, see Mt. Carmel *v.* Wabash County, 50 Ill., 69.

[2] See Mabry *v.* Tarver, 1 Humph., 94, 98; Trapp *v.* White, 35 Texas, 387; Orton *v.* Brown, 35 Miss., 426; Germania *v.* State, 7 Md., 1. The business of a traveling circus not a trade. Speak *v.* Powell, L. R., 9 Exch., 25. The license fee not a tax on property. Orton *v.* Brown, *supra.* See Baker *v.* Cincinati, 11 Ohio, N. S., 534.

[3] Bennett *v.* Birmingham, 31 Penn. St., 15; Commonwealth *v.* Stodder, 2 Cush., 562. For some special questions the following cases may be consulted: St. Charles *v.* Nolle, 51 Mo., 122; Gartside *v.* East St. Louis, 43 Ill., 47; Snyder *v.* North Lawrence, 8 Kans., 82; Cincinnati *v.* Bryson, 15 Ohio, 625.

[4] See Commonwealth *v.* Byrne, 20 Grat., 165. A gas company is a "manufacturing company." Commonwealth *v.* Lowell Gas Light Co., 12 Allen, 75. But an aqueduct company is not. Dudley *v.* Jamaica Pond Aqueduct Co., 100 Mass., 183.

state officers, though neither can tax the compensation received by the officers of the other.[1] And the state may authorize its subdivisions to tax state, county or township offices if it shall be deemed proper to do so.[2]

Other "Privilege" Taxes. Where "privileges" are taxed, any occupation which is not open to all, but can only be exercised under license from some constituted authority, is to be regarded as a privilege.[3] And succession to an inheritance may be taxed as a privilege, notwithstanding the property of the estate is taxed, and taxes on property are required by the constitution of the state to be uniform.[4] Where a tax is laid on all "pursuing any occupation, trade or profession," one keeping a billiard table for profit is included; though if he kept it for amusement merely he would not be.[5] It is no objection to a tax on a business that it operates indirectly as a tax on the consumer.[6] That may perhaps be the very reason why it has been deemed desirable to levy it.

A tax on a business should be laid where the business is carried on; not where the party has his residence, if it is elsewhere.[7]

Taxes on corporations. These are imposed in so many forms

[1] Collector *v.* Day, 11 Wall, 113; *ante*, p. 58. The compensation of a clerk in a postoffice is taxable by the state. Melcher *v.* Boston, 9 Met., 73.

[2] Gilkeson *v.* The Frederick Justices, 13 Grat., 577.

[3] *Caruthers*, J., in French *v.* Baker, 4 Sneed, 193, 195.

[4] Eyre *v.* Jacob, 14 Grat., 422.

[5] Tarde *v.* Benseman, 31 Texas, 277.

[6] Wiley *v.* Owens, 39 Ind., 429.

[7] Bates *v.* Mobile, 46 Ala., 158. See Miner *v.* Fredonia, 27 N. Y., 155; Gardiner, etc., Co. *v.* Gardiner, 5 Greenl., 133. For other cases of business or occupation taxes, see Simmons *v.* State, 12 Mo., 268; St. Louis *v.* Laughlin, 49 id., 456; Carroll *v.* Tuscaloosa, 12 Ala., 173; Gunter *v.* Leckey, 30 id., 591, Portland *v.* O'Niell, 1 Oregon, 218. As to meaning of *profits* or *income* when a tax is laid on results by this designation, see People *v.* Supervisors of Niagara, 4 Hill, 20; Same *v.* Same, 7 id., 504; New Orleans *v.* Hart, 14 La. An., 803; Same *v.* Fassman, id., 865. As to meaning of an insurance company's *surplus*, see State *v.* Parker, 34 N. J., 479; Same *v.* Same, 35 id., 574. A provision in a city charter that its taxes should "be apportioned in the same manner as the state tax," would preclude its discriminating against an occupation in a degree beyond that made against that occupation by the state. Marshall *v.* Snediker, 25 Texas, 460.

that an enumeration is difficult. The following may be mentioned: 1. A specific tax on the franchise. 2. A tax on the property by valuation. 3. A tax on the capital stock. 4. A tax on the business done. 5. A tax on dividends or on profits. Sometimes the franchise is taxed, and also the capital stock or the property; but to tax the capital stock and also the property in which the capital is invested, would be imposing the same burden twice on the same property, and consequently unjust, if not illegal.[1]

[1] The legislature has power to require corporations organized in the state to pay to the treasurer of the state, a tax on the excess of the market value of all their capital stock, over the value of their real estate and machinery otherwise taxable. Commonwealth *v.* Lowell Gas Light Co., 12 Allen, 75; Commonwealth *v.* Hamilton Manuf. Co., id., 298. Such a tax cannot be supported as a tax on property, because not "proportional;" "that is, it is not laid according to any rule of proportion whatever, but is imposed only on the corporations designated in the act, without any reference to the amount required to be raised by taxation for public purposes, or to the actual property held by such corporation subject to taxation, or to the whole amount of property in the commonwealth liable to be assessed for the public service. Commonwealth *v.* Peoples' Savings Bank, 5 Allen, 428, 431; Oliver *v.* Washington Mills, 11 id., 268, 274." Per *Bigelow*, Ch. J., in Commonwealth *v.* Hamilton Manuf. Co., 12 id., 298, 300. It is "in the nature of an excise or duty on the franchise or privilege of each of the corporations designated, to be estimated and measured by ascertaining the excess of the market value of the capital stock or aggregate of the shares, over the value of the real estate and machinery for which each corporation was assessed, in the town or city in which it was established and carried on its business." *Bigelow*, Ch. J., in Commonwealth *v.* Lowell Gas Light Co., 12 Allen, 75, 76. In 12 Allen, 301, the judge shows that this is not equivalent to a tax on property, as the value of the shares may not correspond at all to that. See also Manuf. Ins. Co. *v.* Loud, 99 Mass., 146; Provident Ins. Co. *v.* Massachusetts, 6 Wall., 611; Hamilton Co. *v.* Massachusetts, id., 632; Illinois Mut. Fire Ins. Co. *v.* Peoria, 29 Ill., 180; Coite *v.* Society for Savings, 32 Conn., 173; Society for Savings *v.* Coite, 6 Wall., 594; Coite *v.* Conn. Mut. Life Ins. Co., 36 Conn., 512. That an excise tax may be imposed on corporations chartered in other states, but doing business in the state imposing it, see Attorney General *v.* Bay State Mining Co., 99 Mass., 148. The subject of taxes on foreign insurance companies was much considered in People *v.* Thurber, 13 Ill., 554, per *Caton*, J., and in People *v.* State Treasurer, 31 Mich., 6, per *Graves*, J. It was objected in People *v.* Thurber, that the tax was void because not uniform; that is, because the same sum was not imposed upon each company or agent; but it was well replied that there was no impropriety or injustice in requiring each to contribute to the state revenues in proportion to the amount of business done or money received. That a tax on the market value of the stock of corporations,

Taxation of national banks. By the act of congress of June 3, 1864, the shares of stock held by any person or body corporate in any of the national banks, are allowed to be included in the valuation of personal property "in the assessment of taxes imposed by or under state authority, at the place where such bank

is not applicable to the guaranty stock of a mutual life insurance company, which is redeemable from its earnings, such stock being rather in the nature of a debt of the corporation than stock as generally understood, see Commonwealth *v.* Berkshire Life Ins. Co., 98 Mass., 25. As to the taxation of the capital of mutual life insurance companies, see Coite *v.* Conn. Mut. Life Ins. Co., 36 Conn., 512.

An English joint stock insurance company, clothed with the right of acting independently of the rules that govern an ordinary partnership, is taxable as a "company incorporated or associated." Oliver *v.* Liverpool, etc., Co., 100 Mass., 531; Liverpool, etc., Co. *v.* Massachusetts, 10 Wall., 566.

In Coite *v.* Society for Savings, 32 Conn., 173, 184, in which a tax on a savings institution measured by the amount of its deposits, was contested on the ground that, in effect, it was a tax on United States securities in which the funds of the corporation had been invested, *McCurdy*, J., speaking of the various methods of taxation, says: "Most commonly the tax is laid upon property. But this is not always the most convenient, expedient or just mode. A large portion of the national revenues accrues from a tax on incomes, dividends, licenses, legacies, stamps, etc., irrespective of property. In this state, for many years, and until very lately, the form of taxing lawyers, physicians, traders, tavern keepers, manufacturers and mechanics, was to assess them, either at a fixed sum for each respective class, or at the discretion of the 'listers.' In familiar language, this was called an 'assessment on the faculty.' The present statutes are not free from similar provisions. A capitation tax still remains. The agent, in this state, of an insurance company existing out of the state, is required, in consequence of being allowed to conduct business here, to pay a certain per centage on the amount of his premiums and collections. Auctioneers and express companies are assessed in a like manner. In the case of quarry, mine and ore bed companies (joint stock or incorporated), not only the stock itself, but the franchise is expressly made subject to assessment. By a law of 1862, it is enacted that, for the purposes of taxation, no stock of any railroad company shall be estimated in the list at less than ten per cent. of its par value, although it was then notorious that much of the stock so to be valued was utterly worthless. These examples show that the state has ever adopted, at its own will, different bases of taxation as applied to different subjects, and there is no occasion for surprise that the legislature, in the matter before us, thought proper to impose a tax directly and specifically on these corporations as such, without reference to their assets. There is no reason why they should not contribute their full share to support the government through which they exist and flourish."

As to the taxation of savings societies in general, see Savings Bank *v.* New London, 20 Conn., 111.

is located, and not elsewhere, but not at a greater rate than is assessed upon other moneyed capital in the hands of individual citizens of such state," and not exceeding "the rate imposed upon the shares of any of the banks organized under the authority of the state" where the bank is located; and nothing in the act is to exempt the real estate of such banks "from either state, county or municipal taxes, to the same extent, according to its value, as other real estate is taxed." Under this act, if no tax is imposed by the state on shares in state banks, the shares in the national banks are not taxed at all.[1] This difficulty was met with in states whose laws taxed the capital of banks, but not the shares thereof.[2] The act of congress does not allow of taxation of the capital,[3] nor will it admit of municipal taxation of national bank shares, when the state banks are exempt therefrom.[4] But the fact that two banks, by their charter, are specially taxed, will not preclude the taxation of the shares in the national banks by general law,[5] neither are the shares to be excluded from taxation, because some other classes of moneyed capital are exempt from taxation by law of limited application.[6] It is competent to require that the tax on the shares shall be paid by the bank.[7]

Van Allen *v.* The Assessors, 3 Wall., 573; Bradley *v.* People, 4 id., 459.

[2] Bradley *v.* People, 4 Wall., 459; Smith *v.* First National Bank of Tecumseh, 17 Mich., 479.

[3] Smith *v.* First National Bank of Tecumseh, 17 Mich., 479; Collins *v.* Chicago, 4 Biss., 472. See Smith *v.* Webb, 11 Minn., 500; First National Bank of Hannibal *v.* Meredith, 44 Mo., 500.

[4] Craft *v.* Tuttle, 27 Ind., 332; Wright *v.* Stiltz, id., 338.

[5] Lionberger *v.* Rouse, 43 Mo., 67; S. C. in error, 9 Wall., 468.

[6] Everett's Appeal, 71 Penn. St., 219. The whole subject of taxation under this law received careful examination in Provident Institution *v.* Boston, 101 Mass., 575. And see Tappan *v.* Merchants' National Bank, 19 Wall., 490, opinion by *Waite*, Ch. J.

[7] National Bank *v.* Commonwealth, 9 Wall., 353; Lionberger *v.* Rouse, id., 468; First National Bank *v.* Douglass Co., 1 Cent. Law Jour., 584, per *Dillon*, J. As the federal decisions referred to seem now to have covered the ground of taxation of national banks, we abstain from reference to many state decisions.

CHAPTER XIX.

TAXES UNDER THE POWER OF POLICE.

Difference between taxation and regulation. There are some cases in which levies are made and collected under the general designation of taxes, or under some name employed in revenue laws, to indicate a particular class of taxes, where the imposition of the burden may fairly be referred to some other authority than to that branch of the sovereign power of the state under which the public revenues are apportioned and collected. The reason is, that the imposition has not for its object the raising of revenue, but looks rather to the regulation of relative rights, privileges and duties, as between individuals, to the conservation of order in the political society, to the encouragement of industry, and the discouragement of pernicious employments.[1] Legislation for these purposes, it would seem proper to look upon as being made in the exercise of that authority which is inherent in every sovereignty, to make all such rules and regulations as are needful to secure and preserve the public order, and to protect each individual in the enjoyment of his own rights and privileges by requiring the observance of rules of order, fairness and good neighborhood, by all around him. This manifestation of the sovereign authority is usually spoken of as the police power.

The distinction between a demand of money, under the police power, and one made under the power to tax, is not so much one of form as of substance. The proceedings may be the same in the two cases, though the purpose is essentially different. The one is made for regulation and the other for revenue. If, therefore, the purpose is evident in any particular instance, there can be no difficulty in classifying the case and referring it to the

[1] Mr. Walker, in his Science of Wealth, adds this to Adam Smith's four cardinal rules of taxation: "V. The heaviest taxes should be imposed on those commodities the consumption of which is especially prejudicial to the interests of the people."

proper power. But in what has been said regarding the apportionment of taxes, it has been seen that other considerations than those which regard the production of a revenue are admissible, and that regulation may be kept in view when revenue is the main and primary purpose. The right of any sovereignty to look beyond the immediate purpose to the general effect, neither is nor can be disputed; the government has general authority to raise a revenue and to choose the methods of doing so; it has also general authority in the regulation of relative rights, privileges and duties; and there is no rule of reason, policy or government which can require the legislature, when making laws with the one object in view, to exclude carefully from its attention the other. Nevertheless, cases of this nature are to be regarded as cases of taxation. Revenue is the primary purpose, and the regulation results from the methods of apportionment that are resorted to in obtaining the revenue. Only those cases, where regulation is the primary purpose, can be specially referred to the police power.

Custom has much to do in determining whether certain classes of exactions are to be regarded as taxes or as duties imposed for regulation. If by the common understanding and general custom of the country, a particular duty is regarded as being imposed upon certain individuals, not as their proportionate share in the burdens of government, but because of some special relation to property peculiarly located, or to business peculiarly troublesome or dangerous, so that a requirement that the duty shall be performed by such individuals is usually regarded as only in the nature of regulation of relative obligations and duties through the neighborhood or the municipality, there is no sufficient reason why this may not be considered a mere police regulation, though the proceedings assume the form of taxation, and are even designated by that name. The summoning of the people once a year to put the highways of their neighborhood in order, has sometimes been looked upon as a case of this description; to some extent, at least, in the nature of a police regulation,[1] notwithstanding that, on a failure to obey the summons, the value of the

[1] See State *v.* Halifax, 4 Dev. Law, 345; Sawyer *v.* Alton, 3 Scam., 127, 130; Pleasant *v.* Kost, 290 Ill., 49; Overseers of Amenia *v.* Stamford, 6 Johns., 92; Draining Company Case, 11 La. An., 338, 372.

labor is collected in money. A public purpose, such as is usually accomplished by an expenditure of public moneys, is indeed had in view in such a case; but the custom of requiring highway labor seems to have come down to us from a period when regular taxes were unknown or only collected in kind, and when it was looked upon as a neighborhood duty to keep the roads in order, as it was to prevent riots and arrest criminals, or make compensation for their offenses. A like practice, based upon a similar idea, has prevailed in other countries.

Sidewalk assessments. The cases of assessments for the construction of walks by the side of the streets, in cities and other populous places, are more distinctly referable to the power of police. These foot walks are not only required, as a rule, to be put and kept in proper condition for use by the adjacent proprietors, but it is quite customary to confer by the municipal charters full authority upon the municipalities, to order the walks of a kind and quality by them prescribed, to be constructed by the owners of adjacent lots at their own expense, within a time limited by the order for the purpose, and that in case of their failure so to construct them, it shall be done by the public authorities, and the cost collected from such owners, or made a lien upon their property. When this is done the duty must be looked upon as being enjoined as a regulation of police, made because of the peculiar interest such owners have in the walks, and because their situation gives them peculiar fitness and ability for performing, with promptness and convenience, the duty of putting them in proper state, and of afterwards keeping them in a condition suitable for use. Upon these grounds the authority to establish such regulations has frequently been supported.[1]

[1] The leading case is that of Godard, Petitioner, 16 Pick., 504, 509, in which *Shaw*, Ch. J., speaking of a by-law imposing such an assessment, answers the principal objections to it, and explains its nature as follows:

"Another, and perhaps the most important objection is, that the by-law is one imposing a tax or duty upon the citizens, and it is a violation of the constitution in this, that it is partial, and unequal, and contravenes that fundamental maxim of our social system, that all burdens and taxes laid on the people for the public good shall be equal. But the court are all of the opinion that the by-law in question is not obnoxious to this objection.

"It is not speaking strictly to characterize this city ordinance as a law levying a tax, the direct or principal object of which is, the raising of revenue.

Sewer assessments. There seems to be no legal impediment to a requirement under the police power that lot owners in cities

It imposes a duty upon a large class of persons, the performance of which requires some labor and expense, and therefore indirectly operates as a law creating a burden; but we think it is rather to be regarded as a police regulation, requiring a duty to be performed, highly salutary and advantageous to the citizens of a populous and closely built city, and which is imposed upon them because they are so situated as that they can most promptly and conveniently perform it, and it is laid, not upon a few, but upon a numerous class, all those who are so situated, and equally upon all who are within the description composing the class. It is said to be unequal, because it singles out a particular class of citizens, to wit, the owners and occupiers of real estate, and imposes the duty exclusively upon them. If this were an arbitrary selection of a class of citizens, without reference to their peculiar fitness and ability to perform the duty, the objection would have great weight; as for instance, if the expense of clearing the streets of snow were imposed upon the mechanics, or merchants, or any other distinct class of citizens, between whose convenience and accommodation, and the labor to be done, there is no natural relation. But suppose there is a class of citizens who will themselves commonly derive a benefit from the performance of some public duty, we can see no inequality in requiring that all those who will derive such benefit, shall by a general and equal law be required to do it. Suppose a by-law should require every inhabitant who keeps a cart, truck or other team, or a coach or other carriage, to turn out himself, or send a man, with one or more horses, after a heavy fall of snow, to assist in leveling it. Although other citizens would derive a benefit, yet as these derive some peculiar benefit, accompanied with the ability, I can at present perceive no valid objection to a by-law requiring it, on the ground of inequality. Supposing a general regulation, that at certain seasons of the year, every shopkeeper should sprinkle the sidewalk in front of his own shop, or sweep it, inasmuch as he has a peculiar benefit, and as the duty is equal upon all who come within the description, it seems to us to be equal, in the sense in which the law requires all such burdens to be equal. And it appears to us that the case before us is similar. Although the sidewalk is part of the public street, and the public have an easement in it, yet the adjacent occupant is often the owner of the fee, and generally has some peculiar interest in it, and benefit from it, distinct from that which he enjoys in common with the rest of the community. He has this interest and benefit, often in accommodating his cellar door and steps, a passage for fuel, and the passage to and from his own house to the street. To some purposes, therefore, it is denominated his sidewalk. For his own accommodation, he would have an interest in clearing the snow from his own door. The owners and occupiers of house lots and other real estate, therefore, have an interest in the performance of this duty, peculiar and somewhat distinct from that of the rest of the community. Besides, from their situation, they have power and ability to perform this duty, with the promptness which the benefit of the community requires; and the duty is divided, distributed and apportioned upon so large a number, that it can be done promptly and

and villages shall be at the expense of constructing that portion of the public sewer in front of their respective premises. It is

effectually, and without imposing a very severe burden upon any one. Supposing a by-law should require, what is often done, in practice, that upon an alarm of fire in the night, all householders, on streets leading to and near the fire, should exhibit a light. This would seem to be reasonable. Or that all the owners or occupiers of dwelling houses, having a well and pump, should keep them in repair at their own expense, to be used in case of fire. It would operate partially, but it seems to us not unequal, in the sense in which we are using that term. The city might keep persons ready in every street to light torches and flambeaux in case of fire, and the expense to be paid from the treasury; still it appears to me, that as householders would derive a benefit from the operation of this general regulation, as their local situation puts it peculiarly within their power and ability to perform it without great expense, and as it is equal in its terms, it would not be obnoxious to the charge of being invalid for partiality and inequality.

"In all these cases the answer to the objection of partiality and inequality is, that the duty required is a duty upon the person in respect to the property which he holds, occupies and enjoys, under the protection and benefit of the laws; that it operates on each and all in their turns, as they become owners and occupiers of such estates, and it ceases to be required of them, when they cease to be such holders and occupiers of the estate, in respect to which the duty is required. In this respect it is like a land tax, or house tax, it does not bear upon all citizens alike, but it is not on that account unequal or partial, in the sense contemplated by the declaration of rights, requiring all taxes and burdens to be equal and impartial." The following cases support the same view. Lowell *v.* Hadley, 8 Met., 180; Paxson *v.* Sweet, 13 N. J., 196; Washington *v.* Nashville, 1 Swan, 177; Whyte *v.* Nashville, 2 id., 364; Franklin *v.* Mayberry, 6 Humph., 368; Bonsall *v.* Lebanon, 19 Ohio, 418; Deblois *v.* Barker, 4 R. I., 445; O'Leary *v.* Sloo, 7 La. An., 25; Hart *v.* Brooklyn, 36 Barb., 226; Buffalo City Cemetery Co., *v.* Buffalo, 46 N. Y., 503; Greensburg *v.* Young, 53 Penn. St., 280; Hydes *v.* Joyes, 4 Bush, 464. And see Hudler *v.* Golden, 36 N. Y., 446: Woodbridge *v.* Detroit, 8 Mich., 274, 309, per *Christiancy*, J. The case of Ottowa *v.* Spencer, 40 Ill., 211, 217, is *contra*. In New Jersey, where it is held that the assessment for an improvement on the adjoining land owners, must not exceed the *actual* benefit conferred by such improvement, it is also held that the whole expense of a sidewalk may be assessed upon the lot in front of which it is constructed, regardless of absolute benefits. Van Tassel *v.* Jersey City, 14 Am. L. Reg. (N. S.), 258. In Twycross *v.* Fitchburg R. R. Co., 10 Gray, 293, 295, a lessee's covenant to pay "all taxes or duties," levied or to be levied on the premises during the term, was held not to apply to an assessment for paving the sidewalk in front; that not being a tax or duty levied or to be levied on the premises demised. "It is a permanent improvement of the estate, the benefit of which is to be found in the increased value of the estate, and in the increased rent which it would permanently command." Per *Thomas*, J. It is no objection to a sidewalk tax that a street is not graded. Parker *v.* Challiss, 9 Kans., 155; Challiss *v.*

true, that the levies for the purpose of constructing sewers and of keeping them in repair are commonly spoken of as taxes;[1] but, as has been justly remarked, there is as much reason to subject the owners of land abutting to contribution to their expenditure, as there is to oblige them to pave the footways in front of their grounds, or to keep the same in repair, when the city shall pave the streets adjoining. It should be a charge on the land, just as is the requisition on the owners of land abutting on the streets to clear away the snow at their own expense, which has been determined to be a reasonable provision. It is a charge upon real estate thus situated, and requisite for the comfort and convenience of all the citizens.[2] By this is not meant that the expense of sewers may not be borne by general tax, as indeed is often done: what is meant is only this, that the purpose to be accomplished is of that peculiar nature that the duty to provide for it seems intimately associated with the ownership of adjacent property, the value of which will be increased and the use facilitated by means thereof; and it is therefore within the competency of the legislature to impose upon the owners of such property the duty to make provision for it.

Levee assessments. Assessments for the construction of em bankments or levees, to protect from overflow and destruction

Parker, 11 id., 384. Even when once graded, the grade may be changed at the discretion of the municipal authorities, without affording any legal ground for complaint to the parties affected. Pontiac *v.* Carter, Sup. Ct. Mich. (1875); 2 Am. L. Times, —; 12 Albany L. Jour., p. 88. As a matter of construction, the following cases are important: In Williams *v.* Bruce, 5 Conn., 190, it was decided that the building of a railing on the inner side of a sidewalk could not be compelled under a general authority to require the sidewalk to be constructed. In Wright *v.* Briggs, 2 Hill, 77, it was held that authority to a village council to require adjoining owners to construct sidewalks in front of their premises, would not warrant imposing upon them a tax for improving the street. A power in a municipal charter to "regulate and improve" sidewalks, does not authorize an assessment for their construction. Fairfield *v.* Ratcliffe, 20 Iowa, 396.

[1] See Philadelphia *v.* Tryon, 35 Penn. St., 401; Stroud *v.* Philadelphia, 61 id., 255; Boston *v.* Shaw, 1 Met., 130; Hildreth *v.* Lowell, 11 Gray, 345; Cone *v.* Hartford, 28 Conn., 363; State *v.* Jersey City, 29 N. J., 441.

[2] *Putnam*, J., in Boston *v.* Shaw, 1 Met., 130, 138. In this case it is decided that the levy of a sewer rate by the value of estates is void, as it could not be equal or just.

large tracts of country, are commonly levied on the owners of lands bordering on or lying near the streams or bodies of water from which the danger is anticipated, and are generally looked upon as a species of local tax.[1] But if it should be imposed as a duty upon residents or property owners in the neighborhood of such a danger, that they should turn out periodically, or in emergencies, and give personal attention and labor to the construction of the necessary defenses against overflow and inundation, it is not perceived that there could be any difficulty in supporting such a requirement as one of police, or of resting it upon the same grounds which sustain the regulations in cities, by which duties are imposed on the occupants of buildings, to take certain precautions against fires, not for their own benefit exclusively, but for the protection of the public.[2]

Drainage laws. Similar considerations apply in the case of drainage laws, which are enacted in order to relieve swamps, marshes and other low lands of the excessive waters which detract from their value for occupation and cultivation, and perhaps render them worthless for use, and are likely at the same time to diffuse through the neighborhood a dangerous nuisance. If these may be drained at the expense of the owner, by special tax, there can be no doubt of the right of the state to make it his duty to drain them, as a matter of police regulation; the state coming forward to perform the duty at his expense, in case of its not being suitably or expeditiously performed.[3]

[1] Crowley *v.* Cropley, 2 La. An., 329. See Sessions *v.* Cronklinton, 20 Ohio, N. S., 349; Egyptian Levee Co. *v.* Hardin, 27 Mo., 495; Yeatman *v.* Crandall, 11 La. An., 220; Wallace *v.* Shelton, 14 id., 498; Bishop *v.* Marks, 15 id., 147; Richardson *v.* Morgan, 16 id., 429; McGehee *v.* Mathis, 21 Ark., 40; Jones *v.* Boston, 104 Mass., 461.

[2] It is said by *Elmer*, J., in State *v.* Newark, 27 N. J., 185, 194, that "laws for the drainage and embanking of low grounds, and to provide for the expense for the mere benefit of the proprietors, without reference to the public good, are to be classed, not under the taxing, but the police power of the government; and so also the regulation of fences and party walls."

[3] In State *v.* City Council of Charleston, 12 Rich., 702, 733, the power to require sewers, drains and sidewalks to be constructed by the owners of the property adjacent, is plainly referred to the police power. "From a very early period sewers and pavements have constituted exceptional subjects in reference to assessments. Statutes of drains and sewers were known before

It is not to be doubted that other cases which may have not yet been the subject of judicial consideration, would fall within the same reasons; but it might be presumptuous to attempt an enumeration of them, especially as there can be little or no occasion for doing so, when the taxing power is commonly sufficient to meet all their requirements. A safer ground will be occupied in the consideration of those cases, so often the subject of judicial review, in which burdens in the shape of license fees have been imposed upon business, trades or occupations.

License fees in general. License fees may be imposed: 1. For regulation. 2. For revenue. 3. To give monopolies. 4. For prohibition. The third purpose is inadmissible in any free government, and has not avowedly been had in view at any time in this country, nor in England, since the period immediately preceding the revolution of 1688, so fruitful of arbitrary exactions of every available nature.[1] The fourth purpose is entirely admissible in the case of pursuits or indulgencies which in their general effect are believed to be more harmful than beneficial to society, and which, consequently, the public interest requires should be put an end to. A case of this nature is that of heavy

the time of Henry VIII, when the general statutes on the subject were enacted, and the mode of assessment prescribed. In like manner the act of 1764, provided for assessments for drains or sewers and sidewalks. Various reasons have been assigned for these exceptions. Among others, it has been plainly urged that, as a sanitary regulation, and under the power to abate nuisances, the corporation might require every citizen to drain his own lot, or in case of neglect, exact a penalty; and so by the old act of 1698 (7 Stat. 12), every inhabitant of Charleston was required to mend and raise the sidewalk in front of his house in the manner and to the dimensions therein prescribed, on penalty of forfeiting for each house a penalty to be collected under the warrant of a justice of the peace. In order the better to carry into effect these objects, and to do what each individual might be required to do for himself, the act of 1764 authorized the commissioners of streets to construct drains and level and pave the footways, etc., and to assess the proprietors of lands and houses fronting on the street, etc." *Dunkin*, Chancellor, p. 733.

[1] Taxation for the benefit of individuals is compared to monopolies by *Lowrie*, Ch. J., in Philadelphia Association, etc. *v.* Wood, 39 Penn. St., 67, 82. The very heavy license fees exacted from pawnbrokers in Dublin are said to owe their origin to a purpose to give a monopoly of the business to a few favored retainers of the court. Of course the weight of such fees rests finally on the persons whose necessities make them the pawnbroker's customers.

fees imposed on the keepers of implements of gaming.[1] When, however, prohibition is the object, the end may generally be more directly accomplished by legislation which in its terms is prohibitory, than by the circuitous method of imposing a burden difficult or impossible to be borne; and the direct method is consequently the one usually adopted. But it is often found that the prohibition of an occupation which excites or gratifies the vices or passions of large numbers of people, is met by a resistance so steady and powerful as to render the law wholly ineffectual, when a heavy tax might lessen the evils and possibly in the end make the occupation unprofitable. A belief that this might be the result, has influenced many persons to favor a repeal of the prohibitory liquor laws, and the substitution therefor of laws for the regulation and taxation of the traffic.[2] But it may safely be

[1] State *v.* Doon, R. M. Charlt., 1. The fee in this case was of $1,000, and it was sustained, although it was manifestly imposed for the purposes of prohibition, and its payment would not give to the owner of the table the privilege of making use of it, which was illegal under another statute. The constitution of Arkansas of 1868 provided that "the general assembly shall tax all privileges, pursuits and occupations that are of no real use to society; all others shall be exempt." Art. 10, § 17.

[2] The constitution of Michigan forbids the grant of licenses for the sale of liquors, and for twenty years a statute was in force making the sale, except for medicinal or mechanical purposes illegal, and all contracts connected with such a sale void. The statute did not answer the expectations of those who procured its passage, and in 1875 it was repealed, and a license tax imposed on the dealers in liquors. The law unquestionably had both revenue and regulation in view, but it was contested as unconstitutional. Many objections were made, but the only one important to our present purpose was considered in Youngblood *v.* Sexton, Sup. Ct. Mich., Oct. 1875, and the importance of the principle involved seems to justify quoting at some length from the opinion:

"The objection which appears to be principally relied upon is, that a tax on the traffic in liquors under this law is equivalent to a license of the traffic, and therefore comes directly in conflict with that provision of the constitution which declares that 'the legislature shall not pass any act authorizing the grant of license for the sale of ardent spirits, or other intoxicating liquors.' Const. Art. IV, sec. 7. * *

"The popular understanding of the word license undoubtedly is a permission to do something which, without the license, would not be allowable. This, we are to suppose, was the sense in which it was made use of in the constitution; but this is also the legal meaning. The object of a license, says Mr. Justice *Manning*, is to confer a right that does not exist without a license. Chilvers *v.* People, 11 Mich., 43, 49. Within this definition a mere tax upon

affirmed that prohibition is seldom the purpose of such burdens, and that revenue or regulation — one or both — are the purposes aimed at in the imposition of license fees.

the traffic cannot be a license of the traffic, unless the tax confers some right to carry on the traffic which otherwise would not have existed. We do not understand that such is the case here. The very act which imposed this tax repealed the previous law which forbade the traffic and declared it illegal. The trade then became lawful whether taxed or not; and this law in imposing the tax did not declare the trade illegal in case the tax was not paid. So far as we can perceive, a failure to pay the tax no more renders the trade illegal than would a like failure of a farmer, to pay the tax on his farm, render its cultivation illegal. The state has imposed the tax in each case, and made such provision as has been deemed needful to insure its payment; but it has not seen fit to make the failure to pay a forfeiture of the right to pursue the calling. If the tax is paid the traffic is lawful, but if not paid the traffic is equally lawful. There is consequently nothing in the case that appears to be in the nature of a license. The state has provided for the taxation of a business which was found in existence, and the carrying on of which it no longer prohibits; and that is all.

"But it is urged that by taxing the business the state recognizes its lawful character, sanctions its existence and participates in its profits, all of which is within the real intent of the prohibition of license. The lawfulness of the business, if by that we understand it is no longer punishable, and is capable of constituting the basis of contracts, was undoubtedly recognized when the prohibitory law was repealed; but as the illegality of the traffic depended on the law, so its lawfulness now depends upon its repeal. The tax has nothing to do with it whatever. Now it is not claimed, so far as we are aware, that the repeal of the prohibitory law was incompetent; and, if not, mere recognition of the lawfulness of the traffic cannot make the tax law or any other law invalid. It is only the recognition of an existing and a conceded fact; and the courts could not refuse to recognize it if they would.

"The idea that the state lends its countenance to any particular traffic by taxing it, seems to rest upon a very transparent fallacy. It certainly overlooks or disregards some ideas that must always underlie taxation. Taxes are not favors; they are burdens. They are necessary, it is true, to the existence of government; but they are not the less burdens, and are only submitted to because of the necessity. It is deemed advisable to make careful provision to preclude these burdens becoming needlessly oppressive; but it is conceded by all the authorities that under some circumstances they may be carried to an extent that will be ruinous to individuals. It would be a remarkable proposition, under such circumstances, that a thing is sanctioned and countenanced by the government, when this burden, which may prove disastrous, is imposed upon it, while on the other hand it is frowned upon and condemned when the burden is withheld. It is safe to predict that if such were the legal doctrine, any citizen would prefer to be visited with the untaxed frowns of government rather than with testimonials of approval, which are represented by the demands of the tax-gatherer.

A license is a privilege granted by the state, usually on pay-

"It may be supposed that some idea of special protection is involved when a business is taxed; taxation and protection being reciprocal. If the tax upon any particular thing was the consideration for the thing given to the owner in respect to it, this might be so; but the maxim of reciprocity in taxation has no such meaning. No government ever undertakes to tax all it protects. If a government were to levy only poll taxes. it would not be on the idea that it was to protect only the persons of its citizens, leaving their property open to rapine and plunder. In this state our taxes are derived mainly from real estate; but it has never been suggested that real estate was entitled to special consideration in consequence. In Great Britain, real estate pays a relatively insignificant portion of the taxes, although in the social and political state it is more important than any other property. As a general fact the United States has not taxed real property, and, though during the recent rebellion it taxed most kinds of business for war purposes, the number of subjects taxed has been several times reduced by legislation since, and may reasonably be expected to be further reduced hereafter. But the business taxed is no more protected than the business not taxed; and the fisheries which are favored by bounties are as much protected as either. All this is only an apportionment of taxation by the selection of subjects which, under all the circumstances, it is deemed wise and politic to subject to the burden. Whether a person in respect to his property or his occupation falls within the category of taxables or not, is immaterial as affecting his claim to protection from the government. It is enough for him that the government has selected for itself its own subjects for taxation, and prescribed its own rules. It is his liability to taxation at the will of the government that entitles him to protection, and not the circumstance of his being actually taxed; and the taxation of a thing may be, and often is, when police purposes are had in view, a means of expressing disapproval instead of approbation of what is taxed. * *

"Taxes upon business are usually collected in the form of license fees; and this may possibly have led to the idea that seems to have prevailed in some quarters, that a tax implied a license. But there is no necessary connection whatever between them. A business may be licensed and yet not taxed, or it may be taxed and yet not licensed. And so far is the tax from being necessarily a license, that provision is frequently made by law for the taxation of a business that is carried on under a license existing independent of the tax.

"Such is the case where cities under proper legislative authority tax occupations that are carried on under licenses from the state. Ould *v.* Richmond, 23 Grat., 464; Napier *v.* Hodges, 31 Texas, 287; Cuthbert *v.* Conley, 32 Geo., 211; Wendover *v.* Lexington, 15 B. Monr., 258. The license confers the privilege, but it is not perceived why a privilege thus conferred should not be taxed as much as any other. The federal laws give us illustration of the taxation of illegal traffic. A case in point was that of the taxation of the liquor traffic in the state previous to the repeal of the prohibitory law; the federal law found a business in existence, and it taxed it without undertaking to give it any protection whatever. McGuire *v.* Commonwealth, Wall., 387; Purvear *v.* Commonwealth, 5 Wall, 475. What

ment of a valuable consideration,[1] though this is not essential. To constitute a privilege the grant must confer authority to do something which without the grant would be illegal; for if what is to be done under the license is open to every one without it, the grant would be merely idle and nugatory, conferring no privilege whatever.[2] But the thing to be done may be something lawful in itself, and only prohibited for the purposes of the license; that is to say, prohibited in order to compel the taking out of a license.[3] This is always the case where that which is licensed was not unlawful at the common law.

would have prevented the state from taxing the same traffic at the same time? Is it any more restricted in the selection of subjects of taxation than the general government is? If one may tax and at the same time refuse to protect, may not the other do the same? The only reason suggested for a negative reply to these questions is, that it was the state itself, not the United States, that made the business illegal, and it would be inconsistent and absurd to declare it illegal and at the same time tax it. But how the inconsistency would appear in one case rather than the other, is not apparent. The illegality was declared by competent authority, and yet the federal government taxed the trade, at the same time refusing or being unable to protect it. If protection because of the tax was due to the very thing upon which the tax was imposed, there would be an inconsistency in taxing a prohibited trade; but treating taxation, however and wherever it may fall, as the return for the general benefits of government — for the protection to life, liberty, the social and family relations, as well as to business and property — which is the only legal and proper idea of taxation, there is no inconsistency whatever in making a thing which is not protected one of the measures or standards by which to determine how much the party owning or supporting it ought to pay to the government. If one puts the government to special inconvenience and cost by keeping up a prohibited traffic, or maintaining a nuisance, the fact is a reason for discriminating in taxation against him; and if the tax is imposed on the thing which is prohibited or which constitutes the nuisance, the tax law, instead of being inconsistent with the law declaring the illegality, is in entire harmony with its general purpose, and sometimes may be even more effectual. Certainly, whatever discriminations are made in taxation ought to be in the direction of making the heaviest burdens fall upon those things which are obnoxious to the public interests, whenever that is practicable."

[1] Heise *v.* Columbia, 6 Rich., 404.

[2] Chilvers *v.* People, 11 Mich., 43, 49; Home Ins. Co. *v.* Augusta, 50 Geo., 530.

[3] Requiring a cartman to take out a license under penalty is not void as being in restraint of trade. "The wisdom and expediency of granting such a power to the city were within the legislative power of the state government to decide, and it cannot be said that the ordinance was more than a proper

The grant of a license may be made by the state directly or it may be made indirectly through one of the municipal corporations of the state. Of the indirect grant it is to be observed, that a municipal corporation as such has no inherent power to grant licenses or exact license fees; it must derive all its authority in this regard from the state, and the power must come by direct grant and cannot be taken by implication.

Fees, when a tax. The terms in which a municipality is empowered to grant licenses will be expected to indicate with sufficient precision whether the grant is conferred for the purposes of revenue, or whether, on the other hand, it is given for regulation merely. It is perhaps impossible to lay down any rule for the construction of such grants, that shall be general and at the same time safe; but as all delegated powers to tax are to be closely scanned and strictly construed, it would seem that when a power to license is given, the intendment must be that regulation is the object, unless there is something in the language of the grant, or in the circumstances under which it is made, indicating with sufficient certainty that the raising of revenue by means thereof was contemplated. If a revenue authority is what seems to be conferred, the extent of the tax, when not limited by the grant itself, must be understood to be left to the judgment and discretion of the municipal government, to be determined in the usual mode in which its legislative authority is exercised; but the grant of authority to impose fees for the purposes of revenue would not warrant their being made so heavy as to be prohibitory, thereby defeating the purpose.[1]

Where the grant is not made for revenue, but for regulation merely, a much narrower construction is to be applied. A fee for the license may still be exacted; but it must be such a fee only as will legitimately assist in the regulation; and it should not exceed the necessary or probable expense of issuing the license, and of inspecting and regulating the business which it cov-

regulation of a particular branch of business, for the good order of the city, and the protection of the persons and property of its citizens and the advancement of its prosperity." Brooklyn *v.* Breslin, 57 N. Y., 591, 596, per *Lott*, Com.

[1] *Ex parte* Burnett, 30 Ala., 432; Craig *v.* Burnett, 32 id., 728; Burlington *v.* Insurance Co., 31 Iowa, 102; Kitson *v.* Ann Arbor, 26 Mich., 325; Mason *v.* Lancaster, 4 Bush, 406; Kniper *v.* Louisville, 7 id., 601.

ers.[1] If the state intends to give broader authority, it is a reasonable inference that it will do so in unequivocal terms. But the limitation of the license fee to the necessary expenses will still leave a considerable field for the exercise of discretion, when the amount of the fee is to be determined. The fee, of course, must be prescribed in advance, and when it cannot be determined with any accuracy what the cost of regulation is to be: it must therefore be based upon the estimates, with more or less probability that the result will fail to come anything near a verification of the calculations. Moreover, in fixing upon the fee, it is proper and reasonable to take into the account, not the expense merely of direct regulation, but all the incidental consequences that may be likely to subject the public to cost in consequence of the business licensed. In some cases the incidental consequences are much the most important, and indeed are what are principally had in view when the fee is decided upon. The regulation of the business of huckster, for instance, could seldom be troublesome or expensive, but that of the manufacture and sale of intoxicating drinks could not be measured by anything like the same standard. The business is one that affects the public interest in many ways, and leads to many disorders. It has a powerful tendency to increase pauperism and crime. It renders a large force of peace officers essential, and it adds to the expenses of the courts, and of near-

[1] Freeholders *v.* Barber, 7 N. J., 64; Kip *v.* Patterson, 26 N. J., 298; State *v.* Hoboken, 33 id., 280; State *v.* Roberts, 11 Gill & J., 506; Boston *v.* Schaffer, 9 Pick., 415; Commonwealth *v.* Stodder, 2 Cush., 562; Mobile *v.* Miller, 3 Ala., 137; Bennett *v.* Birmingham, 31 Penn. St., 15; Cincinnati *v.* Bryson, 15 Ohio, 625; Mays *v.* Cincinnati, 1 Ohio, N. S., 268; Baker *v.* Cincinnati, 11 id., 534; Cincinnati Gas Light Co. *v.* State, 18 id., 243; Chilvers *v.* People, 11 Mich., 43; Ash *v.* People, id., 347; Collins *v.* Louisville, 2 B. Monr., 134; St. Louis *v.* Boatmans' Ins. & Trust Co., 47 Mo., 150; State *v.* Herod, 29 Iowa, 123; Burlington *v.* Insurance Co., 31 id., 102; Ward *v.* Maryland, 12 Wall., 429; Dillon, Mun. Corp., § 609. The fact that the license fee is payable into the treasury of the municipality, provided the fee be a reasonable one, does not impress it with the character of a tax. Frankford, etc. R. R. Co., *v.* Philadelphia, 58 Penn. St., 119; Johnson *v.* Philadelphia, 60 id., 445; State *v.* Herod, 29 Iowa, 123. Upon the question when a license fee imposed on the cars of street railways is a tax and when not, the following cases may be consulted with profit in connection with the Pennsylvania cases above cited: New York *v.* Second Avenue R. R. Co., 32 N. Y., 261; Louisville City R. R. Co. *v.* Louisville, 4 Bush, 478; S. C., 2 Withrow's Corp. Cases, 358.

ly all branches of civil administration. It cannot be questioned, therefore, if it is to be licensed by the public authorities, that it is legitimate and proper to take into the account all the probable consequences, or that the payment to be exacted should be sufficient to cover all the incidental expenses to which the public are likely to be put by means of the business being carried on. And all reasonable intendments must favor the fairness and justice of a fee thus fixed; it will not be held excessive unless it is manifestly something more than a fee for regulation.[1]

What may be licensed. Upon this subject it would not be safe to venture upon laying down any rule whatever, as one of limitation. Where revenue is the purpose, enough has been said in other parts of the present work to show that there is practically no limitation whatever. When the license is for regulation merely, the limitation is one of discretion and policy, and the question presented is, whether the business or occupation is one rendering special regulation important for any purpose of protection to the public, or to guard individuals against frauds and impositions. Employments the most necessary and commendable may sometimes need regulations for one or the other of these purposes, and so may the most dearly prized and most essential of fundamental rights or privileges. On this point no illustration could be more appropriate than that of the marriage relation.

[1] See Johnson *v.* Philadelphia, 60 Penn. St., 445; Ash *v.* People, 11 Mich., 347; Burlington *v.* Ins. Co., 31 Iowa, 102. In Burch *v.* Savannah, 42 Geo., 596, 598, the following remarks are made by *McKay*, J. "The license fee for retailing liquors is in no proper sense a tax. Its object is not to raise revenue. It has for many years been thought that this business was one dangerous to the public peace and public morals, and it has been the uniform practice of the country to subject it to regulation, require license from some public functionary before it is engaged in, and to punish as a crime the pursuit of it without a license. The license is part of the public regulations of the country, and the fee is intended rather to prevent the indiscriminate opening of such establishments than to raise the revenue by taxation." And see Thompson *v.* State, 15 Ind., 449; Commonwealth *v.* Byrne, 20 Grat., 165; Straub *v.* Gordon, 27 Ark., 625; Falmouth *v.* Watson, 5 Bush, 660. An objection to a license fee exacted of saloon keepers, etc., that it is unequal and invidious, because the rest of the community are not required to pay similar fees, has no force. Durach's Appeal, 62 Penn. St., 491. Neither has an objection that those taxed are not assessed according to the business done. Youngblood *v.* Sexton, Mich. Sup. Ct., Oct. 1875.

Marriage, between persons of suitable age and discretion, and under proper circumstances, should be esteemed a natural right; but what are suitable age and discretion, and what are the circumstances which should allow or forbid it? There are some cases in which it is as manifestly unfit and pernicious as in others it is proper and suitable; and obviously legislation is essential. In most countries the relation has always been subjected to regulations more or less stringent, among which has been the requirement of a license. Such a license has commonly for its purpose to prevent marriages between persons disqualified by immaturity or mental infirmity, or against the will of those standing in such relation to the parties as to render it proper and reasonable that they should be consulted.

Public amusements may also be forbidden with entire propriety except when licensed, inasmuch as everything of that nature has some tendency to disorder and to increased necessity for police supervision.[1] Perhaps those private amusements in which chance is one of the elements of interest, and which for that reason may beget a desire for gaming, and thus lead to disorders, might also be subjected to regulations of a like nature. The whole subject must be one which presents questions of legislative policy, rather than of strict law.[2]

Lotteries, where permitted, are usually licensed, and sometimes the state which grants the permission and receives a fee therefor, permits its municipalities to exact a license fee also. This it has an undoubted right to do, unless the privilege was obtained from the state on the payment of a bonus, and under legislation which, in terms or by fair construction, would preclude any municipal regulations or exactions.[3] Games of chance or hazard of every

[1] See Sears *v.* West, 1 Murphy, 291; The Germania *v.* State, 7 Md., 1; Orton *v.* Brown, 35 Miss., 426; Mabry *v.* Tarber, 1 Humph. 94; Hodges *v.* Nashville, 2 id., 61; Eldridge *v.* Heneger, 5 Sneed, 257.

[2] In Stevens *v.* State, 2 Ark., 291, it was held that the keeper of a billiard table could not be required to pay a fee as for a privilege. But this was put on the wholly untenable ground that it was unequal, because he was taxed on the table as property; and it was overruled by Washington *v.* State, 13 Ark., 572. And see Straub *v.* Gordon, 27 id., 625.

[3] Wendover *v.* Lexington, 15 B. Monr., 258. Where one holds a license from the state or county, he cannot, without legislation expressly permitting it, be compelled to take out a license in a city as a condition of doing business

description, when made lawful at all, are usually made so under licensed regulations.[1] And though a tax is sometimes levied for revenue upon the keepers of dogs, it is more usual to require the keeping to be licensed; the principal object being to have some person responsible for every animal of the kind that is protected by the law.[2]

Of the occupations upon which license fees are usually imposed, the most conspicuous has already been mentioned; that, namely, of the manufacture and vending of spirituous and malt liquors.[3] Few persons dispute the necessity for the regulation by law of this business; when the legislation has gone to the extent of the entire prohibition, the judiciary has not deemed itself competent to interfere.[4]

Illustrations of other occupations which are commonly supposed to require special regulations, are those of hackmen, draymen, hawkers, auctioneers, etc.[5] A license fee imposed upon "all tran-

within the city limits. Robinson *v.* Franklin, 1 Humph., 156; Hannibal *v.* Guyott, 18 Mo., 575. But where the state law permits it, or where at the time of granting the county or state license a valid city ordinance required a city license, it may be exacted. See Napier *v.* Hodges, 21 Texas, 287; Independence *v.* Noland, 21 Mo., 394.

[1] See Washington *v.* State, 13 Ark., 752; Lewellen *v.* Lockharts, 21 Grat., 570; Tanner *v.* Albion, 5 Hill, 121; State *v.* Hay, 29 Me., 457; State *v.* Freeman, 38 N. H., 426; Commonwealth *v.* Colton, 8 Gray, 488.

[2] See Carter *v.* Dow, 16 Wis., 299; Tenney *v.* Lenz, id., 567; Blair *v.* Forehand, 100 Mass., 136; Morey *v.* Brown, 42 N. H., 373; Mitchell *v.* Williams, 27 Ind., 62.

[3] In Keller *v.* State, 11 Md., 525, an act requiring manufacturers of beer to take out a license for retailing, was objected to as compelling them to pay more than their fair proportion towards the expense of the government; but the court say "the system of legislation to which this act belongs may be vindicated on the plainest grounds of public policy." As to the right in general, see Perdue *v.* Ellis, 18 Geo., 586; Thomasson *v.* State, 15 Ind., 449; Aulainer *v.* Governor, 1 Texas, 653; Smith *v.* Adrian, 1 Mich., 495; Gardner *v.* People, 20 Ill., 43; License Cases, 5 How., 504; License Tax Cases, 5 Wall., 472.

[4] It has been held in Illinois that the corporate authorities of towns, when empowered by their charters to suppress the sale of intoxicating liquors, might declare the unlicensed selling a nuisance. Goddard *v.* Jacksonville, 15 Ill., 588; Byers *v.* Olney, 16 id., 35; Jacksonville *v.* Holland, 19 id., 275; Pekin *v* Smelzil, 21 id., 464; Block *v.* Jacksonville, 36 id., 301. In Texas a fee of $250 required of retailers of liquors has been sustained as only a regulation of police, and not a tax. Baker *v.* Panola County, 30 Texas, 86.

[5] Cincinnati *v.* Bryson, 15 Ohio, 625; Nightingale's Case, 11 Pick., 168;

sient persons keeping stores" in the town imposing it, has been sustained as a police regulation, though called a tax in the legislation which permitted it.[1] The license of street railway cars has been supported under the police power;[2] and so has been the licensing of insurance.[3] Inspection fees are to be referred to the same authority, and are not taxes.[4]

Issuing the license. This is usually done by some administrative officer or board under general regulations. It has been held in Georgia that one applying for a license is entitled to it of right if he complies with the statutory conditions.[5] But this cannot be universally true. In some cases the purpose of the legislation is to limit the number; and then a discretion will be allowed to grant or refuse, just as is done in England in the case of applicants for license to sell liquors. In others the regulations are often made exceedingly stringent. In addition to the payment of the tax a bond for good behaviour is often required, and sometimes a satisfactory showing of good moral character.[6]

White *v.* Kent, 11 Ohio, N. S., 550; Adams *v.* Somerville, 2 Head, 363; State *v.* Crawford, id., 460; Buffalo *v.* Webster, 10 Wend., 99; Brooklyn *v.* Breslin, 57 N. Y., 591.

[1] Wilmington *v.* Roby, 8 Ired., 250. See Wilmington *v.* Patterson, 8 Jones, Law, 182. A statute forbidding sales by sample in the city of Louisville without a license, was sustained against an objection on constitutional grounds in Commonwealth *v.* Smith, 6 Bush, 303; Mork *v.* Commonwealth, id., 397.

[2] Frankford, etc., R. R. Co. *v.* Philadelphia, 58 Penn. St., 119; Johnson *v.* Philadelphia, 60 id., 445; State *v.* Herod, 29 Iowa, 123.

[3] Fire Department *v.* Helfenstein, 16 Wis., 136.

[4] Clarkston *v.* Rogers, 2 McCord, 495. It was decided in East St. Louis *v.* Wider, 46 Ill., 351, that a license fee required of merchants could not be discharged by a tender of evidences of indebtedness of the police commissioners, though that indebtedness was made receivable for *taxes*.

On the general subject of licenses as police regulations see Dillon, Mun. Corp., § 313 to 318, and cases cited; Cooley, Const. Lim., 695 to 697.

[5] State *v.* Justices, 15 Geo., 408; Hill *v.* Decatur, 22 id., 203.

[6] In Whitten *v.* Milledgeville, 43 Geo., 421, a requirement that the applicant for a license to sell liquor should produce the recommendation of four of his nearest neighbors was sustained; a requirement not always possible to be complied with.

The order of a county court to its clerk to issue license to retail spirituous liquors to an applicant, does not, of itself, authorize the applicant to retail, but only authorizes the issuance of the license to do so after the applicant has complied with all the prerequisites of the law. Brown *v.* State, 27 Texas, 335.

Recalling licenses. Under some statutes licenses are permitted to be recalled or revoked for the misbehavior of those who hold them. This in some cases is a very salutary power. They are subject also, like all other statutory privileges, to be terminated by changes in the laws; as a retailer's license, for instance, is terminated by a law totally prohibiting sales.[1]

Collection of license fees. What has already been said regarding the collection of taxes, will preclude the necessity for any extended remarks regarding the collection of these fees. As has been remarked, the payment is usually required in advance. If they are not paid, and the privilege is nevertheless exercised, the statute or ordinance imposing the fee will determine what the consequence shall be, and what proceedings shall be taken. It has been decided that a municipal corporation empowered to grant licenses and to impose a fee therefor, may lawfully make the failure to take out a license and pay the fee subject the offender to the penalty of fine and imprisonment.[2]

Federal licenses. The licenses issued by the federal government for revenue purposes do not supersede state regulations, and consequently must be received subject to all such requirements of license fees as the state may have seen fit to impose.[3] The fed-

[1] On this subject, see Calder *v.* Kirby, 5 Gray, 597; Brimmer *v.* Boston, 102 Mass., 19; Commonwealth *v.* Brennan, 103 id., 70; Baker *v.* Boston, 12 Pick., 183, 194; Brick Presb. Church *v.* New York, 5 Cow., 538; Vanderbilt *v.* Adams, 7 id., 585; People *v.* Morris, 13 Wend., 325; Board of Excise *v.* Barrie, 34 N. Y., 657; State *v.* Holmes, 38 N. H., 225; Hirn *v.* State, 1 Ohio, N. S., 15; Freleigh *v.* State, 8 Mo., 606; State *v.* Sterling, 8 id., 697; Gatzweller *v.* People, 14 Ill., 142; Phalen *v.* Virginia, 8 How., 163; Baxter *v.* Pennsylvania, 10 id., 416. Some courts have been inclined to hold that a license, unless for misconduct, cannot be revoked except on a return of the fee. See Adams *v.* Hackett, 7 Fost., 289, 294; State *v.* Phalen, 3 Harr., 441; Boyd *v.* State, 46 Ala., 329: and certainly repayment would generally be equitable.

[2] See Cincinnati *v.* Buckingham, 10 Ohio, 257; White *v.* Kent, 11 Ohio, N. S., 550; Vandine, Petitioner, 6 Pick., 187; Nightingale, Petitioner, 11 id., 167; Shelton *v.* Mobile, 3 Ala., 540; Chilvers *v.* People, 11 Mich., 43; Brooklyn *v.* Cleves, Lalor, 231; Buffalo *v.* Webster, 10 Wend., 99. *Contra*, Butler's Appeal, 73 Penn. St., 448.

[3] McGuire *v.* Commonwealth, 3 Wall., 387; Purvear *v.* Commonwealth, 5 id., 72; Commonwealth *v.* Thornily, 6 Allen, 445; Commonwealth *v.* Holbrook, 10 id., 300; Commonwealth *v.* Keenan, 11 id., 262; Black *v.* Jeffersonville, 36 Ill., 301; State *v.* Carney, 20 Iowa, 82; State *v.* Stutz, 20 id., 488.

eral government does not issue licenses under the police power, but may do so in some cases under the power to regulate commerce, and in the exercise of other federal powers; but such cases seem to call for no special remark.

CHAPTER XX.

TAXATION BY SPECIAL ASSESSMENT.

One very important species of taxation is that which is exercised in the form of special assessments. The system under which they are levied has been adopted in this country with the general features of that which has prevailed for a long period in England.

The subject of special assessments may be considered under the following heads:

1. The principles which underlie them.
2. The cases in which it is customary to levy them.
3. The objections which are made to them in point of policy.
4. The objections which constitutional principles or provisions are sometimes thought to oppose.
5. The principles of apportionment.
6. The proceedings in levying and collecting them.

1. The principles underlying them. Special assessments are a peculiar species of taxation, standing apart from the general burdens imposed for state and municipal purposes, and governed by principles that do not apply generally. The general levy of taxes is understood to exact contributions in return for the general benefits of government, and it promises nothing to the persons taxed, beyond what may be anticipated from an administration of the laws for individual protection and the general public good. Special assessments, on the other hand, are made upon the assumption that a portion of the community is to be specially and peculiarly benefited, in the enhancement of the value of property peculiarly situated as regards a contemplated expenditure of public funds; and, in addition to the general levy, they demand that special contributions, in consideration of the special benefit, shall be made by the persons receiving it. The justice of demanding the special contribution is supposed to be evident in the fact that the persons who are to make it, while they are made to bear the cost of a public work, are at the same time to suffer no pecuniary loss thereby; their property being increased in value by the expenditure to an amount at least equal to the sum they are required to pay. This is the idea that underlies all these levies. As in the case of all other taxation, it may sometimes happen that the expenditure will fail to realize the expectation on which the levy is made; and it may thus appear that a special assessment has been laid when justice would have required the levy of a general tax; but the liability of a principle to erroneous or defective application cannot demonstrate the unsoundness of the principle itself; and that which supports special assessments is believed to be firmly based in reason and justice.[1]

[1] Kirby *v.* Shaw, 19 Penn. St., 258. "The principle upon which rests that numerous class of statutes which charge lots of ground with the expense of grading and paving the streets in front of them is, that the value of the lots is enhanced by the public expenditure." *Strong*, J., in Schenley *v.* Commonwealth, 36 Penn. St., 29, 57. The principle is that, "when certain persons are so placed as to have a common interest amongst themselves, but in common with the rest of the community, laws may be justly made providing that, under suitable and equitable regulations, those common interests shall be so managed that those who enjoy the benefits shall equally bear the burden." *Shaw*, Ch. J., in Wright *v.* Boston, 9 Cush., 233, 241 — a drain case. "All these municipal taxes for improvement of streets rest for their final reason upon the enhancement of private properties." *Woodward*, J., in McGonigle *v.* Alleghany City, 44 Penn. St., 118, 121. And see, per *Coulter*, J., in Pray *v.* Northern Liberties, 31 Penn. St., 69. The principle is "that the territory subjected thereto would be benefited by the work and charge in question." *Grover*, J., in Litchfield *v.* Vernon, 41 N. Y., 123, 133. "That principle of local taxation which is undisputed, which assesses on the property benefited, or its owner, a tax in proportion to the superadded value of the property caused by the local improvement, of which this property has a peculiar advantage beyond that of others not in like circumstances." *Agnew*, J., in the case of Washington Avenue, 69 Penn. St., 360. See also Lockwood *v.* St. Louis, 24 Mo., 20; Matter of Opening of Streets, 20 La. An., 497; Allen *v.* Drew, 44 Vt., 174, 187. "To pay for the opening of a street in the ratio to the benefit or advantage derived from it is no burthen." *Green*, Ch. J., in Patterson *v.* Society, etc., 24 N. J., 400, quoting with approval, Matter of Mayor, etc., 11 Johns., 80. It is said by *Beck*, J., in Morrison *v.* Hershire, 32 Iowa, 271, 276, that "the power of the city to perform the work does not depend upon the benefits to be derived by property owners. [Citing Warren *v.* Henley, 31 Iowa, 31.] The work is done for the benefit of the public; the assessment for its payment is levied upon the abutting lots, not because of any special benefit their owners derive from the improvement, but because the public good demands it, and the law authorizes special taxation for such objects." In contrast with this, may be

Assessments being a peculiar species of taxation, there must be special authority of law for imposing them. The ordinary grant to a municipal corporation of power to levy taxes for municipal purposes, will not justify any other than the ordinary taxes. This would follow from the general rule which requires a strict construction of all such grants; but the principle has peculiar force when applied to powers in themselves exceptional.[1] And it is always held, that such a power, when plainly granted, is to be construed with strictness,[2] and as strictly pursued by the authorities who are to levy the tax.[3]

2. Cases for assessments. No decision has ever undertaken to enumerate the cases in which special assessments are admissible. The reserve in this regard is wise, as it is obviously impossible to anticipate all the cases in which it might be equitable and proper to levy them; and it is consequently better

cited Lodi Water Co. *v.* Costar, 18 N. J. Eq., 519, cited with approval in Matter of Drainage of Lands, 35 N. J., 497, in which it was decided that where the cost of drainage is assessed upon lands without reference to the fact whether they are benefited to that extent or not, this constitutes an appropriation of private property to public uses. The same principle underlies the decisions in Matter of Albany Street, 11 Wend., 149, and Louisville *v.* Rolling Mill Co., 3 Bush, 416. And see Van Tassel *v.* Jersey City, Sup. Ct. N. J., 14 Am. Law Reg., N. S., 258. In Illinois, to assess without reference to actual benefits, is held to be unconstitutional. St. John *v.* East St. Louis, 50 Ill., 92. And see Lee *v.* Ruggles, 62 id., 427; Ill. Cent. R. R. Co. *v.* Bloomington, 7 Chicago Legal News, 379. In Palmer *v.* Stumph, 29 Ind., 329, an assessment is spoken of as being the adjustment of the shares of a contribution to be made by several towards a common object, according to the benefit received. Taxes, it is said, are impositions for purposes of general revenue; assessments are special and local impositions upon property in the immediate vicinity of an improvement, laid with reference to the special benefit which such property derives from the expenditure. In Hale *v.* Kenosha, 29 Wis., 599, an assessment, as distinguished from other kinds of taxation, is defined in similar language. And see Bridgeport *v.* N. Y. & N. H. R. R. Co., 36 Conn., 255; Alexander *v.* Baltimore, 5 Gill, 383.

[1] See Sharp *v.* Spier, 4 Hill, 76; First Presbyterian Church *v.* Fort Wayne, 36 Ind., 338; Appeal of Powers, 29 Mich., 504; Hitchcock *v.* Galveston, U. S. Circuit, Eastern Dist. of Texas, 2 Central Law Journal, 331.

[2] Reed *v.* Toledo, 18 Ohio, 161; Allentown *v.* Henry, 73 Penn. St., 404.

[3] Smith *v.* Davis, 30 Cal., 536; Taylor *v.* Downer, 31 id., 480. If the statute prescribes how notice shall be given, city authorities cannot substitute one of another character. Chambers *v.* Satterlee, 40 Cal., 497.

and safer that special cases, as they present themselves, be judged upon their special circumstances. The following public purposes have been held to justify special burdens in return for special benefits:

Court House and other Public Buildings. The general rule would require, that these be constructed by the political community that is to own and make use of them. It has, nevertheless, been held in several cases, that a municipality may be permitted to contribute specially, in addition to its share in the general burden, in consideration of the benefits it may receive from having a state or county building located within it.[1] And while, in the adjudicated cases, the expense has generally, if not always, been divided between the state or county and municipality specially taxed, the principle would seem to admit of the whole burden being assumed by the locality peculiarly benefited if the advantages to be reasonably anticipated were sufficient to warrant it.

It is proper to remark of these cases, that they are referred to here only because of the principle that supports them, and not because, in other respects, they differ from the customary taxation. Such an exceptional burden is not laid in the form of a special assessment, but, on the contrary, the municipality which contributes specially to the erection of a public building for the state or county, will do so by voting and raising for the purpose a sum as part of the general taxes for the year. In principle it seems to be special, but in the method of levy and collection it takes its place with the ordinary taxes, and is mingled with them on the same roll.

Streets and Highways. The custom of the country, adopted from England, is to have the ordinary highways, though made for and belonging to the state at large, made, improved and kept in repair by the districts in or through which they are made, except where, for special reasons, the legislature shall otherwise direct. But as these districts are usually the towns — or, where there are no towns, the counties — the expense of the public highways is usually provided for by the general town or county levy, except in the case of important thoroughfares, which are sometimes constructed by the state at large, and except also where

[1] See cases cited *ante*, pp. 114–117.

contributions in labor are demanded for the purpose. As these contributions are usually based on a valuation of property, and if not made, an equivalent in money is collected, the general result, when they are called for, is the same as it would have been had the expense been estimated and an assessment to meet it been made as a part of the general town or county charges.

As to village or city streets, a different practice has prevailed. No doubt, it is entirely competent to put them upon the footing of common highways, and require them to be constructed and kept in repair by a general levy on the city or village;[1] and such must be the course in the absence of any legislation permitting the municipal corporation to levy street taxes on some different basis.[2] But the opening or improvement of a city or village street almost invariably brings to the property in its immediate vicinity an enhancement of value, in which the people of the municipality at large can participate but slightly. It is not surprising that the parties who are to receive the benefit of this enhanced value, are usually the ones who are active in pressing upon the public authorities the importance of these improvements; and while in this there is nothing that is censurable, or that could justify their being singled out for invidious discrimination, yet their relation to the improvement, which induces this action, may very justly be considered when the burden comes to be imposed. That they should pay the cost, or at least some exceptional portion of the cost, in return for special benefits secured, is a belief that has found very general expression in the legislation on this subject.

Special assessments are therefore made for the cost of land required to be taken in opening streets;[3] and when this is done, it

[1] See People *v.* Whyler, 41 Cal., 351, 354, per *Rhoads*, Ch. J.; Sinton *v.* Ashbury, 41 Cal., 525.

[2] Sharp *v.* Spier, 4 Hill, 76.

[3] Matter of 26th Street, 12 Wend., 203; Matter of DeGraw Street, 18 id., 568. In these cases, a basis for an assessment under peculiar circumstances was laid down. Dorgan *v.* Boston, 12 Allen, 223; Nichols *v.* Bridgeport, 23 Conn., 189, and many others are cases of this description. In Sutton's Heirs *v.* Louisville, 5 Dana, 28, it was held not competent to open a street through the grounds of nonassenting parties, offset benefits against the value of land, and render judgment against the owners for the preponderance of benefits. The case, it will be seen, did not take the form of taxation, but of a judicial in-

is not uncommon to provide that one commission or jury shall estimate the value of the lands taken, and the incidental damages, if any, and assess these, together with the costs of the proceeding, upon the lands peculiarly benefited.[1] They are also made for the cost of grading streets,[2] for paving, planking, or otherwise improv-

quisition. For the general principle, see Matter of Pittsburgh District, 2 W. & S., 320; McMasters *v.* Commonwealth, 3 Watts, 292; Pittsburgh *v.* Scott, 1 Penn. St., 309; Alexander *v.* Baltimore, 5 Gill, 383; Powers' Appeal, 29 Mich., 504. In the case last named the whole subject is fully and carefully considered by *Campbell*, J., who points out that, in such cases, where in the same proceeding land is taken for the public use and the cost of the improvement assessed upon adjacent land, the principles which underlie the law of eminent domain must be carefully observed, as well as those which apply to taxation. Where the benefits to the land remaining are equal to the value of the land taken, the owner has no ground for claiming damages. Trinity College *v.* Hartford, 32 Conn., 452; and where they exceed the damages, he may be taxed for the excess. Nichols *v.* Bridgeport, 23 Conn., 189; Holton *v.* Milwaukee, 31 Wis., 27. As to the effect of a constitutional provision in Ohio which entitles the owners of land taken to full compensation without deduction of benefits, see Cleveland *v.* Wick, 18 Ohio, N. S., 303. "It was decided in McMasters *v.* Commonwealth, 3 Watts, 292, that in the opening of streets in a town or city, the damage occasioned to some of the lots might be apportioned and assessed upon others in the neighborhood improved in value thereby. It is there assumed as a well settled principle, employing the words of Chancellor *Walworth*, in Livingston *v.* New York, 8 Wend., 85, that when any particular county, district or neighborhood is exclusively benefited by a public improvement, the inhabitants of that district may be taxed for the whole expense of the improvement, and in proportion to the benefit received by each. The conclusion seemed logically to follow; for if a county, district or town can be assessed for a public improvement, on the ground that they are particularly benefited, there can be no constitutional reason to exempt an individual from assessment on the same principle. It becomes a mere question of expediency, of which the legislature are the competent and exclusive judges, and not of right." *Sharswood*, J., Hammett *v.* Philadelphia, 65 Penn. St., 150.

[1] See for the general principle the important case of Litchfield *v.* Vernon, 41 N. Y., 123. Also Goodrich *v.* Turnpike Co., 26 Ind., 119; Hammett *v.* Philadelphia, 65 Penn. St.. 146, and Livingston *v.* New York, 8 Wend., 85, there quoted. It has been held competent, where land owners dedicate a street through their property, to order it graded and made fit for travel at their expense. State *v.* Dean, 23 N. J., 335; Holmes *v.* Jersey City, 1 Beasl., 299.

[2] Wray *v.* Pittsburgh, 46 Penn. St., 365. It is competent to change the grade and assess the expense against adjoining owners. La Fayette *v.* Fowler, 34 Ind., 140.

ing streets,[1] as well as for altering, widening and extending them.[2] The power to assess the expense of repaving or replanking a street on the adjacent proprietors, who were subjected to the expense of the first construction, has been denied by the supreme court of Pennsylvania;[3] but the authorities in general sustain the right,[4] and it has been well remarked in Louisiana that: "if the first paving of a street is a special benefit to the front proprietor, justifying the imposition upon him of a portion of the expense, while the city pays for the residue as having been incurred for a matter of general utility, so the removal of a dilapidated or insufficient

[1] People *v.* Brooklyn, 4 N. Y., 419; Williams *v.* Detroit, 2 Mich., 560; Indianapolis *v.* Mansur, 15 Ind., 112; La Fayette *v.* Fowler, 34 id., 140; Cleveland *v.* Wick, 18 Ohio, N. S., 303; Chambers *v.* Satterlee, 40 Cal., 497; People *v.* Austin, 47 id., 353; State *v.* Christopher, 12 Wis., 627; *In re* Dugro, 50 N. Y., 513; Morrison *v.* Hershire, 32 Iowa, 271; Gozzler *v.* Georgetown, 9 Wheat., 593; Willard *v.* Presbury, 14 Wall., 676. The authority to assess the expense of paving includes all that is necessary, usual or fit in paving, including curbing. Schenley *v.* Commonwealth, 36 Penn. St., 29.

[2] Jones *v.* Boston, 104 Mass., 461; Hancock Street Extension, 18 Penn. St., 26.

[3] Hammett *v.* Philadelphia, 65 Penn. St., 146. In this case, *Sharswood*, J. (p. 155), says: "The original paving of a street brings the property bounding upon it into the market as building lots. Before that, it is a road, not a street. It is therefore a local improvement, with benefits almost exclusively peculiar to the adjoining properties. Such a case is clearly within the principle of assessing the cost on the lots lying upon it. Perhaps no fairer rule can be adopted than the proportion of feet front, although there must be some inequalities if the lots differ in situation and depth. Appraising their market values, and fixing the proportion according to these, is a plan open to favoritism or corruption, and other objections. No system of taxation which the wit of man ever devised has been found perfectly equal. But when a street is once opened and paved, thus assimulated with the rest of the city and made a part of it, all the particular benefits to the locality, derived from the improvements, have been received and enjoyed. Repairing streets is as much a part of the ordinary duties of the municipality, for the general good, as cleaning, watching and lighting. It would lead to monstrous injustice and inequality should such general expenses be provided for by local assessments." The able dissenting opinion of *Read*, J., contains an interesting review of Pennsylvania legislation on the subject of special assessments, as well as of the adjudications in that and other states.

[4] Willard *v.* Presbury, 14 Wall., 676; McCormack *v.* Patchin, 53 Mo., 33; Gurnee *v.* Chicago, 40 Ill., 165; Williams *v.* Detroit, 2 Mich., 560; Municipality *v.* Dunn, 10 La. An., 57; Bradley *v.* McAtee, 7 Bush, 667; Broadway Baptist Church *v.* McAtee, 8 id., 508.

pavement, and the making of a new and sufficient one in its stead, is a matter of special benefit to the front proprietor, as well as of general utility. The equity is the same in both cases. * * It seems to me that the power to pave the streets is a permanent continuing power, to be exercised when the public good may require it, and that the power to levy a contribution on the property benefited by the paving in front of it, is equally durable and continuing."[1] The cost of curb stones is usually provided for in the same method, and often of sidewalks, though as is shown in a preceding chapter, those conveniences are usually ordered under the police power.[2] And it may be said that, in general, for any improvement whatsoever that tends to make the street more suitable and convenient for the use of the general public,[3] an assessment may be laid.

Drains, Sewers, etc. The expense of constructing drains in order to relieve swamps, marshes and other low lands of their stagnant water, is usually provided for by special assessments. The grounds on which this is done are not always very clearly indicated in the statutes. Sometimes the ground indicated is that the drainage is important to the public health; and in such cases the right to levy assessments for the purpose cannot plausibly be disputed.[4] The special benefits from the enhancement of values

[1] *Slidell*, Ch. J., in Municipality *v.* Dunn, 10 La. An., 57.

[2] See Chapter XIX. And as to special assessments for sidewalks, see State *v.* Fuller, 34 N. J., 227.

[3] It is held in Dean *v.* Carron, 26 N. J., 228, that it is not competent to defeat an assessment for improving a street by showing irregularities in laying it out.

[4] In Reeves *v.* Treasurer of Wood Co., 8 Ohio, N. S., 333, the subject is considered by *Brinkerhoof*, J., and the right to levy an assessment affirmed, though it does not distinctly appear that sanitary objects were had in view. In Woodruff *v.* Fisher, 17 Barb., 224, an assessment made ostensibly for the public health was maintained with some hesitation. Other cases are Anderson *v.* Kerns Draining Co., 14 Ind., 199; Sessions *v.* Crunklinton, 20 Ohio, N. S, 349; Draining Co. Case, 11 La. An., 338; Hagar *v.* Supervisors of Yolo, 47 Cal., 222; O'Reiley *v.* Kankakee Valley Draining Co., 32 Ind., 169. The following were draining cases, in which for the most part only questions of the regularity of assessments were involved: Jordan Association *v.* Wagoner, 33 Ind., 50; Thompson *v.* Draining Co., id., 268; Kinyon *v.* Duchene, 21 Mich., 498; Bench *v.* Otis, 25 id., 29; Atwood *v.* Zeluff, 26 id., 118; Etchinson Association *v.* Bresenback, 39 Ind., 362; Slusser *v.* Rawson, id., 506; Nevins, etc.,

must accrue mainly to the owners of the lands drained, who ought, therefore, to bear the expense. But the authority to levy assessments for draining lands, upon no other consideration than such as pertain to the improvement of the land as property, must, it would seem, be confined within limited bounds. It has been said that "a tax cannot be levied upon any portion of the public for the construction of a drain in which the public are not concerned. Even the owner of the land benefited cannot be taxed to improve it, unless public considerations are involved; but he must be left to improve it or not as he may choose."[1] But where any considerable tract of land, owned by different persons, is in a condition precluding cultivation, by reason of excessive moisture which drains would relieve, it may well be said that the public have such an interest in the improvement, and the consequent advancement of the general interest of the locality, as will justify the levy of assessments upon the owners for drainage purposes. Such a case would seem to stand upon the same solid ground with assessments for levee purposes, which have for their object to protect lands from falling into a like condition of uselessness.[2]

Draining Co. *v.* Alkire, 36 id., 189; People *v.* Jefferson County Court, 56 Barb., 136; People *v.* Haines, 49 N. Y., 587.

[1] People *v.* Supervisors of Saginaw, 26 Mich., 22, 29. That the taking of lands for drains is a taking under the eminent domain, see this case: also People *v.* Nearing, 27 N. Y., 306.

[2] The power to levy assessments for the mere purpose of improving large bodies of lands, is assumed by Chancellor *Walworth*, in French *v.* Kirkland, 1 Paige, 117, and in Philips *v.* Wickham, id., 560. The statutes in question seem to have conferred upon the proprietors of lands *quasi* corporate powers for the purpose. And see Draining Co. Case, 11 La. An., 338. The statute which came under consideration in People *v.* Nearing, 27 N. Y., 306, appears to have had no reference to the public health. The Massachusetts statute of 1847, for the construction of drains in towns, is considered in Wright *v.* Boston, 9 Cush., 233. It is said by *Shaw*, Ch. J., that while the public have some interest in the draining, on the grounds of health and general convenience, it is not mainly with these views that the statutes are framed, but with reference to the benefits to estates taxed. And see Springfield *v.* Gay, 12 Allen, 612; Brewer *v.* Springfield, 97 Mass., 152.

In Hager *v.* Supervisors of Yolo, 47 Cal., 222, 233, *Crockett*, J., answers the objections to such assessments as follows: "It is said, however, that it is not within the constitutional power of the legislature to compel the petitioner to reclaim his lands at his own expense and against his consent. But we think the power of the legislature to compel local improvements, which, in its judg-

As regards sewers and culverts in cities and villages, it is to be remarked that while they are often provided for by special assessments, there is no uniformity of practice in this regard, and perhaps, considering the different offices which sewers perform, being sometimes matters of imperative public necessity, and at others conveniences for a few tenements only, there ought to be

ment, will promote the health of the people, and advance the public good, is unquestionable. In the exercise of this power it may abate nuisances, construct and repair highways, open canals for irrigating arid districts, and perform many other similar acts for the public good, and all at the expense of those who are to be chiefly and more immediately benefited by the improvement. The constitution of the state is not a grant, but a limitation of power; and when an act of legislation is called in question as repugnant to the constitution, those who assail it on this ground must specify the particular provision of that instrument which is violated. The clauses of the constitution which, or some of which, are alleged to have been violated by the act under consideration are: 1st. That which secures to the citizen the right 'to acquire, possess and protect property.' 2d. That which secures to him the right of trial by jury. 3d. That which provides that 'no person shall be deprived of life, liberty or property, without due process of law.' 4th. That which prohibits 'the taking of private property for public use without just compensation.' 5th. The provision that taxation shall be equal and uniform, and that property shall be taxed on the *ad valorem* principle. In my opinion the act in question violates none of these provisions, and the authority to compel local improvements at the expense of those to be immediately benefited, is not taxation, though referable to the taxing power. It has never been held that taxation for general purposes, or for local improvements, is an infringement of that clause of the constitution relating to the acquisition and enjoyment of property; and the right of trial by jury, has no application to proceedings for the collection of taxes. Nor does the enforcement of a valid tax, by whatever method, constitute a taking of property without due process of law, in the sense of the constitution; nor is it a taking of private property for public use, within the perview of that instrument. People *v.* Mayor, etc., of Brooklyn, 4 Comst., 419; Emery *v.* S. F. Gas Co., 28 Cal., 345; Sears *v.* Cottrell, 5 Mich., 251; Murray's Lessee *v.* Hoboken Land Imp. Co., 18 How. (U. S.), 272. It is equally clear that those clauses which provide that taxation shall be equal and uniform throughout the state, and which prescribe the mode of assessment and the persons by whom it shall be made, and that all property shall be taxed, have no application to assessments levied for local improvements. Burnett *v.* Sacramento, 12 Cal., 76; Emery *v.* S. F. Gas Co., *supra*, and cases there cited; Egyptian Levee Co. *v.* Hardin, 27 Mo., 495; Yeatman *v.* Crandall, 11 La. An., 220; Wallace *v.* Shelton, 14 id., 498. 'But we need not rest our decision on the narrow ground that this is strictly a local improvement. On the contrary, the reclamation of the vast bodies of swamp and overflowed land in this state may justly be regarded as a public improvement of great magnitude, and of the utmost importance to the community. If left whollv to individual en-

the diversity that now prevails. That the cost may be assessed upon the adjacent premises under proper legislation, has been often held.[1] And in Connecticut it has been decided that this may be done under a general power to make and maintain highways and streets by special assessments; the sewers which carry off the surface water from the streets, and the filth that would

terprise, it would probably never be accomplished; and in inaugurating so great a work the legislature has pursued, substantially, the same system adopted in other states for the reclamation of similar lands, to wit: by dividing the territory to be reclaimed into districts, and assessing the cost of the improvement on the lands to be benefited. This plan has been adopted in the states of Louisiana, Mississippi and Arkansas, to prevent the annual overflow of the Mississippi by means of levees or embankments, constructed at the expense of the adjacent property. The 'Black Swamp,' in Ohio, has been wholly or partially reclaimed by the same method. A large body of land in Missouri is protected from inundation by similar means. In Massachusetts and Connecticut, swamps and low lands are drained by means of assessments on the property benefited; and in New Jersey the salt marshes have been reclaimed in the same way. In this state, the city of Sacramento, including the ground on which the capitol stands, has been protected from inundation by means of levees, erected at the expense of the inhabitants, in the shape of a tax on the property within the district benefited. In none of these states, so far as we are aware, has the power of the legislature to cause such improvements to be made in this method ever been denied; nor do we see any tenable ground on which it can be questioned."

In England, the sewer assessments are laid with reference to benefits, but they are not necessarily based on sanitary considerations. See Rooke's Case, 5 Rep., 99, b; Keighley's Case, 10 id., 139, a; Case of Isle of Ely, 10 id., 142, b; Dore *v.* Gray, 2 T. R., 358; Masters *v.* Scroggs, 3 M. & S., 447; Netherton *v.* Ward, 3 B. & Ald., 21; Stafford *v.* Hamston, 2 B. & B., 691; Rex *v.* Tower Hamlets, 9 B. & C., 517; Soady *v.* Wilson, 3 Ad. & E., 247; St. Catharine Dock Co. *v.* Higgs, 10 Q. B., 641; Metropolitan Board of Works *v.* Vauxhall Bridge Co., 7 El. & Bl., 964; Hammersmith Bridge Co. *v.* Overseers of Hammersmith, L. R., 6 Q. B., 230. A sewer rate cannot there be laid upon a whole town, but must be against particular estates. Emmerson *v.* Saltmarshe, 7 Ad. & El., 156.

[1] Wright *v.* Boston, 9 Cush., 233; Philadelphia *v.* Tryon, 35 Penn. St., 401; Lipps *v.* Philadelphia, 38 id., 503; Commonwealth *v.* Woods, 44 id., 113; Stroud *v.* Philadelphia, 61 id., 255; Mauch Chunk *v.* Shortz, 61 id., 397; People *v.* Brooklyn, 23 Barb., 166; Cone *v.* Hartford, 28 Conn., 363; St. Louis *v.* Oeters, 36 Mo., 456. For rules for making the assessment, see Clapp *v.* Hartford, 35 Conn., 66. That notwithstanding the whole cost is assessed on adjoining property, the sewer may be made more capacious than present needs require, as a provision for future extensions, see Hungerford *v.* Hartford, 39 Conn., 279, 285.

otherwise accumulate, being regarded rather as improvements of the public highway than as independent works.[1]

Levees. The construction of embankments to protect low lands, bordering upon rivers, from overflow, is a public object of the highest importance to the communities immediately concerned. No doubt general taxation is admissible for this purpose, but the legislation which authorizes special assessments for the construction of embankments, and imposes the cost upon those who, without them, would be the principal sufferers, is probably in most cases wiser and better than would be any provision for general levies. The practice of making local assessments for this purpose has prevailed for many years in the states bordering on the lower Mississippi, and has been sustained against all the objections which have been made to such assessments for other purposes.[2]

Water Pipes in Streets. Of these it has been said that "the benefits are local, as the use of the water must necessarily be mostly restricted to the benefit of the property on [the] lines, both for domestic purposes and the extinguishment of fires. The effect of supplying [the] streets with water is to enhance the value of the dwelling houses thereon. The maintenance of the pipes, and the supplying of water are necessarily a continuing expense," and for these reasons the assessment of the cost upon adjacent property is within the general principle of local assessments.[3]

[1] Cone *v.* Hartford, 28 Conn., 363.

[2] Williams *v.* Cammack, 27 Miss., 209; Alcorn *v.* Hamer, 38 id., 652; Daily *v.* Swope, 47 id., 367; Egyptian Levee Co. *v.* Hardin, 27 Mo., 495. In People *v.* Whyler, 41 Cal., 351, a levy for such a purpose made upon part of a county on the same basis as the ordinary taxes, was held to be a tax, not an assessment. But the basis of apportionment ought not to be very conclusive on this point. It is one peculiarity of assessments, that the measure of supposed benefits may be whatever appears to the legislature most just under the circumstances. See Lockwood *v.* St. Louis, 24 Mo., 20, where a levy made in the same way was sustained as being an assessment, and not in the ordinary sense a tax.

[3] Allentown *v.* Henry, 73 Penn. St., 404, 406, per *Mercur*, J. And see Northern Liberties *v.* Swain, 13 id., 113; Northern Liberties *v.* St. John's Church, id., 104. In Allen *v.* Drew, 44 Vt., 174, 187, *Redfield*, J., explains the principle of such assessments, and says: "It is not easy to see any distinction between an assessment for building a sewer or sidewalk and an aqueduct. They are each in degree a general benefit to the public, and a special benefit to the local property, both in the uses and in the enhanced value of the property.

Lighting Streets with Gas. While lighting the streets is usually provided for by general tax, no reason is perceived why it may not be done by special assessments. Legislation for special assessments exists in several of the states.[1]

Other Special Cases. No doubt the legislature has power to provide for special assessments to meet the expenses of other improvements; and this power is sometimes spoken of, as if it was practically one that was unrestricted.[2] But other cases sanction no such broad doctrine, and justify us, as we think, in saying that, to warrant the levy of local assessments, there must not only exist in the case the ordinary elements of taxation, but the object must also be one productive of special local benefits, so as to make applicable the principles upon which special assessments have hitherto been upheld. A clear case of abuse of legislative authority, in imposing the burden of a public improvement on persons or property not specially benefited, would undoubtedly be treated as an excess of power and void.[3]

3. Objections in point of policy and justice. If the design of the present work embraced the discussion of legislative policy, it would be interesting to give, with some degree of fullness, the views which various judges have expressed regarding the justice of assessing the cost of public improvements upon property supposed to be specially benefited. Some judges have spoken of these assessments as eminently equitable and proper; others seem to have regarded the power to lay them as an extreme power,

The proprietor may, indeed, leave his house tenantless, and his vacant lots unvisited, but the assessment is not for that reason void. Such assessments are justified on the ground that the subject of the tax receives an equivalent."

[1] The subject was somewhat discussed in Jonas *v.* Cincinnati, 18 Ohio, 318, and Creighton *v.* Scott, 14 Ohio, N. S., 438.

[2] See particularly the remarks of *Grover*, J., in Litchfield *v.* Vernon, 41 N. Y., 123, 134.

[3] See Washington Avenue, 69 Penn. St., 352, approving Hammett *v.* Philadelphia, 65 id., 146. In Allen *v.* Drew, 44 Vt., 174, 188, *Redfield*, J., says: "We have no doubt that a local assessment may so far transcend the limits of equality and reason that its exaction would cease to be a tax, or contribution to a common burden, and become extortion and confiscation. In that case it would be the duty of the court to protect the citizen from robbery under color of a better name." Remarks equally decided are made in Louisville *v.* Rolling Mill Co., 3 Bush, 416, 423.

which generally operated oppressively, while still others have undertaken to indicate some line of division of expense, which should be drawn in such cases, between the public and the parties to be specially assessed; putting, for instance, one-half the expense on the former and one-half upon the latter. But, in truth, there is no universal rule of justice upon which such assessments can be made. Sometimes almost the whole benefit accrues to a few. Sometimes the benefit is distributed with something like regularity through the community. An apportionment of the cost that would be just in one case would be unfair and oppressive in another. For this very reason the power to determine when a special assessment shall be made, and on what basis it shall be apportioned, is wisely confided to the legislature, and could not, without the introduction of some new principle in representative government, be placed elsewhere. We dismiss this question, therefore, with the single remark, that with the wisdom or unwisdom of special assessments, when ordered in cases in which they are admissible at all, the courts have no concern, unless there is plainly and manifestly such an abuse of power as takes the case beyond the just limits of legislative discretion.[1]

4. Objections under constitutional principles and provisions. These have been made to special assessments on various grounds.

That they take property without due process of law. If these

[1] Expressions on the subject by judges have been very numerous, but they have been too often general remarks called out by special and somewhat exceptional cases. We refrain from collecting them for the reason expressed in the text; if the matter is of legislative cognizance, the courts and the profession as such have no concern with it. We may, nevertheless, copy what has been said in one case, because it probably expresses the general views which have prevailed in legislation. "Their intrinsic justice strikes every one. If an improvement is to be made, the benefit of which is local, it is but just that the property benefited should bear the burthen. While the few ought not to be taxed for the benefit of the whole, the whole ought [not] to be taxed for the few. A single township in a county ought not to bear the whole county expense; neither ought the whole county to be taxed for the benefit of a single township; and the same principle requires that taxation for a local object, beneficial only to a portion of a town or city, should be upon that part only. General taxation for a mere local purpose is unjust; it burdens those who are not benefited, and benefits those who are exempt from the burden." *Leonard*, J., in Lockwood *v.* St. Louis, 24 Mo., 20, 22.

assessments are made in an exercise of the sovereign taxing power, what has already been said on the subject is equally applicable here.[1] The taxing power proceeds on its own methods, and the rules of the common law bend and conform to them. That these assessments are an exercise of the taxing power, has over and over again been affirmed, until the controversy must be regarded as closed.[2]

That they take property, i. e., money, and appropriate it to the public use without compensation. This objection would seem to fall with the last. If special assessments are taxes, the compensation is conclusively presumed to be received by those who pay them. It is only on the assumption that they are laid in the exercise of the power of eminent domain that the objection could have any force whatever. But the distinction between the two cases is very clear. "Taxation exacts money or services from individuals as and for their respective shares of contribution to any public burden. Private property taken for any public use, by right of eminent domain, is taken, not as the owner's share of contribution to a public burden, but as so much beyond his share. Special compensation is therefore to be made in the latter case, because the government is a debtor for the property so taken; but not in the former, because the payment of taxes is a duty, and creates no obligation to repay otherwise than in the proper application of the tax. Taxation operates upon a community, or upon a class of persons in a community, and by some rule of apportionment. The exercise of the right of eminent domain operates upon an individual, and without reference to the amount or value exacted from any other individual or class of individuals."[3]

[1] *Ante*, Chapter III.

[2] See Pennock *v.* Hoover, 5 Rawle, 291; Pennell's Appeal, 2 Penn. St., 216; Pray *v.* Northern Liberties, 31 id., 69; Gault's Appeal, 33 id., 94; Commonwealth *v.* Woods, 44 id., 113; People *v.* Brooklyn, 4 N. Y., 419; N. Y. Protestant Episcopal School, 31 id., 574; Howell *v.* Buffalo, 37 id., 267; Dorgan *v.* Boston, 12 Allen, 223; Baltimore *v.* Hughes, 1 Gill & J., 480; Baltimore *v.* Cemetery Co., 7 Md., 517; Howard *v.* Independent Church, 18 id., 451; Matter of Dorrance St., 4 R. I., 230; Hoyt *v.* East Saginaw, 19 Mich., 39; Williams *v.* Cammack, 27 Miss., 209; Lexington *v.* McQuillan's Heirs, 9 Dana, 513; Bradley *v.* McAtee, 7 Bush, 667; Scoville *v.* Cleveland, 1 Ohio, N. S., 126; Bridgeport *v.* N. Y. & N. H. R. R. Co., 36 Conn., 255; King *v.* Portland, 2 Ore., 146.

[3] *Ruggles*, J., in People *v.* Brooklyn, 4 N. Y., 419, 424. And see Litchfield *v*

Attention to the distinction here pointed out will make clear the fact that special assessments are not an exercise of the eminent domain. It is certain that when they are levied according to benefits received, they cannot be. The theory of the law is, that full compensation is then received in every instance. It is not, it

Vernon, 41 id., 123, 133, per *Grover*, J.; People *v.* Lawrence, 41 id., 140, per *Mason*, J.; Scoville *v.* Cleveland, 1 Ohio, N. S., 126, 135, per *Ranney*, J.; Matter of Dorrance St., 4 R. I., 230, per *Ames*, Ch. J.; Nichols *v.* Bridgeport, 23 Conn., 189, 205, per *Hinman*, J.; Washington Avenue, 69 Penn. St., 355, 361, per *Agnew*, J. The following cases are also in point: Allen *v.* Drew, 44 Vt., 174, 187; Hill *v.* Higdon, 5 Ohio, N. S., 243; Reeves *v.* Treasurer of Wood Co., 8 id., 333; Malloy *v.* Marietta, 11 id., 636; Peoria *v.* Kidder, 26 Ill., 351; Garrett *v.* St. Louis, 25 Mo., 505; Uhrig *v.* St. Louis, 44 id., 458; Jones *v.* Boston, 104 Mass., 461; State *v.* Fuller, 34 N. J., 227; State *v.* Newark, 35 id., 168, 171; Sutton's Heirs *v.* Louisville, 5 Dana, 28; Lexington *v.* McQuillan's Heirs, 9 Dana, 513; Howell *v.* Bristol, 8 Bush, 493; Holton *v.* Milwaukee, 31 Wis., 27; Woodbridge *v.* Detroit, 8 Mich., 278; Baltimore *v.* Cemetery Co., 7 Md., 517; Griffin *v.* Dogan, 48 Miss., 11. That to tax one exempt from military service in order to procure volunteers, and then exempt others who are liable, is not a taking of private property for public use, see State *v.* Demarest, 32 N. J., 528.

The following case, in which a special assessment was held to be a taking of private property for the public use, is believed to be of sufficient importance to be quoted from at some length. The case is Louisville *v.* Rolling Mill Co., 3 Bush, 416, 423, in which the defendants were assessed the expense of filling up the street in front of their property to an extent that greatly diminished its value, and required the erection of a high wall to protect their buildings. *Williams*, J., states the question to be: "Whether the city has or can have, under our constitutional form of government, the unlimited, absolute, uncontrollable right to order such improvements of the streets as it may deem necessary or beneficial, at the expense of the property holders, and in utter disregard of their interest, and without compensation; for it sometimes does happen that such improvements will not only render the property owned entirely valueless to the owner, but more — take it from him to pay for its own improvement, besides destroying his business, and sometimes cause him to contribute from his other means to its destruction. If cities may exercise this unlimited, uncontrollable, omnipotent power, then the declaration in our bill of rights, 'that absolute, arbitrary power over the lives, liberty and property of freemen exists nowhere in a republic, not even in the largest majority,' becomes meaningless if not absurd. If the filling up the plaintiffs' lot be done so that the improvement of the street may have a sure base upon which to rest, their machinery and building must be removed at enormous costs, else buried under the filling; and if removed, it would not then have a sure, sound basis in this newly filled area for the foundation of such ponderous erections and machinery. If a perpendicular wall be erected by which to confine the filling of the street, then light and air are so essentially ex-

is true, a compensation made in money, but as in every other case of taxation, the person taxed is to receive a benefit from the expenditure of the moneys collected. The benefit which one receives in the enhanced value of his property, from the public

cluded as to prevent its practical working for several of the warmest months of the year; nor can this, by possibility, be remedied by culverts and apertures through the street, for the very potent reason that the lot on the opposite side of the street is also required to be filled correspondingly; and even if it were sure that the owner thereof would erect a perpendicular wall instead of filling, yet he would be entitled to cover his lot with buildings, which would as effectually exclude both light and air, and appellee's passway through their gate would be destroyed. Besides, if all the surrounding streets were improved so as to correspond with this contemplated improvement of Brook, this lot and machinery would be so far below the level of the streets as to render it wholly useless for its present purposes; and the same power that authorizes this improvement of Brook will authorize the improvement of the other streets, and thus, without compensation, plaintiffs' business, not in itself a nuisance, would be broken up, be compelled to remove elsewhere, at enormous expense, lose the profits of their business in the meantime, and then be enormously taxed to pay for the improvements which would be so disastrous to their business. Verily, if this can be done without compensation, private property and private pursuits are held by the slender tenure of the will of others.

"The right of eminent domain — the right to take private property for the public use — is a power almost without limit; but this essential safeguard is thrown around the owner, that the public who wants or needs his property must compensate him for it. Nor does this in any wise impair or conflict with the essential right and power of local government over communities, such as towns and cities, in ordinary cases, to have the streets improved at the expense of the property holders thereon; for, ordinarily, they are most benefited, and it is only requiring them to keep their property in such condition as not to obstruct or injuriously hinder the public; for, legally speaking, each lot owner holds the legal title to one-half the street in his front, subject, it is true, to the public easement; besides, it may ordinarily be, and generally is, only a fair portion of the tax which may justly and legally be laid on him to keep up the streets and public passways, which are so peculiarly beneficial to the realty of all towns and cities; and, moreover, each proprietor may be presumed to have purchased in contemplation of the power in the local authorities, to direct him to erect such improvements as are ordinary and usual. But when, owing to extraordinary facts, none of these presumptions and principles apply, and when, to force the owner to make these improvements is virtually to confiscate his property, or even to permit it to be done, without compensation, is to destroy his property, the question then is, whether it is the constitutional exercise of legitimate legislative power or legislative spoliation.

"In Keasy *v.* Louisville, 4 Dana, 154, this court recognized the full extent

expenditure, is as real and as substantial as that which he receives in the protection afforded to his person and his estate. The difficulty, if any, in the case, must lie back of the nature of compensation, and must apply, rather, to the basis of assessment. If taxation were necessarily, under all circumstances, by values,

of the constitutional and legal rights of city councils to grade and pave, or regrade and repave streets; but it is also guarded as to the abuses of which such powers might be productive, or to which they might be perverted. In that case the street had been graded under the old charter of 1828, a small wooden house had been erected on the lot according to this grade, when, shortly before the suit was brought, the city authorities had caused the grade of the street to be raised about three feet, which necessitated a filling up of Keasy's lot and the raising and reconstructing his house; and for these damages he sued the city. The court said: 'But the public right to regulate the common highways of the city, is of course not *arbitrary* and *unlimited;* far from it. *Private rights must be regarded.* The public, like a common person, must so use its own as not to injure another's property. It cannot take private property for public use without paying a just equivalent, nor can it disturb any personal right of enjoyment. But, without touching the plaintiffs' lot, or in any way encroaching upon it, or interfering with any prescriptive right to light, or to private way, the city had a clear and perfect authority to raise its street higher or sink it lower than the level of his lot, as he would undoubtedly have had to elevate or sink his ground, without touching or otherwise injuring or interfering with the public street.'

"And we think this well expresses the true and furthest extent of constitutional and legal power. As the legal right to the public easement of the streets was in the city council, to be made useful to the public, and held for the common use of all the citizens, there is no doubt but so long as they confined the improvement to the boundary of the street, and interfered with no private right of light, air, or private passway, the incidental injury to the lot owners would be of that class of misfortune to them for which no remedy for the injury is afforded by law. * *

"In this case now under advisement, so far from using its own as not to injure the property of another, and confining the improvement wholly to the street boundary, the general council has ordered the Rolling Mill Co. to fill up its lot so as to support this additional embankment on the street, or to build a perpendicular wall. We are then brought to the inquiry, whether, under the circumstances, this is such an ordinary improvement as every lot owner must be presumed to assent to when he purchases, or, in other words, such as the law contemplates the proper authorities may and likely will make; and therefore every purchase must be presumed to be subordinate to this public right."

(And, after examining the facts and showing that the improvements were made with reference to the grade previously established by the city, that they were expensive, and the proposed improvement instead of benefiting the company would cause irreparable injury, the court proceed:)

it would be conceded that an apportionment by benefits must be inadmissible. But it has already been shown that value is only one of many standards of apportionment; and when others are admissible, it would seem to devolve upon those who deny the right of assessing by benefits, to point out the element of taxation, if any, which is absent when that basis is fixed upon. If apportionment is really made in view of actual benefits in the increased value of property, it is presumptively as fair and equal, and therefore as well supported by the advantages the taxpayer receives from the government, as any other. It must consequently be equally admissible with any other. It cannot be said that the taxpayer has been required to surrender for the public use something beyond his just proportion, when the demand has been made under a rule expressly named to reach that very proportion and no more; a rule, too, that in its basis is so fair that it ought, perhaps, to be preferred to all others, if fairly and honestly applied.[1]

"Our conclusion is, that this improvement is of such an extraordinary character, and so peculiarly injurious to the proprietors of the rolling mill that, so far from making them, at their own expense, damage their property so greatly, it should not at all be done without compensation to them. * * Private property is too sacred, and the individual rights of the citizen are too well guarded, under our constitutional form of government, to be sacrificed at the public behest, without compensation or some overruling public necessity, in cases of emergency, such as vast conflagrations," etc.

[1] The whole argument is briefly summarized in the following extract from an opinion in the Street Case: "But what objection is there to the exertion of such a power? It is said that it takes the property of individuals; that is, their money, for public use, without any compensation therefor. This is not so, either in theory or in fact. If the assessment has been truly and justly made, the fact must be regularly ascertained, to be what the theory of the proceeding supposes it to be, *viz:* that the party whose money is taken is locally and peculiarly benefited, over and beyond the ordinary benefit which, as one of the community, he receives in all public improvements, to the precise extent of the assessment. It is no answer to this, to say that the power may be abused; that is true of every power; and whether this particular power is so liable to be abused, as to make it improper that it should be vested in the city corporations, is a matter of which the legislature must be the sole judge. The legislature saw fit to authorize the city authorities to lay out new streets and public avenues, and instead of throwing the expense on the whole city, to be raised by a general tax, it authorizes the expense of the several new improvements to be assessed upon those who, 'owning or interested in lands, or buildings in said city, will be specially benefited by such lay out, al-

That they violate express constitutional provisions securing uniformity in taxation. These objections have been made under a number of the state constitutions, and require examination separately.[1]

teration or designation, and to apportion among, and to assess to be paid, by such person or persons respectively, the whole, or such part as they shall judge reasonable, of the damages caused by such lay out, alteration or designation.' Now, unless there is some inherent difficulty in ascertaining who are the persons thus specially benefited, we see no more objection to this mode of taxation for a public improvement, than there is in all other modes. From the very nature of the subject, the power of taxation is an arbitrary power, which, when exercised by the government itself, is limited only by the discretion of the legislature, and when exercised by subordinate bodies, is limited by the objects for which the legislature has seen fit to authorize it to be exercised, and by such restrictions as the legislature has seen fit to prescribe, unless, indeed, it is further limited by some constitutional provision. But the only provision that can be found at all, bearing upon this subject, in our constitution, is the one already alluded to, that 'the property of no person shall be taken for public use, without just compensation therefor,' and this has respect to property taken by the right of eminent domain, as where the land itself is taken for a highway or other public work, or where property is directly taken for the use of the government; and has no reference to the collection of taxes where money is taken as the contributive shares of individuals to the public burdens. The rule of taxation authorized by the charter, and which in this particular case, the authorities of Bridgeport adopted, is certainly as equitable as any other. It attempts to apportion each man's tax to the benefit which he is to receive from the improvement for which it is expended. Most of our highways are laid out by the selectmen of the towns, and the expense is borne by the town in which the highway is located, though in regard to many of them, the inhabitants of the towns have a much less interest than the public beyond the local limits of the town; and in regard to many others, they are principally for the accommodation of some, perhaps a small portion of the town's inhabitants. But the towns bear the burden, because the legislature has thrown it upon them. It might, with the same propriety, have thrown it upon the counties, or even upon the lesser territorial corporations; and although injustice may occasionally be done, by compelling a small town to construct an expensive bridge, for the benefit principally of persons outside of its limits, yet the general operation of the law is, perhaps, as equitable as any system that could be devised. At any rate, we have never heard it agitated, as a debatable point, that the system was so unjust as to be unconstitutional or illegal." Per *Hinman*, J., in Nichols *v.* Bridgeport, 23 Conn., 189, 203.

[1] There are provisions in the constitutions of the following states, requiring taxes levied on property to be in proportion to the value: Alabama, Arkansas, California, Florida, Georgia, Illinois, Indiana, Louisana, Maine, Maryland, Michigan, Minnesota, Mississippi, Missouri, Nevada, North Carolina, Oregon, South Carolina, Tennesse, Texas, Virginia and West Virginia. Min-

Alabama. In this state, under a constitutional provision that "all taxes levied on property in this state shall be assessed in exact proportion to the value of such property," it has been decided that assessments for the improvement of a street could only be laid according to value, and that a provision in the city charter, granted before the constitution was adopted, and which authorized such an assessment to be laid on the abutting property was repealed by it.[1]

Arkansas. The constitution provides that "all property shall be taxed according to its value, the manner of ascertaining which to be as the general assembly shall direct, making the same equal and uniform throughout the state. No one species of property shall be taxed higher than another species of property of equal value. The general assembly shall have power to tax merchants, bankers, peddlers and privileges in such manner as may be prescribed by law." This provision applies to the state revenue, and not to taxes levied for local purposes,[2] and does not preclude the assessment of a levee tax on the lands specially benefited.[3]

California. There are provisions in the constitution that "all property in the state shall be taxed in proportion to its value," and that "taxation shall be equal and uniform throughout the state." The constitution also makes provision for conferring the power of taxation and assessment on "municipal corporations." An act of the legislature providing that the expense of a street improvement shall be assessed on property fronting on the street, in proportion to its frontage, has invariably been held not to be in violation of the provisions regarding valuation, equality and uniformity, but as being properly referable to the power of assessment, which had acquired a distinct meaning in other states before being introduced into the constitution of this state.[4]

nesota and Illinois specially provide by their constitutions for the levy of assessments on the property benefited by or fronting on improvements.

[1] Mobile *v.* Dargan, 45 Ala., 310; Mobile *v.* Street Railway Co., 45 id., 322.

[2] Washington *v.* State, 13 Ark., 752.

[3] McGehee *v.* Mathis, 21 Ark., 40.

[4] Burnett *v.* Sacramento, 12 Cal., 76; Blanding *v.* Burr, 13 id., 343; Emery *v.* Gas Co., 28 id., 345; Emery *v.* Bradford, 29 id., 75; Walsh *v.* Mathews, id., 123; Taylor *v.* Palmer, 31 id., 240; Crosby *v.* Lyon, 37 id., 242; Chambers *v.* Satterlee, 40 id., 497. The fact that an assessment is called a tax in the statute will

Illinois. The former constitution of this state contained this section: "That the corporate authorities of counties, townships, school districts, cities, towns and villages may be vested with power to assess and collect taxes for corporate purposes; such taxes to be uniform in respect to persons and property within the jurisdiction of the body imposing the same." This, it was held, forbade an assessment of the cost of improving a street upon the real estate fronting thereon in proportion to frontage; the principle of equality and uniformity applying to local as well as general taxes, and such a special assessment being neither equal nor uniform within the meaning of the constitution. But the opinion was at the same time expressed, that to assess to each lot the special benefit it would derive from the improvement, charging such benefit upon the lot, leaving the residue of the cost to be paid by equal and uniform taxation, would be constitutional.[1] But to make the improvement at the expense of lot owners, without regard to the *actual* benefit received, would not be equal and uniform, and consequently would be forbidden.[2] And so would be an assessment which exempted improvements from its operation.[3]

Indiana. One section of the constitution of this state declares that "the general assembly shall provide by law for a uniform and equal rate of assessment and taxation, and shall prescribe such rules and regulations as shall secure a just valuation for

not preclude its being sustained as an assessment. People *v.* Austin, 47 Cal., 353. A street was improved and city bonds issued therefor, and to pay the same an annual levy was made on the property benefited. *Held* an assessment. Id.

[1] Chicago *v.* Larned, 34 Ill., 203. And see Ottowa *v.* Spencer, 40 id., 211; Chicago *v.* Baer, 41 id., 306; Bedard *v.* Hall, 44 id., 91.

[2] St. John *v.* East St. Louis, 50 Ill., 92. See Lee *v.* Ruggles, 62 id., 427.

[3] Primm *v.* Belleville, 59 Ill., 142. Since the foregoing decisions were made the constitution of 1870 has come into operation, one section of which provides that "the general assembly may vest the corporate authorities of cities, towns and villages with power to make local improvements by special assessment or by special taxation of contiguous property or otherwise. For all other corporate purposes, all municipal corporations may be vested with authority to assess and collect taxes, but such taxes shall be uniform in respect to persons and property within the jurisdiction of the body imposing the same." Art. IX, § 9.

taxation of all property, both real and personal, excepting such only for municipal, educational, literary, scientific, religious or charitable purposes as may be specially exempted by law." Another forbids the passing of local or special laws "for the assessment and collection of taxes for state, county, township or road purposes." These provisions do not preclude street and other local improvements being made, and the expense borne by means of an assessment upon property specially benefited.[1]

Kansas. One provision of the constitution is, that "the legislature shall provide for a uniform and equal rate of assessment and taxation," and another that "provision shall be made by general laws for the organization of cities, towns and villages, and their power of taxation and assessment, etc., shall be so restricted as to prevent abuse of such power." These do not deprive the legislature of power to authorize local improvements of streets at the cost of the adjacent property.[2]

Louisiana. The provision of the constitution that "taxation shall be equal and uniform throughout the state," does not preclude special assessments on property benefited by local improvements.[3]

Massachusetts. The constitution gives full power and authority to the general court, among other things, "to impose and levy proportional and reasonable assessments, rates and taxes upon all the inhabitants of, and persons resident and estates lying within the said commonwealth." This is not violated by authorizing a town, in which the state agricultural college is located, to raise by tax and pay an exceptional portion of the expense.[4] Nor

[1] Goodrich *v.* Turnpike Co., 26 Ind., 119; Bright *v.* McCullough, 27 id., 223; Palmer *v.* Stumph, 29 id., 329. And see La Fayette *v.* Jenners, 10 id., 70; Bank of the State *v.* New Albany, 11 id., 139; Anderson *v.* Draining Co., 14 id., 199; Turpin *v.* Eagle Creek, etc., Co., 48 id., 45.

[2] Hines *v.* Leavenworth, 3 Kans., 186.

[3] Municipality *v.* Dunn, 10 La. An., 57; New Orleans *v.* Elliott, 10 id., 59; Yeatman *v.* Crandall, 11 id., 220; Draining Co. Case, id., 388; Municipality *v.* Guillotte, 14 id., 297; Wallace *v.* Shelton, id., 498; Bishop *v.* Marks, 15 id., 147; Matter of Opening of Streets, 20 id., 497. To divide the expense of an improvement between the city and the property specially benefited is no violation of the rule of uniformity. State *v.* New Orleans, 15 La. An., 354.

[4] Merrick *v.* Amherst, 12 Allen, 500.

does it preclude local, street or drain assessments being laid on the property benefited. This is so well shown by an opinion of the supreme court of Massachusetts, and the opinion itself is of such general application, that we consider it advisable to copy liberally from it:

"It remains for us to consider that branch of the plaintiff's case which involves an inquiry into the validity of the assessment or mode of taxation prescribed by the statute, by means of which the expenses of the proposed improvement are to be defrayed. The broad position assumed by the plaintiff is, that this is a palpable violation of that provision of the constitution, part 2, ch. 1, §1, art. IV, by which the power is given to the legislature to impose only proportional and reasonable taxes. We have already had occasion to consider the force and effect of these words, in connection with other portions of the same article in the constitution, as applied to the imposition of taxes for the public charges of government. As to this class of taxation, the intent seems to be clear to put a restraint on the legislative authority, and to require that taxes levied for general purposes shall be laid on property, so that, taking all estates, real and personal, within the commonwealth, as one of the elements of proportion, each person subject to taxation shall be obliged to pay only such portion of the taxes as the property owned by him bears to the whole sum to be raised. But this conclusion as to taxation for general purposes is drawn mainly from the clause in the constitution which provides that, in order that assessments for such purposes may be made with equality, a valuation of estates shall be taken anew as often, at least, as once in ten years. This requirement seems to indicate very clearly that such taxation, in order to be proportional, shall be laid according to the property owned by each person liable to assessment within the commonwealth. But this provision is in terms limited to the public charges of government; that is, to expenditures incurred for those objects of a public nature for which it is the duty of the government to provide, and the burden of which properly rests and is to be distributed among the whole people of the commonwealth; such, for example, as the charges for carrying on the several departments of the government, for the support of a system of general education, and for the common protection and defense of the people and government of the state. These and other like expenditures, whether incurred by the immediate agents and officers of the state or through the instrumentality of counties or towns, are to be defrayed by assessments laid with equality and in proportion to the property held by each person liable to taxation.

"But there is another large class of expenditures for objects of a public nature, for which it is the proper province of the government to provide, which cannot be deemed to come within the designation of public charges of government, or be held to be a proper subject of general assessment on the whole people of the commonwealth. Take the case of money expended in effecting an improvement of a local character, which, although it may enure, to a certain extent, to the benefit of the public, is nevertheless especially necessary for, and beneficial to, private property in the immediate vicinity. It certainly would not be equitable or just, or tend to an equalization of public burdens, that the cost of such a work should be laid on the whole people, or upon those living remote from the locality, having no property connected with the improvement, and who could derive but little or no benefit or advantage from its construction. The duty of the government to make provision to carry into effect works of such character is clear and unquestionable. Indeed, it is often indispensable for police or sanitary purposes, or the convenience and accommodation of persons living within a certain town or municipality, or a district or section thereof, that money should be expended for purposes of a public nature, but essentially local in their operation and effect. Nor can there be any doubt that ample power to procure the accomplishment of such objects is vested in the legislature, in the exercise of their authority to pass all manner of wholesome and reasonable laws, for the good and welfare of the commonwealth and the subjects thereof. This great and essential attribute of sovereignty would be greatly abridged, if it should be held that the legislature are restricted in their authority to provide means by the levying of taxes for those objects only which would form a proper subject of a general charge on the whole people of the commonwealth, and have no power to authorize assessments for objects of a local character, the execution of which is required by the convenience and necessities of a town or district or neighborhood. We see no reason for construing the provision in the constitution, giving to the legislature the power of imposing proportional and reasonable assessments, rates and taxes, as an inhibition on the levy of a tax for local purposes of a public nature, upon those who will reap the benefit on their estates of a proposed expenditure of money. Such is not the natural or reasonable interpretation of the clause, standing as it does in relation to this class or species of taxation, without other words to qualify or restrict its meaning. As has been already said, it is in regard to the public charges of government that the mode of raising money by the imposition of taxes is specially pointed out, and it is as to these only that a restriction is found on the meaning of the preceding clause, by which the power to levy proportional and reasonable taxes is given. As to all other assessments which may be required by the enactment and execution of wholesome and reasonable laws, no limitation of authority is expressed, and none can be implied except that which arises from the natural and proper import of the words used. It certainly cannot be said that all taxes laid for local purposes of a public nature, on those who would be chiefly and directly benefited by the execution of a proposed work, and in proportion to the degree of benefit or profit which each will receive therefrom, are necessarily either unreasonable or unproportional. Nor can it be contended that the constitution, in regard to this species of taxation, furnishes any fixed rules of proportion, or gives any absolute standard by which to determine whether a particular tax is within the limits of the legitimate exercise of the power granted. Undoubtedly a very wide discretion was intended to be left to the legislature as to the subjects and method of executing the authority conferred on them, of imposing taxes for purposes other than those of a general nature; and yet the power is not wholly without limit. In requiring that taxes should be proportional and reasonable, the framers of the constitution intended to erect a barrier against an arbitrary, unjust, unequal or oppressive exercise of the power.[1] If, for instance, the legislature should arbitrarily designate a certain class of persons on whom to impose a tax, either for general purposes, or for a local object of a public nature, without any reference to any rule of proportion whatever, having no regard to the share of public charges which each ought to pay relatively

[1] Citing Oliver *v.* Washington Mills, 11 Allen, 268.

to that borne by all others, or to any supposed peculiar benefit or profit which would accrue to those made subject to the tax which would not enure to others, so that in effect the burden would fall on those who had been selected only for the reason that they might be made subject to the tax, we cannot doubt that the imposition of it would be an unlawful exercise of power not warranted by the constitution, against the exercise of which a person aggrieved might sue for protection. But no such case is made by the present bill. This part of the plaintiff's case rests on the broad proposition, that the legislature have no power to authorize the assessment of the cost of a work of a public nature, but the construction of which will be of special and peculiar benefit to adjacent property, on the abutting estates in proportion to their value. For the reasons already given, we are of the opinion that such a tax is neither unreasonable, nor unproportional, and that it was competent for the legislature to impose it in the mode prescribed by the statute."[1]

Michigan. The provision that "the legislature shall provide a uniform rule of taxation, except on property paying specific taxes, and taxes shall be levied on such property as shall be prescribed by law," and that "all assessments hereafter authorized shall be on property at its cash value," only relates to the valuation, assessment and taxation of property for general purposes, and consistent with them local assessments may be laid for local improvements, either in proportion to benefits or in proportion to frontage.[2]

Minnesota. Under a provision that "all taxes to be raised in this state shall be as nearly equal as may be, and all property on which taxes are to be levied shall have a cash valuation, and be equal and uniform throughout the state," a special assessment on lands in proportion to the benefits received from the construction of a public road was held inadmissible.[3]

[1] *Bigelow*, Ch. J., in Dorgan *v.* Boston, 12 Allen, 223, 334.

[2] Motz *v.* Detroit, 18 Mich., 495; Hoyt *v.* East Saginaw, 19 id., 39: see Le Fever *v.* Detroit, 2 id., 586; Williams *v.* Detroit, 2 id., 568; Woodbridge *v.* Detroit, 8 id., 274; Warner *v.* Grand Haven, 30 id., 24. As to what are specific taxes, see Walcott *v.* People, 17 Mich., 68; Kitson *v.* Ann Arbor, 26 id., 325.

[3] Stinson *v.* Smith, 8 Minn., 366. Subsequently the clause in the constitution was amended by the addition of the following: "Provided that the legis-

Mississippi. The constitution requires that "taxation shall be equal and uniform throughout the state. All property shall be taxed in proportion to its value, to be ascertained as directed by law." There is nothing in this which takes from the legislature the power to impose a tax on a special district for a local improvement, and municipal corporations may be authorized to assess the expense of a street improvement on the lots fronting on the street.[1] The provision has no application to taxes for local improvements, and it is, therefore, competent to lay a levee tax on lands by the acre instead of by valuation.[2]

Missouri. An assessment for street improvements on a basis of benefits does not contravene the provision of the constitution that "all property subject to taxation shall be taxed in proportion to its value."[3] The same is true of assessments for levee purposes, which need not be made on the basis of valuation.[4]

Ohio. The provision of the constitution that "laws shall be passed taxing by a uniform rule, * * * all real and personal property according to its true value in money," will not preclude the levy and collection of assessments on the basis of benefits in the cases in which they are usually laid.[5]

Oregon. The provision in the constitution that "all taxation shall be equal and uniform," does not preclude an improvement of city streets by means of assessments levied on those to whose benefit the improvements specially inure.[6]

lature may, by general law or special act, authorize municipal corporations to levy assessments for local improvements upon the property fronting upon such improvements, or upon the property to be benefited by such improvements, without regard to cash valuation, and in such manner as the legislature may prescribe."

[1] Williams *v.* Cammack, 27 Miss., 209: see Smith *v.* Aberdeen, 25 id., 458; Alcorn *v.* Hamer, 38 id., 652.

[2] Daily *v.* Swope, 47 Miss., 367.

[3] Garrett *v.* St. Louis, 25 Mo., 505; Uhrig *v.* St. Louis, 44 id., 458: see Neenan *v.* Smith, 50 id., 525.

[4] Egyptian Levee Co. *v.* Hardin, 27 Mo., 495.

[5] Hill *v.* Higdon, 5 Ohio, N. S., 243; Marion *v.* Epler, id., 250; Ernst *v.* Kunkle, id., 520; Reeves *v.* Treasurer of Wood Co., 8 id., 333; Nor. Ind. R. R. Co. *v.* Connelly, 10 id., 159. This provision, however, applies as much to the local taxes, properly so called, as to the state taxes. Zanesville *v.* Richards, 5 Ohio, N. S., 589, 593.

[6] King *v.* Portland, 2 Ore., 146.

Rhode Island. A constitutional provision, that "the burdens of the state ought to be fairly distributed among its citizens," is not inconsistent with an act which provides for the laying out of a street, and the assessment by commissioners of one-half the expense on adjoining proprietors, in proportion to benefits received; the assessment to any one not to exceed the benefits.[1]

Wisconsin. The constitution requires that "the rule of taxation shall be uniform." Also, that "it shall be the duty of the legislature, and they are hereby empowered, to provide for the organization of cities and incorporated villages, and to restrict their power of taxation and assessment," etc. It has been doubted if special assessments on a basis of benefits could be upheld under the provision first quoted; but it has been decided that they may be, when properly authorized under the other.[2]

These are the cases in which the constitutional objections have been most distinctly presented; but many other cases occupy, with more or less fullness, the same ground. The fact very clearly appears that, while there is not such a concurrence of judicial opinion as would be desirable, the overwhelming weight of authority is in favor of the position, that all such provisions for equality and uniformity in taxation, and for taxation by value, have no application to these special assessments. The reasons assigned vary in different cases, but they are no where set forth more clearly or strongly than in the leading case in New York. In that case, speaking of provisions made by the people in their constitutions, it is said: "They have not ordained that taxation shall be general, so as to embrace all persons or all taxable persons within the state, or within any district or territorial division of the state; nor that it must be in the ratio of the value of each man's land, or of his goods, or of both combined; nor that a tax 'must be coextensive with the district, or upon all the property

[1] Matter of Dorrance St., 4 R. I., 230. In the same case it is said that such an act is not invalid by reason of allowing the local authorities a discretion to levy the tax in the method adopted, or some other. And as to assessing by benefits, *Ames*, Ch. J., gives instances of assessments for payment for houses pulled down in populous towns to check the spread of conflagrations, and for the expense of watchmen in compact portions of cities.

[2] Weeks *v.* Milwaukee, 10 Wis., 242; Lumsden *v.* Cross, id., 282; Bond *v.* Kenosha, 17 id., 284.

in a district which has the character of and is known to the law as a local sovereignty.' Nor have they ordained or forbidden that a tax shall be apportioned according to the benefit which each tax payer is supposed to receive from the object on which the tax is expended. In all these particulars the power of taxation is unrestrained.

"The application of any one of these rules or principles of apportionment to all cases, would be manifestly oppressive and unjust. Either may be rightfully and wisely applied to the particular exigency to which it is best adapted.

"Taxation is sometimes regulated by one of these principles, and sometimes by another; and very often it has been apportioned without reference to the locality or to the tax payer's ability to contribute, or to any proportion between the burden and the benefit. The excise laws, and taxes on carriages and watches are among the many examples of this description of taxation. Some taxes affect classes of inhabitants only. All duties on imported goods are taxes on the class of consumers. The tax on one imported article falls on a large class of consumers, while the tax on another affects comparatively a few individuals. The duty on one article consumed by one class of inhabitants is twenty per cent. of its value, while on another, consumed by a different class, it is forty per cent. The duty on one foreign commodity is laid for the purposes of revenue mainly, without reference to the ability of its consumers to pay; as in the case of the duty on salt. The duty on another is laid for the purpose of encouraging domestic manufactures of the same article; thus compelling the community to pay a higher price to one man than he could otherwise have bought the article for from another. These discriminations may be impolitic, and in some cases unjust; but if the power of taxation upon importations had not been transferred by the people of this state to the federal government, there could have been no pretense for declaring them unconstitutional in state legislation.

"A property tax for the general purposes of the government, either of the state at large, or of a county, city or other district, is regarded as a just and equitable tax. The reason is obvious. It apportions the burden according to the benefit more nearly than any other inflexible rule of general taxation. A rich man derives more benefit from taxation, in the protection and improvement of his property, than a poor man, and ought therefore to pay more. But the amount of each man's benefit in general taxation cannot be ascertained and estimated with any degree of certainty, and, for that reason a property tax is adopted instead of an estimate of benefits. In local taxation, however, for special purposes, the local benefits may, in many cases, be seen, traced and estimated to a reasonable certainty. At least, this has been supposed and assumed to be true by the legislature, whose duty it is to prescribe the rules on which taxation is to be apportioned; and whose determination of this matter, being within the scope of its lawful power, is conclusive."[1]

Some of the cases assume the narrow ground, that the constitutional provisions refer solely to state taxation, or that, if they go further, to the general taxation for state, county and municipal purposes; but the view generally expressed is, that though assessments are laid under the taxing power, and are in a certain sense taxes, yet that they are a peculiar class of taxes, and not within the meaning of that term as it is usually employed in our constitutions and statutes.[2] Others are rested on both reasons.

[1] *Ruggles*, J., in People *v.* Brooklyn, 4 N. Y., 419, 427.

[2] On this point see Matter of Mayor, etc. of New York, 11 Johns., 77; Sharp *v.* Spier, 4 Hill, 76; Livingston *v.* New York, 8 Wend., 85; Matter of Furman St., 17 Wend., 649; Nichols *v.* Bridgeport, 23 Conn., 189; Northern Liberties *v.* St. John's Church, 13 Penn. St., 107; Schenley *v.* Allegheny City, 25 id., 128; Wray *v.* Pittsburg, 46 id., 365; Hammett *v.* Philadelphia, 66 id., 146; Washington Avenue, 69 id., 353; Lexington *v.* McQuillan's Heirs, 9 Dana, 513; Barnes *v.* Atchison, 2 Kans., 454; St. Joseph *v.* O'Donohue, 31 Mo., 345; St. Joseph *v.* Anthony, 30 id., 437: Municipality No. 2 *v.* White, 9 La, An., 446; Cummings *v.* Police Jury, 9 id., 503; Richardson *v.* Morgan, 16 id., 429; Matter of Opening of Streets, 20 id., 497; S. C., in Withrow's Corp. Cases, 375; Maloy *v.* Marietta, 11 Ohio St., 636; State *v.* Dean, 23 N, J., 335; State *v.* Jersey City, 24 id., 662; Vasser *v.* George, 47 Miss., 713; Fairfield *v.* Ratcliffe, 20 Iowa, 396; Jones *v.* Boston, 104 Mass., 461; Woodbridge *v.* Detroit, 8 Mich., 274; Alexander *v.* Baltimore, 5 Gill, 383, 397; Baltimore *v.* Cemetery Co., 7 Md., 517; Hale *v.* Kenosha, 29 Wis., 599. An agreement to pay "all taxes and assessments," *held* to embrace street assessments. Oswald *v.* Gilbert, 11 Johns., 443; Codman *v.* Johnson, 104 Mass., 491. One who buys land subject to assessments which by his deed he assumes to pay may nevertheless contest them. State *v.* Jersey City, 35 N. J., 381.

5. The methods of apportionment. Sufficient, perhaps, has been said regarding the principles on which special assessments are levied.[1] The methods which are chosen for giving those principles effect may now receive brief attention.

Although complaint is often made that special assessment operates oppressively and unjustly, and it cannot be denied that in individual cases the complaint is perfectly just, yet on the whole it has a decided advantage over other taxation in the fact that its methods are so flexible, and so easily adapted to the special equity and justice of the several classes of cases. This is shown in the modes of apportionment which are selected under different circumstances.

1. The major part of the cost of a local work is sometimes collected by general tax, while a smaller portion is levied upon the estates specially benefited.

2. The major part is sometimes assessed on estates benefited, while the general public is taxed a smaller portion in consideration of a smaller participation in the benefits.

3. The whole cost in other cases is levied on lands in the immediate vicinity of the work.

In a constitutional point of view either of these methods is ad-

[1] In Alexander *v.* Baltimore, 5 Gill, 388, the general principle underlying these assessments is justly said to be the same with that on which highway taxes are laid. In Nichols *v.* Bridgeport, 36 Conn., 255, 262, *Butler*, J., in considering the question whether a certain act subjecting railroad property to a general tax, and exempting it from all other taxes, would exempt it from special assessments, makes the following remarks: "It is doubtless true that such an assessment of benefits is an exercise of the taxing power, and in a general sense a tax. It was so regarded by this court in Nichols *v.* Bridgeport, 23 Conn., 207, to which we have been referred. But it is never spoken of in the charters of cities and boroughs, or in the general law, or in popular intercourse, as a tax. And although this strictly in a general sense is a tax, it is one of a peculiar nature. It is a *local* assessment imposed occasionally as required, upon a limited class of persons interested in a *local* improvement, and who are assumed to be benefited by the improvement to the extent of the assessment; and it is [imposed and collected as an *equivalent* for that *benefit*, and to pay for the improvement. It has consequently never been regarded as a tax, or termed such in legislative proceedings, in our public or private laws, or in popular intercourse. In all these it is known only and distinctively as "an assessment for benefits," and it cannot safely be assumed that the legislature had such assessments in contemplation when they passed the act of 1864."

misible, and one may be sometimes just, and another at other times. In other cases it may be deemed reasonable to make the whole cost a general charge, and levy no special assessment whatever.[1] The question is legislative, and like all legislative questions may be decided erroneously, but it is reasonable to expect that, with such latitude of choice, the tax will be more just and equal than it would be were the legislature required to levy it by one inflexible and arbitrary rule.[2]

Even after it has been determined how the cost shall be borne, as between the public and the estates benefited, much liberty is allowed in fixing upon the basis of apportionment as between individuals. The two methods between which a choice is commonly made are:

1. An assessment made by assessors or commissioners, appointed for the purpose under legislative authority, and who are to view the estates, and levy the expense in proportion to the benefits which in their opinion the estates respectively will receive from the work proposed.

2. An assessment by some definite standard fixed upon by the legislature itself, and which is applied to estates by a measurement of length, quantity or value.

An assessment by the first method would seem to be most equal and just, because it would be made on actual examination of the lands assessed. The legislature, in such cases, makes the rule, and the proper officers give effect to it in a manner corresponding to the ordinary assessment for a taxation by values. The right thus to assess by benefits has been often affirmed, and can no longer be regarded as a controverted question.[3]

[1] As to the diverse methods, see Wallace *v.* Shelton, 14 La. An., 498.

[2] "General taxation implies a distribution of the burden upon some general rule of *equality*. So a local assessment, or tax for a local benefit, should be distributed among and imposed upon all *equally*, standing in like relation." *Redfield*, J., in Allen *v.* Drew, 44 Vt., 174, 186. The question always is, or should be, what is equal under the circumstances.

[3] McMasters *v.* Commonwealth, 3 Watts, 292; Fenelon's Petition, 7 Penn. St., 173; Hancock Street Extension, 18 id., 26; Schenley *v.* Commonwealth, 36 id., 29; Commonwealth *v.* Woods, 44 id., 113; Wray *v.* Pittsburg, 46 id., 365; Greensburg *v.* Young, 53 id., 280; Allentown *v.* Henry, 73 id., 404; Weber *v.* Reinhard, 73 id., 373; Livingston *v.* New York, 8 Wend., 86; Matter of Twenty-sixth Street, 12 id., 203; Owners of Ground *v.* Albany, 15 id., 374; Matter

When benefits are assessed after this method, the district, within which the tax shall be laid, may be determined in either of two modes:

1. The legislative authority, either of the state, or, when properly authorized, of the municipality, may determine over what territory the benefits are so far diffused as to render it proper to make all lands contribute to the cost; or,

2. The assessors or commissioners who, under the law, are to make the assessment, may have the whole matter submitted to their judgment, to assess such lands as in their opinion are specially benefited, and ought therefore to contribute to the cost of the work.

When the first method is adopted, the legislature exercises directly an undoubted and necessary power, which pertains to it in all matters of taxation; and which is inseparable from the power of apportionment. The whole subject of taxing districts belongs to the legislature; so much is unquestionable.[1] The authority may be exercised directly, or, in the case of local taxes, it may be left to local boards or bodies;[2] but in the latter case the determination will be by a body possessing for the purpose legislative

of Furman Street, 17 id., 649; Matter of De Graw Street, 18 id., 568; People *v.* Brooklyn, 4 N. Y., 419; Wright *v.* Boston, 9 Cush., 233; Dorgon *v.* Boston, 12 Allen, 223; Brewer *v.* Springfield, 97 Mass., 152; Jones *v.* Boston, 104 id., 461; Nichols *v.* Bridgeport, 23 Conn., 189; Cone *v.* Hartford, 28 id., 363; Reid *v.* Toledo, 18 Ohio, 161; Scoville *v.* Cleveland, 1 Ohio N. S., 126; Hill *v.* Higdon, 5 id., 243; Marion *v.* Epler, 5 id., 250; Alexander *v.* Baltimore, 5 Gill, 383; Moale *v.* Baltimore, 5 Md., 314; Baltimore *v.* Cemetery Company, 7 Md., 517; Howard *v.* The Church, 18 id., 457; Bradley *v.* McAtee, 7 Bush, 667; Howell *v.* Bristol, 8 id., 493; State *v.* Newark, 27 N. J., 155; State *v.* Fuller, 34 id., 227; Holton *v.* Milwaukee, 31 Wis., 27; Hoyt *v.* East Saginaw, 19 Mich., 39; Steckert *v.* East Saginaw, 22 id., 104; Brevoort *v.* Detroit, 24 id., 322; Morrison *v.* Hershire, 32 Iowa, 271; Chicago *v.* Larned, 34 Ill., 203; Ottawa *v.* Spencer, 40 id., 211; Chicago *v.* Baer, 41 id., 306; Matter of Dorrance Street, 4 R. I., 230; Garrett *v.* St. Louis, 25 Mo., 505; St. Joseph *v.* O'Donohue, 31 id., 345; St. Louis *v.* Clemens, 36 id., 467; St. Louis *v.* Armstrong, 38 id., 29; Uhrig *v.* St. Louis, 44 id., 458; Burnett *v.* Sacramento, 12 Cal., 76; Emery *v.* Gas Company, 28 id., 345; La Fayette *v.* Fowler, 34 Ind., 140. In State *v.* Charleston, 12 Rich., 702, the right to assess by benefits is denied. The point receives but little consideration, and the decisions to the contrary are not referred to.

[1] Sinton *v.* Ashbury, 41 Cal., 525; and see *ante*, Chapter VII.

[2] Piper's Appeal, 32 Cal., 530.

power, and whose action must be as conclusive as if taken by the legislature itself. It has been repeatedly decided that the legislative act of assigning districts for special taxation on the basis of benefits, cannot be attacked on the ground of error in judgment regarding the special benefits, and defeated by satisfying a court that no special and peculiar benefits are received. If the legislation has fixed the district, and laid the tax for the reason that, in the opinion of the legislative body, such district is peculiarly benefited, that is conclusive.[1] The only exceptions which have been recognized to this rule are those cases in which, under pretense of apportionment, a work of general benefit has been treated as a work of merely local consequence, and the cost imposed on some local community in disregard of the general rules which control legislation in matters of taxation.[2] The authority is sometimes exercised by making several districts for a single work, as indeed is often done in the case of street improvements; it being equally within the power of the legislature to prescribe one district over which the whole cost of the improvement shall be spread, or to make separate districts for the improvement along the several blocks.[3] It has even been held that the improvement of several streets may be treated as one work for the purposes of a special assessment, and the whole cost apportioned by uniform rule throughout one district,[4] and this may perhaps be equally competent with the general assessment throughout a city of the cost of such improvements.

[1] Baltimore *v.* Hughes, 1 Gill & J., 480, 493, per *Buchanan*, Ch. J.; Litchfield *v.* Vernon, 41 N. Y., 123, 133, per *Grover*, J.; People *v.* Lawrence, 41 id., 140; St. Louis *v.* Oeters, 36 Mo., 456; Shaw *v.* Dennis, 5 Gilm., 416; Philadelphia *v.* Field, 58 Penn. St., 320. Compare Wright *v.* Boston, 9 Cush., 233.

[2] Baltimore *v.* Hughes, 1 Gill & J., 480, 492, per *Buchanan*, Ch. J.; Washington Avenue, 69 Penn. St., 352.

[3] Scoville *v.* Cleveland, 1 Ohio, N. S., 126; Creighton *v.* Scott, 14 id., 438; Brevoort *v.* Detroit, 24 Mich., 322; Schenley *v.* Commonwealth, 36 Penn. St., 29.

[4] See *ante*, p. 112. In Arnold *v.* Cambridge, 106 Mass., 352, the expense of constructing sidewalks on two streets was levied by one assessment, and apportioned among the lots abutting on the two streets. The only authority under which this could be done was the statute which empowered the mayor and aldermen, whenever they should deem it expedient to construct sidewalks "in any street," to assess the expense on the abuttors in just proportions. By this the court thought "it was evidently intended by the legislature that the case of each street should be considered separately, and with a view to its

Where the legislature prescribes no limits to the taxing district, but authorizes an assessment on such property as shall appear to be benefited, the report of the assessors or commissioners can alone determine what the district shall be. The subject is referred to them as a matter depending on judgment, after actual inspection; but as they only pass upon the question of fact, the district is to be considered as prescribed by the legislature, when the principle is settled which is to determine it.[1]

Assessments by the Foot Front. In many instances where streets were to be opened or improved, sewers constructed, water pipes laid, or other improvements entered upon, the benefits of which might be expected to diffuse themselves along the line of the improvement in a degree bearing some proportion to the frontage, the legislature has deemed it right and proper to take the line of frontage as the most practicable and reasonable measure of probable benefits; and making that the standard, to apportion the benefits accordingly. Such a measure of apportionment seems at first blush to be perfectly arbitrary, and likely to operate in some cases with great injustice; but it cannot be denied that in the case of some improvements, frontage is a very reasonable measure of benefits; much more just than value could be; and perhaps approaching equality as nearly as any estimate of benefits made by the judgment of men. However this may be, the authorities are well united in the conclusion that frontage may lawfully be made the basis of apportionment.[2]

own special circumstances;" and that, consequently, "the power to treat two sidewalks in two distinct streets as one for the purposes of assessment [was] not given by the statute." In England it is held that separate lines of sewers ought not to be included in one district, when they are on a different level, and no one is of benefit to the district drained by the other. Rex *v.* Tower Hamlets, 9 B. & C., 517.

[1]As to districts depending on the estimates of commissioners, see Appeal of Powers, 29 Mich., 504; Matter of Ward, 52 N. Y., 395.

[2] Pennock *v.* Hoover, 5 Rawle, 291; McGonigle *v.* Alleghany City, 44 Penn. St., 118; Magee *v.* Commonwealth, 46 id., 308; Spring Garden *v.* Wistar, 18 id., 195; Stroud *v.* Philadelphia, 61 id., 255; Covington *v.* Boyle, 6 Bush, 204; State *v.* Elizabeth, 30 N. J., 365; Same *v.* Same, 31 id., 547; State *v.* Fuller, 34 id., 227; Ernst *v.* Kunkle, 5 Ohio St., 520; Upington *v.* Oviatt, 24 id., 232; Barnes *v.* Atchison, 2 Kans., 455; Parker *v.* Challis, 9 id., 155; St. Joseph *v.* Anthony, 20 Mo., 537; Fowler *v.* St. Joseph, 37 id., 228; Neenan *v.* Smith 50 id., 525; Chambers *v.* Satterlee, 40 Cal., 497; Palmer *v.* Stumpf, 29 Ind., 329;

Occasional hardships must inevitably result from the adoption of such a basis, but the question is fairly a debatable one, whether they are likely to be more serious or more frequent than those which are to be anticipated from the selection of some other rule; and this question must be deemed settled by the statute.[1]

The principle of these statutes is the same with that which supports assessments made through the intervention of assessors or commissioners. The benefits, actually or presumptively received, support the tax. Apportioning the cost by the frontage on the improvement is adopted by the legislature as constituting, in the judgment of its members, an apportionment in proportion to benefits as nearly as is reasonably practicable. This we understand to be substantially the view taken by the authorities.[2]

Allen *v.* Drew, 44 Vt., 174; Williams *v.* Detroit, 2 Mich., 560; Motz *v.* Detroit, 18 id., 495; King *v.* Portland, 2 Ore., 146. Many of the cases cited, *ante*, pp. 448-9, recognize the same right.

[1] In Terry *v.* Hartford, 39 Conn., 286, the opening of the street for which a special assessment was made left a narrow strip of land on each side belonging to Terry; so narrow as to be incapable of use, except in connection with the adjacent lands. It was nevertheless assessed heavily for benefits. The case showed that both this and the adjacent land would be largely benefited if used together. The court say, "when we consider that here is land that would be benefited to an amount of more than thirty-six hundred dollars by the laying out of this street, should the annexation be made, and the land adjoining would likewise be benefited to a large amount under the like circumstances, and that no benefit would be conferred on either tract so long as they remain the property of different proprietors, is it reasonable to suppose that there can be any serious obstacle to prevent the one owner from selling and the other from buying, when so great an advantage would result to both from such sale and purchase? A consideration of this character, no doubt, had its proper effect in the determination of the question, whether the land was benefited or not, and the extent of that benefit." See, also, Same *v.* Same, 39 Conn., 291.

The following cases are important: "Bounding or abutting" on a street will include the soil of a private road opening into the street. Pound *v.* Plumstead Board of Works, Law Rep., 7 Q. B., 183. "Adjoining" means, touching or contiguous, as distinguished from lying near or adjacent. Matter of Ward, 52 N. Y., 395, citing Rex *v.* Hodge, 1 M. & M., 371; Peverelly *v.* People, 3 Park. C. R., 59; Holmes *v.* Carley, 31 N. Y., 289. "In front" of a lot construed to embrace, in case of a corner lot, not only the front, commonly so called, but the line of the lot on the side street also. Des Moines *v.* Door, 31 Iowa, 89; Morrison *v.* Hershire, 32 id., 271. A lot is not "fronting" on a street when it is separated from it by a narrow strip. Philadelphia *v.* Eastwick, 35 Penn. St., 75.

[2] See State *v.* Fuller, 34 N. J., 227, 232, per *Bedle*, J.; Schenley *v.* Common-

In some instances a somewhat different method has been adopted for levying the cost of local works. Instead of establishing a taxing district, and apportioning the cost throughout it by some standard of benefit, actual or presumptive, the case of each individual lot fronting on the improvement has been taken by itself, and that lot has been assessed with the cost of the improvement along its front; or perhaps with one-half the cost, leaving the opposite lot to be assessed for the other half. If such a regulation constitutes the apportionment of a tax, it must be supported when properly ordered by or under the authority of the legislature. But it has been denied on what seem the most conclusive grounds that this is permissible. It is not legitimate taxation because it is lacking in one of its indispensable elements. It considers each lot by itself, compelling each to bear the burden of the improvement in front of it, without reference to any contribution to be made to the improvement by any other property, and it is consequently without any apportionment. From accidental circumstances, the major part of the cost of an important public work may be expended in front of a single lot; those circumstances not at all contributing to make the improvement more valuable to the lot thus specially burdened, perhaps even having the opposite consequence. But whatever might be the result in particular cases, the fatal vice in the system is that it provides for no taxing districts whatever. It is as arbitrary in principle, and would sometimes be as unequal in operation, as a regulation that the town from which a state officer chanced to be chosen should pay his salary, or that that locality in which the standing army, or any portion of it, should be stationed for the time being should be charged with its support. If one is legitimate taxation the other would be. In sidewalk cases a regulation of the kind has been held admissible, but it has been justified as a regulation of police, and is not supported on the taxing power exclusively. As has been well said, to compel individuals to contribute money or property to the use of the public, without reference to any common ratio, and without requiring the sum paid by one piece or kind of property, or by one person, to bear any relation whatever to that paid by another, is to lay a forced contribution, not a tax, within

wealth, 36 Penn. St., 29, 57, per *Strong*, J.; Northern Indiana R. R. Co. *v.* Connelly, 10 Ohio, N. S., 159, 165, per *Peck*, J.

the sense of those terms as applied to the exercise of powers by any enlightened or responsible government.[1]

Although, as has been stated, an assessment by frontage is really based upon the idea that the estates taxed receive a benefit in proportion to frontage, yet when the legislature have made benefits the rule of assessment, and provided for assessors or commissioners to ascertain and apportion them, it is not arbitrarily to be assumed that the benefits to any particular lot are in fact in proportion to its front on the improvement. In such cases the assessors or commissioners have a duty to perform, on inspection and examination of the several estates; and a report by them that they have assessed the expense by the foot front, without saying that they find the benefits in that proportion, does not affirmatively show a performance of their duty.[2]

Apportionment by the Acre, as a basis for an assessment has frequently been adopted in levee cases. A statute in Mississippi may be taken as an illustration. It provided for a levee tax, prescribed the district of assessment, and directed the tax to be laid by the acre according to an arbitrary standard of value fixed by the act, as follows: Unimproved lands in a part of the district, five dollars per acre; in the remainder of the district three dollars per

[1] *Christiancy*, J., in Woodbridge *v.* Detroit, 8 Mich., 274, 301. The case of Lexington *v.* McQuillan's Heirs, 9 Dana, 513, is a decision that the improvement of a street cannot be compelled on any such basis. To the same point is Motz *v.* Detroit, 18 Mich., 495. And see St. Louis *v.* Clemens, 49 Mo., 552; Neenan *v.* Smith, 50 id., 525, 531. The case of Warren *v.* Henley, 31 Iowa, 38, is *contra*. Weeks *v.* Milwaukee, 10 Wis., 258, which also seems to be *contra*, appears to be based upon a practice in that state before the constitution was adopted. In the subsequent case of State *v.* Portage, 12 Wis., 562, it was held, under a charter which permitted the expense of an improvement on the abutting lots, in proportion to the front or size of such lots respectively, an ordinance directing that each lot should be charged with the cost of the improvement in front of it was void. "This," says *Paine*, J., speaking of the provision of the charter, "it is obvious is an entirely different principle of assessment from that which charges each lot with the entire expense of the improvement in front of it, and serves to avoid much of the inequality and injustice of the latter system." As to the reasonableness and justice of an assessment by the foot front, compare the remarks of *Carpenter*, J., in Clapp *v.* Hartford, 35 Conn., 66; *Read*, J., in Magee *v.* Commonwealth, 46 Penn. St., 358; *Crozier*, J., in Hines *v.* Leavenworth, 3 Kans., 186.

[2] State *v.* Hudson, 27 N. J., 214; State *v.* Hudson, 29 id., 104, 115; State *v.* Bergen, id., 266; Warner *v.* Grand Haven, 30 Mich., 24.

acre; improved lands in a part of the district twenty dollars per acre, and in the remainder thirty dollars per acre. The act was sustained,[1] as was also a similar statute in Missouri.[2] Street im-

[1] Daily *v.* Swope, 47 Miss., 367. See the previous cases of Smith *v.* Aberdeen, 25 id., 458; Williams *v.* Cammack, 27 id., 209; Alcorn *v.* Hamer, 38 id., 652.

[2] Egyptian Levee Co. *v.* Hardin, 27 Mo., 495. See also the Louisiana and Arkansas cases. Crowley *v.* Copley, 2 La. An., 329; Yeatman *v.* Crandall, 11 id., 220; Wallace *v.* Shelton, 14 id., 498; Bishop *v.* Marks, 15 id., 147; Richardson *v.* Morgan, 16 id,, 429; McGehee *v.* Mathis, 21 Ark., 40. In Wallace *v.* Shelton, *supra*, the levee tax was a specific tax by the acre. *Merrick*, Ch. J., says; "In the case of Layton *v.* The City of New Orleans, 12 La. An., 515, we said that nothing prevented the legislature from adopting different principles as the bases of its legislation. When the different municipalities were consolidated into one city, the legislature adopted the principle, that each municipality ought to pay its own debts; subsequently the legislature adopted the principle that it was equal and just that the city at large should pay the very unequal debts of the different municipalities. It was not in the power of this court to say that the legislation was unconstitutional.

"So here the legislature has established, at different periods, different principles, in regard to the assessments made for the levee district for these parishes, viz: 1st. That it was right, equal and just to levy an *ad valorem* assessment upon the *lands* alone; that the property receiving the advantage should bear the burden. 2d. That in order to protect the *people* from inundation, it was just and equal that they should pay an *ad valorem* assessment upon all of their taxable property in the levee district. 3d. That it costs (as in the Draining Case) as much to protect one acre of land from inundation as it does another; that every acre of land in the district of land subject to overflow will be benefited to a much greater amount than the assessment, and that, therefore, it is just and equal that every acre should pay into the hands of the agents charged with protecting it the same sum as every other acre; and now, by a statute, since this litigation arose; and fourthly, that the second and third principles ought to be combined, and that *the land* ought to be subject to a specific tax, and all other property to an *ad valorem* tax. It is easy to perceive, by examination, that none of these theories can attain absolute equality, or bring about exact justice among the different individuals composing a community subject to assessment. The first and second theories operated harshly upon those persons who occupied high tracts of land, and had already protected themselves by sufficient levees at their own expense; and there may be cases of individual hardships under the third and fourth theories of legislation. But it is not pretended but that the plaintiff is benefited to the full amount of his assessment. The money he pays to the agents appointed to protect his property, is restored to him in the increased value of his lands, and their security from overflow. The argument that he may not wish to sell or cultivate his lands, and that he may prefer that the soil be raised by the overflow each year, cannot be admitted. *Salus populi suprema lex.* The obstinacy of a proprietor

provements in towns are sometimes made at the cost of abutting lots in proportion to their area, in the belief that this is an equally reasonable and just standard of apportionment with any other.[1]

Assessment by Value of Lots. This has sometimes been ordered in levee cases, and also in the case of street improvements. In the latter case, the buildings erected upon the lands are sometimes excluded from the valuation, and very justly so, as the improvements, while increasing largely the market value of land as such, do not usually increase perceptibly the value of the buildings erected upon it.[2]

Property Subject to Assessment. It has been shown in another place, that while these local assessments are laid under a taxing power, they are not taxes in the ordinary understanding of that term, and that, consequently, the usual exemptions from taxation will not preclude the property exempted being subjected to them.[3] But this statement can only be applicable when the assessment is really made on the basis of special benefits which are supposed to be equivalent; for, if it is laid for a work of general utility, in the advantages of which the person assessed participates only as one of the general public, and not as receiving special benefits, it must be considered a general tax, and is improperly designated an assessment. Such has been the conclusion where an assessment was laid upon a railroad company which, by its charter, was exempt from taxation, for the expense of widening a street along

in one case, or the wishes of the capitalist who holds by a speculation in another, cannot be permitted to stand in the way of the safety of a whole community. Courts of justice cannot look to these wishes of parties, but must judge of their liability to assessment and taxation by reference to their property. The argument which would relieve them from the assessment in this case, would relieve them from taxation in every other."

[1] See Clapp *v.* Hartford, 35 Conn., 66; Hines *v.* Leavenworth, 3 Kans., 186.

[2] See Downer *v.* Boston, 7 Cush., 277; Brewer *v.* Springfield, 97 Mass., 152; Creighton *v.* Scott, 14 Ohio, N. S., 438. The levee tax sustained in Williams *v.* Cammack 27 Miss., 209, was laid under an act which provided for a uniform tax of not exceeding ten cents per acre on all lands lying on or within ten miles of the river within a specified county, and of five cents per acre on lands lying ten miles or more from the river. The court say, the act rests upon the same basis with all other taxation. In some cases the assessments have been laid on the value of lots as assessed for ordinary taxes. See People *v.* Whyln, 41 Cal., 351. Lockwood *v.* St. Louis, 24 Mo., 20.

[3] *Ante*, pp. 147–8.

which its track was laid; the assessment upon the company being of such portion of the expense as the commissioners deemed "equitable and just," and not being measured by benefits. "In what respect," it is asked, "does this differ in principle from an ordinary case of taxation? The assessment is not required to be made with any regard to the benefit the improvement may confer upon the company. From all that appears the assessment may have been graduated by a regard to the ability of the company to pay, to the value of its stock, or to the amount of travel that passed through the street upon the railroad. It does not appear that the improvement added any value to the road itself, or to the stock of the company. * * In what mode is the corporation specially benefited over any other inhabitant of the city or traveler through its streets? If the assessment upon the railroad company may be sustained upon the ground of special benefits to the corporation from the increased facilities of travel afforded by widening the street, an assessment may be sustained upon the same ground against the owner of every express wagon or stage coach that travels the street. The assessment in this case is a clear exercise of the taxing power. It is made for a public purpose, and confers no special benefits upon the property of the company."[1] These reasons take the levy out of the category of assessments properly so called, and to which all property specially benefited is liable to be subjected.

Personal property is not commonly thus assessed. The reason is manifest in the fact that special benefits generally accrue almost exclusively to lands. When, however, an exceptional assessment is levied upon a municipality, for the special benefits its people receive from a public building, or other work of the state or of some larger subdivision of the state, the benefits are usually quite as much to business as to real property, and the burden would not be equally distributed if the assessment were not laid on all property subject to ordinary taxation: this course has generally been adopted;[2] though in the case of works commonly classed

[1] State *v.* Newark, 27 N. J., 185, 191, per *Green*, Ch. J. In the same case, an assessment upon houses and lots owned by the company, on the basis of benefits, was supported.

[2] Thomas *v.* Leland, 24 Wend., 68; Kirby *v.* Shaw, 19 Penn. St., 258; Merrick *v.* Amherst, 12 Allen, 500; Marks *v.* Pardue University, 37 Ind., 155;

under the head of "internal improvements," a different course has been sometimes taken, and real estate alone been taxed.

It is no objection to an assessment for a local work that the property assessed is used for a purpose that will not be specially advanced by the improvement; as for instance, that it is dedicated to the purposes of sepulture,[4] or is occupied by a building erected for the purposes of public worship,[1] or is devoted to school or charitable purposes,[3] or constitutes the track of a railroad,[4] or is put to any use to which the market value of the property is unimportant. There is nothing necessarily permanent in any present use; not sufficiently so, at least, to give it a controlling influence in determining principles of taxation. Even public property is often subjected to these special assessments; there being no more reason to excuse the public from paying for such

Gordon *v.* Cornes, 47 N. Y., 608; People *v.* Whyler, 41 Cal., 351; Gilman *v.* Sheboygan, 2 Black, 510.

[1] Baltimore *v.* Cemetery Co., 7 Md., 517. In this case the special objection made was, that to subject the property to liability for paving would endanger its perpetuity as a cemetery; but the force of this, says the court, "whatever it may be, equally applies to all the engagements and liabilities of the corporation. The building of a wall, of a church, or the improvement of the grounds, may superinduce debt and with it disastrous consequences. Although fully sympathizing with the laudable spirit which, with pious zeal and watchfulness, seeks to preserve the undisturbed repose of the dead, we nevertheless feel ourselves bound to declare that we see nothing in the legislation of the state, nor in the nature of the demand itself to exempt the appellees from liability." See to the same effect Buffalo City Cemetery *v.* Buffalo, 46 N. Y., 506.

[2] Matter of Mayor, etc., of New York, 11 Johns., 80; Northern Liberties *v.* St. Johns Church, 13 Penn. St., 104; Second Universalist Society *v.* Providence, 6 R. I., 235; Le Fever *v.* Detroit; 2 Mich., 586; Broadway Baptist Church *v.* McAtee, 8 Bush, 508; Trustees of Church *v.* Ellis, 38 Ind., 3.

[3] Cincinnati College *v.* State, 19 Ohio, 110; Lafayette *v.* Orphan Asylum, 4 La. An., 1; St. Louis Public Schools *v.* St. Louis, 26 Mo., 468; Sheehan *v.* Good Samaritan Hospital, 50 id., 155.

[4] Northern Indiana R. R.. Co. *v.* Connelly, 10 Ohio, N. S., 159; New Haven *v.* Fair Haven, etc., R. R. Co., 38 Conn., 422; Bridgeport *v.* N. Y. & H. R. R. Co., 36 id., 255; Railroad Company *v.* Spearman, 12 Iowa, 112. A street railway company has such an interest in a street where the track is laid as may be specially assessed for benefits for widening the street. Appeal of North Beach, etc., R. R. Co., 32 Cal., 499; Chicago *v.* Baer, 41 Ill., 306. Compare this with State *v.* Newark, 27 N. J., 185.

benefits than there would be to excuse from payment when property is taken under the eminent domain.[1]

6. Proceedings in levying and collecting assessments. These will now require some consideration.

Estimating Benefits. It has been said that, in assessing benefits, the only safe and practicable course, and the one which will do equal justice to all parties, is to consider what will be the influence of the proposed improvement on the market value of the property; what the property is now fairly worth in the market, and what will be its value when the improvement is made.[2] A test of this character should be applied by the legislature before establishing any arbitrary rule of assessment, such for instance, as one which measures benefits by the length of frontage. There can be no justification for any proceeding which charges the land with an assessment greater than the benefits; it is a plain case of appropriating private property to public uses without compensation.[3] It is conceded that the legislative judgment, that a certain district is or will be so far specially benefited by an improvement as to justify a special assessment, is conclusive, and that its determination as to what shall be the basis of the assessment is equally conclusive. To invoke the intervention of a court for relief against the results of its conclusion, is to invoke the judicial authority to give its judgment controlling effect over that of the legislature, in a matter of the apportionment of a tax, which by

[1] See Baltimore *v.* Cemetery Co., 7 Md., 517, 536, per *Le Grand*, Ch. J., St. Louis Public Schools *v.* St. Louis, 26 Mo., 468. But exempting public property from the assessment does not render it illegal. People *v.* Austin, 47 Cal., 353.

[2] *Bronson*, J., in matter of Furman St., 17 Wend., 668, cited with approval in State *v.* Newark, 35 N. J., 157, 167. It is held in Massachusetts that an assessment for the alteration of a street will date from the order for the alteration. Jones *v.* Boston, 104 Mass., 461, citing Parks *v.* Boston, 15 Pick., 198; Meacham *v.* Fitchburg, etc., R. R. Co., 4 Cush., 291; Whitman *v.* Boston, etc., R. R. Co., 7 Allen, 313.

[3] Tide Water Co. *v.* Costar, 18 N. J. Eq., 518; Canal Bank *v.* Albany, 9 Wend., 244; Matter of Canal St., 11 Wend., 155; Matter of Drainage of Lands, 35 N. J., 497; Yeatman *v.* Crandall, 11 La. An., 229; New Orleans *v.* Draining Co., id., 338. It is no objection to an assessment of benefits, that it is made in proportion to value; that may be a proper basis if the commissioners think it just. Piper's Appeal, 32 Cal., 530.

concession on all sides is purely a matter of legislation. This is confessedly inadmissible in any case where the legislative power has not been exceeded by an apportionment merely colorable. An assessment so grossly and palpably unjust and oppressive, as to give demonstration that the legislative judgment had never determined the case on the principles of taxation, must always be open to correction. A man's property is not to be taken from him with impunity, and without redress, by simply calling the appropriation an assessment, when it is not such in its elements.

When the estimate of benefits is referred to assessors, by whatever name they may be called, the same rule of conclusiveness must apply. The remedy of one who considers himself unfairly assessed is to apply for redress to the statutory tribunal, if one is provided with the power to review. In all collateral proceedings, the benefits assessed are conclusively presumed to be received, and the assessment is not open to revisal or review.[1]

[1] Baltimore *v.* Hughes, 1 Gill. & J., 480; Nor. Indiana R. R. Co. *v.* Connelly 10 Ohio, N. S., 159, 165; Commonwealth *v.* Woods, 44 Penn. St., 113; Wray *v.* Pittsburg, 46 Penn. St. 365, 369. Counterclaims of parties for damages cannot be set off against the assessment. Whitney *v.* Boston, 106 Mass., 89. The English sewer cases allow great latitude to the commissioners in the assessment of benefits. They are largely collated in Soady *v.* Wilson, 3 Ad. & El., 248, and it is said by *Lord Denman*, Ch. J., " from Keighley's Case, 10 Rep., 142 *b.* to Rex *v.* Commissioners of Sewers for the Tower Hamlets, 9 B. & C., 517, the doctrine laid down in them all is uniform and undisputed, as applicable to the present question. It rests on the principle, that every one whose property derives benefit from the works of the commissioners, may be assessed to the rates they impose. The benefit is not required to be immediate, nor do the cases, or the commission itself, or the statutes, say anything of the nature or amount of the benefit. Possibly that benefit may be so extremely small, that a jury would not have found the fact stated in the case. But on the other hand the benefit may be of high value, as if a house were inaccessible because surrounded by marshes, and the work of sewerage had made them hard and passable. * * If the commissioners had jurisdiction, this court would not inquire whether they had correctly exercised their judgment, in an action of trespass for levying the rate. But as the jurisdiction results from the fact of benefit being derived, and the case expressly states that some benefit was derived, we think ourselves bound by the finding to say that the defendant had authority to levy the rate, and is consequently entitled to our judgment." It is nevertheless held competent to show, in opposition to the assessment, that no benefit was received. This is on the ground that jurisdiction to make any assessment against a party, depends on his premises being benefited, and the commissioners cannot determine the question of jurisdiction in their own

The broad latitude of legislative and administrative discretion in these cases, undoubtedly opens the door to many abuses, and it may be a reason for carefully criticising the proceedings, in order to see that the law has been strictly observed; but it can constitute no reason for the judiciary taking upon itself the correction of legislative mistakes and errors of judgment. When a judicial review is given of the proceedings of assessors, an opportunity may be afforded for laying down the proper controlling principles; but in other cases it must be assumed that the assessors have had the proper rules in view for their own direction. It is clear that any assessment is wrong which charges lands with a sum beyond the special benefits received. If the cost of any improvement exceeds the local and peculiar benefits, the improvement should either not be made at all, or the excess should be assumed by the public, and become a part of the general levy. In making an assessment of actual benefits, it may undoubtedly be proper to take into consideration the fact of the property being devoted to a permanent use, which for the time being at least, renders the market value of little or no moment. It has already been stated that this does not preclude the property being assessed for benefits. As has been justly remarked of some cases of this nature which have been considered by the courts, when lands were devoted to church or cemetery purposes,[1] "objections to the assessment proceed on the ground that the owner cannot apply the property to any new or different use. When the owner has the unrestrained power of alienation, and the property may be converted to any new use at his pleasure, it is difficult to see how, upon any principle, an exception can be made to the rule regarding only the market value. After the owner has escaped what would otherwise be a great burden, on the ground that he does not intend to use the property in a way which will make the improvement beneficial, he may change his mind, throw the property into the

favor conclusively. Masters *v.* Scroggs, 3 M. & S., 447; Stafford *v.* Hamston, 2 B. & B., 691. See Neave *v.* Weather, 3 Q. B., 984. The American doctrine is clearly the other way. And in England, ratability once established, no question of the amount of benefit is permitted to be raised. Regina *v.* Head, 9 Jur., N. S., 871.

[1] Matter of Mayor, etc., 11 Johns., 77; Matter of Albany Street, 11 Wend., 150.

market, and realize advantages for which others have been made to pay."[1] And the remark is as applicable to those temporarily appropriated to church or other special purposes as to any others. The fact is only a circumstance to be considered by the assessors in making up their estimate.[2]

The fact that a railroad company, or a plankroad or turnpike company has an easement in a public street of a permanent nature, and the right to occupy it for the corporate purposes, does not preclude the street being improved at the expense of adjoining property. It still remains a public street, and subject to the same right of control as before, except as the right is qualified by the easement granted to the private corporation.[3]

Although the assessment for a local improvement must be limited to the cost,[4] yet there is no reason in the nature of things why it should not be made before the work is actually done, and before the cost shall be finally and conclusively determined. It is usually desirable that the collection of the assessment should proceed as the work progresses, that the contractor or workmen may be paid when it is completed. Indeed the charters of very

[1] *Woodhull*, J., in State *v.* Newark, 35 N. J., 157, 167.

[2] The assessment in Nor. Ind. R. R. Co. *v.* Connelly, 10 Ohio, N. S., 159, was *by frontage* on the land appropriated by the railroad company for its track, and was sustained, the court holding that the question of actual benefit was not open for consideration. In Bridgeport *v.* N. Y. & N. H. R. R. Co., 36 Conn., 255, it was denied that the easement of the railroad company in the land occupied for its track could be assessed for benefits for laying out a street along its side. In New Haven *v.* Fair Haven, etc., R. R. Co., 38 Conn., 422, the rails, sleepers, ties and spikes of a street railway company, so laid into and attached to the soil of the street as to become part of the realty, were held properly assessable as real estate for paving the street. The same decision was previously made in Appeal of North Beach, etc., R. R. Co., 32 Cal., 499, where an able opinion was delivered by *Sawyer*, J., who reviews the case of State *v.* Newark, 27 N. J., 186, and points out the difference in the benefits likely to be received by a street railway when the street in which its track is laid is improved, and those which a railway between distant points might be supposed to derive from a like improvement along its track. The assessment in Burlington, etc., R. R. Co. *v.* Spearman, 12 Iowa, 112, was on the depot grounds of the company, for a sidewalk, and seems to have been laid irrespective of the special use.

[3] Bagg *v.* Detroit, 5 Mich., 336; State *v.* Atlantic City, 34 N. J., 99. And see State *v.* New Brunswick, 34 id., 395.

[4] Schenely *v.* Commonwealth, 36 Penn. St, 9.

many cities forbid that any payments shall be made by the corporation, for any street or other local work, except from a fund to be provided by a special assessment made for the purpose; and it is obvious that such works would only be constructed at very serious disadvantage, and at much greater expense, if no payment could be made as the work progressed. It has been said, that in assessing benefits under statutes permitting it, a city common council "is the agent and instrument of the land owners in respect to these improvements. The work is to be conducted and completed under its direction. It is to ascertain how much certain owners are to pay and others receive; to collect the money and see that it is applied to the purposes of the improvement. Its authority must be strictly pursued."[1] But it must also, in order to be enabled to perform its agency to advantage, be allowed to make the assessment, and even the collection if it shall be deemed proper, in advance. It has been repeatedly held that this is admissible.[2] The assessment must of course be made upon an estimate which may be more or less incorrect, as all estimates for public works are likely to be, but the liability to error ought not to defeat a special any more than a general levy for future purposes. If it prove too large it is not fatal,[3] though the excess properly belongs to the lot owners, who would be entitled to have it returned to them.

In assessing benefits the cost of the whole work distributed through the whole district is to be kept in view; the assessors can not restrict themselves in the case of any particular lot to the cost of the improvement in front of it.[4] But at the same time

[1] *Brown*, J., in Howell *v.* Buffalo, 15 N. Y., 512, citing McCullough *v.* Brooklyn, 23 Wend., 458; Lake *v.* Williamsburgh, 4 Denio, 520; Sharp *v.* Spier, 4 Hill, 76.

[2] Manice *v.* New York, 8 N. Y., 120; Henderson *v.* Baltimore, 8 Md., 352; Scoville *v.* Cleveland, 1 Ohio, N. S., 129.

[3] Scoville *v.* Cleveland, 1 Ohio, N. S., 126.

[4] *Ex parte* Mayor of Albany, 23 Wend., 277. See State *v.* Portage, 12 Wis., 567. When in making a street improvement, squares formed by the intersection of other streets are crossed and improved, the city may, if the object in improving the squares, is the improvement of the street, assess the whole expense upon the same property on which the other expenses of the improvements are assessed. Creighton *v.* Scott, 14 Ohio, N. S., 438. See Motz *v.* Detroit, 18 Mich., 495.

they must carefully keep within the district; this is as imperative as it is in ordinary taxation.[1]

As in the case of ordinary taxes, assessments are made either against the land as such, or against the separate interests which individuals have in the land, according as the statute shall prescribe. In either case, there should be a sufficient description of the land for the purpose of identification,[2] and in the latter case, it is imperative that the separate interests be taken notice of in the assessment.[3]

Proceedings in Assessment. These differ too much in different states to be considered in detail. Some general principles may nevertheless be stated. The statute authority must be strictly pursued. This rule is fundamental and imperative. Not that it must be literally followed, but the observance of every one of its substantial requirements must be regarded as a condition precedent to the validity of any assessment.[4] A common requirement

[1] Matter of Livingston Street, 18 Wend., 556; Turpin *v.* Eagle Creek, etc., Gravel Road Co., 48 Ind., 45. A statute provided for viewers to decide upon the expediency of a proposed street extension and to "ascertain and determine what lots in the vicinity of said extension, will probably be benefited by the opening of the said street, and divide and apportion, on equitable principles, the amount that each shall separately contribute to defray the damage incurred," etc. *Held*, that the term "vicinity" is not a matter of eye sight only, but for the judgment also. *Rogers*, J., in Extension of Hancock St., 18 Penn. St., 26, 32.

[2] Sharp *v.* Johnson, 4 Hill, 92.

[3] Matter of De Graw Street, 18 Wend., 568. An assessment to "owners and occupants" for benefits is not the same thing as an assessment on the lands. Sharp *v.* Spier, 4 Hill, 76. Where the assessment is to be of the benefits "beyond that general advantage which all real property in the city may receive therefrom," and the adjudication is that the estates have been benefited certain amounts, this is presumed to have been made as the ordinance contemplates. Jones *v.* Boston, 104 Mass., 461. Where, by the statute, the assessment is authorized upon "the enhanced value of the land," the improvement upon the land must be excluded from consideration. People *v.* Austin, 47 Cal., 353.

[4] Nevins, etc., Draining Co. *v.* Alkire, 36 Ind., 189; *In re* Astor, 50 N. Y., 363; *In re* Cameron, id., 502; Sharp *v.* Spier, 4 Hill, 76; Covington *v.* Casey, 3 Bush, 698; Warner *v.* Grand Haven, 30 Mich., 24; Henderson *v.* Baltimore, 8 Md., 352; Jones *v.* Boston, 104 Mass., 461. A contract for a local improvement need not include the whole work embraced in the resolution providing for it; this is matter of discretion. Emery *v.* San Francisco Gas Co., 31 Cal.,

is that the improvement shall be asked for or assented to by a majority or some other proportion of those who would be taxed. The want of a compliance with this requirement is fatal in any stage of the proceedings.[1] And any decision or certificate of the proper authorities that the requisite application or consent had been made, would not be conclusive, but might be disproved.[2]

Collection of Assessments. These are made as the statute shall prescribe; and what has been said regarding the collection of the ordinary taxes is applicable here.[3]

240. A resolution providing that a street shall be improved "where necessary," is nugatory. Richardson *v.* Heydenfeldt, 46 Cal., 68; People *v.* Clark, 47 id., 456.

[1] Steuart *v.* Baltimore, 7 Md., 500; Henderson *v.* Baltimore, 8 id., 352; Sharp *v.* Spier, 4 Hill, 76; Howard *v.* First Independent Church, 17 Md., 451; Howard *v.* Bristol, 8 Bush, 493; Hitchcock *v.* Galveston, U. S. Circuit, Eastern District of Texas, 2 Central Law Journal, 331, citing Jennings *v.* Moss, 4 Texas, 452; Frazier *v.* Todd, id., 461.

[2] So held in Sharp *v.* Spier, 4 Hill, 76, where the village authorities had decided that the proper autnorities had petitioned for the improvement. And in Henderson *v.* Baltimore, 8 Md., 352, where the statute required the assent in writing of a majority of proprietors of land fronting on the street, before the paving of the street could be ordered, it was held that the assent must appear in fact to have been given; that the certificate of the commissioners that the requisite number of proprietors had assented, was only a *prima facie* warrant of authority, and those who should act under it would do so at their peril. See also People *v.* Batchellor, 53 N. Y., 128, and cases referred to, *ante*, p. 254. Where the statute permitted the improvement of a street and an assessment of expense on the owners fronting thereon, on a petition therefor in writing, by the owners of the larger part of the ground between the points to be improved, provided that the council, by a vote of all the members elect, might order such improvement without such petition. *Held*, that an ordinance not passed by the vote of all, in the absence of such a petition, was invalid. Covington *v.* Casey, 3 Bush, 698. Where the ordinance was required to be passed with "the unanimous consent of the mayor and councilmen in council," and it purported to be passed "by the mayor and board of councilmen," *held* that unanimous consent was to be understood, nothing to the contrary appearing of record. Lexington *v.* Headley, 5 Bush, 508. (The record showed an affirmative vote of all the aldermen, but was silent as to the mayor, though he signed the proceedings.) Compare Hoyt *v.* East Saginaw, 19 Mich., 39. On the point, what is a sufficient ordering of the work, see Wright *v.* Boston, 9 Cush., 233; State *v.* New Brunswick, 30 N. J., 395. There is no power to grade at the public expense where the right of way has not been obtained. Leavenworth *v.* Laing, 6 Kan., 274. And see *ante*, p. 97.

[3] It is no defense to an assessment for improving a street that certain city

It is customary to declare by statute that the assessment shall be a lien on the real estate assessed, and that the lien shall be

officers were interested in the contract. Schenley *v.* Commonwealth, 36 Penn. St., 29.

It has become a common provision in city charters that, in contracting for city improvements, the contractor shall look solely to an assessment against lot owners to be laid for the cost of the improvement. The following decisions have been made under such provisions.

Illinois. Under a contract to look only to the special assessment, the contractor has no other remedy, providing the city is in good faith, and with reasonable diligence, proceeding to make collections by means of such assessments. Chicago *v.* People, 48 Ill., 416. But if the city has no power to make such an assessment, and the improvement has been made without any express contract, the city is liable, upon an implied contract, to pay in the usual way, notwithstanding it was understood the contractor should rely on an assessment. Maher *v.* Chicago, 38 Ill., 266. See, also, Chicago *v.* People, 56 id., 327.

Louisiana. When the contractor for a public work loses his remedy against the land, by reason of the neglect of the authorities to give the proper notice to the owner, or of other fault on their part, an action may be maintained against the municipality for the contract price. Bouligny *v.* Dormenon, 2 Mart. La., N. S., 455; Newcomb *v.* Police Jury, 4 Rob. La., 233; O'Brien *v.* Police Jury, 2 La. An., 355; Michel *v.* Police Jury, 3 id., 123; Same *v.* Same, 9 id., 67. If the municipality contracts with a paver that lot proprietors shall pay a certain portion of the cost of the pavement, and they refuse or neglect to do so, the municipality is liable. Cronan *v.* Municipality No. 1, 5 La. An., 537. So, if by contract the municipality is to pay one-third the cost of a work and the lot owners two-thirds, but, by suit, it is determined that the lot owners can be charged one-third only, the municipality is liable for the two-thirds. Fournier *v.* Municipality No. 1, 5 La. An., 298. As to suits in the name of the corporation for the benefit of the contractor, see New Orleans *v.* Wire, 20 La. An., 500.

Wisconsin. When the contractor is to be paid by certificates, showing the amount chargeable to each lot, which are to be collected as a tax, he cannot maintain an action against the city, but must depend on the collection of the certificates. Whalen *v.* La Crosse, 16 Wis., 271; Finney *v.* Oshkosh, 18 id., 209; Fletcher *v.* Oshkosh, 18 id., 232.

Kentucky. When the contractor has agreed to take and collect the assessments as his pay, he cannot hold the city liable, unless it may be in cases where the whole proceedings are void, or the city neglects its duty; as where it fails to observe the requirements of the charter necessary to make the lot owners liable. Kearney *v.* Covington, 1 Met. (Ky.), 339. For a case of very peculiar contract, see Louisville *v.* Henderson, 5 Bush, 515.

Maryland. Where artesian wells were ordered on a petition, the order reciting: "the petitioners to be responsible for all expenses that may occur in sinking said artesian wells, if a failure should take place in the attempt to procure water," it was *held*, the contractors must look to the petitioners, and not to the city. Ruppert *v.* Baltimore, 23 Md., 184.

enforced by a sale, or by means of some other remedy which the statute prescribes.[1]

Kansas. When, before ordering an improvement, it was necessary that a petition should be presented by a majority of the resident property owners to be affected thereby; and that there should be a stipulation in the contract that the contractor should look to the property owners benefited for his pay, and that the city would not be liable, a contract was let without such petition being presented, and not containing the above stipulation; it was *held*, that the contractor, after failing to collect the amount from the property holders, could not make the city liable for the amount. Leavenworth *v.* Rankin, 2 Kans., 357. But in Kansas, the city is primarily liable to a contractor for grading, and, unless it levies a valid tax and provides some means for enforcing it against the lot owners, it will remain liable. Leavenworth *v.* Mills, 6 Kans., 288.

Indiana. Where the charter provides that the city shall be liable for the paving of so much of the street as is occupied by streets or alleys crossing the same, and that the contractor must look to the owners of the bordering lands for the remainder; *held*, that if the contractor failed to collect from these proprietors, he could not recover the amount from the city. New Albany *v.* Sweeney, 13 Ind., 245. See, also, Johnson *v.* Indianapolis, 16 id., 227.

California. See Lucas *v.* San Francisco, 7 Cal., 463, 474, for a doctrine corresponding to that in the case cited above from Indiana.

Massachusetts. When the contractor for a dike was to be paid from assessments, and after their payment the town was, by statute, liable, it was *held*, there was no liability until such payment. Hendrick *v.* West Springfield, 107 Mass., 541.

Michigan. When by law, and by his contract, the contractor is to look only to a special fund raised by assessment for his compensation, he cannot hold the city liable in the absence of any negligence in levying or collecting the assessment. See Goodrich *v.* Detroit, 12 Mich., 279; Second National Bank *v.* Lansing, 25 id., 207. But the city is liable if it misappropriates the special fund. Chaffee *v.* Granger, 6 Mich., 51; Lansing *v.* Van Gorder, 24 id., 456.

New York. Where, by city charter, the contractor for a city work is to be paid from an assessment levied for the purpose, he cannot maintain a suit against the city before the assessment is collected, in the absence of default on the part of the officers to proceed therewith. Hunt *v.* Utica, 18 N. Y., 442. See Beard *v.* Brooklyn, 31 Barb., 142; Swift *v.* Williamsburg, 24 id., 427.

Minnesota. Where the contractor binds himself to look to the property owners for his pay, but fails to do so, the city is not liable even though it has taken ineffectual steps to make collections from the property owners. Lovell *v.* St. Paul, 10 Minn., 290.

Iowa. If a city agrees to collect the assessment, and fails to do so, it is liable. Morgan *v.* Dubuque, 28 Iowa, 575.

Ohio. If the contractor takes an assignment of the assessment in payment, he cannot look to the city to make up any deficiency in consequence of assessments exceeding the value of lots. Creighton *v.* Toledo, 18 Ohio, N. S., 447.

[1] In People *v.* Brooklyn, 4 N. Y., 419, the assessment was made upon "the

It is no defense to an assessment that the contract for the work was not performed according to its terms. The proper authorities must decide upon this, and if they accept the work, the acceptance, in the absence of frauds, is conclusive. And even fraud, it would seem, could not be accepted as a defense to an assessment, but should be determined in some direct proceeding instituted for the purpose.[1] On this point the following remarks have been made in one case in which an assessment for the construction of a sewer was contested. "It is needless to observe

owners and occupants of all the lands benefited thereby, in proportion to the amount of such benefit." It was made a lien on the land, but was to be collected of the personal property of the owner, and if none, then of the land. As to lien, see also Walsh *v.* Mathews, 29 Cal., 123; Emery *v.* Bradford, id., 75; McMasters *v.* Commonwealth, 3 Watts, 292; Philadelphia *v.* Tryon, 35 Penn. St., 401; Schenley *v.* Commonwealth, 36 id., 29. When the assessment is on land, irrespective of the value of buildings, the lien nevertheless affects the buildings. Wright *v.* Boston, 9 Cush., 233. When an assessment for widening a street is made a lien on the lot in the nature of mortgage, with authority in the city to sell for its satisfaction, and a sale is made which is void, and money refunded, the lien remains, and the sale is no bar to further proceedings to collect. New York *v.* Colgate, 12 N. Y., 149. *Held*, in the same case, that a lien is not barred sooner than a mortgage would be.

[1] Municipality *v.* Guillotte, 14 La. An., 297; Dougherty *v.* Miller, 36 Cal., 83; Taylor *v.* Palmer, 31 id., 240; Cochran *v.* Collins, 29 id., 129: Emery *v.* Bradford, 29 id., 75. In the case last cited, *Sawyer*, J., says: "In this case the contract is admitted by the pleadings to have been performed to the satisfaction of the superintendent. It was a duty devolved upon that officer to determine that question of fact, and he did determine it. There is no fraud charged — nothing but an error in judgment. The law afforded the defendant a remedy in the regular course of the proceeding itself, by which he might have had the error reviewed, and the defect, if any, remedied. He did not avail himself of the remedy, but declined to appeal, and now seeks to review the determination of the superintendent collaterally. We think, by this neglect to appeal, he has acquiesced in the approval of the work by the superintendent, and that his determination is conclusive. The principles applicable to the review of assessments of other taxes would apply here, and such would be the result in respect to ordinary taxes for state, county and municipal purposes. Conlin *v.* Seaman, 22 Cal., 549; Peoria *v.* Kidder, 26 Ill., 358; Aldrich *v.* Cheshire R. R. Co., 1 Foster, 361; Hughes *v.* Kline, 30 Penn. St., 230, 231; Sandford *v.* New York, 33 Barb., 150; Lowell *v.* Hadley, 8 Met., 194; Williams *v.* Holden, 4 Wend., 227, 228; Bouton *v.* Neilson, 3 Johns., 475, 476; Windsor *v.* Field, 1 Conn., 284. It was decided in Nolan *v.* Reese, 32 Cal., 484, that fraud in letting the contract was no defense to an assessment. It might doubtless be a reason for enjoining the execution of the contract, on a bill filed in due season.

that no misconstruction or malconstruction of the work, arising from the incapacity, the honest mistake, or the fraud of the contractor, would invalidate the assessment, or relieve the parties assessed from the obligation to pay it. In this respect the property owners, assessed under the provisions of the law for the cost of a sewer, must stand upon the same footing with parties assessed for taxes for the public benefit. They take the hazard incident to all public improvements, of their being faulty or useless, through the incapacity or fraud of public servants. The pretext that the tax payer shall avoid the payment of his assessment because the funds are injudiciously applied, is the worst form of repudiation." [1]

Collection by Sale of Lands. Lands cannot be sold for such assesments without specific legislation for the purpose. The ordinary authority to sell lands for taxes is not applicable to the case. The reasons for this conclusion are well given in a New York case, from which a quotation is given in the note.[2] But any fail-

[1] *Green*, Chancellor, in State *v.* Jersey City, 29 N. J., 441, 449.

[2] "But it is said that the power to sell lands for these assessments may be found in the seventh section of the act which provides 'that whenever any *tax* of any description on *lands* or *tenements* in the said village shall remain unpaid,' and the collector shall make affidavit 'that the owner or owners of the *premises on which the same is imposed*' cannot be found, or that he has not sufficient personal estate in the village whereon the tax can be levied, the trustees may take order for advertising in a newspaper, for the space of three months 'thereby requiring the owners of *such lands and tenements* respectively,' to pay the tax, and that in case of default, '*such* lands and tenements' will be sold, 'and if, notwithstanding such notice,' the tax shall not be paid, 'then it shall and may be lawful for the said trustees to cause *such* lands and tenements to be sold at auction for a term of years.' Now the first remark upon this section is, that it only authorizes the sale of lands for the payment of a tax; and although it extends to a tax 'of any description,' still it includes nothing but a tax of some kind. Our laws have made a plain distinction between taxes which are burdens or charges imposed upon persons or property, to raise money for public purposes, and *assessments* for city and village improvements, which are not regarded as burdens, but as an equivalent or compensation for the enhanced value which the property of the person assessed has derived from the improvement. This distinction has been made in several statutes, long before Brooklyn was incorporated, and was fully exemplified in the Matter of the Mayor of New York (11 Johns., 77). There, several churches in the city of New York had been *assessed* for the supposed benefit which they would derive from the enlarging of Nassau street, and

ure to give express authority for this purpose must be exceptional and accidental; it is usually conferred with a lien and specific directions for the enforcement. Under some statutes the assessment or list when completed is handed over to the contractor for the work, who proceeds to enforce the lien in his own favor.[1] When this is done, it is generally under provisions of law which impose upon the contractor all responsibility for the collection.

Personal Liability for Assessments. It is customary not only to make the assessment a lien on the land, but also to make it a personal charge against the owner. There is some difficulty in principle in doing this; a difficulty which in two states has been found insurmountable, the courts holding that in principle, at least, it is not permissible.[2]

they denied the legality of the assessment, because it had been expressly enacted that 'no church or place of public worship shall be *taxed* by any law of this state.' But the objection was overruled, and the exemption claimed by the churches denied, on the ground that the assessment could not properly be regarded as a tax. This case apparently goes the whole length of deciding the one now before us. The authority is to sell for a *tax*, and the defendant shows nothing but an assessment for a village improvement. In Bleecker *v.* Ballou, 3 Wend., 263, the question was upon an assessment for pitching and paving a street, and *Savage*, Ch. J., said: 'there is no doubt that the assessment in question was not a *tax*, that being a sum imposed as, is supposed, for some public object.'" Per *Bronson*, J., in Sharp *v.* Spier, 4 Hill, 76, 82. To the same point are McInery *v.* Reid, 23 Iowa, 410; Merriam *v.* Moody's Executors, 25 id., 163; Paine *v.* Spratley, 5 Kans., 525: Leavenworth *v.* Laing, 6 id., 274. In some of the states these assessments are by statute made collectible in the same manner as the ordinary taxes. See Morrison *v.* Hershire 32 Iowa, 271.

[1] See Northern Indiana R. R. Co. *v.* Connelly, 10 Ohio, N. S., 159; Taylor *v.* Palmer, 31 Cal., 240; Chambers *v.* Satterlee, 40 id., 497.

[2] The cases referred to are Taylor *v.* Palmer, 31 Cal., 240, 254, opinion by *Sanderson*, J., and Neenan *v.* Smith, 50 Mo., 525, opinion by *Bliss*, J., afterwards approved in Carlin *v.* Cavender, 56 id., 286, and St. Louis *v.* Brester, id., 350.

"There is a broad distinction, and one of universal recognition, between the foundation upon which is based the right of general taxation for governmental purposes, and that which supports the right of local assessments. The authority to impose either is referred to the taxing power; but the object of one, as giving the authority, widely differs from that of the other. All taxation is supposed to be for the benefit of the person taxed. That for raising a general revenue is imposed primarily for his protection as a member of society, both in his person and his property in general, and hence the amount as-

In the case of the ordinary taxes no sufficient reason exists why those on lands should not be made a personal charge against the owner, if he is a resident and has the usual opportunity to be heard. The taxes are not so much assessed in respect to the particular lands, as the value of the particular lands is taken as the measure of the owner's duty to the state. He is not taxed in consideration of state protection to that particular item of property, but he is taxed for the general protection which the state affords to his life, his liberty, his family and social relations, his property, and the various privileges the law grants to him. If a tax measured by the property should, in its enforcement, take from him more than that property is worth, it would not follow that the state had taken beyond the equivalent rendered. Indeed, the contrary would be almost certainly the fact. It is different in the case of an assessment made upon the basis of benefits. Such an

sessed is against him, to be charged upon his property, and may be collected of him personally. But, on the other hand, local taxes for local improvements are merely assessments upon the property benefited by such improvements, and to pay for the benefits which they are supposed to confer; the lots are increased in value, or better adapted to the uses of town lots, by the improvement. Upon no other ground will such partial taxation for a moment stand. Other property held by the owner is affected by this improvement precisely and only as is the property of all other members of the community, and there is no reason why it should be made to contribute, that does not equally apply to that of all others. The sole object, then, of a local tax being to benefit local property; it should be a charge upon that property only, and not a general one upon the owner. The latter, indeed, is not what is understood by local or special assessment, but the very term would confine it to the property in the locality; for, if the owner be personally liable, it is not only a local assessment, but also a general one as against the owner. The reasonableness of this restriction will appear when we reflect that there is no call for a general execution until the property charged is exhausted. If that is all sold to pay the assessment, leaving a balance to be collected otherwise, we should have the legal amonaly — the monstrous injustice — of not only wholly absorbing the property supposed to be benefited and rendered more valuable by the improvement, but also of entailing upon the owner the loss of his other property. I greatly doubt whether the legislature has the power to authorize a general charge upon the owner of local property which may be assessed for its especial benefit, unless the owners of all taxable property within the municipality are equally charged. As to all property not to be so specially benefited, he stands on the same footing with others; he has precisely the same interests, and should be subject to no greater burdens." Per *Bliss*, J., in Neenan *v.* Smith, 50 Mo., 525, 528.

assessment regards nothing but the benefit that is to be conferred upon the particular estate. The levy is made on the supposition that that estate, having received the benefit of a public improvement, ought to relieve the public from the expense of making it. In such a case, if the owner can have his land taken from him for a supposed benefit to the land, which, if the land is sold for the tax, it is thus conclusively shown he has not received, and he then be held liable for a deficiency in the assessment, the injustice — not to say the tyranny — is manifest. But such a case is liable to occur if assessments are made a personal charge; and cases like it in principle, though less extreme in the injury they inflict, are certain to occur.

The cases are not uncommon in which, on a sale of lands for the payment of a special assessment for a drain or a levee, the whole estate assessed is sold and lost to the owner. Such instances may occur in the case of other improvements. If the statute allows a sale to the highest bidder, the land may be lost to the owner, leaving a balance of the assessment still uncollected. The loss of his lands is incident to a proper exercise of the power of the government, and though severe, can give him no ground for complaint. The assessors have perhaps erred in their judgment; but this may occur in any tax proceeding. The estate was lawfully charged with the supposed benefit, and the charge has been enforced. But where and what are the benefits to the individual, for which he can be called upon to pay any deficiency after a sale of the estate? Unless the whole legal basis of these assessments has been misunderstood by the courts, it would seem that there are none whatever. But the practice of making these assessments a personal charge against resident owners, has been almost universal. The English statutes go so far as to make them a personal charge against "the present or any future owner of the property" assessed until paid.[1] In the United States, personal assessments of this nature have been enforced in a great number of cases.[2] How

[1] Vestry of Bermondsey *v.* Ramsey, Law Rep., 6 C. P., 247; Plumstead Board of Works *v.* Ingoldsby, Law Rep., 8 Exch., 63; affirmed, id., 174.

[2] See New York *v.* Colgate, 12 N. Y., 141; Gilbert *v.* Havermeyer, 2 Sand., 508; Manice *v.* New York, 8 N. Y., 120; People *v.* Nearing, 27 id., 308; Sharp *v.* Johnson, 4 Hill, 76; Cuming *v.* Brooklyn, 11 Paige, 600; McCulloch *v.* Brooklyn, 23 Wend., 459; Gouverneur *v.* New York, 2 Paige, 437; Doughty *v.*

much of this may be due to the fact that the right to make a personal assessment was not contested, can only be matter of conjecture; but at present it must be conceded that the overwhelming weight of authority is in favor of the right.

Hope, 3 Denio, 253; Bennett *v.* Buffalo, 17 N. Y., 383; People *v.* Brooklyn, 4 id., 420; Brewster *v.* Syracuse, 19 id., 118; Bleecker *v.* Ballou, 3 Wend., 263; Litchfield *v.* McComber, 42 Barb., 288; Baltimore *v.* Howard, 6 H. & J., 383; Eschback *v.* Pitts, 6 Md., 71; Clemens *v.* Baltimore, 16 id., 208; Patterson *v.* Society, etc., 24 N. J., 385; Nor. Lib. *v.* St. Johns Church, 13 Penn. St., 104; New Orleans *v.* Wire, 20 La. An., 500; Nichols *v.* Bridgeport, 23 Conn., 190; Lowell *v.* French, 6 Cush., 223; Hill *v.* Higdon, 5 Ohio, N. S., 243; Ernst *v.* Kunkle, id., 529; Creighton *v.* Scott, 14 id., 439; Reeves *v.* Treasurer of Wood Co., 8 id., 333; Le Fever *v.* Detroit, 2 Mich., 586; Lovell *v.* St. Paul, 10 Minn., 290; Hazzard *v.* Heacock, 39 Ind., 172.

CHAPTER XXI.

LOCAL TAXATION UNDER LEGISLATIVE COMPULSION.

The general doctrine. In our discussions hitherto, it has been assumed as a fundamental idea in republican government, that the people who are to pay the taxes must vote them, either directly or by their proper representatives. State taxes must be levied under laws passed by the legislature of the state, and local taxes under the votes of the people concerned or their officers or agents duly authorized.

It has also been assumed that all local powers must have their origin in a grant by the state, which is the source and fountain of authority. The power to tax is no exception to this general rule. Every municipal corporation, and every political division of the state which demands taxes from the people must be able to show due authority from the state to make the demand. The authority in some cases is conferred by the state constitution, but if not found there, it must be given by legislative enactment. No person is compellable to pay taxes for imposing which the authorities are unable to show a legislative grant of power.

If local powers of taxation must come from the state, it might seem to follow as a corollary that the state might at pleasure withhold the grant and exercise the power itself. But in the general framework of our republican governments, nothing is more distinct and unquestionable than that they recognize the existence of local self government, and contemplate its permanency. Some state constitutions do this in express terms, others by necessary implication; and probably in no one of the states has the legislature been entrusted with a power which would enable it to abolish the local governments. It has usually a large authority in determining the extent of local powers, and the framework of local government, but while it may shape the local institutions, it cannot abolish them, and, without substituting others, take all authority to itself.

Local power to tax. Of all the customary local powers, that of taxation is the chief and most valuable. To give local government without this would be a mockery and a cheat. If any state has the power to withhold it, the exercise of such a power would justly be regarded as tyranny. Indeed local taxation is so inseparable an incident to republican institutions, that to abolish it would be nothing short of a revolution.

By local taxation here, we do not mean that which is exercised for state purposes. So far as local officers or local boards are made use of for the levy and collection of state taxes, they cannot be left at liberty to exercise their own discretion in determining whether they will act or abstain from acting. If the state, instead of issuing a separate warrant for the collection of the state taxes, shall see fit to apportion the whole tax among the several townships, leaving the township authorities to collect their several proportions under the same warrants which are issued for the collection of local taxes, there is no reason why the collection of this proportion of the state tax should not be made compulsory. No local community has any inherent right to decide for itself whether it will or will not bear its share of the state burdens, and obviously the state could not afford to confer the right. To do so would leave the state in the same precarious condition that the federal union was found to occupy before the right to tax had been conferred upon it by the constitution; a government without the means of enforcing respect, securing obedience, performing its obligations or perpetuating its existence.[1]

[1] De Tocqueville, who studied American institutions with so much care, and commented upon them with such wisdom, has the following remarks, which bear directly upon the subject now under discussion: "In the nations by which the sovereignty of the people is recognized, every individual has an equal share of power, and participates equally in the government of the state. Why, then, does he obey the government, and what are the natural limits of this obedience? Every individual is always supposed to be as well informed, as virtuous and as strong as any of his fellow citizens. He obeys the government, not because he is inferior to those who conduct it, or because he is less capable than any other of governing himself, but because he acknowledges the utility of an association with his fellow men, and he knows that no such association can exist without a regulating force. He is a subject in all that concerns the duties of citizens to each other; he is free and responsible to God alone for all that concerns himself. Hence arises the maxim that every one is the best and sole judge of his own private interest and that

Compulsory local taxation. But aside from cases of state taxation proper, there are some to which the same principles apply. They are cases in which taxation is usually entrusted to the judgment and discretion of the people to be taxed, but where the interest is really general, and referring the cases to the local community is merely a politic provision for the apportionment of state burdens. Mention of one or two of these cases will sufficiently illustrate the principle.

One of the first and highest of all the duties devolving upon the state is to preserve the public peace. For this purpose,

society has no right to control a man's actions, unless they are prejudicial to the common weal, or unless the common weal demands his help. This doctrine is universally admitted in the United States. I shall hereafter examine the general influence which it exercises on the ordinary actions of life. I am now speaking of the municipal bodies. The township, taken as a whole and in relation to the central government, is only an individual like any other, to whom the theory I have just described is applicable. Municipal independence in the United States is, therefore, a natural consequence of this very principle of the sovereignty of the people. All the American republics recognize it more or less; but circumstances have peculiarly favored its growth in New England.

"In this part of the union, political life had its origin in the townships, and it may almost be said that each of them originally formed an independent nation. When the kings of England afterwards asserted their supremacy, they were content to assume the central power of the state. They left the townships where they were before, and, although they are now subject to the state, they were not at first, or were hardly so. They did not receive their powers from the central authority, but, on the contrary, they gave up a portion of their independence to the state. This is an important consideration, and one which the reader must constantly recollect. The townships are generally subordinate to the state only in those interests which I shall term *social*, as they are common to all the others. They are independent in all that concerns themselves alone; and amongst the inhabitants of New England, I believe that not a man is to be found who would acknowledge that the state has any right to interfere in their town affairs.

"The towns of New England buy and sell, prosecute, or are indicted, augment or diminish their rates, and no administrative authority ever thinks of offering any opposition.

"There are certain social duties, however, which they are bound to fulfill. If the state is in need of money, a town cannot withhold the supplies; if the state projects a road, the township cannot refuse to let it cross the territory; if a police regulation is made by the state, it must be enforced by the town; if a uniform system of public instruction is enacted, every town is bound to establish the schools which the law ordains." Democracy, ch. v.

peace officers are chosen, judges selected, the militia organized, and the executive armed with very high powers to meet the contingencies of riot and disorder. In some cases, a state police force has been established as assistant to, and in some degree to supersede the ordinary officers; but in general, the belief has prevailed that the public peace and good order were better preserved by apportioning the duty among the several municipal divisions, retaining only a state supervision over all. This apportionment is made by general laws, under which counties, towns, etc., choose their own peace officers, and levy the necessary taxes to meet the expense of a local administration of police laws; and by municipal charters which confer large police powers upon the bodies incorporated.

But if the local authorities were allowed unlimited discretion to levy or refuse to levy the necessary taxes for the support of the local police force, it might possibly happen, that from neglect or refusal to do so, one part of the state might be left a prey to disorder and violence, to the general detriment of the state at large. Of course, no state could safely, for a single day, tolerate such a condition of affairs. A city or township could no more be left at liberty to decline taxation for police purposes, when the police laws and police force, and the tax which supports them, are made by law local, than if all were general. The police organization of the state is really general, however it may vary in different localities, and the obligation to support it is general, however it may be apportioned. To this effect are the decisions.[1] And within the reason of these decisions would fall all cases in which the municipal corporations or subdivisions of the state are called upon to tax their people for the erection and repair of court houses and jails, by means of which the police laws are rendered effectual. Such calls must, of course, be responded to.

[1] People *v.* Draper, 15 N. Y., 532; Baltimore *v.* State, 15 Md., 476; People *v.* Mahaney, 13 Mich., 481; People *v.* Common Council of Detroit, 28 Mich., 228, 236; People *v.* Common Council of Chicago, 51 Ill., 17. It was decided in Taylor *v.* Board of Health, 31 Penn. St., 73, that a board of health for a city district was a state functionary, and that a tax allowed to be levied by such a board on immigration was "not a legitimate tax for mere local purposes, and it was not applied to such; for the guarding of the frontiers of a state against importation of pestilence is not a local purpose. The whole regulation was general in its purposed benefits, though necessarily local in its execution."

Elsewhere, in this work, the public highways have been spoken of as matters of general concern to the people of the whole state. In a certain sense they are of local concern, because the local organizations construct and support them, but they are constructed for the general benefit and use of all the people, and only turned over to the localities as a matter of apportionment. This being the case, any township, city or county, that neglects its duty in this regard, may be compelled by the interference of the state, and on state account, to perform it.[1] This doctrine applies to the common highways; whether it can be extended to exceptional means of passage and transportation will be considered further on.

Wherever a system of public instruction is established by law, to be administered by local boards, who levy taxes, build school houses, and employ teachers for the purpose, it can hardly be questioned that the state, in establishing the system, reserves to itself the means of giving it complete effect and full efficiency in every township and district of the state, even though a majority of the people of such township or district, in a want of a proper appreciation of its advantages, should refuse to take upon themselves the expense necessary to give them a participation in its benefits. Possibly judicial proceedings might be available in some such cases, where a state law for the levy of local taxes for educational purposes had been disobeyed; but the legislature would be at liberty to choose its own method for compelling the performance of the local duty.[2]

[1] That the legislature, in laying out a road through several towns, has authority to apportion between them the expense of construction, see Harwich *v.* County Commissioners, 13 Pick., 60; Hingham and Quincy Company *v.* Norfolk County, 6 Allen, 353; Salem Turnpike, etc., Corporation *v.* Essex County, 100 Mass., 282; Commonwealth *v.* Newburyport, 103 id., 129; Waterville *v.* Kennebeck County, 59 Me., 80; Shaw *v.* Dennis, 5 Gilm., 405. It has been held that the legislature may order a reapportionment when justice requires it. Cambridge *v.* Lexington, 17 Pick., 222; Attorney General *v.* Cambridge, 16 Gray, 247.

[2] It is noticeable that in those states in which a general system of public instruction has longest prevailed, the municipalities have not been disposed to find fault because they were required to maintain schools; but the complaint, when there has been any, has come from single individuals, who have complained that the local powers of taxation were exercised with unreason-

Those cases in which the state interferes to compel a political corporation or body, which exists and exercises authority by its permission, to meet its contract obligations and pay its just debts, may be defended on two grounds: *First*, that it is the right and the duty of the state to see that the powers it confers are not abused, to the injury of those who have relied upon them. *Second*, that when a political corporation has contracted a debt or incurred an obligation, it has already taken the initiatory step in taxation, and has, in effect, given its consent that the subsequent steps, so far as they may be essential to the discharge of such debt or obligation, may be taken. No matter, therefore, what the purpose of any lawful municipal contract; the taxation to perform it must be regarded as taxation by consent of the people who made it. And while the general law usually makes provision for such cases, by means of suits at law and perhaps executions, circumstances sometimes render it entirely proper that more speedy remedies be provided; and of these the most speedy and effectual might possibly be a special tax upon the delinquent municipality, ordered by the state, and perhaps levied through state agencies.[1] Nor would the power of the state in this regard be confined to obligations of a strictly legal nature; for the difference between a legal and moral obligation is frequently no more than this: that the one has a remedy provided for its enforcement, and the other has not. No question, for example, can fairly be raised of the right of the state, after it has formed two municipal governments where one existed before, and apportioned the debts and property of the old organization between the two new ones, to require and compel the payment of any balance found equitably due.[2] Another case is where the state requires one of its corporations to reimburse to

able liberality for this purpose. The cases of Cushing *v.* Newburyport, 10 Met., 508; Stewart *v.* Kalamazoo, 30 Mich., 69, and Horton *v.* School Commissioners, 43 Ala., 598, may be referred to. The contest has been made on other grounds in other states: see Kinney *v.* Zimpleman, 36 Texas, 554; Commissioners of Schools *v.* Alleghany Co., 20 Md., 439.

[1] See Dunovan *v.* Green, 57 Ill., 63; a case of the levy of a tax by the state upon the municipality to provide for municipal obligations.

[2] Harrison *v.* Bridgeton, 16 Mass., 16; Layton *v.* New Orleans, 12 La. An., 515; People *v.* Alameda, 26 Cal., 641; People *v.* Power, 25 Ill., 187; *ante*, p. 176, note 2

the officers expenses they have incurred in an honest, though mistaken effort to perform their official duty.[1] Another is where a municipal corporation is compelled, by means of taxation, to make compensation for losses sustained within its limits at the hands of mobs and rioters. It has been thought from very early times that that political division of the county which failed to exert its authority for the effectual suppression of disorder, by means whereof innocent parties suffered from lawlessness and violence within its boundaries, might justly be required to make good the losses, and that its diligence in maintaining the empire of the laws would be quickened by the requirement.[2] Such legislation is, in effect, only a part of the state police system, under which the municipal divisions are severally looked to for the preservation of the public peace within their respective limits.[3] And speaking generally, it may be affirmed that in any case in which compulsory taxation is found necessary, in order to compel a municipal corporation or political division of the state to perform properly and justly any of its duties as an agency in state government, or to fulfill any obligation legally or equitably resting upon it in consequence of any corporate action, the state has ample power to direct and levy such compulsory taxation, and the people to be taxed have no absolute right to a voice in determining whether it shall be levied, except as they may be heard through their representatives in the legislature of the state.[4]

[1] See the extreme case of Guilford *v.* Supervisors of Chenango, 18 Barb., 615; S. C. in error, 13 N. Y., 143, questioned in People *v.* Tappan, 29 Wis., 664, 687. In Sinton *v.* Ashbury, 41 Cal., 525, 530, *Crockett*, J., asserts in strong terms the power of the legislature to compel a municipal corporation "to pay a demand, when properly established, which in good conscience it ought to pay, even though there be no legal liability to pay it."

[2] Darlington *v.* New York, 31 N. Y., 164. This case was decided under a law passed before the mischief was done; but no reason is perceived why the equity of such a claim might not be recognized by legislation adopted afterwards.

[3] See *In re* Pennsylvania Hall, 5 Penn. St., 204; People *v.* Chicago, 51 Ill., 17; Wider *v.* East St. Louis, 55 Ill., 133, 137; Fauria *v.* New Orleans, 20 La. An., 400; S. C., 2 Withrow's Corp. Cas., 374.

[4] It is competent, by special statute, to compel one county to levy a tax in order to refund to another county the fair proportion of the expenses which have been incurred by the latter in trials concerning the distribution of the

Doubtful cases. Where a county is divided and property and debts are to be apportioned, political considerations are involved, and the legislature must directly or indirectly pass upon them. But when demands are asserted against municipal corporations, growing out of contracts, or upon such grounds as might give rights of action against individuals, it is at least questionable whether the legislature may pass upon the facts, adjudge the corporation liable, and proceed to enforce payment by taxation. Such action, as against a natural person, would be clearly judicial, and therefore beyond the legislative competency; and it could only be sustained in the case of municipal corporations on the doctrine that their powers and rights are wholly at the legislative disposal; a doctrine dangerous in government, and, as we think, unsound in constitutional law. The opinion has sometimes been expressed that these corporations were entitled to the constitutional benefits of an ordinary trial.[1] But this is denied in other cases, and perhaps a hearing before some court or board of audit might be all the corporation could demand.[2] But such a hearing, if local municipal government is a matter of substance, they must be entitled to. It is not believed that the liability of the corporation must be made to turn on legal questions purely. On the contrary, it is more consistent with the dignity and honor of government that all demands against the public shall be settled on broad grounds of equity, instead of being tested by technical rules; and auditing boards are generally, with the utmost propriety, empowered to govern their action by equitable considerations. This only is maintained; that the legislature is not a proper auditing board as between the municipalities and third persons, though it may undoubtedly prescribe the rule of liability for all cases.

proceeds of sales of property lying in both. Lycoming *v.* Union, 15 Penn. St., 166.

[1] See Sanborn *v.* Rice County, 9 Minn., 273; People *v.* Haws, 37 Barb., 440; Plimpton *v.* Somerset, 33 Vt., 283; Gage *v.* Graham, 57 Ill., 144; State *v.* Tappan, 29 Wis., 664.

[2] *In re* Pennsylvania Hall, 5 Penn. St., 204; Borough of Dunmore's Appeal, 52 id., 374; Layton *v.* New Orleans, 12 La. An., 515. Compare Commonwealth *v.* Pittsburgh, 34 Penn. St., 496. In Vasser *v.* George, 47 Miss., 713, 720, *Simrall*, J., claims very broad authority for the legislature in adjusting claims against municipalities.

Nature of municipal corporations. Before considering some other cases, it may be well to refer briefly to the general nature of municipal corporations. Primarily these are public and their powers governmental. They are created for convenience, expediency and economy in government, and, in their public capacity, are and must be at all times subject to the control of the state which has imparted to them life, and may at any time deprive them of it. But they have or may have another side, in respect to which the control is in reason, at least, not so extensive. They may be endowed with peculiar powers and capacities for the benefit and convenience of their own citizens, and in the exercise of which they seem not to differ in any substantial degree from the private corporations which the state charters. They have thus their public or political character, in which they exercise a part of the sovereign power of the state for governmental purposes, and they have their private character in which, for the benefit or convenience of their own citizens, they exercise powers not of a governmental nature, and in which the state at large has only an incidental concern, as it may have with the action of private corporations. It may not be possible to draw the exact line between the two, but provisions for local conveniences for the citizens, like water, light, public grounds for recreation, and the like, are manifestly matters which are not provided for by municipal corporations in their political or governmental capacity, but in that *quasi* private capacity in which they act for the benefit of their corporators exclusively.[1] In their public, political capacity, they have no discretion but to act as the state which has created them shall, within constitutional limits, command, and the good government

[1] This two-fold nature of municipal corporations has often been commented upon and been made the ground of important decisions. See Bailey *v.* New York, 3 Hill, 531; Milhau *v.* Sharp, 15 Barb., 212, 213, per *Edwards*, P. J.; Lloyd *v.* New York, 5 N. Y., 369, 375, per *Jones*, J.; Storrs *v.* Utica, 17 N. Y. 104; People *v.* Batchellor, 53 id., 128, per *Grover*, J.; Western Savings Fund Society *v.* Philadelphia, 31 Penn. St., 175; Touchard *v.* Touchard, 5 Cal., 306; Holland *v.* San Francisco, 7 id., 361; San Francisco Gas Co. *v.* San Francisco, 9 id., 453; Western College *v.* Cleveland, 12 Ohio, N. S., 375, 377, per *Gholson*, J.; Jones *v.* New Haven, 34 Conn., 1, 12; Hewison *v.* New Haven, 37 id., 475, 483; Detroit *v.* Corey, 9 Mich., 165; People *v.* Hurlbut, 24 id., 44; People *v.* Common Council of Detroit, 28 Mich., 228, 238; Hasbrouck *v.* Milwaukee, 13 Wis., 37; Atkins *v.* Randolph, 31 Vt., 226.

of the state requires that the power should at all times be ample to compel obedience, and that it should be capable of being promptly and efficiently exercised. In the capacity in which they act for the benefit of their corporators merely, there would seem to be no sufficient reason for a power in the state to make them move and act at its will, any more than in the case of any private corporation. With ample authority in the state to mould, measure and limit their powers at discretion, and to prevent any abuse thereof, their action within the prescribed limits, in matters of importance to themselves only, it would naturally be supposed, should be left to the judgment of their citizens and of their chosen officers.

And this has been the view on which the several state legislatures have in general acted. The largest liberty of action has been permitted to municipal action in matters of local concern, and very seldom has the disposition been evinced to interfere any further than was deemed necessary to prevent an oppressive exercise of local powers, and to confine them to proper local purposes. And in those cases in which municipal corporations have been allowed to vote taxes for purposes not strictly local, but on the grounds of special local benefit, the legislation has seldom gone beyond giving permission to vote them if the electors of the locality should elect to do so. Whenever the legislation has gone further than this, the courts have generally held that the legislative power of control had been exceeded. In a leading case in Vermont, the legislature provided for the appointment, by a county commissioner, of a town agent, who should be empowered to purchase liquors on the credit of the town, and sell the same for such purposes as were admissible under what was known as the prohibitory liquor law, accounting to the town for the proceeds. The act was held invalid; the court declaring that "courts that have gone farthest in sustaining laws of state legislatures, against the restrictive provisions of state constitutions, repudiate entirely the idea that a person, whether natural or artificial, can be compelled by legislative enactment to become a party to, or to be subjected to liability upon a contract."[1] A like doctrine has been strongly

[1] Atkins *v.* Randolph, 31 Vt., 226, 236, per *Barrett*, J. In this case, Chief Justice *Black* is quoted, who, in that opinion of his in Sharpless *v.* Philadelphia, 21 Penn. St., 147, 165, which asserts legislative supremacy in matters of

asserted in Massachusetts, where in a case in which the legislature had taken steps looking to the establishment of a pecuniary demand against a municipal corporation, without its consent, the court declared — having the municipal corporation in view as the party to be charged — that "it is not in the power of the legislature to create a debt from one person to another, without the consent, express or implied, of the person to be charged," and that if the attempt were made, "it would not be within the power of any judicial court to enforce such an act."[1] A similar ruling was made in Maine in a similar case.[2] In Wisconsin, the power of the legislature to force taxation upon the people for objects not within the customary grant of local powers for governmental purposes, has been pointedly denied in cases in which the objects contemplated were presumptively of great local importance and value; one case, being that of an improvement of the city harbor,[3] and another that of a state normal school, to be located in the city, whose money, collected for local school purposes, the state directed should be appropriated to its erection.[4] In Michigan, the author-

taxation in very strong, if not extravagant language, nevertheless, interposes this caution: "I do not say, however, that a contract between two individuals, or two corporations, can be made by the legislature. That would not be legislation. Besides it would be impossible, in the nature of things; for the essence of a contract is the agreement of the parties."

1 Hampshire *v.* Franklin, 16 Mass., 76, 84, per *Parker*, Ch. J. And see Richland *v.* Lawrence, 12 Ill., 1, 8.

2 Brunswick *v.* Litchfield, 2 Greenl., 28, 32; Bowdoinham *v.* Richmond, 6 id., 112.

3 Hasbrouck *v.* Milwaukee, 13 Wis., 37. In this case, *Dixon*, Ch. J., speaking of the power of the legislature to make a contract for a municipal corporation against its will, says: "It is certainly unnecessary at this day to enter into an argument or to cite authorities to show that, under a constitutional government like ours, the legislature has no such power." This decision is defended in an able opinion by the same learned judge, in Mills *v.* Charlton, 29 Wis., 413. See also Knapp *v.* Grant, 27 id., 147; State *v.* Tappan, 29 id., 664.

4 State *v.* Haben, 22 Wis., 660, per *Dixon*, Ch. J. "Was it competent" it was inquired in this case, "for the legislature, without the assent of the city or its inhabitants, thus to divert the funds raised and in the hands of the treasurer for the purpose of erecting a suitable high school building, and to declare that they should be appropriated, not for that purpose, but for the purpose of purchasing a site for a state normal school in the city? We are clearly of the opinion that it was not. It is well settled as to all matters pertaining to

ity of the state to appoint agents who, without the consent of a city, might issue obligations binding upon it for the purchase and embellishment of a public park for its citizens, was denied on like grounds.[1] In Kansas, where county officers had issued to a creditor of the county the county bonds, bearing a rate of interest higher than was permitted by the law under which the debt was contracted, it was decided that the legislature had no power to validate the bonds; this being in effect the making of a new contract to which the county had not assented.[2] In Illinois, similar decisions have been based upon a narrower ground. The constitution of the state provides that "the corporate authorities of counties, townships, school districts, cities, towns and villages, may be vested with power to assess and collect taxes for corporate purposes;" and this, it is held, by implication precludes the levy

vested rights of property, whether real or personal, and to the obligation of contracts, that municipal corporations are as much within the protection of the federal constitution as private individuals are. The legislature cannot divest a municipal corporation of its property without the consent of its inhabitants, nor impair the obligation of a contract entered into with or in behalf of such corporation."

[1] People *v.* Common Council of Detroit, 28 Mich., 228. And see People *v.* Hurlbut, 24 id., 44. In this last case, in answer to an objection that there was no express saving of municipal rights in the state constitution, the following remarks are made (p. 107): "Some things are too plain to be written. If this charter of state government which we call a constitution were all there was of constitutional command; if the usages, the customs, the maxims, that have sprung from the habits of life, modes of thought, methods of trying facts by the neighborhood, and mutual responsibility in neighborhood interests, the precepts which have come from the revolutions which overturned tyrannies, the sentiments of manly independence and self control which impelled our ancestors to summon the local community to redress local evils, instead of relying upon king or legislature at a distance to do so; if a recognition of all these were to be stricken from the body of our constitutional law, a lifeless skeleton might remain, but the living spirit, that which gives it force and attraction, which makes it valuable and draws to it the affections of the people, that which distinguishes it from the numberless constitutions, so called, which in Europe have been set up and thrown down within the last hundred years, many of which, in their expression, have seemed equally fair and to possess equal promise with ours, and have only been wanting in the support and vitality which these alone can give; this living and breathing spirit, which supplies the interpretation of the words of the written charter, would be utterly lost and gone."

[2] Shawnee County *v.* Carter, 2 Kans., 115.

of local taxes, or the contracting of local debts, by agencies created by the legislature, and not being the corporate authorities of the locality to be taxed, or to be bound by the debts.[1] While as has been said, the ground chosen in those cases is narrow, the decisions are nevertheless of very general application, for the terms in which authority over the municipal corporations is conferred by other constitutions, though not the same, will generally be found open to similar implications. A similar decision has been made in Tennessee.[2]

In one or two states an inclination has been manifested to accept, in its broadest signification, the language in which an unrestricted authority in the legislature over the whole subject of taxation is usually spoken of when there is no occasion for pointing the limitations. It has already been shown by the citation of a large number of cases that no such unrestricted power exists, and it may safely be asserted that it ought not to exist. It is not difficult to give the most reckless robbery for private purposes the forms of constitutional action, and it is as easy to call it a tax as it was in former periods to call those exactions which were enforced by prisons and physical suffering and the quartering of a ruthless soldiery upon the people by the gentle name of benevolences. Taxation is a fearful power, but, like other legislative powers in representative government, it has its checks and balances. It is certainly limited as to purposes, and, as has been

[1] People *v.* Chicago, 51 Ill., 17; People *v.* Salomon, id., 37; Harward *v.* Drainage Co., id., 130; Lovingston *v.* Wider, 53 id., 302; People *v.* Canty, 55 id., 33; Wider *v.* East St. Louis, id., 133; Sleight *v.* People, Sup. Ct. Ill., 1875, 7 Chicago Legal News, 292.

[2] Pope *v.* Phifer, 3 Heisk., 682, in which an able opinion is delivered by *Freeman*, J. See also, State *v.* Leffingwell, 54 Mo., 458; People *v.* Hastings, 29 Cal., 449. The case in Heiskell involved the validity of an act of the legislature appointing a state board for the levy of county taxes in a few counties named. The court held the act invalid, as being inconsistent with the right of local taxation which by implication was considered retained and intended to be perpetuated by the constitution. And after commenting upon the maxim that taxation and representation go together, the court query concerning the board in question: "Can it be believed for a moment that the power was ever intended to be delegated by the people to the legislature to authorize such a body, so appointed and constituted, to perform the functions assigned to them in this act? We think no reasonable man can come to such a conclusion."

generally believed, by local rights immemorially existing and universally recognized.

A recent case in Alabama is of importance as bearing upon this question just mentioned. An act of the legislature of that state constituted a board, consisting of the president of the court of county commissioners of revenue of Mobile county, the mayor of Mobile, the president of the bank of Mobile, the president of the Mobile chamber of commerce and one citizen of the county of Mobile to be appointed by the governor, who, and their successors, were to be commissioners for the purpose of improving the river, harbor and bay of Mobile. The county commissioners of revenue were directed to issue to said board bonds to the amount of $1,000,000, binding upon the county, to be made payable as they should determine, and "to levy such tax as may be deemed proper to pay such bonds." The constitution provides that "No power to levy taxes shall be delegated to individuals or private corporations;" but the act was nevertheless sustained in an opinion that does little more than to allude to the very important question arising under the state constitution, and avoids the discussion of general principles.[1]

A case which was more considered was decided a few years since in New York. An act of the legislature had named commissioners, authorized them to lay out and construct roads in two townships named, at a cost per mile not exceeding $20,000, exclusive of bridges. The sum necessary to be raised to meet the expense was to be obtained by a sale of town bonds, to be issued by the town officers on the requisition of the commissioners, and by the latter sold. The roads, it will be seen, were local roads, to be constructed by state agents at the cost of the towns; neither

[1] President and Commissioners, etc., *v.* State, 45 Ala., 399. The case in which the question arose was a proceeding in mandamus against the county commissioners of revenue, to compel them to issue bonds under the act to the harbor improvement board. In answer to the objection that here was a case of delegation of the power to tax, which by the constitution was forbidden, *Safford*, J., delivering the opinion of the court, says: "even if it be a delegation of the taxing power to individuals or private corporations, that portion of the act only need be vitiated." We should understand from this that the court did not regard the conferring upon this board the power of making the improvement, and of demanding and making use of bonds binding upon the county, for the purpose, as being equivalent to a delegation of the power to tax.

the people of the towns nor the local officers being consulted or allowed any authority whatever in the premises, or even the privilege of being heard. The work was exceptionally if not extravagantly expensive, and it is difficult to conceive of any justifiable ground for forcing upon an unwilling people an expense of this description, when no corresponding burdens were imposed on other localities. The court of appeals, however, felt constrained to uphold this legislation, basing their decision upon the ground of a general power in the legislature over the subject of taxation, which in this particular was not restricted by any express provision of the state constitution.[1]

Conceding this to be sound doctrine, it must nevertheless be called hard doctrine. Such legislation stands wholly apart and distinct from all the ordinary provisions for the construction and support of highways. The customary regulations are made on some rule of apportionment, and this case had no rule but the special legislative determination.[2] And it may well have been regarded by the people concerned as specially objectionable, because depriving them of one of the privileges intended to be secured to them by the state constitution. That instrument had provided that local officers should be chosen by the voters of the locality,[3] and it doubtless intended that they should be left to exercise the usual local powers. While this appointment of commissioners for roads in the two towns avoided a violation of the words of the constitution, the violation of its spirit, unless the roads were in importance something more than ordinary town highways, would seem to be undoubted. It is a well known principle, however, that a legislative violation of the spirit of the constitution does not ordinarily permit of judicial correction.

A case in Pennsylvania in which the legislature provided for the construction of an exceptionally expensive road at the cost of

[1] People *v.* Flagg, 46 N. Y., 401.

[2] In Goodrich *v.* Turnpike Co., 26 Ind., 119, an act "to allow county commissioners to organize turnpike companies," which permitted the cost of constructing the turnpike to be assessed upon the real estate within three-fourths of a mile of the proposed road, was sustained. This was an exceptional method, but not unknown to the law, and it was neither oppressive nor was the whole matter taken out of the hands of the local authorities.

[3] Const. of N. Y., art. X, § 2.

the people living on and near the same without their consent, and not, as the court found, for the local but for the general benefit, must be regarded as opposed to the one in New York. The court held that, on the general principles governing taxation, the legislature had no such power.[1] And this decision finds, as we think, strong support in a recent decision of the court of appeals of Kentucky; a court whose decisions in matters of taxation are always able and strong. The case there was one of a city assessment. It was denied that the legislature possessed the power to require a certain portion of one street in a city to be improved in a manner exceptionally expensive, at the cost of abutting owners and without their consent, when by the law as to all the other streets, the owners of the larger proportion of the frontage must petition for such an improvement before it could be ordered.[2] The case was one of an invidious assessment, as were those in Pennsylvania and New York. "A law," it is said by the court, "imposing taxation on the general public, the evident intent and legitimate results of which are to equalize the burden so far as practicable, will not be held as violative of the fundamental law, merely because that desirable end may not be attained. But when, as in this case, the most probable if not the necessary consequence of the law is to produce the most oppressive inequality, and to compel a small minority of tax payers to provide, at their sole expense, an improvement of general utility and public interest, the construction of which costs more than double as much as the character of such improvements in general use, and from which, when constructed, the general public derives almost as much advantage as themselves, it assumes the character of an attempted exercise of arbitrary power over the property of this minority; it becomes in a constitutional sense a taking and appropriation of their private property to the public use without compensation, and it cannot be sustained, so long as the safeguards placed around the citizen by our fundamental law are respected and upheld. No such power over the property of the citizen can be constitutionally exercised by any department of our state government; and whenever it is attempted, it is the imperative duty of the judi-

[1] Matter of Washington Avenue, 69 Penn. St., 352.

[2] Howell *v.* Bristol, 8 Bush, 493, per *Lindsay*, J.

ciary to interpose in behalf of those whose constitutional rights are being thereby prejudicially affected." Whatever may be thought of the relative soundness of these decisions in matters of law, those which deny the power to levy such invidious burdens are most likely to conduce to equality and fairness in matters of local taxation, and with just purposes and purity in legislation. It is difficult to conceive of a more corrupting power than that of voting taxes by those who are not to feel them, especially when the expenditure may be confided to those who have no interest, personally or as corporators, and who will presumably be concerned only to the extent that they can make a personal profit of the taxes which others are to pay.

In another recent case in New York, it is decided that the legislature may require a village to levy a special tax to be expended in the construction of a state educational institution at that locality.[1] This decision is based upon the sovereign power of the state to tax and apportion the public burdens; a power which, unless it is subject to implied limitations, would enable the legislature of a state to require its capital town to construct the state house, another town to construct the state prison, and so on, to the entire relief of the state at large. It has been seen that a decision in Wisconsin is opposed to the one just cited, and that derives strong support in more recent cases in Illinois.[2]

The New York cases which have been mentioned find abundant justification in an earlier case in the same state, and could not well have been decided otherwise without rejecting that as an authority. The facts in that case were the following:

Certain citizens of Utica, in order to secure the connection of the Chenango with the Erie at their place, entered into a bond, conditioned to pay to the state some $38,000, the estimated increased expense in bringing the canal to that point, instead of to another which had been proposed. Having thereby secured the location, the legislature then interfered for their relief, and required the amount of the obligation to be assessed as a tax upon

[1] Gordon *v.* Cornes, 47 N. Y., 608.

[2] Livingston County *v.* Weider, 64 Ill., 427, is specially referred to. This case is commented on and explained in Burr *v.* Carbondale, Sup. Ct. Ill., 1874, 6 Chicago Legal News, 350, in which it was held competent to *permit* a locality to vote special aid to a state building.

the real estate of the city of Utica. Was this a constitutional tax? The supreme court of the state held that it was. "The general purpose of raising the money by tax was to construct a canal, a public highway, which the legislature believed would be a benefit to the city of Utica as such; and independently of the bond, the case is the ordinary one of local taxation to make or improve a highway."[1]

How far the principle of this case can be carried beyond the exact state of facts upon which it was decided, is a question of the highest interest. Would it, for instance, have been within the power of the legislature to compel the city of New York to bear the whole cost of the Erie canal? or to construct at its own cost the Erie railroad? Or might the whole cost of the Hoosac tunnel be thrown upon Boston? Or might Chicago or St. Louis be compelled to construct a system of railways through the state, on the ground, that in the opinion of the legislature the railways would specially benefit the city which was made a terminus? If a power to require such expenditures can rest in the hands of any legislature, restrained only by a sense of the responsibility of its

[1] Thomas *v.* Leland, 24 Wend., 65, 67, per *Cowen*, J. Under the principles of this decision, it might, perhaps, be held that the legislature had the power to require the refunding by the munipalities of commutation moneys, or moneys paid to procure substitutes, where the effect was to relieve the municipality from a draft. The purpose of the payment, so far as it went to aid the government by money or men, was public; and yet as such payments are made by parties for their own advantage, a law levying taxation to refund them is judicially declared to resemble "an imperial rescript," rather than constitutional taxation. *Thompson*, J., in Tyson *v.* School Directors, 51 Penn. St., 9, 22. In Perkins *v.* Milford, 59 Me., 315, 318, *Appleton*, Ch. J., in denying the authority to authorize the refunding of commutation moneys by towns, says: "The money was voluntarily paid, and without expectation of repayment. It was a gift — so understood, so intended by all the parties subscribing. It was no advance or loan to the town, with the expectation of repayment. Whether the gift was to the soldiers enlisting, or to the town, makes no difference. The naked question recurs, Can the town raise money to give to individuals? This is not a gift to any public purpose. It is a gift as a recompense for past generosity. If a town can give to A., it can give to B. If it can give little, it can give much. If it can give, then every man holds his estate subject to the will of the majority, who can give away as much or little as they please. Taxation is for public purposes, and for those the right of the government to impose taxes is unlimited. Taxation is imposed by the state to meet its exigencies. But taxes to meet the plaintiff's claims would be taxes for a private purpose, for a gift to an individual."

members to their constituents, there is always a possibility that the members may at some time discover that a majority of the constituencies would be pleased to see the power exercised.[1]

Another recent case in New York seemed to interpose a check to the unlimited power of the legislature over the taxation of municipal corporations. The point of the decision was, that towns could not be compelled to give aid to railroad corporations by subscribing to their stock. The decision was an able one, and made by the court of last resort.[2] But this decision, so far as in the nature of things it would be possible, was shortly afterwards qualified, and, as it would seem, overruled by the assistant court, called the commission of appeals. The case decided by this court asserts a power in the legislature broader and more absolute than has ever been applied in this country, by any court of corresponding dignity, whose decisions have fallen under our notice. The point of the decision was, that where the legislature had once empowered a commissioner, appointed for a town, but not by it or by any town officer or authority, to subscribe for the town to the stock of a railroad corporation, on the condition precedent of obtaining the assent of a majority of the resident tax-payers, the legislature had full power afterwards to remove the condition and empower the commissioner to bind the town by a subscription without it. "As it is obvious," say the court, "that all the property of a town, as an artificial being, is public property, and must usually have proceeded from the exercise of the power of taxation, and as the private rights of individuals residing in the town can only be affected through the exercise of the power of taxation, it follows that the substantial power of the

[1] In Freeland *v.* Hastings, 10 Allen, 570, 580, *Bigelow*, Ch. J., speaking of the right of the state to apportion among the municipalities the expense of highways, etc., says: "Perfect equality in the allotment of public burdens is unattainable. If they are distributed on just principles, applicable alike to all on whom they are imposed; if no undue discrimination is made among those on whom a charge or duty is laid; if no tax is assessed which is disproportionate, or 'without the assent of the people or their representatives,' substantial equality will be attained, and no legal or constitutional right or privilege will be violated or evaded." This seems to us an admirable statement of the principles governing the imposition by the state of burdens upon the municipalities.

[2] People *v.* Batchellor, 53 N. Y., 128, opinion by *Grover*, J.

legislature, through the power of taxation, is broad enough to sustain the requirement to a town to aid in the construction of a railroad, in the construction of which, in the judgment of the legislature, it has a public interest. And if it may do this directly by the imposition of a tax, and the direct and immediate employment of the money raised, it is not perceived how the issuing of bonds, with the only contingency of taxation to follow, can be beyond the legislative power; nor how the more remote possibility of becoming chargeable by reason of holding stock, can alter the case." [1]

As the commissioner who made the subscription was not a town officer, nor a town agent with the town's consent, it is manifest that he was able to accomplish what was said by the eminent Pennsylvania judge, whose views have been quoted, to be "impossible in the nature of things"—a contract without the consent of the parties.[2]

It must, we should suppose, be conceded that the doctrine that the legislature may do anything to which it gives the form of taxation, and which is not expressly forbidden by the constitution, is necessarily corrupting in practice. It constitutes a standing invitation to corrupt classes of the state to flock to the state capital with schemes for enriching themselves at the expense of localities; and it would be remarkable if they were not often successful. Perhaps, if the state were owner of important public works, a more tempting attraction might thereby be presented, and the municipalities be left unmolested. But even this might prove otherwise, for the evils of vicious legislation are likely to increase and multiply in every direction, when once it is admitted that they are subject to no legal restraints, and that the central authority may legislate on local matters which concern only the locality, and, concerning which, the members acting will know nothing, except as interested parties may undertake to inform or misinform them.

[1] *Johnson*, Com., in Duanesburgh *v.* Jenkins, 57 N. Y., 177, 187. The decision in the case reversed the decision in supreme court made by Judges *James*, *Bockes*, *Rosecrans* and *Potter*.

[2] *Black*, Ch. J., in Sharpless *v.* Philadelphia, 21 Penn. St., 147, 165. See also what is said by *Mellen*, Ch. J., in Bowdoinham *v.* Richmond, 6 Greenl., 112, 114.

All the property of a municipal coporation may be assumed to come from taxation. If any of it comes from gift or grant, it is not believed that the nature of its ownership is any different on that account, unless the gift or grant was charged with a trust. It is public property, but public for the purposes of the municipality, and not for the purposes of the state. If any of it has been raised for special purposes, under state authority, the state may compel its proper application. The state must have a power of direction, also, in cases where municipal powers are so modified as to preclude the contemplated purpose being followed; but it is believed to be an unsound doctrine that the legislature of the state may, for that reason or any other, apply it to state uses, or even to local uses, against the consent of the people concerned. Mr. Justice *Story* early expressed the view that the legislature, changing, modifying, enlarging or restraining the local powers, must secure the property for the uses of those for whom, and at whose expense, it was originally purchased.[1] There can be little doubt that this is the view that has been generally acted upon, and that any other is, to say the least, less safe, either to the general interests of the state or of the municipalities. It is very true, as has often been said, the fact that a power is liable to abuse, is no argument against its existence; it would only constitute a reason which should influence the people to expressly withhold the grant of power when framing their constitution. But when it is considered that the states in general have not been accustomed to exercise such a power, and that its existence is inconsistent with any substantial constitutional protection to local self-government — that feature of the American representative system which has

[1] Terrett *v.* Taylor, 9 Cranch, 43, 52. "It may also be admitted," he says, in Dartmouth College *v.* Woodward, 4 Wheat., 518, 594, "that corporations for mere public government, such as towns, cities and counties, may, in many respects, be subject to legislative control. But it will hardly be contended that, even in respect to such corporations, the legislative power is so transcendent, that it may, at its will, take away the private property of the corporation, or change the uses of its private funds acquired under the public faith. Can the legislature confiscate to its own use the private funds which a municipal corporation holds under its charter, without any default or consent of the corporators?" And again, on p. 698, he says of the state: "It cannot recall its own endowments granted to any hospital, or college, or city, or town."

usually been looked upon as the corner stone of all, and must leave the municipalities at the mercy of legislative majorities, it may justly be questioned whether the recognition of the power is not an innovation. It is not to be forgotten that the power in question is "a power to destroy"— an expression which loses none of its force when applied to municipal corporations — and that it is capable of being exercised in legitimate modes to the destruction of private fortunes. And the subject seems to invite the remark, as bearing upon the question whether the early New York decision, which has been referred to, was not a departure from sound principle, that if the legislature of the state may vote the local taxes, or take the moneys which have been raised by taxation for local purposes, and appropriate them to other purposes in their discretion, on any assumption that, as they have now become public funds, they must be at the state's disposal; then the maxim that taxation and representation go together, would seem to be merely a glittering generality, promising much, but assuring nothing. For any reliance upon responsibility to constituents, as a check upon extravagant taxation and reckless misappropriation, becomes useless, and indeed worse than useless, because deceptive, if the constituency in general, instead of bearing the burden of evil legislation, may actually, in some cases, have the general burden diminished by the selection of particular communities for exceptional and invidious taxation. And any principle in representative government may well be considered obsolete when, as applied, it only removes the substantial responsibility and restraining power from the constituency concerned to a distant central authority.[1]

[1] On this general subject, reference is made to the case of Sleight *v.* People, Sup. Ct. Ill. (1875), 7 Chicago Legal News, 292. The facts were, that a railway was built through four townships — Oxford, Clover, Weller and Galva — of Henry county. Two of these townships — Weller and Galva — subscribed for capital stock and issued their bonds in payment of the subscription. The charter of the railroad company provided that "the taxes to be collected from said railroad company for county and township purposes, by the several counties and townships through which said railroad runs, shall be paid to and set apart by the county treasurer as a sinking fund to redeem the principal of the bonds issued by any township or townships in said county." On behalf of the railroad company, the claim was made that the entire tax collected from the railroad company, for county and township purposes, in the several townships through which the railroad runs, should be paid to and set

CHAPTER XXII.

THE REMEDIES OF THE STATE AGAINST COLLECTORS OF TAXES.

Remedies in general. It has been seen that the law sometimes provides for very summary proceedings for the enforcement of the duty to pay taxes, and that the legislative competency to do so has been very fully sustained. With much greater reason may the law provide summary remedies against those who, having collected taxes, neglect or refuse to pay them over to the proper authority. Whatever hardships there may be in forcing summary payment by the person who is simply negligent in paying his dues, there can be none in requiring speedy accounting and settlement by one who has, by his office, become custodian of the public

apart by the treasurer of the county as a sinking fund, to be applied *pro rata*, in redeeming the principal of the bonds issued by the towns of Weller and Galva.

In the opinion of the court, by *Schofield*, J., it is said: "A tax cannot be levied for county or township purposes on property which is not subject to the jurisdiction of the authority levying the tax; and the property of the railway company in the county and in each township must be subject to the same taxation as other taxable property there situated, for county and township purposes; and no property can be held for the payment of a county or township tax which is not levied for a corporate purpose.

"Without undertaking to define what is a corporate purpose, it is very certain that a tax imposed for the payment of a debt not incurred by the authority imposing the tax, and for the payment of which it is in no wise responsible, is not for a corporate purpose.

"Neither Henry county, nor the towns of Oxford or Clover, made any subscription to the capital stock of this railway company, or incurred any indebtedness by issuing bonds or otherwise on account thereof. Nor are they either indebted to the towns of Weller or Galva.

"Neither Henry county, nor the towns of Oxford or Clover, could therefore levy and collect a tax in excess of the amount needed for their respective corporate purposes, and equal to the amount claimed for this sinking fund, because such a tax would not be for a corporate purpose.

"But the claim here made is for the taxes actually levied and collected for county and township purposes, from the railway company, in the towns of Oxford and Clover. If this amount shall be taken, then there must necessa-

funds; and whatever evils may be anticipated in the case of individual neglects are likely to be multiplied many fold, if one who has collected from numerous persons may then neglect or refuse to pay over his collections until it shall suit his convenience to do so.

The remedies which are at the service of the public authorities, and one or more of which are usually made use of, are the following:

Suit at the Common Law. The state, or any of its municipalities, for whom moneys have actually been collected, may pursue its delinquent collector by suit at the common law, if under the circumstances that remedy shall be deemed adequate and suitable.[1] Where expedition is not important and the party is responsible, this may be all that is essential. Such a suit the collector can defend only on such grounds as would constitute a defense to a like suit as between other parties who stand in the relation of principal and agent. It would be for money received by the collector for the use of the public; and he would not be permit-

rily be a deficiency to that extent in the county and township revenues, which will have to be supplied by additional taxation. The property liable to taxation in one municipality will thus be compelled to bear a burden of taxation imposed by the corporate authority of a different municipality, and this, too, without its consent, and in the absence of any presumptive corresponding benefits. The principle upon which alone this can be sustained is, that the legislature may, in its pleasure, impose debts upon counties and townships, and require their payment without regard to the wishes of the inhabitants and tax payers of such counties and townships; for it is evident that the practical result is precisely the same, whether it is said the taxes levied for county and township purposes on the property of the railway company in the towns of Oxford and Clover shall be set apart for the payment of the bonds issued by the towns of Weller and Galva, or that the county and these townships shall pay a sum equal to the amount out of their revenues for the same purpose. In either event, it is taking so much of the revenues of the county and of the towns of Oxford and Clover to pay the debts of the towns of Weller and Galva. But it has been repeatedly held by this court, that the legislature is powerless to impose a debt upon a municipaliy against its consent; and those cases must be deemed conclusive on the questions involved here. The People *v.* The Mayor, etc., 51 Ill, 18; People *v.* Salomon, id., 38; People *v.* Chicago, id., 580; Madison Co. *v.* People, 58 id., 463; Hessler *v.* The Drainage Commissioners, 53 id., 105; Lovingston *v.* Wider, id., 302."

[1] Adams *v.* Farnsworth, 15 Gray, 423; Helvey *v.* Huntington Co., 6 Blackf., 317; Wentworth *v.* Gove, 45 N. H., 160; Spencer *v.* Perry, 18 Mich., 394.

ted to rely on technical objections which might be made to the right of the public to the money. If he receives the money to the use of the public, he should account for it; and it is immaterial that those who have paid it might successfully have resisted the collection from them. It has been elsewhere shown [1] that a collector *de facto*, or even an intruder, will not be permitted to resist the demand of the state upon him for taxes collected, by showing that he collected them without due authority. And it has been held that although a bond to perform the duties of an office would be void if there were, by law, no such office in existence, yet an irregular appointment of a person to an office which is established by law is valid as a contract to perform the duties of the office, and entitles the public to demand the fulfillment of the engagement.[2] The principles here stated are applicable not merely to the case of a defect in the official authority, but to the case also in which defects, either technical or substantial, might have been urged to the tax the officer has enforced.[3] The substantial fact is that he has received money for the state, and having done so, it is not his privilege to pause and question the right of the state to receive it; but he should pay it over, and leave those from whom it was received to present a claim to the state for the refunding, if they deny its right to retain it.[4] Even an unconstitutional tax, once collected, the collector has no right to retain, but should account as in other cases.[5] The action in

[1] *Ante*, pp. 191, 192. See in addition to the cases there cited, Ford *v.* Clough, 8 Greenl., 334; Johnson *v.* Goodridge, 15 Me., 29; Orono *v.* Wedgewood, 44 Me., 49; Trescott *v.* Moan, 50 Me., 347; State *v.* Woodside, 8 Ired., 104; Lyndon *v.* Miller, 36 Vt., 329.

[2] United States *v.* Maurice, 2 Brock., 98.

[3] Williams *v.* Holden, 4 Wend., 223; Moore *v.* Alleghany City, 18 Penn. St., 55.

[4] Commonwealth *v.* Philadelphia, 27 Penn. St., 497.

[5] In Waters *v.* State, 1 Gill, 302, and Smyth *v.* Titcomb, 31 Me., 272, it was decided not to be a good defense to a suit to recover taxes collected, that the tax itself was unconstitutional. In O'Neal *v.* School Commissioners, 27 Md., 221, there was a like ruling as to a tax claimed to have been unlawfully levied. In State *v.* Baltimore and Ohio R. R. Co., 34 Md., 344, this doctrine was applied to a railroad company which, being required to pay to the state one-fifth of the fares on a certain branch, collected the fares, but declined to pay, alleging the unconstitutionality of the tax. See also State *v.* Cunningham, 8 Blackf., 339.

these cases is for the money had and received to the use of the public. The like action will not lie for a mere neglect to perform the official duty to collect; but an action on the case would be the appropriate remedy.[1]

Collector's Bond. It is a customary precaution to require of any collector of public moneys that he shall give bond to secure a proper accounting. The form, or at least the requisites, of such a bond, are commonly prescribed by statute, and statute remedies cannot be had upon it unless it is a good bond under the statute. But it is always lawful for one who has a duty to perform to a third person or the public, to give sureties for the performance thereof; and a bond by a public collector, which is not in the statutory form, may nevertheless be a good bond at the common law, upon which the usual common law remedies will be available.[2] On this ground suits have been sustained upon bonds which were given to one body or official board, when the statute required them to be given to another,[3] and also upon those which were so defective in any of their requisites as not to constitute a sufficient statutory bond. Of course if the bond is given to an obligee different from that named in the statute, suit upon it must be brought in the name which appears in the obligation.[4] What has been said of the liability of the collector, to account for moneys received, is as applicable in a suit on any such bond, as in a suit for money had and received; he cannot defend by showing that those who voluntarily have paid to him could not legally have been compelled to do so.[5]

[1] Charleston *v.* Stacey, 10 Vt., 562.

[2] Claasen *v.* Shaw, 5 Watts, 468; Freeman *v.* Davis, 7 Mass., 200; Morse *v.* Hodsden, 5 id., 317; Burroughs *v.* Lowder, 8 id., 372; Sweetser *v.* Hay, 2 Gray, 49; Horn *v.* Whittier, 6 N. H., 88; Treasurer *v.* Bates, 2 Bailey, 362, 375; Governor *v.* Allen, 8 Humph., 176; Walker *v.* Chapman, 22 Ala., 116.

[3] Van Hook *v.* Barnett, 4 Dev., 268; Justices of Christian *v.* Smith, 2 J. J. Marsh., 472. And see Supervisors of St. Joseph *v.* Coffinbury, 1 Mich., 355; People *v.* Johr, 22 Mich., 461, 462; Mallory *v.* Miller, 2 Yerg., 113. The rulings in the federal courts are that a bond taken from a collector of taxes is good as a common law bond, though not required by law, or though not in statutory form when a bond is required. Dixon *v.* U. S., 1 Brock., 177; Postmaster General *v.* Rice, Gilpin, 554; United States *v.* Howell, 4 Wash., C. C., 620; United States *v.* Tingey, 5 Pet., 115.

[4] Stevens *v.* Hay, 6 Cush., 229. See Walker *v.* Chapman, 22 Ala., 116.

[5] See cases cited, *ante*, p. 498. Also Kelly *v.* Savage, 20 Me., 199.

The liability on the bond must, however, be governed by its condition. It has been held that when sureties undertake for the collection of all rates for which the collector shall have "sufficient warrant under the hands of the assessors," a recovery cannot be had upon the bond for taxes collected without such warrant; the cases not being within the terms of the undertaking.[1] But where the sureties undertake that the collector shall "faithfully perform his duty, and pay over the moneys collected," they are liable for the moneys collected by him, whether with warrant or without.[2]

It is not the business of the collector to question the fairness or propriety of any tax which has been committed to him for collection. If the assessment is excessive, the party assessed must make the objection, and not the assessor. His duty is to collect the list committed to him, and he cannot excuse himself for any failure to exhaust his authority in collecting, on the pretense that the person taxed should not have been assessed at all, or should have been assessed otherwise than as he was.[3] Nor is it a sufficient answer to a suit for neglect of duty, that the party taxed being poor, any proceedings by distress would not have been available.[4] His duty in such a case is to exhaust his power in an effort to collect; and the legal evidence of the inability of the person taxed to pay the amount will then be furnished by his return.

A collector may always refuse to proceed in the collection of a tax for the collection of which his authority is insufficient. While he is bound to account for all sums voluntarily paid to him by persons taxed, he is under no obligation to commit trespass in the attempted exercise of a void authority; and it is always a defense to him and his sureties, that the process committed to him would not have protected him in its execution.[5] Undoubtedly, also, the

[1] Foxcroft *v.* Nevens, 4 Greenl., 72.

[2] Johnson *v.* Goodridge, 15 Me., 29; State *v.* Woodside, 8 Ired., 104. And see Ford *v.* Clough, 8 Greenl., 334; Orono *v.* Wedgewood, 44 Me., 49; Trescott *v.* Moan, 50 Me., 347; Williamstown *v.* Willis, 15 Gray, 427.

[3] See Williams *v.* Holden, 4 Wend., 223; Moore *v.* Allegheny City, 18 Penn. St., 55.

[4] Gorham *v.* Hall, 57 Me., 58, 62, citing Colerain *v.* Bell, 9 Met., 499, 503. The same doctrine is laid down in Treasurers *v.* Hilliard, 8 Rich., 412.

[5] Reynolds *v.* Lofton, 18 Geo., 47; Barlow *v.* The Ordinary, 47 id., 639;

collector may decline to proceed in the collection of a tax illegally levied; as any person may refuse to recognize any illegal authority, or to obey an unconstitutional law. But he takes upon himself a great responsibility when he assumes to question the validity of a statute, or of the acts of his superiors. In any case he ought to be the last person to raise the question, and then only when necessary to his own protection. So long as the persons taxed voluntarily make payment of the tax, it is his duty to proceed with the collection.

The collector should receive for the taxes money only, unless the statute permits him to receive something different. Money is always understood in tax laws when nothing else is mentioned.[1] The collector is not at liberty to use his office as a means of speculation, and therefore cannot buy up demands against the public and turn them in when he comes to account.[2] Even if such demands are by law made receivable for taxes, they are not available to him in his settlement, unless he actually received them in payment.[3] And what the collector receives he must, at his peril, safely keep and account for. It is no defense, when he is sued for a failure to account, that the moneys have been stolen from him, or otherwise lost, without fault or negligence on his part.[4] This seems a very harsh rule, but it is, without question, a very necessary one.

When the time arrives for the collector to account and pay over his collections, no demand is necessary in order to fix upon him and his sureties a liability for failure to do so; but they may be sued at once, as soon as a default has occurred.[5]

Liability of Sureties. In general the liabilities of sureties on

Cheshire *v.* Howland, 13 Gray, 321; Adams *v.* Farnsworth, 15 id., 423; Weimer *v.* Bunbury, 30 Mich., 201.

[1] See Johnson *v.* United States, 5 Mason, 425; United States *v.* Morgan, 11 How., 154; Miltenberger *v.* Cooke, 18 Wall., 421.

[2] Frier *v.* State, 11 Fla., 300: and see Cheshire *v.* Howland, 13 Gray, 321.

[3] Commonwealth *v.* Rodes, 5 T. B. Monr., 319. The collector has no right to receive in payment of taxes the draft of his creditor upon himself. Elliott *v.* Miller, 8 Mich., 132.

[4] United States *v.* Prescott, 3 How., 578; United States *v.* Morgan, 11 id., 154; Morbeck *v.* State, 28 Ind., 86; Muzzy *v.* Shattuck, 1 Denio, 233.

[5] State *v.* McIntosh, 9 Ired., 307; State *v.* Woodsides, 9 id., 496.

these official bonds are the same as those on other undertakings for third persons. The undertaking of a surety is always looked upon as *strictissimi juris*, and cannot be extended beyond the exact terms of his undertaking. His position is essentially different from that of the officer himself. The latter, in accepting his position, has the obligation imposed upon him by law to perform its duties; but the former has only entered into a contract, and consented to be bound by the terms of that, but by nothing else. The law creates no obligation for him whatever.[1] A very important consequence resulting from this fact is, that if any alteration is made in the contract of the surety without his consent, it discharges him, because it is no longer his contract.[2] And this would be the case even though the alteration tended to diminish the surety's responsibility, instead of to increase it; on the plain principle that the law cannot, where a party has made one contract, charge him with another, upon any such untenable ground as that it would have been for his interest to have made the substituted contract instead of the other.[3]

In one particular, however, it is possible there may be an important difference between this undertaking and the ordinary contract of suretyship: in general an extension of time granted to the principal for the performance of his obligation will discharge the surety; but the rule, we should say, did not apply to the sureties of a collector of taxes, at least, so far as the extension of time to make collections is concerned; such an extension being supposed beneficial to them, rather than the contrary. But whether beneficial or not, such an undertaking ought to be regarded as

[1] Miller *v.* Stewart, 9 Wheat., 681, 702; United States *v.* Boyd, 15 Pet., 187; Leggett *v.* Humphreys, 21 How., 66; Swanson *v.* Ball, Hempst., 39; Walsh *v.* Bailie, 10 Johns., 180.

[2] Gass *v.* Stinson, 2 Sumn., 453; Smith *v.* United States, 2 Wall., 219.

[3] "The alteration of the bond, after it was executed by the defendants, and without their consent, discharged them from all liability under it. It does not now truly represent the obligation into which they entered. That obligation was that Jonathan Eldridge should act faithfully as collector of a tax of $2,572.82, which had been already assessed; by the alteration of the bond, the obligation which it purported to impose on the defendants was, that the said Eldridge should act faithfully as collector of a tax of $2,490.01, which was assessed after the bond was executed. This obligation they never consented to incur." *Metcalf*, J., in Doane *v.* Eldridge, 16 Gray, 254.

made subject to any provisions of law that might influence the obligation or the duties of the officer for which the sureties have undertaken.[1] But on this point there is some conflict of opinion.[2]

The repeal of the law under which the bond was given does not affect the responsibility of the sureties, whose contract remains in full force as before.[3]

In many cases it is made the duty of some auditing board or other authority to examine the collector's accounts periodically, and come to a settlement with him for previous collections. Undoubtedly all such boards or authorities should perform their duty, and give the sureties such benefit as might accrue to them therefrom; but the legal view of provisions of law imposing such

[1] The point was made in State *v.* Carlton, 1 Gill, 249, 257. *Stephen*, J.: "The condition of the bond is, that the principal shall well and truly account for and pay over to the treasurer the several sums of money which he shall receive, or be answerable for by law, 'at such times as the law shall direct.' The extension of the time of payment, therefore, by the legislature was no change or alteration of the terms of the contract, but was warranted and authorized by the express language of the condition of the bond upon which the suit was instituted. The principle, therefore, that time given to the principal debtor by the creditor, without the consent of the sureties, will operate their discharge, cannot be applied in this case. The terms of the condition of the bond reserved to the state a right to grant the indulgence by law, if she thought fit to do so, without affecting in any manner the liability of the sureties. But it is not necessary to rely upon the condition of the bond alone, for the reversal of the judgment of the court below. A similar question was brought before the court of appeals for the eastern shore from Worcester county, several years ago, and the court then decided that the granting of indulgence by law to the principal collector did not operate to discharge his sureties. The law was not considered as binding or obligatory upon the state, but alterable by the legislature at their pleasure, whenever the interest or the convenience of the state might require it."

[2] In a recent decision the supreme court of Tennessee has decided that sureties are discharged under such circumstances. Johnson *v.* Harker, 2 Central Law Journal, 625. The court of appeals of West Virginia had previously decided the other way. Bennett *v.* The Auditor, 2 W. Va., 441, per *Brown*, Prest.

[3] Tucker *v.* Stokes, 3 S. & M., 124. That a collector's bond is for the security of the public only, and private citizens have no remedy upon it, see Brown *v.* Phipps, 6 id., 51. A collector gave a general official bond conditioned to pay over all tax moneys collected by him. A statute afterwards provided for a special tax, and authorized the county board to require of the collector a further bond, which they failed to do. *Held*, that the sureties on the general bond were liable for the special tax. State *v.* Hathorn, 36 Miss., 491. See also Stevenson *v.* Bay City, 26 Mich., 44.

duties is, that they are made, not for the protection of sureties, but of the public. The sureties undertake for the conduct of the principal, and cannot require the state to protect them against his misconduct or neglect. If, therefore, they suffer from neglects which are not only his neglects, but also those of some other public officer or board, the loss must be borne by themselves. If periodical settlements would tend to their advantage, they will be expected to look after them in their own interest.[1]

Summary remedies. So far, we have spoken of obligations and remedies, in providing for which no serious question of legislative power could well arise. But in the case of collectors of the public revenue, it has sometimes been thought important to compel them to place themselves under obligations and subject themselves to liabilities not demanded in other cases. Provisions of the following import are often met with:

1. That the statement of accounts by the state auditor or other public accountant shall, as between the state and its collector, be conclusive.

2. That, when the collector is in default, process in the nature of an execution may be issued against him by his superior officer, without any judicial finding, or any hearing, and this process shall be collected of the property of the collector and his sureties.

3. That, on application to some specified court, summary judgment may be taken against the collector on motion, without other process than short notice to show cause.

Upon this is to be remarked, that the justification of such remedies must be found in the contract relations established between the state and the collector, by the acceptance of office by the latter while such provisions are in force, and between the

[1] United States *v.* Kirkpatrick, 9 Wheat., 720; United States *v.* Van Zandt, 11 id., 184; United States *v.* Nicholl, 12 id., 505; Dox *v.* Postmaster General, 1 Pet., 318; State *v.* Atherton, 40 Mo., 209; Christian, *Ex parte*, 23 Ark., 641; Christian *v.* Ashley County, 24 id., 142; State *v.* Bates, 36 Vt., 387, 398; Detroit *v.* Weber, 26 Mich., 284. As to the liability of sureties in different bonds where the collector was his own successor for several terms, and the sureties in the several bonds were not the same, and defaults existed in each term, see United States *v.* Eckford, 17 Pet., 251; S. C., 1 How., 250; Detroit *v.* Weber, 29 Mich., 24.

state and the obligors in the official bond, by their giving the bond under the statute which provides this summary remedy. The bond, in such a case, is to be read as if the provisions of the statute were set forth at large in it, and had thereby received the express assent of the parties.[1] And this removes the difficulty that would otherwise exist were the rights of a party to be concluded without giving him the opportunity of a judicial hearing.

It has been affirmed in Kentucky, that it is competent to make the auditor's statement of the amount of taxes evidence against the sheriff who acted as collector of taxes, in a proceeding against him for an accounting, and also in favor of the sheriff and against his deputy, who received the list to collect; and to give a summary remedy against both.[2] And, in another case, it was more distinctly decided that the auditor's statement must be conclusive where the statute so declares. "We acknowledge," it is said, "that this * * does curtail the privilege of defense to be made by a collector, and places him on a footing different from that of other defendants in our courts, and we have no doubt that it is necessary to do so for the security of the revenue, and that, without it, not only great confusion would be produced in the finances of the state, but many frauds would be practiced on the treasury. If this defense of tender and refusal, or discount, or whatever it may be called, is allowed, what will soon be the consequence? The collectors need never settle their accounts with the proper department; for, if they do, it will only acquit them of costs. [And, after suggesting the probable evil results, it is added]: To prevent this, the state has selected its own auditor, and required every claim to pass through his hands before any can be allowed, or any debtor be released. This rigor with regard to officers of the revenue is not new in the science of government."[3]

[1] Murray *v.* Hoboken Land Co., 18 How., 272; People *v.* Van Eps, 4 Wend., 387, 390; Lewis *v.* Garrett's Adm'r, 6 Miss., 434; Chaffee *v.* Thomas, 5 Mich., 53; Pratt *v.* Donovan, 10 Wis., 378; Philadelphia *v.* Commonwealth, 52 Penn. St., 451; Whitehurst *v.* Coleen, 53 Ill., 247.

[2] Johnson *v.* Thompson, 4 Bibb, 294. The point arose only incidentally in this case.

[3] *Mills*, J., in Commonwealth *v.* Rodes, 5 T. B. Monr., 318, 324, citing, in support of his views, the action of the federal government in making tran-

In other cases, similar statutes have been enforced without any question being made of the competency to adopt them.[1]

A summary distress warrant against the collector and his sureties can only be awarded where the bond is in accordance with the statute, and where all the statutory conditions exist. The process being extraordinary and in derogation of the common law, the steps leading to it must all have been taken; and if it is issued under any other circumstances than those under which the statute gives it, the officer issuing it will be a trespasser.[2] The liability is *strictissimi juris*, and cannot be extended a single step beyond the statutory permission. The same remark may be made of the case of application for judgment on motion. The statute must be strictly pursued, as the ordinary legal intendments do not apply in aid of the proceedings in such a case.[3] But where the statute has been strictly pursued, the summary remedies have been sustained by the courts without hesitation. "The federal government," it is said by an able jurist of Georgia, "may summarily enforce the collection of its revenue out of defaulting receivers or other duly appointed agents. Upon like

scripts from the books of the treasury evidence of delinquencies. For similar expressions, see Waldron *v.* Lee, 5 Pick., 323; Smyth *v.* Titcomb, 31 Me., 272. It was held, in Board of Justices *v.* Fennimore, Cox, 242, that a committee of the county commissioners did not conclude the collector by their settlement with him, but he might show errors on being sued for the balance. In Texas, the controller's statement of accounts is not evidence in a suit against the collector. Albright *v.* The Governor, 25 Texas, 687. This would be the rule anywhere in the absence of an express statute making it evidence.

[1] See Prather *v.* Johnson, 3 H. & J., 487; Billingsley *v.* State, 14 Md., 369.

[2] Weimer *v.* Bunbury, 30 Mich., 201; S. C., 2 Am. Law Times, 37.

[3] Nabors *v.* The Governor, 3 Stew. & Port., 15. And see Walker *v.* Chapman, 22 Ala., 116; Graham *v.* Reynolds, 45 id., 578. As to the recitals in the record, see Hardaway *v.* The County Court, 5 Humph., 557. Where the statute authorizes summary judgment against the collector and his sureties, the collector is a necessary party, and if he be dead, the summary remedy is gone. Governor *v.* Powell, 23 Ala., 579. If the bond is taken to the county trustee when it should have been to the governor, the summary remedy cannot be had. Mallory *v.* Miller, 2 Yerg., 113. And see Broughton *v.* State, 7 Humph., 193. So a bond dated fourteen months after the collection is *prima facie* not the statutory bond, and motion for judgment on it should be denied. De Soto County *v.* Dixon, 34 Miss., 150. But the fact that the penalty of the bond is smaller than the statute requires is no objection to it. Mabry *v.* Tarver, 1 Humph., 94.

principles the state may collect taxes immediately out of the defaulting citizen; for that purpose the tax collector is authorized to issue execution. These powers of the government are founded in an imperious necessity. They are necessary to the preservation of the government, to the administration of the law, indeed to a maintenance of all the rights of the people. If the government were forced to submit the case of every defaulting tax payer and tax gatherer and financial agent to a jury, with the delays and uncertainties attending a judicial investigation, it could not command its revenue, it could not be administered." [1]

The necessity for a strict compliance with the statute in the issue of such process is seen in the further fact that the officer who issues it is usually a mere ministerial officer, without judicial power. As has been said in a case from which quotation has already been made, and in which by statute an inferior court issued the process, "The inferior courts have judicial powers, but I apprehend that this is not one. They act as mere agents of the state. They are instructed by the act to issue execution for the amount which appears to be due. There is no issue to try; there is no judgment to be pronounced. As *auditors*, it is their business to ascertain the amount due, and then to issue execution. So the state treasurer is the mere agent of the state. His business is to state the collector's account, and if he is in arrear, to issue execution." [2]

Precisely the same reasons sustain those acts of the legislature which forbid the courts interfering with the process which is issued in revenue cases. If it is important that the party in default should be precluded from a resort to dilatory proceedings of one kind, it is equally important that the power to interpose others

[1] *Lumpkin*, J., in Tift *v.* Griffin, 5 Geo., 185, 191. The learned judge comments in this case upon the claim that the tax collector was entitled to a trial by jury, and declares that the case is, and always has been, and must be an exception to the right of jury trial. And see Waldron *v.* Lee, 5 Pick., 323; Smyth *v.* Titcomb, 31 Me., 272; Bassett *v.* The Governor, 11 Geo., 207; Harper *v.* Commissioners, 23 id., 566; Daggett *v.* Everett, 19 Me., 373; Fremont *v.* School District, 33 id., 482; Cruikshanks *v.* Charleston, 1 McCord, 360; Prather *v.* Johnson, 3 H. & J., 487; Billingsley *v.* State, 14 Md., 369; Hobson *v.* Commonwealth, 1 Duv., 172; Weimer *v.* Bunbury, 30 Mich., 201.

[2] Tift *v.* Griffin, 5 Geo., 185, 193. It is added that if the duty were judicial, it would make no difference, because it is exceptional.

should not be allowed to them.[1] Here again is a rule which seems severe, but the statutes which prescribe it do not go beyond those which have been sustained by the courts, in which is taken away the right to maintain replevin for property taken for taxes, or to take any other proceedings calculated to embarrass the collector's action. The legal view of such statutes is, that while they take away a specific remedy, they nevertheless leave to the party other remedies which are adequate to do him eventually full justice.[2]

Even as regards the summary proceedings, however, there are some principles which will constitute protection to the collector and his sureties. One of these must be, that they can only be proceeded against on notice with a hearing on the question of delinquency. We say nothing here of the evidence which may be

[1] Eve *v.* State, 21 Geo., 50; Scofield *v.* Perkerson, 46 id., 350, 360. In this last case, *Warner*, Ch. J., after considering the legislative act in question, proceeds to say: "But it is said if there is not judicial interference, the complainants will be remediless. The 7th section of the act before cited points out the remedy, which negatives the idea that it was to be by judicial interference. The principle is, that the state must collect her revenue for the support of government through the action of the executive department thereof, whether derived from taxes or from her other sources of revenue, without any judicial interference therewith. The courts will not presume that the state, in the exercise of her sovereign prerogative in the collection of her revenue, will do injustice to any of her citizens for her own benefit. The complainants, at the time they signed the official bonds of their principal, must be presumed to have done so with a full knowledge of the law applicable to their liability thereon, and as to the manner of its enforcement against them for the default of their principal. The issuing the executions by the comptroller general in this case, being the act of the executive department of the government having the exclusive jurisdiction over that subject matter, the courts have no legal right, judicially, to interfere with the exercise of that jurisdiction, for the reasons alleged, either in the original bills of the complainants or in their amended bills, but on the contrary, are expressly prohibited from doing so."

[2] It has been decided in Georgia that the governor may be authorized to vacate the commission of a defaulting tax collector and fill the vacancy. "The running of the state machinery is so intimately connected with its treasury, and may be said to be so dependent upon it, and it is of such transcendent importance to its citizens and the public, that it cannot be subjected to the ordinary rules governing in other cases." *Trippe*, J., in State *v.* Frazier, 48 Geo., 137. But the remedy by summary judgment for taxes collected cannot be had against one who has been ousted on *quo warranto* as a usurper. Hartley *v.* State, 3 Kelley, 233, 237.

received on the hearing; of its quality or its conclusiveness; but the principle, that one is not to be condemned unheard, should be considered inviolable. The hearing will of course be summary, and a substituted notice might be sufficient where, in proper cases, the law so provides. Another is, that there shall be some official showing of the delinquency; something of an authoritative character, and based upon documents, returns or records, which show the facts. It has been decided in one case that an officer who could have no better evidence of a collector's default than the legal presumption that another officer, whose business it was to deliver to the collector the proper tax rolls and warrant, had performed that duty, could not be empowered to issue execution on such a presumption, since the like presumption would be equally strong in favor of the collector, and should consequently protect him.[1] It was also decided in the same case that any such summary process — at least where the statute had prescribed no form — should show on its face the existence of all the facts necessary to give jurisdiction to issue it.[2]

[1] Weimer *v.* Bunbury, 30 Mich., 201; S. C., 2 Am. Law Times, 37. In this case the supreme court of Michigan fully sustained the power to provide for this summary process, but held that a county treasurer, in whose office there was no evidence that the collector had ever had the tax warrant, and no evidence of delinquency, except the mere fact that the time for making return of taxes collected and delinquent had expired, could not be authorized to issue execution against the collector. Compare Commonwealth *v.* Wilson, Myers (Ky.), 127.

[2] Weimer *v.* Bunbury, 30 Mich., 201. In this case, speaking of the statutory provisions, the court say: "It was necessary in this case that the state and county taxes should be properly apportioned to the city of Niles, and that the city treasurer should have executed to the county treasurer the proper bond. The supervisors must subsequently have delivered to the city treasurer, tax rolls, with state, county, city, school, and other taxes extended thereon, with warrants annexed giving him proper legal authority to collect the same, and directions as to what disposition he was to make of the several taxes he should collect. All these were necessary prerequisites, without which the city treasurer could not be subjected to this summary process. Treating the city treasurer's official bond to the county treasurer as an agreement that a summary execution may issue when a default occurs, its terms cannot be extended so as to subject the city treasurer and his sureties to this extraordinary process, when the default is on the part of another officer. The city treasurer is not in default if he never receives the tax roll; and though he may be liable in a proper form of action for any tax moneys actually received by him, it is

The conclusion to be drawn from the authorities appears to be, that the officer, by accepting the public trust, submits himself to the laws which provide remedies for the enforcement of his duties, with this restriction, that final process is not to be issued against him unless the officer issuing it has evidence that a default has

clear that he does not agree, by his bond or otherwise, to become responsible for all the moneys called for by the tax roll, if no warrant accompanies it empowering him to enforce payment. In other words, he must have in his hands the statutory means for collection before he can be in default for not collecting. And when summary process of this nature is issued against him, it must show on its face all the facts which are necessary to constitute a default; for nothing can be taken by intendment in favor of a proceeding like this, which is in derogation of common law principles, and therefore must depend for its validity upon a strict conformity to the statute. As in the case of the process of all other inferior and special tribunals not proceeding according to the course of the common law, the county treasurer's warrant must show the facts which presumptively would make out a case in which he had jurisdiction to issue it. Nichols *v.* Walker, Cro. Car., 394; Rex *v.* Manning, 1 Burr., 377; Rex *v.* Mayor, etc., of Liverpool, id., 2244; Frary *v.* Dakin, 7 Johns., 75; Mills *v.* Martin, 19 id., 733; People *v.* Koeber, 7 Hill, 39; Dakin *v.* Hudson, 6 Cow., 221; Bridge *v.* Ford, 4 Mass., 642; Barrett *v.* Crane, 16 Vt., 246; Brewster *v.* Hyde, 7 N. H., 211; Chandler *v.* Nash, 5 Mich., 409; Platt *v.* Stewart, 10 id., 260; Hart *v.* Newsom, 14 id., 233. In this case the county treasurer has no record back of the warrant which shows the default, and consequently any question which might be made regarding the support of the warrant by such a record is not in the case.

"What does the county treasurer's precept show in this case? It begins with a recital that the city treasurer is in default 'in the payment to the county treasurer of the taxes apportioned to said city of Niles for the year 1872.' Here is the statement of a legal conclusion without the recital of a single fact to support it. It is a judgment without preliminary accusation or finding. It is difficult to conceive of a proceeding more defective in the statement of jurisdictional facts. Nothing is said of any tax rolls, nothing of any tax warrants; but upon the naked fact that taxes have been apportioned to the city of Niles, which have not been paid over to the county treasurer, the sheriff is to proceed to levy and collect the same of the property of the city treasurer and his sureties. Nor do the subsequent recitals in the precept support this preliminary declaration of the city treasurer's default. The subsequent recitals show two facts only; that certain persons became sureties on the bond of the city treasurer to the county treasurer, and that 'there remains now due and unaccounted for from the said Thomas A. Bunbury, as such city treasurer as aforesaid, the sum of four thousand eight hundred and seventy-two dollars and sixty-two cents.' Now the city treasurer might be in default for this amount without being liable to this process, for, the taxes unpaid might be city, school, highway, or special taxes, with which the county treasurer has no concern. It may be doubtful, therefore, if this statement would

occurred. And so far as the officer himself is concerned, as his obligation does not spring from contract, but comes from the law itself, he may perhaps be subjected to such change of remedies, or provision for new remedies, as may be made by changes in the statute after his appointment or election. But summary remedies cannot be given against sureties except as they have assented to them, either expressly by their bond, or by implication in giving the bond under a statute which provides for them. And changes in the statute law which, if applied to their contract, would subject them to further responsibility, or to other remedies unknown to the common law, could not be applied at all.

The same principle seems to apply here as to the remedy by suit against the collector: while he cannot be compelled to make an illegal collection, or be rendered liable for neglect to do so, yet if he actually collects a tax, he cannot defeat the summary proceeding by showing that the tax was unauthorized.[1]

show a default, even if it were recited that tax rolls and warrants were duly delivered; but it is clear it could be of no service in the absence of such a recital. It follows that the county treasurer's precept was not fair on its face; that is to say, it did not contain recitals sufficient to show that it was lawfully issued."

[1] Palmer *v.* Craddock, Myers (Ky.), 182. An act authorizing the treasurer to issue execution against persons making default in listing their property for taxation was considered in State *v.* Allen, 2 McCord, 55. But this seems to be going a great way.

CHAPTER XXIII.

ENFORCING OFFICIAL DUTY UNDER THE TAX LAWS.

Under any system of taxation, most careful provisions are essential to ensure obedience to the law on the part of those who are entrusted with its administration. The serious consequences that ensue when any important provision of law is overlooked or disregarded are sufficient to render such regulations prudent, and the perpetual temptations which invite officers to disobedience or evasion of the law must admonish the government of their necessity. It is to be borne in mind also that tax laws, however necessary, do not enlist the affections of the people, and that the public sympathy does not accompany the officers in the performance of their duties. On the contrary, the people submit to taxation as a hard necessity; and as every individual is likely to be impressed with a conviction that the laws seldom or never operate with equality or justice, he is also likely to be entirely willing to make his case one that shall escape the heavy burdens. The tax official is therefore expected to enforce the law against a community, the members of which excuse to themselves an evasion of its provisions on the ground that even then they perform their duties as nearly as do the others upon whom the like duty rests; and will feel, if compulsory steps are taken against them, something like a sense of personal wrong. The difficulty is complicated by the fact that the officers who make the assessments are chosen by the people assessed, and as the local assessments are usually made the basis for state taxation, their people will expect them to make the valuations sufficiently low to protect them against unfair assessments elsewhere. The sense of official duty must be strong and the firmness considerable that can resist under such circumstances the pressure for some departure from the strict rule of law; and the conclusive evidence that it is not always resisted is found in the notorious fact, that men who take solemn oath to perform to the best of their ability the duty of assessing property at its fair cash value are accustomed to assess it at from one-fourth to two-fifths only, justifying their disobedience of the law on the general disobedience of others. The provision for a state equalization as a correction of this evil does not appear to cure this demoralizing disregard of law and official oaths, nor does any legal process seem adequate to the case.

Of the securities relied upon for the performance of duty by tax officials, besides those which may be found in the character of the officials themselves, or that may rest in the power of removal, the following may be mentioned.

1. *The Official Oath.* Upon this much less reliance is placed than formerly, for the reason, perhaps, that the community has come to tolerate — it may almost be said to demand — a disregard or evasion of its provisions, when the apparent interest of the district seems to require it. Moreover, as has been shown in another place, an official oath is not absolutely essential, and if neglected, the proceedings may still be valid. The oath is consequently of little or no importance, and probably might be abolished without detriment to the public service; certainly without detriment to the public morals.[1]

2. *An Official Bond.* This is usually required of collectors only. The value of this depends on the law, on its terms and on the sureties, and there is no occasion to add here to what has been said in another place.

3. *Penalties for Neglect of Duty.* Of these great use is made. They are either penalties to be recovered in a civil action, or they are imposed as criminal punishments. For the cases of various officers connected with the public revenue system, particularly collectors, appraisers and other officers or agents in the internal revenue and customs service of the United States, it has been found necessary to go further, and to make some criminal misconduct and delinquencies punishable as felonies.

4. *Common Law Remedies.* These lie back of those given by

[1] Sufficient evidence of this is furnished too often by the further fact that men appointed from the ranks of respectability to perform duties under the internal revenue and other tax laws are found in very many cases to pay not the least regard to official obligations or official oaths, and use the position as one of vantage for the purposes of public plunder.

statute. The most useful and efficient of them all is that which is afforded by the writ of *mandamus.*

Mandamus: its nature. The writ of *mandamus* is a summary writ, issuing from the proper court, which commonly is the highest court of common law jurisdiction of the state, commanding the officer or body to whom it is addressed to perform some specific duty, which the party applying for the writ is entitled of right to have performed.[1] The award of the writ rests in the discretion of the court, which will allow or deny it according as in its opinion justice requires,[2] and it is in general a sufficient reason for denying it that another adequate remedy exists. Thus, it has been refused when applied for to compel the board of supervisors to audit and allow to one wrongfully assessed the tax he had paid; he having, in that case, an adequate remedy by suit against the assessors who had assessed him without jurisdiction.[3] The writ is not awarded to control the exercise of a discretionary authority, and it is therefore usually said that a judicial duty cannot be enforced by means of it. Such a statement is not accurate; a judicial duty is as susceptible of being enforced by the process as any other when the right is clear, and when the judicial officer, if he obey the law, has no option, but must do some specific thing which the law requires of him. The more accurate statement would be, that a judicial officer, or one exercising a judicial or discretionary authority, cannot be coerced in his judgment or compelled to exercise his discretion in a particular manner by means of this writ. But when a judge or other officer has no discretion as regards the particular act to be done, and a refusal to do some specific thing would be a wrongful denial of a right or a remedy, *mandamus* is a proper and suitable process to compel him to perform his duty.[4]

[1] 3 Bl. Com., 110; Commonwealth *v.* Pittsburgh, 34 Penn. St., 496, 509, per *Strong*, J.; Marathon *v.* Oregon, 8 Mich., 372, 378, per *Campbell*, J.; *Ex parte* Nelson, 1 Cow., 417, 423, per *Savage*, Ch. J.; High on Extraordinary Remedies, ch. I.

[2] Weber *v.* Zimmerman, 23 Md., 45; Stickney *Ex parte*, 40 Ala., 160; People *v.* Judge of Wayne Circuit, 19 Mich., 296.

[3] People *v.* Supervisors of Chenango, 11 N. Y., 563.

[4] See *Ex parte* Bradley, 7 Wall., 364; Stafford *v.* Union Bank, 17 How., 275; *Ex parte* Burr, 9 Wheat., 529; *Ex parte* Bradstreet, 7 Pet., 634. A singular

It will not only lie, therefore, to compel an auditing board to proceed to the consideration of an account, and to pass upon it in some manner, but if the charges are legal, and it is the clear duty

case of overlooking this distinction is seen in *Ex parte* Ostrander, 1 Denio, 679; the more singular from the fact that it in effect overruled several previous cases in the same state. The case was one in which the court of common pleas had wrongfully dismissed an appeal; and the supreme court held the reinstatement could not be compelled by *mandamus*, even though the party wronged had no other remedy, because the common pleas had cognizance of the matter. And this, too, though the court found the dismissal to have been "in manifest violation of the provisions of the statute on that subject," and "an exercise of a power which the court did not possess." The previous cases of *Ex parte* Caykendoll, 6 Cow., 52; People *v.* Superior Court, 5 Wend., 114, and People *v.* N. Y. Common Pleas, 19 Wend., 118, which are plainly opposed to this, are not noticed in the opinion; but the case has often since been cited as authority, probably because the general principle which it lays down but misapplies — that a judicial *discretion* will not be controlled by this writ — is manifestly sound. We say misapplied, because, as the supreme court found, the common pleas had no discretion in the premises, and were clearly guilty of abuse. Recent New York cases place the doctrine on safer ground. In Howland *v.* Eldredge, 43 N. Y., 457, 461, *Grover*, J., says of judicial tribunals: "They may, by *mandamus*, be compelled to proceed and determine the matter, but they cannot be compelled to decide in any particular way. If they could, it would no longer be their judgment or discretion, but that of the court awarding the writ." Applying this rule to auditing boards, the court often compels them to allow claims which are legal demands, after they have once decided they will not do so. See People *v.* Supervisors of Delaware, 45 N. Y., 196, 200, per *Folger*, J., who cites Hull *v.* Supervisors of Oneida, 19 Johns., 259; Wilson *v.* Supervisors of Albany, 12 id., 416. In the still later case of People *v.* Supervisors of Otsego, 51 N. Y., 401, 407, *Earl*, Com., explains the rule more fully, and shows how little foundation there is for the doctrine of *Ex parte* Ostrander, that a judicial body cannot be compelled to undo wrongful action by means of this writ. An extract from the decision in this case will be given further on.

Ex parte Bradley, 7 Wall., 364, is in striking contrast to Ostrander's case. An attorney, as the court found, had been unlawfully disbarred by an inferior court. "We agree," says Mr. Justice *Nelson*, "that this writ does not lie to control the judicial discretion of the judge or court, and hence where the action complained of rested in the exercise of this discretion, the remedy fails. But this discretion is not unlimited, for if it be exercised with manifest injustice, the Court of King's Bench will command its due exercise. Tapping on Mandamus, 13, 14. It must be a sound discretion and according to law. As said by Chief Justice *Taney*, in *Ex parte* Secomb, 19 How., 13: 'The power, however, is not an arbitrary and despotic one, to be exercised at the pleasure of the court, or from passion, prejudice or personal hostility.' And by Chief Justice *Marshall*, in *Ex parte* Burr, 9 Wheat., 530: 'The court is not inclined

of the board under the statute to make the allowance, that duty the members may be compelled to perform by means of this writ.[1]

to interpose unless it were in a case where the conduct of the circuit or district court was irregular or was flagrantly improper.'" The judge who dissents in the case does so on other grounds. The following cases may be referred to as supporting like views: *Ex parte* Conway, 4 Ark., 302; Wright *v.* Johnson, 5 id., 687; *Ex parte* Pile, 9 id., 336; Day *v.* Justices of Fleming, 3 B. Monr., 198; Applegate *v.* Applegate, 4 Met. (Ky.), 236; Castello *v.* St. Louis County Court, 28 Mo., 259; Roberts *v.* Holsworth, 5 Halst., 57; Merced Mining Co. *v.* Fremont, 7 Cal., 130; Ortman *v.* Dixon, 9 id., 23; People *v.* Bacon, 18 Mich., 247; People *v.* Judge of Wayne Circuit Court, 22 id., 493; People *v.* Pearson, 1 Scam., 458; Illinois Central R. R. Co. *v.* Rucker, 14 Ill., 353; Stephenson *v.* Mausony, 4 Ala., 317; Hudson *v.* Daily, 13 id., 722; *Ex parte* Lowe, 20 id., 330; Shadden *v.* Sterling, 23 id., 518; *Ex parte* Thornton, 46 id., 384. Other Alabama cases make a more liberal use of this writ than would be sanctioned in other states. The whole doctrine may be thus summarized: If a body having judicial powers shall refuse to proceed to do what the law requires, it may be compelled to do it by this writ. If it has done an act which the law does not authorize, its duty is to undo it on request, and this duty may be compelled by this writ. But if it has acted in a matter which by the law was committed to its judgment or discretion, *mandamus* will not lie to correct its errors, for judgment and discretion are not to be controlled or coerced by this process.

[1] Bright *v.* Supervisors of Chenango, 18 Johns., 242; Hull *v.* Supervisors of Oneida, 19 id., 259; People *v.* Supervisors of New York, 32 N. Y., 473; People *v.* Supervisors of Otsego, 51 id., 401; People *v.* Supervisors of Macomb, 3 Mich., 475; Gunn's Adm'r *v.* Pulaski County, 3 Ark., 427. Where the county court is to order a surveyor's report to be recorded "unless it see some objection to the report," the duty may be compelled by *mandamus.* Delancy *v.* Goddin, 12 Grat., 266; Randolph *v.* Stalnoker, 13 id., 523. In People *v.* Supervisors of Otsego, *supra*, *Earl*, Com., considers the question somewhat fully, and answers the objections usually made to the employment of the writ in cases where the supervisors are to audit and allow accounts. The following is an extract from the opinion, p. 407:

"But it is claimed on the part of the appellant, that it has done all it can be compelled to do by *mandamus;* that it has heard the relator's claim, and determined it adversely to him. It is true that boards of supervisors have a certain judicial discretion to exercise in reference to claims presented to them, which cannot be controlled by *mandamus.* They are to investigate and determine the facts as to any disputed claim, and if it is unliquidated, they are to determine the amount to be paid. But the law is supposed to be plain, and they are presumed to understand it, and they have no right to reject a claim as illegal, which the law plainly requires them to allow. If they do, they can be compelled to the allowance by *mandamus.* (People *v.* Supervisors of New York, 11 Abb. Pr., 114; People *v.* Board of Supervisors of New York, 32 N.

In the application of these principles to the case of assessors it will be manifest that they cannot be controlled in their judgment, as to the amount they shall assess against a person or his property. The doctrine is shortly stated by the supreme court of Massachusetts, in a case in which county commissioners had declined to abate a tax on behalf of one who claimed to have been over-

Y., 473; People *v.* Board of Supervisors of New York, 21 How. Pr., 322; People *v.* Supervisors of St. Lawrence, 30 id., 178; Hill *v.* The Supervisors of Oneida, 19 Johns., 259; People *v.* Supervisors of New York, 1 Hill, 362.) Where supervisors refuse to audit and allow a legal claim, on the ground that it is illegal, they do not exercise the discretion which the law vests in them; and hence, in such case, they can be compelled by *mandamus* to exercise their discretion upon the facts and the amount to be allowed.

"Now, let us see what was done in this case. The relator, in the affidavits upon which the order to show cause was based, showed clearly and particularly that it owned the United States stocks; that it was assessed upon them and paid the taxes claimed. These facts showed that it had a claim which, under the special act of 1867, the board of supervisors was bound to determine; and if it found the facts to be true, then it had no discretion left, and was bound to cause the money paid to be refunded. These facts were not disputed. When the claim was presented, it was referred to a committee. It does not appear that the committee or the board of supervisors made any investigation whatever of the facts pertaining to the claim, although the statutes furnish ample power to make such investigation (Laws of 1845, ch. 180; Laws of 1858, ch. 190). The committee, in their report, speak of the taxes as 'collected and paid,' and then state that the county and towns 'cannot, in justice, refund said taxes,' thus substantially admitting that the taxes had been paid as claimed. They do not report that they have examined and inquired into the facts, or that any of the statements contained in the affidavit of complainant were untrue. They simply report that they have examined the claims, and that it would be unjust for the county and towns to refund the taxes. Then the board of supervisors adopted a resolution reported by the committee, that the claim was invalid, and that the same be disallowed. There was no determination by the board of supervisors that the relator was not assessed just as alleged, and that it did not pay the taxes just as claimed by it. The claim was evidently rejected simply because it was unjust and illegal. The legislature had determined that the claim for taxes illegally exacted, as mentioned in the act, was both just and legal; and the only questions to be determined by the board of supervisors, in reference to which it had any discretion, were, whether the complainant had such claims, and the amount of them. This case is, therefore, brought within the rule laid down in Hill *v.* Supervisors of Oneida (*supra*): 'Where the supervisors of a county refuse to allow a claim for services as a county charge, this court, if it be a legal charge, may instruct and guide the supervisors in the execution of their duty by a writ of *mandamus*, and compel them to admit the claim as a county charge.'"

rated. "If the commissioners," it is said, "had refused to hear and determine upon the complaint, this court would have issued a *mandamus* requiring them to do it. But the question whether the petitioner's taxes should be abated or not, was a judicial question. And although it is within the province of this court to require the commissioners to decide the question, yet we have no power to decide it for them, or to determine what decision they shall make. No judicial officer, in determining a matter legally submitted to his discretion, can ever be required to be governed by the dictates of any judgment but his own. We are clearly of opinion that in refusing to abate the petitioner's taxes, the commissioners acted judicially, upon a subject of which they had final jurisdiction, and in which the exercise of their discretion cannot be revised by any other tribunal."[1] A like view has been expressed in Pennsylvania, in a case in which an inferior court had issued the writ to compel school directors to exonerate a person taxed. "This," it is said, "was an unprecedented application of the writ of *mandamus*. It is not the ordinary official duty of school directors to exonerate taxes, but rather to levy and collect them. If they were backward in the exercise of this official function, *mandamus* might be used to stir them up. But when they have set themselves in motion, and are proceeding to discharge the duty imposed by law, they are no longer subject to *mandamus*. Exoneration is a discretionary power incidental to their office, and in this instance would seem to have been exercised by a refusal to grant the relief asked for. We have no power to control a discretion vested in them, and no appeal lies from them to judicial tribunals."[2] This rule undoubtedly applies to all classes of assessments, and to all other actions of assessors which they are to perform according to the dictates of their own judgment. In New York, where a statute made it the duty of town assessors when a majority of tax payers, owning more than one-half the taxable property of the town had signed a certain paper, to make affidavit of the fact for a certain purpose important

[1] Gibbs *v.* County Commissioners of Hampden, 19 Pick., 298, citing Chase *v.* Blackstone Canal Co., 10 id., 244; United States *v.* Lawrence, 3 Dallas, 42.

[2] *Woodward*, J., in School Directors of Bedford *v.* Anderson, 45 Penn. St., 388. 390.

to the town, a mandamus to compel them to perform the duty was held unauthorized. "The affidavit of the assessors must be in accordance with what they believe to be the fact, otherwise they incur the moral guilt of perjury, irrespective of any determination the court may have made thereon. By the seventeenth section of the act, false swearing by the assessors is made perjury, and, should it turn out that they are right and the court wrong in their views, the only ground upon which they could escape conviction would be that the affidavit was not their voluntary act, but the result of coercion, which they had no power to resist. If this appeared upon the face of the affidavit, it is entirely clear that in no legal sense would it be their affidavit at all, but a mere nullity. It follows that there is no remedy provided by the act for the correction of errors into which the assessors may fall, in respect to the matter referred to their determination. The statute having declared it to be their duty to make the affidavit when the fact exists, the court have power, by *mandamus*, to compel them to proceed and examine the evidence and determine the fact, and if, from their determination, it appears that the requisite consent has been given, to make an affidavit in accordance therewith. This is the universal rule in respect to all subordinate courts and tribunals clothed with the exercise of judgment or discretion. They may by *mandamus* be compelled to proceed and determine the matter, but cannot be compelled to decide in any particular way. If they could it would no longer be their judgment or discretion, but that of the court awarding the writ. Their determination is conclusive, unless some mode of review is provided."[1]

For like reasons, operating with still greater force, the writ cannot be employed to compel the performance of duties of a political nature. Such would be the duty of determining what taxes should be levied by a municipal corporation for the current needs of the year, in respect to which no previous imperative duty was fixed upon the municipality, in consequence of previous indebtedness or otherwise. If this writ were to be employed for such purposes, the courts and not the people, would in effect exercise the local political powers.[2]

[1] Howland *v.* Eldredge, 43 N. Y., 457.

[2] See Union County Court *v.* Robinson, 27 Ark., 116, where the endeavor was made to compel school district authorities to increase the school levy which

On the other hand, the writ will lie to compel assessors to strike from the assessment roll nontaxable property which they have included in it. Here is a clear case of excess of jurisdiction; nothing is submitted to their discretion, because by the law the subject matter of the controversy is put beyond their authority, and they can lawfully neither list it, nor value it.[1] And the writ will lie to compel the refunding of taxes charged upon exempt property, where by statute the officers are directed to refund it, even though the exemption depends upon matters of fact which they are to inquire into and pass upon. The refunding in such a case is a mere ministerial duty; the officers are supposed to know the law, and it is their duty to apply it to the facts as they find them.[2] A similar ruling has been made in the case of a state officer who had the power by law to reject illegal taxes which had been returned to him; and he was required by this writ to reject taxes on lands which were exempt from the levy, though there was no specific statute commanding it.[3] And if assessors omit from the roll property which is taxable, they may be compelled to insert it on the roll on the application of the proper law officer of the state.[4] The relief in all such cases is based on the

the people had voted for the year, on a showing that it was insufficient for the support of proper schools.

[1] People *v.* Assessors of Barton, 44 Barb., 148; People *v.* Olmsted, 45 id., 644. Compare Miltenberger *v.* St. Louis County Court, 50 Mo., 172, which possibly would appear *contra* if all the facts were given, but the statement of the case is somewhat imperfect. The case cites Dunklin County *v.* District Court, 23 Mo., 449, and State *v.* La Fayette County Court, 41 id.. 221, which are cases of a different nature.

[2] People *v.* Supervisors of Otsego, 51 N. Y., 401. The case was one of taxation of national securities, which, under the law and the decisions of the courts, were not within the jurisdiction of the assessors. It was made the duty of the supervisors to refund the tax, which they could only do on a showing of facts. The board adopted a resolution that the claim was invalid, and that it be disallowed, but this was a manifest evasion of duty.

[3] People *v.* Auditor General, 9 Mich., 134. The duty of the auditor general to reject taxes in this case, depended upon the date when the patents for the lands issued; a fact only to be brought to his knowledge by evidence, but which made the duty clear when it was proved. In that regard the case resembled People *v.* Supervisors of Otsego, 51 N. Y., 401.

[4] People *v.* Shearer, 30 Cal., 645. The case was one in which possessory rights in the public lands were held to be taxable, and ordered to be placed

clear legal right of the public or of a private party to have performed a certain act which the officer refuses to perform; and it is immaterial what is the nature of the duty, if in the particular case the officer has no discretion. Such cases are in pointed contrast to those in which the attempt is made to control the judgment or discretion of assessors, or of the appellate board of review, after an appeal has been taken to it.[1] But the assessor, when he has a mere ministerial duty to perform, like that of the delivery to the officer of a correct copy of the assessment roll in a case where he has assumed to make unauthorized changes, may be compelled on this writ to perform it.[2]

A suitable case for the employment of the writ is where it is found necessary to compel county commissioners to proceed to the hearing of an appeal from an assessment, where the hearing is of right under the statute.[3] It will lie to compel the proper officer to issue a distress warrant against a defaulting collector; though it is said that if it is manifest from an inspection of the proceedings that the collector has no authority to collect the tax, by reason of its illegality, or that the persons assessed, on being compelled to pay it, would have a remedy back for restitution, the court will not grant a process, to enforce a collection that would be fruitless and oppressive.[4] So the remedy by this writ

upon the roll. Possibly a private individual might have been relator in this case. See People *v.* Halsey, 53 Barb., 547; S. C., on appeal, 37 N. Y., 344.

[1] Gibbs *v.* County Commissioners, 19 Pick., 298. See Miltenberger *v.* St. Louis County Court, 50 Mo., 172.

[2] People *v.* Ashbury, 44 Cal., 616.

[3] This seems to be recognized in James *v.* Bucks County, 13 Penn. St., 72, where, however, the party had deprived himself of the right to be heard. And see Virginia, etc., Company *v.* County Commissioners, 5 Nev., 341.

[4] Smyth *v.* Titcomb, 31 Me., 272, 281, per *Howard*, J. See, also, Waldron *v.* Lee, 5 Pick., 323, which covers all the same ground. A ruling like this in principle was made in People *v.* Halsey, 53 Barb., 547; S. C., on appeal, 37 N. Y., 344. The case was one in which a county treasurer had assumed to question an assessment, as being unjust, and had refused to issue his warrant for the collection of the tax. The court held that he had no discretion in the premises, and ordered a *mandamus* to issue. It was also decided in the same case that a private individual, having a common interest with the rest of the community in the collection of the tax, might be relator in the proceeding. On this last point *Fullerton*, J., in 37 N. Y., 344, 348, says: "Inasmuch as the people themselves are the plaintiffs in a proceeding by *mandamus*, it is not of

may be had to compel a board of supervisors to assess upon the county the amount due to it from the state, after it has been adjusted and settled by the competent authority;[1] or to compel a county trustee to levy a tax to pay the damages awarded in a proceeding for the construction of a county road; it being his duty under the law to do so.[2]

The purchaser at a tax sale may have *mandamus* to compel the delivery to him of the proper certificate as evidence of his purchase,[3] or of a proper deed, if the one delivered to him is defective.[4] And the owner, whose title has been cut off by a tax sale, may have *mandamus* to compel the payment to him of any surplus moneys received on the sale.[5] But *mandamus* never lies to coerce the performance of legislative duties, either by the legislature of the state or by any inferior and subordinate body; not only because legislation is foreign to judicial duties, but also because, in its nature, legislative action is discretionary. But where ministerial action is required of a body, which also exercises legislative functions, its performance may be compelled by

vital importance who the relator should be, so long as he does not officiously intermeddle in a matter with which he has no concern. The office which a relator performs is merely the instituting a proceeding in the name of the people, and for the general benefit. The rule, therefore, as it is sometimes stated, that a relator in a writ of *mandamus* must show an individual right to the thing asked must be taken to apply to cases where an individual interest alone is involved, and not to cases where the interest is common to the whole community. This is the rule adopted in many of the states. Hamilton *v.* The State, 3 Ind., 452; State *v.* County Judge, 7 Iowa, 186; State *v.* Bailey, id., 390; County of Pike *v.* State, 11 Ill., 202. The rule is different in other states. Heffner *v.* The Commonwealth, 28 Penn. St., 108; The People *v.* The Regents of the University, 4 Mich., 98; The People *v.* The Inspectors of State Prison, id., 187; Arberry v. Beavers and others, 6 Texas, 457; Zebulon Sanger *v.* Commissioners of Kennebec, 25 Me., 291. But the practice which has so long prevailed here, though never, so far as I can discover, passed upon directly by the court of last resort, where the objection was raised, seems to be a reasonable and convenient one, and ought now to be considered as settled."

[1] People *v.* Supervisors of Jackson, 24 Mich., 237.

[2] Huntington *v.* Smith, 25 Ind., 486.

[3] State *v.* Magill, 4 Kans., 415. See State *v.* Bowker, id., 114.

[4] Clippinger *v.* Fuller, 10 Kans., 377.

[5] People *v.* Hammond, 1 Doug. (Mich.), 276.

this writ as well as if the act were to be performed by an individual. But the writ will not be awarded to the executive of the nation or state; such officer being an independent department of the state, as much so as the judiciary itself.[1]

These references sufficiently indicate the general nature of the cases in which the writ of *mandamus* may afford the proper remedy. It will be seen, that it is awarded as well on behalf of the public authorities, to compel performance of the successive official duties, under the revenue laws, as on behalf of private parties, whose rights have not been regarded in taxation or in any of the proceedings which are to result in taxation. On behalf of the state, the writ may issue against officers of corporations where a duty is imposed upon them under the tax laws; such, for instance, as that of furnishing a list of the stockholders for assessment,[2] or of paying over a tax on dividends which have been declared by the corporation.[3] But it will never be issued until the duty has become fixed; and, therefore, it will not lie to compel the levy of a tax for a balance of accounts which still remains to be adjusted by the proper statutory authority.[4] The writ cannot confer an authority to do an act which could not voluntarily have been done; and, therefore, cannot require an official act by one after he has gone out of office,[5] nor by one who, though elected, has never qualified and entered upon the performance of his duties.[6] Nor will the writ issue in advance of

[1] There are conflicting cases on this point which are collected in High on Extraordinary Remedies, §§ 118–124; and in Dillon on Mun. Corp., § 671 and note. Also in the recent Michigan and Texas cases. People *v.* Governor, 29 Mich., 320; Bledsoe *v.* International R. R. Co., 40 Texas, 537; Keuchler *v* Wright, 40 id., 600.

[2] Insurance Co. *v.* Baltimore, 23 Md., 296, 309.

[3] State *v.* Mayhew, 2 Gill, 487. See Person *v.* Warren R. R. Co., 32 N. J., 441, which was one of *mandamus* to the lessee of a road to compel the payment of a tax upon it.

[4] State *v.* Rice, 35 Wis., 178.

[5] State *v.* Perrine, 34 N. J., 254. That where proceedings have been begun against a board, they may be continued against their successors, see Bassett *v.* Barbin, 11 La. An., 672. But the levy of a tax cannot be compelled after the time fixed by law, for the levy has expired. Ellicott *v.* Levy Court, 1 Har. & J., 359.

[6] State *v.* Beloit, 21 Wis., 280.

the time for the performance of a duty, on any assumption that it will not be performed in due season.[1]

One of the most common cases in which the writ of *mandamus* is employed in tax matters is, where it has become the clear duty of the authorities to levy a tax for general purposes, or for the payment of some demand, and they refuse to do so.[2] In such cases the remedy may be had on behalf of the state or the muncipality concerned, or by any individual whose demand the tax should pay. Thus, if one has recovered a judgment against a muncipality which can only be paid by means of taxation, the levy of a tax to pay it may in proper cases be compelled.[3] It is customary to make express provision by statute for such cases, and when the statute requires the levy of a tax, the case is clear. When the statute does not expressly require it, the duty may perhaps be equally plain if the muncipality has been clothed with the requisite power; but it cannot be compelled to levy a tax in excess of the restrictions which are imposed upon it by charter or by the general law.[4] But it may not be essential that a judg-

[1] Commissioners of Schools *v.* County Commissioners, 20 Md., 449; State *v.* Burbank, 22 La. An., 298. A *mandamus* will not be issued to compel the spreading of a tax on the roll in advance of the time when it is to be done. On the contrary, it will be assumed that the officer will perform his duty when the time comes. Zanesville *v.* Richards, 5 Ohio, N. S., 589, 593.

[2] See Manor *v.* McCall, 5 Geo., 522; Beaman *v.* Board of Police, 42 Miss., 237; Commissioners of Schools *v.* County Commissioners, 20 Md., 449; *Ex parte* Common Council of Albany, 3 Cow., 358; Whiteley *v.* Lansing, 27 Mich., 131; Morgan *v.* Commonwealth, 55 Penn. St., 456; Robinson *v.* Supervisors of Butte County, 43 Cal., 353.

[3] Knox County *v.* Aspinwall, 24 How., 376; Supervisors *v.* United States, 4 Wall., 435; Von Hoffman *v.* Quincy, 4 id., 535; Galena *v.* Amy, 5 id., 705; Walkley *v.* Muscatine, 6 id., 481; Riggs *v.* Johnson County, id., 166; Weber *v.* Lee County, id., 210; United States *v.* Keokuk, id., 514; Benbow *v.* Iowa City, 7 id., 313; Mayor, etc., *v.* Lord, 9 id., 409; Supervisors *v.* Durant, id., 415; State *v.* Madison, 15 Wis., 33; State *v.* Beloit, 20 id., 79; State *v.* Milwaukee, id., 87; Watertown *v.* Cady, id., 501; State *v.* Racine, 22 id., 258; Hasbrouck *v.* Milwaukee, 25 id., 122; Whiteley *v.* Lansing, 27 Mich., 131; Coy *v.* Lyons City, 17 Iowa, 1; Boynton *v.* Newton, 34 id., 510; Huntington *v.* Smith, 25 Ind., 486; Olney *v.* Harvey, 50 Ill., 453; Lutterloh *v.* Commissioners, 65 N. C., 403; Gooch *v.* Gregory, id., 142; Gorgas *v.* Blackburn, 14 Ohio, 252; Frank *v.* San Francisco Co., 21 Cal., 668; Flagg *v.* Palmyra, 33 Mo., 440; State *v.* Hug, 44 id., 116; Commonwealth *v.* Allegheny Co., 37 Penn. St., 277, 290.

[4] United States *v.* Burlington, 2 Am. Law. Reg, N. S., 394, per *Miller*, J. of the Federal Supreme Court. And see note to same case by Judge Dillon.

ment should have been recovered, in order that the duty to levy a tax may be imperative. If the amount of the demand is absolutely fixed and determined as it would be by judgment, and the law makes it the duty of the proper officers to levy a tax for its payment as a settled demand, this is sufficient, and *mandamus* may issue if performance of the duty is neglected or refused.[1] Indeed it has been held in the case of bounty bonds, which by the law under which they were issued were "a valid and lawful claim against the township," to "be paid in the same manner as the ordinary township expenses" are paid, that is to say, by the levy of a tax by the township officers, an action upon the bonds would not lie; *mandamus* being the appropriate and also the adequate remedy.[2]

The federal courts have no general power to issue the writ of *mandamus* to compel the performance of duties under the state tax laws. That belongs to the province of the state courts. It has nevertheless been held in many cases, that they might issue the writ in order to compel municipalities to levy taxes for the satisfaction of judgments which had been rendered in such courts, and which the local authorities neglected or refused to provide for by taxation, though clothed by law with full author-

[1] Schoolbred *v.* Charleston, 2 Bay, 63; Wilkinson *v.* Cheatham, 43 Geo., 258; Clark Co. Court *v.* Turnpike Co., 11 B. Monr., 143; Rodman *v.* Justices of Larue, 3 Bush, 144; People *v.* Supervisors of Columbia, 10 Wend., 363; People *v.* Bennett, 54 Barb., 480; People *v.* Supervisors of Otsego, 51 N. Y., 401; Robinson *v.* Supervisors of Butte, 43 Cal., 353; Tarver *v.* Commissioners, 17 Ala., 527; Pegram *v.* Commissioners, 64 N. C., 557; State *v.* Smith, 11 Wis., 65; State *v.* Clinton County, 6 Ohio, N. S., 280; Cass *v.* Dillon, 16 id., 38; State *v.* Harris, 17 id., 608; Columbia County *v.* King, 13 Fla., 451; Commonwealth *v.* Pittsburgh, 34 Penn. St., 496; United States *v.* Sterling, 2 Bissell, 408.

[2] *Campbell*, J. in Dayton *v.* Rounds, 27 Mich., 82, citing People *v.* Township Board of La Grange, 2 Mich., 187; Marathon *v.* Oregon, 8 id., 372; People *v.* Auditors of Wayne, 5 id., 223; People *v.* Porter, 18 id., 101. See also Robinson *v.* Butte County, 43 Cal., 353. In this case it is said if the officers order a levy which is not sufficient to pay what is due on such a demand, a relevy may be compelled by *mandamus*. When the proper tax has been levied, so that it has become the duty of the treasurer to make payment on presentation of the obligations, it is not necessary for the holder to have an order from the county commissioners for the purpose, and consequently they will not be compelled to issue one. State *v.* McCrillis, 4 Kans., 250.

ity to do so.[1] The extent of the federal jurisdiction in state tax cases is pointed out in recent decisions of the federal supreme court, and it is shown to be purely exceptional.[2] In some cases, under state laws, these courts have appointed commissioners to levy a tax when the local officers have refused to provide for it.[3] But for this purpose the proper statutory authority must exist.[4]

[1] See Knox County *v.* Aspinwall, 24 How., 376, and other cases cited in note 3, p. 524. And see High on Extraordinary Remedies, § 392.

[2] Rees *v.* Watertown, 19 Wall., 107, opinion by *Hunt*, J.; Heine *v.* Levee Commissioners, id., 655, opinion by *Miller*, J. The opinion of Mr. Justice *Bradley*, in the case last named, is reported in 1 Woods' Reports, 246.

[3] Supervisors *v.* Rogers, 7 Wall., 175, cited and explained in Rees *v.* Watertown, 19 id., 107, 117.

[4] Rees *v.* Watertown, 19 Wall., 107.

CHAPTER XXIV.

THE REMEDIES FOR EXCESSIVE AND ILLEGAL TAXATION.

Reference has already been made by us to the principle which in this country has been adopted from the Great Charter, that no person shall be deprived of his property except by the law of the land, or, as it is sometimes expressed, by due process of law; and it has been stated that this principle is as much applicable in the case of taxation as in any other case. It has also been said that however summary and apparently arbitrary are the methods and processes in tax cases, they cannot deprive the citizen, when his property is taken in the course of their enforcement, of a trial of the right to take it, before some impartial judicial tribunal to which the public authorities must justify their proceedings. What the tribunal shall be, and what the proper remedy to seek in it, may depend on the tax law itself, and on the stage which the proceedings have reached before a remedy is sought.

Abatement of taxes. There are always methods in which one who is wrongfully assessed for taxation, or unequally taxed, may have abatement of the assessment or tax without resort to the customary legal remedies. While the assessor still has the list or roll in his hands uncompleted, he may abate any assessment on his own motion, or on application, when satisfied that it is either wholly or in part illegal or unjust. No statute could be necessary for this. But when the assessment has passed from his hands, the right to an abatement must in general depend upon the statute. No doubt the legislature might abate taxes, and probably the proper legislative authority of a municipality might do the same as regards a municipal tax, where no legislative or constitutional provision was in the way; but taxing officers or boards must have special authority to warrant their doing so. In the absence of special authority, they are to accept the assessment as legal and just, and levy and collect the taxes accordingly.

The remedy usually given is by

Reviews and appeals. The reviews may perhaps be directed to be had by the assessors themselves; the appeals will of course be to some court or appellate board. The abatement may be total, where one is unlawfully taxed, or taxed for exempt property or property he does not own,[1] or it may be partial, where the complaint is only that the valuation is excessive.[2] In either case, one applying for an abatement must comply strictly with the provisions of the statute which confers the right.[3]

When the tax is illegal, one is not obliged to apply for an abatement, unless the statute makes that the sole remedy; but he may contest the tax when attempt is made to collect it. But for a merely excessive or unequal assessment, where no principle of law is violated in making it, and the complaint is of an error of judgment only, the sole remedy is an application for an abatement, either to the assessors or to such statutory board as has been provided for hearing it. If fraud is charged, equity may interfere, but equity has no jurisdiction under its general powers to correct a merely unequal or unjust assessment when there is a statutory board that may do so.[4] And this principle is applicable

[1] State *v.* Ormsby County, 7 Nev., 392. Authority to abate taxes for over-valuation will not embrace a case where one complains that he is assessed for property he does not own. Walker *v.* Cochran, 8 N. H., 166.

[2] State *v.* Powers, 24 N. J., 406; Phillips *v.* Stevens Point, 25 Wis., 594.

[3] State *v.* Parker, 34 N. J., 49; State *v.* Bishop, id., 45; Otis Co. *v.* Ware, 8 Gray, 509.

[4] Stafford *v.* Albany, 6 Johns., 1; S. C., 7 id., 541; Matter of Beekman St., 20 id., 269; Matter of Canal St., 11 Wend., 154; Matter of Mount Morris Square, 2 Hill, 14; Matter of Canal and Walker Sts., 12 N. Y., 406; Petition of Eager, 46 id., 100; Western R. R. Co. *v.* Nolan, 48 id., 513; Kimber *v.* Schuylkill Co., 20 Penn. St., 366; Hughes *v.* Kline, 30 id., 227; Wharton *v.* Birmingham, 37 id., 371; Clinton School District's Appeal, 56 id., 315; Stewart *v.* Maple, 70 id., 221; Everitt's Appeal, 71 id., 216; County Court *v.* Marr, 8 Humph., 634; Holton *v.* Bangor, 23 Maine, 264; Stickney *v.* Bangor, 30 id., 404; Gilpatrick *v.* Saco, 57 id., 277; Gravel Road Co. *v.* Black, 32 Ind., 468; Richardson *v.* Scott, 47 Miss., 236. See Brook *v.* Shelton, 47 id., 243; Weaver *v.* State, 39 Ala., 535; Andrews *v.* Rumsay, Sup. Ct. Ill. (1875), 7 Chicago Legal News, 321, citing Chicago, etc., R. R. Co. *v.* Frary, 22 Ill., 34; Munson *v.* Minor, 22 id., 594; Cook County *v.* Chicago, etc., R. R. Co., 35 id., 460; Du Page County *v.* Jenks, 65 id., 278. When a person is liable to taxation in personal or real estate in a particular district, his sole remedy for excessive valuation, or for including in the assessment property of which he is not the owner, or for which he is not liable to taxation, is by application

to the determination of boards of equalization. If they are properly constituted, there is no appeal from their determination in matters of judgment, where the statute gives none.[1] For a merely *irregular* assessment the statutory remedy is also the exclusive remedy. It is supposed to be adequate to all the requirements of justice, and it is the party's own folly if he fails to avail himself of it.[2] And if he appeals to the statutory tribunal and is dissatisfied with its judgment, he is nevertheless concluded by it.[3]

An assessment made without jurisdiction is of course illegal, and may be disregarded on that ground.[4] And the action of an appellate board is held not to be binding where the board itself has disobeyed the law, to the prejudice of parties. If, by law, it is to meet at one time, but meets at another, when parties have

to the assessors for an abatement. Bourne *v.* Boston, 2 Gray, 494, 496, citing Howe *v.* Boston, 7 Cush., 273; Lincoln *v.* Worcester, 8 id., 55: compare Lee *v.* Templeton, 6 Gray, 579. This doctrine applied to one properly taxed for real estate in a town, but improperly taxed for other real estate not in the town. Salmond *v.* Hanover, 13 Allen, 119. But compare Bailly *v.* Buell, 59 Barb., 158.

[1] Rhodes *v.* Cushman, 45 Ind., 85. No fraud was charged, but error only.

[2] Windsor *v.* Field, 1 Conn., 279; Hughes *v.* Kline, 30 Penn. St., 230; Aldrich *v.* Railroad Co., 21 N. H., 359; Conlin *v.* Seaman, 22 Cal., 546; Chambers *v.* Satterlee, 40 id., 497, 519; Emery *v.* Bradford, 29 id., 75; Nolan *v.* Reese, 32 id., 484; Peoria *v.* Kidder, 26 Ill., 351; Deane *v.* Todd, 22 Mo., 90. In Maryland, it is said if the party fails to avail himself of the remedy given by statute, he cannot come into equity unless he makes out a very clear case; by which is meant, doubtless, a case within the ordinary jurisdiction of equity. Church *v.* Baltimore, 6 Gill, 391; O'Neal *v.* Bridge Co., 18 Md., 1.

[3] Weaver *v.* State, 39 Ala, 535. Suit will not lie at law for the levy of an irregular or excessive assessment which might be corrected on review or appeal. Wright *v.* Boston, 9 Cush., 233; Bourne *v.* Boston, 2 Gray, 494; Commonwealth *v.* Cary, etc., Co., 98 Mass., 19. When special appeal to a subordinate court is given there can be no appeal thence to the supreme court unless expressly given, but *certiorari* will lie to review regularity. Kimber *v.* Schuylkill Co., 20 Penn. St., 366. Where the right is given to any person to appeal from a special assessment, the city against whom an assessment is made may appeal. Matter of Opening of Streets, 20 La. An., 497.

[4] See Commonwealth *v.* Cary, etc., Co., 98 Mass., 19; Weller *v.* St. Paul, 5 Minn., 95. An act that proceedings on the sale of land for local improvements shall not be questioned collaterally, but may, *at any time*, be reviewed by *certiorari*, or other proper proceeding, in the supreme or circuit court, sustained. State *v.* Jersey City, 35 N. J., 381. And see Smith *v.* Cleveland, 17 Wis., 556.

neither actual nor constructive notice to appear, its action is invalid; and so it will be if the statute requires notice to be given of its meetings, and the notice does not appear by the record of the board to have been given.[1]

Refunding taxes. This is only an abatement, made after the tax has been paid or enforced. A general right exists in the state to refund any tax collected for its purposes, and a corresponding right probably exists in the common council, or other proper boards, of cities, villages, towns, etc., to refund to individuals any sums paid by them as corporate taxes, which are found to have been wrongfully exacted, or are believed to be for any reason inequitable. But no executive or ministerial officer could have any such authority, unless expressly given by law.

Remedy by certiorari. At the common law the writ of *certiorari* lies to remove into the supreme court of judicature the proceedings of inferior tribunals, in order that their errors may be corrected when it is alleged that they have exceeded their jurisdiction. In some of the states, considerable use has been made of this writ in tax cases, sometimes with, and sometimes without, statutory regulations. When the writ is by statute, a broader scope may be, and usually is, given to it than it has at the common law.[2] The common law writ is not one of right, but is granted on the special facts; and the court has a discretion to refuse to grant it in any case, when great mischiefs might be likely to follow the setting aside the proceedings complained of.[3] It may even dismiss the writ after it has been granted, without a consideration of the merits, if, in the opinion of the court, it was granted

[1] Nixon *v.* Ruple, 30 N. J., 58. In Kelly *v.* Corson, 12 Wis., 610, the effect of errors in the action of a board of equalization was considered by *Cole*, J., and the conclusion reached, that errors committed by the board when acting in good faith will not invalidate their action, or give a right of action to one who cannot show that he was injured thereby.

[2] When the relief sought by the applicants would affect all other tax payers and residents of a town equally with themselves, in arresting the collection of an alleged illegal tax, it has been held that it should be denied unless applied for by all. Libby *v.* West St. Paul, 14 Minn., 248.

[3] In Fractional School District *v.* The Joint Board, 27 Mich., 3, the writ was refused when applied for to review the proceedings in establishing a school district, fifteen months after the action had been taken; the district in the meantime having organized and taken upon itself corporate functions.

improvidently.[1] The writ must be applied for in due season, and before the proceeding, which it is desired to review, has passed beyond the control of the tribunal in which it was taken. If, therefore, the writ is issued to review the action of assessors, after the assessment roll has passed from their hands into the hands of the supervisor, it will be dismissed for that reason.[2] The writ is not awarded to review political action, and, therefore, the action of a town or any other municipality, or of any of the local boards, in determining upon the purposes for which taxes shall be levied, or the time and manner of levying them, when that is committed to their judgment, or of causing the sums to be levied, or the objects of expenditure, or anything of a like nature, is not subject to review by means of it.[3] The writ will be refused where an appeal is given which affords an adequate remedy, or, in other words, which is not so restricted in its scope as to preclude the party from a review of the errors of which he complains.[4] It will

[1] Magee *v.* Cutler, 43 Barb., 239; People *v.* Supervisors of Allegany, 15 Wend., 198; Susquehanna Bank *v.* Supervisors of Broome, 25 N. Y., 312; Matter of Lantis, 9 Mich., 324. The writ should not be allowed where the purpose is merely to enable a party to recover back taxes paid, by procuring a reversal of the proceedings. People *v.* Commissioners of Taxes, 43 Barb., 494; People *v.* Reddy, id., 539.

[2] People *v.* Delaney, 49 N. Y., 655. See People *v.* Supervisors of Queens, 1 Hill, 195, 199.

[3] People *v.* Supervisors of Allegany, 15 Wend., 198; Benton *v.* Taylor, 46 Ala., 388. See Dwight *v.* Springfield, 4 Gray, 107; Dillon, Mun. Corp., §§ 739-743.

[4] The New York decisions on the subject of the remedy of *certiorari* are very numerous, and in People *v.* Betts, 55 N. Y., 600, 602, they are reviewed by *Folger*, J., in the following language: "The office of a common law *certiorari* is, in strictness, merely to bring up the record of the proceedings of an inferior court or tribunal, to enable the court of review to determine whether the former has proceeded within its jurisdiction; and not to correct mere errors in its proceedings. People *v.* Commissioners of Highways, etc., 30 N. Y., 72. True, it has been sometimes intimated, and sometimes held, that in the absence of any other remedy, and to prevent a failure of justice, the party will be suffered by it to bring up, not only the naked question of jurisdiction, but the evidence, as well as the ground or principles on which the inferior body acted, and the questions of law on which the relator relies. Susquehanna Bank *v.* Supervisors, etc., 25 N. Y., 312; Baldwin *v.* Buffalo, 35 id., 380; Swift *v.* Poughkeepsie, 37 id., 511. Many cases are cited in the People *v.* Assessors, 39 N. Y., 81, and it is there held that the office of the writ extends to the review of all questions of jurisdiction, power and authority of inferior

not lie to review any merely discretionary action of any tribunal;[1] nor is it within the proper scope of the writ to review the decisions of inferior tribunals on the merits. The court awarding it, therefore, will not look into the evidence on which the inferior tribunal may have acted, except so far as may be necessary to the determination of any jurisdictional question that may depend upon it.[2] The proper office of the writ is to ascertain whether

tribunals to do the acts complained of, and to all questions of regularity of their proceedings. In People *v.* Assessors, 40 N. Y., 154, it is held that the writ may bring up for review, the decision that a given state of facts is not legally sufficient to compel a board of assessors to the conclusion that certain property was not liable to assessment: in other words, a decision of law. See also People *v.* Board, etc., 39 N. Y., 506; Freeman *v.* Ogden, 40 id., 105; People *v.* Hamilton, 39 id., 107; Western R. R. Co. *v.* Nolan, 48 id., 513. In People *v.* Delaney, 49 N. Y., 655, inclining the other way, it was held that a departure by assessors from the statutory standard for estimating the value of property on the assessment roll cannot be corrected on *certiorari*. In People *v.* Supervisors, etc., 51 N. Y., 442, it was held that it was the office of a *certiorari* to review the determinations of inferior boards where a claim was rejected, as not just or legal. And in People *v.* Allen, 52 N. Y., 538, a *certiorari* brought up for review the decision of the defendants upon a question of law. It is thus seen that the office of a common law writ of *certiorari* has been somewhat enlarged since the decision in 30 N. Y., *supra*. But it will also be seen that it is in cases where the relator has no other available remedy, and where injustice would be done if the writ was not permitted to do its work. The rule still remains unimpaired, at least in principle, that where there is a remedy by appeal, the writ will be confined to its original and more appropriate office. Storm *v.* Odell, 2 Wend., 287. See also *In re* Mt. Morris Square, 2 Hill, 14, 27." To the foregoing may be added People *v.* Nearing, 27 N. Y., 306. That *certiorari* does not lie where there is an adequate remedy by appeal, see Withowski *v.* Skalowski, 46 Geo., 41; Peacock *v.* Leonard, 8 Nev., 84, 157, 247; State *v.* Apgar, 31 N. J., 358; Macklot *v.* Davenport, 17 Iowa, 379; State *v.* Bentley, 23 N. J., 532. When in assessing upon abutting lots the expense of a local improvement, a jury is allowed on their demand to parties dissatisfied with the assessment, the demand for a jury is the proper remedy for an excessive assessment and not *certiorari*. Jones *v.* Boston, 104 Mass., 461, citing North Reading *v.* County Commissioners, 7 Gray, 109: and see Whiting *v.* Boston, 106 Mass., 89.

[1] The action of the auditor general in charging back certain taxes to a county in his settlement with it, being within his official discretion, cannot be reviewed on *certiorari*. Supervisors of Midland *v.* Auditor General, 27 Mich., 165.

[2] Matter of Mount Morris Square, 2 Hill, 14, 27, per *Cowen*, J., citing Rex *v.* Moreley, 2 Burr., 1040, 1042; Philadelphia and Trenton R. R. Co., 6 Whart., 25, 41. And see Jackson *v.* People, 9 Mich., 111; Low *v.* Galena, etc., R. R. Co.,

the inferior tribunal has acted in a case of which it had jurisdiction, and has lawfully exercised its jurisdiction in what it has assumed to do: to keep the inferior tribunal within the limits of the law, and not to make its judgments conform to the opinion of the superior tribunal on the facts.

The following conclusions are deduced by the authorities from these general principles: That the writ does not lie to the collector of taxes or any other mere ministerial officer to review either his action, or any of the prior action on which his own was based;[1] that assessments cannot be revised and set aside on this writ on the ground merely that they are excessive or unequal;[2] or that the assessors have erred in any matter of judgment, or have been guilty of irregularities in the exercise of their authority, not being of a nature to deprive them of jurisdiction or to take from the party complaining any substantial right.[3] The discretionary ac-

18 Ill., 324; Commissioners *v.* Supervisors of Carthage, 27 Ill., 140; Central Pacific R. R. Co. *v.* Placer Co., 43 Cal., 365; Swift *v.* Poughkeepsie, 37 N. Y., 511; People *v.* Assessors of Brooklyn, 39 id., 81. See the general subject considered: Carson *v.* Martin, 26 N. J., 594; Gaertner *v.* Fond du Lac, 34 Wis., 497; People *v.* Assessors of Brooklyn, 39 N. Y., 81, 88; People *v.* Assessors of Albany, 40 N. Y., 154. While valuations are not subject to review on *certiorari*, if the assessors enter on the roll property not subject to taxation, and refuse on application to strike it out, the action, it is held, may be reviewed in this mode. People *v.* Ogdensburg, 48 N. Y., 390. *Mandamus* would seem, however, to be a more appropriate remedy. The writ will lie in the case of a warrant issued by a justice of the peace to collect militia penalties. State *v.* Kirby, 6 N. J., 143.

[1] People *v.* Supervisors of Queens, 1 Hill, 195. This was a case in which counsel moved for a *certiorari*, prohibition, *mandamus*, "or some other writ, instrument, process, order or proceeding," to review the action of town auditors in allowing a large sum against the town, for the expense of certain suits which it was claimed were not a proper charge against it. The errors complained of all originated in this allowance. The tax roll was at the time in the collector's hands, and the court held that no relief could be given in any of the modes proposed.

[2] Owners of Ground *v.* Albany, 15 Wend., 374; People *v.* Ogdensburgh, 48 N. Y., 390; Jones *v.* Boston, 104 Mass., 461; Randle *v.* Williams, 18 Ark., 380; State *v.* Kingsland 23 N. J., 85; State *v.* Ross, id., 517; State *v.* Danser, id., 552; State *v.* Powers, 24 id., 400; State *v.* Manchester, 25 id., 531.

[3] Jones *v.* Boston, 104 Mass., 461; People *v.* Fredricks, 48 Barb., 173; Newark *ads.* State, 32 N. J., 453; State *v.* Newark, id., 491; Matter of Mount Morris Square, 2 Hill, 14. If a corporation, in opening a street and assessing the expense, act within the scope of the authority conferred upon it, and

tion of a county board in equalizing the assessments of the county, like the assessments themselves, is not subject to review on this process.[1] In the following cases action may be set aside on *certiorari:* Where the assessment is erroneous in point of law, either because the assessors have adopted some inadmissible basis in making it, or because they have disregarded any of the mandatory provisions of statute on which parties assessed have a right to rely for their protection;[2] where errors of a like character are committed by any appellate jurisdiction which is empowered by statute to review, revise or equalize the assessments;[3] and where muni-

comply with the forms prescribed by the statute, the proceedings will not be reversed on *certiorari*, though its own by-laws may have been disregarded. *Ex parte* Mayor, etc., of Albany, 23 Wend., 276. But where there are questions of jurisdiction in the appointment of commissioners to make the assessment, *certiorari* will lie. Patchin *v.* Brooklyn, 13 Wend., 664. An assessment will not be set aside because of its including property not taxable with that which is, if the whole valuation is not excessive for that which is taxable. State *v.* Haight, 35 N. J., 178.

[1] Smith *v.* Supervisors of Jones Co., 30 Iowa, 531; People *v.* Supervisors of Allegany, 15 Wend., 198; People *v.* Supervisors of Queens, 1 Hill, 195.

[2] See Newburyport *v.* County Commissioners, 12 Met., 211 (where the question was whether the commissioners were not legally bound to assess at the valuation which the tax payer had given in the list which he had furnished as required by law); Heywood *v.* Buffalo, 14 N. Y., 534; Genesee, etc., Bank *v.* Livingston Co., 53 Barb., 223; Hatch *v.* Buffalo, 38 N. Y., 276; People *v.* Ogdensburgh, 48 id., 390; State *v.* Clothier, 30 N. J., 351 (where it is held that *certiorari* may be brought though the tax has been collected by distress and sale: But see, as to this, National Bank of Chemung *v.* Elmira, 53 N. Y., 49); Ohio, etc., R. R. Co. *v.* Lawrence Co., 27 Ill., 50; State *v.* McClurg 27 N. J., 253 (where it is decided that if an excessive tax is assessed it will be set aside for the excess only); State *v.* Quaife, 23 N. J., 89 (where a similar ruling was had); State *v.* Newark, 27 id., 185 (where, on *certiorari*, an assessment was set aside which assumed to be made by benefits, where from the nature of the case there could be no benefits); California, etc., R. R. Co., *v.* Supervisors of Butte, 18 Cal., 671; Swann *v.* Cumberland, 8 Gill, 150; Buckner *Ex parte*, 4 Eng. (Ark.) 73; Carroll *v.* Mayor, 12 Ala., 173.

[3] In New York, where street assessments were to be submitted to the common council for confirmation, and that body was empowered to alter the same in such manner as, in its opinion, justice might require, the act of confirmation was held to be an exercise of judicial authority, and subject to be removed into the supreme court by *certiorari*. Leroy *v.* New York, 20 Johns., 430; Starr *v.* Rochester, 6 Wend., 564; Matter of Mount Morris Square, 2 Hill, 14; People *v.* New York, 5 Barb., 43; People *v.* Brooklyn, 9 id., 535. So in Massachusetts, the proceedings of county commissioners in reviewing assess-

cipal bodies in levying assessments for local improvements exceed their authority, or lay down erroneous principles to govern the action of the assessors or commissioners who are to make them.[1]

In reviewing a case on *certiorari* the court is confined to the record of the tribunal reviewed. Extrinsic evidence cannot be received to contradict or control it.[2] If the tax is rendered illegal by facts not appearing of record, some other remedy must be sought.[3] On *certiorari* the court will not set aside the whole of a tax proceeding if justice can be done to the party without doing so,[4] unless, perhaps, where by law, in case it is vacated, there can be a new assessment; in which case, vacating the whole may be most likely to accomplish the general purposes of the law for making the levy.[5]

ments on appeal were held reviewable in this mode. See Parks *v.* Boston, 8 Pick., 218; Gibbs *v.* County Commissioners, 19 id., 298; Newburyport *v.* County Commissioners, 12 Met., 211; Lincoln *v.* Worcester, 8 Cush., 55, 61. A similar ruling in New Jersey: State *v.* Falkinburge, 15 N. J., 320; State *v* Parker, 34 id., 49. And in Missouri: State *v.* St. Louis County Court, 47 Mo., 594; State *v.* Dowling, 50 id., 134. And see Floyd *v.* Gilbreath, 27 Ark., 675.

[1] In New Jersey, it is said that the action of municipal bodies in levying assessments for local improvements must be kept strictly within the limits assigned to them by the statute, and if the assessments appear not to be within those limits, they shall not only be liable to reversal on *certiorari*, but also be held void and insufficient to support a title professing to be founded on them. State *v.* Jersey City, 35 N. J., 381; State *v.* Hudson City, 29 id., 104, 475.

[2] Charlestown *v.* County Commissioners, 109 Mass., 270. See Hatch *v.* Buffalo, 38 N. Y., 276.

[3] Floyd *v.* Gilbreath, 27 Ark., 675; Hatch *v.* Buffalo, 38 N. Y., 276.

[4] State *v.* Kingsland, 23 N. J., 83, 88. In this case, *Carpenter*, J., says: "But though this vote was illegal, we do not think we are bound to proceed under this writ, and set the vote and proceedings aside. The money has been collected and disbursed under that vote without objection, so far as it appears, except on the part of the prosecutor, Cornelius Van Vorst. Much inconvenience might result from such judgment to the township, while, on the other hand, it is not necessary for the protection of Mr. Van Vorst, whose grievance will be redressed under another writ. The power of the court to restrain such proceedings, and which was exerted in the case of The State *v.* Albright, is indisputable. But there are cases when the court will not interfere with the assessment of taxes, from regard to the public inconvenience, and particularly when not necessary for the protection of any individal who may complain. The writ will, in the discretion of the court, under such circumstances, be refused or dismissed. King *v.* King, 2 T. R., 235; Lawton *v.* Commissioners of Highways, 2 Caines, 182; *Ryerson*, J., 3 Green, 323."

[5] State *v.* Bergen, 34 N. J., 438. But whether on *certiorari* the court will set

Enjoining collection. To entitle a party to relief in equity against an illegal tax, he must by his bill bring his case under some acknowledged head of equity jurisdiction. The illegality of the tax alone, or the threat to sell property for its satisfaction, can not, of themselves, furnish any ground for equitable interposition.[1] In ordinary cases a party must find his remedy in the courts of law, and it is not to be supposed he will fail to find one adequate to his proper relief. Cases of fraud, accident or mistake, cases of cloud upon the title to one's property, and cases where one is threatened with irremediable mischief, may demand other remedies than those the common law can give, and these in proper cases may be afforded in the courts of equity.

The available remedy in equity, when any is admissible, is commonly that by injunction. It is probable that this remedy has many times been awarded in equity with too little regard to any other consequences than those which concerned the individual applying for it. But the personal consequences are not the only ones which must be kept in view in these cases. When the illegalities complained of affect only the person complaining, an injunction which restrains the collection as to him may cause no considerable mischief, and may very properly be awarded if a sufficient case is made out; but when they affect the whole tax levy, as they often do, a court should be extremely cautious in awarding, on the complaint of one person, or even of several, a process which may reach the cases of others not complaining, and which may seriously embarrass all the operations of the government depending on the source of revenue which by means of it would be

aside an assessment after an act of the legislature to confirm it, even though that act be invalid, see State *v.* Apgar, 31 id., 358.

[1] Dows *v.* Chicago, 11 Wall, 108; Hannewinkle *v.* Georgetown, 15 id., 547; Savings and Loan Society *v.* Austin, 46 Cal., 415, 488; Floyd *v.* Gilbreath, 27 Ark., 675; Mooers *v.* Smedley, 6 Johns. Ch., 27; Messeck *v.* Supervisors of Columbia, 50 Barb., 190; Hanlon *v.* West Chester County, 57 id., 383; Heywood *v.* Buffalo, 14 N. Y., 534; Susquehanna Bank *v.* Broome County, 25 id., 312; McDonald *v.* Murphree, 45 Miss., 705; Sayre *v.* Tompkins, 23 Mo., 443; First National Bank of Hannibal *v.* Meredith, 44 id., 500; Barrow *v.* Davis, 46 id., 394; McPike *v.* Pew, 48 id., 525; U. P. R. R. Co. *v.* Lincoln County, 2 Dill., 297; Weaver *v.* State, 39 Ala., 535; Cook County *v.* Chicago, etc., R. R. Co., 35 Ill., 460. But see Williams *v.* Pinney, 25 Iowa, 436; Jeffersonville *v.* Patterson, 32 Ind., 140; Burnes *v.* Leavenworth, 2 Kans., 454; Warden *v.* Supervisors, 14 Wis., 618.

stopped. "How," it has been justly remarked, "could a government calculate with any certainty upon the revenues, if the collection of the taxes was subject to be arrested in every instance in which a tax payer or tax collector could make out *prima facie* a technical case for arresting such collection? Far better is it * * to let the individual pay to the government what it demands of him, at the time of the demand, as he will be certain of getting it back with interest, after more or less delay, if it was not due."[1] So serious have been the embarrassments by an improvident employment of the writ of injunction and other obstructive process, that the legislature has in some cases deemed it necessary to interpose and forbid the issue of injunction, replevin or other specified writs, the tendency of which would be to embarrass collections.[2] The courts also have sometimes imposed conditions to equitable remedies in cases where they deemed the public interest to demand it. Thus where an injunction has been applied for to restrain the collection of a tax, partly legal and partly not, the court has made the payment of the legal a condition precedent,[3]

[1] *Benning*, J., in Eve *v.* State, 21 Geo., 50. This approved in Cody *v.* Lennard, 45 id., 85, where it was held that the act providing that "no replevin shall lie, or any judicial interference be had in any levy or distress for taxes under this law, but the party injured shall be left to his proper remedy in any court of law," was valid. The party must pay the tax, even though illegal, and pursue his remedy against the collector. See also Scofield *v.* Perkerson, 46 Geo., 350.

[2] That restraining collection of taxes may be prohibited, see Pullan *v.* Kinsinger, 2 Abb. U. S., 94; 9 Am. L. Reg., N. S., 557.

[3] Conway *v.* Waverley, 15 Mich., 257; Palmer *v.* Napoleon, 16 id., 176; Hersey *v.* Milwaukee County, 16 Wis., 185; Bond *v.* Kenosha, 17 id., 284; Myrick *v.* La Crosse, 17 id., 442; Mills *v.* Johnson, 17 id., 598; Mills *v.* Charleston, 29 id., 400; Dean *v.* Borchsenius, 30 id., 236; O'Kane *v.* Treat, 25 Ill., 557; Taylor *v.* Thompson, 42 id., 9; Briscoe *v.* Allison, 43 id., 291; Reed *v.* Tyler, 56 id., 288; Barnett *v.* Cline, 60 id., 205; Harrison *v.* Haas, 25 Ind., 281; Roseberry *v.* Huff, 27 id., 12; Board of Commissioners *v.* Elston, 32 id., 27; Adams *v.* Castle, 30 Conn., 404; Morrison *v.* Hershire, 32 Iowa, 271; Corbin *v.* Woodbine, 33 id., 297; Shelton *v.* Dunn, 6 Kans., 128; Lawrence *v.* Killam, 11 id., 499; Twombly *v.* Kimbrough, 24 Ark., 459; Frazer *v.* Siebern, 16 Ohio, N. S., 614. If the tax is excessive by reason of the list not including some lots which should have been embraced, the collection will not be enjoined until the amount really chargeable to complainant has been paid. Ottowa *v.* Barnes, 10 Kans., 270. If the bill shows precisely the amount of the excess of the taxes which are claimed to be illegal, and only asks to have the collection of the illegal taxes restrained, the bill will not be dismissed for want of

and it has been strongly intimated, in a case where it was alleged that by fraud the assessment had been made too high, that the payment of what the party conceded would be his just proportion, ought to be required before injunction should issue, in order that the proceeding may be as little as possible injurious to the public interest.[1]

Personal Taxes. When a tax is assessed as a personal charge against the party taxed, or against his personal property, it is difficult to suggest any ground of equitable jurisdiction. Presumptively the remedy at law is adequate. If the tax is illegal and the party makes payment, he is entitled to recover back the amount. The case does not differ in this regard from any other case in which a party is compelled to pay an illegal demand; the illegality alone affords no ground for equitable interference, and the proceedings to enforce the tax by distress and sale can give none, as these only constitute an ordinary trespass. To this point the decisions are numerous.[2] The exceptions to this rule, if any, must be of cases which are to be

a formal offer to pay the legal taxes. Clement *v.* Everest, 29 Mich., 19. Compare Board of Commissioners *v.* Elston, 32 Ind., 27. If the legal and illegal taxes are so blended that they cannot be distinguished, a prohibition may go for the whole. State *v.* Hodges, 14 Rich., 256.

[1] Merrill *v.* Humphrey, 24 Mich., 170; Frazer *v.* Siebern, 16 Ohio, N. S., 614. Where a bill is filed praying that the levy of state, county and township taxes be restrained, alleging them all to be invalid, if complainant fails to show any illegality in the state and county taxes, the bill will be dismissed. Pillsbury *v.* Auditor General, 26 Mich., 245.

[2] Brewer *v.* Springfield, 97 Mass., 152; Durant *v.* Eaton, 98 id., 469; Loud *v.* Charlestown, 99 id., 208; Whiting *v.* Boston, 106 id., 89; Hunnewell *v.* Charlestown, 106 id., 350; Rockingham Savings Bank *v.* Portsmouth, 62 N. H., 17; Ritter *v.* Patch, 12 Cal., 298; Berri *v.* Patch, 12 id., 299; Worth *v.* Fayetteville, Winst. Eq. (N. C.), 70; Williams *v.* Detroit, 2 Mich., 560; Conley *v.* Chedic, 6 Nev., 222; Van Cott *v.* Supervisors of Milwaukee, 18 Wis., 247; Greene *v.* Mumford, 5 R. I., 492; McCoy *v.* Chillicothe, 3 Ohio, 370; Dodd *v.* Hartford, 25 Conn., 232; Sayre *v.* Tompkins, 23 Mo., 443; Barrow *v.* Davis, 46 id., 394; McPike *v.* Peru, 48 id., 525; Hopkins *v.* Lovell, 47 id., 102; Leslie *v.* St. Louis, 47 id., 474; Lockwood *v.* St. Louis, 24 id., 20; Fowler *v.* St. Joseph, 37 id., 228; Deane *v.* Todd, 22 id., 90. The doctrine of these cases is very succinctly stated by *Bigelow*, Ch. J., in Brewer *v.* Springfield, 97 Mass., 152, 154. "Until the plaintiffs have been compelled to pay the tax which they allege to have been illegally assessed upon them, they have suffered no wrong. When they have paid it they can recover it back by an action at law, which would furnish them an adequate and complete remedy." See also Brooklyn *v.* Messerole, 26 Wend., 132.

classed under the head of irreparable injury; as when the enforcement of a tax might destroy a valuable franchise;[1] or when property is levied upon which possesses a peculiar value to the owner beyond any possible market value it can have;[2] and other like cases where the recovery of damages would be inadequate redress. It must be conceded, however, that the cases in some states go further, and sustain the remedy by injunction in all cases of illegal taxation; proceeding in doing so upon the ground that "when officers or individuals have no legal authority to lay a tax, and they assume the right; or when persons are vested with the legal authority to lay a tax for a specified purpose, but instead of exercising that power they proceed to impose a tax which the law has not authorized, or lay it for fraudulent or unauthorized purposes; then a court of equity will interpose to afford preventive relief, by restraining the exercise of powers perverted to fraudulent or oppressive purposes."[3] But in the large majority of cases in which taxes are illegal, there is no fraud, actual or intended, and the illegality consists in an erroneous construction of powers, or in the unintentional omission of some necessary proceeding, or in other defect not inconsistent with good faith on the part of officers; and it seems a great stretch of equitable principles to treat such a case as one of legal fraud, and to be remedied on that ground. The equitable jurisdiction in these cases has grown up somewhat imperceptibly, and perhaps owes its origin as much to an idea that municipal officers, in the authority which affects the property of the people, are exercising a trust over which equity may properly assume a supervision, as to any supposed fraud, actual or constructive, which may be involved in their illegal action.[4] In view of the conflict in the de-

[1] Osborne *v.* Bank of United States, 9 Wheat., 738, where an officer was enjoined from enforcing a heavy state tax unlawfully laid on a branch of the Bank of the United States, on the ground that to enforce it would drive the bank from the state and work irreparable mischief. See Foote *v.* Linck, 5 McLean, 616.

[2] See Henry *v.* Gregory, 29 Mich., 68, 70.

[3] Drake *v.* Phillips, 40 Ills., 388, 393, per *Walker*, Ch. J. See also Foote *v.* Milwaukee, 18 Wis., 270; Toledo, etc., R. R. Co. *v.* La Fayette, 22 Ind., 262; Commissioners of Clay Co. *v.* Markle, 46 id., 96; Knight *v.* Flatrock, etc., Co., 45 id., 134; Shoemaker *v.* Grant Co., 36 id., 175; Riley *v.* Western Union Telegraph Co., 47 id., 511; Spencer *v.* Wheaton, 14 Iowa, 38; St. Clair Board's Appeal, 74 Penn. St., 252.

[4] Mr. High, in his valuable Treatise on the Law of Injunctions, says: "It will

cisions regarding the basis of equitable jurisdiction, it seems advisable to classify somewhat the cases which have been decided, indicating, wherever necessary, the points of divergence.

Preliminary Action. The action of the proper authorities in voting a tax cannot be restrained on the ground that they are voting more than is necessary for the purpose;[1] nor on an allegation that there is an intent to appropriate some portion of the sum voted to a purpose not authorized by law;[2] nor because complainant is injured by unreasonable delay in doing the work for which the tax is laid,[3] nor can the making of an assessment be enjoined, the act being judicial.[4]

Excessive Assessments. For excessive assessments, when fraud is not charged, there can be no relief in equity. The remedy must be such as the statute has given.[5]

Irregular Taxation. A tax will not be restrained on the ground merely that it is irregular or erroneous. Errors in the assessment do not render the tax void, nor, as a general rule, do they constitute any reason whatever against its being strictly enforced. But however that may be in any particular case, the law has provided

be found on examination that courts of equity have been inclined, in the case of assessments by municipal corporations, to relax somewhat the stringency of the rule of noninterference as applied to the collection of state taxes. Though it is difficult to perceive any sufficient reason for such distinction, yet the distinction itself remains." § 369.

1 Wharton *v.* School Directors, 42 Penn. St., 358. The levy of a tax within the limits of legislative authority is an act of sound discretion, and cannot render the board ordering it liable to the parties whose property is taken for its satisfaction. Moore *v.* School Directors, 59 Penn. St., 232.

2 Truesdell's Appeal, 58 Penn. St., 148. The principle was involved in Morgan *v.* Graham, 1 Woods, 124, in which it was attempted to restrain state officers from issuing bonds under what was alleged to be an unconstitutional law.

3 Whiting *v.* Boston, 106 Mass., 89.

4 Western R. R. Co. *v.* Nolan, 48 N. Y., 513.

5 Kimber *v.* Schuylkill, 20 Penn. St., 366; Hughes *v.* Kline, 30 id., 227; Everett's Appeal, 71 id., 216; Hutchinson *v.* Pittsburgh, 72 id., 320. An injunction would seem to be the appropriate remedy where a town makes discriminations in the discounts on taxes, this not rendering the tax illegal. Toby *v.* Wareham, 2 Allen, 594. Equity can not relieve on the ground of the tax having become burdensome by depreciation of property. White Sulphur Springs Co. *v.* Robinson, 3 W. Va., 542.

remedies for all such mere irregularities and errors as do not go to the foundation of the tax, and parties complaining must be confined to these. In this the authorities are agreed.[1] But it is not a mere irregularity when one is denied his legal right to work out a road tax, and the amount is demanded in money,[2] nor when a tax once paid is demanded a second time;[3] nor when property is unlawfully exempted from taxation, thereby increasing the burden upon complainant;[4] nor when property which is exempt from taxation by law is assessed;[5] nor when one's assessment has been increased without giving him the notice to which by law he is entitled. In all these cases the party taxed is denied a substantial right, or his tax is unlawfully increased beyond his due proportion, and his right to an adequate remedy is unquestionable. If, however, the tax is a personal tax only, it will appear from the references to decisions, which have already been made, that in a majority of the states the remedy by injunction would not be given, and the party would be turned over to his suit at law.[7]

[1] Dows *v.* Chicago, 11 Wall., 108; Hughes *v.* Kline, 30 Penn. St., 227; Clinton, etc., Appeal, 56 id., 315; Chicago, etc., R. R. Co. *v.* Frary, 22 Ill., 34; State *v.* Bremond, 38 Texas, 116; Jones *v.* Summer, 27 Ind., 510; Center, etc., Co. *v.* Black, 32 id., 468; Ottowa *v.* Walker, 21 Ill., 605; Metz *v.* Anderson, 23 id., 463; O'Neal *v.* Virginia, etc., Co., 18 Md., 1; Mills *v.* Gleason, 11 Wis., 470; Mills *v.* Johnson, 17 id., 598; Brooklyn *v.* Messerole, 26 Wend., 132; Marklot *v.* Davenport 17 Iowa, 379; West *v* Whittaker, 37 id., 598; Dodd *v.* Hartford, 25 Conn., 232; Greene *v.* Mumford, 5 R. I., 472; Lawrence *v.* Killam, 11 Kans., 499; Smith *v.* Leavenworth, 9 id., 296; Kansas Pacific R. R. Co. *v.* Russel, 8 id., 558; Merrill *v.* Gorham, 6 Cal., 41. If equity should give relief on the ground of a mere irregularity, it would require payment of the tax as a condition. Savings and Loan Society *v.* Ordway, 38 Cal., 679. Equity will not relieve on the ground of a very slight excess in the levy. Smith *v.* Leavenworth, 9 Kans., 296. Nor on the ground of an illegal tax collected of complainant in former years. Fremont *v.* Mariposa County, 11 Cal., 361.

[2] Miller *v.* Gorman, 38 Penn. St., 309.

[3] Commonwealth *v.* Supervisors of Colby, 29 Penn. St., 121. To entitle one to relief from double taxation, it must appear that he has paid once. Savings and Loan Society *v.* Austin, 46 Cal., 415.

[4] Illinois Central R. R. Co. *v.* McLean County, 17 Ill., 291; Mott *v.* Pennsylvania R. R. Co., 30 Penn. St., 9. See what is said on this subject, *ante*, Chapter VI.

[5] Morris, etc., Co. *v.* Jersey City, 1 Beas. Ch., 227.

[6] Darling *v.* Gunn, 50 Ill., 424; Cleghorn *v.* Postlewaite, 43 id., 428.

[7] To the point that equity will give no relief in tax cases where the remedy

Tax upon Lands. When a tax is assessed against the owner of lands, and is a personal charge upon him, and not a lien upon the land, there can be no grounds for equitable interference which would not exist in the case of a tax assessed upon personalty.[1] In those states in which a personal tax would be restrained if illegal, a tax upon land constituting a personal charge would be restrained also. In other states it would not be, unless some special ground of equity jurisdiction was shown.

Cloud upon Title. If the tax is a lien upon lands, it may then constitute a cloud upon the title; and one branch of equity jurisdiction is the removal of apparent clouds upon the title, which may diminish the market value of the land, and possibly threaten a loss of it to the owner. A cloud upon one's title is something which constitutes an apparent incumbrance upon it, or an apparent defect in it; something that shows *prima facie* some right of a third party, either to the whole or some interest in it. An illegal tax may or may not constitute such a cloud. If the alleged tax has no semblance of legality; if, upon the face of the proceedings, it is wholly unwarranted by law, or for any reason totally void, so that any person inspecting the record and comparing it with the law is at once apprised of the illegality, the tax, it would seem, could neither constitute an incumbrance, nor an apparent defect of title; and, therefore, in law, could constitute no cloud. If this be so, the jurisdiction which is exercised by courts of equity, to relieve parties by removing clouds upon their titles, could not attach in such a case. And so it has been held in many cases.[2]

at law is adequate, the following additional cases may be referred to. Weaver *v.* State, 39 Ala., 535; Dodd *v.* Hartford, 25 Conn., 232; Magee *v.* Denton, 5 Blatch., 130; Missouri River, etc., R. R. Co. *v.* Wheaton, 7 Kans., 232.

[1] See Williams *v.* Detroit, 2 Mich., 560; Brewer *v.* Springfield, 97 Mass., 152; Greene *v.* Mumford, 5 R. I., 474; Hunnewell *v.* Charlestown, 106 Mass., 350; Henry *v.* Gregory, 29 Mich., 68.

[2] Messerole *v.* Brooklyn, 8 Paige, 198; Wiggin *v.* N. Y., 9 id., 16; Van Doren *v.* N. Y., id., 388; Livingston *v.* Hollenbeck, 4 Barb., 9, 16; Van Rensselaer *v.* Kidd, 4 id., 17; Bouton *v.* Brooklyn, 15 id., 375; Cox *v.* Clift, 2 N. Y., 118; Scott *v.* Onderdonk, 14 id., 9; Hatch *v.* Buffalo, 38 id., 276; Newell *v.* Wheeler, 48 id., 486; Dean *v.* Madison, 9 Wis., 402; Head *v.* James, 13 id., 641; Shepardson *v.* Supervisors of Milwaukee, 28 id., 593; Milwaukee Iron Co. *v.* Hubbard, 29 id., 51; Floyd *v.* Gilbreath, 27 Ark., 675; Mobile, etc., R. R. Co. *v.* Peebles, 47 Ala., 317; Robinson *v.* Gaar, 6 Cal., 273; Bucknall *v.* Story, 36 id., 67; Ewing *v.* St. Louis, 5 Wall., 413; Hannewinkle *v.* Georgetown, 15 id., 547.

When, however, the illegality or fatal defect does not appear on the face of the record, but must be shown by evidence *aliunde*, so that the record would make out a *prima facie* right in one who should become purchaser, and the evidence to rebut this case may possibly be lost, or be unavailable from death of witnesses or other cause, or when the deed given on a sale of the lands for the tax would by statute be presumptive evidence of a good title in the purchaser, so that the purchaser might rely upon that for a recovery of the lands until the illegalities were shown, the courts of equity regard the case as coming within their ordinary jurisdiction, and have extended relief on the ground that a cloud on the title existed or was imminent. The cases on this point are numerous, and in considerable variety, as would be anticipated in view of the different tax systems under which they have been made.[1]

[1] Hannewinkle *v.* Georgetown, 15 Wall., 547; Dows *v.* City of Chicago, 11 id., 108; Dean *v.* Madison, 9 Wis., 402; Weeks *v.* Milwaukee, 10 id., 242; Jenkins *v.* Rock County, 15 id., 11; Mitchell *v.* Milwaukee, 18 id., 92; Crane *v.* Janesville, 20 id., 305; Grimmer *v.* Sumner, 21 id., 179; Hamilton *v.* Fond du Lac, 25 id., 490; Siegel *v.* Outagamie County, 26 id., 70; Judd *v.* Fox Lake, 28 id., 583; Shepardson *v.* Milwaukee, 28 id., 593; Wals *v.* Grosvenor, 31 id., 681; Conway *v.* Waverley, 15 Mich., 257; Palmer *v.* Rich, 12 id., 414; Scofield *v.* Lansing, 17 id., 437; Kenyon *v.* Duchene, 21 id., 498; Shell *v.* Martin, 19 Ark., 139; Chaplin *v.* Holmes, 27 id., 414; Polk *v.* Rose, 25 Md., 153; Weller *v.* St. Paul, 5 Minn., 95; Gage *v.* Rohrbach, 56 Ill., 262; Gage *v.* Billings, 56 id., 268; Reed *v.* Tyler, 56 id., 288; Gage *v.* Chapman, 56 id., 311; Barnett *v.* Cline, 60 id., 205; Reed *v.* Reber, 62 id., 240; Lee *v.* Ruggles, 62 id., 427; Moers *v.* Smedley, 6 Johns. Ch. 28; Pettit *v.* Shepherd, 5 Paige, 493; Oakley *v.* Trustees of Williamsburg, 6 id., 262; Hanlon *v.* Supervisors of Westchester, 57 Barb., 383; Van Doren *v.* New York, 9 Paige, 388; Scott *v.* Onderdonk, 14 N. Y., 9; Ward *v.* Dewey, 16 id., 519; Hatch *v.* Buffalo, 38 id., 276; Allen *v.* Buffalo, 39 id., 386; Overing *v.* Foote, 43 id., 290; Crooke *v.* Andrews, 40 id., 547; Newell *v.* Wheeler, 48 id., 486; Heywood *v.* Buffalo, 14 id., 534; Lapp *v.* Morrill, 8 Kans., 678; Harmer *v.* Boling, 8 Cal., 384; Cohen *v.* Sharp, 44 id., 29; Ward *v.* Ward, 2 Hayw., 226; Leigh *v* Everheart's Executors, 4 T. B. Monr., 379; Harrison *v.* Haas, 25 Ind., 281; Morris Canal, etc., Co. *v.* Jersey City, 1 Beas. Ch. 227; Lockwood *v.* St. Louis, 24 Mo., 20; Fowler *v.* St. Joseph, 37 id., 228; Morrison *v.* St. Paul, 9 Minn., 108; Weber *v.* San Francisco, 1 Cal., 455; Robinson *v.* Gaar, 6 id., 273; Hardenburg *v.* Kidd, 10 id., 403; Bern *v.* Patch, 12 id., 299; Pixley *v.* Huggins, 15 id., 127; Burr *v.* Hunt, 18 id., 303; Bucknall *v.* Story, 36 id., 67; Houghton *v.* Austin, 47 id., 646; Arrington *v.* Liscom, 34 id., 365; Coulson *v.* Portland, Deady, 481; Huntington *v.* Central Pacific R. R. Co., 2 Sawyer, 503. It is no answer to the bill in such a case that the tax might have been collected from personal property. Scofield *v.* Lansing, 17 Mich., 437. The cloud upon the title is presumptively removed when personal

There are many cases, however, which ignore the distinction between proceedings void on their face for illegality, and proceedings which, though illegal in fact, are on their face presumptively valid. Such cases, if they do not give relief on the ground of illegality alone, will give it on the ground that any sale of the land under proceedings which assume to be by authority of law, and are conducted by public officers empowered to make such sales, is such a cloud upon the title of the owner as he ought, in equity, to be relieved against, if the officers are proceeding unlawfully, and have no authority in fact.[1]

Quieting Title after a Sale. If land has been actually sold and conveyed for a tax, the original owner remaining in possession may have the validity of the sale tested by a bill in equity, filed for the purpose of quieting his title. This is the general rule. Courts of law cannot give him relief in such a case, as he can not bring ejectment, being himself in possession; and no other form of action is given by the common law for such a case. And where the case has proceeded to sale and conveyance, even though the defects in the title are apparent of record, and the deed is not *prima facie* evidence of title, it may perhaps be possible to distinguish the case from one in which the void proceedings are only impending. While they are in progress, it may be assumed that the officers will pause in their illegal action before any sale is reached; but when the proceedings have reached that point, and a conveyance has been given, which, though void, may affect the market value of the land, there would seem to be no very conclusive reason why equity should not interfere and decree a cancelment of the void claim.[2] If the tax purchaser has entered into

property sufficient to satisfy the tax is levied upon. Henry *v.* Gregory, 29 Mich., 68.

[1] See Burnett *v.* Cincinnati, 3 Ohio, 73; Culbertson *v.* Cincinnati, 16 id., 574; Ottowa *v.* Walker, 21 Ill., 605, and cases cited; Chicago, etc., R. R. Co. *v.* Frary, 22 id., 34; Barnard *v.* Hoyt, 63 id., 341; Holland *v.* Baltimore, 11 Md., 186; Baltimore *v.* Porter, 18 id., 284; Litchfield *v.* Polk Co., 18 Iowa, 70; Leslie *v.* St. Louis, 47 Mo., 474. And see Blackwell cn Tax Titles, 483; High on Injunctions, ch. VII., where the cases are collected with the author's usual industry and care. The occupant of lands, though he be not the owner, may file a bill to remove the cloud cast by an illegal tax. Barnard *v.* Hoyt, 63 Ill., 341.

[2] See Yancey *v.* Hopkins, 1 Mumf., 419; Holland *v.* Baltimore, 11 Md., 186;

possession of the land, the original owner has an adequate remedy by suit at law in ejectment; and to this he must resort.[1] When neither party has actual possession, if the statute has authorized the action of ejectment to be brought on the constructive possession, which either may claim by virtue of the conveyances which he holds, the suit at law would appear to be the adequate remedy in such a case also.[2]

Joint Complaint by Several Persons Taxed. When the supposed illegality in a tax affects a single person only, or affects him in a peculiar manner, distinguishing his case from that of others, he can not unite with others in a suit to restrain its collection. A joint bill by two or more parties, setting out distinct grounds on which each sought relief, would be dismissed as multifarious.[3] But where the illegality extends to the whole assessment, or where it affects, in the same manner, a number of persons, so that the question involved can be presented without confusion by one bill filed by all or any number of those thus affected, there seems to be no sufficient reason why a joint bill should not be permitted. The reasons favoring it are, that it avoids the necessity of a multiplicity of suits, and the attendant trouble and expense; and the objection that the interests of complainant are several is suffi-

Polk *v.* Rose, 25 id., 153; Almony *v.* Hicks, 3 Head, 39; Head *v.* Fordyce, 17 Cal., 149; Hartford *v.* Chipman, 21 Conn., 488; Fonda *v.* Sage, 48 N. Y., 173. If complainant by his bill makes out a case for relief, it is not necessary for him to aver that he has paid the taxes. Polk *v.* Rose, 25 Md., 153.

[1] The court of chancery is not the proper tribunal for settling titles to land generally. Munson *v.* Munson, 28 Conn., 582; Thayer *v.* Smith, 9 Met., 470; Sunderton *v.* Thompson, 2 Dev. Ch., 539; Devaux *v.* Detroit, Har. Ch., 98; Blackwood *v.* Van Vleet, 11 Mich., 252.

[2] Parish *v.* Eager, 15 Wis., 532; Bonnell *v.* Roane, 20 Ark., 114; Scott *v.* Watkins, 22 id., 556. It is not competent to give relief in equity against the party in actual possession; he having a constitutional right to a trial by jury. Tabor *v.* Cook, 15 Mich., 322. See Springer *v.* Rosette, 47 Ill., 223. As to bill by tax purchaser, and what he must aver, see Belcher *v.* Mhoon, 47 Miss., 613.

[3] Kerr *v.* Lansing, 17 Mich., 34; Hudson *v.* Atchison County, 12 Kans., 140; compare Cutting *v.* Gilbert, 5 Blatch., 259. One person cannot file a bill to restrain the collection of a tax from another. Missouri River, etc., R. R. Co. *v.* Wheaton, 7 Kans., 232. To a bill filed by a stockholder to restrain illegal taxation of the corporation, the corporation must be made a party. Davenport *v.* Dows, 18 Wall., 626.

ciently met by the fact that complete justice may be done to all in one suit on the single issue; whereas, if the parties did not join, the same issue must be passed upon in separate suits brought by the several complainants. Although there has been some hesitation in sanctioning such bills, the weight of authority is decidedly in favor of supporting them, and this method of redress is now most commonly resorted to where the case is appropriate for it.[1]

But the mere saving of the expense of several suits at law, where each of the complainants has an adequate remedy, is no ground for sustaining a joint suit in equity where no other ground of equitable relief is apparent. This is well explained by the supreme court of Connecticut, in a case in which a joint petition was filed to restrain the collection from several complainants of sewer assessments made upon their lands severally, and which were claimed to be illegal. "The multiplicity of suits, which the petition seeks to avoid, does not injuriously affect any one of the petitioners. No one of them has occasion to expect any such multiplicity affecting himself. One suit is all that any one of them has to fear, and the object of this bill would seem to be to relieve these parties severally from that one suit, and to consolidate the apprehended litigation. In other words, to enforce a consolidation rule by means of the extraordinary powers of the court of chancery. If the assessment were against one person only, it is not claimed that he could transfer from a court of law to a court of equity the question of his liability. But how is the condition of any one

[1] Bull *v.* Read, 13 Grat., 78; Johnson *v.* Drummond, 20 id., 419; Floyd *v* Gilbreath, 27 Ark., 675; Stevens *v.* Rutland, etc., R. R. Co., 29 Vt., 545; Holmes *v.* Baker, 16 Gray, 259; Mott *v.* Pennsylvania R. R. Co., 30 Penn. St., 39; Page *v.* Allen, 58 id., 338; Manly *v.* Raleigh, 4 Jones Eq., 370; Galloway *v.* Jenkins, 63 N. C., 147; Kerr *v.* Lansing, 17 Mich., 34; Scofield *v.* Lansing, 17 id., 437; Motz *v.* Detroit, 18 id., 495; Webster *v.* Harwinton, 32 Conn., 131; Terret *v.* Sharon, 34 id., 105; Sherman *v.* Carr, 8 R. I., 431; Upington *v.* Oviatt, 24 Ohio, N. S., 232; Vanover *v.* The Justices, 27 Geo., 354; Baltimore *v.* Porter, 18 Md., 284; La Fayette *v.* Cox, 5 Ind., 38; Baltimore *v.* Sill, 31 Md., 375; Nill *v.* Jenkinson, 15 Ind., 425; Oliver *v.* Keightley, 24 id., 514; Harward *v.* St. Clair, etc., Company, 51 Ill., 130; Hooper *v.* Ely, 46 Mo., 505; Steiner *v.* Franklin County, 48 Mo., 167; Barr *v.* Deniston, 19 N. H., 170; McMillan *v.* Lee County, 3 Iowa, 311; Mandeville *v.* Riggs, 2 Pet., 482; King *v.* Wilson, 1 Dillon, 555; Coulson *v.* Portland, Deady, 481. For a case under the Kansas statute, see Wyandotte, etc., Bridge Co. *v.* Wyandotte County, 10 Kans., 326.

of these petitioners the worse because others are assessed for the same improvement? It would undoubtedly be convenient to try the questions relating to these warrants in one comprehensive law suit. But it does not seem to the court that the case presented by the bill is one of such irreparable injury, or of inadequate relief at law, as to warrant us in taking it away from the legal tribunals." [1]

Fraud. A tax founded on an assessment which, from corrupt and malicious motives, is made excessive, may be enjoined.[2] So may any other tax which is rendered unequal and unfair by fraudulent practices of the officers, or in which the party is deprived by like practices of important rights which the law intends to secure to him; such, for instance, as the right of appeal from an assessment, or to be heard by the board of review before his assessment should be raised.[3]

Bills of Interpleader. It is possible for cases to arise in which the same sum of money is demanded as a tax under conflicting claims by different officers — or, in city cases under peculiar ordinances, by a contractor and an officer. Conflicting claims may also arise where one is taxed as representing another, in the capacity of agent, trustee or otherwise, or as officer of a corporation representing the shareholders, and where the person beneficially interested contests the tax. Such cases may possibly justify a bill of interpleader, as the most ready method of determining to whom the custodian of the fund is under obligation to make payment.[4]

[1] *Seymour*, J., in Dodd *v.* Hartford, 25 Conn., 232, 238. And see Sheldon *v.* School District, id., 224. Compare Savings and Loan Association *v.* Austin, 46 Cal., 415; Houghton *v.* Austin, 47 id., 646; Central Pacific R. R. Co. *v.* Corcoran, 48 id., 65.

[2] Albany, etc., R. R. Co. *v.* Canaan, 16 Barb., 244; Lefferts *v.* Calumet, 21 Wis., 688; Milwaukee Iron Co. *v.* Hubbard, 29 id., 51; Merrill *v.* Humphrey, 24 Mich., 170; Republic Life Ins. Co. *v.* Pollak, Sup. Ct. Illinois, 7 Chicago Legal News, 357.

[3] See Cleghorn *v.* Postlewaite, 43 Ill., 428; Darling *v.* Gunn, 50 id., 424. Each of these was a case in which an assessment was increased without notice to the person assessed, and the collection was enjoined. The case is not distinctly put on the ground of fraud, it being sufficient under the Illinois decisions that the party had been illegally deprived of his right to be heard before his assessment should be increased.

[4] See Thomson *v.* Ebbets, Hopk. Ch., 272; Mohawk and H. R. R. Co. *v.* Clute, 4 Paige, 384.

Illegal Corporate Action. The cases are hopelessly divided on the question, whether individual tax payers may file a bill on their own behalf to restrain unlawful municipal action, when it constitutes the preliminary step leading to taxation. Such, for instance, as the contracting of a debt *ultra vires*, the allowance of an illegal claim, the consent to a collusive judgment, or the misappropriation of the public moneys. On the one hand it is insisted that, until a tax is actually laid, the grievance, if any, is purely a public grievance, and public grievances must be redressed on the application of the proper public authorities; that individuals can proceed in equity only when their interests are separate and individual; and such interests are only affected by the unlawful action when a tax is laid and has become an individual charge against the several persons taxed.[1] On the other hand, it is said that the case is to be distinguished from the cases of public wrongs, in which the general public are alike concerned; that the tax payers constitute a class specially damaged by the unlawful act, in the increase of the burden of taxation upon their property. They have, therefore, a special interest in the subject matter of the suit distinct from that of the general public.[2] The decided preponderance of authority is in support of the right of the tax payers to file bills on their own behalf in such a case. The jurisdiction of equity may be sustained on the ground that the injury which would be done by the unlawful municipal action would be irreparable; and this would meet any objection on the ground that the parties would have a remedy at law when the tax came to be levied. In most cases the injury would be irreparable, and it might become so in all; as misappropriation of corporate funds cannot render a subsequent tax illegal, even though levied for the very purpose of meeting the deficiency thereby caused;[3] and consequently, all remedy may be lost if the misappropriation is not enjoined. It may be lost also in any case in which a corporate

[1] Doolittle *v.* Supervisors of Broome, 18 N. Y., 155; Roosevelt *v.* Draper, 23 id., 318; Miller *v.* Grandy, 13 Mich., 540; Conklin *v.* Commissioners, 13 Minn., 454; Morgan *v.* Graham, 1 Woods, 124. In Massachusetts, a remedy is given by statute. Cooley *v.* Granville, 10 Cush., 56, and many subsequent cases were brought under statutes conferring jurisdiction.

[2] *Bartol*, Ch. J., in Baltimore *v.* Gill, 31 Md., 375, 394.

[3] See Wright *v.* Dunham, 13 Mich., 414.

debt is evidenced by some negotiable instrument given under an authority to contract in that form, and is put into circulation. The effective remedy must usually in such cases be preliminary to the threatened illegal action; and though the state may interfere in such cases through its proper law officer, to restrain an abuse of the limited powers it has granted,[1] its right to do so is commonly held not to preclude redress on the application of individual tax payers.[2]

Delay in Proceedings. It has been held in Massachusetts that persons taxed for school purposes, when the district has been illegally constituted, may unite in a bill to restrain the collection of the tax, notwithstanding a delay of thirteen months since the illegal action to establish the district, and notwithstanding in the meantime a tax has been levied and collected, and other important action has been had by the district.[3] In Michigan, after several years had elapsed, the court refused to permit the regularity of the organization to be attacked in equity, and the cases referred to in the opinion tend strongly in the direction of holding that, on grounds of public policy, it should not be suffered, even after a short delay, if the district, in the mean time, had become peaceably organized, and was in the exercise of authority as such.[4]

Actions at Law against Assessors. When questions are re-

[1] See Attorney General *v.* Detroit, 26 Mich., 263, and cases cited.

[2] See Mandeville *v.* Riggs, 2 Pet., 482; Dodge *v.* Woolsey, 18 How., 331; Sharpless *v.* Philadelphia, 21 Penn. St., 147; Mercer County *v.* Pittsburgh, etc., R. R. Co., 27 id., 389; Page *v.* Allen, 58 id., 338; New London *v.* Brainard, 22 Conn., 552; Webster *v.* Harwinton, 32 id., 131; La Fayette *v.* Cox, 5 Ind., 38; Oliver *v.* Keightley, 24 id., 514; Terrett *v.* Sharon, 34 Conn., 105; Barr *v.* Deniston, 19 N. H., 170; Merrill *v.* Plainfield, 45 id., 126; Colton *v.* Hanchett, 13 Ill., 615; Drake *v.* Phillips, 40 id., 388; Rice *v.* Smith, 9 Iowa, 570; McMillan *v.* Lee County, 3 id., 311; Grant *v.* Davenport, 36 id., 396; Fleming *v.* Mershon, id., 413; Wade *v.* Richmond, 18 Grat., 583; Douglass *v.* Placerville, 18 Cal., 643; Stevens *v.* Rutland, etc., R. R. Co., 29 Vt., 546; Gifford *v.* New Jersey R. R. Co., 10 N. J. Eq., 171; Baltimore *v.* Gill, 31 Md., 375; Hooper *v.* Ely, 46 Mo., 505; Steines *v.* Franklin County, 48 id., 167: see also Gray *v.* Chapin, 2 Sim. & Stu., 267; Bromley *v.* Smith, 1 Sim., 8.

[3] Holmes *v.* Baker, 16 Gray, 259. The opinion barely refers to the delay, saying that "The plaintiffs have been guilty of no delay or negligence which should deprive them of a remedy by injunction against the future illegal proceedings of the defendant."

[4] Stewart *v.* Kalamazoo, 30 Mich., 69, citing People *v.* Maynard, 15 id., 463; Fractional School District *v.* The Joint Board, 27 id., 3.

ferred to the decision of an officer selected for the purpose of deciding them, and who, in making the decision, must act upon his own judgment, it is of the highest importance, that in their consideration, he shall be entirely unembarrassed by any possible consequences to himself, and left free to the exercise of an unbiased judgment. He must, consequently, be wholly exempt from responsibility to private parties who may be dissatisfied with his conclusions, and who might be disposed, if the law permitted it, to cause them to be reviewed in a collateral proceeding, instituted before some other tribunal for the recovery of compensation for damages sustained in consequence of an erroneous judgment. This principle is so plain and reasonable that it meets with universal assent, and is applied in all cases where functions of a judicial nature are exercised. "They who are entrusted to judge ought to be free from vexation, that they may determine without fear; the law requires courage in a judge, and therefore provides security for the support of that courage."[1] "Judges have not been invested with this privilege for their own protection merely; it is calculated for the protection of the people by insuring to them a calm, steady and impartial administration of justice."[2] And this principle of protection is not limited in its application to the judges of courts, but extends to all officers who have duties to perform which in their nature are judicial, and which are to be performed according to the dictates of their judgment. Instances of this nature are the decisions of highway officers, that a person claiming exemption from a road assessment is not exempt in fact,[3] or that one assessed is in default

[1] Barnardiston *v.* Soane, 6 How. St. Tr., 1096, per *North*, Ch. J.

[2] Taaffe *v.* Downes, 3 Moore, P. C., 36, n. See Floyd *v.* Barker, 12 Rep., 23; Mostyn *v.* Fabrigas, Cowper, 161; Garnett *v.* Farrand, 6 B. & C., 611; Mills *v.* Collett, 6 Bing., 85; Holroyd *v.* Bean, 2 B. & Ald., 473; Pike *v.* Carter, 3 Bing., 78; Dicas *v.* Lord Brougham, 6 C. & P., 249; Lowther *v.* Earl of Radnor, 8 East, 113; Basten *v.* Carew, 3 B. & C., 652; Yates *v.* Lansing, 5 Johns., 282, 291; S. C. 9 id., 395; Stewart *v.* Hawley, 21 Wend., 552; Weaver *v.* Devendorf, 3 Denio, 117; Vail *v.* Owen, 19 Barb., 22; Hill *v.* Sellick, 21 id., 207; Wilkes *v.* Dinsman, 7 How., 89; Hoggett *v.* Bigley, 6 Humph., 236; Walker *v.* Hallock, 32 Md., 239; Gordon *v.* Farrar, 2 Doug., Mich., 411; Wall *v.* Trumbull, 16 Mich., 228; Gregory *v.* Brooks, 37 Conn., 365; Bradley *v.* Fisher, 13 Wall., 335; Fuller *v.* Gould, 20 Vt., 644; Wilson *v.* Marsh, 34 id., 352.

[3] Harrington *v.* Commissioners, etc., 2 McCord, 400.

for not working out the assessment,[1] or that a road should or should not be laid out on a prescribed line;[2] to the appraisement of damages when property is taken under the eminent domain;[3] to action of inspectors of elections who are to decide questions of fact which determine the qualifications of voters;[4] of school directors in deciding upon the removal of a teacher;[5] of corporate authorities in passing upon questions of suspension of members;[6] of members of a township board in deciding upon the allowance of claims;[7] and the like. In many of these cases it will be perceived that the officer who is held exempt is one who, in the main, performs ministerial functions only; but this is unimporant, if in the particular case complained of he was exercising a discretionary authority, or one which, by law, was confided to his deliberate judgment.[8]

No question can be made that these principles apply to the case of assessors.[9] The proper remedy for erroneous decisions on their part is not by suit at law to hold them to personal responsibility. "In the imperfection of human nature," it has been said by an eminent judge, "it is better that an individ-

[1] Freeman *v.* Cornwall, 10 Johns., 470.

[2] Sage *v.* Laurain, 19 Mich., 137.

[3] Van Steenburgh *v.* Bigelow, 3 Wend., 42.

[4] Gordon *v.* Farrar, 2 Doug. (Mich.), 511; Jenkins *v.* Waldron, 11 Johns., 121; Miller *v.* Rucker, 1 Bush, 135; Carter *v.* Harrison, 5 Blackf., 138; Rail *v* Potts, 8 Humph., 225; Peavy *v.* Robbins, 3 Jones L., 339; Caulfield *v.* Bullock, 18 B. Monr., 494; Elbin *v.* Wilson, 33 Md., 135; Friend *v.* Hamill, 34 id., 298; Geotchens *v.* Mathewson, 5 Lans., 214.

[5] Burton *v.* Fulton, 49 Penn. St., 151.

[6] Harman *v.* Tappenden, 1 East, 555.

[7] Wall *v.* Trumbull, 16 Mich., 228.

[8] Jenkins *v.* Waldron, 11 Johns., 121; Weaver *v.* Devendorf, 3 Denio, 117; Wall *v.* Trumbull, 16 Mich., 228.

[9] Dillingham *v.* Snow, 5 Mass., 547; Easton *v.* Calendar, 11 Wend., 90; Weaver *v.* Devendorf, 3 Denio, 117; Vail *v.* Owen, 19 Barb., 22; Brown *v.* Smith, 24 id., 419; People *v.* Reddy, 43 id., 539; Vose *v.* Willard, 47 id., 320; Bell *v.* Pearce, 48 id., 51; Barhyte *v.* Shepherd, 35 N. Y., 238; Western R. R. Co. *v.* Nolan, 48 id., 513; Pentland *v.* Stewart, 4 Dev. & Bat., 386; Steam Navigation Co. *v.* Wasco County, 2 Oregon, 209; Macklot *v.* Davenport, 17 Iowa, 379; Muscatine Western R. R. Co. *v.* Horton, 38 id., 33; Walker *v.* Hallock, 32 Ind., 239; Lilienthal *v.* Campbell, 22 La. An., 600; Wall *v.* Trumbull, 16 Mich., 238.

ual should occasionally suffer a wrong, than that the course of justice should be impeded and fettered by constant and perpetual restraints and apprehensions on the part of those who are to administer it."[1] And the remark is as true of assessors as it is of the judges of courts; it is of the highest importance that they should be protected in the honest exercise of their judgment.[2]

Assessors are therefore not liable for an excessive assessment, even though it may be made such by erroneously including in the estimate property not belonging to the party assessed, or not within the district.[3] Nor are they liable for erroneously listing for taxation persons or property which, though within their jurisdiction, are not taxable,[4] or for an error of judgment, influenced

[1] *Lord Tenterden*, Ch. J., in Garnett *v.* Ferrand, 6 B. & C., 611.

[2] That while the assessors are protected, the collector who collects the tax is protected also, as well as the town, county, etc., to which the money is paid over, see Holton *v.* Bangor, 23 Me., 264; Gilpatrick *v.* Saco, 57 id., 277; Wharton *v.* Birmingham, 37 Penn. St., 371; Ontario Bank *v.* Bunnell, 10 Wend., 186; Little *v.* Greenleaf, 7 Mass., 236; Osborne *v.* Danvers, 6 Pick., 98; Bates *v.* Boston, 5 Cush., 93; Howe *v.* Boston 7 id., 274; Lincoln *v.* Worcester, 8 id., 57; Greene *v.* Mumford, 4 R. I., 313; People *v.* Arguello, 37 Cal., 524; Glascow *v.* Rowse, 43 Mo., 479.

[3] Stickney *v.* Bangor, 30 Me., 404; Hemingway *v.* Machias, 33 id., 445; Brown *v.* Smith, 24 Barb., 419; Dow *v.* Backer, 61 id., 597.

[4] Huggins *v.* Hinson, 1 Phil. N. C., 126; Vail *v.* Owen, 19 Barb., 22; Easton *v.* Calendar, 11 Wend., 90; Weaver *v.* Devendorf, 3 Denio, 117; Brown *v.* Smith, 24 Barb., 419; Bell *v.* Pierce, 48 id., 51; Barhyte *v.* Shepherd, **35** N. Y., 238, 255. Compare National Bank of Chemung *v.* Elmira, 53 id., 49. A contrary decision was made in Gridley *v.* Clark, 2 Pick., 402, but the point was not discussed. Afterwards statutes were passed in that state to protect assessors in some cases. As, where through mere error and while acting with integrity and fidelity, they assessed a person not taxable. See Baker *v.* Allen, 21 Pick., 382; Durant *v.* Eaton, 98 Mass., 469. So the statute of 1823 provided that assessors shall not be responsible for the assessment of any tax upon the inhabitants of any city, town, district, parish or religious society of which they are assessors, when thereto required by the constituted authorities thereof, but the liability, if any, shall rest solely with such city, etc. *Held*, under this, that assessors were not liable for errors of law committed without fraud or intentional wrong. Ingraham *v.* Doggett, 5 Pick., 451; Devinnels *v.* Parsons, 98 Mass., 470. But where the regular assessment has been made for the year, and without authority of law they make another, they are liable. Inglee *v.* Bosworth, 5 Pick., 498. And see further, Gage *v.* Currier, 4 id., 399; Freeman *v.* Kenney, 15 id., 44; Suydam *v.* Keys, 13 Johns., 444; People *v.* Supervisors of Chenango, 11 N. Y., 573; Lyman *v.* Fiske, 17 Pick., 231; Baker *v.* Allen, 21 id., 382; Griffin *v.* Rising, 11 Met., 345. The above statute held not

by which they omit from their roll persons or property which ought to be taxed, thereby increasing the tax upon others.[1] And the rule is general, applying to all errors of law and mistakes of fact in the exercise of their lawful authority.[2]

But to bring one within this rule of protection, he must be careful not to assume a jurisdiction which the law does not confer upon him. If persons assume to be assessors when they are not, they may justly be held responsible as trespassers;[3] and the lawful assessor, if he assumes an authority to decide upon the rights of others in cases which the law has not confided to his judgment, is in general responsible to the same extent as if he possessed no official character whatever. The office protects him only when he keeps within the limits which have been prescribed for his official action; when he exceeds those he lays aside his official character, and must rely for his protection on the same principles behind which citizens in private life must defend themselves. A case in illustration is that of the assessment of a personal tax upon persons who are not resident within the district, and consequently not subject to the jurisdiction of the assessors.[4] Others are

to apply to school districts. Little *v.* Merrill, 10 Pick., 543; Taft *v.* Wood, 14 id., 362. An act exempting assessors from responsibility except "only for the want of integrity and fidelity on their own part," held not to protect them for assessing a school tax for a district having no legal existence. Bassett *v.* Porter, 4 Cush., 487; S. C., 10 id., 418; Dickinson *v.* Billings, 4 Gray, 42. But in such a suit it does not devolve on the assessors to prove a legal organization. The organization in fact, and action as a district, are sufficient *prima facie.* Stevens *v.* Newcomb, 4 Denio, 437.

[1] Dillingham *v.* Snow, 5 Mass., 559. Where taxes were irregularly assessed and paid over to the county and town, and the assessors, to avoid suit, refunded it to the taxpayers, and the town voted to refund to them, this was held a good promise as to the town tax, but not as to the others. Nelson *v.* Milford, 7 Pick., 18. As to the liability of assessors for refusing to assess the plaintiff, whereby he lost his right to vote, see Griffin *v.* Rising, 11 Met., 339.

[2] Assessors held not liable to a parish for negligence in not levying a tax equal to the amount voted by the parish, where they acted under an honest belief that they were carrying out the views of the parish. First Parish in Sherburne *v.* Fiske, 8 Cush., 264. Nor for neglect to take the oath of office. Id.

[3] Allen *v.* Archer, 49 Me., 346. A tax levied without an assessment is of course void. Shewalter *v.* Brown, 35 Miss., 423.

[4] Mygatt *v.* Washburn, 15 N. Y., 316; Wade *v.* Matterson, 4 Lans., 159; Hennan *v.* Stevens, 43 Me., 437; Martin *v.* Mansfield, 3 Mass., 419; Ware *v.* Perci-

where they spread upon the roll a sum never lawfully voted,[1] or a sum in excess of that which by law is to be levied for the year, or in excess of that which has been lawfully voted;[2] or a sum which has been voted for an unlawful purpose.[3]

Possibly, the assessors should be held liable also if, by neglect of duty, they deprive the taxpayer of the opportunity of being heard before the board of review.[4] The distinction which runs

val, 61 Me., 391; S. C., 14 Am. Rep., 565; Agry *v.* Young, 11 Mass., 220; Gage *v.* Currier, 4 Pick., 399; Sumner *v.* Dorchester, 4 id., 361; Inglee *v.* Bosworth, 5 id., 498; Freeman *v.* Kenney, 15 id., 44; Lyman *v.* Fiske, 17 id., 231; Henry *v.* Edson, 2 Vt., 499; Fairbanks *v.* Kittridge, 24 id., 9; Bailey *v.* Buell, 59 Barb., 158; Bennet *v.* Buffalo, 17 N. Y., 383; Clark *v.* Norton, 49 id., 243; Westfall *v.* Preston, 49 Barb., 349; Dorwin *v.* Strickland, 57 N. Y., 492. But where one is assessed in the wrong town by his own request, he cannot maintain an action against the assessors for so assessing him. Pease *v.* Whitney, 8 Mass., 93.

[1] As where a school tax is levied which was voted at a meeting not legally called: Bussey *v.* Leavitt, 12 Me., 378; Baldwin *v.* McClinch, 1 id., 102; Colby *v.* Russell, 3 id., 227; Mussy *v.* White, 3 id., 290; Gardiner *v.* Gardiner, 5 id., 133; Paine *v.* Ross, 5 id., 400; Johnson *v.* Goodrich, 15 id., 29; Barnard *v.* Argyle, 20 id., 296; Kellar *v.* Savage, 20 id., 199; Withrington *v.* Eveleth, 7 Pick, 106; Little *v.* Merrill, 10 id., 543. A tax list made out before a tax is voted is void. Mead *v.* Gale, 4 Hill, 109; S. C., 2 Denio, 232. This was a case in which a tax had been voted and the vote afterwards repealed, and at a later meeting the repealing vote itself repealed. *Held*, that the tax was to be regarded as voted at the date of the last meeting. But assessors are not bound to go behind the records to see that a meeting was properly called. Saxton *v.* Nimms, 14 Mass., 315; Libby *v.* Burnham, 15 id., 144.

[2] Libby *v.* Burnham, 15 Mass., 144; Joyner *v.* School District, 3 Cush., 567; Drew *v.* Davis, 10 Vt., 506; Grafton Bank *v.* Kimball, 20 N. H., 107.

[3] Stetson *v.* Kempton, 13 Mass., 271; Drew *v.* Davis, 10 Vt., 506. The liability in such cases, however, would probably depend upon the position the assessor occupies under the statutes of his state relatively to the vote. If the assessor is himself to take from the township records the sums voted, and spread them upon the roll, or if they are certified to him in detail, so that he is necessarily informed before he is required to act officially what sums are legal and what illegal, it seems clear that he cannot fall back upon the vote for his protection. But if, on the other hand, some other officer is required to certify to him in gross the sums voted, and he is then to spread the amount on the roll, this certificate, if in due form, like process fair on its face, should constitute his sufficient protection, and he cannot be held bound to inquire for illegalities behind it. See Wall *v.* Trumbull, 16 Mich., 228; Parish *v.* Golden, 35 N. Y., 462.

[4] See Thames Manufacturing Co. *v.* Lathrop, 7 Conn., 550. In this case, it appeared that the law required the assessment list to be filed for inspection

through the cases is between an unlawful assumption of authority which has not been conferred, and a mistaken, erroneous or irregular exercise of authority actually possessed; the former will render any officer liable irrespective of the good faith of his action; for the latter he is, in general, not liable at all.[1] The law which governs the whole subject is summed up in few words in a leading case decided in Massachusetts: "When judicial officers, deriving their authority from the law, mistake or err in the execution of their authority, in a case clearly within their jurisdiction, which they have not exceeded, we know of no law declaring them trespassers *vi et armis*. If the law were otherwise respecting assessors, who, when chosen, are compellable to serve or pay a fine, hard indeed would be their case. But the same law must apply to them as to inferior judicial officers. If, there-

by the first of December. It was not filed until the twentieth of that month, but this was ten days before the meeting of the board of relief. *Held*, that the selectmen who took out a tax warrant on this list, by virtue of which the property of a person taxed was seized, were liable in trespass. See note on this case in 25 Vt., 27. In New York, where by statute, the last assessment roll of the township was to govern in levying a school tax, except as changes were made, of which notice was to be given to the parties affected before the assessment was completed, it was held, that the omission of this notice did not render the assessors liable as trespassers. Randall *v.* Smith, 1 Denio, 214, citing with approval Eaton *v.* Callendar, 11 Wend., 90, where trustees of a school district were held not liable, though they had erroneously added collection fees to the amount to be raised, and omitted to assess three individuals; the court holding, that the apportionment of the tax was to a certain extent a judicial act, and that, "though the trustees may err in point of law or in judgment, they should not be either civilly or criminally answerable, if their motives are pure." The court distinguish Alexander *v.* Hoyt, 7 Wend., 89, in which the school assessment was made from a town assessment not finished and afterwards changed, and where the trustees were held to be trespassers.

[1] In many cases, jurisdiction depends on questions of fact; as where, for instance, the question is one of residence. But these questions the assessor must decide correctly at his peril; he cannot, by his own error, obtain a jurisdiction which the law has not conferred. Dorwin *v.* Strickland, 57 N. Y., 492. Where the assessor increased the valuation of a person's property, after the list had passed beyond his control, he was held liable. Bristol Manufacturing Co. *v.* Gridley, 28 Conn., 201. That an irregular assessment affords no cause of action against assessors, see Sanford *v.* Dick, 15 Conn., 447; Sprague *v.* Bailey, 19 Pick., 436. National banks, not being taxable as such by the states, are not within the jurisdiction of assessors, who are liable if they assess them. National Bank of Chemung *v.* Elmira, 53 N. Y., 49, citing many cases.

fore, the persons acting as assessors have been duly chosen and qualified to execute that office, if the sum assessed has been legally ordered to be assessed, if the assessment be made and the warrant of collection be issued by them or a major part of them, in due form of law, if the poll and estate of the party complaining of the assessment be legally taxable, he cannot, in our opinion, maintain an action against them as trespassers *vi et armis* for any error or mistake of theirs in the exercise of their discretion."[1]

It has been made a question whether these principles should apply to a case where these officers are accused of having been actuated by malice, and where the impelling motive has been to inflict injury upon the parties assessed. It has already been seen that assessments, purposely made excessive through evil motive, may be reached and corrected in equity. But to subject every tax officer to the necessity of being compelled to justify his motives to the satisfaction of others, under a penalty of personal responsibility, is perhaps to go beyond what is necessary to the protection of tax payers; and in matters depending on judgment of values, would be so dangerous to the officers that it is doubtful if sound policy could sanction it. In a leading case in New York it is declared that the question of motive is not to be raised in a suit against assessors who have kept within their jurisdiction. "The assessors," it is said, "were judges acting clearly within the scope and limit of their authority. They were not volunteers, but the duty was imperative and compulsory; and acting, as they did, in the performance of a public duty, in its nature judicial, they were not liable to an action, however erroneous or wrongful their determination may have been. This case might be disposed of on narrow ground, for there was no evidence to justify the conclusion that the defendants acted maliciously in fixing the value of the property of the plaintiff, or of any one else; and surely it will not be pretended they were liable for a mere error of judgment. But I prefer to place the decision on the broad ground, that no public officer is responsible, in a civil suit, for a judicial determination, however erroneous it may be, and however malicious the motive which produced it. Such acts, when corrupt, may be punished criminally, but the law will not allow

[1] *Parsons*, Ch. J., in Dillingham *v.* Snow, 5 Mass., 559.

malice and corruption to be charged in a civil suit against such an officer, for what he does in the performance of a judicial duty. The rule extends to judges from the highest to the lowest; to jurors, and to all public officers, whatever name they may bear, in the exercise of judicial power. It of course applies only where the judge or officer had jurisdiction of the particular case, and was authorized to determine it. If he transcends the limits of his authority, he necessarily ceases, in the particular case, to act as a judge, and is responsible for all consequences. But with these limitations, the principle of irresponsibility, so far as respects a civil remedy, is as old as the common law itself."[1]

Action against supervisors. The supervisors of townships in some states act in several capacities. They are members of the township board, and as such pass upon claims against the township; they meet in convention and constitute the county board which audits the county claims and votes the county taxes, and perhaps they act as assessors also, and issue process for the collection of the taxes after they have been properly spread upon the roll. Thus their action in each of these capacities may affect the tax payer; but the cases must be rare in which the party aggrieved could go back of the supervisor's action as assessor, if that was not in itself illegal, and maintain an action against him as supervisor for something done in another capacity. Thus, it has been held in New York that supervisors who issue a tax warrant, having jurisdiction to do so, are not liable in trespass for having included in the levy a sum improperly allowed by them to a county officer.[2] The like decision has been made in Michigan, where a supervisor was sued for placing upon the roll allowances unlawfully made by the township board of which he was a member.[3] But in Michigan, the supervisor who undertakes to justify the issuing of a tax warrant, does not make out his justification by proving his official character merely; he must show

[1] *Beardsley*, J., in Weaver *v.* Devendorf, 3 Denio, 117, 120. Compare Baker *v.* State, 27 Ind., 485; Walker *v.* Hallock, 32 id., 239; Gregory *v.* Brooks, 37 Conn., 365; Burton *v.* Fulton, 49 Penn. St., 151; Pike *v.* Megoun, 44 Mo., 491, 497; Auditor *v.* Atchison, etc., R. R. Co., 6 Kans., 500.

[2] Parish *v.* Golden, 35 N. Y., 462.

[3] Wall *v.* Trumbull, 16 Mich., 228. See Smith *v.* Crittenden, id., 152; Cunningham *v.* Mitchell, 67 Penn. St., 78.

that the sums to be levied have been certified to him by the competent authorities, and that the assessment roll has come to him from the board of supervisors as provided by law. These are prerequisites to his jurisdiction to issue any tax warrant.[1] And if a tax is assessed on lands as a personal charge against a resident, the description on the roll must be sufficient to identify the land; and if not, that particular assessment will be void and its enforcement will render him liable.[2] In Iowa, township trustees are held not liable for a refusal to issue a certificate of compliance with the conditions upon which a tax has been voted in aid of a corporation, unless they act willfully and corruptly.[3]

Resisting collection. It is stated on a preceding page that if a tax is unlawful, the person taxed may resist the exaction instead of submitting to it and bringing suit afterwards. This is only a statement of a general principle of the common law, which recognizes the individual liberty of every person to that extent. Where, however, the tax warrant on its face discloses no illegality, it has been held that resistance to the officer is not permitted, notwithstanding illegalities lie back of it; and it can seldom be advisable or even safe to do otherwise than submit to the process and seek the proper remedy afterwards. But where lands are sold, the peaceful and quiet remedy which consists in retaining possession, and leaving the purchaser to resort to his suit at law, is usually all that is necessary, and under the statutes of limitation will, after a time, become completely effectual, unless the purchaser resorts to the courts for a remedy on his own behalf.[4]

[1] Clark *v.* Axford, 5 Mich., 182.

[2] Atwell *v.* Zeluff, 26 Mich., 118.

[3] Muscatine Western R. R. Co. *v.* Horton, 38 Iowa, 33.

[4] We have referred, on a preceding page, to the decisions in Wisconsin, that the holder of a tax deed of lands is to be considered constructively in possession, where the land is unoccupied. The rule was laid down in Sydnor *v.* Palmer, 29 Wis., 226, that, under statutes of limitations, "evidence of adverse possession is always to be strictly construed, and every presumption is to be made in favor of the true owner." In Wilson *v.* Henry, 35 Wis., 241, 245, this rule is explained as applying to the holder of the tax title when he claims by constructive possession, and the "true owner" is in such case to be regarded as the original owner, notwithstanding any technical defects that may be found in his claim of title. This just and reasonable rule was applied to the facts of the particular case in the following language: "The plaintiff seeks

Liability of collector. In general, any mere ministerial officer to whom process is issued, which proceeds from an officer, board or other body having authority to issue process of that nature, which process is legal in form and contains nothing on its

to cut off the remedy and destroy the right of the true owner, and to show an indefeasible title in himself, by virtue of an adverse constructive possession of the land for three years next after the recording of his tax deed. Within the rule, the evidence of such adverse constructive possession must be strictly construed, and the defendant may avoid the bar and defeat the right asserted by the plaintiff on this ground, by showing any actual occupation and use of the premises under his title for any portion of the three years so required to perfect the title of the plaintiff, or to debar the remedy of the defendant. This principle has already been settled by this court in the case of Lewis *v.* Disher, 32 Wis., 504, and it is needless to add to the discussion which will there be found. The court there say: 'In order that the claimant by tax deed may assert or acquire title to unoccupied land in that way, or by lapse of time under the statute, it must appear that the land remained and was continuously unoccupied for the whole period during which the statute was running. Any intervention and actual occupancy during the time by the former owner, or any person for him, disengages the bar of the statute, and relieves the former owner from the conclusive effect which would otherwise be given to the tax deed.' But, as will be seen from the same decision, and others by this court, with which counsel are familiar, the effect of an actual possession taken and held by the former owner, during the whole or any considerable portion of the three years, is not only to disengage the bar of the statute, when resorted to in favor of the grantee by tax deed, but also to create a bar against him, and in favor of the title of such former owner. It operates in favor of the true or former owner thus entering and holding, to cut off the remedy of the grantee by tax deed, and to annul his title, whatever it may have been. In view of these well settled principles, this court is of opinion that it was error for the court below to reject the offer of proofs made by the defendants on the trial." The offer is recited, and consisted in substance of a proposal to show that persons mined for lead on the land in controversy during what was called the mining season, in the winter, recognizing the defendant's right, and paying rent to him; also that a custom exists where this land is situate, making it obligatory upon the land owner to hold mineral diggings for the miner operating them during the summer season, though the miner does not work during such summer season upon such diggings. And it is then added: "The time included in the foregoing offer embraced the whole period of the three years from and after the recording of the plaintiff's tax deed; and the facts, if established, would divest the plaintiff of all constructive possession during the same period. They would not only disprove and destroy his constructive possession, but they would turn the statute of limitation against him by showing the actual possession and occupancy of the former owner, thus cutting off any title acquired under the tax deed, unless the plaintiff saw fit to bring his action to recover the possession within the three years. The offer, if proved

face to notify or fairly apprise him that it is issued without authority, will be protected in serving it, even though, in fact, it was issued without authority of law. This is a rule, not only essential to the protection of such officers, but absolutely required also for the due dispatch of public business.[1] It would seem to be impolitic in a very high degree to compel such an officer to ascertain, at his peril, the illegalities that might lie back of a pro-

as made, would have shown that the plaintiff was thus under the necessity of bringing his action, and that, not having done so, he had lost his title, if any, acquired by the tax deed, and could not maintain this action, which was not instituted until after the expiration of the three years. It would have sustained the plea or answer of the statute of limitations made by the defendants, so as to protect them and the title under which they claim against the present action, and the right now set up by the plaintiff."

[1] Ford *v.* Clough, 8 Me., 334; Kellar *v.* Savage, 20 id., 199; Tremont *v.* Clark, 33 id., 482; State *v.* McNally, 34 id., 210; Caldwell *v.* Hawkins, 40 id., 526; Bethel *v.* Mason, 55 id., 501; Judkins *v.* Reed, 48 id., 386; Nowell *v.* Tripp, 61 id., 426; Savacool *v.* Boughton, 5 Wend., 171; McGuinty *v.* Herrick, id., 240, 243; Wilcox *v.* Smith, id., 231; Alexander *v.* Hoyt, 7 id., 89; Beach *v.* Furman, 9 Johns., 228; Warner *v.* Shed, 10 id., 138; Reynolds *v.* Moore, 9 Wend., 35, 36; Coon *v.* Congden, 12 id., 496, 499; Bennett *v.* Burch, 1 Denio, 141; Patchin *v.* Ritter, 27 Barb, 34; Webber *v.* Gray, 24 Wend., 485; Abbott *v.* Yost, 2 Denio, 86; Dunlap *v.* Hunting, id., 643; Cornell *v.* Barnes, 7 Hill, 35; People *v.* Warren, 5 id., 440; Sheldon *v.* Van Buskirk, 2 N. Y., 473; Chegaray *v.* Jenkins, 5 N. Y., 376; Turner *v.* Franklin, 29 Mo., 285; Glascow *v.* Rouse, 43 id., 479; St. Louis Building, etc., Ass'n *v.* Lightner, 47 id., 393; State *v.* Dulle, 48 id., 282; Walden *v.* Dudley, 49 id., 419; Holden *v.* Eaton, 8 Pick., 436; Colman *v.* Anderson, 10 Mass., 105; Sprague *v.* Bailey, 19 Pick., 436; Upton *v.* Holden, 5 Met., 360; Lincoln *v.* Worcester, 8 Cush., 55; Aldrich *v.* Aldrich, 8 Met., 102; Hays *v.* Drake, 6 Gray, 387; Howard *v.* Proctor, 7 id., 128; Williamstown *v.* Willis, 15 id., 427; Cheever *v.* Merritt, 5 Allen, 563; Underwood *v.* Robinson, 106 Mass., 296; Brainerd *v.* Head, 15 La. An., 489; Blanchard *v.* Goss, 2 N. H., 491; Henry *v.* Sargent, 13 id., 321; State *v.* Weed, 21 id., 262; Rice *v.* Wadsworth, 27 id., 104; Kenniston *v.* Little, 30 id., 318; Kelley *v.* Noyes, 43 id., 209; Moore *v.* Alleghany City, 18 Penn. St., 55; Billings *v.* Russell, 23 id., 189; Dennis *v.* Shaw, 5 Gilm., 405; Hill *v.* Figley 25 Ill., 156; Allen *v.* Scott, 13 id., 80; State *v.* Jervey, 4 Strobh., 304; Cunningham *v.* Mitchell, 67 Penn. St., 78; Loomis *v.* Spencer, 1 Ohio, N. S., 153; Thames Manuf'g Co. *v.* Lathrop, 7 Conn., 550; Watson *v.* Watson, 9 id., 140; Neth *v.* Crofut, 30 id., 580; Grumon *v.* Raymond, 1 id., 40; Prince *v.* Thomas, 11 id., 472; Burton *v.* Fulton, 49 Penn. St., 151; McLean *v.* Cook, 23 Wis., 364; Noland *v.* Busby, 28 Ind., 154; Le Roy *v.* East Saginaw City Railway Co., 18 Mich., 233; Lott *v.* Hubbard, 44 Ala., 593; State *v.* Lutz, 65 N. C., 503; Gore *v.* Martin, 66 id., 371; Bird *v.* Perkins, Sup. Ct. Mich., Oct. Term, 1875; Erskine *v.* Hohnbach, 14 Wall., 613.

cess apparently legal, and it might be justly expected to force prudent men to decline the office altogether, or to proceed with such hesitation and circumspection as sometimes to render the process of little or no avail.[1] The general rule is, that such an officer is legally protected against any illegalities, except those committed by himself, and it is not illegal for him to execute process which comes to him as a ministerial officer, from other officers whose action he has no authority to revise or review.[2] He is consequently not liable to one who is unlawfully taxed, by reason of not residing within the district for which the tax is levied;[3] nor does the fact that sums are included in the warrant, which were never lawfully voted, render him liable.[4] And he is protected in executing his warrant by arrest, notwithstanding the person taxed has been discharged in bankruptcy.[5]

[1] In Vermont the ruling is different, and a treasurer sued in trespass, for taking goods on a warrant of distress, for taxes, cannot rely on a valid warrant, but must show that all the previous proceedings were legal. "It has never been considered in this state that the tax bill and warrant were of themselves any sufficient justification to the officer. Neither the vote of the town, nor the assessment of the tax by the selectmen, is in the nature of the proceedings of a court, either of general or special jurisdiction. The legality of all the proceedings must be shown by the collector." *Redfield*, J., in Collamer *v.* Drury, 16 Vt., 574, 578. To the same point are Downing *v.* Roberts, 21 Vt., 441; Hathaway *v.* Goodrich, 5 id., 65; Spear *v.* Tilson, 24 id., 420; Shaw *v.* Peckett, 25 id., 423. See also Downer *v.* Woodbury, 19 id., 329; Wheelock *v.* Archer, 26 id., 380. But the rule seems to be the reverse of this in that state, when suit is brought for taxes, for then it is held the burden is upon the defendant to impeach the regularity and validity of the list. Macomber *v.* Center, 44 Vt., 235, citing Willson *v.* Seavey, 38 id., 221.

[2] Erskine *v.* Hohnbach, 14 Wall., 613: Nowell *v.* Tripp, 61 Me., 426; S. C., 14 Am. Rep., 572; Moore *v.* Alleghany City, 18 Penn. St., 55.

[3] Savacool *v.* Boughton, 5 Wend., 171; Nowell *v.* Tripp, 61 Me., 426; S. C., 14 Am. Rep., 572; Holden *v.* Eaton, 8 Pick., 436.

[4] Lincoln *v.* Worcester, 8 Cush., 55; Abbott *v.* Yost, 2 Denio, 86.

[5] Aldrich *v.* Aldrich, 8 Met., 102; Wilmarth *v.* Burt, 7 id., 257. The collector having a warrant from an authority of competent jurisdiction to issue it, cannot inquire into the precedent steps. Cunningham *v.* Mitchell, 67 Penn. St., 78. He may even officially receive voluntary payments where his authority is defective. State *v.* Woodside, 8 Ired., 104; Same *v.* Same, 9 id., 496; Johnson *v.* Goodridge, 15 Me., 29; Orono *v.* Wedgewood, 44 id., 49; Trescott *v.* Moan, 50 id., 347; Sandwich *v.* Fish, 2 Gray, 298; Cheshire *v.* Howland, 13 id., 321; Williamstown *v.* Willis, 15 id., 427. Compare Waters *v.* State, 1 Gill, 302; O'Neal *v.* School Commissioners, 27 Md., 227; Commonwealth *v.*

It is not easy to lay down any general rule as to what will constitute a defect in the process which should put the collector on his guard. Where the law required the assessment roll to be attached to the warrant, and the certificate attached thereto was not in accordance with the law, it was *held*, that the warrant could not be said to be fair on its face, and the collector was liable for executing it.[1] The same ruling was made where the warrant showed on its face that a certain tax included in it could not lawfully have been placed in the list for that year.[2] And so where the affidavit which was required to be attached to the roll after the time for reviewing the assessments had expired, appeared to be made prematurely.[3] So where the warrant was issued by a justice of the peace, where, by law, it should have been issued by the supervisors.[4] But mere clerical errors may be overlooked in any case.[5]

Philadelphia, 27 Penn. St., 497; Moore *v.* Alleghany City, 18 id., 55. If the collector's warrant was sufficient when property is seized under it, a subsequent alteration, by the magistrate who signed it, for the purpose of making it a warrant for another tax, will not invalidate the collector's action. Goodwin *v.* Perkins, 39 Vt., 598.

[1] Van Rensselaer *v.* Witbeck, 7 N. Y., 517.

[2] Eames *v.* Johnson, 4 Allen, 382. So the collector was held liable in collecting a personal tax from a bank which, by law, was taxable on its realty only. American Bank *v.* Mumford, 4 R. I., 478. Compare National Bank of Chemung *v.* Elmira, 53 N. Y., 49, and cases cited. That, however, was a suit against the town after the money had been paid over.

[3] Westfall *v.* Preston, 49 N. Y., 349. See, also, National Bank of Chemung *v.* Elmira, 53 id., 49; Gale *v.* Mead, 4 Hill, 109.

[4] Chalker *v.* Ives, 55 Penn. St., 81. And see Hilbish *v.* Hower, 58 id., 93.

[5] Process issued to one as "constable and collector" will be sufficient, if in fact he was authorized to act as collector when it was issued to him. Hays *v.* Drake, 6 Gray, 387. And a collector is not a trespasser in seizing property by virtue of two warrants, if either of them is sufficient. Id. A warrant attached to a tax list, and signed by the supervisors, was *held* to be fair on its face, though they failed to add the official title to their names. Sheldon *v.* Van Buskirk, 2 N. Y., 473. A warrant issued in pursuance of law for the collection of a tax from one who has removed from the township, is sufficient, though it fails to recite the fact of removal. Cheever *v.* Merritt, 5 Allen, 563. And see Sherman *v.* Torrey, 99 Mass., 472; Hubbard *v.* Garfield, 102 id., 72. So it will protect the officer where the only defect is a failure to insert the direction to sell distrained goods within seven days, according to law. King *v.* Whitcomb, 1 Met., 328. And for other cases, where questions of validity

But though a valid process will protect an officer against personal responsibility, it will not enable him to build up a title to property seized by virtue of it, either general or special. While, therefore, he might have a perfect defense to a suit brought against him in trespass, for seizing property, he might not successfully defend an action of replevin, or any other action in which the legal title to the property, or the legal right to possession, was the question at issue. In any such action it would not be sufficient for him that the process under which he acted appeared to be valid on its face, but it should be valid in fact.[1] This is an important distinction, which is sometimes overlooked.

It has been decided that if taxes are collected by color of law, and actually paid over by the collector according to the command of his warrant, that officer is not liable for the amount at the suit of the tax payer, though it turn out that the authority under which he acted was void for unconstitutionality or other reason.[2] This seems but reasonable, since the tax payer still has his remedy, as will be seen further on.

If the collector levies distress for a tax and afterwards abuses his authority, the warrant becomes no protection to him, and he is held to be a trespasser *ab initio*. This rule has been applied in one case where the collector sold the property at half its value within two hours after seizure, and without giving public notice of the time and place of sale.[3] It has been applied also where the collector, after a sale on which he had received a surplus, failed to render to the owner an account in writing of the sale and charges, as required by the statute under which the sale was made.[4]

of process have been raised, see Mussey *v.* White, 3 Me., 290; Bachelder *v.* Thompson, 41 Me., 539; Stephens *v.* Wilkins, 6 Penn. St., 260; Bank of Chenango *v.* Brown, 26 N. Y., 467; Barnard *v.* Graves, 13 Met., 85. And see *ante*, pp 304, 305.

[1] Earl *v.* Camp, 16 Wend., 562; Beach *v.* Botsford, 2 Doug. (Mich.), 199; Le Roy *v.* East Saginaw, 18 Mich., 233.

[2] Dickens *v.* Jones, 6 Yerg., 483; Crutchfield *v.* Wood, 16 Ala., 702; Lewis County *v.* Tate, 10 Mo., 650. In Wood *v.* Stirman, 37 Texas, 584, however, it was decided that where a county treasurer collects taxes without authority of law, he alone is liable, and not his sureties or the county, though the money may have been actually paid in to the county treasury, and disbursed as other county funds.

[3] Blake *v.* Johnson, 1 N. H., 91.

[4] Blanchard *v.* Dow, 32 Me., 557.

And the collector is liable as a trespasser *ab initio*, if he keeps the distress until after the time limited by law for making sale, and then sells it;[1] or if, having sold enough to satisfy the tax, he proceeds to sell more.[2]

The rules which have been given apply to collectors under the internal revenue laws of the United States, who are protected in like manner in the collection of taxes committed to them by lists fair on their face.[3] The case of the collector of customs duties is

[1] Pierce *v.* Benjamin, 14 Pick., 356, 360, citing Purrington *v.* Loring, 7 Mass., 388; Nelson *v.* Merriam, 4 Pick., 249. See to the same effect Brackett *v.* Vining, 49 Me., 356; *contra*, Ordway *v.* Ferrin, 3 N. H., 69. Where a collector of taxes, after seizing property as a distress and advertising it for sale, neglected to sell it at the time appointed, but afterwards again advertised it the requisite period, and sold it upon such new advertisement: *Held*, that neither the neglect to sell at the appointed time, nor the subsequent sale, could make him a trespasser *ab initio*. Souhegan Nail, etc., Factory *v.* McConike, 7 N. H., 309.

[2] Williamson *v.* Dow, 32 Me., 559. But in such a case he is trespasser only as to the excess. Leckins *v.* Goodale, 61 Me., 400; S. C., 14 Am. Rep., 568. Compare Polk *v.* Rose, 25 Md., 153. If an officer under two rate bills, one valid and the other invalid, seizes no more property than he is authorized to by virtue of the valid process, and sells the same for more than enough to satisfy the valid process, and then appropriates the excess to satisfy the invalid process, such misapplication does not render the officer a trespasser *ab initio*. To make him a trespasser *ab initio*, the wrongful act must be done to the property taken, not to the fund realized from a legal sale. Wilson *v.* Seavey, 38 Vt., 221, 230. For the law as to what will render one a trespasser *ab initio*, see the Six Carpenters' Case, 8 Coke, 290; S. C., 1 Smith's Leading Cases, 162 and notes; Van Brundt *v.* Schenck, 11 Johns., 377; S. C., 13 Johns., 413. If one whose property is unlawfully seized and sold by the collector causes it to be bid in for himself and appropriates it to his own use, he can recover in an action against the collector only what he paid for the property on the sale; as that was the extent of his injury. Hurlburt *v.* Green, 41 Vt., 490.

[3] Erskine *v.* Hohnbach, 14 Wall., 613, 616. In this case Mr. *Justice Field* states the rule of protection very clearly and concisely as follows: "Whatever may have been the conflict at one time in the adjudged cases, as to the extent of protection afforded to ministerial officers, acting in obedience to process or orders issued to them by tribunals or officers invested by law with authority to pass upon and determine particular facts, and render judgment thereon, it is well settled now that if the officer or tribunal possess jurisdiction over the subject matter upon which judgment is passed, with power to issue an order or process for the enforcement of such judgment, and the order issued thereon to the ministerial officer is regular on its face, showing no departure from the law, or defect of jurisdiction over the person or property affected, then, and in such case, the order or process will give full and entire

different. He has no tax warrant or other process to protect him, and he proceeds at his peril in demanding and receiving what he claims to be demandable as duties. If he collects illegal or excessive duties, and they are paid under protest, he is liable to the party paying for the amount;[1] but he is excused if he pays over the moneys before protest is made.[2]

Liability of town, county, etc. The town, village, city or county for which a tax has been levied and collected, may also, under some circumstances, be liable to an action at the suit of parties from whom the tax has been exacted. The authorities warrant us in specifying the following as the conditions on which any such action may be maintained:

1. The tax must have been illegal and void, and not merely irregular.

2. It must have been paid under compulsion or the legal equivalent.

3. It must have been paid over by the collecting officer, and have been received to the use of the municipality.

And to these should perhaps be added:

4. The party must not have elected to proceed in any remedy he may have had against the assessor or collector.[3]

For a merely irregular assessment, it has already been stated in several places, the remedy of the party is that which the statute may give him. Irregularities do not make a tax void, nor commonly do they attach to it any circumstance of inequality or injus-

protection to the ministerial officer in its regular enforcement against any prosecution which the party aggrieved thereby may institute against him, although serious errors may have been committed by the officer or tribunal in reaching the conclusion or judgment upon which the order or process is issued:" citing Savacool *v.* Boughton, 5 Wend., 170; Earl *v.* Camp, 16 Wend., 563; Chegaray *v.* Jenkins, 5 N. Y., 376; Sprague *v.* Burchard, 1 Wis., 457. To the same effect is Haffin *v.* Mason, 15 Wall., 671. And see Cutting *v.* Gilbert, 5 Blatch., 259; Nelson *v.* Carman, id., 511; Braun *v.* Sauerwein, 10 Wall., 218; The Collector *v.* Hubbard, 12 id., 1; Coblens *v.* Abel, 1 Woolw., 293.

[1] Elliott *v.* Swartwout, 10 Pet., 137; Maxwell v. Griswold, 10 How., 242.

[2] Elliott *v.* Swartwout, 10 Pet., 137.

[3] In Ware *v.* Percival, 61 Me., 391, the person illegally assessed sued the town and recovered satisfaction. Afterwards he sued the assessors, but his first revovery and satisfaction were held conclusive. See same case, 14 Am. Rep., 565.

tice. When a municipal corporation is sued for money collected and paid over to it as a tax, the idea on which the suit is predicated is, that the corporation has received that which, in justice, it ought not to retain. But the merely irregular action of the officers in their proceedings in assessing and levying the tax do not show injustice; there must be something further in the case which either exempts the party from the tax altogether, or which, because of illegality or inequality, deprived the officers of jurisdiction. Municipalities do not guaranty to their people correct action on the part of their officers, and if they did, no one would be entitled to rely upon the guaranty until he was injured. Irregular action does not necessarily injure the parties concerned; and where it does, the remedies given by review or appeal are supposed to afford full redress. Any further remedy must proceed upon the idea that the tax is void; a mere nullity.[1] That a tax voluntarily paid cannot be recovered back, has been held by the authorities with very few exceptions.[2] It is immaterial in such a case that the tax has been illegally laid, or even that the law under which it was laid was unconstitutional.[3]

[1] Wright *v.* Boston, 9 Cush., 233, 241, per *Shaw*, Ch. J., citing Preston *v.* Boston, 12 Pick., 7; Boston, etc., Glass Co. *v.* Boston, 4 Met., 181; Howe *v.* Boston, 7 Cush., 273; Lincoln *v.* Worcester, 8 id., 55; approved in Rogers *v.* Greenbush, 58 Me., 390. If an illegal state tax is collected and paid over, the state becomes trustee of the moneys for the persons paying it, and their remedy is to ask the law-making power to make the proper appropriation. Shoemaker *v.* Grant County, 36 Ind., 175. If the state has any auditing board competent to allow such claims, their power might be adequate to the case. When the town collector collects a state, county and town tax levied on property not taxable, if the town is sued, the recovery will be limited to what was paid over to it for its own use, and will not embrace the state and county taxes. Vermont Central R. R. Co. *v.* Burlington, 28 Vt., 193. See, also, Spear *v.* Braintree, 24 id., 414; Slack *v.* Norwich, 32 id., 818; Matheson *v.* Mazomanie, 20 Wis., 191.

[2] Smith *v.* Readfield, 27 Me., 145; New York, etc., R. R. Co. *v.* Marsh, 12 N. Y., 308; Walker *v.* St. Louis, 15 Mo., 563; Christy's Administrators *v.* St. Louis, 20 id., 143; Hospital *v.* Philadelphia County, 24 Penn. St., 229; Phillips *v.* Jefferson County, 5 Kans., 412; Wabaunsee County *v.* Walker, 8 id., 431; Corkle *v.* Maxwell, 3 Blatch., 413; Elliott *v.* Swartwout, 10 Pet., 137.

[3] Taylor *v.* Board of Health, 31 Penn. St., 73; Barrett *v.* Cambridge, 10 Allen, 48. And see Forbes *v.* Appleton, 5 Cush., 115. Money paid to secure a license, issued on the petition of the party, is voluntarily paid, and cannot be recovered back, even though no power existed to require it. Mays *v.* Cincinnati, 1 Ohio,

The principle is an ancient one in the common law, and is of general application. Every man is supposed to know the law; and if he voluntarily makes a payment which the law would not compel him to make, he cannot afterwards assign his ignorance of the law as the reason why the state should furnish him with legal remedies to recover it back. Especially is this the case when the officer receiving the money, who is chargeable with no more knowledge of the law than the party making payment, is not put on his guard by any warning or protest, and the money is paid over to the use of the public in apparent acquiescence in the justice of the exaction. Mistake of fact there cannot well be in such a case; as the illegalities which render such a demand a nullity must appear from the records, and the taxpayer is just as much bound to inform himself what the records show or do not show, as are the public authorities. The rule of law is a rule of public policy also; it is a rule of quiet as well as of good faith, and precludes the courts being occupied in undoing the arrangements of parties which they have voluntarily made, and into which they have not been drawn by fraud or accident, or by any excusable ignorance of their legal rights and liabilities.[1]

N. S., 268, citing Brisbane *v.* Dacres, 5 Taunt., 143; Elliott *v.* Swartwout, 10 Pet., 150; Clark *v.* Dutcher, 9 Cow., 674; Robinson *v.* Charleston, 4 Rich., 317; Smith *v.* Readfield, 27 Me., 145. To the same effect is Ligonier *v.* Ackerman, 46 Ind., 552. In California it is held that a tax imposed by city ordinance, without authority of law, may be recovered back, even though paid without protest. Galveston *v.* Snyder, 39 Texas. 236, citing Marshall *v.* Snediker, 25 id., 460; Baker *v.* Panola County, 30 id., 86.

[1] Parties who have acquiesced in a tax for eleven years, *held* to have yielded forever their right to question the law which imposed it. Commonwealth *v.* Philadelphia, 27 Penn. St., 497. In Kentucky it has been held that where a party pays taxes illegally assessed without knowledge of the illegality, he may recover back, though he made no protest. Underwood *v.* Brockman, 4 Dana, 309; Ray *v.* Bank of Kentucky, 3 B. Monr., 510; Louisville *v.* Zanone, 1 Met. (Ky.), 151; Covington *v.* Powell, 2 id., 226. But in Iowa it has been held that a tax, paid under ignorance that the law under which it was levied was invalid, could not on that ground be recovered back. Kraft *v.* Keokuk, 14 Iowa, 86; Espy *v.* Fort Madison, id., 226. And see Lester *v.* Baltimore, 29 Md., 415. A competent authority, having jurisdiction, assessed the plaintiffs for personal property. They complained, and appealed to the courts. Before the court of appeals rendered a final decision, the officer having charge of the collection of taxes gave notice to the plaintiffs, requiring payment, and stating that if the tax was not paid, a warrant would issue to collect the same.

All payments of taxes are supposed to be voluntary which are not made under protest or under the apparent compulsion of legal process.[1] When a protest is relied upon, nothing very formal is requisite; "taxes illegally assessed may always be recovered back, if the collector understands from the payer that the tax is regarded as illegal, and that suit will be instituted to compel the refunding." [2]

A payment made to release goods from seizure is a payment on compulsion,[3] and so is payment after threat of distress of

Thereupon the plaintiffs paid the tax. There being no warrant, seizure, or threatened seizure, payment of money to free the property from the possession of another, or ignorance of facts, it was *held*, that it was a purely voluntary payment, and no action would lie to recover back the same. Union Bank *v.* New York, 51 Barb., 159.

[1] Where a town offers a discount to those who make payment promptly, a payment made to obtain this discount has been held to be voluntary, though made under protest. Lee *v.* Templeton, 13 Gray, 476. In Connecticut it has been decided that if one's land is sold for a tax after protest, and he buys it in, this purchase must be regarded as a voluntary payment, and will give him no right of action. Sheldon *v.* School District, 24 Conn., 88. In Taylor *v.* Board of Health, 31 Penn. St., 73, taxes levied under an unconstitutional law had been demanded and paid for a series of years, and the law being then held void, suit was brought to recover back. The taxes were in the shape of head money on immigrants, and were collected of consignees of ships, without process. *Lowrie*, J.: "If the matter complained of here was a wrong, then the state did it in the only way a state can do a wrong — by its public functionaries. The suit is not against the state, and could not be; but it is against the executive officer of the state; for in this matter the board of health was nothing else. A state imposes certain taxes, and orders a certain officer to collect them and apply them in a certain way, and if he does so, how can the state compel him to refund them to the taxpayer? Will it be said that in this case the order was void, and therefore the officer acted on his own authority and at his own risk? The plaintiff cannot well say that, seeing that he paid voluntarily, and without attempting to deny the duty or to warn the officer that he must proceed at his own risk. Had he given such warning, the validity of the tax would have been tested by the superior officers of the collector. He paid without dispute, and thus assented to the collection of the tax for public purposes, and of course, to the application of it; and he has no shadow of equity against the collecting functionary." In Busby *v.* Noland, 39 Ind., 234, it is said that one who pays without protest is estopped from disputing the legality of the tax.

[2] *Chase*, Ch. J., in Erskine *v.* Van Arsdale, 15 Wall., 75, 77.

[3] Briggs *v.* Lewiston, 29 Me., 472. But it was held in this case that the costs paid were not recoverable back. And see Dow *v.* Sudbury, 5 Met., 73; Shaw

goods;[1] and much more would be the satisfaction of the demand by actual sale of goods distrained;[2] and it seems that if the officer calls upon the person taxed, and "demands a sum of money under a warrant directing him to enforce it, the party of whom he demands it may fairly assume that if he seeks to act under the warrant at all, he will make it effectual. The demand itself is equivalent to a service of the writ on the person. Any payment is to be regarded as involuntary, which is made under a claim involving the use of force as an alternative; as the party of whom it is demanded cannot be compelled or expected to await actual force, and cannot be held to expect that an officer will desist after making a demand. The exhibition of a warrant directing forcible proceedings, and the receipt of money thereon, will be in such case equivalent to actual compulsion."[3]

The proper action against a corporation, in these cases, is assumpsit for money had and received; the liability not attaching

v. Becket, 7 Cush., 442; though if the suit were brought against the officers in a proper case, it would be otherwise. Shaw *v.* Becket, *supra.*

[1] Grim *v.* School District, 57 Penn. St., 433, citing Henry *v.* Horstick, 9 Watts, 414; Caldwell *v.* Moore, 11 Penn. St., 60; Allentown *v.* Saeger, 20 id., 421. And see Guy *v.* Washburn, 23 Cal., 111. A payment is not voluntary where the payer lays down money, but forbids the collector to take it. Bellinger *v.* Gray, 51 N. Y., 610. And see Greenabaum *v.* King, 4 Kans., 332.

[2] Hurley *v.* Texas, 20 Wis., 634.

[3] *Campbell*, J., in Atwell *v.* Zeluff, 26 Mich., 118, citing Boston, etc., Glass Co. *v.* Boston, 4 Met., 181. And see Amesbury, etc., Manuf'g Co. *v.* Amesbury, 17 Mass., 461; Preston *v.* Boston, 12 Pick., 7; George *v.* School District, 6 Met., 497; Joyner *v.* School District, 3 Cush., 567; Lincoln *v.* Worcester, 8 id., 55. Upon the right to maintain this action in general, see Henry *v.* Chester, 15 Vt., 460; Allen *v.* Burlington, 45 id., 202; Richards *v.* Stogsdell, 21 Ind., 74; Hubbard *v.* Brainard, 35 Conn., 563; Goddard *v.* Seymour, 30 Conn., 394; Callaway *v.* Milledgeville, 48 Geo., 309; Wilkey *v.* Pekin, 19 Ill., 160; Allentown *v.* Saeger 20 Penn. St., 421. The question what constitutes a voluntary payment was quite fully discussed, and the English authorities cited in Baker *v.* Cinncinnati, 11 Ohio, N. S., 534, and Taylor *v.* Board of Health, 31 Penn. St., 73. The latter case quotes particularly Fullan *v.* Down, 6 Esp., 26; Valpy *v.* Manly, 1 C. B., 594; Parker *v.* G. W. Railway Co., 7 M. & G., 253; Morgan *v.* Palmer, 2 B. & C., 729. In Carleton *v.* Ashburnham, 102 Mass., 348, the maxim that where two acts are done at the same time, the one shall take effect first which ought in strictness to have been done first, in order to give it effect (Claflin *v.* Thayer, 13 Gray, 459), was applied to a simultaneous payment of tax and delivery of a protest against its exaction.

until the money is paid over, and being then based upon the receipt of the money, and not upon the illegalities which preceded it.[1] The recovery will of course be limited to the money received; while in an action of trespass against the assessors, or trespass or trover against the collector, the party might recover such actual damages as he could show he had sustained.[2] It is possible that in the case of municipal corporations existing under special charters, the rule may be different. If such corporations, in the exercise of their legislative power, order the collection of an illegal tax, and process is issued to their officers for its collection, such officers may well be regarded as the agents of the corporation in the execution of the process, and the corporation held liable in

[1] A town is not liable for any mistake or misfeasance of the assessors or collector by means whereof one has been compelled to pay a tax wrongfully levied, the money not having been paid into the treasury of the town. These officers are not, in a legal sense, the agents of the town in its corporate capacity, in performing duties under the tax laws. Lorillard of Monroe, 12 Barb., 161, and 11 N. Y., 372. And see People *v.* Supervisors of Chenango, 11 N. Y., 563; Preston *v.* Boston, 12 Pick., 7; Chapman *v.* Brooklyn, 40 N. Y., 372; Newman *v.* Supervisors of Livingston, 45 N. Y., 676. When one is illegally assessed a tax afterwards abated, and is arrested by the collector, the payment by the town to the collector of the cost of the arrest is not such a ratification of the act as to render the town liable. Perley *v.* Georgetown, 7 Gray, 464. In a suit against a town to recover back an illegal tax, the town cannot defend by showing that the assessors were not legally elected. Sudbury *v.* Heard, 103 Mass., 543. On the other hand, it is no ground for recovering back a tax, that it was collected by one who was not collector *de jure* where he was such *de facto*. Williams *v.* School District, 21 Pick., 75. Where a tax has been collected and paid over to a city, and is afterwards set aside, suit will lie against the city to recover it back, even though the assessors were not appointed or controlled by the corporation. Bank of Commonwealth *v.* New York, 43 N. Y., 184. See also Chapman *v.* Brooklyn, 40 id., 372; Newman *v.* Supervisors of Livingston, 45 id., 676: compare Swift *v.* Poughkeepsie, 37 id., 511. If the tax is charged to the collector in a general settlement with him, this is equivalent to a payment into the treasury. County Commissioners *v.* Parker, 7 Minn., 267; Slack *v.* Norwich, 32 Vt., 819; Babcock *v.* Granville, 44 id., 325.

[2] Dow *v.* Sudbury, 5 Met., 73; Shaw *v.* Becket, 7 Cush., 442. And see Inglee *v.* Bosworth, 5 Pick., 498, per *Morton*, J.; Ware *v.* Percival, 61 Me., 391, per *Appleton*, Ch. J. If the proceedings in the collection of a tax are wholly void, and the person taxed neither has been nor can be disturbed in his possession, there is no ground for an action against the town, as the plaintiff has lost nothing. Such would be the case of a void sale of shares in a corporation. Noyes *v.* Haverhill, 11 Cush., 338.

tort if the officer resorts to compulsory measures for its enforcement.[1]

A demand is not necessary before bringing suit to recover back illegal taxes.[2] Interest is recoverable from the date of demand, but not before.[3] If only a part of the tax was illegal, the recovery will be limited to that part, if capable of being distinguished.[4]

[1] Howell *v.* Buffalo, 15 N. Y., 512. See Conrad *v.* Ithaca, 16 id., 158; West *v.* Brockport, id., 116, note; Bennett *v.* Buffalo, 17 id., 383; Sheldon *v.* Kalamazoo 24 Mich., 383.

[2] Look *v.* Industry, 51 Me., 375. See Pierce *v.* Benjamin, 14 Pick., 356.

[3] Boston, etc., Glass Co. *v.* Boston, 4 Met., 181. See Atwell *v.* Zeluff, 26 Mich., 118, 120.

[4] Torrey *v.* Millbury, 21 Pick., 64. See this case commented on in Lincoln *v.* Worcester, 8 Cush., 55. Whether cost of the proceedings to collect the tax can be recovered from the town, see Briggs *v.* Lewiston, 29 Me., 472; Dow *v.* Sudbury, 5 Met., 73; Shaw *v.* Becket, 7 Cush., 442. The following illustrations of illegal taxes recovered back may be cited: One who pays a personal and poll tax in a town of which he is not a resident may recover it back, if paid under the threat of a warrant, notwithstanding he was properly taxed for real estate in that town. This would not be regarded as a case of excessive taxation from which the party should appeal; the tax on the personalty and poll being wholly unauthorized. Preston *v.* Boston, 12 Pick., 7. Further, as to the recovery of a town, etc., by nonresidents unlawfully taxed within it, see Hathaway *v.* Addison, 48 Me., 440; Sumner *v.* Dorchester, 4 Pick., 361; Inglee *v.* Bosworth, 5 id., 498; Dow *v.* Sudbury, 5 Met., 73; Lee *v.* Boston, 2 Gray, 484; Dickinson *v.* Billings, 4 id., 42; People *v.* Supervisors of Chenango, 11 N. Y., 563. It has been held that if school taxes are levied unlawfully in a district by vote of the town, they may be recovered back of the town. Powers *v.* Sanford, 39 Me., 183. If a nonresident is taxed on personalty in a town where he does not reside, his right to recover it back cannot be affected by the fact of his having real estate in the town which was omitted from the list. Hathaway *v.* Addison, 48 Me., 440. Where an inhabitant is wrongfully taxed on property held in trust for him abroad, and has no property taxable to him, he may recover back of the town a tax assessed to and paid by him in respect of the property so held in trust. Dorr *v.* Boston, 6 Gray, 131, relying upon Preston *v.* Boston, 12 Pick., 7. When by law the personal estate of corporations is assessed in the shares of the company, but the assessors tax to the corporation both their personal and real estate, and they pay the taxes, they may recover back the tax on the personalty. Dunnel Manuf. Co. *v.* Pawtucket, 7 Gray, 277. For further cases, see Perry *v.* Dover, 12 Pick., 206; Joyner *v.* School District, 3 Cush., 567; Huckins *v.* Boston, 4 Cush., 543; Bacon *v.* School District, 97 Mass., 421; Mathewson *v.* Mazomanie, 20 Wis., 191; Hurley *v.* Texas, id., 634; James *v.* New Orleans, 19 La. An., 109; Hill *v.* Supervisors of Livingston, 12 N. Y., 52; Atwater *v.* Woodbridge, 6 Conn., 223; Adam *v.* Litchfield, 10 id., 127; Gillette *v.* Hartford, 31 id., 351;

A municipal corporation or body, for whose benefit taxes are enforced, does not warrant to the purchaser the title to property sold for their satisfaction, or the legality of the proceedings on which the sale was based. The purchaser in such a case buys at his own risk, and at his peril investigates the proceedings. This is a general rule in tax sales.[1]

A misapplication by a corporation, actual or threatened, of moneys collected by taxation, will give no right of action to an individual to recover his proportion of the tax. The money, when collected and paid to the corporation, belongs to it, and not to those from whom it has been collected. For misapplication there may be remedies on behalf of the public, and perhaps individual taxpayers may enjoin it; but a suit to recover the moneys must be based upon an individual right to it, which could not exist in the case.[2]

Remedy by replevin. In some cases, one whose goods have been seized for the satisfaction of a tax may recover them by writ of replevin. But to justify this process the tax must be absolutely void, and not merely unjust, excessive or irregular. The case must consequently be brought within the rules already laid down, regarding the invalidity of tax levies, or the suit in replevin must fail. The liability of this process to vexatious use is so considerable, that it has been deemed proper in some of the states, on grounds of public policy, to provide that replevin shall not lie for property distrained for taxes. Taking away this remedy would still leave to the party all the other remedies which are applicable to the case; and he may therefore still contest the

Nicodemus *v.* East Saginaw, 25 Mich., 456; Supervisors of Stephenson *v.* Manny, 56 Ill., 160; Lauman *v.* Des Moines County, 29 Iowa, 310; Allen *v.* Burlington, 45 Vt., 202; Judd *v.* Fox Lake, 28 Wis., 583; First Ecclesiastical Society *v.* Hartford, 38 Conn., 274; Foster *v.* County Commissioners, 7 Minn., 140.

[1] Lynde *v.* Melrose, 10 Allen, 49; Packard *v.* New Limerick, 34 Me., 266. In Vermont, it is otherwise by statute. See Saulters *v.* Victory, 35 Vt., 351.

[2] Withrington *v.* Harvard, 8 Cush., 66; Moore *v.* School Directors, 59 Penn. St., 232; Wright *v.* Dunham, 13 Mich., 414. A tax on corporate dividends cannot be disputed by creditors of the corporation on the ground of its having been declared when the corporation was insolvent. Pennsylvania Bank Assignees' Account, 39 Penn. St., 103.

validity of the tax in a suit to recover the money after it has been paid, or in an action to recover the value of his goods, if the tax was collected by distress and sale.[1] And it has been held that a statute taking away the remedy by replevin is not to be held applicable to a third person whose goods are seized for a tax for which he is no way liable;[2] nor to one who was not liable to be assessed for taxation.[3]

Where replevin is allowed, it cannot be maintained by the party taxed unless the whole tax is illegal; as it must assume that the seizure of the goods is without warrant of law.[4]

Estoppel. Under some circumstances, a party who is illegally assessed may be held to have waived all right to a remedy by a course of conduct which renders it unjust and inequitable to others that he should be allowed to complain of the illegality. Such a case would exist if one should ask for and encourage the levy of the tax of which he subsequently complains; and some of the cases referred to in the note go far in the direction of holding, that a mere failure to give notice of objections to one who, with the knowledge of the person taxed, as contractor or otherwise, is expending money in reliance upon payment from the taxes, may have the same effect.[5] But the duty to speak

[1] Dudley *v.* Ross, 27 Wis., 679; Macklot *v.* Davenport, 17 Iowa, 379.

[2] Traverse *v.* Inslee, 19 Mich., 98. Compare Atlantic, etc., R. R. Co., *v.* Cleino, 2 Dillon, 175; Cardinel *v.* Smith, Deady, 197.

[3] Stockwell *v.* Vietch, 15 Ab. Pr., 412. See Ross *v.* East Saginaw, 18 Mich., 233. As to such statutes in general, see O'Reiley *v.* Good, 42 Barb., 521; McClaughry *v.* Cratzenburgh, 39 Ill., 117; Mt. Carbon, etc., R. R. Co., *v.* Andrews, 53 id., 176; Yancey *v.* New Manchester, etc., Manuf. Co., 33 Geo., 622; Cady *v.* Lennard, 45 id., 85. Where mere irregularities are complained of, replevin will not be the appropriate remedy. Buell *v.* Ball, 20 Iowa, 282; Bilbo *v.* Henderson, 21 id., 56, and cases cited.

[4] Brackett *v.* Whidden, 3 N. H., 17; Emerick *v.* Sloan, 18 Iowa, 139.

[5] Weber *v.* San Francisco, 1 Cal., 455; Kellogg *v.* Ely, 15 Ohio, N. S., 64; Tash *v.* Adams, 10 Cush., 252; Motz *v.* Detroit, 18 Mich., 495; Warner *v.* Grand Haven, 30 id., 24; Peoria *v.* Kidder, 26 Ill., 351; Sleeper *v.* Bullen, 6 Kans., 300; Pease *v.* Whitney, 8 Mass., 93; La Fayette *v.* Fowler, 34 Ind., 140. In Indiana it is held that one who has seen a public improvement go on without objection, until it is accepted as completed by the city, cannot afterwards enjoin the collection of the assessment on the ground that the work was not done according to contract. Evansville *v.* Pfisterer, 34 Ind., 36. Or that the whole proceeding was invalid. La Fayette *v.* Fowler, 34 Ind., 140, citing Hel-

ought to be very imperative to make mere silence operate as an estoppel.[1]

Remedy by mandamus. A summary remedy by the writ of *mandamus* may be had by parties illegally assessed in a few cases, which are more particularly referred to in another chapter.[2] They embrace cases in which the property or subject taxed is not taxable by law, and the remedy is given by compelling the proper officer to strike off the assessment or to discharge the tax.[3] But an excessive assessment is not to be corrected by means of the writ, it not lying to correct mere errors of judgment in the exercise of judicial or discretionary powers.[4]

Remedy by prohibition. The common law writ of prohibition lies to keep inferior courts within their jurisdiction, and is inapplicable to tax cases, except, perhaps, under very peculiar statutes. A statutory remedy has been given in some states under this name.[5]

Quo warranto. This is the process by means of which usurpations of corporate franchises may be inquired into. It may doubtless be made available on behalf of the state in some cases where powers of taxation are unlawfully claimed, but is not adapted to the redress of individual wrongs under the revenue

lenkamp *v.* La Fayette, 30 id., 192; Palmer *v.* Strumph, 29 id., 329. And see Sleeper *v.* Bullen, 6 Kans., 300. One contesting a drainage proceeding, but admitting before the supervisors that the land is swamp and overflowed is estopped from disputing that fact on *certiorari*. Hagar *v.* Supervisors of Yolo, 47 Cal., 222.

[1] Where city property is assessed by city officers and sold as individual property, this does not estop the city from setting up its title. St. Louis *v.* Gorman, 29 Mo., 593. Taxing lots as private property whose boundaries include part of what is actually used as a street does not estop the city from claiming it as a street. Ellsworth *v.* Grand Rapids, 27 Mich., 250.

[2] Chapter XXIII.

[3] See People *v.* Barton, 44 Barb., 148; People *v.* Olmstead, 45 id., 644; People *v.* Supervisors of Otsego, 51 N. Y., 401; People *v.* Auditor General, 9 Mich., 134.

[4] Howland *v.* Eldridge, 43 N. Y., 457; School Directors *v.* Anderson, 45 Penn. St., 388; Gibbs *v.* Hampden Co. Commissioners, 19 Pick., 298; Miltenberger *v.* St. Louis County Court, 50 Mo., 172.

[5] See People *v.* Supervisors of Queens, 1 Hill, 195; Talbot *v.* Dent, 9 B. Monr., 526; State *v.* Gary, 33 Wis., 93.

laws. It has been held not to be the proper process to correct corporate action, where a city, instead of establishing remunerative water rates to pay the interest and part of the principal of the water loan — which it was claimed was its duty to do annually — established nominal rates only, and levied a tax on the city at large to pay the debt and interest.[1]

Conclusion. It will be apparent from what has appeared in this chapter, that many serious errors may be committed and many wrongs done in the exercise of the power to tax, which the parties wronged must submit to, because the law can afford them no redress whatever. All injuries which result from an exercise of political or legislative authority are to be included in this category; and these are often the most serious which, in matters of taxation, the people are visited with. In all such cases, the authority of the judiciary is confined to an inquiry into the jurisdictional question, and if it appears that the political or legislative body has kept within the limits of its authority, the judiciary must pause there, and admit its incompetency to inquire into wrongs which, within those limits, may have been committed. The wrongs which spring from errors on the part of assessors are, in a large proportion of all the cases, as little susceptible of correction, unless the legislature shall have provided a remedy by statute. Courts of equity have but a limited jurisdiction, extending to few cases besides those in which the impelling motive on the part of the assessors has been to do injustice and inflict injury. The chief protection of the citizen must at last be sought in the intelligence and integrity of public officers, and where these fail, as too often they do, the injury must frequently prove irreparable.

[1] Attorney General *v.* Salem, 103 Mass., 138. Neither is a bill in equity the proper remedy for such a case. Carlton *v.* Salem, 103 Mass., 141.

INDEX.

A.

B.

C.

D.

E.

F.

G.

H.

I.

J.

K.

L.

M.

N.

O.

P.

Q.

R.

S.

T.

U.

V.

W.

Y.

www.ingramcontent.com/pod-product-compliance
Ingram Content Group UK Ltd.
Pitfield, Milton Keynes, MK11 3LW, UK
UKHW041448071026
15587UKWH00010B/661

9 781584 773825